IMAGINING SOCIOLOGY

IMAGINING SOCIOLOGY

An Introduction with Readings

Catherine Corrigall-Brown

OXFORD
UNIVERSITY PRESS

OXFORD
UNIVERSITY PRESS

Oxford University Press is a department of the University of Oxford.
It furthers the University's objective of excellence in research, scholarship,
and education by publishing worldwide. Oxford is a registered trade mark
of Oxford University Press in the UK and in certain other countries.

Published in Canada by
Oxford University Press
8 Sampson Mews, Suite 204,
Don Mills, Ontario M3C 0H5 Canada

www.oupcanada.com

Library and Archives Canada Cataloguing in Publication

Corrigall-Brown, Catherine, author
Imagining sociology / Catherine Corrigall-Brown.

Includes bibliographical references and index.
ISBN 978-0-19-900877-3 (paperback)

1. Sociology—Textbooks. 2. Canada—Social conditions—
Textbooks. I. Title.

HM586.C68 2016   301   C2015-906396-5

Cover image: Tyrone Trevor/Getty Images

Oxford University Press is committed to our environment.
Wherever possible, our books are printed on paper
which comes from responsible sources.

Printed and bound in The United States of America

1 2 3 4 — 19 18 17 16

Contents

Chapter 6: Gender at the Intersections   160

PART 3: The Role of Institutions

Chapter 7: Language and the Media   192

Chapter 8: The Family   220

Chapter 9: Education   246

Chapter 13: Social Movements   362

From the Publisher

Oxford University Press is delighted to present Catherine Corrigall-Brown's *Imagining Sociology: An Introduction with Readings*. This exciting new work brings sociology to life through a fresh, dynamic treatment of core topics that incorporates important readings in the field and ample opportunities for applied learning. This innovative approach empowers students to see how sociology can help them make sense of the world—and is sure to spark their sociological imaginations!

Key Features

▶ **Fully integrated readings** allow students to engage directly with classic and contemporary sociological works. These well-curated readings illuminate concepts and theories under discussion and highlight the discipline's roots as well as its current findings.

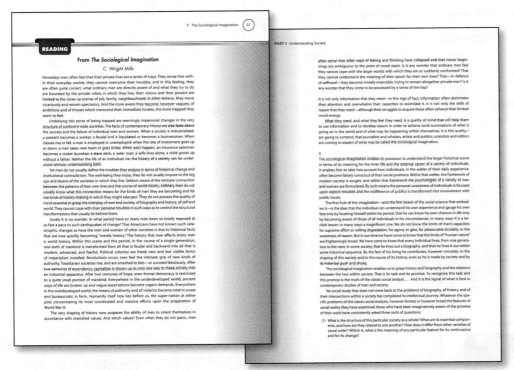

▶ **Critical reading questions** draw out key points and encourage students to develop their own conclusions about sociological ideas and issues.

1. What does Mills mean by "neither the life of an individual nor the history of a society can be understood without understanding both"? How could you understand your own life better by knowing more about history? How do individual biographies shape history? Think of a concrete example of this connection between individual biography and larger social history.

2. What do the terms *personal troubles* and *public issues* mean? How could we understand the issues of gender inequality, poverty, and crime as either a personal trouble or a public issue? How does labelling these problems a personal trouble or a public issue shape the kinds of solutions we would propose to solve them?

CRITICAL Reading Questions

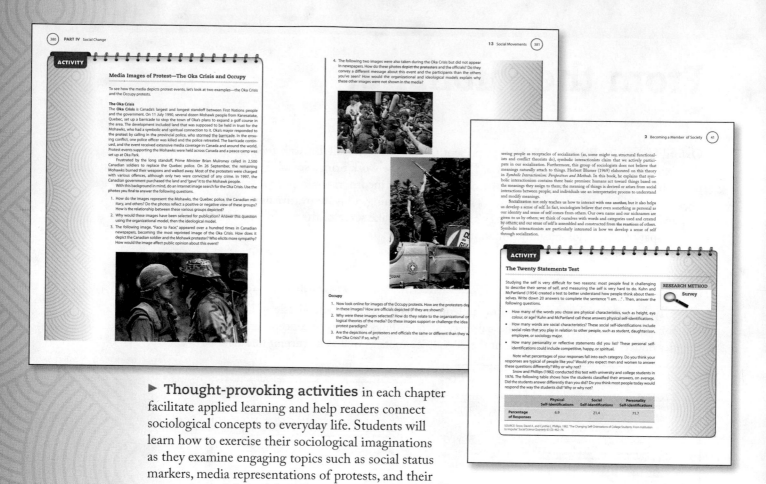

▶ **Thought-provoking activities** in each chapter facilitate applied learning and help readers connect sociological concepts to everyday life. Students will learn how to exercise their sociological imaginations as they examine engaging topics such as social status markers, media representations of protests, and their own ecological footprint.

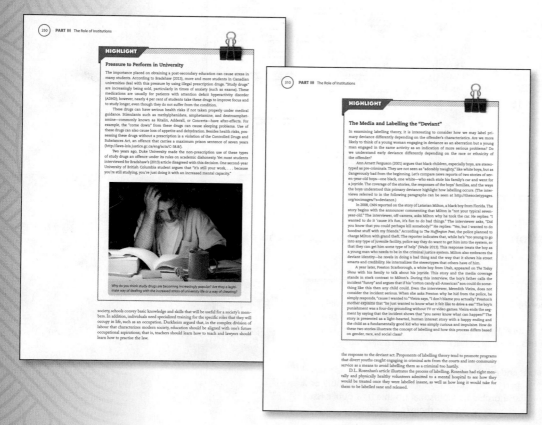

▶ **Highlight boxes** discuss relevant topics such as world hunger, women and political rights, and family violence, providing students with deeper insight into the issues, themes, and theories explored in each chapter.

PHOTO 10.2 Katy Perry performs at the 2013 American Music Awards in Los Angeles. Do you agree that her use of Japanese symbols is cultural commodification? Should performers be able to use cultural symbols in this way? Why or why not?

► **Contemporary and Canadian coverage**—including examples from recent events and popular culture, the latest research in the field, and Canadian cases and data—gives students a current and relevant overview of the discipline.

► **Theory integrated throughout** the text helps students easily relate theoretical concepts to the various sociological issues discussed in each chapter.

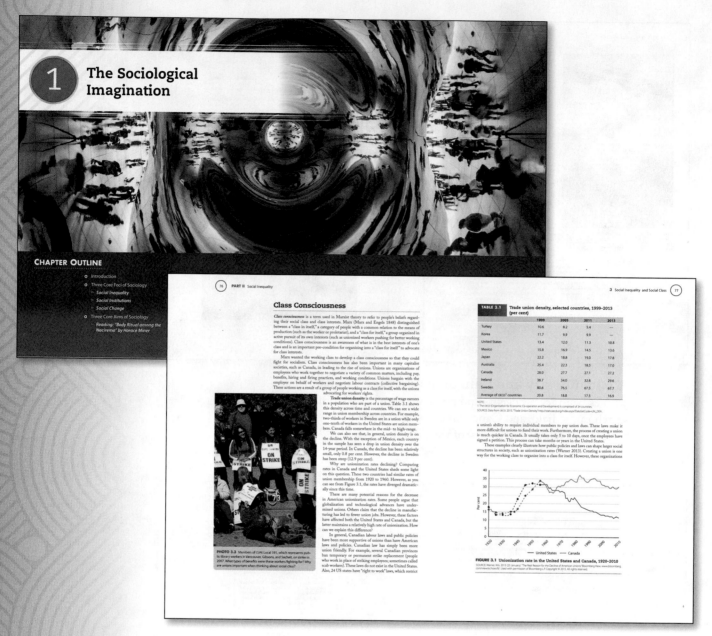

▶ **A vibrant four-colour design**—featuring an array of photos, maps, tables, and graphs—reflects the vitality of the field and helps students visualize data trends and essential issues and concepts.

▶ **A research methods icon** indicates whether a study discussed in the text involved surveys, experiments, interviews, or participant observation, helping students identify how sociologists use quantitative and qualitative methods in their research.

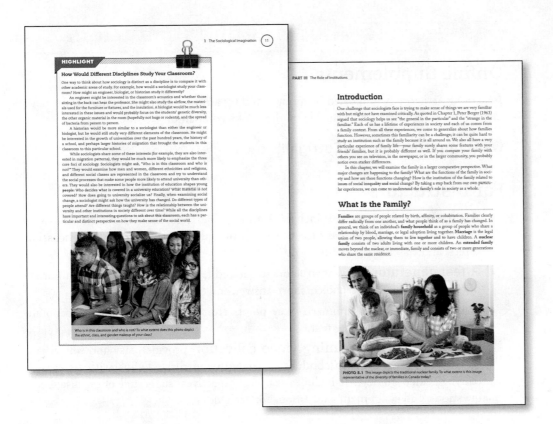

▶ **A lively and accessible writing style** grabs students' attention and makes even the most complex concepts easy to understand.

▶ **Helpful pedagogical features,** including chapter outlines, lists of key terms, and further readings, enhance student comprehension and offer avenues for learning beyond the classroom.

Resources for Students and Instructors

Online Supplements

Imagining Sociology is supported by an outstanding array of ancillary materials for both instructors and students, all available on the book's companion website:

www.oupcanada.com/CorrigallBrown

For Instructors

- **An instructor's manual** includes learning objectives, chapter overviews, lists of key concepts, sample answers to critical reading questions and activities, discussion topics, and classroom activities.
- **A test generator** allows instructors to sort, edit, import, and distribute hundreds of questions in multiple-choice, short-answer, and true/false format.
- **PowerPoint slides** summarize key points from every chapter and incorporate figures and tables from the text.
- **OUP's sociology streaming video collection** provides easy and immediate access to a variety of videos, both feature-length and curated clips, with an accompanying video guide that includes learning objectives, suggested clips, discussion questions, and assignment suggestions for each video.

For Students

- **A comprehensive online study-guide** provides chapter summaries, self-assessment quizzes, annotated lists of readings and web resources, and other material designed to enhance student learning.
- **A list of relevant web links for in-chapter activities** allows students to easily access online activity components.

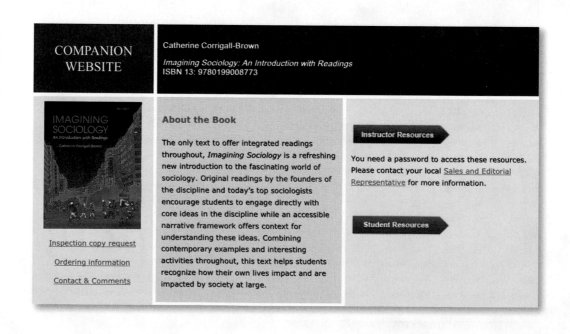

Preface

I remember signing up for my first sociology class. I needed one more course to complete my schedule in my first year of university and a friend suggested that I take sociology. Even though I had never heard of sociology and did not know what it would entail, I took the class. I was forever changed.

That course fundamentally altered the way I think about the world around me. Sociology provided me with a lens to understand our complex society. I learned that, while we all have a lifetime of experiences within society, the importance of that society is often hard to understand because we are so immersed in it. Sociology helped me understand how society as a whole shaped my life and the world around me.

By teaching sociology for many years, I have had the pleasure of helping students discover their sociological imagination, the key lens we use to understand the connection between individuals and society. It is a delight to see them start to use the theories, ideas, and research in our discipline to help make sense of the world around them. We can use these ideas to answer pressing questions such as "Why is there poverty?" "Why do men and women earn different amounts of money?" "How do race and ethnicity shape our lives?" "How does social change happen?"

This book aims to bring sociology to life. Original readings by the founders of the discipline and today's top sociologists illuminate the concepts and theories in the text. These readings highlight the discipline's roots as well as its current foci and findings. Critical thinking questions, which follow every reading, facilitate further thought and help you apply the reading's main concepts. The book also includes highlight boxes, which explore various theories and issues and provide deeper insight into the concepts discussed in each chapter. Key terms are defined in a glossary.

Each chapter also contains activities that help you connect the theories and ideas of sociology to your life. For example, what can you learn about socialization by looking at the toys you played with as a child? How can comparing your grandparents' education with your own help you understand the larger social changes in educational attainment in Canada? What do the curricula of your high-school classes tell you about the values of society and how they are changing? How are protest events depicted in the media and how does this portrayal shape how you think about protesters?

As the systematic study of human society, sociology covers a lot of ground. This book is divided into four sections. Part I introduces the sociological imagination, the process of socialization, and how we learn to fit into society and develop a sense of identity. Part II focuses on social inequality, a core area of sociology. This section examines social class, social status, race, ethnicity, gender, and sexuality. We also discuss the global inequality between countries. Understanding how inequalities between people and countries arise, perpetuate, and can be reduced is fundamental to sociology and is a primary theme of this book. Part III assesses several core institutions of society, including the media, family, education, work, and deviance. Sociology as a discipline encourages us to understand how individual choices can be structured or limited by larger social forces. Institutions are one such force that can shape the kind of lives we lead and larger patterns of social inequality.

We end the book by examining social change. It is clear that there is much inequality in society and a myriad of social problems in Canada and around the world. In Part IV, we learn about the role of the state, social movements, and other avenues for creating social change. It is certainly possible to make a more equal and just world. In fact, social change is a constant phenomenon that has helped us to address many social problems.

The diversity of people in your sociology class is a testament to how society can change and become more equal. However, much more can be done! Learning about social change will conclude this book, and hopefully ignite your sociological imagination.

Acknowledgements

My sociological imagination has been shaped by the many wonderful professors who taught me at the University of Victoria, Western University, and the University of California, Irvine. My colleagues at the University of British Columbia and Western University have helped build on this foundation and deepened my interest and enjoyment of sociology. They have all shaped my understanding of and fascination with the discipline, which I hope to pass on to sociology students.

I am indebted to the wonderful people at Oxford University Press who have helped this project come to fruition. Suzanne Clark, Tanuja Weerasooriya, Janna Green, Lisa Ball, Darcey Pepper, Danielle Pacey, and Isabelle Zerafa have deftly guided this project through its many stages and their hard work is much appreciated. This book has also been strengthened by the wonderful work of four students who have helped me to make it as accessible and animated as possible. I thank Mabel Ho, Kevin Hennessy, Joseph Jamil, and Paige Lougheed for their invaluable assistance. I also join Oxford University Press in thanking the following reviewers for their comments on the manuscript: Janet M.C. Burns (University of New Brunswick), Stephen Decator (St. Clair College), Riva Lieflander (University of Toronto), Greg Nepean (University of Guelph), Sharon Roberts (Renison University College), Anita van Wyk (University of the Fraser Valley), and one reviewer who chose to remain anonymous.

Most importantly, I thank my wonderful husband, Steve Weldon, for his endless support of this project and all my work. I also gratefully acknowledge my parents, Melodie and Hans, for their encouragement, and my sister, Sarah, for her inspiration.

This book is dedicated to my son, Leo. He was born into a challenging world but one filled with possibilities. May it become more equal and just as he grows.

For Leo

PART I

Understanding Society

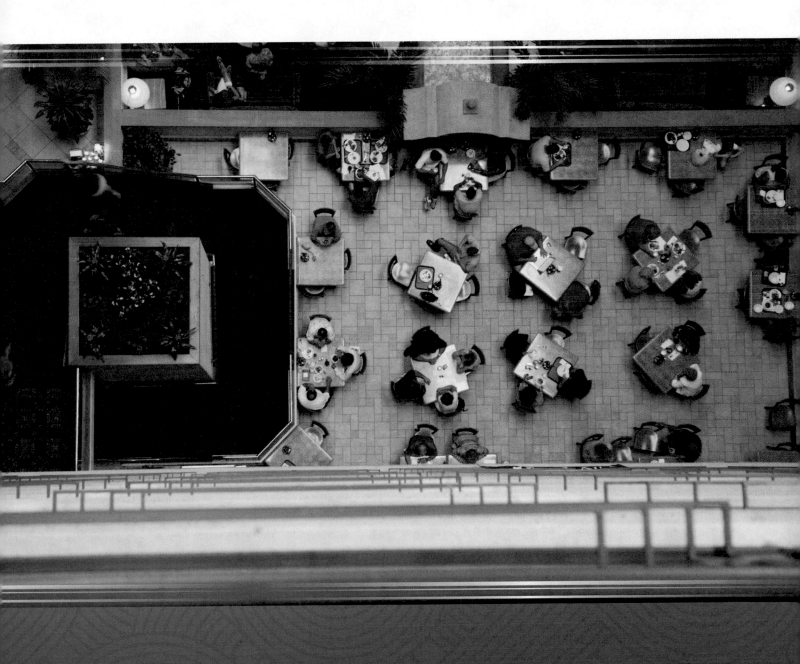

1 The Sociological Imagination

CHAPTER OUTLINE

Introduction

The word *sociology* was first coined by Auguste Comte, who believed that this new discipline had the potential to bring together all the sciences and to improve society. Comte was, in part, inspired to create this new area of study because he lived in a period of rapid social change (1798–1857). Industry was replacing agricultural ways of life, democracies were emerging from monarchies, and populations were migrating from the countryside to the cities. Wanting to make sense of this immense social change, Comte sought to understand how society worked and how all these changes might transform society and the people living in it.

Before and after Comte, individuals from all disciplines have been interested in explaining how society operates and why it sometimes does not work as well as we think it could. For example, philosophers as far back as Socrates and Plato wondered what makes a good society. But sociology is different in that it studies society in a systematic way. In fact, what defines sociology as a discipline is that it focuses on the systematic study of human society. This definition begs the question, "What is society?"

Society is the largest-scale human group that shares a common geographic territory and common institutions. Societies are not necessarily the same as states. In fact, many states contain a number of different societies. For example, Canada is sometimes thought to contain two distinct societies, with Quebec reflecting a different society than the rest of Canada. This idea is reinforced by the existence of many distinct institutions in the province. For example, Quebec's legal system is based on the Napoleonic code, whereas the other provinces and territories use the British system of common law.

Society is based on and requires social interaction between its members. These interactions can occur in a variety of settings and on a number of different levels, such as in neighbourhoods, schools, or workplaces. Such connections are important because they create shared understandings and are the basis of continued co-operation between the members of a society. These interactions also work to socialize newcomers, either those who emigrated from other parts of the world or young people who are learning how to behave within our society. Through this socialization, we teach others the written and unwritten rules and values of our society. We also use this interaction between members to monitor and regulate each other, making sure that we all follow the society's rules and expectations.

Interactions within society happen in patterned ways—for example, most people go to the same coffee shop every morning and have the same conversation with the barista. These routines, expectations, and behaviours are established over time so that ongoing co-operation between people is possible (Charon 2012). Imagine if you replied to the barista's question of "How are you?" with a long story about your new sociology course or your indecision about whether to go on another date with someone. He would probably be quite surprised at your unusual behaviour in this situation because the routine is that you simply say, "Fine, thank you." By responding in an unexpected way, you challenge the common expectations of how this social interaction should take place. The fact that most interactions in society are predictable establishes a common set of understandings of how our society works and how we are supposed to behave in it.

Interactions in society are also shaped by culture. **Culture** is a system of behaviour, beliefs, knowledge, practices, values, and materials. Cultures shape how we behave and the physical elements of our society. Our culture affects a myriad of elements of our lives, from how we set up cities to how we dress. It is clear from this definition that culture is contested—we certainly don't all agree on how we should act or what we should believe. These distinctions can exist between the dominant culture and subcultures or countercultures.

The **dominant culture** is able to impose its values, beliefs, and behaviours on a given society because of its political and economic power. Think about the "human interest" stories discussed on talk shows. They tend to be of interest to the people with a lot of money or power: what to buy, how to decorate a home, what to wear, or which stocks to buy or sell. These stories are based on the values of the dominant culture—that it is important to look attractive and fashionable, own an impressive home, and make a lot of money. There are many people who disagree with these foci in our culture. A **counterculture** is a group that rejects certain elements of the dominant culture. For example, anti-consumerist groups are countercultural. They reject our society's dominant focus on the importance of acquiring and consuming mass amounts of products in order to show our status and worth.

Subcultures also differ from the dominant culture, but they do not necessarily oppose it the way that countercultures do. For example, minor differences in occupational groups can create subcultures. Lawyers' daily routines, values, and style of dress might differ significantly from those of plumbers. Students involved in fraternities or sororities, those on sports teams, or those in fine arts programs might also be quite different from each other in their behaviours and dress.

Culture is often divided into high and popular culture. When people say that someone is "cultured," they tend to mean that the person participates in **high culture**, the culture of a society's elite. In general, this type of culture may be difficult to appreciate without having been taught to enjoy and understand it. **Popular** (or **low**) **culture** is the culture of the majority. In the world of music, opera and classical music are high culture, while rap and pop are popular culture. In literature, classic novels and plays (think Austen or Shakespeare) are high culture; romance and spy novels are popular culture (Jason Bourne is just one of the masses).

Photo 1.1 shows the humorous intersection of high and popular culture. The novel *Pride and Prejudice and Zombies* is an obvious play on the high culture works of Jane Austen and the popular culture interest in zombies. This cultural product juxtaposes the two types of culture to illustrate the disjuncture between them. Austen would certainly be surprised to see her heroines interacting with zombies!

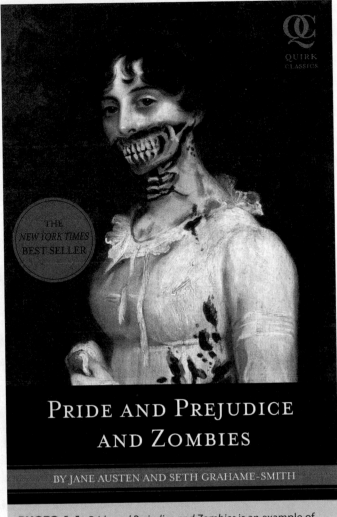

PHOTO 1.1 *Pride and Prejudice and Zombies* is an example of the merging of high and popular culture.

Three Core Foci of Sociology

As we learned earlier, sociology is the systematic study of human society. Sociologists can study a wide variety of things; in fact, almost anything in human society can be examined with a sociological perspective. However, most of sociology focuses on three core areas: the study of social inequality, the role of social institutions, and the study of social change.

Social Inequality

The study of **social inequality** is at the core of sociology. Generally, inequality is the gap between the advantaged and disadvantaged in society. More precisely, inequality is based on the "differences between people . . . that are *consequential* for the lives they lead, most particularly for the rights and opportunities they exercise and the rewards or privileges they enjoy" (Grabb 2006: 2; emphasis in original).

HIGHLIGHT

When Social Patterns Are Broken—Harold Garfinkel and Breaching Experiments

Harold Garfinkel (1991) was interested in the unexamined ways that we follow the rules of our society. He argued that people unknowingly create and recreate the rules of society every day. He thought that we could not really see or understand these rules until they are broken. Individuals are constantly interacting with one another, guided by a set of expectations regarding how they should act in a given situation. However, we are not always able to articulate, or even notice, these rules because they are taken for granted. To examine these accepted ways of producing social order in society, Garfinkel developed what he called **breaching experiments**. In a breaching experiment, the researcher breaks

RESEARCH METHOD

Experiment

Socially "awkward" behaviours can inspire sociologists to ask what we consider "normal" or "acceptable" behaviours. What are some of the unspoken social rules that you must follow in your life as a student to appear normal?

People differ from one another in an almost infinite number of ways. For example, humans have different eye colours, are different heights, and write with either their right or left hand (or both). While these are all differences among people, they are not particularly consequential in a person's life. Differences that are more important, and that have been the basis of most sociological inquiry, include social class, gender, race, and ethnicity. These topics have been of interest to sociologists since the beginning of the discipline. More recently, sociologists—and society in general—are starting to see the importance of other differences, such as sexual orientation, age, immigration status, disability, and ability. All these differences can be very important for the lives that individuals lead.

Characteristics such as our gender, race, or age can shape the rights, opportunities, rewards, or privileges that individuals enjoy. Examples include the right to vote and the opportunity to attend university or college. Women were not afforded the right to vote in federal elections in Canada until 1921 and First Nations people were not fully enfranchised until 1960. Therefore, being female or being First Nations had important consequences for the political rights that these individuals received. Rewards and privileges include access to good jobs and safe housing. We know, for example, that Canadians who a social rule to reveal the unrecognized way that all individuals co-operate to maintain the smooth functioning of social interactions and social order. Garfinkel—or, more often, his graduate students—would break a social rule and then see how people reacted. By creating disorder, he hoped to demonstrate how social order is usually maintained.

In one experiment, Garfinkel instructed his students to act as guests in their parents' homes during their holiday visit. The students were to be excessively polite, ask permission to use the restroom, and pretend not to know the people in the household. By behaving like strangers, the students undermined the expectations of how children should act toward their parents. Students reported that parents were upset and confused by the behaviour—some were even quite angry at being treated so formally.

Garfinkel also did many experiments in grocery stores. He had students take items from other people's carts. Shoppers initially assumed that a mistake had been made. Perhaps the students thought the cart was their own? However, the students would tell the other shopper that they simply found it easier to take items from another cart instead of walking the aisles. This behaviour is not explicitly forbidden—grocery stores have no signs saying not to take things from someone else's cart and the items have not yet been purchased. However, the shoppers often were angry at having their carts raided.

Although many people find encounters with rule breakers frustrating, it is a long-standing part of comedy. The movie *Borat* is essentially one long breaching experiment. The titular character, a native of Kazakhstan, travels across the United States, breaking social norms. In one scene, he walks the streets of New York City and starts talking to strangers. Some of them get so unnerved that they literally run away from him. Television shows such as *The Big Bang Theory* and *Just for Laughs: Gags* are also based on the humour in seeing other people break social rules. When Sheldon from *The Big Bang Theory* does something unusual, such as not allowing anyone to sit in his seat on the couch, we find it humorous because social rules dictate that we allow guests to sit where they please. It is only by breaking the social rule, or seeing others do so, that we can see what the social rule is and why following it makes society run smoothly.

What kinds of experiments could you conduct that would breach the social order? How could you behave differently in your day-to-day life to show the unexamined rules that we usually follow in society?

are of a lower social class are much less likely than those in a higher class to live in a safe neighbourhood with good amenities (e.g. parks and schools nearby).

Inequality between people exists in all societies. When sociologists look at inequality, they are interested in a number of key questions. Why does inequality exist? How is inequality generated, maintained, and reproduced? What are the implications of inequality? How can inequality be reduced? These and other important questions form the basis of the sociological study of inequality.

While the existence of inequality is universal, the type and amount differ across societies and over time. Different societies exhibit varying levels of inequality, with some societies being much more unequal than others. For example, the traditional caste system in India, which makes it almost impossible for people to move out of the social status of their birth, is much more unequal than modern Canadian society. Inequality also increases and decreases within a single society. Even India's rigid caste system has been challenged over time. The Indian government passed legislation to fight the discrimination experienced by the lowest caste group, the untouchables. There has also been a rise in marriage between castes, which was historically unthinkable but has reduced prejudice and inequality between groups. Finally, inequality is based on different factors across societies—some societies have a lot of racial inequality but little class differentiation, while others have little racial inequality but strict class hierarchies.

Many people wonder if our society is becoming more or less equal. This question is extremely difficult to answer because it depends on the kind of inequality being examined and on the measures used. For simplicity's sake, we will examine income and assess whether inequality based on this factor is increasing or decreasing across social class, race, and gender groups.

There is a great deal of evidence that class inequality is increasing in Canada. We can see this trend if we compare the richest 20 per cent of families with the poorest 20 per cent (each called a quintile). In a totally equal society, each group would earn 20 per cent of the society's entire income. We know that this is certainly not the case, as there are some people who are much richer than others in this country. This inequality increased from the 1970s until the 1990s and has remained relatively high since. In 2011, Canadian families in the top 20 per cent received 9.2 times the income of families in the bottom 20 per cent (Statistics Canada 2011a).

The growing divide between Canada's rich and poor does not tell the whole story of inequality in this country. Other types of inequality are declining. For example, if we compare the earnings of individuals based on their ethnicity or race, there is less inequality now than there was in the past. Let's compare visible minorities with non-visible minorities. **Visible minorities** are defined by the Government of Canada as "persons, other than Aboriginal peoples, who are non-Caucasian in race or non-white in colour" (Government of Canada 1995, 2). The use of the word *visible* is significant because Canada has important historical political divisions based on language (English vs French) and religion (Catholics vs Protestants), which are "invisible" traits.

In 2000, visible minorities born in Canada made 28.8 per cent less income than did Canadians who are not visible minorities. While the situation is certainly not equal, it is better than it was in 1990, when the figure was 29.9 per cent. In other words, the inequality between the incomes of Canadian-born visible minorities and non-minorities is declining. Visible minorities born outside the country made 15.2 per cent less in 2000 than non-visible minorities born outside Canada, down from 17.0 per cent in 1990 (Samuel and Basavarajappa 2006). Although the imbalance is improving, we clearly have a long way to go before such inequality is eradicated.

Income inequality based on gender has both increased and decreased. In 1991, Canadian women working full-time made 68.7 per cent of what their male counterparts did. This number increased to 72.3 per cent in 1996 but then dropped to 70.5 per cent in 2003 (Samuel and Basavarajappa 2006). It increased again to 74 per cent in 2011 (Pay Equity Commission 2012). This example shows the challenges of changing inequality. The task would be even more difficult if we looked beyond simple income to experiences of discrimination and prejudice or educational and work opportunities. It is no surprise, then, that so many sociologists are concerned with such an important and elusive topic.

In addition to measuring and assessing social inequality, sociologists often study why and how inequality persists. We know that all societies have inequality. But why is this the case? How does inequality endure? How can it be reduced? This book examines all these questions. In particular, we will learn more about inequality that arises from social class, race, ethnicity, and gender.

Social Institutions

Social institutions are the norms, values, and rules of conduct that structure human interactions. Institutions are not just physical places or buildings but also the social arrangements for how things are done. For example, the institution of education is not just a school or classroom; it is a set of larger arrangements that organize how people will receive education and what they will learn. There are five core institutions in modern Canadian society: the family, education, religion, the economy, and government. Other institutions, such as the mass media, medicine, science, and the military, are also important parts of Canadian society.

Institutions are standardized ways of doing something. In institutions, actions become regularized, patterned, and reproduced. When you consider education, you might think of your specific teachers, your class experience, or the schools you attended. Such details are certainly important aspects of your education. However, the institution of education is far more than these parts. It is based on the routine and patterned ways that education is delivered and assessed. For example, the material that you learned in elementary and secondary school was not simply the choice of your teachers. The institution of education sets a curriculum and decides, for example, that all students in grade 9 will read Shakespeare's *Romeo and Juliet*. Our education system is also based on teaching students from roughly 8:30 to 3:30, 5 days a week for 10 months of the year. All these routines are established by the institution of education in Canada and structure how education functions across the country.

Institutions are important because they generally help society run smoothly. They do so in part by socializing us and thereby teaching us the rules of our society. When you first go to school, you learn that you must sit quietly in class and raise your hand when you want to speak. These rules are important and help later schooling and other social interactions function. Imagine if everyone just wandered around the room during your university classes—the result would certainly be a chaotic environment.

However, institutions can also serve a negative function by maintaining and reinforcing inequality. In fact, one of the main reasons that inequality tends to persist is the role of social institutions. Because standardized methods become routine, they can reinforce some of the differences between people. For example, if your university or college has very high tuition, students of lower social classes might not be able to attend the school. In this way, the institution is partly responsible for people from lower social classes being less likely to get the degrees that would allow them to increase their social standing.

PHOTO 1.2 What do you think of when someone mentions the Canadian government? Do you think of politicians or places such as Parliament Hill in Ottawa?

Institutions can also be an avenue for social change. We know that individuals from lower social classes are much less likely to get a university or college degree than those from higher social classes. Many social programs instituted by the Government of Canada have tried to address this imbalance. The Veterans Rehabilitation Act (VRA), passed in 1944, included a program that helped World War II veterans receive a post-secondary education by paying their full tuition and living expenses for up to four years. The idea was that helping soldiers get an education would help them return to civilian life. Over 120,000 veterans—mostly men—received this support. Research estimates that, as a result of the program, men of the postwar period had an average of 0.2 to 0.4 more years of education and had higher wages over the course of their lives than they otherwise would have had (Lemieux and Card 1998).

Social Change

Social change is the third core area of sociology. Sociologists examine how, as we have just seen, social institutions can perpetuate inequality or create social change. If society is based on interactions among people, it can change just as people do.

One major institution in modern Canadian society that has changed greatly is religion. **Secularization**—the process of a religion losing its authority over individuals and social life in general—is a frequently discussed social change. Core founders of sociology, such as Karl Marx, Max Weber, and Émile Durkheim, all argued that the modernization of society would inevitably coincide with a decline in religiosity. Karl Marx was quite happy about this shift, as he thought that religion was an "opiate" of the masses, something that just dulled our pain and senses so that we would not resist the great social inequality that we experience in our lives. Durkheim was more likely to lament this decline; he thought religion was an important part of the glue that holds individuals together in society. Weber looked at how new rational systems, such as science and bureaucracies, would make religious answers to our questions less relevant (Collins 1994). These perspectives illustrate how sociologists have always been interested in religion's role in society. (We will learn much more about these three sociologists in the following chapters.)

The study of secularization seeks to explain how and why religious values, practices, and institutions are losing their power in modern society. It is certainly true that religion is currently less integral to many functions of Canadian society than it was in the past. For example, traditionally, many schools were run by religious institutions. You can still attend a religious school, but most schools in Canada are now operated by the state and are non-religious. Religious institutions were also once the main provider of charitable and welfare services, running orphanages, soup kitchens, and hospitals. Now, the government primarily performs such functions. Many religious institutions are still involved with these activities and raise money for these causes; however, the control of these services rests mostly in the hands of the state.

PHOTO 1.3 At this nineteenth-century hospital in Quebec, Catholic nuns took care of patients and did many of the tasks that nurses perform today. This photo illustrates the role that religious institutions traditionally played in healthcare in Canada.

HIGHLIGHT

How Would Different Disciplines Study Your Classroom?

One way to think about how sociology is distinct as a discipline is to compare it with other academic areas of study. For example, how would a sociologist study your classroom? How might an engineer, biologist, or historian study it differently?

An engineer might be interested in the classroom's acoustics and whether those sitting in the back can hear the professor. She might also study the airflow, the materials used for the furniture or fixtures, and the insulation. A biologist would be much less interested in these issues and would probably focus on the students' genetic diversity, the other organic material in the room (hopefully not bugs or rodents), and the spread of bacteria from person to person.

A historian would be more similar to a sociologist than either the engineer or biologist, but he would still study very different elements of the classroom. He might be interested in the growth of universities over the past hundred years, the history of a school, and perhaps larger histories of migration that brought the students in this classroom to this particular school.

While sociologists share some of these interests (for example, they are also interested in migration patterns), they would be much more likely to emphasize the three core foci of sociology. Sociologists might ask, "Who is in this classroom and who is not?" They would examine how men and women, different ethnicities and religions, and different social classes are represented in the classroom and try to understand the social processes that make some people more likely to attend university than others. They would also be interested in how the institution of education shapes young people: Who decides what is covered in a university education? What material is not covered? How does going to university socialize us? Finally, when examining social change, a sociologist might ask how the university has changed. Do different types of people attend? Are different things taught? How is the relationship between the university and other institutions in society different over time? While all the disciplines have important and interesting questions to ask about this classroom, each has a particular and distinct perspective on how they make sense of the social world.

Who is in this classroom and who is not? To what extent does this photo depict the ethnic, class, and gender makeup of your class?

Canadians are also becoming less religious. In 1991, 12.5 per cent of Canadians reported not being affiliated with any religion. This number had increased to 16.5 per cent by 2001 and to 24.0 per cent by 2011 (Statistics Canada 2011b). This decline is fairly typical of the general secularization occurring across North America and Europe. However, some sociologists have questioned if it is a universal trend or just a tendency in a certain set of countries that also share other characteristics, such as level of development, in common.

In fact, **religiosity** (a measure of how religious a person is) is increasing in many parts of the world. Scott M. Thomas, a British scholar who looks at trends in religiosity, finds that religion is actually quite healthy around the world (Bibby 2011). Between 1950 and 2000, the number of Catholics in the world doubled from fewer than 500 million to over a billion. The great attention paid to the selection of Pope Francis in 2013 attests to the strength and wide reach of the modern Catholic Church. There is also a dramatic increase in the spread of evangelical Protestantism, which now has 700 million adherents worldwide (Bibby 2011).

The discussion of religion's changing role illustrates a number of key elements in the study of sociology. Religion is an important institution in society, whose set of organized beliefs establish how we, as a society, will attempt to meet our basic social needs. It provides norms, values, and rules of conduct for individuals and helps to structure human interactions. Religion's changing role shows the larger social transformations that are at the heart of the study of sociology. Finally, the changing nature of religion depends on the social context in which it is examined.

Three Core Aims of Sociology

When looking at sociology's core areas, sociologists aim to do three main things. They try to see general themes in everyday life. They seek to assess critically what seems familiar and common sense. And, they examine how individuals both shape society and are shaped by society.

Everyone has a lifetime of experiences in society. From all these experiences, we come to generalize about how society functions and how people behave in it. However, sometimes this familiarity can be a challenge—it can be difficult to study society because it is all around us. It is like a fish trying to study water. However, sociology, as the systematic study of human society, pushes us to make sense of all our experiences and what we see around us and to come up with general ideas of how society functions.

In *Invitation to Sociology*, Peter Berger (1963) calls on us to see "the general in the particular." Put another way, sociologists should look for general patterns in particular people's behaviour. We may know some women who are very successful in large companies and have a great deal of responsibility in their jobs, but we see that most CEOs and Members of Parliament are men. This information suggests that there is a general pattern of women being less likely than men to hold positions of power. We can now ask ourselves why this might be the case: Is it that fewer women choose to enter business or politics or is there discrimination in these professions? Through systematic study, we can answer these types of questions.

The following reading by Horace Miner helps us with this first core aim of sociology. In this article, Miner describes the Nacirema culture. He outlines their rituals, customs, and practices and encourages us to see the general themes in the particular group.

Berger (1963) also called on us to see the "strange in the familiar." He said that the first wisdom of sociology is that things are not what they seem. When we travel to other countries, we expect to have some sort of culture shock—to see people eating different food, performing different customs, and wearing different clothing. Berger said that, when we study our own society, it should also be a culture shock minus the

Body Ritual among the Nacirema

Horace Miner

The anthropologist has become so familiar with the diversity of ways in which different peoples behave in similar situations that he is not apt to be surprised by even the most exotic customs. In fact, if all of the logically possible combinations of behaviour have not been found somewhere in the world, he is apt to suspect that they must be present in some yet undescribed tribe. This point has, in fact, been expressed with respect to clan organization by Murdock (1949: 71). In this light, the magical beliefs and practices of the Nacirema present such unusual aspects that it seems desirable to describe them as an example of the extremes to which human behaviour can go.

Professor Linton first brought the ritual of the Nacirema to the attention of anthropologists 20 years ago (1936: 326), but the culture of this people is still very poorly understood. They are a North American group living in the territory between the Canadian Cree, the Yaqui, and Tarahumare of Mexico, and the Carib and Arawak of the Antilles. Little is known of their origin, although tradition states that they came from the east. According to Nacirema mythology, their nation was originated by a culture hero, Notgnihsaw, who is otherwise known for two great feats of strength—the throwing of a piece of wampum across the river Pa-To-Mac and the chopping down of a cherry tree in which the Spirit of Truth resided.

Nacirema culture is characterized by a highly developed market economy which has evolved in a rich natural habitat. While much of the people's time is devoted to economic pursuits, a large part of the fruits of these labours and a considerable portion of the day are spent in ritual activity. The focus of this activity is the human body, the appearance and health of which loom as a dominant concern in the ethos of the people. While such a concern is certainly not unusual, its ceremonial aspects and associated philosophy are unique.

The fundamental belief underlying the whole system appears to be that the human body is ugly and that its natural tendency is to debility and disease. Incarcerated in such a body, man's only hope is to avert these characteristics through the use of the powerful influences of ritual and ceremony. Every household has one or more shrines devoted to this purpose. The more powerful individuals in the society have several shrines in their houses and, in fact, the opulence of a house is often referred to in terms of the number of such ritual centres it possesses. Most houses are of wattle and daub construction, but the shrine rooms of the more wealthy are walled with stone. Poorer families imitate the rich by applying pottery plaques to their shrine walls.

While each family has at least one such shrine, the rituals associated with it are not family ceremonies but are private and secret. The rites are normally only discussed with children, and then only during the period when they are being initiated into these mysteries. I was able, however, to establish sufficient rapport with the natives to examine these shrines and to have the rituals described to me.

The focal point of the shrine is a box or chest which is built into the wall. In this chest are kept the many charms and magical potions without which no native believes he could live. These preparations are secured from a variety of specialized practitioners. The most powerful of these are the medicine men, whose assistance must be rewarded with substantial gifts. However, the medicine men do not provide the curative potions for their clients, but decide what the ingredients should be and then write them down in an ancient and secret language. This writing is understood only by the medicine men and by the herbalists who, for another gift, provide the required charm.

The charm is not disposed of after it has served its purpose, but is placed in the charm-box of the household shrine. As these magical materials are specific for certain ills, and the real or imagined maladies of the people are many, the charm-box is usually full to overflowing. The magical packets are so numerous that people forget what their purposes were and fear to use them again. While the natives are very vague on this point, we can only assume that the idea in retaining all the old magical materials is that their presence in the charm-box, before which the body rituals are conducted, will in some way protect the worshipper.

Beneath the charm-box is a small font. Each day every member of the family, in succession, enters the shrine room, bows his head before the charm-box, mingles different sorts of holy water in the font, and proceeds with a brief rite of ablution. The holy waters are secured from the Water Temple of the community, where the priests conduct elaborate ceremonies to make the liquid ritually pure.

In the hierarchy of magical practitioners, and below the medicine men in prestige, are specialists whose designation is best translated [as] "holy-mouth-men." The Nacirema have an almost pathological horror of and fascination with the mouth, the condition of which is believed to have a supernatural influence on all social relationships. Were it not for the rituals of the mouth, they believe that their teeth would fall out, their gums bleed, their jaws shrink, their friends desert them, and their lovers reject them. They also believe that a strong relationship exists between oral and moral characteristics. For example, there is a ritual ablution of the mouth for children which is supposed to improve their moral fibre.

The daily body ritual performed by everyone includes a mouth-rite. Despite the fact that these people are so punctilious about care of the mouth, this rite involves a practice which strikes the uninitiated stranger as revolting. It was reported to me that the ritual consists of inserting a small bundle of hog hairs into the mouth, along with certain magical powders, and then moving the bundle in a highly formalized series of gestures.

In addition to the private mouth-rite, the people seek out a holy-mouth-man once or twice a year. These practitioners have an impressive set of paraphernalia, consisting of a variety of augers, awls, probes, and prods. The use of these objects in the exorcism of the evils of the mouth involves almost unbelievable ritual torture of the client. The holy-mouth-man opens the client's mouth and, using the above-mentioned tools, enlarges any holes which decay may have created in the teeth. Magical materials are put into these holes. If there are no naturally occurring holes in the teeth, large sections of one or more teeth are gouged out so that the supernatural substance can be applied. In the client's view, the purpose of these ministrations is to arrest decay and to draw friends. The extremely sacred and traditional character of the rite is evident in the fact that the natives return to the holy-mouth-men year after year, despite the fact that their teeth continue to decay. . . .

The medicine men have an imposing temple, or *latipso*, in every community of any size. The more elaborate ceremonies required to treat very sick patients can only be performed at this temple. These ceremonies involve not only the thaumaturge but a permanent group of vestal maidens who move sedately about the temple chambers in distinctive costume and headdress.

The *latipso* ceremonies are so harsh that it is phenomenal that a fair proportion of the really sick natives who enter the temple ever recover. Small children whose indoctrination is still incomplete have been known to resist attempts to take them to the temple because "that is where you go to die." Despite this fact, sick adults are not only willing but eager to undergo the protracted ritual purification, if they can afford to do so. No matter how ill the supplicant or how grave the emergency, the guardians of many temples will not admit a client if he cannot give a rich gift to the custodian. Even after one has gained admission and survived the ceremonies, the guardians will not permit the neophyte to leave until he makes still another gift.

The supplicant entering the temple is first stripped of all his or her clothes. In every-day life the Nacirema avoids exposure of his body and its natural functions. Bathing and excretory acts are performed only in the secrecy of the household shrine, where they are ritualized as part of the body-rites. Psychological shock results from the fact that body secrecy is suddenly lost upon entry into the *latipso*. A man, whose own wife has never seen him in an excretory act, suddenly finds himself naked and assisted by a vestal maiden while he performs his natural functions into a sacred vessel. This sort of ceremonial treatment is necessitated by the fact that the excreta are used by a diviner to ascertain the course and nature of the client's sickness. Female clients, on the other hand, find their naked bodies are subjected to the scrutiny, manipulation, and prodding of the medicine men.

Few supplicants in the temple are well enough to do anything but lie on their hard beds. The daily ceremonies, like the rites of the holy-mouth-men, involve discomfort and torture. With ritual precision, the vestals awaken their miserable charges each dawn and roll them about on their beds of pain while performing ablutions, in the formal movements of which the maidens are highly trained. At other times they insert magic wands in the supplicant's mouth or force him to eat substances which are supposed to be healing. From time to time the medicine men come to their clients and jab magically treated needles into their flesh. The fact that these temple ceremonies may not cure, and may even kill, the neophyte in no way decreases the people's faith in the medicine men.

There remains one other kind of practitioner, known as a "listener." This witch-doctor has the power to exorcise the devils that lodge in the heads of people who have been bewitched. The Nacirema believe that parents bewitch their own children. Mothers are particularly suspected of putting a curse on children while teaching them the secret body rituals. The counter-magic of the witch-doctor is unusual in its lack of ritual. The patient simply tells the "listener" all his troubles and fears, beginning with the earliest difficulties he can remember. The memory displayed by the Nacirema in these exorcism sessions is truly remarkable. It is not uncommon for the patient to bemoan the rejection he felt upon being weaned as a babe, and a few individuals even see their troubles going back to the traumatic effects of their own birth.

In conclusion, mention must be made of certain practices which have their base in native esthetics but which depend upon the pervasive aversion to the natural body and its functions. There are ritual fasts to make fat people thin and ceremonial feasts to make thin people fat. Still other rites are used to make women's breasts larger if they are small, and smaller if they are large. General dissatisfaction with breast shape is symbolized in the fact that the ideal form is virtually outside the range of human variation. A few women afflicted with almost inhuman hypermammary development are so idolized that they make a handsome living by simply going from village to village and permitting the natives to stare at them for a fee.

Reference has already been made to the fact that excretory functions are ritualized, routinized, and relegated to secrecy. Natural reproductive functions are similarly distorted. Intercourse is taboo as a topic and scheduled as an act. Efforts are made to avoid pregnancy by the use of magical materials or by limiting intercourse to certain phases of the moon. Conception is actually very infrequent. When pregnant, women dress so as to hide their condition. Parturition takes place in secret, without friends or relatives to assist, and the majority of women do not nurse their infants.

Our review of the ritual life of the Nacirema has certainly shown them to be a magic-ridden people. It is hard to understand how they have managed to exist so long under the burdens which they have imposed upon themselves. But even such exotic customs as these take on real meaning when they are viewed with the insight provided by Malinowski when he wrote (1948: 70):

Looking from far and above, from our high places of safety in the developed civilization, it is easy to see all the crudity and irrelevance of magic. But without its power and guidance early man could not have mastered his practical difficulties as he has done, nor could man have advanced to the higher stages of civilization.

REFERENCES CITED

Linton, Ralph. 1936. *The Study of Man*. New York: D. Appleton-Century.

Malinowski, Bronislaw. 1948. *Magic, Science, and Religion*. Glencoe, IL: Free Press.

Murdock, George P. 1949. *Social Structure*. New York: Macmillan.

CRITICAL
Reading
Questions

1. What group is Horace Miner really talking about in this classic article?

2. Miner mentions a number of interesting elements of Nacirema culture. What is he referring to when he talks about shrine rooms, charm-boxes, holy-mouth-men, mouth-rites, the *latipso*, and the listener?

3. Miner says that the Nacirema feel that the "human body is ugly and its natural tendency is to debility and disease" and that this group has a "pervasive aversion to the natural body and its functions." Do you think this is true? What evidence could you find to support or contradict this assertion?

4. What is the main point of this article? How does this article help you develop a more critical sociological perspective, particularly an ability to see the strange in the familiar?

geographic displacement. In other words, the sociologist travels at home, with shocking results. Miner's article illustrates how we can work to see the strange in the familiar when confronted with a society and culture (even our own).

The final goal of sociology is to see the dual process of how we shape society and how society shapes us. People create institutions in society in many ways, such as by passing laws and electing leaders who decide how some of these institutions will run. The institutions then influence individuals and the society in which we live. Émile Durkheim's famous study of suicide illustrates this relationship.

Émile Durkheim and the Study of Suicide

Although Comte coined the term *sociology*, no universities offered courses or did research in sociology during his lifetime. Émile Durkheim, who was born in France in 1858, was one of the original proponents of creating a field of sociology that would have a significant presence at universities. He argued that sociology was different from philosophy, a popular discipline at the time, because it would focus on empirical research. He claimed that sociology was distinct from psychology, another well-established discipline of the period, because it prioritizes the social over the individual. To help establish this new discipline, Durkheim created *L'Année Sociologique*, an annual review of French sociology that became the country's most influential publication of its kind. He also wrote a number of significant books using the sociological perspective and method he was advocating, including *The Division of Labour in Society* (1893), *The Rules of the Sociological Method* (1895), *On the Normalcy of Crime* (1895), *Suicide* (1897), and *The Elementary Forms of Religious Life* (1912).

For Durkheim, sociology was a unique discipline because it was to be based on the study of **social facts**, the external social structures, norms, and values that shape individuals' actions. As Durkheim (1897/1951, 37–8) explained, the "sociological methods as we practice it rests wholly on the basic principle that social facts must be studied as things, that is, as realities external to the individual." He believed that society is something more than just a group of individuals and the individual in society is "dominated by a moral reality greater than himself" (38).

To illustrate his concept of social facts and the way the sociological method could work, Durkheim conducted a study of suicide. The topic was chosen quite deliberately. At first glance, suicide seems like an obviously individual act; a person's choice to take his own life is often explained in terms of the person's own psychology. For example, we often think that people commit suicide because they are depressed or unhappy. While Durkheim acknowledged that psychology might matter, he argued that psychology alone

HIGHLIGHT

Getting to Know Émile Durkheim

▶ Durkheim was part of the Army of Justice, a group of intellectuals who fought what they considered the unfair execution of a French captain accused of treason.

▶ Durkheim's early death was attributed to his "loss of spirit and well-being" after his son's death in World War I.

▶ Durkheim wrote three of sociology's most influential works (*Suicide*, *The Rules of Sociological Method*, and *The Division of Labor in Society*) within a five-year period.

▶ Durkheim did not make it into the École normale supérieure until his third attempt.

cannot explain suicide. "Admittedly," he wrote, "under similar circumstances, the degenerate is more apt to commit suicide than the well man; but he does not necessarily do so because of his condition" (Durkheim 1897/1951, 81). He asked the following question: If suicide is strictly an individual psychological decision, why are suicide rates different for men and women, for Protestants and Catholics, and across countries? These differences can be explained only by social facts, elements of society that are beyond the individual.

Durkheim began his study not by looking at an individual's decision to commit suicide but by comparing the rates of suicide across groups of people. This systematic study of suicide led him to argue that there are four **types of suicide**, which differ based on the level of integration or regulation in a society as a whole. Societies differ in individuals' integration into the society. In societies with extremely low levels of integration, individuals commit egoistic suicide, whereas in societies with extremely high levels of integration, they commit altruistic suicide. Societies also differ in their level of regulation, the degree of external constraint on individuals. When regulation is excessively low, individuals commit anomic suicide; when it is excessively high, they commit fatalistic suicide. In essence, Durkheim argued that the conditions of society as a whole are so powerful that they influence even this most personal decision for individuals.

Durkheim believed that the best part of individuals—their morals, values, and sense of purpose—come from society. When individuals do not feel integrated into society, this can lead to egoistic suicide. Being a part of society can give our lives meaning, and participating in religion is one way that many people derive such meaning. Despite this important potential function, not all religions are equally effective at integrating individuals. For example, Durkheim found that Protestants were much more likely than Catholics to commit suicide, despite the fact that both religions prohibit and condemn suicide with equal fervour. He argued that this difference was partly because the Protestant Church is less effective than the Catholic Church at integrating its members. Protestantism focuses on individual faith, and adherents are encouraged to read and interpret the Bible on their own. Catholicism, however, places more emphasis on participating in church activities that are run by a clearly defined hierarchy of leaders. This feature encourages Catholics to interact with one another and to rely on the church to interpret religious teachings for them, both of which increase the amount of social interaction between members and the integration they feel.

In order to support this argument, Durkheim compared countries that are mostly Protestant (Prussia, Denmark, and Saxony) with those that are mostly Catholic (Spain, Portugal, and Italy). He found that the average suicide rate in the Protestant countries was 190 per million persons, whereas it was only 58 per million persons in the Catholic countries (Durkheim 1897/1951, 152). The larger social context of Protestantism was associated with a suicide rate over four times as high as the social context of Catholicism. However, some might argue that other differences between these countries might account for the different suicide rates. In order to test this claim, Durkheim compared the rates across regions of Switzerland, a nation with both Catholic and Protestant areas. Even within

ACTIVITY

Suicide in Canada

Can we still use Durkheim's insights to understand suicide rates today? The first chart shows suicide rates in Canada by gender and family type. The second chart lists countries by their level of religiosity and suicide rates. Examine the data and answer the following questions.

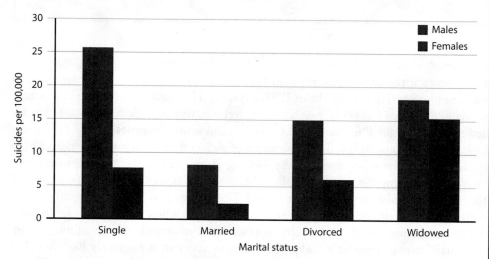

Suicide rates per 100,000, Canada, 2007

SOURCE: Statistics Canada, Canadian Vital Statistics Death Database; Statistics Canada, CANSIM, table 051-0010.

Suicide rates and religiosity by country, 2005–2006		
Country	**Religiosity**	**Suicide Rate**
Philippines	79	2.10
India	76	10.65
Guatemala	75	2.15
Brazil	69	4.35
Ireland	63	9.75
United States	61	11.05
Chile	54	10.45
Canada	49	11.65
Israel	44	6.25
France	30	18.30
Japan	29	24.20
Russia	28	36.15

SOURCE: Adapted from Pelham, Brett, and Zsolt Nyiri. 2008 (3 July). "In More Religious Countries, Lower Suicide Rates: Lower Suicide Rates Not a Matter of National Income." www.gallup.com/poll/108625/more-religious-countries-lower-suiciderates.aspx.

1. How do gender and family type relate to suicide? How does Durkheim's theory about certain social conditions leading to suicide explain the suicide rates among Canadian men and women in different family situations?

2. How is religiosity related to suicide rates across countries? Would Durkheim be surprised that more religious countries tend to have lower levels of suicide? Why or why not? How would he explain this relationship?

3. In general, countries that are very religious have low levels of suicide and countries that are not very religious have higher levels. But Israel has a relatively low rate of suicide given its low level of religiosity and India has a relatively high rate of suicide given its high rate of religiosity. How can you explain these unusual cases? Can you use Durkheim's theory? Why or why not?

this one country, the suicide rate of Protestants was four to five times higher than that of Catholics (155). This data support Durkheim's argument that those who are less integrated are more likely to commit suicide and some religions are more effective at integrating their adherents than others.

While a lack of integration in society can lead to suicide, Durkheim argued that excessively integrated societies can also have high suicide rates. Highly integrated societies can include cults, in which adherents sometimes commit mass suicide. For example, a mass suicide of 39 Heaven's Gate members occurred in California in 1997. Terrorists who martyr themselves for a cause are also examples of how being excessively integrated into a society, so much so that a person thinks only about the group's needs, can be associated with suicide.

According to Durkheim, levels of regulation in society are also associated with suicide. In a society with very little regulation, individuals can come to feel anomic, a term Durkheim used to refer to a feeling of rootlessness or normlessness. When the rules and regulations of society are weak or unclear, individuals feel free to do anything they please. While this freedom sounds good, a lack of regulation can reduce an individual's feeling of meaning and connection to others. Durkheim argued that a lack of regulation can occur in either good times, such as economic booms, or bad times, such as economic depressions. Any temporary disruption in the social order makes the collectivity unable to exercise its authority over the individual. In these times, the old rules and standards for behaviour no longer apply, but new rules and standards have not yet been created. This situation can lead to anomic suicide.

The final type of suicide discussed by Durkheim, fatalistic suicide, occurs when there is excessive regulation in society. Durkheim named this type of suicide but did not spend much time discussing it in his work. He did say, however, that it occurs among "persons with futures pitilessly blocked and passions violently choked by oppressive discipline" (1857/1951, 276). For example, a slave might commit suicide because she feels she has no other option and her life is totally controlled by another.

The brilliance of Durkheim's study is in the way it shows how a phenomenon that is generally thought of as a psychological process, the decision to commit suicide, is shaped by the structure of the society in which a person lives. By examining the integration and regulation in a society, we can predict its suicide rate. Or, by comparing across groups of people, we can predict who will be more or less likely to commit suicide based on the propensity of their group to be integrated into or regulated by society. For example, Durkheim compared the suicide rates of men and women and found that men are more likely to commit suicide in part because they tend to be less integrated into society. In the same way, he found that unmarried individuals are more likely to commit suicide because they are less integrated into families.

Durkheim's work, while highly influential, has sparked criticism and debate. Some later researchers argue that there is a logical error in the research: Durkheim explained micro-level individual behaviour (the act of suicide) with macro-level country statistics (suicide rates). Despite this potential problem, the work illuminates the connection between individuals and the society in which they live, which is at the heart of sociology.

The Sociological Imagination

In Canadian society, most people believe that individuals shape their own destiny. To a certain extent, this is true—we, as individuals, make decisions every day that shape the kind of life we lead. For example, you made decisions about whether to attend university or college, how hard to work in your classes, where to live when attending school, and what type of summer job you want. But, of course, many factors influence these decisions.

Let's examine your decision about a summer job. If your parents are willing and able to help pay for your education, you might not have to work in the summer or you might choose to take an unpaid internship, which would be impossible if you needed to pay your own tuition. In this way, your individual choice of whether you work and what type of job you get is, to some degree, structured by the wealth and support of your parents. The reason we might be interested in how your individual choices are constrained is that it might shape later outcomes for you. For example, students who have completed an unpaid internship might find it easier to get a good job after graduation, as they will have gained skills and social contacts while working. Students who have wealthy parents (and therefore don't need a summer job) are more likely than other students to have time to do an internship, which can perpetuate inequality in society over time.

This example illustrates how individual choices (sometimes called agency) are structured in society. We have the ability to make decisions, but our choices are often shaped or limited by larger social forces, such as our family, our social class, the economy, the education system, and gender norms. Many sociologists have tried to make sense of this complicated relationship between an individual's agency and society's constraints. Marx famously said that "[people] make their own history, but they do not make it as they please; they do not make it under self-selected circumstances, but under circumstances existing already, given and transmitted from the past" (in Tucker 1978: 595).

C. Wright Mills (1959/2000) also tried to tackle these complicated issues with what he called the **sociological imagination**. Mills called on us to try to see the connections between our individual lives and the larger society in which we live. He argued that we can really understand our own lives and biographies only if we understand the larger history of our society. Once we make these connections, we will be able to see the relationship between our own **personal troubles** (problems that we face as individuals) and larger **public issues** (social problems that arise in society).

First published in 1959, Mills's *The Sociological Imagination* is one of the most widely read sociology books of all time. The sociological imagination is at the core of sociology. In fact, it is the inspiration for the title of this textbook. The following excerpt, from Chapter 1 of the book, discusses the links between personal and public.

PHOTO 1.4 C. Wright Mills, the author of *The Sociological Imagination*, is pictured here on his motorcycle. Using the social imagination, we can see how society as a whole can shape our individual experiences and how our own personal biographies are related to larger historical processes.

From *The Sociological Imagination*

C. Wright Mills

Nowadays men often feel that their private lives are a series of traps. They sense that within their everyday worlds, they cannot overcome their troubles, and in this feeling, they are often quite correct: what ordinary men are directly aware of and what they try to do are bounded by the private orbits in which they live; their visions and their powers are limited to the close-up scenes of job, family, neighbourhood; in other milieux, they move vicariously and remain spectators. And the more aware they become, however vaguely, of ambitions and of threats which transcend their immediate locales, the more trapped they seem to feel.

Underlying this sense of being trapped are seemingly impersonal changes in the very structure of continent-wide societies. The facts of contemporary history are also facts about the success and the failure of individual men and women. When a society is industrialized, a peasant becomes a worker; a feudal lord is liquidated or becomes a businessman. When classes rise or fall, a man is employed or unemployed; when the rate of investment goes up or down, a man takes new heart or goes broke. When wars happen, an insurance salesman becomes a rocket launcher; a store clerk, a radar man; a wife lives alone; a child grows up without a father. Neither the life of an individual nor the history of a society can be understood without understanding both.

Yet men do not usually define the troubles they endure in terms of historical change and institutional contradiction. The well-being they enjoy, they do not usually impute to the big ups and downs of the societies in which they live. Seldom aware of the intricate connection between the patterns of their own lives and the course of world history, ordinary men do not usually know what this connection means for the kinds of men they are becoming and for the kinds of history-making in which they might take part. They do not possess the quality of mind essential to grasp the interplay of man and society, of biography and history, of self and world. They cannot cope with their personal troubles in such ways as to control the structural transformations that usually lie behind them.

Surely it is no wonder. In what period have so many men been so totally exposed at so fast a pace to such earthquakes of change? That Americans have not known such catastrophic changes as have the men and women of other societies is due to historical facts that are now quickly becoming "merely history." The history that now affects every man is world history. Within this scene and this period, in the course of a single generation, one-sixth of mankind is transformed from all that is feudal and backward into all that is modern, advanced, and fearful. Political colonies are freed; new and less visible forms of imperialism installed. Revolutions occur; men feel the intimate grip of new kinds of authority. Totalitarian societies rise, and are smashed to bits—or succeed fabulously. After two centuries of ascendancy, capitalism is shown up as only one way to make society into an industrial apparatus. After two centuries of hope, even formal democracy is restricted to a quite small portion of mankind. Everywhere in the underdeveloped world, ancient ways of life are broken up and vague expectations become urgent demands. Everywhere in the overdeveloped world, the means of authority and of violence become total in scope and bureaucratic in form. Humanity itself now lies before us, the super-nation at either pole concentrating its most coordinated and massive efforts upon the preparation of World War III.

The very shaping of history now outpaces the ability of men to orient themselves in accordance with cherished values. And which values? Even when they do not panic, men often sense that older ways of feeling and thinking have collapsed and that newer begin-nings are ambiguous to the point of moral stasis. Is it any wonder that ordinary men feel they cannot cope with the larger worlds with which they are so suddenly confronted? That they cannot understand the meaning of their epoch for their own lives? That—in defence of selfhood—they become morally insensible, trying to remain altogether private men? Is it any wonder that they come to be possessed by a sense of the trap?

It is not only information that they need—in this Age of Fact, information often dominates their attention and overwhelms their capacities to assimilate it. It is not only the skills of reason that they need—although their struggles to acquire these often exhaust their limited moral energy.

What they need, and what they feel they need, is a quality of mind that will help them to use information and to develop reason in order to achieve lucid summations of what is going on in the world and of what may be happening within themselves. It is this quality, I am going to contend, that journalists and scholars, artists and publics, scientists and editors are coming to expect of what may be called the sociological imagination.

1

The sociological imagination enables its possessor to understand the larger historical scene in terms of its meaning for the inner life and the external career of a variety of individuals. It enables him to take into account how individuals, in the welter of their daily experience, often become falsely conscious of their social positions. Within that welter, the framework of modern society is sought, and within that framework the psychologies of a variety of men and women are formulated. By such means the personal uneasiness of individuals is focused upon explicit troubles and the indifference of publics is transformed into involvement with public issues.

The first fruit of this imagination—and the first lesson of the social science that embod-ies it—is the idea that the individual can understand his own experience and gauge his own fate only by locating himself within his period, that he can know his own chances in life only by becoming aware of those of all individuals in his circumstances. In many ways it is a ter-rible lesson; in many ways a magnificent one. We do not know the limits of man's capacities for supreme effort or willing degradation, for agony or glee, for pleasurable brutality or the sweetness of reason. But in our time we have come to know that the limits of "human nature" are frighteningly broad. We have come to know that every individual lives, from one genera-tion to the next, in some society; that he lives out a biography, and that he lives it out within some historical sequence. By the fact of his living he contributes, however minutely, to the shaping of this society and to the course of its history, even as he is made by society and by its historical push and shove.

The sociological imagination enables us to grasp history and biography and the relations between the two within society. That is its task and its promise. To recognize this task and this promise is the mark of the classic social analyst. . . . And it is the signal of what is best in contemporary studies of man and society.

No social study that does not come back to the problems of biography, of history, and of their intersections within a society has completed its intellectual journey. Whatever the spe-cific problems of the classic social analysts, however limited or however broad the features of social reality they have examined, those who have been imaginatively aware of the promise of their work have consistently asked three sorts of questions:

(1) What is the structure of this particular society as a whole? What are its essential compon-ents, and how are they related to one another? How does it differ from other varieties of social order? Within it, what is the meaning of any particular feature for its continuance and for its change?

(2) Where does this society stand in human history? What are the mechanics by which it is changing? What is its place within and its meaning for the development of humanity as a whole? How does any particular feature we are examining affect, and how is it affected by, the historical period in which it moves? And this period—what are its essential features? How does it differ from other periods? What are its characteristic ways of history-making?

(3) What varieties of men and women now prevail in this society and in this period? And what varieties are coming to prevail? In what ways are they selected and formed, liberated and repressed, made sensitive and blunted? What kinds of "human nature" are revealed in the conduct and character we observe in this society in this period? And what is the meaning for "human nature" of each and every feature of the society we are examining?

Whether the point of interest is a great power state or a minor literary mood, a family, a prison, a creed—these are the kinds of questions the best social analysts have asked. They are the intellectual pivots of classic studies of man in society—and they are the questions inevitably raised by any mind possessing the sociological imagination. For that imagination is the capacity to shift from one perspective to another—from the political to the psychological; from examination of a single family to comparative assessment of the national budgets of the world; from the theological school to the military establishment; from considerations of an oil industry to studies of contemporary poetry. It is the capacity to range from the most impersonal and remote transformations to the most intimate features of the human self— and to see the relations between the two. Back of its use there is always the urge to know the social and historical meaning of the individual in the society and in the period in which he has his quality and his being.

That, in brief, is why it is by means of the sociological imagination that men now hope to grasp what is going on in the world, and to understand what is happening in themselves as minute points of the intersections of biography and history within society. In large part, contemporary man's self-conscious view of himself as at least an outsider, if not a permanent stranger, rests upon an absorbed realization of social relativity and of the transformative power of history. The sociological imagination is the most fruitful form of this self-consciousness. By its use men whose mentalities have swept only a series of limited orbits often come to feel as if suddenly awakened in a house with which they had only supposed themselves to be familiar. Correctly or incorrectly, they often come to feel that they can now provide themselves with adequate summations, cohesive assessments, comprehensive orientations. Older decisions that once appeared sound now seem to them products of a mind unaccountably dense. Their capacity for astonishment is made lively again. They acquire a new way of thinking, they experience a transvaluation of values: in a word, by their reflection and by their sensibility, they realize the cultural meaning of the social sciences.

2

Perhaps the most fruitful distinction with which the sociological imagination works is between "the personal troubles of milieu" and "the public issues of social structure." This distinction is an essential tool of the sociological imagination and a feature of all classic work in social science.

Troubles occur within the character of the individual and within the range of his immediate relations with others; they have to do with his self and with those limited areas of social life of which he is directly and personally aware. Accordingly, the statement and the resolution of troubles properly lie within the individual as a biographical entity and within the scope of his immediate milieu—the social setting that is directly open to his personal experience and to some extent his willful activity. A trouble is a private matter: values cherished by an individual are felt by him to be threatened.

Issues have to do with matters that transcend these local environments of the individual and the range of his inner life. They have to do with the organization of many such milieux into the institutions of a historical society as a whole, with the ways in which various milieux overlap and interpenetrate to form the larger structure of social and historical life. An issue is a public matter: some value cherished by publics is felt to be threatened. Often there is a debate about what that value really is and about what it is that really threatens it. This debate is often without focus if only because it is the very nature of an issue, unlike even widespread trouble, that it cannot very well be defined in terms of the immediate and everyday environments of ordinary men. An issue, in fact, often involves a crisis in institutional arrangements, and often too it involves what Marxists call "contradictions" or "antagonisms."

In these terms, consider unemployment. When, in a city of 100,000, only one man is unemployed, that is his personal trouble, and for its relief we properly look to the character of the man, his skills, and his immediate opportunities. But when in a nation of 50 million employees, 15 million men are unemployed, that is an issue, and we may not hope to find its solution within the range of opportunities open to any one individual. The very structure of opportunities has collapsed. Both the correct statement of the problem and the range of possible solutions require us to consider the economic and political institutions of the society, and not merely the personal situation and character of a scatter of individuals.

Consider war. The personal problem of war, when it occurs, may be how to survive it or how to die in it with honour; how to make money out of it; how to climb into the higher safety of the military apparatus; or how to contribute to the war's termination. In short, according to one's values, to find a set of milieux and within it to survive the war or make one's death in it meaningful. But the structural issues of war have to do with its causes; . . . with its effects upon economic and political, family and religious institutions, with the unorganized irresponsibility of a world of nation-states.

Consider marriage. Inside a marriage a man and a woman may experience personal troubles, but when the divorce rate during the first four years of marriage is 250 out of every 1,000 attempts, this is an indication of a structural issue having to do with the institutions of marriage and the family and other institutions that bear upon them.

Or consider the metropolis—the horrible, beautiful, ugly, magnificent sprawl of the great city. For many upper-class people, the personal solution to "the problem of the city" is to have an apartment with private garage under it in the heart of the city, and 40 miles out, a house by Henry Hill, garden by Garrett Eckbo, on a hundred acres of private land. In these two controlled environments—with a small staff at each end and a private helicopter connection—most people could solve many of the problems of personal milieux caused by the facts of the city. But all this, however splendid, does not solve the public issues that the structural fact of the city poses. What should be done with this wonderful monstrosity? Break it all up into scattered units, combining residence and work? Refurbish it as it stands? Or, after evacuation, dynamite it and build new cities according to new plans in new places? What should those plans be? And who is to decide and to accomplish whatever choice is made? These are structural issues; to confront them and to solve them requires us to consider political and economic issues that affect innumerable milieux.

In so far as an economy is so arranged that slumps occur, the problem of unemployment becomes incapable of personal solution. In so far as war is inherent in the nation-state system and in the uneven industrialization of the world, the ordinary individual in his restricted milieu will be powerless—with or without psychiatric aid—to solve the troubles this system or lack of system imposes upon him. In so far as the family as an institution turns women into darling little slaves and men into their chief providers and unweaned dependents, the problem of a satisfactory marriage remains incapable of purely private solution. In so far as the overdeveloped megalopolis and the overdeveloped automobile are built-in features of the overdeveloped society, the issues of urban living will not be solved by personal ingenuity and private wealth.

What we experience in various and specific milieux, I have noted, is often caused by structural changes. Accordingly, to understand the changes of many personal milieux we are required to look beyond them. And the number and variety of such structural changes increase as the institutions within which we live become more embracing and more intricately connected with one another. To be aware of the idea of social structure and to use it with sensibility is to be capable of tracing such linkages among a great variety of milieux. To be able to do that is to possess the sociological imagination. . . .

CRITICAL Reading Questions

1. What does Mills mean by "neither the life of an individual nor the history of a society can be understood without understanding both"? How could you understand your own life better by knowing more about history? How do individual biographies shape history? Think of a concrete example of this connection between individual biography and larger social history.

2. What do the terms *personal troubles* and *public issues* mean? How could we understand the issues of gender inequality, poverty, and crime as either a personal trouble or public issue? How does labelling these problems a personal trouble or a public issue shape the kinds of solutions we would propose to solve them?

3. Mills questions the role of the physical and natural sciences in this chapter. He says that, in some cases "they have raised more problems . . . than they have solved, and the problems that they have raised lie almost entirely in the area of social not physical affairs" (Mills 1959/2000, 15). How could the problem of climate change illustrate this point? What are the social ways we could prevent or ameliorate the effects of climate change?

ACTIVITY

The History and Biography of Higher Education in Canada

C. Wright Mills emphasized how individual biographies and the history of society are inextricably linked. With this idea in mind, let's examine higher education in Canada. By examining your own personal biography, we can see how you came to higher education. Mills, however, pushed us to understand our own personal biographies as they relate to the history of society as a whole. We can begin to see this connection between biography and history by comparing your personal story with the biographies of your parents and grandparents and with the Canadian population as a whole. Through these comparisons, we can gain insight into how access to higher education has changed and how larger historical changes in society might have affected you and your family. Throughout this activity, keep in mind Mills's distinction between the role of history and biography.

1. Begin by tracing the educational attainment of your family. What are your parents' and grandparents' highest levels of education? Compare the educational pathways of the males and females in your family. Do both sides of your family have similar types and amounts of education? Try to explain why the different people in your

continued

family (parents and grandparents, male and female, both sides of your family) attained the education that they did.

2. The following figures outline the percentage of males and females enrolled in American and Canadian universities in the 1960s (roughly when your grandparents might have gone to university) until recently (your generation's university attendance). The latter figure shows the male and female rates of attendance over time. Looking at the overall statistics of university enrolment in Canada and the United States, how has the number and type of people attending university changed? What major trends do you observe in the chart? What types of larger historical changes in society have led to these changes in university enrolment? How have larger social processes created these changing patterns?

3. How does knowing the larger historical trends in Canadian society help you to better understand the biographies of your family members? How does knowing your own family's biography help you to better understand the historical trends you observe in the data on Canadian society?

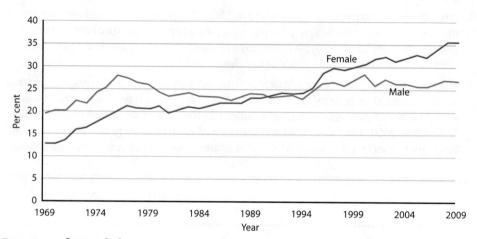

Per cent of US adults ages 25–29 with a bachelor's degree or higher, 1969–2009

SOURCE: Kevin Pollard, "The Gender Gap in College Enrollment and Graduation," (Washington, DC: Population Reference Bureau, 2011).

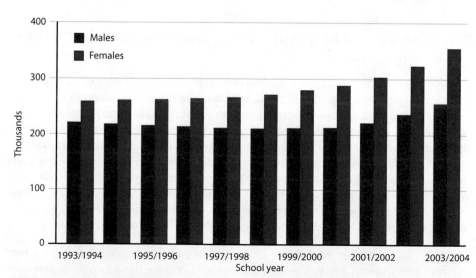

Full-time undergraduate university enrolment, Canada, by sex

SOURCE: Statistics Canada, CANSIM table 477-0013.

Understanding the connection of your own biography and the history of society is a fundamental part of Mills's sociological imagination. As did many sociologists before and since him, Mills strived to see the connection between individual experiences and the structure of society as a whole. Throughout this book, keep these ideas in mind and try to see how your own life and experiences are shaped by the society in which you live.

HIGHLIGHT

Is Sociology Just Common Sense?

Because we all live within society, it is sometimes hard to see how there could be much to learn in sociology. Can't we just use our own experiences to make sense of the social world? Isn't sociology really just common sense? Randall Collins (1992), a famous sociologist, notes that obvious social questions may not have obvious or simple answers. Sociology's greatest strength, he argues, is precisely its potential for penetrating the superficial observation of everyday life and finding the fundamental social processes hidden beneath.

For example, many people wonder what makes a romantic couple compatible. Common sense tells us that "opposites attract." However, it also tells us that "birds of a feather flock together." If both of these axioms are common sense and are based on our life experience, how can we make sense of which idea is the better explanation of compatibility? Much systematic research has been conducted in sociology to answer just this question, and this research comes to a clear consensus that, while it may seem like opposites attract, most couples share similar characteristics. In fact, the **homophily** principle structures social relationships of every type, including marriage, friendship, and work relationships. Most people have personal networks that are very homogeneous, which is partly why most romantic partners are similar to one another. They are most likely to be similar in race and ethnicity, with age, religion, education, and occupation following, in roughly that order. In addition, couples are also most often similar in terms of their attitudes and values.

There are many reasons why most people romantically couple with and marry people who are similar to them. The most important reason is simple geography. Most people have more contact with those who are like them. For example, one of the main reasons that people tend to date and marry others of similar age is because of the age-based structure of schooling. The fact that schools group ages together into classrooms induces homophily. As many people meet romantic partners and select mates while they are attending school and are most likely to meet and interact with others of their age group in these settings, it is not surprising that they are most likely to choose a partner in their age group.

Partners are also most likely to come from the same social class or status. This is, in part, because our social class often determines the neighbourhood where we grow up and live. People with more money and higher status occupations tend to live in more expensive neighbourhoods, where other upper-class people live. They are also more likely to attend elite private schools, where they meet others of their social class. And they are more likely to work in fields such as the law, business, or medicine, where other people of their class are located. These social networks bring people of the same class into contact with one another and provide opportunities to create friendships.

The finding that most relationships, be they romances, friendships, or acquaintances, tend to be between people who are similar can be very important for

continued

According to the homophily principle, friends and romantic partners tend to have similar interests and to come from similar backgrounds. This group of friends shares an interest in food and conversation and probably comes from similar ethnic and class backgrounds. What similarities and dissimilarities can you find between you and your friends?

understanding how society works. If people tend to know others like themselves, they might be less likely to be open or tolerant of people who are different from them. It also might limit the amount and diversity of information people receive, as they are generally just in contact with people who have the same opinions and experiences. Considering what we think we know about society and examining it in a systematic way can help us to better understand the world around us. This is what sociology is all about.

Research Methods: How Do Sociologists Study Society?

Sociologists conduct research to explain systematically how society operates and to create accurate and objective understandings of the social world. They use this information to answer questions about individual behaviour and the functioning of society as a whole. Sociologists, and other social scientists, have a variety of different research techniques that make up the sociological toolkit.

Sociology and the other social sciences include two major types of research: qualitative and quantitative (although many researchers use both types of methods). **Quantitative research** focuses on things that can be counted. This research examines how variables relate to one another and tests these relationships with statistical models. For example, a quantitative researcher interested in crime might look at records of all individuals arrested for committing crimes. They could record the age, sex, ethnicity, and incomes of each person arrested and use statistical models to generalize about what types of people are more or less likely to be arrested for a crime. Quantitative research focuses on measuring social phenomena and using statistical models to assess the patterns of association among these variables. Because these types of techniques require a large number of cases to test for the relationships between variables effectively, quantitative research often must examine relationships at a high level of abstraction.

One of the major ways that quantitative research is conducted is with surveys. **Survey research** involves giving questionnaires to a large number of people to learn about their characteristics, attitudes, or behaviours. The census, collected by Statistics Canada for the Government of Canada, is an example of a survey. In the census, Statistics Canada asks Canadians about themselves, including their age, gender, and income. We can use this data to examine many types of questions. For example, we can study if men make more money than women do, how this discrepancy might differ across professions, and if it is increasing or decreasing over time. This information is quite important for understanding gender inequality and for choosing a career.

Experiments are another major quantitative method. In experiments, the researcher looks at the effect of some factor, sometimes called a treatment, on individual behaviour. This approach involves comparing two groups—the experimental group and the control group. The experimental group is given the treatment, while the control group is not. If we wanted to understand the effect of money as an incentive for learning, we could bring two groups of students to a lab. We would have all the students learn a list of words. Half the students would be paid money for each correct word they learned; the others would receive nothing. Presuming that the students in each group were the same in terms of important characteristics (such as their intelligence and incomes), if the students who were told they would be paid for correct answers did better on the task than those not given this incentive, we would conclude that paying students to achieve was a useful way to increase performance. Garfinkel's **breaching experiments**, discussed earlier in the chapter, are a particular kind of experiment.

Qualitative research tends to examine a smaller number of cases in more detail and emphasizes social processes. Instead of focusing on counting phenomena, qualitative researchers often examine the meaning of action for individuals and groups. Sociologists use a variety of qualitative techniques. However, two major qualitative methods in sociology are interviewing and participant observation. **Interviewing** is a qualitative method in which a researcher asks each participant the same set of questions and records his or her responses. Interviews allow the researcher to ask questions that require longer answers and to ask follow-up questions to get more detail. For example, interviews might be quite useful if you are interested in how going to university or college changes the way young people see themselves. To understand how various elements of university life, such as living in a dorm, taking classes, joining campus groups, and making friends, can shape an individual's identity, you might want to give individuals more time to explain these complicated changes and to ask follow-up questions to probe for more information.

Participant observation (or **ethnography**) is another core qualitative method. The researcher actively engages with a group of individuals and works to understand their lives and experiences through intensive involvement with them over an extended period. For example, if you wanted to understand how young people pick up others in a bar, you might go to the same bar every Saturday night and watch as young men and women introduce themselves to one another. By observing them, you could see what types of men and women are the most likely to approach others and who are most likely to be approached. You could also see how couples interact with one another in the context of the bar. While you could, of course, survey or interview people about their pick-up practices, you could certainly learn additional things by watching these interactions happen in person. In fact, as a researcher, you might gain insights that the people had not considered (we might not be the best assessors of our own pick-up techniques).

These four core sociological methods are all good ways to understand the social world. No one method is the best method of research. All these techniques are simply tools. Just as it would be ridiculous to argue that a hammer is a better tool than a saw (it depends on whether you want to join things together or cut something in half), it does not make sense to argue which method is the best. Each method is more or less useful for understanding different types of phenomena, and it is always useful to have as many tools in our toolkit as possible.

Throughout this book, we will learn about studies using each of these core methods. A marginal icon 🔍 indicates the specific method. When you come across these studies in this class and others, think about how another method might be more or less able to answer the same questions and about what else we might learn through another method of research.

Summary

We began this chapter, and this book, by introducing sociology as a discipline focused on the systematic study of human society. Sociologists focus on three core areas of study: social inequality, social institutions, and social change. When looking at these three areas, sociologists aim to see general themes in everyday life, critically examine the familiar world around them, and understand how society shapes individuals while individuals also shape society. We have come to better understand these ideas through examining Harold Garfinkel's breaching experiments, Horace Miner's article on the Nacirema, Émile Durkheim's study of suicide, and C. Wright Mill's concept of the sociological imagination. Mills encourages us to connect our own individual biography with the history of society and to see how our personal troubles are connected to larger public issues. Through this lens of the sociological imagination, we can make sense of how society works and how the individual is connected to the society in which she lives. Finally, we learned some of the major qualitative and quantitative ways that sociologists conduct research—something that will be highlighted throughout the book.

Key Terms

breaching experiments 29
counterculture 5
culture 4
dominant culture 4
experiment 29
high culture 5
homophily 27
interview 29
participant observation (ethnography) 29
personal troubles 20
popular (or low) culture 5
public issues 20
qualitative research 29

quantitative research 28
religiosity 12
secularization 10
social fact 16
social inequality 5
social institutions 8
society 4
sociological imagination 20
sociology 4
subculture 5
survey research 29
types of suicide 17
visible minority 8

For Further Reading

Berger, Peter. 1963. *Invitation to Sociology*. Garden City, NY: Doubleday.

Collins, Randall. 1992. *Sociological Insight: An Introduction to Non-Obvious Sociology*, 2nd edn. New York: Oxford University Press.

Durkheim, Émile. 1897/1951. *Suicide: A Study in Sociology*. New York: Free Press.

Kuhn, Thomas S. 1995. *The Structure of Scientific Revolutions*. Chicago: University of Chicago Press.

Mills, C. Wright. 1959/2000. *The Sociological Imagination*. New York: Oxford University Press.

2 Becoming a Member of Society

CHAPTER OUTLINE

Introduction

Former British prime minister Margaret Thatcher famously declared, "There is no such thing as society . . . there are individual men and women, and there are families" (Keay 1987). This is a bold statement. While Thatcher was willing to admit that individuals do, at least, have families, she asserted that there is no higher level of organization or collectivity of importance beyond individuals and their immediate relatives.

Sociologists would argue that Thatcher missed something crucial. Most of us feel a loyalty to some society, be it our birthplace (e.g. Canada, China, Chile) or our ethnic group (e.g. Italian Canadians, Iraqi Canadians, Indonesian Canadians). We also feel society's constraints guiding our actions and beliefs. We can see that society shapes our behaviours, such as how to eat a meal or what to say to elders. But how does society enable and constrain our actions?

The Individual and Society

Émile Durkheim, whose study of suicide was discussed in Chapter 1, said that society soars above us, exerts a constraining influence on us, and regulates collective activity. At the same time, society enables us to understand the rules that govern social behaviour and helps us get along with one another. This chapter examines how we become a member of society through socialization, an important process that both facilitates our existence in society and constrains our actions. We will discuss how we, as individuals, come to fit into society through socialization, why this process is important, and how it happens throughout our lives.

Durkheim's first published article, excerpted in the following pages, was a review of the German sociologist Albert Schaeffle's *Bau und Leben des Sozialen Körpers: Erster Band*. Written when Durkheim was 27 years old, the article lays the foundation for his influential theory of society, which he continued to develop over the course of his career. The review begins with a discussion of Jean-Jacques Rousseau's ideas of human nature. A famous philosopher and political theorist, Rousseau (1712–1778) began his theories of human nature by thinking about what humans would be like before society existed. Rousseau (2011) thought that humans could exist before there were societies and that they would be "happy savages" who did not interact with one another or have language. He asserted that the stage before society existed, between the primitive idea of humans as brute animals and the modern extreme of decadent civilization, was the best stage in human development. He imagined that

> nothing is so gentle as man in his primitive state, when placed by nature at an equal distance from the stupidity of brutes and the fatal enlightenment of civil man. . . . The more one reflects on it, the more one finds that this state was the least subject to upheavals and the best for man, and that he must have left it only by virtue of some fatal chance happening that,

PHOTO 2.1 Émile Durkheim is often considered one of the founding fathers of sociology. Here he sits, perhaps pondering society!

for the common good, ought never to have happened. The example of savages, almost all of whom have been found in this state, seems to confirm that the human race had been made to remain in it always; that this state is the veritable youth of the world; and that all the subsequent progress has been in appearance so many steps toward the perfection of the individual, and in fact toward the decay of the species. (64, 74)

For Rousseau, society corrupts humans and leads to our "decay."

Durkheim fundamentally disagreed with these ideas for a number of reasons. First, he thought that humans cannot exist without society or develop without interaction with other humans. In addition, he argued that society is good for people because it helps them feel connected to one another. In fact, Durkheim's definition of what it means to be human is fundamentally social; he posited that part of what makes us human is our interactions with and dependence on one another. While Rousseau might have been able to imagine a world of humans before society, Durkheim claimed that it is impossible to have humans without society because society is what makes us human.

READING

Review of Albert Schaeffle, *Bau und Leben des Sozialen Körpers: Erster Band*

Émile Durkheim

I

. . . Society is not a simple collection of individuals, it is an entity which preceded those who comprise it at present and which will survive them, which acts more on them than they on it, which has its own life, own consciousness, own interests and destiny. But what is its nature? . . .

We are not dealing with man as Rousseau conceived of him—that abstract being, born to solitude, renouncing it only very late and by a sort of voluntary sacrifice, and then only as the issue of a well-deliberated covenant. Every man is, on the contrary, born for society and in a society. What proves this is not only his marvelous aptitude for defining himself within it and, consequently, for uniting himself with it; still more, it is his inability to live in isolation. What remains if, from the sum of our knowledge, our sentiments, and our customs we take away all that comes to us from our ancestors, our masters, and the milieu in which we live? We will have removed at the same time all that makes us truly men. But aside from all that thus reaches us from outside, there is within us, or so it appears, something intimate and personal which is our own creation; this is our ideal. This is, in the final analysis, a world in which the individual reigns supreme and into which society does not penetrate. Doesn't the cult of the ideal presuppose an entirely internal life, a spirit turned inward on itself and detached from other things? Is idealism not at once the most elevated and the most prideful form of egoism? Quite the contrary, there is no more powerful link for uniting men to one another. For the ideal is impersonal; it is the common possession of all mankind. It is toward this dimly glimpsed goal that all the forces of our nature converge. The more we are clearly aware of it, the more we feel that we are in solidarity with each other. This is precisely what distinguishes human society from all others; it alone can be moved by this need for a universal ideal. . . .

IV

There exists a social consciousness of which individual consciousness are, at least in part, only an emanation. How many ideas or sentiments are there which we obtain completely on our own? Very few. Each of us speaks a language which he has not himself created: we find it ready-made. Language is, no doubt, like the clothing in which thought is dressed up. It is not, however, everyday clothing, not flattering to everyone's figure, and not the sort that anyone can wear to advantage. It can adapt itself only to certain minds. Every articulated language presupposes and represents a certain articulation of thought. By the very fact that a given people speaks in its own way, it thinks in its own way. We take in and learn at the same time. Similarly, where do we get both the rules of reasoning and the methods of applied logic? We have borrowed all these riches from the common capital. Finally, are not our resolutions, the judgments which we make about men and about things, ceaselessly determined by public mores and tastes? That is how it happens that each people has its own physiognomy, temperament, and character. That is how it happens that at certain moments a sort of moral epidemic spreads through the society, one which, in an instant, warps and perverts everyone's will. All these phenomena would be inexplicable if individual consciousness were such independent monads.

But how are we to conceive of this social consciousness? Is it a simple and transcendent being, soaring above society? The metaphysician is free to imagine such an indivisible essence deep within all things! It is certain that experience shows us nothing of the sort. The collective mind (*l'esprit collectif*) is only a composite of individual minds. But the latter are not mechanically juxtaposed and closed off from one another. They are in perpetual interaction through the exchange of symbols; they interpenetrate one another. They group themselves according to their natural affinities; they coordinate and systematize themselves. In this way is formed an entirely new psychological being, one without equal in the world. The consciousness with which it is endowed is infinitely more intense and more vast than those which resonate within it. For it is "a consciousness of consciousness" (*une conscience de consciences*). . . .

We can, therefore, affirm that a collective consciousness is nothing but an integrated system, a harmonic consensus. And the law of this organization is the following: each social mass gravitates about a central point and is subject to the action of a directing force which regulates and combines the elementary movements. Schaeffle calls this force authority. The various authorities are subordinated one to another in their turn, and that is how a new life, at once unified and complex, arises out of all the individual activities.

Authority can be represented by a man or by a class or by a slogan. But whatever form it takes, it is indispensable. What would become of individual life without innervation? We would have chaos. Always and everywhere it is faith that provides the force of authority. If we obey when authority commands, it is because we believe in it. Faith can be freely given or imposed; with progress, it will no doubt become more intelligent and more enlightened, but it will never disappear. If, by the use of violence or trickery, it is suffocated for a time, either the society breaks apart or new beliefs are reborn without delay—beliefs less correct and worse than those which preceded them because they are less ripe and not so well tested, because, pressed by the necessity of living, we seize upon the first beliefs to happen along, without examining them. What's more, faith is nothing to be embarrassed about. We cannot know everything or do everything for ourselves; this is an axiom which every day becomes more true. It is, therefore, quite necessary that we address ourselves to someone else, someone more competent. Why stake our honour on being self-sufficient? Why not take advantage of the division of labour?

Authority is, nonetheless, a terrible thing if it is tyrannical. Everyone must be able to criticize it and need submit to it only voluntarily. If the masses are reduced to passive obedience, they will ultimately resign themselves to this humiliating role; they will become, little by little, a sort of inert matter which will no longer resist events, which can be moulded at will, but from which it will no longer be possible to wrest the slightest spark of life. Yet the basis of a people's force is the initiative of the citizens; it is the activity of the masses. Authority directs social life but neither creates it nor replaces it. It coordinates its movements, but presupposes their existence. . . .

A broad-minded individual can, almost at the same time, think one thing and its opposite; but he cannot at once act and abstain from acting. One must choose between two courses of action. It is, therefore, necessary that someone in the society be charged with choosing and deciding. Some authority is no doubt also necessary to coordinate individual intellects and sensitivities. But this authority has no precise organization; it is established here or there according to needs and circumstances. It is, moreover, only consultative. On the other hand, that authority which is charged with guarding the interests of the country is made to command and must be obeyed. That is why it is concentrated at certain determinate points of the territory and belongs only to certain clearly designated persons. In the same way, the principles which regulate collective activity are not indecisive generalizations or vague approximations but positive laws, the formulation of which is sharply delineated once and for all.

However, the role of the public is not purely passive submission: it participates in this activity even though it does not direct it. The laws do not owe their existence to the solitary will of the legislator. They are immanent in society just as the laws of gravity are immanent in physical bodies. The state does not create the former any more than the scientist creates the latter. Law and morality are simply the conditions of collective life; it is, therefore, the people who make them, so to speak, and the people who determine them just by living. The legislator states and formulates them. Moreover, he is not indispensable. If he does not intervene, the law nonetheless exists in the form of custom—half unconscious, it is true, but no less efficacious for that. It loses its precision, not its authority. Moreover, most collective resolutions are directly prepared and almost imposed by public opinion. Once a question becomes the order of the day, opposing sides are organized, engage in battle, and fight for the majority. To be sure, in well-constituted societies, this entire movement, once it arrives on the threshold of social consciousness, stops there. At that point, the organ of the will begins to function. But who cannot see that the matter has already been decided, just as the human will has already been predetermined, by the time that deliberation is cut off? It is the stronger side which triumphs.

But If we concede so large a role to individual wills, will they not impart to the social body all sorts of disordered movements? This fear would be legitimate if egoism was man's only natural sentiment. If everyone pursued only his personal ends, the society would be done for; torn in all directions, it would soon break apart. But at the same time that we love ourselves, we love others. We have a certain sense of solidarity (*Gemeinsinn*) which prevents us from ignoring others and which predisposes us without difficulty to devotion and sacrifice. Of course, if we believe that society is an invention of men, an artificial combination, then there is reason to fear that it will perpetually be torn apart. For so fragile a bond can be broken at any moment.

Man is free, Rousseau said, and yet everywhere he is in chains. If this is true, there is reason to fear that at any moment he will break his chains. But this savage individualism is not part of nature. The real man—the man who is truly a man—is an integral part of a society which he loves just as he loves himself, because he cannot withdraw from it without becoming decadent.

V

Social psychology can ultimately be reduced to the special study of the nervous system: it is a chapter of histology. Schaeffle passes from the tissues to the organs.

Every organ is formed by the combination of five functional tissues . . . These five elements are combined in different ways and in different proportions, but they are all necessary and are found everywhere. The Church, whose ends are not of this world, still has its economic organization; the shop and the factory have their intellectual lives. . . .

Social life does not take place in the penumbra of the unconscious; everything happens in broad daylight. The individual is not led by instinct; rather, he has a clear conception of the group to which he belongs and the ends which it is appropriate to pursue. He compares, discusses, and yields only to reason. Faith itself is but the free submission of an intellect which comprehends the advantages and the necessity of the division of labour. That is why there is something free and willed about the social organization. Societies are not, to be sure, the product of a contract, and they cannot be transformed from one day to the next. But, on the other hand, they are not the product of a blind necessity, and their history is not a fatal evolution. Consciousness are perpetually open to ideas and, consequently, to change. They can, therefore, escape their first impulse and modify the given direction, or, at any rate, if they persist in the original course, it is because they wished to. Finally, what sets human societies entirely apart is their remarkable tendency toward universality. Animal societies never extend beyond a tiny space, and colonies of a single species always remain distinct, often even enemies. Human societies (*les nations*), on the contrary, become more and more confused with one another; national characteristics, races, and civilizations mix and inter-penetrate. Already science, art, and religions have no country. Thus, little by little a new society emerges from all the isolated and distinct groups, a society in which all others will fuse, and which will end by one day including the entire human race. . . .

CRITICAL Reading Questions

1. Durkheim begins his article by stating that society is not simply a collection of individuals; society has "its own life, own consciousness, own interests and destiny." What does he mean by society's consciousness and interests? Give examples of both.

2. Durkheim suggests that individuals have very few ideas that are completely their own. What does this statement mean?

3. How do ideas become the great truths of science, dogmas of religion, or prescriptions of fashion? How do these ideas become accepted as "true"?

4. Where do laws come from, according to Durkheim?

Socialization

While Durkheim and Rousseau might have disagreed about what humans would be like without society, they agreed that humans are shaped by their society. Current sociological work remains focused on how this shaping occurs. How do we come to learn how to fit into society? We gain this knowledge through **socialization**, the lifelong process of learning our society's norms, customs, and ideologies. This process also provides us with the skills necessary for participating in society, thereby helping us both to fit into society and to develop a sense of identity and self.

Socialization is understood differently depending on your theoretical perspective. Sociology has three core theoretical perspectives that will be used throughout this book: structural functionalism, conflict theory, and symbolic interactionism.

Structural functionalism, which was particularly popular in the early years of the discipline, is mainly interested in explaining how society functions effectively. Structural functionalists such as Durkheim look at how different structures or institutions in society work together to create consensus and social cohesion. A common analogy, popularized by structural functionalist Herbert Spencer, is that the parts of society are like organs in the human body. Just as the body is made up of various parts that need to function together properly for it to be healthy, the parts of society need to work well together for society to run smoothly. The body's purpose is to survive; therefore, its subsystems (e.g. the respiratory system or central nervous system) have to co-operate and maintain the

HIGHLIGHT

What Are People Like without Society?

Most sociologists would argue that individuals could not exist without society. One way to see the importance of society for individuals is to look at situations where children have grown up without other people (i.e. outside society). Children who have had little contact with others from a young age—because they were lost or abandoned in the wilderness or were confined and denied social interaction by abusive adults—are referred to as feral children. Such cases are, fortunately, quite rare. Two cases, those of Anna and Genie, are famous examples of feral children. What can the experiences of these young women tell us about the importance of social interaction and socialization for children?

Born to a single, mentally ill woman in 1932, Anna lived in her grandfather's attic. She was not allowed to talk with anyone and had no social contact with others. When she was found at the age of six, she "had no glimmering of speech, absolutely no ability to walk, no sense of gesture, not the least capacity to feed herself even when the food was put in front of her, and no comprehension of cleanliness. She was so apathetic that it was hard to tell whether or not she could hear" (Davis 1940, 434). Because of this abusive and neglectful treatment, Anna was removed from her home and was placed in a special school, where she worked with a number of healthcare professionals and slowly learned to walk and talk. However, because of her poor physical health, she died from jaundice at 10 years of age.

Genie had been locked in a basement room from age 1 to 13. She was chained either to an infant potty or to a crib by her father. He discouraged her from making noise and made only barking, animal-like sounds in her presence. He forbade her mother (whom he also abused) from seeing or talking to her. When Genie was discovered in 1970, she was unable to speak, walk, chew solid food, or focus her eyes beyond 12 inches (Rigler 1993). With help from various professionals, she learned to walk, dress, and eat properly and she developed a limited vocabulary. However, she could never communicate beyond the level of a typical three- or four-year-old. Throughout the 1980s and 1990s, she was moved through a number of foster homes. In some of these homes, she experienced further abuse, which eroded the advances made in her speech and socialization. As of 2008, Genie was living in California in her sixth foster home, as a ward of the state, and was, again, speechless.

The stories of Anna and Genie highlight the fact that babies do not naturally become functioning adults. We learn how to walk, talk, and behave by interacting with others. In fact, we do not even develop physically without interaction with others—lack of such interaction partly contributed to the girls' poor physical health. Social interaction, then, is critical to both our social and physical development.

system as a whole. For the structural functionalists, society's purpose is also to survive and reproduce itself. All the subsystems of society (e.g. the family or the education system) must work well together to keep society running smoothly.

Structural functionalists consider socialization an extremely significant part of how society functions effectively. From this perspective, socialization is a top-down process. When children internalize social rules and values through socialization and learn to conform to the **roles** (the behaviours, beliefs, and norms performed in social situations) and expectations of society, they learn how to be a part of society. Talcott Parsons, who was a prominent structural functionalist and was highly influenced by Durkheim, discussed the importance of socialization in his book *Family, Socialization, and Interaction Process*. According to Parsons (1955), we must all learn society's rules and values; when we all understand them, there is social conformity and consensus. The more thoroughly members of society accept and adopt the dominant rules and values, the more smoothly society will function.

Structural functionalists see socialization as a process that helps to create solidarity. However, some sociologists argue that this perspective takes a rather rosy picture of how individuals are socialized into society. They claim that socialization is not always a harmonious process and that fitting into society as it is might not be such a great thing. **Conflict theory** sees society and socialization in a very different way. Instead of focusing on cohesion as the foundation of society, conflict theorists suggest that human behaviour and social relations result from the underlying conflicts that exist between competing groups.

Conflict theory was developed by Karl Marx, who understood society as being based on the conflict between social classes—particularly the clash between individuals who own the means of production (capitalists) and those who do not (workers). (We will learn more about Marx in Chapter 3, where we discuss social class and status.) Many later sociologists have extended Marx's theory and applied it to conflicts based on social differences beyond class. For example, you can use this theory to explain relations between men and women, between different ethnic or racial groups, or between rich and poor countries. A common theme in this perspective is that some individuals and groups have more power than others and the struggle over that power is a key element of social life.

Both conflict theorists and structural functionalists agree that socialization helps to re-create society as it is now. But whereas structural functionalists see this recreation as positive, conflict theorists see it as negative. They ask the following questions: Who has the power to shape how individuals are socialized? How does socializing people to fit into society as it is benefit some groups over others? How does socialization help or hinder social inequality?

RESEARCH METHOD

Interviews

Melvin Kohn's (1959) study of parental socialization and social class illustrates how conflict theorists might think about socialization. Kohn examined how parental social class shapes the values that parents encourage in their children. While most parents agree that children should be taught a general set of values, their opinions on the most important values are shaped by their social class.

Kohn (1959) interviewed 400 families—half from the working class and half from the middle class. He found significant differences when comparing the values emphasized by the mothers from these two groups. Middle-class mothers were more likely to focus on the importance of internal feelings and self-direction. For example, they tended to value empathy, happiness, self-control, and curiosity for both their sons and daughters. Working-class mothers, however, were more likely to emphasize the importance of values that lead to conformity among their children. For example, neatness and obedience were much more likely to be highly valued by working-class mothers than by middle-class mothers. Working-class mothers also had very different expectations for boys and girls. For boys, they valued school performance and ambition highly; for girls, they tended to emphasize the importance of neatness and good manners.

How do these findings affect our understanding of socialization? A conflict theorist would highlight how the different values could reinforce the pre-existing inequality between these two social classes. Valuing curiosity and happiness instead of conformity and obedience has real implications for the types of jobs that these children will be prepared to do. Most professional jobs require ambition and curiosity and could not be done well by someone who is merely obedient. The working-class mothers also perpetuate gender inequality by encouraging their sons to perform well in school and their daughters to be polite. These different traits could certainly lead to different career outcomes for boys and girls.

Like structural functionalists, conflict theorists tend to think of socialization as mostly a top-down process. Some sociologists argue, however, that children also learn from one another and from their shared experiences. For example, kids on the playground learn songs and games from one another. **Symbolic interactionism** examines how socialization is negotiated through our connections with other people. Instead of seeing people as receptacles of socialization (as, some might say, structural functionalists and conflict theorists do), symbolic interactionists claim that we actively participate in our socialization. Furthermore, this group of sociologists does not believe that meanings naturally attach to things. Herbert Blumer (1969) elaborated on this theory in *Symbolic Interactionism: Perspectives and Methods*. In this book, he explains that symbolic interactionism contains three basic premises: humans act toward things based on the meanings they assign to them; the meaning of things is derived or arises from social interactions between people; and individuals use an interpretative process to understand and modify meanings.

Socialization not only teaches us how to interact with one another, but it also helps us develop a sense of self. In fact, sociologists believe that even something as personal as our identity and sense of self comes from others. Our own name and our nicknames are given to us by others; we think of ourselves with words and categories used and created by others; and our sense of self is assembled and constructed from the reactions of others. Symbolic interactionists are particularly interested in how we develop a sense of self through socialization.

The Twenty Statements Test

Studying the self is very difficult for two reasons: most people find it challenging to describe their sense of self, and measuring the self is very hard to do. Kuhn and McPartland (1954) created a test to better understand how people think about themselves. Write down 20 answers to complete the sentence "I am. . .". Then, answer the following questions.

RESEARCH METHOD

Survey

- How many of the words you chose are physical characteristics, such as height, eye colour, or age? Kuhn and McPartland call these answers physical self-identifications.

- How many words are social characteristics? These social self-identifications include social roles that you play in relation to other people, such as student, daughter/son, employee, or sociology major.

- How many personality or reflective statements did you list? These personal self-identifications could include competitive, happy, or spiritual.

Note what percentages of your responses fall into each category. Do you think your responses are typical of people like you? Would you expect men and women to answer these questions differently? Why or why not?

Snow and Phillips (1982) conducted this test with university and college students in 1976. The following table shows how the students classified their answers, on average. Did the students answer differently than you did? Do you think most people today would respond the way the students did? Why or why not?

	Physical Self-Identifications	Social Self-Identifications	Personality Self-Identifications
Percentage of Responses	6.9	21.4	71.7

SOURCE: Snow, David A., and Cynthia L. Phillips. 1982. "The Changing Self-Orientations of College Students: From Institution to Impulse." *Social Science Quarterly* 63 (3): 462–76.

Two important symbolic interactionists who were interested in socialization and the development of self were George Herbert Mead and Charles Horton Cooley. Mead (1934) argued that children develop their sense of self through four **stages of role-taking**. In the first, or preparatory stage, children learn to use language and other symbols by imitating the **significant others** in their lives. Significant others are key individuals—primarily parents and, to a lesser degree, older siblings and close friends—after whom young children model themselves. Children in this stage simply copy other people's actions or behaviours. For example, when you smile at a baby, she will often smile back. Babies do not necessarily understand what you are doing or why; they simply imitate your actions. They also mimic their parents by wanting to hold the objects they see their parents using, such as keys, even though they don't understand how to use such items.

The second stage, in which children pretend to be other people, is called the role-taking stage. Children engage in role-playing games, thus exhibiting a number of behaviours they see performed by various people in their lives. For example, many children like to play house by performing the role of mother or father. In these roles, they might cook, clean, or care for children (in the form of dolls).

By about seven years of age, children move into the third stage, the game stage. Games are different from play because they involve complex rules and require children to take the role of several other people simultaneously. For example, if you are a pitcher in a baseball game, you have to think about what you are doing while simultaneously understanding what the batter, the first baseman, and the catcher are supposed to do. You also have to remember all the rules of the game, such as when a player is allowed to run from base to base, when a player is out, and when an inning is over. Understanding all these roles and rules at once is quite complicated.

The final stage involves taking the role of the generalized other. Children in this stage are able to think of how they generally appear to other people instead of how they appear to one specific significant other, such as their mother or father. Do people tend to think of you as shy, smart, or mischievous? Understanding how a generalized other will think of you requires that you be able to take the perspective of people you may not know well or at all.

Through all these stages, individuals learn about themselves and the society in which they live. This development is not a simple matter of learning a list of rules. Instead, children have to interact with other people in order to understand the roles that these other people play, their own roles, and how they should fit into relationships with others. They must negotiate how they see themselves and their place in society through interacting with other people.

Mead's theory highlights the importance of significant and generalized others in the process of socialization. Other theorists call these various groups of people **agents of socialization** because they guide us through the process of becoming a member of society and help to shape the people we become. There are many different agents of socialization, but we tend to consider the family, peer groups, the education system, the mass media, and religion to be the most important. Each of these groups teaches us how we are supposed to behave as adults in society, to perform different roles, and to function effectively within society and social groups. We sometimes learn from agents of socialization through direct teaching, such as when

PHOTO 2.2 What are these children emulating? Where might they have learned these behaviours? What other mimicking behaviours have you noticed among small children?

we learn math or reading in school. However, much socialization takes the form of latent learning, which occurs when we imitate role models, such as the people we see on TV.

Charles Horton Cooley (1902) said that our sense of self is assembled and constructed from the reactions of others. He called this process the **looking-glass self**. When we look at other people, they act as a mirror that helps us to understand how we appear. In essence, we look to others to better understand who we are.

The idea behind Cooley's theory is that we refine our sense of self in light of other's reactions. In fact, we develop a self-image based on the messages we get from others (as we understand them). This development occurs in three main steps: we imagine how others see us; we imagine how others judge our appearance; and we refine this appearance based on how we interpret such judgments. In other words, our understanding about who we are depends largely on how we see ourselves evaluated by others. Just as we see our physical body reflected in a mirror, we also see our social selves reflected in other people's reactions to us.

This process might become problematic. Consider a person with an eating disorder. While this person might be a normal and healthy body weight, she might see herself as overweight and might think that others also see her in this way, even when they do not. Other people are clearly valuable sources of information about us, but we are not always good at reading what they think about us. For example, when people laugh after we say something, we cannot always tell if they are ridiculing us or if they think we just told a funny joke. As a result, we could respond to a false impression of how we appear to others. In addition, it is not always a good idea to let other people's opinions of us shape how we feel about ourselves.

Cooley's concept of the looking-glass self has all the hallmarks of the symbolic interactionist perspective. It focuses on how we attach meaning to things (including ourselves) through interacting with other people. This theory is based on the idea that we learn about ourselves through interacting with others in society. Think of how these processes were not possible for Anna and Genie (see p. 39). Children who do not interact with others cannot learn to be a member of society or develop a sense of self.

Socialization is a lifelong process. In its earliest stage, called **primary socialization**, we learn how to become a member of society by discovering the attitudes, values, and actions that are culturally and socially appropriate. It helps to think of primary socialization as the process by which individuals learn the unwritten rules of a society, such as how to have a conversation. Family members are very important in this primary socialization as they are the first people we encounter in our lives.

Much of what we learn at this stage is not explicitly taught. Instead, it is learned through observation and imitation. For example, no one specifically tells us how far we should stand from other people when we talk with them. We learn this information by observing how our parents and other adults engage in conversations. We might not even be able to say the specific acceptable distance between conversation partners—is it 20 or 40 centimetres? But we can definitely tell if someone is standing too close or too far away. People who stand too close seem aggressive and rude. People who stand too far away seem uninterested and pompous. Primary socialization teaches us these types of unwritten rules.

Next, we go through **secondary socialization**, where we learn the appropriate behaviours and attitudes of a subculture within our larger society. For example, secondary socialization could occur when individuals join a soccer team. When they join this smaller group, they cannot simply apply the rules they learned in primary socialization. They certainly could not seek the kind of nurturing relationship they have with their parents from their team members. Along with having to alter their behaviour to fit into this new group, they also have to learn new behaviours that will mark them as a member of the group. For example, they learn how to interact with teammates, do team cheers, wear the uniform, and playfully trash talk the other team. The main difference between primary and secondary socialization is one of scale. Primary socialization

HIGHLIGHT //

Applying the Three Core Theories

One of the challenges of sociology is seeing social phenomena from different theoretical perspectives. Think of theories as lenses. If you put on sunglasses with purple lenses, the world looks purple. If you change to a pair with green lenses, the same world looks green. When you look at an issue through a structural functionalist lens, you will see it in a different way than if you were looking through a lens of conflict theory or symbolic interactionism. For example, each theory would understand prostitution in very different ways.

Structural functionalists often argue that, if a structure in society no longer serves a function, it will be eliminated. The fact that prostitution is a long-standing reality in society must mean, from a structural functionalist perspective, that it serves some function. For example, some suggest that prostitution is a way for people to earn an income if they are not able to work in other professions. You could also argue that prostitution might keep marriages together because spouses would not have to engage in long or numerous extra-marital affairs to satisfy their sexual interests (although this hypothesis is certainly controversial).

Although there is some logic to how structural functionalists might explain why prostitution exists in society, this theory misses certain things. Conflict theory would try to understand prostitution by asking how the practice is rooted in conflict, power, and inequality. What types of people are most likely to turn to prostitution to make money? Why are other forms of employment not available to them? What is the power relationship between the prostitute and the customer?

Symbolic interactionists would ask still different questions. How do prostitutes use their clothing and behaviour to indicate that they are sex workers without actually saying so (which is illegal)? How do prostitutes and customers negotiate the meaning of their sexual interaction and what that interaction means to each participant?

While these theories are presented as distinct and separate, sociological work often incorporates multiple theories when trying to understand the social world. For

Sex workers use various strategies and physical habits to communicate to potential clients that they offer sexual services. These visual cues are important because they allow prostitutes to attract customers without having to say explicitly that they are engaging in prostitution.

example, it is clear that prostitution is based on power inequalities and that the interactions between prostitutes and customers are negotiated. Moreover, prostitution serves certain functions for some members of society (while obviously serving as a dysfunction for others). The best way to understand the social world is to see how various theories and theoretical approaches can help us make sense of phenomena.

refers to the process of becoming a member of larger society, while secondary socialization refers to the process of socializing someone to be a member of a smaller group within that society.

Primary and secondary socialization usually occur during the early years of an individual's life. As we age, we have to learn to play new roles. Two types of socialization that occur later in life, when life changes such as entering a new profession or family situation require people to incorporate new roles, are anticipatory socialization and resocialization.

Anticipatory socialization refers to the process in which individuals "rehearse" potential roles that they may have to take on in the future, such as mother, father, or a new position at work. We can see this in Mead's theory of the development of the self—children play at being parents in order to rehearse for a role they might later perform. We continue to rehearse roles later in life. For example, medical students often practise interacting with patients to learn good bedside manner. Anticipatory socialization gives us a chance to prepare for a new role before we even begin to play it in real life. This way, we are ready for all the behaviours and responsibilities that the role will entail once we are expected to perform it.

People are also sometimes resocialized, whereby they take on new roles and discard former behaviours, attitudes, and values. In **resocialization**, we do not just add a new role to all the other roles we play, we replace an old role with a new one. For example, adults who retire face the prospect of resocialization when they have to discard their former patterns of working and the identity attached to their occupation and take on the new role of a retiree. Resocialization is sometimes a voluntary process, such as when a person has a religious conversion, moves to a new country, or joins the military. Other times, individuals are forced to change roles. Involuntary resocialization can include role changes such as leaving prison, being fired, or being forced to enter a rehab facility. A person does not have a choice about whether or not to leave prison, but he must discard the "prisoner" role for a new one in this situation.

The process of resocialization can be difficult, but many things can ease this transition. For example, ex-convicts sometimes move to halfway houses after they leave prison. Instead of having to manage on their own, they are assisted with reintegrating into society by having a structure that helps them to find work, re-establish an independent routine, and organize their time. They replace their old role as prisoners with a new role as regular members of society.

Helen Rose Fuchs Ebaugh (1988) both experienced and wrote about resocialization. Ebaugh was a Catholic nun who left the order and married later in life. This major transformation led her to think more critically about how people generally transition from one role to another. She argues that changing roles is a common experience in modern society. In earlier societies, individuals often spent their whole lives in the same town, with one partner, one job, and a very limited set of experiences. Today, people move from city to city, change jobs, partner and re-partner, and experience a multitude of other social role changes. To understand these changes, Ebaugh interviewed 185 people who were experiencing a wide range of social transformations, such as leaving jail, divorcing, leaving jobs as police officers or doctors, retiring, and changing sexual identity. Her research illustrated common stages of what she calls the "role exit process," regardless of the discarded role. Individuals move from being disillusioned with a particular identity to searching for alternative roles, experiencing a turning point that triggers their decision to exit a past role, and, finally, creating an "ex" identity.

RESEARCH METHOD

Interviews

How Do Toys Socialize Us?

Even things as innocuous as toys are important parts of socialization. You've probably noticed that many children play with gender-specific toys. Playing with dolls, action figures, or other gendered toys is part of how children become socialized into their gender roles. While sex (being male or female) is assigned at conception and involves physical trait differences, gender (ideas of femininity and masculinity) are learned. **Gender socialization** is the process of learning how to behave in a way that is consistent with the gender rules and norms of your society. The play that we engage in as children is an important part of our learning to act in ways that our society deems appropriately masculine or feminine.

For example, playing with a Barbie or G.I. Joe teaches children something about what a boy or girl should be like in society. Think about what you do with a Barbie doll. Mostly, you simply dress her up, change her hair, and buy her accessories, such as cars and dream houses. This play reinforces the idea that physical appearance is very important for women and that material goods can help them define and demonstrate who they are. Even the newer versions of Barbie, including Doctor Barbie and Astronaut Barbie, are only distinguishable from the original by clothing and accessories. Apparently, all it takes to be a doctor is a nice lab coat and a stethoscope!

What about G.I. Joe, the "real American hero"? Do you dress him and change his hair, as you do with Barbie? No—you can't even change G.I. Joe's outfit because it is painted on. Instead, you fight with him, reinforcing the idea that men should be aggressive and strong and that they become heroes by being violent and physically powerful. It is important to note that there is much discussion about Barbie's physical shape being an unrealistic ideal for women (which is certainly true) but little discussion of G.I. Joe's physicality, which is also unrealistic (unless you have no neck and an upper body like an upside-down triangle).

To see what toys today's children play with, visit websites such as Toys R Us (www.toysrus.ca) and then answer the following questions:

1. What types of things are these toys teaching?

2. Are boys and girls encouraged to play with different types of toys? What might be the impact of such encouragement?

3. Do toys that were traditionally gender neutral (such as Lego) now seem gendered? If so, how?

It is clear that socialization in general, and gender socialization in particular, starts very young. However, we are taught and retaught how to act according to our gender throughout our lives. Think about the beauty products that you use. Deodorant, shampoo, and razors are essentially the same across brands, but they are marketed to and priced for men and women very differently. Using the following websites as starting points, explore the Internet and your local drugstore to look at these different products and their advertisements.

Deodorant	Men: Axe (www.theaxeeffect.com)
	Women: Secret (www.secret.com)
Shampoo	Men: American Crew (www.americancrew.com)
	Women: Herbal Essences (www.herbalessences.com)
Razors	Men: Gillette (www.gillette.com)
	Women: Quattro (www.quattroforwomen.com)

Now answer these questions:

1. How are these products marketed to men and women differently?
2. What could these products and advertisements be teaching us about the ways women and men should act?
3. What products, if any, did you find that do not follow gender stereotypes?

Aging and Socialization

As we've discussed, the process of learning how to become a member of society and developing an identity is shaped by the society in which we live. While it may feel like growing up is just a natural biological process that remains unchanged, the culture and institutions of our society shape this process. The sociological study of aging focuses on both the social aspects of how individuals age and concerns with the general aging of the population as a whole. The experience of aging, and moving through the life-course, depends on social factors such as changes in public policies and programs, overarching cultural values, and norms. In addition, our understanding of the aging process, and its different stages, has changed over time.

One way that our cultural understanding of aging has changed is in the concept of childhood as a life-stage. The historian Steven Mintz (2004) explains that, prior to the eighteenth century, there was no idea of childhood as a separate period of life—children were just small adults in waiting. By the middle of the century, "childhood was increasingly viewed as a separate stage of life that required special care and institutions to protect it" (3). For example, child labour laws emerged to protect children, as a group, from the harsh realities of working in factories. During the nineteenth century, the growing acceptance of this new ideal of childhood was evident among the middle class. Young people began living in the parental home for longer periods and were expected to obtain more formal schooling. This period also saw an increasing consciousness about young people's emotional and psychological development. These changes culminated in the development of the concept of adolescence around the beginning of the twentieth century.

The notion of adolescence as a period between childhood and adulthood, in which young people learn about themselves and form identities, is a historical invention. Our modern conception of adolescence is that it is a period when young people are rebellious, prone to dramatic displays, and engage in violent and risky behaviour. Think of how television shows such as *Glee*, *Pretty Little Liars*, and *The Vampire Diaries* depict adolescents as impulsive, tempestuous, and emotional.

One of the first and most important scholarly works that challenged our current ideas about adolescence as a time of turmoil and stress was *Coming of Age in Samoa* (1928) by anthropologist Margaret Mead (no relation to our friend George Herbert). To see if our Western understanding of adolescence was a natural and biological phenomena or a social creation, she compared the transition to adulthood in American society with the same period in Samoan society. If young Samoans also experienced adolescence as a time of "storm and stress," Mead would have additional evidence that such turmoil was simply the natural experience of this period of life. However, if she found that adolescence was not such a stressful period in Samoa, it would lead us to question the assumption that young people will be dramatic, rebellious, and in search of their identity at this stage.

RESEARCH METHOD

Participant Observation

PHOTO 2.3 Margaret Mead (centre) poses for a photograph with two unidentified Samoan women. Through her research, Mead found that adolescent Samoan girls were free of the "teen angst" experienced by Westerners. Think about how teenagers are currently depicted in the Western media. Does the media tend to depict this period as one of stress and anxiety?

Mead (1928) engaged in participant observation in three villages in Samoa. She lived in these villages and (with the help of an interpreter) interviewed 68 young women between the ages of 9 and 20. She found that, compared with Western societies, adolescence in Samoa was not a stressful time. She attributed this finding to cultural differences between Samoa and Western countries. While Mead's book on this research was very popular and generally well received, some argued that she failed to recognize the change that occurred in Samoan society. Despite these concerns, the research highlights how something that appears natural could be a product of the culture and institutions of our society.

Popular movies and television shows often focus on the struggles that young people have when transitioning to adulthood. Movies such as *Failure to Launch*, with Matthew McConaughey and Sarah Jessica Parker, are based on a widespread modern social phenomenon whereby it takes longer for young people to be considered full adults and to take on full adult responsibilities.

Sociologists have long been interested in how individuals move through life stages and how larger institutions of society can shape these transitions. The following article examines the transition to adulthood in modern society. When reading this article, think about how our ideas about becoming an adult have changed, how these changes are related to larger historical transformations in society, and how these changes are experienced differently by women and men.

Furstenberg and colleagues highlight how larger social and historical changes impact young people's transition to adulthood. They also illuminate how these social changes can transform our understanding of what it means to be an adult. The article was based on data from the United States, but similar trends are occurring in Canada.

Growing Up Is Harder to Do

Frank F. Furstenberg, Jr, Sheela Kennedy, Vonnie C. McLoyd,
Rubén G. Rumbaut, and Richard A. Settersten, Jr

In the past several decades, a new life stage has emerged: early adulthood. No longer adolescents, but not yet ready to assume the full responsibilities of an adult, many young people are caught between needing to learn advanced job skills and depending on their family to support them during the transition.

In the years after World War II, Americans typically assumed the full responsibilities of adulthood by their late teens or early twenties. Most young men had completed school and were working full-time, and most young women were married and raising children. People who grew up in this era of growing affluence—many of today's grandparents—were economically self-sufficient and able to care for others by the time they had weathered adolescence. Today, adulthood no longer begins when adolescence ends. Ask someone in their early twenties whether they consider themselves to be an adult, and you might get a laugh, a quizzical look, a shrug of the shoulders, or a response like that of a 24-year-old Californian: "Maybe next year. When I'm 25."

Social scientists are beginning to recognize a new phase of life: early adulthood. Some features of this stage resemble coming of age during the late nineteenth and early twentieth centuries, when youth lingered in a state of semi-autonomy, waiting until they were sufficiently well off to marry, have children, and establish an independent household. However, there are important differences in how young people today define and achieve adulthood from those of both the recent and the more distant past.

This new stage is not merely an extension of adolescence, as has been maintained in the mass media. Young adults are physically mature and often possess impressive intellectual, social, and psychological skills. Nor are young people today reluctant to accept adult responsibilities. Instead, they are busy building up their educational credentials and practical skills in an ever more demanding labour market. Most are working or studying or both, and are developing romantic relationships. Yet, many have not become fully adult—traditionally defined as finishing school, landing a job with benefits, marrying, and parenting—because they are not ready, or perhaps not permitted, to do so. For a growing number, this will not happen until their late twenties or even early thirties. In response, American society will have to revise upward the "normal" age of full adulthood, and develop ways to assist young people through the ever-lengthening transition. . . .

Changing Notions of Adulthood

Traditionally, the transition to adulthood involves establishing emotional and economic independence from parents or, as historian John Modell described it, "coming into one's own." The life events that make up the transition to adulthood are accompanied by a sense of commitment, purpose, and identity. Although we lack systematic evidence on how adulthood was defined in the past, it appears that marriage and parenthood represented important benchmarks. Nineteenth-century American popular fiction, journalism, sermons, and self-help guides rarely referred to finishing school or getting a job, and only occasionally to leaving home or starting one's own household as the critical turning point. On the other hand, they often referred to marriage, suggesting that marriage was considered, at least by middle-class writers, as the critical touchstone of reaching adulthood.

By the 1950s and 1960s, most Americans viewed family roles and adult responsibilities as nearly synonymous. In that era, most women married before they were 21 and had at least one child before they were 23. For men, having the means to marry and support a family was the defining characteristic of adulthood, while for women, merely getting married and becoming a mother conferred adult status. As Alice Rossi explained in 1968: "On the level of cultural values, men have no freedom of choice where work is concerned: they must work to secure their status as adult men. The equivalent for women has been maternity. There is considerable pressure upon the growing girl and young woman to consider maternity necessary for a woman's fulfillment as an individual and to secure her status as an adult."

Research conducted during the late 1950s and early 1960s demonstrated widespread antipathy in America toward people who remained unmarried and toward couples who were childless by choice. However, these views began to shift in the late 1960s, rendering the transition to adulthood more ambiguous. Psychologists Joseph Veroff, Elizabeth Douvan, and Richard Kulka found that more than half of Americans interviewed in 1957 viewed someone who did not want to get married as selfish, immature, peculiar, or morally flawed. By 1976, fewer than one-third of a similar sample held such views. A 1962 study found that 85 per cent of mothers believed that married couples should have children. Nearly 20 years later, just 40 per cent of those women still agreed, and in 1993 only 1 in 5 of their daughters agreed. Arland Thornton and Linda Young-Demarco, who have studied attitudes toward family roles during the latter half of the twentieth century, conclude that "Americans increasingly value freedom and equality in their personal and family lives while at the same time maintaining their commitment to the ideals of marriage, family, and children." While still personally committed to family, Americans increasingly tolerate alternative life choices.

To understand how Americans today define adulthood, we developed a set of questions for the 2002 General Social Survey (GSS), an opinion poll administered to a nationally representative sample of Americans every two years by the National Opinion Research Center. The survey asked nearly 1,400 Americans aged 18 and older how important each of the following traditional benchmarks was to being an adult: leaving home, finishing school, getting a

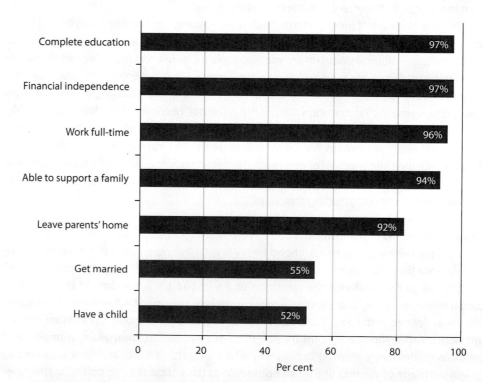

Per cent of Americans who say that an event is at least somewhat important to being considered an adult

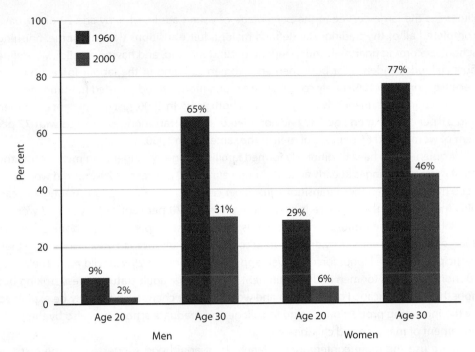

Per cent completing transition to adulthood in 1960 and 2000 using traditional benchmarks (leaving home, finishing school, getting married, having a child, and being financially independent)

full-time job, becoming financially independent from one's parents, being able to support a family, marrying, and becoming a parent.

The definition of adulthood that emerges today does not necessarily include marriage and parenthood. As shown in [the figure], the most important milestones are completing school, establishing an independent household, and being employed full-time—concrete steps associated with the ability to support a family. Ninety-five per cent of Americans surveyed consider education, employment, financial independence, and the ability to support a family to be key steps on the path to adulthood. Nonetheless, almost half of GSS respondents do not believe that it is necessary to actually marry or to have children to be considered an adult. As a young mother from San Diego explained, having a child did not make her an adult; instead she began to feel like an adult when she realized that "all of us make mistakes, but you can fix them and if you keep yourself on track . . . everything will come out fine." Compared with their parents and grandparents, for whom marriage and parenthood were virtually a pre-requisite for becoming an adult, young people today more often view these as life choices, not requirements.

The Lengthening Road to Adulthood

Not only are the defining characteristics of adulthood changing, so is the time it takes to achieve them. To map the changing transitions to adulthood, we also examined several national surveys that contain information on young adults both in this country and abroad. Using U.S. Census data collected as far back as 1900, we compared the lives of young adults over time. We also conducted about 500 in-depth interviews with young adults living in different parts of the United States, including many in recent immigrant groups.

Our findings, as well as the work of other scholars, confirm that it takes much longer to make the transition to adulthood today than decades ago, and arguably longer than it has at any time in America's history. [The figure above], based on the 1960 and 2000 US censuses, illustrates the large decline in the percentage of young adults who, by age 20 or 30, have completed all of the traditionally defined major adult transitions (leaving home, finishing school, becoming financially independent, getting married, and having a child). We define financial independence for both men and women as being in the labour force; however, because women in 1960 rarely combined work and motherhood, married full-time mothers are also counted as financially independent in both years. In 2000, just 46 per cent of women and 31 per cent of men aged 30 had completed all five transitions, compared with 77 per cent of women and 65 per cent of men at the same age in 1960.

Women—who have traditionally formed families at ages younger than men—show the most dramatic changes at early ages. Although almost 30 per cent of 20-year-old women in 1960 had completed these transitions, just 6 per cent had done so in 2000. Among 25-year-olds (not shown), the decrease is even more dramatic: 70 per cent of 25-year-old women in 1960 had attained traditional adult status, in 2000 just 25 per cent had done so. Yet, in 2000, even as they delayed traditional adulthood, 25-year-old women greatly increased their participation in the labour force to levels approaching those of 25-year-old men. The corresponding declines for men in the attainment of traditional adult status are less striking but nonetheless significant. For both men and women, these changes can largely be explained by the increasing proportion who go to college and graduate school, and also by the postponement of marriage and childbearing.

If we use the more contemporary definition of adulthood suggested in [the first figure]—one that excludes marriage and parenthood—then the contrasts are not as dramatic. In 2000, 70 per cent of men aged 30 had left home, were financially independent, and had completed their schooling, just 12 points lower than was true of 30-year-old men in 1960. Nearly 75 per cent of 30-year-old women in 2000 met this standard, compared to nearly 85 per cent of women in 1960. Nonetheless, even these changes are historically substantial, and we are not even taking into account how many of these independent, working, highly educated young people still feel that they are not yet capable of supporting a family.

The reasons for this lengthening path to adulthood, John Modell has shown, range from shifting social policies to changing economic forces. The swift transition to adulthood typical after World War II was substantially assisted by the government. The GI Bill helped veterans return to school and subsidized the expansion of education. Similarly, government subsidies for affordable housing encouraged starting families earlier. At the same time, because Social Security was extended to cover more of the elderly, young people were no longer compelled to support their parents. The disappearance or reduction of such subsidies during the past few decades may help to explain the prolongation of adult transitions for some Americans. The growing cost of college and housing forces many youth into a state of semi-autonomy, accepting some support from their parents while they establish themselves economically. When a job ends or they need additional schooling or a relationship dissolves, they increasingly turn to their family for assistance. Thus, the sequencing of adult transitions has become increasingly complicated and more reversible.

However, the primary reason for a prolonged early adulthood is that it now takes much longer to secure a full-time job that pays enough to support a family. Economists Timothy Smeeding and Katherin Ross Phillips found in the mid-1990s that just 70 per cent of American men aged 24 to 28 earned enough to support themselves, while fewer than half earned enough to support a family of three. Attaining a decent standard of living today usually requires a college education, if not a professional degree. To enter or remain in the middle class, it is almost imperative to make an educational commitment that spans at least the early twenties. Not only are more Americans attending college than ever before, it takes longer to complete a degree than in years past. Census data reveal that from 1960 to 2000, the percentage of Americans aged 20, 25, and 30 who were enrolled in school more than doubled. Unlike during the 1960s, these educational and work investments are now required of women as well as men. It is little wonder then that many young people linger in early adulthood, delaying marriage and parenthood until their late twenties and early thirties.

Those who do not linger are likely those who cannot afford to and, perhaps as a result, views on how long it takes to achieve adulthood differ markedly by social class. Less-educated and less-affluent respondents—those who did not attend college and those at the bottom one-third of the income ladder—have an earlier expected timetable for leaving home, completing school, obtaining full-time employment, marriage, and parenthood. Around 40 per cent of the less well-off in the GSS sample said that young adults should marry before they turn 25, and one-third said they should have children by this age. Far fewer of the better-off respondents pointed to the early twenties, and about one-third of them said that these events could be delayed until the thirties. These social class differences probably stem from the reality that young people with more limited means do not have the luxury of investing in school or experimenting with complex career paths. . . .

RECOMMENDED RESOURCES

Modell, John. *Into One's Own: From Youth to Adulthood in the United States 1920–1975*. Berkeley, CA: University of California Press, 1989.

Smeeding, Timothy, and Katherin Ross Phillips. "Cross-National Differences in Employment and Economic Sufficiency." *Annals of the American Academy of Political and Social Science* 580 (2002): 103–33.

Thornton, Arland, and Linda Young-DeMarco. "Four Decades of Trends in Attitudes toward Family Issues in the United States: The 1960s through the 1990s." *Journal of Marriage and the Family* 63 (2001): 1009–37.

CRITICAL Reading Questions

1. What are the trends for women and men making the transition to adulthood? How do our understandings of these trends depend on the definition of adulthood?

2. How has our idea of what it takes to be considered an adult changed? How is this definition different for women and men?

3. How have larger historical and government policy changes affected the transition to adulthood?

Grant and McFarland (2012) shed some light on how young Canadians transition to adulthood and how this process is shaped by struggles with employment and rising debt. Based on data collected by Vital Signs and the Community Foundation of Canada, they report that the jobless rate among people 15 to 24 years of age had reached a two-year high of 15 per cent in 2012. If we take a broader measure of youth unemployment to include all those people who are no longer looking for work because they are too discouraged by the job market, the number reaches 19.6 per cent, the highest level for any September in 15 years. In addition, among those who have found work, the availability of good, stable jobs with benefits is limited. In the first eight months of 2012, 28.6 per cent of 20- to 24-year-olds were working in temporary jobs. This figure represents a steady increase since 1997, when it was 21.5 per cent. These temporary jobs are much less likely to pay good wages, have benefits, or allow young people to become fully financially independent.

These employment numbers are problematic, partly because of the rising debt young people are incurring, particularly as a result of prolonged periods of schooling. The average household debt among Canadians between 18 and 25 in 2011 was $74,100. This amount is a record high compared with the $44,500 of average debt in 2002. Because of this high rate of debt and low rate of full-time employment, 42.3 per cent of Canadians in their twenties were still living with their parents.

While these numbers are certainly discouraging, it is important to note that young people's difficulties with transitioning to adulthood are, in part, structured by the changing social and economic nature of contemporary times. Concerns with integrating young people into the economy are not new. For example, in Chapter 1, we discussed the reintegration of young World War II veterans. Government programs that provided funding for education, housing, and other social programs were instrumental at alleviating the possible high level of unemployment among this group. Could our current government enact policies to assist young people in accessing higher education and entering the workforce?

As stated earlier, aging research is centrally concerned with different phases of the life-course and changes in our understanding of these phases. This research also examines the general aging of the population as a whole and its implications for society. It is clear that Canadian society is aging. In 1971, the median age for Canadians was 26.2 (meaning half our population was older and half was younger than this age). By 2011, the median age had risen to 39.9 years (Statistics Canada 2011c).

The fastest growing age group in the Canadian population is seniors. This trend is expected to continue for the next several decades, mainly due to low fertility rates and increasing life expectancies. The increase is so notable that, by 2051, about 25 per cent of Canadians will be over the age of 65 (see Figure 2.1).

The aging of the population as a whole has serious social and economic implications. The growth of the senior portion of the population will have major implications for both pensions and healthcare. For example, the Old Age Security (OAS) program and the Guaranteed Income Supplement (GIS), which are government benefits given to low-income seniors, cost $27.1 billion and $7.7 billion, respectively, in 2009 (Library of Parliament 2011). These figures are projected to quadruple by 2036. In terms of healthcare, an aging population can also be quite expensive. While seniors account for only 14 per cent of the population, they consume nearly 44 per cent of the annual healthcare costs. As the population grows, these costs will rise. With the increased size of the over over-65 group, there is also a decreased proportion of working-age individuals to support these social services. Figure 2.2 illustrates this changing age structure in Canada.

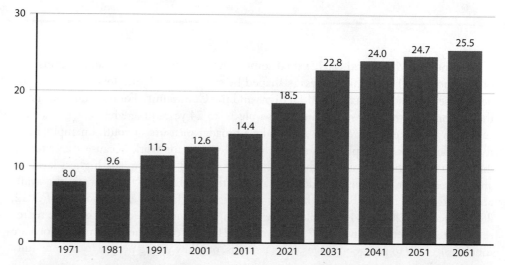

FIGURE 2.1 Percentage of population 65 years and over, Canada, historical (1971–2011) and projected (2012–2061)

NOTE: Population projections use a medium-growth scenario (M1) based on interprovincial migration trends from 1981 to 2008. For further information, see Statistics Canada. *Population Projections for Canada, Provinces and Territories (2009–2036)*. (Cat. No. 91-520 XIE).
SOURCE: Employment and Social Development Canada. 2015. "Canadians in Context—Aging Population." http://www4.hrsdc.gc.ca/.3ndic.1t.4r@-eng.jsp?iid=33.

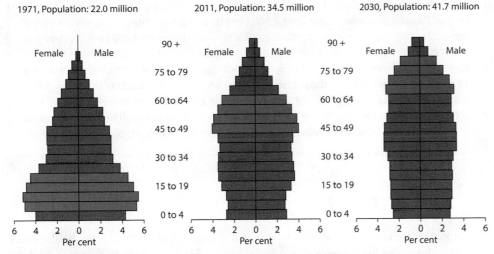

1971, Population: 22.0 million   2011, Population: 34.5 million   2030, Population: 41.7 million

FIGURE 2.2 The age structure of the Canadian population, 1971–2030 (projected)

SOURCE: Department of Finance Canada. 2012. "Economic and Fiscal Implications of Canada's Aging Population." http://fin.gc.ca/pub/eficap-rebvpc/report-rapport-eng.asp#Toc02.

HIGHLIGHT

From American Secretary to King Peggy—Taking on a New Role

Individuals play a variety of different roles in their daily lives. I am a daughter, a spouse, a professor, and a runner. Each of these roles involves a number of different behaviours, beliefs, and norms. Two roles in Peggielene Bartels's life include extremely different behaviours. In August 2008, Bartels was an administrative assistant who lived in a one-bedroom apartment in Washington, DC (Sesay and Kermeliotis 2013). One night, she received a call from her cousin who lives in a small village in Ghana. He told her that the previous king of Otuam, who was Bartels's uncle, had just died and she had been appointed the new king by the village elders.

Peggielene Bartels inhabits two very different roles depending on whether she is in the United States or in Ghana. Consider your own life: How does the role you play change depending on where you are and with whom you interact?

continued

Over only a few days, Bartels was transformed into King Peggy, the first female king of Otuam. She now reigns over 7,000 people. Since becoming king, she has lived two extremely separate lives. In Washington, she continues to work as a secretary at the Ghanaian Embassy. She says: "When I am in the United States I do everything by myself. I do my own laundry, I do my own cooking, I do my own driving and I do my own bed when I wake up in the morning" (Sesay and Kermeliotis 2013). In Ghana, how-ever, she is a "gold crown-wearing, scepter-holding king who lives in a refurbished pal-ace." Her subjects call her "Nana"—an honorary title given to royalty—and bow when they see her. The village residents cook for her and carry her from place to place.

The Performance of Social Roles

An important part of socialization is the process of learning to perform roles. Shakespeare thought a lot about how people play roles in society. In *As You Like It*, he wrote: "All the world's a stage, And all the men and women merely players." Canadian sociologist Erving Goffman (1922–1982) shared this view when he created the **dramaturgical perspective**, seeing social life as a stage and individuals as actors portraying roles.

Goffman is considered one of the most influential sociologists of the twentieth cen-tury. He believed that, when we meet others, we work to influence their impression of us (Goffman 1959). In essence, we want to manage the impression that we give to others. We can do this by changing our setting or appearance. While we try to shape our conver-sation partner's impression of us, she tries to form the most accurate impression possible. Like other symbolic interactionists, Goffman was interested in how individuals interact with others to create an impression and to gauge the impressions given off by others.

Goffman also believed that individuals in social interaction try to "smooth it out," to make it easier and more comfortable for everyone. In order to do this, individuals con-stantly work to avoid embarrassing themselves or others. The challenge is that the behav-iours that are appropriate or least likely to cause embarrassment differ across situations. For example, it is acceptable to yell and sing loudly at a football game but probably not in class. Therefore, we must learn to tailor how we act based on the situation. We must be able to take our stage of action into account when deciding how to behave and then modify our behaviour accordingly.

For example, if you have a job interview, you might practise parts of your perform-ance in advance, thinking of how you would answer questions that might be asked. You would certainly think about your clothing and appearance, as you want to look like you fit in the new workplace. If everyone wears a suit, perhaps you should too. If the interview is for a creative job, such as at an advertising agency or media company, you would perhaps choose to present a more artistic self. Clearly, you have to manage the impression you give, and the props you use to do so, based on the social situation.

In social interaction, as in the theatre, there is a front stage where we perform. This is where actors work to make a positive impression on others. But there is also a back stage that includes the private places where individuals do not feel they are being watched. Essentially, the back stage has no audience to try to impress.

The concepts of front stage and back stage are easy to see in many social settings. Think about restaurant workers. How are they different when they are front stage in the restaurant (where they are serving tables for patrons) versus back stage (in the kitchen or dishwashing area)? Workers tend to maintain a calm demeanour and a cheerful dis-position in the front of the restaurant, while they might grumble and spit in the food in the back stage. Although we often prepare for the front stage by thinking about what impression we hope to make, we are sometimes caught out of "character" when some-one unexpectedly sees us in our back stage. For example, a customer walking past a restaurant's kitchen to get to the washroom may see the servers in their back stage, perhaps having a drink or chatting.

The following reading is from Goffman's most famous book, *The Presentation of Self in Everyday Life* (1959). In this excerpt, Goffman explains the dramaturgical model, which has been very influential in many areas of sociology. As you read the following pages, consider what this theory tells us about social interaction and socialization. How do we learn to interact with others? How is this process like the theatre?

READING

The Presentation of Self

Erving Goffman

When an individual enters the presence of others, they commonly seek to acquire information about him or to bring into play information about him already possessed. They will be interested in his general socio-economic status, his conception of self, his attitude toward them, his competence, his trustworthiness, etc. Although some of this information seems to be sought almost as an end in itself, there are usually quite practical reasons for acquiring it. Information about the individual helps to define the situation, enabling others to know in advance what he will expect of them and what they may expect of him. Informed in these ways, the others will know how best to act in order to call forth a desired response from him.

For those present, many sources of information become accessible and many carriers (or "sign-vehicles") become available for conveying this information. If unacquainted with the individual, observers can glean clues from his conduct and appearance which allow them to apply their previous experience with individuals roughly similar to the one before them or, more important, to apply untested stereotypes to him. They can also assume from past experience that only individuals of a particular kind are likely to be found in a given social setting. They can rely on what the individual says about himself or on documentary evidence he provides as to who and what he is. If they know, or know of, the individual by virtue of experience prior to the interaction, they can rely on assumptions as to the persistence and generality of psychological traits as a means of predicting his present and future behaviour.

However, during the period in which the individual is in the immediate presence of the others, few events may occur which directly provide the others with the conclusive information they will need if they are to direct wisely their own activity. Many crucial facts lie beyond the time and place of interaction or lie concealed within it. For example, the "true" or "real" attitudes, beliefs, and emotions of the individual can be ascertained only indirectly, through his avowals or through what appears to be involuntary expressive behaviour. . . .

The expressiveness of the individual (and therefore his capacity to give impressions) appears to involve two radically different kinds of sign activity: the expression that he gives, and the expression that he *gives off*. The first involves verbal symbols or their substitutes which he uses admittedly and solely to convey the information that he and the others are known to attach to these symbols. This is communication in the traditional and narrow sense. The second involves a wide range of action that others can treat as symptomatic of the actor, the expectation being that the action was performed for reasons other than the information conveyed in this way. As we shall have to see, this distinction has an only initial validity. The individual does of course intentionally convey misinformation by means of both of these types of communication, the first deceit, the second feigning. . . .

Let us now turn from the others to the point of view of the individual who presents himself before them. He may wish them to think highly of him, or to think that he thinks highly of them, or to perceive how in fact he feels toward them, or to obtain no clear-cut impression; he may wish to ensure sufficient harmony so that the interaction can be sustained, or to defraud, get rid of, confuse, mislead, antagonize, or insult them. Regardless of the particular objective which the individual has in mind and of his motive for having this objective, it will be in his interests to control the conduct of the others, especially their responsive treatment of him.[1] This control is achieved largely by influencing the definition of the situation which the others come to formulate, and he can influence this definition by expressing himself in such a way as to give them the kind of impression that will lead them to act voluntarily in accordance with his own plan. Thus, when an individual appears in the presence of others, there will usually be some reason for him to mobilize his activity so that it will convey an impression to others which it is in his interests to convey. Since a girl's dormitory mates will glean evidence of her popularity from the calls she receives on the phone, we can suspect that some girls will arrange for calls to be made, and Willard Waller's finding can be anticipated:

> It has been reported by many observers that a girl who is called to the telephone in the dormitories will often allow herself to be called several times, in order to give all the other girls ample opportunity to hear her paged.[2]

Of the two kinds of communication—expressions given and expressions given off—this report will be primarily concerned with the latter, with the more theatrical and contextual kind, the nonverbal, presumably unintentional kind, whether this communication be purposely engineered or not. As an example of what we must try to examine, I would like to cite at length a novelistic incident in which Preedy, a vacationing Englishman, makes his first appearance on the beach of his summer hotel in Spain:

> But in any case he took care to avoid catching anyone's eye. First of all, he had to make it clear to those potential companions of his holiday that they were of no concern to him whatsoever. He stared through them, round them, over them—eyes lost in space. The beach might have been empty. If by chance a ball was thrown his way, he looked surprised; then let a smile of amusement lighten his face (Kindly Preedy), looked round dazed to see that there *were* people on the beach, tossed it back with a smile to himself and not a smile *at* the people, and then resumed carelessly his nonchalant survey of space.
>
> But it was time to institute a little parade, the parade of the Ideal Preedy. By devious handlings he gave any who wanted to look a chance to see the title of his book—a Spanish translation of Homer, classic thus, but not daring, cosmopolitan too—and then gathered together his beach-wrap and bag into a neat sand-resistant pile (Methodical and Sensible Preedy), rose slowly to stretch at ease his huge frame (Big-Cat Preedy), and tossed aside his sandals (Carefree Preedy, after all).
>
> The marriage of Preedy and the sea! There were alternative rituals. The first involved the stroll that turns into a run and a dive straight into the water, thereafter smoothing into a strong splashless crawl towards the horizon. But of course not really to the horizon. Quite suddenly he would turn on to his back and thrash great white splashes with his legs, somehow thus showing that he could have swum further had he wanted to, and then would stand up a quarter out of water for all to see who it was.
>
> The alternative course was simpler, it avoided the cold-water shock and it avoided the risk of appearing too high-spirited. The point was to appear to be so used to the sea, the Mediterranean, and this particular beach, that one might as well be in the sea as out of it. It involved a slow stroll down and into the edge of the water—not even noticing his toes were wet, land and water all the same to *him*!—with his eyes up at the sky gravely surveying portents, invisible to others, of the weather (Local Fisherman Preedy).[3]

The novelist means us to see that Preedy is improperly concerned with the extensive impressions he feels his sheer bodily action is giving off to those around him. We can malign Preedy further by assuming that he has acted merely in order to give a particular impression, that this is a false impression, and that the others present receive either no impression at all, or, worse still, the impression that Preedy is affectedly trying to cause them to receive this particular impression. But the important point for us here is that the kind of impression Preedy thinks he is making is in fact the kind of impression that others correctly and incorrectly glean from someone in their midst. . . .

There is one aspect of the others' response that bears special comment here. Knowing that the individual is likely to present himself in a light that is favourable to him, the others may divide what they witness into two parts; a part that is relatively easy for the individual to manipulate at will, being chiefly his verbal assertions, and a part in regard to which he seems to have little concern or control, being chiefly derived from the expressions he gives off. The others may then use what are considered to be the ungovernable aspects of his expressive behaviour as a check upon the validity of what is conveyed by the governable aspects. In this a fundamental asymmetry is demonstrated in the communication process, the individual presumably being aware of only one stream of his communication, the witnesses of this stream and one other. For example, in Shetland Isle one crofter's wife, in serving native dishes to a visitor from the mainland of Britain, would listen with a polite smile to his polite claims of liking what he was eating; at the same time she would take note of the rather rapidity with which the visitor lifted his fork or spoon to his mouth, the eagerness with which he passed food into his mouth, and the gusto expressed in chewing the food, using these signs as a check on the stated feelings of the eater. The same woman, in order to discover what one acquaintance (A) "actually" thought of another acquaintance (B), would wait until B was in the presence of A but engaged in conversation with still another person (C). She would then covertly examine the facial expressions of A as he regarded B in conversation with C. Not being in conversation with B, and not being directly observed by him, A would sometimes relax usual constraints and tactful deceptions, and freely express what he was "actually" feeling about B. This Shetlander, in short, would observe the unobserved observer.

Now given the fact that others are likely to check up on the more controllable aspects of behaviour by means of the less controllable, one can expect that sometimes the individual will try to exploit this very possibility, guiding the impression he makes through behaviour felt to be reliably informing.[4] . . . A specific illustration may be cited from Shetland Isle. When a neighbour dropped in to have a cup of tea, he would ordinarily wear at least a hint of an expectant warm smile as he passed through the door into the cottage. Since lack of physical obstructions outside the cottage and lack of light within it usually made it possible to observe the visitor unobserved as he approached the house, islanders sometimes took pleasure in watching the visitor drop whatever expression he was manifesting and replace it with a sociable one just before reaching the door. However, some visitors, in appreciating that this examination was occurring, would blindly adopt a social face a long distance from the house, thus ensuring the projection of a constant image. . . .

In everyday life, of course, there is a clear understanding that first impressions are important. . . . When the interaction that is initiated by "first impressions" is itself merely the initial interaction in an extended series of interactions involving the same participants, we speak of "getting off on the right foot" and feel that it is crucial that we do so. . . .

In stressing the fact that the initial definition of the situation projected by an individual tends to provide a plan for the co-operative activity that follows—in stressing this action point of view—we must not overlook the crucial fact that any projected definition of the situation also has a distinctive moral character. It is this moral character of projections that will chiefly concern us in this report. Society is organized on the principle that any individual who possesses certain social characteristics has a moral right to expect that others will value and treat him in an appropriate way. Connected with this principle is a second, namely that an individual who implicitly or explicitly signifies that he has certain social characteristics ought in fact to be what he claims he is. In consequence, when an individual projects a definition of the situation and thereby makes an implicit or explicit claim to be a person of a particular kind, he automatically exerts a moral demand upon the others, obliging them to value and treat him in the manner that persons of his kind have a right to expect. He also implicitly foregoes all claims to be things he does not appear to be[5] and hence foregoes the treatment that would be appropriate for such individuals. The others find, then, that the individual has informed them as to what is and as to what they *ought* to see as the "is."

One cannot judge the importance of definitional disruptions by the frequency with which they occur, for apparently they would occur more frequently were not constant precautions taken. We find that preventive practices are constantly employed to avoid these embarrassments and that corrective practices are constantly employed to compensate for discrediting occurrences that have not been successfully avoided. When the individual employs these strategies and tactics to protect his own projections, we may refer to them as "defensive practices"; when a participant employs them to save the definition of the situation projected by another, we speak of "protective practices" or "tact." Together, defensive and protective practices comprise the techniques employed to safeguard the impression fostered by an individual during his presence before others. It should be added that while we may be ready to see that no fostered impression would survive if defensive practices were not employed, we are less ready perhaps to see that few impressions could survive if those who received the impression did not exert tact in their reception of it.

In addition to the fact that precautions are taken to prevent disruption of projected definitions, we may also note that an intense interest in these disruptions comes to play a significant role in the social life of the group. Practical jokes and social games are played in which embarrassments which are to be taken unseriously are purposely engineered.[6] Fantasies are created in which devastating exposures occur. Anecdotes from the past—real, embroidered, or fictitious—are told and retold, detailing disruptions which occurred, almost occurred, or occurred and were admirably resolved. There seems to be no grouping which does not have a ready supply of these games, reveries, and cautionary tales, to be used as a source of humour, a catharsis for anxieties, and a sanction for inducing individuals to be modest in their claims and reasonable in their projected expectations. The individual may tell himself through dreams of getting into impossible positions. Families tell of the time a guest got his dates mixed and arrived when neither the house nor anyone in it was ready for him. Journalists tell of times when an all-too-meaningful misprint occurred, and the paper's assumption of objectivity or decorum was humorously discredited. Public servants tell of times a client ridiculously misunderstood form instructions, giving answers which implied an unanticipated and bizarre definition of the situation.[7] Seamen, whose home away from home is rigorously he-man, tell stories of coming back home and inadvertently asking mother to "pass the fucking butter."[8] Diplomats tell of the time a near-sighted queen asked a republican ambassador about the health of his king.[9]

To summarize, then, I assume that when an individual appears before others he will have many motives for trying to control the impression they receive of the situation. . . .

NOTES

1. Here I owe much to an unpublished paper by Tom Burns of the University of Edinburgh. He presents the argument that in all interaction a basic underlying theme is the desire of each participant to guide and control the responses made by the others present. A similar argument has been advanced by Jay Haley in a recent unpublished paper, but in regard to a special kind of control, that having to do with defining the nature of the relationship of those involved in the interaction.

2. Willard Waller, "The Rating and Dating Complex," *American Sociological Review*, 2, 730.

3. William Sansom, *A Contest of Ladies* (London: Hograth, 1956), 230–31.

4. The widely read and rather sound writings of Stephen Potter are concerned in part with signs that can be engineered to give a shrewd observer the apparently incidental cues he needs to discover concealed virtues the gamesman does not in fact possess.

5. This role of the witness in limiting what it is the individual can be has been stressed by Existentialists, who see it as a basic threat to individual freedom. See Jean-Paul Sartre, *Being and Nothingness*, trans. by Hazel E. Barnes (New York: Philosophical Library, 1956).

6. Goffman, op. cit., pp. 319–27.

7. Peter Blau, "Dynamics of Bureaucracy" (PhD dissertation, Department of Sociology, Columbia University, forthcoming, University of Chicago Press), pp. 127–29.

8. Walter M. Beattie, Jr., "The Merchant Seaman" (unpublished MA Report, Department of Sociology, University of Chicago, 1950), p. 35.

9. Sir Frederick Posonby, *Recollections of Three Reigns* (London: Eyre & Spottiswoode, 1951).

CRITICAL Reading Questions

1. What is Goffman's distinction between expressions that one gives and expressions that one gives off? What is Goffman referring to when he uses the terms *face-to-face interaction*, *projective techniques*, *defensive practices*, and *protective practices/tact*?

2. a. Suppose you are about to visit or e-mail your professor to ask a question about the upcoming exam. In terms of the expressions you give and expressions you give off, how could you ensure that your professor infers that you are a smart student?

   b. Suppose you are preparing for a date that you have been looking forward to for several days. Your goal is to have fun and to ensure that your partner infers that you are a cool person. How might you accomplish this goal?

   c. Is there a difference between how you would act in each situation? Why or why not? Which is the "real" you?

3. Goffman seems to imply that individuals have considerable control over how others perceive them and that these perceptions are largely the result of face-to-face interactions. What are some other factors that might influence the perceptions others have of an individual? For example, how might power, inequalities, or history influence perceptions?

Summary

In this chapter, we have learned how socialization helps individuals become members of society. Socialization is important because it is the process of both learning the rules and norms of society and developing a sense of identity. Sociologists from different theoretical traditions look at this process in a variety of ways. Structural functionalists, such as Durkheim and Parsons, tend to focus on how socialization helps society run smoothly and creates social cohesion. Conflict theorists, such as Marx, focus on how socialization may reinforce the inequality in society. Symbolic interactionists, such as George Herbert Mead, Cooley, and Goffman, see socialization as something that is negotiated throughout social life.

Socialization is generally understood as a complicated, lifelong process that is shaped by a variety of individuals and institutions. For example, many different agents of socialization, such as the family and peer groups, help to form the people we become as adults. This process is also shaped by the culture and history of our society as a whole. Looking at the invention of adolescence and the changing transition to adulthood highlights how our understanding of the way that individuals become adults has changed.

Key Terms

agents of socialization 42

anticipatory socialization 45

conflict theory 40

dramaturgical perspective 56

gender socialization 46

looking-glass self 43

primary socialization 43

resocialization 45

roles 39

secondary socialization 43

significant others 42

socialization 38

stages of role-taking 42

structural functionalism 38

symbolic interactionism 40

For Further Reading

Blumer, Herbert. 1969. *Symbolic Interactionism: Perspective and Method.* Englewood Cliffs, NJ: Prentice-Hall.

Cooley, Charles Horton. 1902. *Human Nature and the Social Order.* New York: Scribner's.

Goffman, Erving. 1959. *The Presentation of Self in Everyday Life.* New York: Anchor Books.

Mead, George Herbert. 1934. *Mind, Self, and Society.* Chicago: University of Chicago Press.

Parsons, Talcott. 1955. *Family, Socialization, and Interaction Process.* Glencoe, IL: Free Press.

PART II

Social Inequality

Social Inequality and Social Class

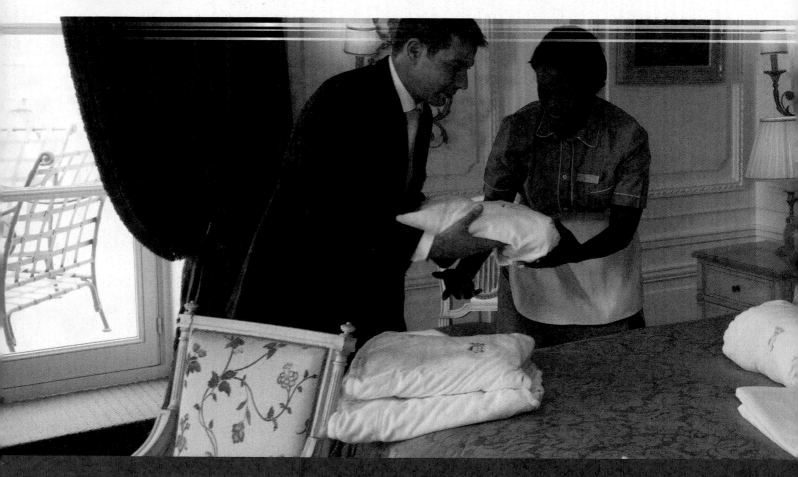

Introduction

Do you think of yourself as middle class, working class, upper class, or some other group? If you are like most Canadians, you see yourself as middle class. In fact, 56 per cent of Canadians describe themselves this way. An additional 18 per cent say they are upper-middle class and 19 per cent say they are lower-middle class (Environics 2012). Considering these numbers, what does it mean to be middle class in Canadian society? Why do people choose to describe themselves as members of this class?

In this chapter, we will explore what two of the founders of sociology—Karl Marx and Max Weber—thought about social class. We will also examine the significance of social status and social mobility in Canada. Social class and social status are important because they shape our opportunities, from the neighbourhoods we grow up in to the schools we attend and the types of jobs we get. While most Canadians do not think much about the matter of social class, it shapes the kind of life we lead.

Karl Marx and Social Class

Karl Marx (1818–1883) is one of the most important figures in the development of sociology and, as mentioned in Chapter 2, is the founder of conflict theory. He is also a significant figure outside sociology; his ideas shaped many historical events and are still debated today. Governments espousing Marxist ideology came to power in the Union of Soviet Socialist Republics (USSR or Soviet Union) in 1922 and the People's Republic of China in 1949. Marx's writings also inspired the rise of many of the world's labour unions and workers' parties, which advocate for workers' rights and safer working conditions.

It may surprise some that Marx's parents were middle class and relatively wealthy. Marx studied at the University of Bonn and the University of Berlin. In 1843, he moved to Paris, where he met Friedrich Engels. He and Engels collaborated on their work throughout their lives. In 1849, Marx was exiled and moved to London with his family. His work was both academic and political. He also campaigned for socialism and in worker's groups, such as the International Workingmen's Association.

Marx argued that the core struggle in all societies is **class struggle**: conflicts between those who own the means of production (capitalists) and those who simply own their own labour power (workers). He called capitalism, the economic system in which businesses are privately owned and goods are sold on the market for profit, the "dictatorship of the **bourgeoisie**." For Marx, capitalism is controlled and run by a small group of wealthy business owners. He argued that, like all previous economic systems, it is founded on internal tensions that make it unsustainable. He predicted that capitalism would eventually be replaced by socialism, an alternative economic system featuring a collective ownership of the means of production. In socialism, power is held by the working class. Marx referred to this system as the "dictatorship of the **proletariat**" or a "workers' democracy." He also theorized that socialism would be replaced by communism, a completely classless society (Marx and Engels 1848).

Marx actively fought for the implementation of socialism, arguing that academics should play an important part in toppling capitalism and causing revolutionary social change. In fact,

PHOTO 3.1 Karl Marx's work encourages us to think critically about how social class shapes our lives and society as a whole.

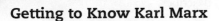

HIGHLIGHT

Getting to Know Karl Marx

- While he was a student at the University of Bonn, Marx was a member of the Poets' Club and a co-president of the Trier Tavern Club drinking society.

- In university, Marx was in a duel with another student.

- Marx married Jenny von Westphalen, a Prussian baroness, in 1843. Their relationship was controversial because of their different social classes and ethnic origins. They had seven children and, by all accounts, a very happy marriage.

- In 1837, Marx wrote a short novel, a play, and a series of love poems to his wife. All remain unpublished.

in the final line of his *Theses on Feuerbach*, a work first published in 1888 and co-edited with Engels, Marx (2004; emphasis added) says that "the philosophers have only *interpreted* the world, in various ways. The point, however, is to *change* it." Marx sought to be part of that change by promoting the development of a socialist economic system.

Marx's view of the world emphasizes the economy's role in social life. Marx argued that historical periods are distinguished by the mode of production of goods and services that dominates the time. The mode of production is the way that we make things in our society. For example, in early feudalism (i.e. the seventeenth and eighteenth centuries) the nobility owned land, including farms, homes, and villages, and peasants worked the land, mainly using human and animal energy. The mode of production creates the distinctions and relationships between classes in a society. The feudal system led to certain relationships between the nobility and the peasantry. Peasants were tied to their landlords, who gave them a place to live and protection in exchange for their labour.

Classes, for Marx, are groups of people who play different roles in the productive system. Capitalism has two main classes: the bourgeoisie (capitalist) and the proletariat (workers). The bourgeoisie are the people who own the means of production and **property**, which is any resource that can be used to produce things of value and to generate wealth. Land is an important type of property because it allows the owner to grow food or raise animals that can be sold. Other types of property include businesses or factories, in which an owner can produce goods such as shoes, clothing, or other products to sell. Essentially, the bourgeoisie owns the means of producing more wealth.

The proletariat does not own the means of production. Members of the proletariat own only their capacity to labour (either physically or mentally), which they must sell to the capitalist. Thus, the proletariat must work in the capitalists' factories or on their farms to make a wage (a fraction of the profits from the bourgeoisie's sales, set by the bourgeoisie) to survive.

Marx argued that classes are relational and are defined by their relationship to both the means of production and to each other. Capitalists cannot exist without workers to labour in their factories; at the same time, workers must have somewhere to sell their labour to make money to live. However the relationship between these two groups is coercive by nature. Workers are beholden to the capitalist, who can pay them low wages and give them poor working conditions. Marx argued that capitalism functions and continues to exist through this perpetual exploitation of the worker's labour and subsequent oppression.

Class Struggles

Despite the power differentiation between the bourgeoisie and proletariat, the two classes clearly depend on one another. The capitalist cannot have a functioning factory or farm without workers. And the worker needs the capitalist to make a wage in order to live. But the relationship between the two is by nature unequal, which inevitably leads to class struggles. As Marx (Marx and Engels 1848, 57) describes,

> The history of all hitherto existing society is the history of class struggles. Freeman and slave, patrician and plebian, lord and serf, guildmaster and journeyman, in a word, oppressor and oppressed, stood in constant opposition to one another, carried on an uninterrupted, now hidden, now open fight, a fight that each time ended, either in a revolutionary reconstitution of society at large, or in the common ruin of the contending classes.

According to Marx, class struggles exist because the classes want different things and have different interests. For example, capitalists want to make as much money as they can from their factories or farms. They must pay wages so that workers will be able to live and come back to work. However, they want to extract the most **surplus value**—the excess value that workers produce beyond the cost of their labour—from the workers that they can. In other words, surplus value is the amount of money that capitalists get to keep after paying their workers' wages. It is not surprising that capitalists want as much of this surplus as possible, which means keeping wages low, having workers work quickly, and setting long work hours. As Marx (1867/2000, 218) said, "the rate of surplus value is . . . an exact expression of the degree of exploitation of labour power by capital, or of the labourer by the capitalist."

Workers want very different things than capitalists do. They want to make a good wage that allows them to live and support their families. They want to work under safe conditions and for decent hours. These desires can conflict with the capitalist's attempt to make large profits, which could include creating more cost-effective yet more dangerous workplaces.

Marx wrote many academic books about the problems created by capitalism and about a possible socialist future. As discussed earlier, he was also interested in helping to overthrow capitalism. He worked to help encourage a worker's revolution by explaining the perils of capitalism and the benefits of socialist and communist systems to a wider audience. In 1848, the Communist League commissioned Marx and Engels to write a short pamphlet outlining capitalism's main issues. The following is an excerpt from the result, *The Communist Manifesto*.

READING

Manifesto of the Communist Party

Karl Marx and Friedrich Engels

I. Bourgeois and Proletarians[1]

. . . In the earlier epochs of history, we find almost everywhere a complicated arrangement of society into various orders, a manifold gradation of social rank. In ancient Rome we have patricians, knights, plebeians, slaves; in the Middle Ages, feudal lords, vassals, guild-masters, journeymen, apprentices, serfs; in almost all of these classes, again, subordinate gradations.

The modern bourgeois society that has sprouted from the ruins of feudal society has not done away with clash antagonisms. It has but established new classes, new conditions of oppression, new forms of struggle in place of the old ones.

Our epoch, the epoch of the bourgeoisie, possesses, however, this distinctive feature: it has simplified the class antagonisms: Society as a whole is more and more splitting up into two great hostile camps, into two great classes directly facing each other: Bourgeoisie and Proletariat.

From the serfs of the Middle Ages sprang the charted burghers of the earliest towns. From these burgesses the first elements of the bourgeoisie were developed.

The discovery of America, the rounding of the Cape, opened up fresh ground for the rising bourgeoisie. The East-Indian and Chinese markets, the colonization of America, trade with the colonies, the increase in the means of exchange and in commodities generally, gave to commerce, to navigation, to industry, an impulse never before known, and thereby, to the revolutionary element in the tottering feudal society, a rapid development.

The feudal system of industry, under which industrial production was monopolized by closed guilds, now no longer sufficed for the growing wants of the new markets. The manufacturing system took its place. The guild-masters were pushed on one side by the manufacturing middle class; division of labour between the different corporate guilds vanished in the face of division of labour in each single workshop.

Meantime the markets kept ever growing, the demand ever rising. Even manufacture no longer sufficed. Thereupon, steam and machinery revolutionized industrial production. The place of manufacture was taken by the giant, Modern Industry, the place of the industrial middle class, by industrial millionaires, the leaders of whole industrial armies, the modern bourgeois.

Modern Industry has established the world market, for which the discovery of America paved the way. This market has given an immense development to commerce, to navigation, to communication by land. This development has, in its turn, reacted on the extension of industry; and in proportion as industry, commerce, navigation, railways extended, in the same proportion the bourgeoisie developed, increased its capital, and pushed into the background every class handed down from the Middle Ages.

We see, therefore, how the modern bourgeoisie is itself the product of a long course of development, of a series of revolutions in the modes of production and of exchange.

Each step in the development of the bourgeoisie was accompanied by a corresponding political advance of that class. An oppressed class under the sway of the feudal nobility, an armed and self-governing association in the medieval commune;[2] here independent urban republic (as in Italy and Germany), there taxable "third estate" of the monarchy (as in France), afterwards, in the period of manufacture proper, serving either the semi-feudal or the absolute monarchy as a counterpoise against the nobility, and, in fact, cornerstone of the great monarchies in general, the bourgeoisie has at last, since the establishment of Modern Industry and of the world market, conquered for itself, in the modern representative State, exclusive political sway. The executive of the modern State is but a committee for managing the common affairs of the whole bourgeoisie.

The bourgeoisie, historically, has played a most revolutionary part.

The bourgeoisie, wherever it has got the upper hand, has put an end to all feudal, patriarchal, idyllic relations. It has pitilessly torn asunder the motley feudal ties that bound man to his "natural superiors," and has left remaining no other nexus between man and man than naked self-interest, than callous "cash payment." It has drowned the most heavenly ecstasies of religious fervour, of chivalrous enthusiasm, of philistine sentimentalism, in the icy water of egotistical calculation. It has resolved personal worth into exchange value, and in place of the numberless indefeasible chartered freedoms, has set up that single, unconscionable freedom—Free Trade. In one word, for exploitation, veiled by religious and political illusions, it has substituted naked, shameless, direct, brutal exploitation.

The bourgeoisie has stripped of its halo every occupation hitherto honoured and looked up to with reverent awe. It has converted the physician, the lawyer, the priest, the poet, the man of science, into its paid wage-labourers.

The bourgeoisie has torn away from the family its sentimental veil, and has reduced the family relation to a mere money relation. . . .

The bourgeoisie cannot exist without constantly revolutionizing the instruments of production, and thereby the relations of production, and with them the whole relations of society. Conservation of the old modes of production in unaltered form, was, on the contrary, the first condition of existence for all earlier industrial classes. Constant revolutionizing of production, uninterrupted disturbance of all social conditions, everlasting uncertainty and agitation distinguish the bourgeois epoch from all earlier ones. All fixed, fast-frozen relations, with their train of ancient and venerable prejudices and opinions, are swept away, all new-formed ones become antiquated before they can ossify. All that is solid melts into air, all that is holy is profaned, and man is at last compelled to face with sober senses, his real conditions of life, and his relations with his kind.

The need of a constantly expanding market for its products chases the bourgeoisie over the whole surface of the globe. It must nestle everywhere, settle everywhere, establish connections everywhere. . . .

The bourgeoisie, by the rapid improvement of all instruments of production, by the immensely facilitated means of communication, draws all, even the most barbarian, nations into civilization. The cheap prices of its commodities are the heavy artillery with which it batters down all Chinese walls, with which it forces the barbarians' intensely obstinate hatred of foreigners to capitulate. It compels all nations, on pain of extinction, to adopt the bourgeois mode of production; it compels them to introduce what it calls civilization into their midst, i.e., to become bourgeois themselves. In one word, it creates a world after its own image.

The bourgeoisie has subjected the country to the rule of the towns. It has created enormous cities, has greatly increased the urban population as compared with the rural, and has thus rescued a considerable part of the population from the idiocy of rural life. Just as it has made the country dependent on the towns, so it has made barbarian and semi-barbarian countries dependent on the civilized ones, nations of peasants on nations of bourgeois, the East on the West.

The bourgeoisie keeps more and more doing away with the scattered state of the population, of the means of production, and of property. It has agglomerated population, centralized means of production, and has concentrated property in a few hands. The necessary consequence of this was political centralization. Independent, or but loosely connected provinces, with separate interests, laws, governments, and systems of taxation, became lumped together into one nation, with one government, one code of laws, one national class-interest, one frontier, and one customs-tariff.

The bourgeoisie, during its rule of scarce 100 years, has created more massive and more colossal productive forces than have all preceding generations together. Subjection of Nature's forces to man, machinery, application of chemistry to industry and agriculture, steam navigation, railways, electric telegraphs, clearing of whole continents for cultivation, canalization of rivers, whole populations conjured out of the ground—what earlier century had even a presentiment that such productive forces slumbered in the lap of social labour?

We see then: the means of production and of exchange, on whose foundation the bourgeoisie built itself up, were generated in feudal society. At a certain stage in the development of these means of production and of exchange, the conditions under which feudal society produced and exchanged, the feudal organization of agriculture and manufacturing industry, in one word, the feudal relations of property became no longer compatible with the already developed productive forces; they became so many fetters. They had to be burst asunder; they were burst asunder.

Into their place stepped free competition, accompanied by a social and political constitution adapted to it, and by the economical and political sway of the bourgeois class. . . .

The weapons with which the bourgeoisie felled feudalism to the ground are now turned against the bourgeoisie itself.

But not only has the bourgeoisie forged the weapons that bring death to itself; it has also called into existence the men who are to wield those weapons—the modern working class—the proletarians.

In proportion as the bourgeoisie, i.e., capital, is developed, in the same proportion is the proletariat, the modern working class, developed—a class of labourers, who live only so long as they find work, and who find work only so long as their labour increases capital. These labourers, who must sell themselves piecemeal, are a commodity, like every other article of commerce, and are consequently exposed to all the vicissitudes of competition, to all the fluctuations of the market.

Owing to the extensive use of machinery and to division of labour, the work of the proletarians has lost all individual character, and consequently, all charm for the workman. He becomes an appendage of the machine, and it is only the most simple, most monotonous, and most easily acquired knack, that is required of him. Hence, the cost of production of a workman is restricted, almost entirely, to the means of subsistence that he requires for his maintenance, and for the propagation of his race. But the price of a commodity, and therefore also of labour,[3] is equal to its cost of production. In proportion, therefore, as the repulsiveness of the work increases, the wage decreases. Nay more, in proportion as the use of machinery and division of labour increases, in the same proportion the burden of toil also increases, whether by prolongation of the working hours, by increase of the work exacted in a given time or by increased speed of the machinery, etc.

Modern industry has converted the little workshop of the patriarchal master into the great factory of the industrial capitalist. Masses of labourers, crowded into the factory, are organized like soldiers. As privates of the industrial army they are placed under the command of a perfect hierarchy of officers and sergeants. Not only are they slaves of the bourgeois class, and of the bourgeois State; they are daily and hourly enslaved by the machine, by the overlooker, and, above all, by the individual bourgeois manufacturer himself. The more openly this despotism proclaims gain to be its end and aim, the more petty, the more hateful and the more embittering it is.

The less the skill and exertion of strength implied in manual labour, in other words, the more modern industry becomes developed, the more is the labour of men superseded by that of women. Differences of age and sex have no longer any distinctive social validity for the working class. All are instruments of labour, more or less expensive to use, according to their age and sex.

No sooner is the exploitation of the labourer by the manufacturer, so far, at an end, that he receives his wages in cash, than he is set upon by the other portions of the bourgeoisie, the landlord, the shopkeeper, the pawnbroker, etc.

The lower strata of the middle class—the small tradespeople, shopkeepers, and retired tradesmen generally, the handicraftsmen and peasants—all these sink gradually into the proletariat, partly because their diminutive capital does not suffice for the scale on which Modern Industry is carried on, and is swamped in the competition with the large capitalists, partly because their specialized skill is rendered worthless by new methods of production. Thus the proletariat is recruited from all classes of the population. . . .

But with the development of industry the proletariat not only increases in number; it becomes concentrated in greater masses, its strength grows, and it feels that strength more. The various interests and conditions of life within the ranks of the proletariat are more and more equalized, in proportion as machinery obliterates all distinctions of labour, and nearly everywhere reduces wages to the same low level. The growing competition among the bourgeois, and the resulting commercial crises, make the wages of the workers ever more fluctuating. The unceasing improvement of machinery, ever more rapidly developing, makes their livelihood more and more precarious; the collisions between individual workmen and individual bourgeois take more and more the character of collisions between two classes.

Thereupon the workers begin to form combinations (Trades Unions) against the bourgeois; they club together in order to keep up the rate of wages; they found permanent associations in order to make provision beforehand for these occasional revolts. Here and there the contest breaks out into riots.

Now and then the workers are victorious, but only for a time. The real fruit of their battles lies, not in the immediate result, but in the ever-expanding union of the workers. This union is helped on by the improved means of communication that are created by modern industry and that place the workers of different localities in contact with one another. It was just this contact that was needed to centralize the numerous local struggles, all of the same character, into one national struggle between classes. But every class struggle is a political struggle. And that union, to attain which the burghers of the Middle Ages, with their miserable highways, required centuries, the modern proletarians, thanks to railways, achieve in a few years.

This organization of the proletarians into a class, and consequently into a political party, is continually being upset again by the competition between the workers themselves. But it ever rises up again, stronger, firmer, mightier. It compels legislative recognition of particular interests of the workers, by taking advantage of the divisions among the bourgeoisie itself. Thus the ten-hours' bill in England was carried. . . .

The lower-middle class, the small manufacturer, the shopkeeper, the artisan, the peasant, all these fight against the bourgeoisie, to save from extinction their existence as fractions of the middle class. They are therefore not revolutionary, but conservative. Nay more, they are reactionary, for they try to roll back the wheel of history. If by chance they are revolutionary, they are so only in view of their impending transfer into the proletariat, they thus defend not their present, but their future interests, they desert their own standpoint to place themselves at that of the proletariat. . . .

Hitherto, every form of society has been based, as we have already seen, on the antagonism of oppressing and oppressed classes. But in order to oppress a class, certain conditions must be assured to it under which it can, at least, continue its slavish existence. The serf, in the period of serfdom, raised himself to membership in the commune, just as the petty bourgeois, under the yoke of feudal absolutism, managed to develop into a bourgeois. The modern labourer, on the contrary, instead of rising with the progress of industry, sinks deeper and deeper below the conditions of existence of his own class. He becomes a pauper, and pauperism develops more rapidly than population and wealth. And here it becomes evident, that the bourgeoisie is unfit any longer to be the ruling class in society, and to impose its conditions of existence upon society as an overriding law. It is unfit to rule because it is incompetent to assure an existence to its slave within his slavery, because it cannot help letting him sink into such a state, that it has to feed him, instead of being fed by him. Society can no longer live under this bourgeoisie, in other words, its existence is no longer compatible with society.

The essential condition for the existence, and for the sway of the bourgeois class, is the formation and augmentation of capital; the condition for capital is wage-labour. Wage-labour rests exclusively on competition between the labourers. The advance of industry, whose involuntary promoter is the bourgeoisie, replaces the isolation of the labourers, due to competition, by their revolutionary combination, due to association. The development of Modern Industry, therefore, cuts from under its feet the very foundation on which the bourgeoisie produces and appropriates products. What the bourgeoisie, therefore, produces, above all, is its own gravediggers. Its fall and the victory of the proletariat are equally inevitable.

NOTES

1. By bourgeoisie is meant the class of modern Capitalists, owners of the means of social production and employers of wage-labour. By proletariat, the class of modern wage-labourers who, having no means of production of their own, are reduced to selling their labour-power in order to live. [*Engels, English Edition of 1888*]

2. "Commune" was the name taken, in France, by the nascent towns even before they had conquered from their feudal lords and masters local self-government and political rights as the "Third Estate." Generally speaking, for the economical development of the bourgeoisie, England is here taken as the typical country; for its political development, France. [*Engels, English edition of 1888*]

    This was the name given their urban communities by the townsmen of Italy and France, after they had purchased or wrested their initial rights of self-government from their feudal lords. [*Engels, German edition of 1890*]

3. Subsequently Marx pointed out that the worker sells not his labour but his labour power.

CRITICAL
Reading
Questions

1. What significant changes occurred with the rise of the bourgeoisie class?
2. Do you agree that class is the most important dimension of inequality? Why or why not?
3. The final stage proposed by Marx and Engels was a communist society without classes. Do you think a society or group of people could ever exist without some form of hierarchy? Why or why not?
4. Is social class still relevant? Why or why not?

It seems clear from Marx's discussion that capitalism can create many problems for workers and that the inequality between those who own the means of production and those who own only their labour power can be severe. However, it is also clear that there are many more workers than there are capitalists. Why don't the workers simply rise up and ask for better wages, working conditions, and other benefits? Why don't they start the revolution Marx dreamed about? Marx outlined a number of reasons for the lack of such an uprising and for the difficulties in uniting to fight oppression.

One of the main reasons that workers do not join together is the role of ideology. **Ideologies** are sets of conscious and unconscious ideas or beliefs that govern and guide people's lives. Marx (2004, 64) said that the dominant ideologies in any historical epoch are those of the dominant class in that period: "The ideas of the ruling class are in every epoch the ruling ideas, i.e., the class which is the ruling material force of society, is at the same time its ruling intellectual force."

Most of us were raised within capitalist societies and therefore cannot see the many ideologies and assumptions upon which this system is based. Ideologies such as meritocracy, individualism, progress, evolution, expansion, and development are fundamentally intertwined with our economic system, yet they often seem natural and invisible so they end up being accepted by those within the society.

For example, Canadian society has a strong belief in meritocracy, the idea that people will achieve based on their own merit. This ideology supports the idea that wealthy people earned their money from working hard and that those with less money must have not worked as hard or be less deserving. From a Marxist perspective, we can see that this ideology benefits the bourgeoisie by legitimizing the fact that they have money, highlighting the hard work and intelligence it took to get that money, and making it seem that anyone could achieve this status with effort and perseverance. It helps encourage the proletariat (the rest of us) to buy into the system of capitalism because it promotes the belief that we too can become rich and successful if we work hard enough. However, this ideology ignores the many other factors that determine one's social position. An individual's social class, which shapes his or her educational opportunities and social connections, also plays an important role in determining financial and other types of success.

PHOTO 3.2 Meritocracy is a very important ideology in Canadian society. We tend to believe that smart and hard-working people will make more money and be more successful than other people. To what extent is this true about someone like Donald Trump? How hard did he work to attain his success?

Marx would argue that other ideologies, such as individualism and progress, also benefit the dominant class and legitimize the economic and social system as it is.

Marx claimed that workers in capitalism develop a **false consciousness**, a willingness to believe in ideologies that support the ruling class but are actually disadvantageous to working-class interests. Ideologies such as individualism and meritocracy all support and serve the interests of the dominant class. They blunt the working class's desire to unite and call upon capitalists and governments to be more responsive to their needs. Social institutions, such as the education system, mass media, and the family, teach us these ideologies and help to perpetuate them.

For Marx, even the government is simply a tool of capitalism because capitalists use the state to further their own interests. In fact, Marx (1975) argued that the state is used to sustain the class system that benefits the ruling class. Consequently, he argues that the state does not reflect the interest of the vast majority of people, the workers. This situation is complicated in a democracy by the fact that the workers have the right to vote. The small group of capitalists has to persuade the larger group of workers to accept the concentration of power in the former's hands. This is done, in part, by the capitalist control of ideas through avenues such as the media and school curriculums. Through these mechanisms, the capitalist tries to persuade the workers that the current system is the optimal way of running society and is simply the "natural" way for things to be organized. However, Marx argued that, when these softer ways of convincing people about the benefits of capitalism fail, the ruling class uses more coercive methods, such as the police, military, or the judicial system, to defend this system.

Marx and Engels demonstrated that, far from being inevitable, the current organization of the economy is socially constructed and can be changed. The means of production—in our case, capitalism—determines the resulting social systems, relations, class struggles, and ideologies in society. In essence, Marx and Engels argued that all aspects of society, from overarching power structures (i.e. the way the government is run) to daily individual experiences with exploitation (i.e. workers in factories) form as a result of the economic system or means of production.

Marx's ideas have formed how many sociologists and others think about social class. However, these ideas have not gone without criticism. Many people argue that there are no longer simply two classes and they criticize him for seeing the economic world as such a sharp distinction between capitalists and workers. In some ways, this criticism is unfair. Marx (1907) identified two smaller and, in his opinion, less important class groupings: the petite bourgeoisie and the lumpenproletariat. The petite bourgeoisie ("little bourgeoisie") are small-scale capitalists, such as shopkeepers and managers. People in this group do not necessarily sell their labour like proletariats but neither do they buy the labour of others like the capitalists (Marx and Engels 1848). They often work alongside the labour they buy from others, unlike large-scale capitalists who do not work with labourers. For example, a petite bourgeoisie who owns a small coffee shop might, like his employees, make coffee. However, the owner of Starbucks, a large bourgeoisie, would not. Marx said that the petite bourgeoisie would disappear over time, mostly because they would eventually fall into the proletariat class.

The lumpenproletariat (translated roughly as "slum workers") is the lowest layer of the working class and includes beggars, prostitutes, petty criminals, and the chronically unemployed (Marx 1907). Marx largely dismissed this group, feeling that its members were highly unlikely to join what he hoped would be a workers' revolution.

Keeping Marx's classes in mind, where would physicians fit? This occupational group makes a relatively high salary yet does not own the means of production. Under Marx's conceptual framework, they would be considered proletariats. However, some theorists argue that physicians are not in the same fundamentally exploitative relationship with capitalists as the proletariat class that Marx discussed.

Economic systems have changed since Marx's time. He wrote in an era of industrial capitalism, when most individuals working in the formal labour market were employed in manufacturing. Today, however, most people work in other industries. In 2014, 78 per cent of Canadians had service jobs (e.g. retail, health, and education), with only 22 per cent working in the manufacturing sector (Statistics Canada 2014). As you can see, changes in the structure of the economic system complicate Marx's theories of class stratification.

HIGHLIGHT

Ideology and Positive Thinking

The Secret is a best-selling 2006 self-help book by Rhonda Byrne. Based on "the law of attraction," the book claims that positive thinking can create life-changing results, such as increased wealth, health, and happiness. The book has sold almost 20 million copies in 46 languages. Here are a few examples of Byrne's advice.

> Money is magnetic energy. You are a magnet attracting to you all things, via the signal you are emitting through your thoughts and feelings. To become a powerful money magnet:
>
> - Be clear about the amount of money you want to receive. State it and intend it! Don't think about how much money you earn, but how much you want to receive.
> - Visualize and imagine yourself spending all the money you want, as though you already have it.
> - Speak, act, and think from the mindset of being wealthy now. Eliminate thoughts and words of lack such as "I can't afford it," "It is too expensive."
> - Do whatever it takes for you to feel wealthy.
> - Do whatever it takes to feel good. The emotions of joy and happiness are powerful money magnets. Be happy now! (thesecret.tv/teachings-summary html)

It is hard to argue that positive thinking is a bad thing—everyone likes a person with a positive attitude! But is there a danger in these kinds of teachings? Consider the advice in this book and answer the following questions:

1. How does the ideology of *The Secret* help perpetuate capitalism?
2. Who does this ideology benefit?
3. Why would people believe in these ideologies?
4. What risks can these ideologies pose for individuals, social groups, and society as a whole?

Class Consciousness

Class consciousness is a term used in Marxist theory to refer to people's beliefs regarding their social class and class interests. Marx (Marx and Engels 1848) distinguished between a "class in itself," a category of people with a common relation to the means of production (such as the worker or proletariat), and a "class for itself," a group organized in active pursuit of its own interests (such as unionized workers pushing for better working conditions). Class consciousness is an awareness of what is in the best interests of one's class and is an important pre-condition for organizing into a "class for itself" to advocate for class interests.

Marx wanted the working class to develop a class consciousness so that they could fight for socialism. Class consciousness has also been important in many capitalist societies, such as Canada, in leading to the rise of unions. Unions are organizations of employees who work together to negotiate a variety of common matters, including pay, benefits, hiring and firing practices, and working conditions. Unions bargain with the employer on behalf of workers and negotiate labour contracts (collective bargaining). These actions are a result of a group of people working as a class for itself, with the unions advocating for workers' rights.

Trade union density is the percentage of wage earners in a population who are part of a union. Table 3.1 shows this density across time and countries. We can see a wide range in union membership across countries. For example, two-thirds of workers in Sweden are in a union while only one-tenth of workers in the United States are union members. Canada falls somewhere in the mid- to high-range.

We can also see that, in general, union density is on the decline. With the exception of Mexico, each country in the sample has seen a drop in union density over the 14-year period. In Canada, the decline has been relatively small, only 0.8 per cent. However, the decline in Sweden has been steep (12.9 per cent).

Why are unionization rates declining? Comparing rates in Canada and the United States sheds some light on this question. These two countries had similar rates of union membership from 1920 to 1960. However, as you can see from Figure 3.1, the rates have diverged dramatically since this time.

There are many potential reasons for the decrease in American unionization rates. Some people argue that globalization and technological advances have undermined unions. Others claim that the decline in manufacturing has led to fewer union jobs. However, these factors have affected both the United States and Canada, but the latter maintains a relatively high rate of unionization. How can we explain this difference?

In general, Canadian labour laws and public policies have been more supportive of unions than have American laws and policies. Canadian law has simply been more union friendly. For example, several Canadian provinces ban temporary or permanent strike replacement (people who work in place of striking employees; sometimes called scab workers). These laws do not exist in the United States. Also, 24 US states have "right to work" laws, which restrict

PHOTO 3.3 Members of CUPE Local 391, which represents public library workers in Vancouver, Gibsons, and Sechelt, on strike in 2007. What types of benefits were these workers fighting for? Why are unions important when thinking about social class?

TABLE 3.1	Trade union density, selected countries, 1999–2013 (per cent)			
	1999	**2005**	**2011**	**2013**
Turkey	10.6	8.2	5.4	—
Korea	11.7	9.9	9.9	—
United States	13.4	12.0	11.3	10.8
Mexico	15.8	16.9	14.5	13.6
Japan	22.2	18.8	19.0	17.8
Australia	25.4	22.3	18.5	17.0
Canada	28.0	27.7	27.1	27.2
Ireland	38.7	34.0	32.6	29.6
Sweden	80.6	76.5	67.5	67.7
Average of OECD[1] countries	20.8	18.8	17.5	16.9

NOTE:

1. The OECD (Organisation for Economic Co-operation and Development) is comprised of 34 countries.

SOURCE: Data from OECD. 2015. "Trade Union Density." http://stats.oecd.org/Index.aspx?DataSetCode=UN_DEN .

a union's ability to require individual members to pay union dues. These laws make it more difficult for unions to fund their work. Furthermore, the process of creating a union is much quicker in Canada. It usually takes only 5 to 10 days, once the employees have signed a petition. This process can take months or years in the United States.

These examples clearly illustrate how public policies and laws can shape larger social structures in society, such as unionization rates (Warner 2013). Creating a union is one way for the working class to organize into a class for itself. However, these organizations

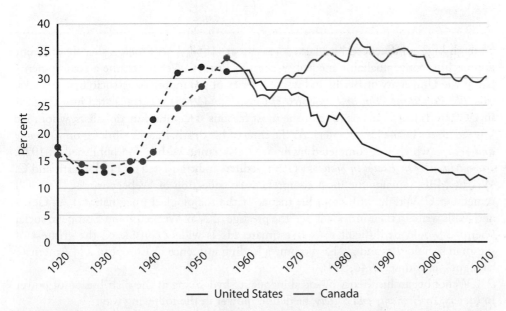

FIGURE 3.1 Unionization rate in the United States and Canada, 1920–2010

SOURCE: Warner, Kris. 2013 (23 January). "The Real Reason for the Decline of American Unions." Bloomberg View. www.bloomberg.com/view/echoes/8/. Used with permission of Bloomberg L.P. Copyright © 2015. All rights reserved.

face challenges, such as ideological barriers presented by the ruling classes, and structural impediments enacted by them, such as laws.

Class struggle between workers and capitalists can be overt. When workers strike, create a union, or lead a revolution, they are open and clear about their unhappiness with the power inequality between themselves and capitalists. Marx advocated for overt struggles against the capitalist system. However, workers can also engage in more covert actions to undermine capitalism, capitalists, and their workplaces. As Hollander and Einwohner (2004, 545) explain:

> overt resistance is behaviour that is visible and readily recognized by both targets and observers as resistance and, further, is intended to be recognized as such. This category includes collective acts such as social movements . . . as well as individual acts of refusal. . . . We use the term covert resistance to refer to acts that are intentional yet go unnoticed (and, therefore, unpunished) by their targets, although they are recognized as resistance by other, culturally aware observers.

Imagine that you think your boss or company is treating you very poorly. Perhaps you are paid a low wage, have to work a lot of unpaid overtime, have to adjust to changing schedules at the last minute, are forced to work in unsafe conditions, are harassed at work, or are belittled by your boss. You have the option of overt resistance, but you fear losing your job or being punished. Instead, you show your unhappiness by engaging in more covert actions. Perhaps you work a little more slowly than you have to or waste time at work. You spend a few extra minutes checking your e-mail or texting people. Perhaps you undermine your boss by talking about her with other co-workers or you don't quite follow the rules—you give customers free refills or you don't wear the proper uniform. You might push this covert resistance so far that you actually steal from your work by taking extra food or products from the workplace. You justify this action by telling yourself that you're just levelling the playing field. This sort of resistance aims at regaining dignity from organizations that violate workers' interests and undermine their autonomy. Have you engaged in any of these activities at work? Are they ever justified? If so, in what context?

Max Weber and Social Status

Though highly influenced by Marx, Max Weber (1864–1920) took a slightly different approach to conceptualizing inequality. Born in Prussia, Weber became a faculty member at the University of Berlin and wrote a series of groundbreaking sociological works. His *The Protestant Ethic and the Spirit of Capitalism* (1905) was translated into English in 1930 by Talcott Parsons (one of the most famous structural functionalists, whom we learned about in the last chapter). At the time of his death, he was working on *Economy and Society*, which was completed by his wife, Marianne Weber, and published in 1922. *From Max Weber: Essays in Sociology* (1991), edited and translated by H.H. Gerth and C. Wright Mills, remains the most comprehensive collection of Weber's works. (You will remember C. Wright Mill from his theory of the sociological imagination.) As Gerth and Mills write in their introduction, "the prestige of Max Weber among European social scientists would be difficult to over-estimate. He is widely considered the greatest of German sociologists and . . . has become a leading influence in European and American thought" (in Shimer 1946, 374).

Weber began his theory of social inequality by looking at the distribution of power in society. In *Economy and Society*, he defines **power** in the following way:

> In general, we understand by "power" the chance of a man or of a number of men to realize their own will in a communal action even against the resistance of others who are participating in the same action (in Gerth and Mills 1991, 180).

HIGHLIGHT

Getting to Know Max Weber

- Max Weber's full name is Karl Emil Maximillian Weber. With these two additional names, is it any surprise that he, Karl Marx, and Emile Durkheim became the three founding fathers of sociology?

- For Christmas 1876, Weber gave his parents two of his historical essays: "About the Course of German History, with Special Reference to the Positions of the Emperor and the Pope" and "About the Roman Imperial period from Constantine to the Migration of Nations." Quite a present from a 12-year-old!

- During his first years as a student at the University of Berlin, Weber spent much of his time "drinking and fencing"—a dangerous combination.

- Weber suffered from depression and insomnia and spent the summer and fall of 1900 in a sanatorium. He described his ongoing ordeal in his biography, which was later destroyed by his wife because she feared that public knowledge of his mental illness would tarnish his legacy.

While he agreed with Marx that economic power is very important, Weber argued that many other, non-economic factors are significant parts of who has power in society and who does not. Ideas and interests that emerge from politics, religion, and other institutions also shape who has power in society. Contrary to Marx, Weber contended that these other areas of power are not simply secondary to the economy. He posited that there are three primary bases of power in society: economic class (income, wealth), social status (prestige, honour), and party (political power). For Weber, classes are about power in the economic order, status groups are about power in the social order, and parties are about power oriented toward influencing communal action.

Both Weber and Marx defined class based on an individual's relationship to the economy. Classes, for Weber, are groups of people who share a similar position with respect to the ownership of property or goods. They are economic categories developing out of human interaction in a market, a system of competitive exchange whereby people buy and sell things of value in pursuit of profit. According to Weber, a class is a group of people sharing a common situation in this market and, therefore, having common interests. The main division for Weber was between the classes with property and those without. So far, this description sounds very similar to Marx's theory of class, discussed earlier in the chapter. The difference between Marx and Weber lies in the finer details of their ideas about class and the divisions they see. Weber said that class can be differentiated into the kinds of property and services that an individual can offer in a market. Whereas Marx described two main groups, Weber claimed that there were four classes: large capitalists, small capitalists, specialists, and the working class.

Large capitalists own large factories, farms, or other businesses that employ large numbers of workers; small capitalists (what Marx called the petite bourgeoisie) own smaller businesses with fewer employees. Specialists, such as doctors, lawyers, and professors, have marketable skills and training that they sell to the capitalist through their labour. The working class, which is similar to Marx's proletariat, are manual labourers. They do not have specialized education or training; therefore, they have less power and freedom in the labour market than specialists do.

Weber's second main basis of power is status. **Status groups** have a "style of life" and are based on social honour and prestige that is expressed in our interactions with each other. This kind of recognition can be formal—such as when we refer to a person with a special title or give them a degree to mark their status. The title "doctor" or "lawyer" denotes a particular type of education and occupation and cannot simply be given to

PHOTO 3.4 Working conditions in sweatshops, such as this one, can be quite dangerous and unsafe. Why are we more likely to find these types of sweatshops in developing countries?

anyone. However, status can also be informal, such as when we respect older people even if they have no specific title or position of authority. Social honour may be either positive or negative, in that an individual may be given a high level of social esteem or honour or may be disrespected because he or she is seen to fall into an undesirable social category.

In general, people of high social class tend to have high status. For example, a CEO of a large company is from the upper, capitalist class and also has a lot of status. He is likely to have a lifestyle that involves a large house, designer clothing, and luxury goods. Such people are accorded respect and esteem by others. Conversely, those with low social class tend to have low social status. People who work in fast-food restaurants, for example, have a low social class and receive little status or respect in society.

It is important to note that social class and social status do not always correspond. For example, priests and rabbis have extremely high social status. They are accorded

ACTIVITY

Social Status Markers

Let's examine Weber's concept of "style of life" by looking at wealthy people as a status group. Go to this book's companion website and watch the videos "Becoming a WASP," "Passing for Upper Class," and "How to Marry a Millionaire," and then answer the following questions:

1. What social status markers are discussed in the videos?

2. Which markers are purely financial? What other types of markers are not based on money alone?

3. How have the markers of social status changed since these videos were made? How have they remained the same? If you displayed all the markers suggested in the videos, would you easily fit into a wealthy, upper-class environment? Why or why not?

4. How are markers of social status different across groups of people? Give some examples of the distinct social markers in your group of friends and with others your age. How do people your age mark social status?

much distinction and esteem and are deferred to in a variety of social settings. Yet they are not necessarily of the upper social class. They are not capitalists who own the means of production; in fact, many of them make very little money. At the other end of the spectrum, plumbers or electricians might make a good salary and be self-employed (making them petite bourgeoisie or capitalists). However, people in these jobs are not generally accorded the respect or status given to a priest or rabbi. Weber's ideas encourage us to think about how social class and social status are distinct constructs.

Status groups can be formed from a variety of dimensions. For example, men and women form different status groups. They have distinct "styles of life" and are accorded different levels of esteem. Sexual orientations, education levels, ethnicities, religions, and neighbourhood affiliations could also be status groups. Hence, individuals can be a part of many different status groups but are in only one social class.

Weber's last main dimension of power is party. **Parties** are organizations that attempt to influence social action and that focus on achieving some goal in the sphere of power. Parties are not simply political parties, such as the Liberals, NDP, Greens, Conservatives, or Bloc Québécois. Parties also include groups aimed at improving specific social problems (e.g. a block watch or a parent–teacher group), environmental groups (e.g. Greenpeace, World Wildlife Fund) or even sporting and recreation organizations.

As the preceding discussion shows, the theories of Marx and Weber have certain similarities and differences. Are their theories compatible? Which is more useful in helping to understand modern Canadian society?

Income Inequality in Canada

Many sociologists examine income inequality in Canada by using the concept of **socio-economic status (SES)**. SES is a measure of an individual's or family's social and economic position relative to others. It is a composite scale that includes measures of income, educational attainment, and occupational prestige. Income refers to any wages, salaries, profits, rents, dividends, or pensions a person receives per year. Educational attainment is the highest level (grade or degree) a person has completed. Occupational prestige is measured by the educational attainment required, the income earned, and the associated skills of one's job. SES is typically divided into three categories—high, middle, and low.

You can see that SES incorporates ideas about social class and social status, as discussed by Marx and Weber. The concept also makes it possible to deal with some of the disjunctions that sometimes occur between class and status. Recall the earlier example of a plumber. SES can reconcile the apparent contradiction between a plumber's high wages and low occupational status.

One way to think about income inequality in Canada is to look at it over time. Much of the information on this topic (and much of the data presented in this book) comes from Statistics Canada, a government body that collects information about Canadian citizens and immigrants. This information is essential in helping us understand the population and its various groups in areas such as health, income, and educational opportunities. Figure 3.2 shows Statistic Canada data regarding the average income of Canadians in the top and bottom 20 per cent income groups. As you can see, the period before 1996 was fairly stagnant in terms of inequality; since this time, the gap between the rich and poor has widened. Figure 3.3 compares the income of the top 20 per cent of earners with other income groups. This chart shows that families in the top 20 per cent of income earn between 7.2 and 9.5 times more than families in the bottom 20 per cent.

These two figures clearly show growing income inequality in Canada. How concerned should we be about this issue? If there is a lot of **social mobility** (movement on a stratification system, such as the class system) in Canada, income inequality is less of a problem. If the rich are getting richer because they are working harder and people can

RESEARCH METHOD

Survey

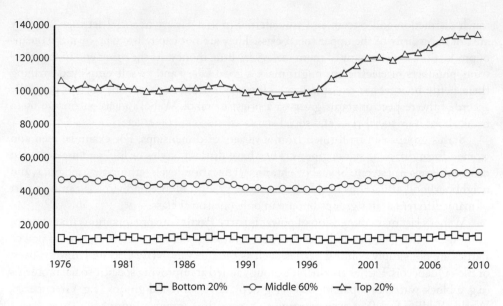

FIGURE 3.2 Average after-tax income by income group, Canada, 1976–2010 (2010 constant dollars)

SOURCE: HRSDC calculations based on Statistics Canada. 2012. *Market, Total and After-Tax Income, by Economic Family Type and After-Tax Income Quintiles, 2010 Constant Dollars, Annual* (CANSIM Table 202-0703). Ottawa: Statistics Canada.

move from one class to another through hard work, the gap between the rich and the poor is less concerning.

This idea is an example of an **achievement-based stratification system**. In this system, people's rank depends on their accomplishments; those who work hard and are diligent achieve high social status or class. Conversely, an **ascription-based stratification system** determines an individual's rank by her ascribed characteristics (i.e. the features she is born with). If people of certain ethnicities, religions, or sexes hold certain ranks in society simply because of who they are (not what they have done), they live in an

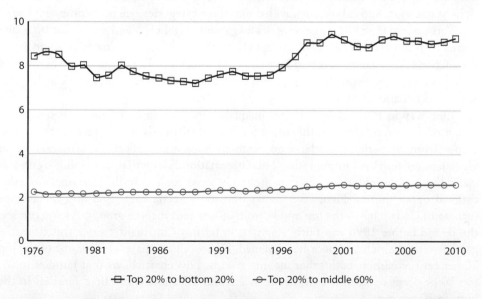

FIGURE 3.3 Average income of the top 20 per cent group relative to other groups, Canada, 1976–2010

NOTE: Average incomes were calculated using the average after-tax family income.
SOURCE: HRSDC calculations based on Statistics Canada. 2012. *Market, Total and After-Tax Income, by Economic Family Type and After-Tax Income Quintiles, 2010 Constant Dollars, Annual* (CANSIM Table 202-0703). Ottawa: Statistics Canada.

ascription-based system. Apartheid in South Africa was such a system. The minority white population ran the country, while the black majority was oppressed because of their skin colour.

We are all born with an SES determined by our parents' income, occupational status, and education. But the extent to which a society is achievement- or ascriptive-based depends on its level of social mobility. There are two types of social mobility—intergenerational and intragenerational. Intergenerational mobility occurs between generations. Your parents or grandparents might be working class, but you are middle or upper class. Intragenerational mobility occurs within a single generation. Perhaps your parents were born into the working class but became middle class during their lifetime.

Many studies compare social mobility across countries. Some measure **intergenerational income elasticity**—the statistical relationship between a parent's and child's economic standings. The higher the number, the less social mobility a society has and the greater the role of parental features in predicting a child's economic standing. Lower numbers indicate that children's economic standing is the result of their individual talents and capabilities. Of the nine developed countries studied by Corak (2006), Denmark, Norway, Finland, and Canada have the lowest intergenerational income elasticity (the most social mobility); the UK, the United States, and France have the highest (the least social mobility; see Figure 3.4).

In his article on social mobility, Barrie McKenna (2012) explains a series of new studies that "turns conventional wisdom on its head" by showing that Americans enjoy less economic mobility than do Canadians. The United States is the richer country, but it is less equal and has less social mobility. McKenna suggests that, in the United States, "inequality is inherited, much like hair and eye colour."

RESEARCH METHOD

Survey

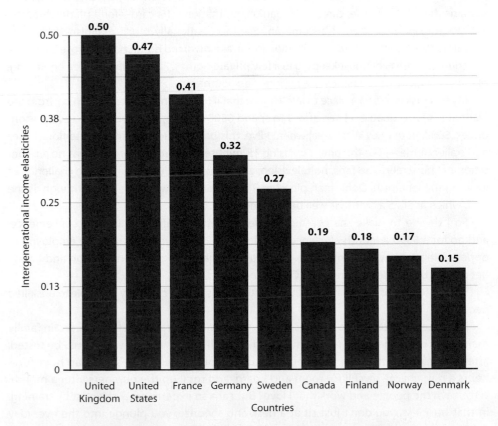

FIGURE 3.4 Intergenerational income elasticities for nine developed countries

SOURCES: Economic Mobility Project; Corak, Miles. 2006. "Do Poor Children Become Poor Adults? Lessons from a Cross Country Comparison of Generational Earnings Mobility." *Research on Economic Inequality* 13 (1): 143–88.

According to Corak (2006), Canadian public policy and tax systems account for Canadians being as much as three times more economically mobile than Americans. He explains that "what distinguishes the two countries is what's happening at the tails . . . Rich kids grow up to be rich adults and poor kids stay poor. In Canada, that's not so much the case. . . . even the poorest of Canadian children have access to good schools, quality health care and decent homes" (McKenna 2012). While social mobility is higher in Canada, people still have difficulty moving up the social stratification system and great inequality continues to exist.

As previously stated, each of us grows up in a particular class. The people we know also tend to be in the same class because we live in the same neighbourhoods, go to the same schools, or have similar circles of friends. For this reason, it is sometimes hard to truly understand how other people experience social class and inequality. To highlight these issues, Barbara Ehrenreich, a journalist and *New York Times* best-selling author, lived the life of the working poor in North America. Her account of this life first appeared as an article in *Harper's* and was subsequently published in book form. The following pages describe one of her experiences as a minimum-wage worker.

RESEARCH METHOD

Participant Observation

READING

From *Nickel-and-Dimed: On (Not) Getting By in America*

Barbara Ehrenreich

At the beginning of June 1998 I leave behind everything that normally soothes the ego and sustains the body—home, career, companion, reputation, ATM card—for a plunge into the low-wage workforce. There, I become another, occupationally much diminished "Barbara Ehrenreich"—depicted on job-application forms as a divorced homemaker whose sole work experience consists of housekeeping in a few private homes. I am terrified, at the beginning, of being unmasked for what I am: a middle-class journalist . . .

My first task is to find a place to live. I figure that if I can earn $7 an hour—which, from the want ads, seems doable—I can afford to spend $500 on rent, or maybe, with severe economies, $600. In the Key West area, where I live, this pretty much confines me to flophouses and trailer homes—like the one, a pleasing 15-minute drive from town, that has no air-conditioning, no screens, no fans, no television, and, by way of diversion, only the challenge of evading the landlord's Doberman pinscher. The big problem with this place, though, is the rent, which at $675 a month is well beyond my reach. . . .

So I decide to make the common trade-off between affordability and convenience, and go for a $500-a-month efficiency 30 miles up a 2-lane highway from the employment opportunities of Key West, meaning 45 minutes if there's no road construction and I don't get caught behind some sun-dazed Canadian tourists. . . .

But is it really possible to make a living on the kinds of jobs currently available to unskilled people? . . .

It may seem excessive to put this proposition to an experimental test. As certain family members keep unhelpfully reminding me, the viability of low-wage work could be tested, after a fashion, without ever leaving my study. I could just pay myself $7 an hour for 8 hours a day, charge myself for room and board, and total up the numbers after a month. Why leave the people and work that I love? But I am an experimental scientist by training. In that business, you don't just sit at a desk and theorize; you plunge into the everyday chaos of nature, where surprises lurk in the most mundane measurements. Maybe, when I got into it, I would discover some hidden economies in the world of the low-wage worker. After all, if 30 per cent of the workforce toils for less than $8 an hour, according to the

EPI [Economic Policy Institute], they may have found some tricks as yet unknown to me. Maybe—who knows? . . .

On the morning of my first full day of job searching, I take a red pen to the want ads, which are auspiciously numerous. Everyone in Key West's booming "hospitality industry" seems to be looking for someone like me—trainable, flexible, and with suitably humble expectations as to pay. I know I possess certain traits that might be advantageous—I'm white and, I like to think, well-spoken and poised—but I decide on two rules: One, I cannot use any skills derived from my education or usual work—not that there are a lot of want ads for satirical essayists anyway. Two, I have to take the best-paid job that is offered me and of course do my best to hold it; no Marxist rants or sneaking off to read novels in the ladies' room. . . .

So I put on what I take to be a respectful-looking outfit of ironed Bermuda shorts and scooped-neck T-shirt and set out for a tour of the local hotels and supermarkets. Best Western, Econo Lodge, and HoJo's all let me fill out application forms, and these are, to my relief, interested in little more than whether I am a legal resident of the United States and have committed any felonies. . . .

At "The Palms," let's call it, a bouncy manager actually takes me around to see the rooms and meet the existing housekeepers, who, I note with satisfaction, look pretty much like me . . . Mostly, though, no one speaks to me or even looks at me except to proffer an application form. At my last stop, a palatial B&B, I wait 20 minutes to meet "Max," only to be told that there are no jobs now but there should be one soon, since "nobody lasts more than a couple weeks." (Because none of the people I talked to knew I was a reporter, I have changed their names to protect their privacy and in some cases perhaps, their jobs.)

Three days go by like this, and, to my chagrin, no one out of the approximately 20 places I've applied calls me for an interview. I had been vain enough to worry about coming across as too educated for the jobs I sought, but no one even seems interested in finding out how overqualified I am. . . . At one of the big discount hotel chains, . . . I go, as usual, for housekeeping and am sent, instead, to try out as a waitress at the attached "family restaurant," a dismal spot with a counter and about 30 tables that looks out on a parking garage and features such tempting fare as "Pollish [sic] sausage and BBQ sauce" on 95-degree days. Phillip, the dapper young West Indian who introduces himself as the manager, interviews me with about as much enthusiasm as if he were a clerk processing me for Medicare, the principal questions being what shifts can I work and when can I start. I mutter something about being woefully out of practice as a waitress, but he's already on to the uniform: I'm to show up tomorrow wearing black slacks and black shoes; he'll provide the rust-colored polo shirt with HEARTHSIDE embroidered on it, though I might want to wear my own shirt to get to work, ha ha. At the word *tomorrow*, something between fear and indignation rises in my chest. I want to say, "Thank you for your time, sir, but this is just an experiment, you know, not my actual life."

So begins my career at the Hearthside, I shall call it, one small profit centre within a global discount hotel chain, where for two weeks I work from 2:00 till 10:00 p.m. for $2.43 an hour plus tips. . . . For the next eight hours, I run after the agile Gail, absorbing bits of instruction along with fragments of personal tragedy. . . .

At least Gail puts to rest any fears I had of appearing overqualified. From the first day on, I find that of all the things I have left behind, such as home and identity, what I miss the most is competence. Not that I have ever felt utterly competent in the writing business, in which one day's success augurs nothing at all for the next. But in my writing life, I at least have some notion of procedure: do the research, make the outline, rough out a draft, etc. As a server, though, I am beset by requests like bees: more iced tea here, ketchup over there, a to-go box for table 14, and where are the high chairs, anyway? Of the 27 tables, up to 6 are usually mine at any time, though on slow afternoons or if Gail is off, I sometimes have the whole place to myself. There is the touch-screen computer-ordering system to master, which is, I suppose, meant to minimize server–cook contact, but in practice requires constant verbal fine-tuning: "That's gravy on the mashed, okay? None on the meatloaf," and so forth—while the cook scowls as if I were inventing these refinements just to torment him. Plus, something I had forgotten in the years since I was 18: about a third of a server's job is "side work" that's invisible to customers—sweeping, scrubbing, slicing, refilling, and restocking. If it isn't all done, every little bit of it, you're going to face the 6:00 p.m. dinner rush defenceless and probably go down in flames. I screw up dozens of times at the beginning, sustained in my shame entirely by Gail's support—"It's okay, baby, everyone does that sometime"—because, to my total surprise and despite the scientific detachment I am doing my best to maintain, I care. . . .

Ten days into it, this is beginning to look like a livable lifestyle. I like Gail, who is "looking at 50" but moves so fast she can alight in one place and then another without apparently being anywhere between them. I clown around with Lionel, the teenage Haitian busboy, and catch a few fragments of conversation with Joan, the svelte fortyish hostess and militant feminist who is the only one of us who dares to tell Jack [the cook] to shut the fuck up. I even warm up to Jack when, on a slow night and to make up for a particularly unwarranted attack on my abilities, or so I imagine, he tells me about his glory days as a young man at "coronary school"—or do you say "culinary"?—in Brooklyn, where he dated a knock-out Puerto Rican chick and learned everything there is to know about food. I finish up at 10:00 or 10:30, depending on how much side work I've been able to get done during the shift, and cruise home to the tapes I snatched up at random when I left my real home . . . Midnight snack is Wheat Thins and Monterey Jack, accompanied by cheap white wine on ice and whatever AMC has to offer. To bed by 1:30 or 2:00, up at 9:00 or 10:00, read for an hour while my uniform whirls around in the landlord's washing machine, and then it's another eight hours spent following Mao's central instruction, as laid out in the Little Red Book, which was: Serve the people.

I could drift along like this, in some dreamy proletarian idyll, except for two things. One is management. If I have kept this subject on the margins thus far it is because I still flinch to think that I spent all those weeks under the surveillance of men (and later women) whose job it was to monitor my behaviour for signs of sloth, theft, drug abuse, or worse. Not that managers and especially "assistant managers" in low-wage settings like this are exactly the class enemy. In the restaurant business, they are mostly former cooks or servers, still capable of pinch-hitting in the kitchen or on the floor, just as in hotels they are likely to be former clerks, and paid a salary of only about $400 a week. But everyone knows they have crossed over to the other side, which is, crudely put, corporate as opposed to human. Cooks want to prepare tasty meals; servers want to serve them graciously; but managers are there for only one reason—to make sure that money is made for some theoretical entity that exists far away in Chicago or New York, if a corporation can be said to have a physical existence at all. . . .

Managers can sit—for hours at a time if they want—but it's their job to see that no one else ever does, even when there's nothing to do, and this is why, for servers, slow times can be as exhausting as rushes. You start dragging out each little chore, because if the manager on duty catches you in an idle moment, he will give you something far nastier to do. So I wipe, I clean, I consolidate ketchup bottles and recheck the cheesecake supply, even tour the tables to make sure the customer evaluation forms are all standing perkily in their places—wondering all the time how many calories I burn in these strictly theatrical exercises. . . .

The other problem, in addition to the less-than-nurturing management style, is that this job shows no sign of being financially viable. You might imagine, from a comfortable distance, that people who live, year in and year out, on $6 to $10 an hour have discovered some survival stratagems unknown to the middle class. But no. It's not hard to get my co-workers to talk about their living situations, because housing, in almost every case, is the principal source of disruption in their lives, the first thing they fill you in on when they arrive for their shifts. After a week, I have compiled the following survey:

- Gail is sharing a room in a well-known downtown flophouse for which she and a roommate pay about $250 a week. Her roommate, a male friend, has begun hitting on her, driving her nuts, but the rent would be impossible alone.

- Claude, the Haitian cook, is desperate to get out of the two-room apartment he shares with his girlfriend and two other, unrelated, people. As far as I can determine, the other Haitian men (most of whom only speak Creole) live in similarly crowded situations.

- Annette, a 20-year-old server who is 6 months pregnant and has been abandoned by her boyfriend, lives with her mother, a postal clerk.

- Marianne and her boyfriend are paying $170 a week for a one-person trailer.

- Jack, who is, at $10 an hour, the wealthiest of us, lives in the trailer he owns, paying only the $400-a-month lot fee. . . .

- Tina and her husband are paying $60 a night for a double room in a Days Inn. This is because they have no car and the Days Inn is within walking distance of the Hearthside. When Marianne, one of the breakfast servers, is tossed out of her trailer for subletting (which is against the trailer-park rules), she leaves her boyfriend and moves in with Tina and her husband.

- Joan, who had fooled me with her numerous and tasteful outfits (hostesses wear their own clothes), lives in a van she parks behind a shopping centre at night and showers in Tina's motel room. The clothes are from thrift shops.

It strikes me, in my middle-class solipsism, that there is gross improvidence in some of these arrangements. When Gail and I are wrapping silverware in napkins—the only task for which we are permitted to slt—she tells me she is thinking of escaping from her roommate by moving into the Days Inn herself. I am astounded: How can she even think of paying between $40 and $60 a day? But if I was afraid of sounding like a social worker, I come out just sounding like a fool. She squints at me in disbelief, "And where am I supposed to get a month's rent and a month's deposit for an apartment?" I'd been feeling pretty smug about my $500 efficiency, but of course it was made possible only by the $1,300 I had allotted myself for start-up costs when I began my low-wage life: $1,000 for the first month's rent and deposit, $100 for initial groceries and cash in my pocket, $200 stuffed away for emergencies. In poverty, as in certain propositions in physics, starting conditions are everything.

There are no secret economies that nourish the poor; on the contrary, there are a host of special costs. If you can't put up the two months' rent you need to secure an apartment, you end up paying through the nose for a room by the week. If you have only a room, with a hot plate at best, you can't save by cooking up huge lentil stews that can be frozen for the week ahead. You eat fast food, or the hot dogs and Styrofoam cups of soup that can be microwaved in a convenience store. . . .

So unless I want to start using my car as a residence, I have to find a second, or alternative, job. I call all the hotels where I filled out housekeeping applications weeks ago—the Hyatt, Holiday Inn, Econo Lodge, HoJo's, Best Western, plus a half dozen or so locally run guest-houses. Nothing. Then I start making the rounds again, wasting whole mornings waiting for some assistant manager to show up, even dipping into places so creepy that the front-desk clerk greets you from behind bulletproof glass and sells pints of liquor over the counter. But either someone has exposed my real-life housekeeping habits—which are, shall we say, mellow—or I am at the wrong end of some infallible ethnic equation: most, but by no means all, of the working housekeepers I see on my job searches are African Americans, Spanish-speaking, or immigrants from the Central European post-Communist world, whereas servers are almost invariably white and monolingually English-speaking. When I finally get a positive response, I have been identified once again as server material. Jerry's, which is part of a well-known national family restaurant chain and physically attached here to another budget hotel chain, is ready to use me at once. The prospect is both exciting and terrifying, because, with about the same number of tables and counter seats, Jerry's attracts three or four times the volume of customers as the gloomy old Hearthside. . . .

On my first day, in fact, I am hurt by my sister servers' coldness. My mentor for the day is an emotionally uninflected 23-year-old, and the others, who gossip a little among themselves about the real reason someone is out sick today and the size of the bail bond someone else has had to pay, ignore me completely. On my second day, I find out why. "Well, it's good to see you again," one of them says in greeting. "Hardly anyone comes back after the first day." I feel powerfully vindicated—a survivor—but it would take a long time, probably months, before I could hope to be accepted into this sorority.

I start out with the beautiful, heroic idea of handling the two jobs at once, and for two days I almost do it: the breakfast/lunch shift at Jerry's, which goes till 2:00, arriving at the Hearthside at 2:10, and attempting to hold out until 10:00. In the 10 minutes between jobs, I pick up a spicy chicken sandwich at the Wendy's drive-through window, gobble it down in the car, and change from khaki slacks to black, from Hawaiian to rust polo. There is a problem, though. When during the 3:00 to 4:00 p.m. dead time I finally sit down to wrap silver, my flesh seems to bond to the seat. I try to refuel with a purloined cup of soup, as I've seen Gail and Joan do dozens of times, but a manager catches me and hisses "No eating!" though there's not a customer around to be offended by the sight of food making contact with a server's lips. So I tell Gail I'm going to quit, and she hugs me and says she might just follow me to Jerry's herself.

But the chances of this are minuscule. She has left the flophouse and her annoying roommate and is back to living in her beat-up old truck. But guess what? she reports to me excitedly later that evening: Phillip has given her permission to park overnight in the hotel parking lot, as long as she keeps out of sight, and the parking lot should be totally safe, since it's patrolled by a hotel security guard! With the Hearthside offering benefits like that, how could anyone think of leaving? . . .

I make the decision to move closer to Key West. First, because of the drive. Second and third, also because of the drive: gas is eating up $4 to $5 a day, and although Jerry's is as high-volume as you can get, the tips average only 10 per cent, and not just for a newbie like me. Between the base pay of $2.15 an hour and the obligation to share tips with the busboys and dishwashers, we're averaging only about $7.50 an hour. Then there is the $30 I had to spend on the regulation tan slacks worn by Jerry's servers—a setback it could take weeks to absorb. (I had combed the town's two downscale department stores hoping for something cheaper but decided in the end that these marked-down Dockers, originally $49, were more likely to survive a daily washing.) Of my fellow servers, everyone who lacks a working husband or boyfriend seems to have a second job . . . Without the 45-minute commute, I can picture myself working 2 jobs and having the time to shower between them.

So I take the $500 deposit I have coming from my landlord, the $400 I have earned toward the next month's rent, plus the $200 reserved for emergencies, and use the $1,100 to pay the rent and deposit on trailer number 46 in the Overseas Trailer Park, a mile from the cluster of budget hotels that constitute Key West's version of an industrial park. Number 46 is about 8 feet in width and shaped like a barbell inside, with a narrow region—because of the sink and the stove—separating the bedroom from what might optimistically be called the "living" area, with its two-person table and half-sized couch. . . .

When my month-long plunge into poverty is almost over, I finally land my dream job— housekeeping. I do this by walking into the personnel office of the only place I figure I might have some credibility, the hotel attached to Jerry's, and confiding urgently that I have to have a second job if I am to pay my rent and, no, it couldn't be front-desk clerk. "All right," the personnel lady fairly spits, "So it's housekeeping," and she marches me back to meet Maria, the housekeeping manager, a tiny, frenetic Hispanic woman who greets me as "babe" and hands me a pamphlet emphasizing the need for a positive attitude. The hours are nine in the morning till whenever, the pay is $6.10 an hour, and there's one week of vacation a year. I don't have to ask about health insurance once I meet Carlotta, the middle-aged African-American woman who will be training me. Carla, as she tells me to call her, is missing all of her top front teeth.

On that first day of housekeeping and last day of my entire project—although I don't yet know it's the last—Carla is in a foul mood. We have been given 19 rooms to clean, most of them "checkouts," as opposed to "stay-overs," that require the whole enchilada of bed-stripping, vacuuming, and bathroom-scrubbing. When one of the rooms that had been listed as a stay-over turns out to be a checkout, Carla calls Maria to complain, but of course to no avail. "So make up the motherfucker," Carla orders me, and I do the beds while she sloshes around the bathroom. For four hours without a break I strip and remake beds, taking about four and a half minutes per queen-sized bed, which I could get down to three if there were any reason to. We try to avoid vacuuming by picking up the larger specks by hand, but often there is nothing to do but drag the monstrous vacuum cleaner—it weighs about 30 pounds—off our cart and try to wrestle it around the floor. Sometimes Carla hands me the squirt bottle of "BAM" (an acronym for something that begins, ominously, with "butyric"; the rest has been worn off the label) and lets me do the bathrooms. No service ethic challenges me here to new heights of performance. I just concentrate on removing the pubic hairs from the bath-tubs, or at least the dark ones that I can see. . . .

I can do this two-job thing, Is my theory, if I can drink enough caffeine . . . At eight, Ellen [a co-worker at Jerry's] and I grab a snack together standing at the mephitic end of the kitchen counter, but I can only manage two or three mozzarella sticks and lunch had been a mere handful of McNuggets. I am not tired at all, I assure myself, though It may be that there is simply no more "I" left to do the tiredness monitoring. What I would see, if I were more alert to the situation, is that the forces of destruction are already massing against me. There is only one cook on duty, a young man named Jesus ("Hay-Sue," that is) and he is new to the job. And there is Joy, who shows up to take over in the middle of the shift, wearing high heels and a long, clingy white dress and fuming as if she'd just been stood up in some cocktail bar.

Then it comes, the perfect storm. Four of my tables fill up at once. Four tables is nothing for me now, but only so long as they are obligingly staggered. As I bev table 27, tables 25, 28, and 24 are watching enviously. As I bev 25, 24 glowers because their bevs haven't even been ordered. Twenty-eight is four yuppyish types, meaning everything on the side and agonizing instructions as to the chicken Caesars. Twenty-five is a middle-aged black couple, who complain, with some justice, that the iced tea isn't fresh and the tabletop is sticky. But table 24 is the meteorological event of the century: 10 British tourists who seem to have made the decision to absorb the American experience entirely by mouth. Here everyone has at least two drinks—iced tea and milk shake, Michelob and water (with lemon slice, please)—and a huge promiscuous orgy of breakfast specials, mozz sticks, chicken strips, quesadillas, burgers with cheese and without, sides of hash browns with cheddar, with onions, with gravy, seasoned fries, plain fries, banana splits. Poor Jesus! Poor me! . . .

Much of what happened next is lost in the fog of war. Jesus starts going under. The little printer on the counter in front of him is spewing out orders faster than he can rip them off, much less produce the meals. Even the invincible Ellen is ashen from stress. I bring table 24 their reheated main courses, which they immediately reject as either too cold or fossilized by the microwave. When I return to the kitchen with their trays (three trays in three trips), Joy confronts me with arms akimbo: "What is this?" She means the food—the plates of rejected pancakes, hash browns in assorted flavours, toasts, burgers, sausages, eggs. "Uh, scrambled with cheddar," I try, "and that's . . . ""NO," she screams in my face. "Is it a traditional, a super-scramble, an eye-opener?" I pretend to study my cheque for a clue, but entropy has been up to its tricks, not only on the plates but in my head, and I have to admit that the original order is beyond reconstruction. "You don't know an eye-opener from a traditional?" she demands in outrage. All I know, in fact, is that my legs have lost interest in the current venture and have announced their intention to fold. I am saved by a yuppie (mercifully not one of mine) who chooses this moment to charge into the kitchen to bellow that his food is 25 minutes late. Joy screams at him to get the hell out of her kitchen, please, and then turns on Jesus in a fury, hurling an empty tray across the room for emphasis.

I leave. I don't walk out, I just leave. I don't finish my side work or pick up my credit-card tips, if any, at the cash register or, of course, ask Joy's permission to go. And the surprising thing is that you can walk out without permission, that the door opens, that the thick tropical night air pans to let me pass, that my car is still parked where I left it. There is no vindication in this exit . . . just an overwhelming, dank sense of failure pressing down on me and the entire parking lot. I had gone into this venture in the spirit of science, to test a mathematical proposition, but somewhere along the line, in the tunnel vision imposed by long shifts and relentless concentration, it became a test of myself, and clearly I have failed. . . .

When I moved out of the trailer park, I gave the key to number 46 to Gail and arranged for my deposit to be transferred to her. She told me that Joan is still living in her van and that Stu had been fired from the Hearthside. . . .

In one month, I had earned approximately $1,040 and spent $517 on food, gas, toiletries, laundry, phone, and utilities. If I had remained in my $500 efficiency, I would have been able to pay the rent and have $22 left over (which is $78 less than the cash I had in my pocket at the start of the month). During this time I bought no clothing except for the required slacks and no prescription drugs or medical care (I did finally buy some vitamin B to compensate for the lack of vegetables in my diet). Perhaps I could have saved a little on food if I had gotten to a supermarket more often, instead of convenience stores, but it should be noted that I lost almost four pounds in four weeks, on a diet weighted heavily toward burgers and fries. . . .

CRITICAL Reading Questions

1. What are the challenges to living on minimum wage? Is working for minimum wage sustainable? Why or why not?

2. What physical, psychological, and emotional problems come with the work Ehrenreich performed?

3. In her book, Ehrenreich writes that her experiences as a white woman were different than the experiences of men, visible minorities, and others. How do you think race, ethnicity, and gender impacted Ehrenreich's experience of low-wage labour?

4. Ehrenreich often notes that her experiences are different from those of "real" minimum-wage workers. What advantages did Ehrenreich have that other minimum-wage workers might not?

5. This article was published in 1999 and is based on experiences in the United States. How would this situation be different in Canada? How have things changed?

6. How does this reading help us to understand the problems with living on minimum wage? What does it tell us about the issue that other means, such as a survey or interview, would not reveal?

Poverty

Poverty—a state in which resources (material or cultural) are lacking—is a serious social problem in the world. We can think about this issue in terms of relative poverty, the deprivation of one individual in comparison with another, or absolute poverty, the life-threatening deprivation of an individual. Approximately a billion people, or 20 per cent of the global population, live in absolute poverty. Both types of poverty are important concerns in Canada. People who are homeless or who are unable to buy food, clothing, and other necessities live in absolute poverty. Many more people in Canada live in a state of precarious employment that is not necessarily life-threatening but places them in relative deprivation.

ACTIVITY

Creating Low-Income Cut-Offs (LICOs)

Defining poverty is a challenge because there are different thresholds (such as absolute and relative poverty) and because it is context dependent. Statistics Canada (2006) created **low-income cut-offs (LICOs)** to indicate the point at which a family spends more of its income on food, shelter, and clothing than an average family. These levels vary by family and community size; the LICOs in the following table represent the amount of money a person has to earn to be above the low-income threshold in Canada.

Low-income cut-offs (LICOs) before tax, Canada, 2011					
	Community Size				
Family Size	**Rural**	**<30,000**	**30,000–99,999**	**100,000–499,999**	**500,000+**
1 person	16,038	18,246	19,941	20,065	23,298
2 people	19,966	22,714	24,824	24,978	29,004
3 people	24,545	27,924	30,517	30,707	35,657
4 people	29,802	33,905	37,053	37,283	43,102
5 people	33,800	38,454	42,025	42,285	49,102
6 people	38,122	43,370	47,398	47,692	55,378
7+ people	42,443	48,285	52,770	53,097	61,656

SOURCE: Statistics Canada. 2012. "Low Income Lines, 2010 to 2011." Ottawa: Minister of Industry, 26. http://www.statcan.gc.ca/pub/75f0002m/75f0002m2012002-eng.pdf

1. Select a community size and a household size. For example, you could use your current living situation or the one you plan to have in the future. Using the table, determine the amount of money you need to live above the corresponding LICO. How much money would you have to make per hour (based on a 40-hour week) to pass that threshold?

2. The table below lists the minimum wage for each Canadian province and territory.

continued

Minimum wage by province, 2015	
Province	**Minimum Wage (in dollars)**
Alberta	11.20
British Columbia	10.45
Manitoba	11.00
New Brunswick	10.30
Newfoundland and Labrador	10.50
Northwest Territories	12.50
Nova Scotia	10.60
Nunavut	11.00
Ontario	11.25
Prince Edward Island	10.50
Quebec	10.55
Saskatchewan	10.50
Yukon	10.86

SOURCE: http://srv116.services.gc.ca/dimt-wid/sm-mw/rpt4.aspx?lang=eng.

a. Will working full-year, full-time allow you to live above the LICO? Could you take a vacation or time off if you or your family are ill? How much flexibility will you have in your work? Do you have health benefits for yourself and your family (i.e. dental, sick leave, prescriptions)?

b. Look up the rent for an apartment or house in your community. Could you afford this rent, along with food and clothing, on the amount of money indicated in the LICO? Is the LICO a reasonable measure of what you would need to survive in your community? Why or why not?

c. The LICO is based on the amount of money needed to pay for shelter, food and clothing. What other expenses are not included? How much do they cost? Are the costs likely to differ depending on your age, gender, and family situation? Why or why not?

Ehrenreich's article and the LICO activity demonstrate that living on minimum wage is a real struggle. In addition, many people are unable to find work or are unable to work because of health or other problems. These, and many other factors, lead to poverty. Almost 1 in 10 Canadians live in poverty, but one's propensity to live in this condition is not equally distributed. Table 3.2 compares the poverty rate among different groups of Canadians.

The table shows that the average poverty rate in the country decreased from 1981 to 2010, although it was at its highest level in 1996. Women are more likely than men to live in poverty, but the discrepancy between these two groups has decreased. New immigrants are also much more likely to live in poverty than the overall population, and people who live within families are much less likely to live in poverty than those who are single or who are lone parents. This last finding is not surprising when you consider that individuals living within families can share expenses (such as rent and car costs) and can rely on one another in times of resource scarcity (such as when one person loses a job or falls ill).

Poverty among the elderly is an interesting example of how social policies affect the lived experiences of individuals. As shown in Figure 3.5, poverty among this group

TABLE 3.2	Poverty rate by group, Canada, 1981–2010				
Persons in low income	**1981**	**1989**	**1996**	**2007**	**2010**
Sex					
Male	9.9	8.8	14.2	9.0	8.7
Female	13.3	11.6	16.2	9.3	9.3
Immigrant Status					
New Immigrant	12.6	14.2	32.8	16.9	17.6
Marital Status					
In Families	8.8	7.6	12.0	6.0	5.9
Unattached Individuals	35.5	29.0	36.1	27.6	26.9
Age					
Under 18	12.6	11.9	9.5	9.0	8.2
18–64	9.8	9.3	15.0	9.9	10.1
Over 65	21.0	11.3	9.7	4.8	5.3
National Average	11.6	10.2	15.2	9.1	9.0

SOURCES: Adapted from Citizens for Public Justice. 2012. *Poverty Trends Scorecard*, 5. www.cpj.ca/files/docs/poverty-trends
-scorecard.pdf; AMSSA. 2013. *The Intersection of Poverty and Immigration in BC and Canada.* www.amssa.org/files/Info_Sheet/.

was very high in the early and mid-1900s. To deal with this extremely important social issue, the Government of Canada instituted the **Canada Pension Plan (CPP)** in 1966. The first group to benefit from this plan turned 65 in 1976 and began to take the CPP at that time. We all pay CPP on each of our paycheques throughout our working lives (you probably noticed these deductions). When you reach the normal retirement age of 65, the CPP provides regular pension benefit payments to you. Everyone in Canada will get this benefit when they retire at 65.

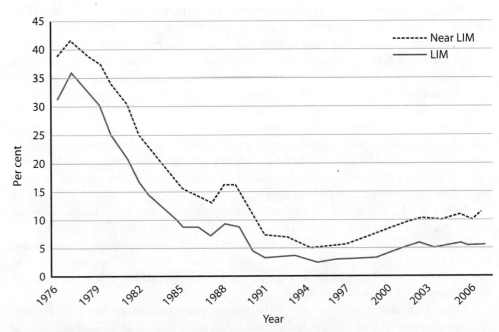

FIGURE 3.5 Canada's elderly poverty rate (per cent)

SOURCE: Tabulations by Tristat Resources using Statistics Canada SCPs and SLIDs. www.fin.gov.on.ca/en/consultations/pension/
dec09report.html#_Toc246235732.

PHOTO 3.5 Breakfast programs for school children are one way to address the symptoms of poverty (in this case, hunger) among at-risk groups (in this case, children). What other kinds of social programs try to minimize poverty's effects?

This program vastly reduced poverty among the elderly from around 33 per cent before the program was instituted (eligible citizens began collecting the pension in 1976) to 4 per cent in 1994, although poverty in this group is rising again (see Figure 3.5). These numbers illustrate that the CPP is very successful. Think about what programs we could institute to reduce poverty among other at-risk groups, such as children, women, new immigrants, First Nations people, or single-parent families.

The **cycle of poverty** refers to how poverty tends to perpetuate itself and is therefore likely to continue for an individual or group unless there is some outside intervention. The cycle of poverty is perpetuated by such factors as low (or no) income, little education, lack of sufficient housing and other material resources, insufficient social connections, and/or poor health. All these disadvantages compound to create a cycle that is very difficult to break and makes it extremely challenging for individuals to escape poverty.

For example, if you are poor and living on the street, you might be looking for a job. However, a job search is difficult when you do not have an address to put on your resumé, a computer to print a resumé, or clean clothes to wear to an interview. Children who come from poor families might find it hard to get out of this situation because it is difficult for them to do well in school without proper food, clothing, or supplies. In these ways, poverty can be a a self-perpetuating cycle.

In her article, Ehrenreich notes that living in poverty is very inefficient and expensive. If you do not have enough money to pay monthly rent up front, you might have to pay daily rates at a hotel or motel, which is considerably more expensive. If you cannot afford a car, you might not be able to get to supermarkets. As a result, you would have to buy groceries in small quantities at a corner store or eat out, which is less efficient and more expensive than cooking at home.

Ehrenreich also outlines some of the serious consequences to living in poverty. Perhaps the most obvious is that individuals living in poverty tend to have inadequate housing—housing that is unsafe, in poor repair, too small, or temporary. This housing tends to be in neighbourhoods with high crime rates, high levels of traffic, few public spaces (such as parks), and poor social services (such as schools, libraries, or community centres). Moreover, poverty is associated with inadequate nutrition, poor healthcare, poor physical and mental health, increased stress, and shorter life spans. Tjepkema, Wilkins, and Long (2013) found that, between 1991 and 2006, people with the lowest 20 per cent of income were 67 per cent more likely to die in that period than were those in the richest 20 per cent.

Summary

This chapter explored the importance of social class, social status, and inequality in Canadian society. Karl Marx understood social class as being based on an individual's relationship to the means of production—you are either a capitalist who owns the means of production or a worker who owns only your labour power. Max Weber added the importance of social status (the honour and prestige accorded to various groups) to Marx's ideas. Modern Canadian society tends to use socio-economic status to talk about social inequality. Based on income, education, and occupational prestige, this concept considers issues of class and status. The chapter also discussed issues of social mobility in Canada, comparing mobility across countries. Finally, we examined the important social issue of poverty in Canada. The activity on LICOs showed how we define poverty and how various groups are more or less likely to live in poverty.

Key Terms

achievement-based stratification system 82
ascriptive-based stratification system 82
bourgeoisie (capitalist) 66
Canada Pension Plan (CPP) 93
class 67
class consciousness 76
class struggle 66
cycle of poverty 94
false consciousness 74
ideology 73
intergenerational income elasticity 83

low-income cut-offs (LICOs) 91
party 81
poverty 91
power 78
proletariat (worker) 66
property 67
social mobility 81
socio-economic status (SES) 81
status group 79
surplus value 68
trade union density 76

For Further Reading

Ehrenreich, Barbara. 2001. *Nickel and Dimed: On (Not) Getting By in America*. New York: Metropolitan Books.
Gerth, H.H., and C. Wright Mills (eds.). 2009. *From Max Weber: Essays in Sociology*. New York: Routledge.
Giddens, Anthony. 1981. *The Class Structure of Advanced Societies*. London: Unwin Hynman.
Marx, Karl, and Frederick Engels. 1848. "Manifesto of the Communist Party." In *Marx/Engels Selected Works, Volume One*, 98–137. Moscow: Progress Publishers.
Tilly, Charles. 1999. *Durable Inequality*. Berkeley, CA: University of California Press.

Introduction

Globalization appears to be all around us. Its implications are complicated, and its promise or danger is understood differently depending on the theoretical lens used to examine it. In this chapter, we will discuss three core theories of globalization (modernization, world systems, and world society). We will also look at global inequality and examine how we can measure it, how it has changed, and how we can help alleviate it. Let's begin by thinking about globalization.

What Is Globalization?

We have all heard that we live in a globalized world. But what does this mean? What is globalization, how does it happen, and what effects does it have on Canada and other countries? **Globalization** is a process of increasing interconnectedness of people, products, ideas, and places. Globalization has several causes; for example, improvements in transportation systems and in communication and information technologies are particularly important factors. These developments facilitate the easy movement of people, products, and ideas, which can lead to political, economic, social, and cultural integration.

Globalization increases interconnectedness in three main ways. First, material or physical connections increase. The movement of goods, people, and money across national borders is relatively fluid. These increased flows are facilitated by shared global infrastructure. For example, physical global infrastructure, such as international transportation and banking systems, are shared across countries and make increased interaction and the exchange of goods and money relatively easy. In addition, normative similarities such as trade tariff agreements and friendly relations between countries develop from global infrastructure.

The importance of this physical interconnectedness is evident when we travel to different countries. Twenty years ago, people travelling from Canada to Europe had to take traveller's cheques or the currency of each country they would be visiting (e.g. British pounds, French francs, German marks, Italian lira). Now, we can all simply use our bankcard at any bank in Europe or pay with our credit card at any store or restaurant. The international banking system has facilitated European travel, and the use of the euro, the common currency of many European countries, makes moving between nations easier than ever before. (No more converting currencies in our heads!)

Second, globalization entails a spatio-temporal element; places that once felt very far away now feel much closer. We can get on a plane and be halfway around the world in a few hours or we can use technology such as Skype to talk to or e-mail friends who live in other cities or countries. The impact of distant events also becomes more relevant to our day-to-day lives. Tsunamis or famines occurring in other lands seem more real to us because we can easily (and almost instantly) see pictures or videos of them. The 9/11 terrorist attacks occurred around 9:00 a.m., yet many people did not hear about them until that afternoon or evening. Social media such as Twitter informed people of the Boston Marathon bombing minutes after it occurred in 2013.

This spatio-temporal convergence is the basis of theorist Marshall McLuhan's concept of the global village. The ease of international communication has allowed us to form an increasingly interconnected and unified global community, where we can easily interact and learn about faraway people and places. Through media such as the Internet, we can join Facebook groups, read blogs, or follow the Twitter feeds of people from other countries or continents. We can learn about world events and share updates about our lives instantaneously. McLuhan believed that this increased shared interaction creates a greater global responsibility for social betterment through heightened awareness. (We will learn more about McLuhan in Chapter 7.) An example of this idea is the Kony 2012 video, which exposed the brutality of militia leader Joseph Kony in Africa. The video has been viewed over 100 million times on YouTube; individuals from various countries have commented on the video, tweeted about the cause, or shared the link on Facebook to raise awareness, despite the fact that the situation did not directly affect them.

Another example of the spatio-temporal element of globalization is the impact that distant wars and conflicts can have on our daily lives. These effects can range from stricter airport security to higher gas prices. The latter helps to show the spatio-temporal element of globalization. Everyone has heard the complaint that the price of gas is rising. Oil companies, the news media, and other observers note that these prices are rising because of the conflicts in the Middle East, where much of the world's oil deposits exist. This relationship illustrates the globalized nature of world economies, as an overseas conflict affects our daily activity of buying gas.

The world's oil supply is a globalized commodity market. Canada produces a lot of oil—in fact, Alberta has the world's third largest oil reserves (behind only Saudi Arabia and Venezuela). Canada has 170.2 billion barrels, or about 11 per cent of the global oil reserve, and uses about 860 million barrels of oil a year (Alberta Energy 2014). These figures indicate that we have enough oil to meet our current use. If Canadians got all their oil from Alberta, global conflicts should not affect the price of gas in Canada. In other words, it should not matter that there are tensions or wars in the Middle East if we ship oil from Alberta to the other provinces and territories. However, all our oil, along with the oil from the Middle East and other regions, goes onto the global market and we compete with other countries to purchase it. As a result, international conflicts outside our control cause prices in Canada to fluctuate, despite our access to our own oil supply.

Finally, globalization has a cognitive element that involves the dissemination of ideas and culture throughout the world. This diffusion creates a situation in which cultural models can become increasingly similar across countries. If you have ever been in a remote location in another country and heard a Taylor Swift song on the radio or seen a McDonald's, you have witnessed the global dispersion of culture.

One positive example of the dissemination of cultural ideals is the spread of the concept of human rights. Most people would agree that individuals have the right to not suffer intentional and unwanted physical harm (unless provoked or legally necessary), to choose how to spend their time (within reasonable constraints), to have access to clean water and other resources necessary for survival, and to practise the religion of their choice. The first major human rights legislation, the International Declaration of Human Rights, was passed by the United Nations General Assembly in 1948. At that time, 48 countries signed the declaration, supporting the idea of human rights internationally. More recently, the United Nations (UN) passed the Convention on the Rights of Persons with Disabilities, which was signed by 91 countries and ratified in 2008. These two conventions illustrate the increased international support for the idea of human rights and the global spread of this cultural norm.

PHOTO 4.1 Oil pipeline construction can have important consequences for the Canadian and world economy, the environment, and domestic and international politics. How does this development illustrate the three main dimensions of globalization?

However, sharing ideas and cultural models is not always positive. Hearing a Taylor Swift song or seeing a McDonald's abroad would be a happy surprise to some and a disappointment to others. Other cultural ideals, such as consumerism and materialism, also spread from country to country. Bennett and colleagues (2004) found that Western ideals of beauty have significant reach, affecting many women and girls in other parts of the world. They compared young Ghanaian women with a very low body mass index (BMI) with a friend who had a normal index. Each young woman completed a survey on her eating habits and self-image. The researchers found that the rise in eating disorders in Ghana was partly explained by the low-weight girls' desire to conform to Western beauty standards. Other studies also report an increase in eating disorders among ethnic Fijian girls following the introduction of Western television. In essence, weight concerns and anorexia became more common as exposure to Western media increased.

<table>
<tr><td>**RESEARCH METHOD**</td></tr>
<tr><td>Survey</td></tr>
</table>

Understanding Globalization

It is important to recognize that globalization does not occur in one direction—we are not simply becoming more globalized. In other words, globalization is not a process of linear evolution but one that involves regressions and advances. The world is generally becoming more interconnected, but there are still times when countries or individuals become more isolationist. For example, a country might raise taxes on imported goods, restrict the amount of foreign content on television, or increase the barriers to entering its territory. Globalization is also not always a harmonious process. Not all individuals agree that becoming more interconnected is a good idea or is beneficial for all. For some countries, increased globalization can lead to a waning of culture, increased unemployment, and loss of autonomy over national services and resources. Academics, politicians, and the public continue to debate globalization's potential advantages and disadvantages, and concerned citizens and social movements encourage, contest, and challenge this process.

Globalization is a complicated process that can greatly affect individuals, communities, countries, and the world. Theorists have advanced several ways to understand it, including modernization theory, world systems theory, and world society theory. The following sections examine these approaches and the ways these different theoretical lenses can help us to shed light on different aspects of globalization.

Modernization Theory

Modernization theory attempts to isolate the features that predict which societies will progress and develop. This theory argues that a society's internal features, including its economic, social, and cultural systems, can either help or hinder development. It also claims that certain traditional sets of values and processes hinder certain countries' development. This theory argues that, by emulating the more "successful" advanced nations, all countries can develop. Modernization theory claims that countries are poor because they cling to traditional and inefficient attitudes, technologies, and institutions. In contrast, modern societies embrace industrial capitalism, advanced technologies, and modern institutions. With enough time and the help of "correct" behaviours, all societies can become modernized and develop like Western societies.

Moreover, modernization theory encourages all countries to strive to modernize in the same way that Western Europe and North America did. This process requires that societies go through a set of established stages. W.W. Rostow (1991) describes these steps in his famous book, *The Stages of Economic Growth: A Non-Communist Manifesto* (a play on the title of Marx and Engels's *Communist Manifesto*). Rostow argues that all societies start as traditional societies, which emphasize the importance of history and tradition. Traditional societies are static and rigid in that they have very little economic

HIGHLIGHT ///

Modernization Theory and Émile Durkheim

Modernization theory takes some of its ideas from Émile Durkheim (1960), who was interested in the social evolution of societies. He argued that, like organisms, societies progress through several stages: they start simple and evolve into more complex forms of organization.

Sociologists often focus on social problems, but Durkheim was more interested in how society functions fairly effectively, even when people have conflicting interests. In particular, he was interested in explaining social solidarity, a feeling of unity among people in a society. How do we explain this harmony? How has the foundation of such solidarity changed as societies have altered?

Durkheim argued that early societies were based on **mechanical solidarity**. Each unit (such as a family) basically provided for its own production and consumption needs, and subunits could survive in isolation from one another. A family might live on a small subsistence farm, where it would grow its own crops and make its own clothes, candles, and soap. In these societies, each unit could survive on its own—a family did not need to rely on anyone else to make goods for it or provide it with services. However, these societies were held together by a shared sense of collective consciousness, the shared beliefs and sentiments that created solidarity between people. For example, most people in a village or town were of the same religion and thus had a shared set of beliefs about appropriate behaviours and attitudes.

Modern societies tend to be comprised of people who are quite different from one another. There is no common adherence to a collective conscience—people are from different religions, cultural traditions, or philosophies, especially in a country as multicultural as Canada. As a result, individuals are guided by distinct norms and values that weaken the overall collective consciousness. This period is also associated with an increased division of labour, with more and more people engaging in specialized tasks and activities. Some people are teachers, some farmers, others architects. Because different people perform different functions in society, no group can survive on its own. Farmers have food, but they probably cannot build their own houses or educate their children; they need architects and teachers, just as the architects and teachers need farmers to grow their food. These societies are based on **organic solidarity**: because people are dissimilar and specialized, they depend on one another to provide what they cannot supply for themselves.

Given recent technological advancements, are we still in Durkheim's period of organic solidarity? In our daily lives, we encounter numerous scenarios where we use machines to perform a function instead of relying on another human. We bank online or use an ATM rather than wait for a teller; we get our own soft drink at a fast-food restaurant rather than wait for a cashier to do it for us; we even check out our own groceries at the supermarket. Even more complex tasks are being replaced by technological media. For example, we self-diagnose our ailments on WebMD rather than consult a doctor or purchase Rosetta Stone to learn a language rather than take a course.

mobility and prioritize stability over change. They are based on subsistence agriculture (the growing of crops to feed the farmer's own livestock and family) or hunting and gathering. These societies, such as those in the feudal systems of medieval Europe, focus on spiritual richness but lack material abundance.

As the demand for raw materials increased, these traditional societies could not keep up. They were pushed to develop more productive, commercial agriculture and to create **cash crops** (crops to be sold instead of consumed by the producers). Widespread technological advances, including the development of irrigation systems and ports, led to increased productivity and the broader dissemination of goods. All these changes facilitated an increase in social mobility and put the previous social equilibrium, which had existed for centuries, in flux. This period is called the pre-conditions to takeoff (Rostow 1991).

The second period is economic takeoff, during which manufacturing becomes more efficient and increases in size and scale. Because of this mass productivity, societies are able to produce goods for both domestic consumption and export. Markets emerge as people produce goods to trade with others for profit. This phase is also a time of rising individualism, which is focused on individual material enrichment and can undermine family ties and time-honoured norms and values.

Next, societies move toward technological maturity. In this period, all sectors of society become involved in market production, and international trade rises. Economies become increasingly diversified, with many different goods and services produced and sold. This period is also associated with a great reduction in absolute poverty. Cities grow as people leave rural villages in search of jobs and economic opportunities in urban areas. The rise of individualism and an increased sense of efficacy generate social movements demanding greater political rights to, for example, provide universal basic education and increase the rights of various groups, such as women and minorities.

The final period of development is mass consumption. The mass production that occurred in the last period stimulates this stage. People soon feel that they need the new diversity of products available and consume those goods accordingly. Because consumers

PHOTO 4.2 Black Friday, held the day after American Thanksgiving, is an extreme example of concentrated mass consumption. Retailers offer extreme sales and special deals to encourage the consumption of goods beyond basic needs. In 2013, US consumers spent more than $57 billion on this one day. Black Friday has come to Canadian stores, even though Canadians celebrate Thanksgiving a month earlier. How does Black Friday illustrate the mass consumption that occurs in modern society?

now have more disposable income, they are able to consume more. Canadian society currently resides in this stage.

Modernization theorists argue that, for most of human history, the whole world was poor. In fact, countries began moving out of poverty only a few centuries ago. From this perspective, it is the current affluence in some modern countries that demands an explanation. How have some countries been able to move out of poverty? During the Middle Ages, a proliferation of exploration and trade brought wealth to a growing share of people in Western Europe. The Industrial Revolution and the growth of capitalism also created vast new wealth. This affluence was initially concentrated in the hands of the few; however, the industrial system was so productive that its benefits soon expanded to include a growing number of people. Today, middle-income countries in Latin America and Asia are also industrializing and becoming wealthier as a result.

If industrialization has such potential to reduce poverty, why isn't the whole world moving in this direction? Modernization theory points to tradition as the greatest barrier to development. Traditional family values, gender roles, and cultural models can hinder the adoption of new technologies and procedures. But not all societies seek new technology or embrace new methods of production; many people resist such advances because they see them as threats to their social and cultural systems and beliefs.

However, modernization theorists argue that traditional societies should embrace modern technologies and production methods. A specific change that would help countries develop is to focus on cash crops of high-yield agricultural products. As mentioned earlier, traditional societies are based on subsistence farming, while more developed countries sell their crops for profit. Most farms in Canada and other developed countries currently practise **monocropping**, an economically efficient and profitable method of repeatedly growing one high-yield crop. Farmers using this technique can purchase specialized equipment and design their fields and irrigation systems for the specific crop. By adopting this method, they can use the profits to purchase consumer goods and other products that would improve their lives. In theory, the process would lead to more economic productivity and to Rostow's period of economic takeoff.

Monocropping not only leads to prosperity, but it can also increase short-term food production. However, it has certain disadvantages. Relying on cash crops can be volatile and unsustainable. Prices for major cash crops are set on a global scale; therefore, nations, regions, or individual producers of these crops are at the market's mercy. (This situation is similar to Canadian oil being put on the global market and its price being affected by global production and conflict.) Monocropping is also controversial because it has long-term environmental disadvantages. It can damage the soil, lead to the growth of parasites, and increase crop vulnerability to opportunistic insects and plants.

Modernization theory as a whole has been criticized on a number of different fronts. Some argue that it fails to recognize that rich nations industrialized from a position of global strength, colonizing other countries and taking their resources. As a result, the countries that colonized early were able to accumulate wealth, while the colonized countries were exploited and became poorer. In other words, the European takeoff period was fuelled by the resources (including natural resources and human resources in the form of forced slavery) taken from other countries. Colonization was hugely problematic at the time and is now an unrealistic (and undesirable) avenue for development. Furthermore, the idea that poor countries remain poor because of "backward" ways or a refusal to embrace technologies or progress suggests that all countries have the same resources and opportunities to develop, which is surely not the case.

Modernization theory is also criticized for being ethnocentric, or judging other cultures by the standards of one's own. Many question whether it is fair to measure other countries against Western standards or to assume that the Western mode of doing things is best. Western notions of development have led to many problems, such as environmental degradation and materialism. Is it, then, good to push other countries to become more like Western nations?

ACTIVITY

The Ecological Footprint

We can get a sense of how much we impact the natural environment by calculating our **ecological footprint**—the amount of land and sea necessary to supply the resources a human population consumes and to process the waste it produces. We can use this information to estimate how much of the earth (or how many earths) it would take to support an individual or country if everybody followed a given way of life (www.footprintnetwork.org).

Go to this book's companion website to access a test that calculates your ecological footprint. When you have completed the test, answer the following questions:

1. How many earths would there have to be for everyone to live your lifestyle?

2. Where did most of your footprint come from—carbon, food, housing, or goods and services? Were you surprised at the areas where you had the largest and smallest footprints? If so, why?

3. How did your footprint compare with others from your country? Why is your footprint larger or smaller than the average Canadian's?

4. What advice does the test give for reducing your footprint? What other methods could you use to reduce it? Discuss which ways would be easiest and which would be hardest.

Now let's look at a bigger picture and compare ecological footprints in different parts of the world. The figure below shows the relationship between a country's footprint and its **Human Development Index (HDI)**, a number that combines a variety of measures regarding the health and quality of life in a country (e.g. life expectancy, education, and income). Examine the figure and then answer the following questions.

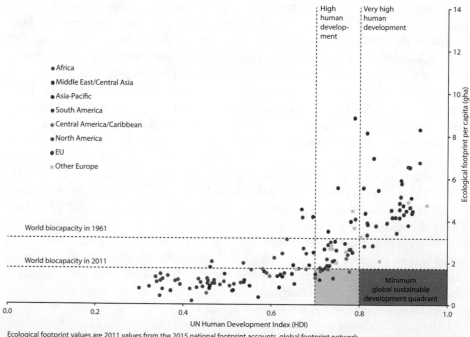

Ecological footprint values are 2011 values from the 2015 national footprint accounts, global footprint network
HDI 2011 values are from the 2014 human development report, UNDP

Human welfare and ecological footprints compared

SOURCE: Ecological Footprint values are 2011 values from the 2015 National Footprint Accounts, Global Footprint Network
HDI 2011 values are from the 2014 Human Development Report, UNDP.

1. Which regions have the largest ecological footprints and which have the smallest? How do the world's regions differ in their human development and in their ecological footprint?

2. How is a country's human development related to its ecological footprint? Why do you think this relationship exists?

World Systems Theory

Developed by Immanuel Wallerstein (2011) as a critique of modernization theory, **world systems theory** highlights the inherent inequality that occurs through globalization and global development. World systems theory understands globalization in a very different way than modernization theory does; it sees the world as a transnational division of labour between core, semi-periphery, and periphery countries.

Core countries are the most powerful nations in the world. Their power is based on their economic diversification, high level of industrialization, high-skill labour, and focus on the manufacturing of goods instead of simply extracting raw resources for export. These nations dominate new technologies and industries and can exert significant economic and military influence over other countries. Core countries have been traditionally found in the northwest of Europe; however, Canada, the United States, and Japan are now part of the core.

Periphery countries are the least powerful of the three types. They are not economically diversified and are only minimally industrialized. These countries focus on extracting raw materials for export to core countries. Periphery nations, which are concentrated in Latin America and sub-Saharan Africa, are attractive to core countries' business interests because they tend to have lax labour and environmental laws.

Semi-periphery countries, such as China, India, Brazil, and South Africa, combine characteristics of the core and periphery. They are often countries moving toward industrialization and economic diversification. Canada was once a semi-periphery country, when its economy was focused on resource extraction and it had very low levels of industrialization.

As the example of Canada's shift from the periphery to the core highlights, countries can gain power over time. They can also lose power. Many countries, such as the Netherlands and the United Kingdom, have had the distinction of being superpowers for a time. However, this status is hard to maintain.

World systems theory is based on Marxist principles. Think of the core countries as the capitalists. They benefit from the labour of the proletariat countries (the periphery) in a number of ways. First, companies in the core take the resources from the periphery countries, such as the United States extracting oil from the Middle East. Second, they use periphery countries' labour power and pay very low wages (which they cannot do in their own countries because of unions and labour laws). A classic example is companies such as Nike or Walmart, both American corporations, outsourcing their labour to countries such as Bangladesh or China. Third, core countries pollute periphery countries and deplete their resources. Companies from the core might clear forests to make space for factories, which decreases air quality. As with labour exploitation, environmental protection laws prohibit companies from engaging in these practices in their own countries. Finally, the capitalists in core countries sell the goods produced in the periphery to the workers in the periphery. These wealthy owners bring the resulting profits back to the core countries. In this way, poorer nations keep getting poorer and can never catch up economically.

According to world systems theorists, the unequal trade relations between the core and periphery countries create many problems for those in the latter. Periphery countries are pressured to produce a small variety of cash crops that are oriented to export (as the modernization theorists encourage). For example, these countries might be encouraged

ACTIVITY

Commodity Chains and Global Inequality

Chances are that the clothing you wear, the computer you use, and the car or bus you take to school are made in countries other than Canada. Goods come to Canada through **commodity chains**, which gather resources, transform them into commodities, and distribute them to consumers. This process is a natural part of globalization.

Greg Linden, Kenneth Kraemer, and Jason Dedrick (2009) were interested in the commodity chains of an Apple iPod. They examined where the product originated and where its value went. They write: "An iPod is designed and marketed by a US company, assembled by Taiwanese manufacturers in China, and includes key parts from Japanese, Korean and US suppliers" (140). This list does not even scratch the surface regarding the places where the raw materials—silicon, copper, gold, aluminum—and chemicals come from; they could, for example, originate in the United States, Canada, Russia, Brazil, India, Zambia, or others. Most of the profit, however, goes to the United States, with very little remaining in the countries where the iPod is made (see the following table).

The geography of $190 of the captured value in a single $299 video iPod						
	Country of Final Sale	United States	Japan	Korea	Taiwan	Total
Distribution and Retail	75					75
Apple		80				80
Top 10 Components		7	27	1	5	40
TOTAL	75	87	27	1	5	195

SOURCE: Linden, Greg, Kenneth L. Kraemer, and Jason Dedrick. 2009. "Who Captures Value in a Global Innovation Network? The Case of Apple's iPod." *Communications of the* ACM 52 (3): 140–4.

For this activity, choose a product (either a Starbucks coffee and cup or a Nike shoe) and look at its manufacturing and delivery routes. What stops (farms, factories, regions, countries) contribute to making the finished product? Use the Internet to research where your chosen product comes from and how it is made. Then check the CIA's *World Factbook* online (or access the direct link on this book's companion website) for information about the countries involved in making the product. Click on the economy, people, and government links to examine the conditions in these countries, including average life expectancy, infant mortality rate, unemployment rate, percentage of the population living below the poverty line, and inequality. With this information in mind, why do you think that your product was made in those countries? What is the implication of this process for global inequality?

to produce coffee beans for export instead of fruits and vegetables, which could feed the local population. In addition, periphery countries are urged to extract natural resources in their raw formats and export them to core countries, where they are processed (e.g. mined stones set in rings or furniture built out of raw lumber) to make a profit. This process destroys the local environment in peripheral countries.

Local industries in the periphery cannot compete with companies from the core. As a result, few local businesses develop in the periphery and workers must buy their processed goods from the core countries at high cost, creating more debt. For example, periphery countries sell cheap resources and raw materials to the core. To do so, they must buy expensive fertilizers, pesticides, and mechanical equipment from the core. This downward cycle leads the periphery to become poorer as the core becomes richer. Just as in Marx's theory, poor and rich countries depend on one another, but the benefits of their relationship are skewed toward the rich core nations.

World systems theory argues that resources flow from the periphery to the core and ideas and procedures flow in the opposite direction. For example, the flow of news and entertainment media privileges the core's needs and interests. News about the core is reported everywhere in the periphery, while news about the periphery is rarely reported in the core. Thus, people in the periphery know a lot about processes and current events in core countries. Barack Obama's inauguration was reported all over the world; however, the armed conflict in Peru that killed approximately 70,000 people from 1980 to 2000 was rarely covered in core media outlets. This lack of dialogue perpetuates exploitation and global inequality, as those with the means to help create change (such as core country citizens) are usually unaware of events in the periphery.

Like all theories, world systems theory has been criticized. For example, many people note that foreign trade has assisted some countries. Trade with rich countries has helped the economies of Singapore, Hong Kong, and Japan. Others also argue that, as modernization theory predicts, foreign investment stimulates growth, not economic decline. Furthermore, the ability of countries to move into the core counters the claim that globalization will lead to increased poverty in the periphery.

In this chapter's first reading, Daina Stukuls Eglitis asks why rich nations don't do more to reduce world poverty. This is a great question—most people in core countries believe that global poverty is a significant social issue. However, global poverty continues and may even be worsening. How do we explain this trend? Eglitis argues that people in rich countries benefit from global poverty. This argument is difficult to accept, especially for those who live in a rich country.

READING

The Uses of Global Poverty: How Economic Inequality Benefits the West

Daina Stukuls Eglitis

Why don't rich nations do more to reduce the severe poverty that paralyzes much of the world? This selection argues that people in rich countries, including the United States, actually benefit from global poverty in a number of ways.

In the global village, there stand a wide variety of homes, from the stately mansion on the hill, to the modest abode blessed with electricity and running water, to the adequate but un-heated (or uncooled) hut, to the flood-prone, tattered shanty cobbled together from gath-ered scrap. Those who live on the hill are aware of their neighbours, as their neighbours are aware of them. Most inhabitants of the global village recognize that wealth and the accom-panying opportunities for education, healthcare, and consumption are not evenly divided and that a substantial gap exists between the more and less materially blessed populations. Not everyone agrees on why that is the case. . . .

What have been the responses of well-off states to this global class system with its extremes of wealth and poverty? Not surprisingly, perhaps, political rhetoric has consistently elevated the goal of spreading the prosperity enjoyed by the advanced industrial states of the West around the globe. . . .

If shared global prosperity was the goal, it seems safe to say that while there was some modest progress made in areas like Latin America, Eastern Europe, and parts of Asia, "we" did not really succeed, because the global wealth gap is still massive and growing. The rich countries remain rich, and the poor countries, for the most part, remain trapped in desperate, dire poverty. This has not changed. . . .

Western rhetoric, assistance programs, and advice seem to support the goal of global prosperity and its extension to the 1.3 billion who live on less than $1 per day and those millions or even billions more who eke out a sparse existence just above the threshold of absolute poverty. But the reality of prosperity has touched only a relative few countries, while the struggle to meet basic needs touches many more. Social indicators like the GNI PPP [gross national income purchasing power parity] highlight the differences we find in our village. But what explains them? Why does global poverty exist and persist? Why does a global class system with a thin layer of rich states and a broad strata of poor countries exist and persist? What explains why some villagers inhabit houses on the mount while others squat in mud huts below? Possible answers are many. This article explores one way of understanding the yawning gap between the planet's wealthiest and poorest states.

In 1971, sociologist Herbert Gans published an article entitled "The Uses of Poverty: The Poor Pay All."[1] In the article, Gans utilized a conservative theoretical perspective in sociology, functionalism, to inquire about the persistence of poverty in America. The functionalist perspective takes as its starting point the position that essentially all institutions and social phenomena that exist in society contribute in some manner to that society—that is, they are functional for society. If they did not contribute to the social order, the functionalists maintain, they would disappear. Using this perspective, functionalists may inquire about, for instance, the functions, both obvious and hidden (or manifest and latent, to use sociologist Robert Merton's terms), of institutions like the education system or the family or social phenomena like punishment for deviance. These social theorists assume that institutions or phenomena exist because they are functional, and hence their guiding question is, What function do they serve?

Gans posed a similar question about poverty, asking, What are the uses of poverty? Clearly, the notion that poverty is functional for society as a whole is ludicrous: Who would suggest that it is functional for those who endure economic deprivation? So Gans offered a modified functionalist analysis: ". . . instead of identifying functions for an entire social system, I shall identify them for the interest groups, socio-economic classes, and other population aggregates with shared values that 'inhabit' a social system. I suspect that in a modern heterogeneous society, few phenomena are functional or dysfunctional for the society as a whole, and that most result in benefits to some groups and costs to others."

Gans sought to explain the existence and persistence of poverty in modern, wealthy America by highlighting the way that the existence of poverty has benefits for the non-poor—not just "evil" individuals like the loan shark or the slumlord, but for "normal" members of nonpoor classes. He identified 13 "uses" of poverty, including the notions that the existence of a poor class "ensures that society's 'dirty work' will be done," that the poor buy goods others do not want and thus prolong the economic usefulness of such goods," and "the poor can be identified and punished as alleged or real deviants in order to uphold the legitimacy of conventional norms." He was not arguing that poverty is good. He was suggesting that understanding poverty's existence and persistence means recognizing that the poor have positive social and economic functions for the nonpoor. Thus, one would conclude that the elimination of poverty, while elevated as a societal goal, would be, in practice, costly to the nonpoor.

While Gans's theoretically based inquiry into poverty was focused on America's poor, the same question might be asked about the existence of global poverty: What are the "uses" of global poverty for the better-off countries of the world economic system? The purpose of such an inquiry would be, as it was in Gans's inquiry, not to use a functionalist analysis to legitimate poverty or the highly skewed distribution of wealth in the global system, but to contribute to a deeper understanding of why it continues to exist by explaining how its persistence confers benefits on well-off states and their inhabitants.

The argument is not that advanced states are consciously conspiring to keep the poor states destitute: well-off countries have historically sought to offer help to less developed countries. In reality, however, there are limited incentives for the better-off states to support the full industrial and technological (and even democratic) development of all the states in the global system. To the degree that the existence of a class of poor states is positively functional for wealthy states, we can begin to imagine why development and assistance programs that help ensure survival, but not prosperity, for poor populations are quite characteristic of Western policy.

This article notes 11 "uses" of global poverty. Global poverty is not, from this perspective, functional for the global community as a whole. The notion that the poverty of billions who live in economically marginal states is globally "useful" would be absurd. But it is not absurd to ask how the existence of a class of poor states serves wealthy states. In fact, asking such a question might contribute to a better understanding of the dual phenomena of global poverty and the global "class" system.

Point 1: The existence of global poverty helps ensure the wealth of affordable goods for Western consumers.

The cornucopia of decently priced goods of reasonable quality enjoyed by Western consumers is underpinned by the low-wage work done in low-income countries. The labels on the clothing you are wearing right now likely contain the familiar words "Made in China" or perhaps "Made in Pakistan." Your clothing is probably of reasonable quality, and you likely paid a reasonable (but not necessarily cheap) price for it.

The Western consumer of textiles such as off-the-rack clothing is a beneficiary of a globalized manufacturing process that has seen the movement of manufacturing to low-wage areas located in poor states that provide ready pools of workers needy enough to labour for a pittance. In China, the average hourly wage of apparel workers is about 23 cents. This benefits the consumer of that apparel. The worker herself (workers in this industry are usually female) derives less benefit: the average hourly wage needed to meet basic needs in China, according to Women's Edge, an advocacy group, is 87 cents.[2] . . .

Stories about low-wage workers in developing countries have, in recent years, emerged in the Western press and provoked some expressions of outrage and the formation of groups like United Students Against Sweatshops. These expressions have been small and limited. Imagine, however, the outrage if popular sports shoes, already pricey, climbed another $50 in cost as a result of manufacturers opting for well-paid, unionized labour. Or imagine if the price of a head of iceberg lettuce, America's favourite vegetable, suddenly doubled in price to $3.00. Which outrage would be more potent?

Point 2: The existence of global poverty benefits Western companies and shareholders in the form of increased profit margins.

Labour costs typically constitute a high percentage of a company's expenditures. By reducing labour costs, companies can both keep prices reasonable (which benefits, as noted, the consumer) and raise profit margins. Not surprisingly, then, companies are not likely to locate in—and are more likely to leave—locations where wages are relatively high. The use of poor female workers in the Third World is, in this respect, especially "beneficial" to companies. Women comprise about 80 per cent of workers in Export Processing Zones and are often paid 20 per cent to 50 per cent less than male counterparts. The less costly the workforce, the greater the opportunity for profit. Not coincidentally, countries with an ample supply of poor workers willing to work for miserable wages are also countries with lax safety and environmental regulations, which also keeps down the costs to the Western employer and pushes up the profits. Hence, companies benefit directly from the existence of economically deprived would-be workers willing (or not in a position to be unwilling) to work for paltry wages in potentially hazardous, or at least very unpleasant, conditions.

Point 3: The existence of global poverty fosters access to resources in poor states that are needed in or desired by the West.

Poor states may sell raw goods at low prices to Western states, which can transform the resource into a more valuable finished product. The position of the poor states in the world economy makes it less likely that they can derive the full benefit of the resources they possess for the government and people. The case of oil in resource-rich but desperately poor Nigeria is an example. Seven major foreign oil companies operate in Nigeria, all representing interests in wealthy states. The vast majority of benefits from Nigeria's oil has accrued not to the country's people, but to the companies (and consumers) of the wealthy states. . . .

Point 4: The existence of global poverty helps support Western medical advances.

The poor provide a pool of guinea pigs for the testing of medicines developed for use primarily in the West. The beneficiaries are not the poor themselves but Western consumers of advanced medicine (60 per cent of profits are made in the United States, which leads the world in drug consumption) and the pharmaceutical companies, which stand astride a $350 billion (and growing) industry. A series of reports in *The Washington Post* in December 2000 documents the disturbing practice of conducting drug trials on ill inhabitants of poor states. For instance, an unapproved antibiotic was tested by a major pharmaceutical company on sick children during a meningitis epidemic in Nigeria. The country's lax regulatory oversight, the sense among some doctors that they could not object to experiment conditions for political or economic reasons, the dearth of alternative healthcare options, combined with the desire of the company to rapidly prepare for the market a potential "blockbuster" drug underpinned a situation in which disease victims were treated as test subjects rather than patients. This case highlights the way that nonpoor states actually benefit from the existence of poor states with struggling, sick populations. . . .

Point 5: The existence of global poverty contributes to the advancement of Western economies and societies with the human capital of poor states.

Poorer states like India have become intellectual feeders of well-educated and bright individuals whose skills cannot be fully rewarded in less developed states. The magnetic draw of a better life in economies that amply reward their human capital pulls the brightest minds from their countries of origin, a process referred to as "brain drain." Advanced economies such as the United States and England are beneficiaries of brain drain. The United States has moved to take advantage of the pool of highly educated workers from the developing world. . . .

Point 6: The existence of global poverty may contribute to the pacification of the Western proletariat, or "Workers of the World, A Blue Light Special!"

To some degree, the broad availability of good, inexpensive merchandise may help obscure class divisions in the West, at least in the arena of consumption. It is clear that those with greater wealth can consume more high-quality goods, but low-end "designer" merchandise is accessible to the less well-off in cathedrals of consumption such as Wal-Mart. At K-Mart, for instance, Martha Stewart peddles her wares, intended to transform "homemaking chores . . . into what we like to call 'domestic art.'" Thanks in part to the low-wage workers in places like China, these goods are available to the unwashed masses (now washed by Martha's smart and cozy towels) as well as to better-situated homemakers. Consumption appears to be one of the great equalizers of modern society. (It is worth noting, though, that many members of the Western working class are also "victims" of global poverty, since many jobs have gone abroad to low-wage areas, leaving behind, for less educated workers, positions in the less remunerative and less secure service industry or leaving former industrial workers jobless.)

Point 7: Global poverty benefits the West because poor countries make optimal dumping grounds for goods that are dangerous, expired, or illegal.

Wealthy countries and their inhabitants may utilize poorer states as repositories for dangerous or unwanted material such as nuclear waste. The desperation of cash-strapped states benefits better-off countries, which might otherwise have difficulty ridding themselves of the dangerous by-products of their industrial and consumer economies. For instance, in December 2000, the Russian Parliament, in an initial vote on the issue, overwhelmingly supported the amendment of an environmental law to permit the importation of foreign nuclear waste. The alteration of the law was supported by the Atomic Ministry of the Russian Federation, which suggested that over the next decade, Russia might earn up to $21 billion from the importation of spent nuclear fuel from states like Japan, Germany, and South Korea. Likely repositories of the radioactive refuse are Mayak and Krasnoyarsk, already among the most contaminated sites on the planet. . . .

Point 8: The existence of global poverty provides jobs for specialists employed to assist, advise, and study the world's poor and to protect the "better-off" from them.

Within this group of specialists we find people in a variety of professions. There are those who are professional development workers, operating through organizations like the United States Agency for International Development (USAID) . . .

Academics in fields as diverse as economics, sociology, international affairs, political science, and anthropology study, write about, and "decipher" the lives of the poor and the condition of poor states. Texts on development, articles debating why poverty persists, and books from university presses are only some of the products of this research. Journalists and novelists can build careers around bringing colourful, compelling representations of the poor to the warm living rooms of literate, well-off consumers. Still others are charged with the task of protecting wealthy states from "invasions" of the poor: US border patrols, for instance, employ thousands to keep those seeking better fortunes out of US territory.

Point 9: Global poverty benefits inhabitants of wealthy countries, who can feel good about helping the global poor through charitable work and charitable giving.

From the celebrity-studded musical production "We are the World" to trick-or-treating for UNICEF, those who inhabit the wealthy corners of the world feel good about themselves for sharing their good fortune. The website of World Vision, a faith-based charity that offers the opportunity to sponsor poor children, features a speak-out area for contributors. On that site, a young Canadian sponsor wrote, "A few days ago I woke up early and turned the TV on . . . looking at those children made me realize I could help them. I thought if I have enough money to pay for the Internet, cellphone, and a couple of other things I didn't need, I said to myself, [then] why not give that money to people who need it instead of spending it all in (sic) luxury and things that are not really important. . . . I immediately picked up the phone and called to sponsor a child! I am happy. I can help someone who needs it!"[3]

Apparently, we need not feel guilt about consuming many times what the unfortunate inhabitants of the world's poor states do if only we are willing to give up a few of our luxuries to help them . . .

A related point is that the poor we see on television or hear about in news or music give those of us in wealthy countries the opportunity to feel good about ourselves, regardless of our position in the socio-economic structure of our own states. . . .

Point 10: The poverty of less developed states makes possible the massive flow of resources westward.

Imagine if large and largely poor countries like China, Nigeria, and India consumed at US rates. At present, Americans consume a tremendously disproportionate share of the world's resources. With their profligate use of all manner of resources, most notably fossil fuels, Americans are the greediest consumers of natural resources on the planet. On both an absolute and per capita basis, most world resources flow westward. Notably, a 4 October 2000 article in *The Seattle Times* reported that bicycles, long a characteristic and popular means of transport for Chinese commuters, are losing popularity: "Increasingly, young Chinese are not even bothering to learn to ride bikes, because growing wealth has unleashed a plethora of transportation choices, public and private."[4] The new transportation of choice is still largely public buses or private taxis: the Chinese have not yet graduated to mass private cars. But it is interesting to ponder whether there would be enough (affordable) oil for everyone if the Chinese, with their growing population and prosperity, became a country of two-vehicle families or developed a taste and market for gas-guzzling sports utility vehicles. In this case, the West likely benefits from the fact that few can afford (at least at present) to consume at the rate its people do.

Point 11: The poorer countries, which reproduce at rates higher than Western states, are useful scapegoats for real and potential global environmental threats.

What is the bigger environmental threat to our planet? Is it the rapid growth of the populations of developing states or the rapid consumption of resources by the much smaller populations of developed states? The overdevelopment of the West may well be the bigger threat, though the growth of populations in Third World countries, which is often linked to conditions of underdevelopment, such as a lack of birth control and the need to have "extra" children as a hedge against high child mortality rates, makes an attractive alternative explanation for those who would not wish to fault the SUV-driving, disposable-diaper using, BBQ-loving American consumer for threats to the global environment. While some Western policy-makers express concern about the environmental threats emerging from rapid population growth or the use of "dirty" technology in developing states, there is comparably little serious attention given to the global threat presented by the profligate consumption by Western states. The poor divert attention from the environmental problems caused by Western overconsumption.

I have talked about 11 ways that the continued existence of global poverty benefits those who reside in wealthy states. The argument I have offered to explain the persistence of a strata of poor states and the yawning global gap highlights the idea that while global poverty (and the status quo) is beneficial to the wealthy West, serious steps to alleviate it will not be taken.

It is surely the case that poverty does not have to exist. But while we in the West derive the benefits and bonuses of these economic inequalities, it seems likely that our efforts to support, advise, and assist the less developed states will remain at levels that are financially and politically convenient and feasible, and will target survival rather than true prosperity for those outside our gated, privileged, greedy Western neighbourhood. In Gans's words, "Phenomena like poverty can be eliminated only when they become dysfunctional for the affluent or powerful, or when the powerless can obtain enough power to change society."

NOTES

1. *Social Policy*, July/August 1971.
2. Information on issues of trade and Chinese women is available at http://www.womensedge.org. The information cited is from the April 2000 web issue of *Notes from the Edge*.
3. The charity's website address is http//www.worldvision.org.
4. The article is cited at the website of the Competitive Enterprise Institute: http://www.cei.org/CHNReader.asp?ID=1227.

1. How does this article use ideas from structural functionalism (see Chapter 2)?

2. The quote on page 108 claims that global poverty benefits (is "functional" for) only some people in the world. Who benefits from global poverty and how?

3. How does this article use ideas from conflict theory (see Chapter 2)?

4. Of the 11 functions of global poverty outlined in this article, which three do you think the most convincing or important? Which three are the least convincing or important? Give reasons to support your answers.

World Society Theory

The third theory of globalization that we will examine is **world society theory.** John W. Meyer and colleagues (1997) originated this theory, which focuses on the importance of global institutions and cultural models in shaping the behaviour of nations, organizations, and individuals. In contrast to world systems and modernization theory, the world society tradition explains global change as the consequence of emerging global institutions and a "world culture" since World War II.

World society theory argues that countries are becoming increasingly similar. They are coming to see things in a way that is consistent with Enlightenment ideals of progress, science, human rights, and modernization. As a result, both individuals and nation-states tend to adopt common cultural frames or perspectives, resulting in one world culture. While this theory emphasizes the positive elements of globalization, such as the spread of ideals of human rights, science, and tolerance, it is important to note that negative ideas, such as consumerism, materialism, and violence, can also become common cultural frames.

World society theory is rooted in comparative education research conducted in the 1970s. Researchers noted that education systems in sub-Saharan Africa were surprisingly like the education systems in Western Europe and North America, despite the vast cultural, economic, and social differences in the societies as a whole. Theorists sought to explain these similarities by arguing that they resulted from some underlying dominant, legitimatized, or taken-for-granted views. In this way, education systems were based on cultural models that spread across countries and provided blueprints for what a good education system should be (Meyer et al. 1997). International organizations are a very important part of the institutionalization of these cultural models.

One cultural ideal that has spread in modernity is individualism and individual rights. At the end of World War II, focus turned from the rights of groups (corporatism) to rights for individuals as the ultimate motivators and beneficiaries of society (individualism). This shift led to many social changes. For example, the rise and spread of capitalist ideologies are based on an individual worker's (or capitalist's) ability to make a wage (or profit). Democracy is based on the idea of one person, one vote.

The world society framework can help us to understand certain globalization processes. For example, Frank, Camp, and Boutcher (2010) examined the changing regulations of sex and sexuality (including laws about adultery, sodomy, child sexual abuse, and rape). They found that, between 1945 and 2005, the criminal regulations concerning adultery and sodomy drastically diminished; those regarding rape and child sexual abuse expanded. During the period under study, 68 per cent of the laws about adultery and 81 per cent of those about sodomy lessened or eliminated state punishment for these acts. This change is in stark opposition to the laws about child sexual abuse and rape—85 per cent of the laws about child sexual abuse and 98 per cent of the laws about rape criminalized or increased the punishment for these two crimes.

Frank and colleagues (2010) suggest that we can understand these changes using world society theory. Early laws regulating sex and sexuality focused on the perceived needs of society as a whole, namely, the procreative functions of sex. Therefore, sexual activity that was procreative and could lead to "legitimate" heirs (e.g. heterosexual, unprotected sex between husbands and wives) was protected. Under this type of social focus, sexual activity that was non-procreative (sodomy or homosexuality) or that undermined the family (adultery) was heavily regulated.

Today, laws about sexuality focus on protecting an individual's autonomy. As such, laws regarding issues of consent prevail. Rape and child sexual abuse laws are much more common now. These laws are based on the ideas of individual rights and the need for individual consent, which is absent in instances of rape and abuse. Other sexual acts, such as adultery and sodomy, are less of a concern in many societies, as they are seen to occur between consenting adults and to not violate a person's individual rights. Frank and colleagues (2010) argue that the rising regulation of rape and child sexual abuse (and the declining regulation of adultery and sodomy, both of which were previously illegal in most countries) indicates a widespread international change in norms about individualism.

Canadian laws on marital rape are a case in point. Before 1983, there was (legally) no such thing as marital rape in Canada. It was thought impossible for a man to rape his wife because rape was defined as an act that occurred outside marriage. A judge explained the situation in this way: "The intercourse which takes place between husband and wife is not by virtue of any special consent on her part, but is mere submission to an obligation imposed on her by law" (Frank et al. 2010, 872). Marital exemptions to rape laws basically focused on corporatist needs (the need of society to create babies) over the individual rights of women to consent to sexual activity. The law was eventually changed to prioritize women's right to give or deny consent.

Is Globalization a Good Thing?

As you can see from this discussion, the effects of globalization are both beneficial and detrimental to individuals and countries. Some believe that globalization does and will continue to have positive results, while others stress the negative consequences.

To see how globalization is portrayed, Peer Fiss and Paul Hirsch (2005) examined newspaper coverage of the concept. They looked at all articles about globalization published in *The New York Times*, *The Wall Street Journal*, or *The Washington Post* between January 1984 and December 1998. They considered not only the number of articles on globalization but also the tone. Positive coverage focused on the increased opportunities, benefits, and gains that globalization could bring. Negative coverage focused on issues of poverty, unemployment, and economic crisis. Neutral coverage discussed the process of globalization as a gradual, continuing trend without commenting on its benefits or problems.

The researchers found that, in 1986, the three newspapers published only 35 articles on globalization. Of these articles, 10 per cent had a positive view, 2 per cent had a negative view, and an overwhelming 88 per cent were neutral. By 1997, the coverage had increased dramatically, to approximately 400 articles. A majority (53 per cent) of the pieces were negative, 20 per cent were positive, and 25 per cent were neutral. Clearly, our understanding of globalization has shifted from neutral to negative.

A more recent survey, conducted by World Public Opinion (2007), shows that citizen attitudes toward globalization differ greatly by country. While citizens in some countries, including China, South Korea, Thailand, and Israel, have extremely positive attitudes toward globalization, citizens from other countries, such as Mexico, Russia, and the Philippines, are much more skeptical (see Figure 4.1). Canada was not part of this survey. How might Canadians have responded? Why did some of the periphery countries express positive attitudes?

Global Inequality

In Chapter 3, we learned about income inequality in Canada. It is clear that income is unevenly distributed in Canada and, over time, the richest Canadians earn an increasingly larger share of all income made in the country. Not only are there inequalities in income within countries, but there are also wide, and even starker, disparities between countries. Modernization, world systems, and world society theories have different perspectives on the promise and pitfalls of globalization, but they all see these vast inequalities.

According to the UN, the three richest people in the world own more than the combined gross domestic product (GDP; all goods and services produced in a country in a year) of the 54 least developed countries. Furthermore, the richest 1 per cent of the world's population earns as much income as the bottom 57 per cent. The top 20 per cent earns more than 70 per cent of the world's total income, compared with just 2 per cent of the total income going to the bottom 20 per cent (Ortiz and Cummins 2011). These statistics present an extremely high level of income inequality between individuals and countries. Although some progress has been made, UNICEF estimates that, at the same rate of change, it would take more than 800 years for the bottom billion people to achieve 10 per cent of the world's income. This conclusion is particularly troublesome, as approximately 50 per cent of children live below the $2-a-day international poverty line.

One way to compare income inequality across countries systematically is with the **Gini index**, developed by the Italian sociologist Corrado Gini. This index measures income inequality on a scale of 0 to 1; 0 represents perfect equality in a society (all individuals in the society make the same income) and 1 represents the maximum level of inequality in a society (one person receives all the society's income). In other words, the lower the Gini index, the more equal the country.

Figure 4.2 shows the Gini levels of most countries in the world. We can see that Canada is a relatively equal society, with a Gini of 0.32 (CIA, 2013). The Scandinavian countries and many other nations in Western and Eastern Europe are just as equal (Sweden is the most equal society in the world; its Gini index is 0.23). Countries in Africa and South and Central America, as well as the United States, are the most unequal countries. However, Africa has a huge amount of variability in terms of inequality—from the very high level in South Africa (the second most unequal place in the world, with a Gini of 0.63) to the very low level in Ethiopia (0.33 Gini index—almost as equal as Canada).

Inequality is quite high throughout the world, but has it increased or decreased? It might surprise you to learn that, between 1820 and 2005, the global Gini index rose from 0.50 to 0.68 (see Table 4.1). This change indicates that global inequality is increasing.

The Gini index measures inequality by comparing the incomes of the richest and the poorest in a society or across countries. However, we can also compare inequalities in health, education, employment, or a variety of other measures. Table 4.2 compares the wealth, inequality, health, and well-being outcomes, including **infant mortality rate**, for

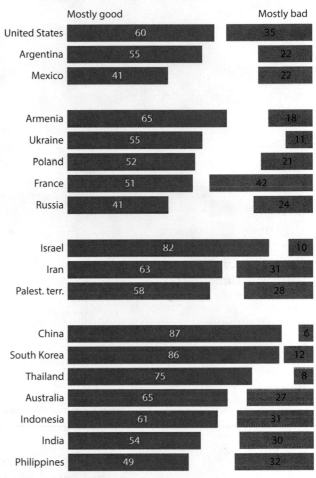

Views of Globalization

...Do you believe that globalization, especially the increasing connections of our economy with others around the world, is mostly good or mostly bad for [survey country]?

FIGURE 4.1 Views of globalization

SOURCE: World Public Opinion. 2007 (25 April). "World Public Favors Globalization and Trade but Wants to Protect Environment and Jobs." www.worldpublicopinion.org/pipa/articles/btglobalizationtradera/349.php?lb=btgl.

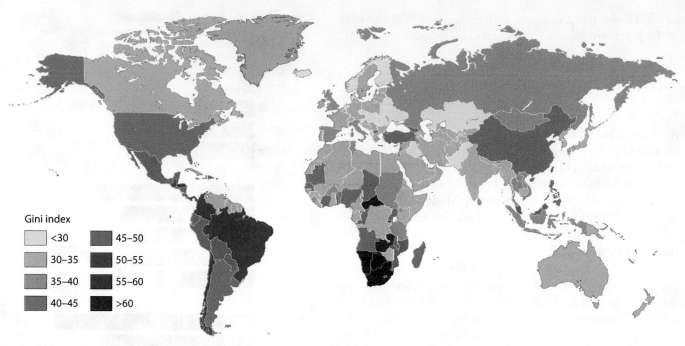

FIGURE 4.2 Gini index

SOURCE: Kiersz, Andy. 2014 (November). "Here Are the Most Unequal Countries in the World." *Business Insider.* www.businessinsider.com/
gini-index-income-inequality-world-map-2014-11.

seven countries. These nations spend different amounts on healthcare and have different levels of inequality (as measured by their Gini indices).

People who live in countries with higher GDP (i.e. more wealth) generally have better health; they live longer and fewer children die in their first year. In addition, governments in rich countries tend to spend more money on healthcare—Sweden, Canada, Japan, and the United States spend more than Mexico, South Africa, and India. However, more spending does not always buy better health. The United States spends about twice as much per person on healthcare than Japan and 1.5 times more than Canada, yet it has a higher rate of infant mortality and shorter life expectancy than the other two countries.

One of the main reasons for this situation is that wealthy countries differ significantly in terms of their levels of equality. The Gini indices in Table 4.2 indicate that the gap between the rich and the poor is greater in the United States than it is in Canada, Japan, or Sweden. In general, research shows that the higher the level of inequality in a country, the less healthy its population. A country's healthcare system also influences this relationship. Sweden, Canada, and Japan all have universal healthcare systems administered by their respective governments. The United States has no such system; therefore, access is very different across groups of Americans.

Another interesting comparison is between India and South Africa. People living in India are doing much better in terms of general well-being. While South Africa has a GDP five times higher than India, South Africans live 15 years less on average, partly because of the extreme inequality in the country.

Inequality in a society can have serious and wide reaching implications. Richard Wilkinson and Kate Pickett (2010) argue that more equal societies do better in a variety of ways than less equal ones. Furthermore, equal societies are not simply better for those at the bottom of the social hierarchy, but the society as a whole functions

TABLE 4.1	Estimated global Gini indices, 1820–2005
Year	**Gini**
1820	0.50
1950	0.64
1980	0.66
2005	0.68

SOURCE: Evan Hildebrand for the Food and Agriculture Organization of the United Nations Economic and Social Development Department .

TABLE 4.2	GDP, health spending, and Gini by country					
	Wealth and Inequality in Country			**Health and Well-Being Outcomes**		
	GDP (in millions)	**Health as per cent of GDP**	**Gini Index**	**Human Development**	**Life Expectancy**	**Infant Mortality Rate**
Sweden	57,113	9.6	23.0	0.956	80.5	2.73
Canada	50,343	11.4	32.1	0.961	80.3	4.78
United States	48,111	17.6	45.0	0.951	77.9	5.90
Japan	45,902	9.5	37.6	0.953	82.3	2.17
Mexico	10,047	6.5	48.2	0.829	75.6	16.26
South Africa	8,070	9.2	65.0	0.674	50.8	42.15
India	1,508	4.2	36.8	0.554	65.5	44.60

SOURCE: Adapted from World Bank data. GDP: http://data.worldbank.org/indicator/NY.GDP.MKTP.CD; Health as percentage of GDP: http://data.worldbank.org/indicator/SH.XPD.TOTL.ZS; Gini index: http://data.worldbank.org/indicator/SI.POV.GINI.

better. The researchers compiled information from 20 sets of data collected by the UN, the World Bank, the World Health Organization, and the US Census. They found, for example, that crime rates are closely tied to inequality. In particular, violent crime tends to be much more prevalent in countries, regions, and cities with high levels of inequality. Figure 4.3, which shows the homicide rate by country, illustrates this point.

Wilkinson and Pickett (2010) also maintain that everyone, not just the poor, is adversely affected by inequality. For example, Britain and the United States have relatively high levels of inequality and very high levels of mental health problems—25 per

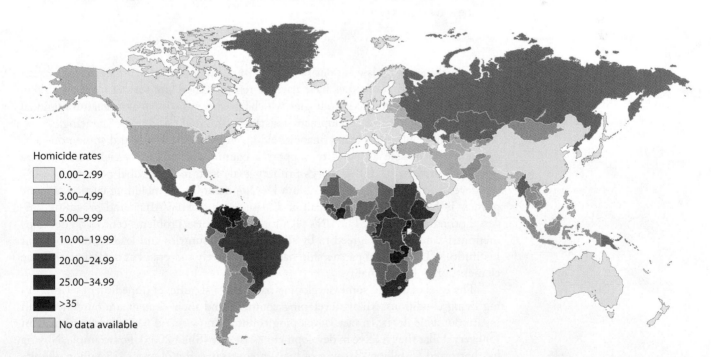

Homicide rates
- 0.00–2.99
- 3.00–4.99
- 5.00–9.99
- 10.00–19.99
- 20.00–24.99
- 25.00–34.99
- >35
- No data available

FIGURE 4.3 Homicide rates by country, 2010 (or latest available year)

SOURCE: UN Office on Drugs and Crime. 2011. *2011 Global Study on Homicide: Trends, Contexts, Data*, 11. www.unodc.org/documents/data-and-analysis/statistics/Homicide/Globa_study_on_homicide_2011_web.pdf.

cent of Brits and more than 25 per cent of Americans report experiencing mental health problems in any given year. The relatively more equal countries of Japan, Germany, Sweden, and Italy have far fewer mental health problems, with less than 10 per cent of citizens per year reporting mental health issues. Inequality also leads to consumerism, isolation, and anxiety, experiences that are associated with mental illness. Thus, according to Wilkinson and Pickett, the structures of these unequal societies lead to higher levels of mental health problems for both the rich and the poor—problems that cannot be solved through individual mental health solutions because they are inextricably linked to the unequal nature of these societies as a whole.

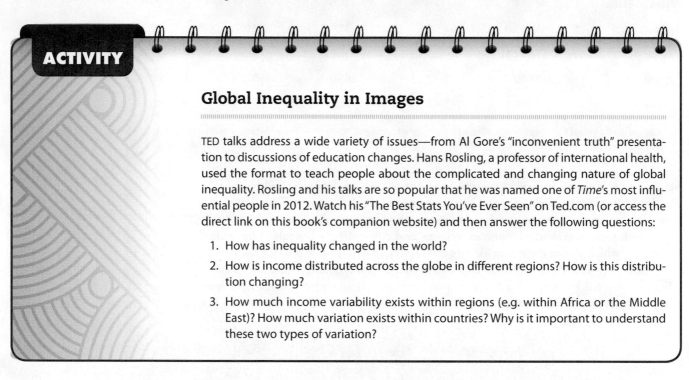

ACTIVITY

Global Inequality in Images

TED talks address a wide variety of issues—from Al Gore's "inconvenient truth" presentation to discussions of education changes. Hans Rosling, a professor of international health, used the format to teach people about the complicated and changing nature of global inequality. Rosling and his talks are so popular that he was named one of *Time*'s most influential people in 2012. Watch his "The Best Stats You've Ever Seen" on Ted.com (or access the direct link on this book's companion website) and then answer the following questions:

1. How has inequality changed in the world?

2. How is income distributed across the globe in different regions? How is this distribution changing?

3. How much income variability exists within regions (e.g. within Africa or the Middle East)? How much variation exists within countries? Why is it important to understand these two types of variation?

Global inequality is a serious problem that many individuals, organizations, countries, and international bodies have tried to resolve. There are several ways to address global inequality. Three main strategies, which have been the focus of much international and domestic debate, are development assistance, debt relief, and microfinancing.

Development assistance is financial aid given by governments and some non-governmental charitable agencies to support a country's economic, social, and political development. One of this strategy's primary goals is to reduce global poverty. The UN has developed a set of eight Millennium Development Goals, including cutting extreme poverty in half, reducing the spread of diseases such as HIV/AIDS, and providing universal primary education. The UN's plan for tackling these problems centres on development assistance, a plan agreed to by all the world's countries and leading development institutions. This type of partnership has been relatively successful at dealing with some elements of global inequality.

The level of debt in some developing nations is a significant impediment to improving living conditions. Many developing countries and their citizens are burdened with insurmountable debts. In fact, developing countries now spend $13 on debt repayment for every dollar they receive in development assistance (Shah 2005). For example, Nigeria has borrowed $5 billion. Because of high interest rates, it still owes $28 billion, despite having already repaid $16 billion. A country's debt works just like a personal credit card debt. Once the balance reaches a certain point, the monthly payments go toward the interest and it becomes impossible to pay off the principal.

The Scarcity Fallacy—Why Is There World Hunger?

The UN's Food and Agriculture Organization (FAO) estimates that, between 2012 and 2014, nearly 805 million people, or 1 in 9 people in the world, suffered from chronic undernourishment (World Hunger Education Service 2015). Many people argue that famine is the result of natural disasters, inefficient production of food, and excessive population growth within particular regions. Large-scale environmental changes, particularly global climate change, also cause long-term food shortages. Put another way, famine is simply the result of a lack of food. If we could increase food production, we would eradicate famine.

This argument seems quite convincing. However, much research suggests that famine is actually an issue of affordability and accessibility. Sociologists Stephen Scanlan, J. Craig Jenkins, and Lindsey Peterson (2010, 34) argue that "social inequalities, distribution systems, and other economic and political factors create barriers to food access" and food security problems for individuals.

Studies suggest that hunger is often connected to high pricing relative to income and difficulty of access. For example, members of a remote community might have to drive great distances to purchase food items or might be restricted to shopping at one highly priced retailer. People who live in Canada's North, such as these residents of Ellesmere Island, experience a higher-than-average cost of living due to the high cost of transporting food so far north.

Because scarcity and problems of access and affordability call for radically different solutions, it is important to determine which causes hunger. If scarcity is the cause, we can eliminate hunger only by reducing it. We could, for example, increase food yields by introducing more efficient technologies and farming methods or facilitate the movement of goods from the farm to the consumer. According to Scanlan and colleagues (2010), though, food is more plentiful today than it ever has been. In fact, we are living in a time of global food surpluses. If, as the researchers claim, hunger is caused by access problems, what types of solutions could we develop to deal with this problem?

PHOTO 4.3 The UN is actively working to reduce global poverty. Its Millennium Development Goals are one way that individuals and countries can come together to deal with the challenging social problem of global inequality.

PHOTO 4.4 Villagers in Palaro, Uganda, attend a microfinance training session with the Community Action Fund for Women in Africa (CAFWA). Microfinance attempts to address global poverty and inequality. Why might microfinancing be more effective than traditional bank loans at reducing poverty?

With so much money going to debt repayment (particularly interest), developing countries have less money to spend on important social programs that would improve their citizens' lives, such as education, healthcare, and other government services. As well, increasing globalization and international privatization of resources force poorer countries to sell off their profitable national institutions to help pay off the debt, which creates higher unemployment and problems for their future GDP. In response to these problems, international campaigns have called on richer countries to forgive the debt of developing nations. For example, Jubilee 2000 brought together citizens from 40 countries to call for the cancellation of Third World debt by 2000. Make Poverty History has also been lobbying for debt relief for developing countries. In Chapter 13, we will learn more about how such social movements can help to create social change.

In many ways, global poverty seems almost insurmountable. One new, innovative way of dealing with the problem is **microfinancing**. The following article explains this strategy, its benefits, and some concerns regarding its practice.

READING

The Record of Microfinance:
The Effectiveness/Ineffectiveness of Microfinance Programs as a Means of Alleviating Poverty

Jon Westover

...

Introduction

Poverty has different meanings to different people and is the source of much debate in the public arena. This is largely due to the fact there are many potential causes of poverty, ranging from those that could be categorized as causes stemming from one's personal choices and actions, causes stemming from structural constraints and inequalities in society, and causes that arise from government welfare entitlement programs. As a result of such a wide and diverse array of potential poverty causes, there are an equally large number of proposed policy interventions and solutions designed to eradicate the problem of poverty, some addressing each of the different areas mentioned above. One potential solution that has been increasing in popularity, and controversy, in recent years is the area of microfinance. However, despite the increased popularity, what is the record of such programs? Furthermore, what is the effectiveness/ineffectiveness of such programs on reducing poverty? Finally, what are the predominant methodological approaches in the microfinance literature? As with any intervention strategy, as the number of microfinance programs instituted throughout the world continues to increase, formal investigation into the effectiveness of such programs is important.

In this paper I will provide evidence from the existing literature on microfinance to show the current performance record of such programs and the effectiveness/ineffectiveness of such programs on reducing poverty....

Review of Literature

...

BACKGROUND TO MICROFINANCE

Poverty is a worldwide epidemic. [The figure] below illustrates that though extreme poverty rates have been declining across many regions of the world in recent decades, high rates still persist. Furthermore, it is estimated that about one-sixth (500 million of an estimated 3

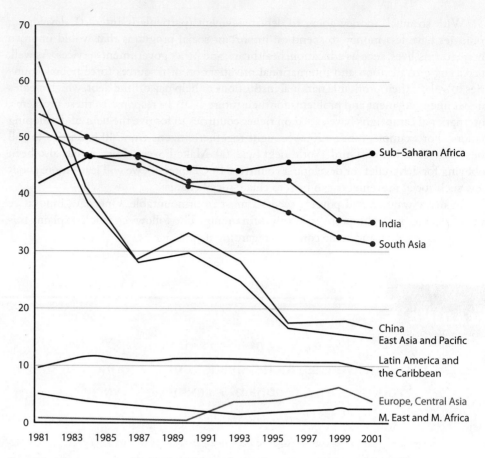

Extreme poverty rates in world regions (per cent below $1.08/day at 1993 PPP)

SOURCE: www.worldbank.org/research/povmonitor/.

billion) of poor people throughout the world have access to formal financial services (World Bank, 2005). This represents a large gap in access to such services.

One approach to reducing this gap that has increased in popularity in recent years has been the formation of microfinance institutions (an estimated 7,000 microfinance institutions serving approximately 16 million poor individuals in developing countries) (World Bank, 2005). However, [the following figure] illustrates the large gap that still persists between need and the access of microfinance services available to the world's poorest families.

The idea of microfinance started in Bangladesh around 1976 with Muhammad Yunus and Grameen Bank (recently awarded the Nobel Peace Prize for his work). Microfinance refers to financial services offered to low SES individuals that are excluded from the traditional financial system (considered "unbankable"—lacking collateral, steady employment, and a verifiable credit history). Aspects of microfinance, such as microcredit, are designed to help lift individuals, families, and communities out of poverty by providing small amounts of start-up capital for entrepreneurial projects, which will then presumably help individuals to generate income, build wealth, and exit poverty.

One aspect of microfinance that distinguishes it from the traditional financial system is the "joint liability concept," where groups of individuals, usually women, group together to apply for loans, and hold joint accountability for repayment of the loan. The premise is that providing low SES individuals access to financial services will better enable poor households to move away from subsistence living, to a future-oriented outlook on life and an increased investment in nutrition, education, and living expenses. Furthermore, microfinance is unique

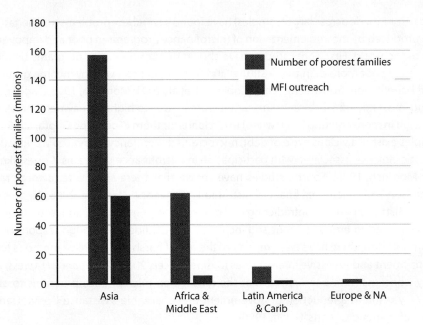

Access to microfinance services

SOURCE: www.unitus.com/wwd_whatismf.asp.

as a development tool because of its potential to be self-sustaining (both reducing poverty and maintaining a profitable business) (Business Week, 2005).

REPORTED STRENGTHS/POSITIVE IMPACTS OF MICROFINANCE PROGRAMS

A variety of studies have found a few key strengths and positive impacts produced by the implementation of microfinance programs in poor and impoverished areas of the world. First, microfinance programs can be an effective way to provide low-cost financial services to poor individuals and families (Miller and Martinez, 2006; Stephens and Tazi, 2006). Second, such programs have been shown to help in the development and growth of the local economy as individuals and families are able to move past subsistence living and increase disposable income levels (Khandker, 2005).

In addition, many studies (primarily microfinance institution impact studies and academic researcher qualitative or case studies) have shown that microfinance programs were able to reduce poverty through increasing individual and household income levels, as well as improving healthcare, nutrition, education, and helping to empower women. For example, standard of living increases, which help to eradicate extreme poverty and hunger, have occurred at both the individual and household levels as a result of microfinance programs (Khandker, 2005). Furthermore, it has been demonstrated by some research that microfinance programs increase access to healthcare, making preventative healthcare measures more affordable to the poor. In addition, more children are being sent to school and staying enrolled longer (Morduch, 1998). Finally, it has been shown that such programs can help borrowers to develop dignity and self-confidence in conjunction with loan repayment, and self-sufficiency as a means for sustainable income becomes available. Since microfinance services are primarily focused on women, it is argued that this leads to the empowerment of women and the breaking down of gender inequalities, through providing opportunities for women to take on leadership roles and responsibilities (Goetz and Gupta, 1995).

REPORTED PROBLEMS/NEGATIVE IMPACTS OF MICROFINANCE PROGRAMS

In contrast to the various positive impacts and strengths of microfinance programs listed above, other studies (more quantitative, with appropriate treatment/control frameworks and comparisons made across larger samples) have found several key problems and negative impacts produced by the implementation of microfinance programs in poor and impoverished areas of the world. First, some studies have shown that microfinance programs benefit the moderately poor more than the destitute, and thus impact can vary by income group (better-off benefit more from microcredit) (Copestake et al., 2001; Morduch, 1998; Dugger, 2004). Second, most microfinance programs target women (due to higher repayment rates), which may result in men requiring [their wives] to get loans for them (Goetz and Gupta, 1995). Third, examples exist of a vicious cycle of debt, microcredit dependency, increased workloads, and domestic violence associated with participation in microfinance programs (Copestake et al., 2001; Morduch, 1998). Fourth, studies have shown that there are low repayment rates in comparison with traditional financial institutions (Miller and Martinez, 2006; Stephens and Tazi, 2006), thus possibly contradicting one of the key strengths listed above, that such programs can lead to empowerment and increased self-confidence through responsible loan repayment. Fifth, there have been reports of the use of harsh and coercive methods to push for repayment and excessive interest rates (*Business Week*, 2005; *The Financial Express*, 2005). Finally, concerns have been raised that the reliance on microfinance programs to aid the poor may result in a reduction of government and charitable assistance ("privatization of public safety-net programs") (Neff, 1996).

MICROFINANCE AS A MEANS TO ALLEVIATE POVERTY?

Based on the findings reported above, there are mixed conclusions as to the overall impact of microfinance institutions. This leads us to the key question of this paper: What is the effectiveness/ineffectiveness of microfinance programs on reducing poverty? Some studies have found marked decreases in overall poverty levels, including declining levels of extreme poverty (Khandker, 2005), while other studies do not find the same direct effect (Morris and Barnes, 2005; Kan, Olds, and Kah, 2005; Goetz and Gupta, 1996). Still, other studies provide mixed results (Copestake, Bhalotra, and Johnson, 2001; Morduch, 1998). Thus, the academic literature is mixed in regards to the specific impact that microfinance has on alleviating poverty. In what follows, I will review these studies, briefly discussing the study designs and key findings.

MICROFINANCE HELPS TO ALLEVIATE POVERTY

The only study, among those selected for review in this paper, that was both more rigorous in design and reported very clear and direct effects of microfinance programs on poverty was Khandker's 2005 article, "Microfinance and Poverty: Evidence Using Panel Data from Bangladesh." This research examined 1,638 households that participated in two waves of the BIDS–World Bank 1991/92 and 1998/99 survey in Bangladesh. Khandker found that moderate poverty in the sample villages declined 17 per cent between the two waves of the survey, and extreme poverty declined 13 per cent. Among those households that participated in the microfinance programs, the poverty rate declined 20 per cent in the same period, with more than half of the nearly 3 per cent annual moderate poverty decline among participants attributed to the microfinance programs alone. He further found that access to microfinance programs contributed to the reduction of both moderate and extreme poverty of individuals (particularly women) as well as for the village as a whole—where inflow of microfinance funds to rural areas impacted the local economy—and raised per capita household consumption for both participants and nonparticipants.

MICROFINANCE DOES NOT HELP TO ALLEVIATE POVERTY

Despite the very positive results reported by Khandker, other studies reported more findings that were much muddier. Kah, Olds, and Kah (2005) studied the evolution, sustainability, and management of 10 microcredit institutions in Gossas, Senegal, using a mixed-methods approach to study design, utilizing socio-economic surveys, semi-structured interviews, and ethnographic research over a period of three years. They found that microcredit institutions have helped to create some positive change, but that there was no clear and marked evidence of poverty reduction that was attributable to the microfinance programs studied and stated that the expectations of what microcredit can do to help lift communities out of poverty is "a bit too optimistic" (p. 146).

Morris and Barnes (2005) attempted to provide an overall assessment of the impact of microfinance, and examined the impacts of three microfinance programs in Uganda (FINCA, FOCCAS, and PRIDE). Utilizing survey data collected via random sample from each of the three program areas (for both program clients and non-clients), baseline data was first collected in the winter of 1997, and then the survey was repeated in the winter of 1999 to assess impact. The researchers did not find that microfinance programs help to alleviate poverty in program areas, though results from these impact studies indicated positive impacts of these microfinance programs on both program participants' entrepreneurial business endeavours and within their own households. The authors further found that microfinance programs help to reduce financial vulnerability of poor individuals through the diversification of available income sources and the accumulation of assets. . . .

REFERENCES

Copestake, James, Bhalotra, Sonia, and Johnson, Susan. 2001. "Assessing the Impact of Microcredit: A Zambian Case Study." *The Journal of Development Studies*, Vol. 37 (4), pp. 81–100.

Dugger, Celia W. 2004. "Debate Stirs over Tiny Loans for World's Poorest." *The New York Times*.

Goetz, Anne Marie, and Gupta, Rina Sen. 1996. "Who Takes the Credit? Gender, Power and Control over Loan Use in Rural Credit Programmes in Bangladesh." *World Development* Vol. 24 (1), pp. 45–63.

Kah, Jainaba M. L., Olds, Dana L., and Kah, Muhammadou M. O. 2005. "Microcredit, Social Capital, and Politics." *Journal of Microfinance*, Vol. 7 (1), pp. 121–151.

Khandker, Shahidur R. 2005. "Microfinance and Poverty: Data from Bangladesh." *The World Bank Economic Review*, Vol. 19 (2), pp. 263–286.

"Large NGOs Becoming Rockefellers." *The Financial Express*, 22 November 2005.

"Micro Loans, Solid Returns: Microfinance Funds Lift Poor Entrepreneurs and Benefit Investors." *Business Week*, 9 May 2005.

Miller, Jared, and Martinez, Renso. "Championship League: An Overview of 80 Leading Latin American Providers of Microfinance." *Microbanking Bulletin*, April 2006.

Morduch, Jonathan. 1998. "Does Microfinance Really Help the Poor? New Evidence from Flagship Programs in Bangladesh." MacArthur Network, Princeton University.

Morris, Gayle, and Barnes, Carolyn. 2005. "An Assessment of the Impact of Microfinance." *Journal of Microfinance*, Vol. 7 (1), pp. 40–54.

Neff, Gina. 1996. "Microcredit, Microresults." *The Left Business Observer* Vol. 74.

Stephens, Blaine, and Tazi, Hind. "Performance and Transparency: A Survey of Microfinance in South Asia." *Microbanking Bulletin*, April 2006.

1. What is microfinancing? When and by whom was this concept invented?
2. Who has access to microfinancing? Why might this alternative to traditional banks be important for this group?
3. What are the benefits of microfinancing?
4. What are some potential problems with microfinancing?
5. Choose a microfinancing opportunity from http://lendahand.finca.org/ that you think will help someone move out of poverty. Why do you think it is a particularly effective opportunity?

CRITICAL Reading Questions

Summary

Sociologists are fundamentally concerned with inequality. In Chapter 3, we learned how social class and social status can create inequalities within a country. In this chapter, we extended our focus to examine how inequality can arise between countries. Understanding how our world is becoming increasingly globalized can help us to make sense of how global inequality has arisen and how we can work to reduce it. The three theoretical lenses we covered in this chapter (modernization theory, world systems theory, and world society theory) understand globalization differently, but they all note the inequality resulting from this process. We also discussed ways to measure and compare global inequality, such as the Gini and human development indices. We ended this chapter by exploring three ways to relieve global inequality: development assistance, debt relief, and microfinancing programs.

Key Terms

cash crops 101

commodity chain 106

core countries 105

ecological footprint 104

Gini index 115

globalization 98

Human Development Index (HDI) 104

infant mortality rate 115

mechanical solidarity 101

microfinancing 121

modernization theory 100

monocropping 103

organic solidarity 101

periphery countries 105

semi-periphery countries 105

world society theory 113

world systems theory 105

For Further Reading

Durkheim, Émile. 1960. *Division of Labour in Society*. Glencoe, IL: Free Press.

Krücken, Georg, and Gili S. Drori (eds). 2009. *World Society: The Writings of John W. Meyer*. Oxford: Oxford University Press.

Sassen, Sasia. 2007. *A Sociology of Globalization*. New York: Norton.

Wallerstein, Immanuel. 2011. *The Modern World System*. Berkeley, CA: University of California Press.

Wilkinson, Richard, and Kate Pickett. 2010. *The Spirit Level: Why More Equal Societies Almost Always Do Better*. New York: Bloomsbury.

5 The Social Construction of Race and Ethnicity

CHAPTER OUTLINE

The Consequences of Social Constructions

The theory of social construction highlights the ways that the social categories we consider natural and unchanging, such as race and ethnicity, are in fact socially created. It helps us to understand how the norms, rules, and categories of our society come to be and how they can change. Although social constructionists argue that race is not a "real" thing—that there is no biological basis for racial categories and they change over time—our social construction of race has real consequences for individuals in society. Being defined as one race or another can shape the type of neighbourhood you are likely to live in, the job that you are likely to get, and the perceptions that others will likely have of you.

The idea that social constructions have real consequences is called the **Thomas principle**. According to W.I. Thomas and D.S. Thomas (a husband and wife team of sociologists), "If [people] define situations as real, then they are real in their consequences" (1928, 52). For example, ghosts are not real. But when a little boy cannot sleep at night because he is worried that there are ghosts under his bed, they have real consequences. It does not matter that, when you look under the bed, there are no ghosts. Not being able to sleep is a real consequence of a social construction.

A humorous example of how our perceptions can be more real than reality is the famous toilet paper crisis of 1973. At that time, there was a lot of anxiety over oil shortages. When people heard of possible shortages, they would often stock up on gas or other commodities. On an episode of *The Tonight Show*, host Johnny Carson started his monologue by saying, "You know what's disappearing from the supermarket shelves? Toilet paper. There's an acute shortage of toilet paper in the United States." After the show aired, 20 million people immediately went to the grocery store and bought large quantities of the product (Crockett 2014). By the next day, most stores were out of toilet paper. The situation was so dire that Carson was forced to explain that the story was a joke. This clarification did little to help; once shoppers saw the empty shelves, they felt compelled to buy more. Even though there was no "real" shortage, seeing the low quantities of toilet paper at the store made people anxious and want to stock up. The perception that the story was real was more important than the fact that toilet paper was in abundant supply. The "shortage" lasted three weeks, until the shelves could be resupplied.

On a much more serious note, racism is a real consequence of our socially constructed ideas about race. It does not matter that race is not based in biology. **Racism** is an organized system of race-based group privilege that operates at every level of society and is held together by a sophisticated ideology of "race" supremacy (Cazenave and Maddern 1999, 42). Racism leads to both privileges and sanctions. Privileges include the white privilege discussed in the box on page 144. Sanctions include restrictions and limitations on people in certain racial categories. For example, in 1885 the Canadian government imposed a head tax on Chinese immigrants. In 1923, the Chinese Immigration Act went further, stopping all immigration from China except for special groups such as clergy and business people.

PHOTO 5.3 Journalist, activist, and lobbyist Wong Foon Sien (1899–1971) was a key challenger of the Canadian government's discrimination against Chinese immigrants and their descendants in the first half of the twentieth century. He was instrumental in the 1947 repeal of the Chinese Immigration Act. What other activists have challenged discriminatory government policies?

TABLE 5.1	Income and education by ethnic group, Canada, 2006		
Ethnic Group	**Average Income ($)**	**High-School Graduation (percentage)**	**Bachelor's or Higher Education (percentage)**
Japanese	45,116	90	33
White	37,752	76	17
Chinese	33,081	79	33
South Asian	31,102	79	29
Filipino	29,491	89	33
Arab	29,441	82	35
Black	28,231	79	16
West Asian	26,279	81	32
Latin American	26,241	77	19
Korean	25,929	88	41
Aboriginal	25,924	52	6

SOURCE: Adapted from Statistics Canada. 2008. 2006 Census. Cat # 97-564-XCB2006009.666; 97-564-XCB2006009-111111.

To understand the racial and ethnic inequality that occurs in Canada, we can examine how groups vary in terms of education and income. Table 5.1 compares income and education for several ethnic groups (that people self-identified with on the census). We can see that Japanese Canadians have the highest incomes, followed by white Canadians. First Nations people have the lowest incomes, making an average of $12,000 less than white Canadians per year.

Most people believe that Canada is a meritocracy and, as a result, expect that ethnic groups with high levels of education should have relatively high incomes. This correlation is certainly true for some groups in the table. Japanese Canadians, for example, have both the highest incomes and highest high-school graduation rate. However, white Canadians make very high incomes (the second highest in the table) but are among the lowest levels of high-school and university graduate rates. Filipino Canadians and Korean Canadians have very high graduation rates, yet make very low incomes compared with other groups.

There are a variety of explanations for this discrepancy. We could point to racism and discrimination, which is certainly an important part of the picture (and something we will be discussing later in the chapter). Another explanation is the Canadian immigration system, which attracts immigrants with high levels of education but often limits their ability to perform the jobs for which they were trained. We will discuss these important issues at the end of this chapter, when we talk about immigration and multiculturalism in Canada.

First Nations People in Canada

First Nations is a Canadian term of ethnicity that refers to the Indigenous people who are neither Inuit nor Métis (indigenousfoundations.arts.ubc.ca). The use of the term *First* is important because it highlights that First Nations people were the original residents of what is now Canada. *Nations* recognizes that the bands residing across Canada have

HIGHLIGHT

White Privilege

One of the interesting challenges in studying inequality—be it racial, ethnic, class, gender, or other—is that it requires us to examine the disadvantages of various groups in society. This task is difficult because it goes against our society's dominant ideology that we live in a meritocracy, where the smartest and hardest-working people are the ones who get ahead. How do we reconcile this view with the reality that, based on characteristics they do not control (social class, race, gender), some groups have more advantages than others?

Another reason that it is challenging to think about inequality is that it forces us to consider not only the disadvantages that some groups face but also the advantages that accrue to other groups. For example, we cannot think about the disadvantages to the poor without thinking of the advantages our society gives to the rich, the disadvantages to visible minorities without thinking of the advantages given to whites, or the disadvantages given to gays and lesbians without thinking of the advantages given to heterosexuals.

Peggy McIntosh (1988) wrote an interesting article in which she challenged herself to not only think about the disadvantages that visible minorities face but also to enumerate the advantages that she, as a white American, experiences in her daily life. She talks about these advantages of white privilege as an **invisible knapsack**—"an invisible package of unearned assets that I can count on cashing in each day, but about which I was 'meant' to remain oblivious. White privilege is like an invisible weightless knapsack of special provisions, maps, passports, codebooks, visas, clothes, tools, and blank checks" (1). Here are some examples of the privileges she experiences:

- I can if I wish arrange to be in the company of people of my race most of the time.
- I can be pretty sure that my neighbours will be neutral or pleasant to me.
- I can turn on the TV or open a paper and see people of my race widely represented.
- When I am told about our national heritage or about "civilization," I am shown that people of my colour made it what it is.
- I can go to a shop and find the music of my race, into a supermarket and find my staple foods, into a salon and find someone who can cut my hair.
- I can do well in a challenging situation without being called a credit to my race.
- I am never asked to speak for all people of my race.
- I can easily buy posters, postcards, picture books, cards, dolls, and toys featuring people of my race.
- I can take a job with an affirmative action employer without having co-workers suspect I got it because of my race.
- I can choose blemish cover or bandages in "flesh tone" and have them more or less match my skin (2–3).

With this list in mind, what are the potential problems of ignoring white privilege? How is white privilege similar to male privilege, heterosexual privilege, or middle-class privilege? How is it different?

institutions, governments, and cultural practices that are part of all nations (such as the Canadian nation). The pluralization denotes the vast diversity of this country's 663 First Nations groups, including their various languages, cultural practices, and traditions. First Nations, Inuit, and Métis people make up 4.3 per cent of the total population of Canada (Statistics Canada 2013). (*Inuit* is a general term for Aboriginal people living in the Artic; Métis people have both First Nations and European ancestors.)

Early encounters between Europeans and First Nations were trading relationships. The Royal Proclamation of 1763 recognized what it referred to as "Indian" nations or tribes and extended sovereignty over Indian people. This proclamation instructed colonial governments to respect Indian land and resulted in many treaties between First Nations people and, following Confederation, the Canadian government. There were relatively few treaties in British Columbia, however, which created land claim disputes that continue to this day.

The Indian Act of 1876 outlined whom the Government of Canada deemed to be "Indian" people and allowed it to regulate many aspects of their lives. The government worked actively in this period to attempt to assimilate First Nations people by restricting their cultural practices. For example, from 1876 to 1996, 150,000 First Nations children were forced to leave their homes and attend residential schools, which tried to resocialize them and destroy their culture. There was also rampant physical, sexual, and psychological abuse at these schools. According to the UN's Convention on the Prevention and Punishment of the Crime of Genocide (1948), forcibly moving children of one group to another is an act of genocide.

The residential schools also restricted the use of First Nations languages. Children in the schools were not allowed to speak their native language but were forced to speak English or French. This rule is partly responsible for First Nations languages being in danger of dying out. All but 3 of the original 65 languages are currently considered at risk of extinction. While 87 per cent of First Nations people had a native language as their mother tongue in 1951, only 20 per cent do so today (Norris 2014). Language is a critical part of cultural transmission, especially in groups that primarily pass culture from one generation to the next orally. We will discuss the important role of language further in Chapter 8.

The Canadian government also limited First Nations political rights. First Nations people did not have the right to vote in federal elections in Canada until 1960 and in provincial elections in Quebec until 1969, far later than any other racial or ethnic group in the country (see the box on p. 147). Working on land claims and participating in potlatches, an important cultural and economic practice in many First Nations communities, were illegal until 1951.

The consequences of these injustices are evident in the long-term inequality experienced by Canada's First Nations people. Along with Métis and Inuit people, First Nations individuals and families make roughly 70 per cent of the national average income in Canada (see Figure 5.1), up from 56 per cent in 1996. This is a significant gap. Poverty rates in First Nations communities are also staggeringly high. In 2010, the poverty rate of 15.2 per cent among First Nations people was well above the national average of 9.0 per cent (Statistics Canada 2011b). However, the child poverty rate reveals the starkest inequality between First Nations people and other Canadians. Poverty rates are two to three times higher for First Nations children than they are for other children. In Manitoba and Saskatchewan, almost two in three status First Nations children live below the poverty line (see Figure 5.2).

While these statistics are alarming and should be cause for considerable concern, a number of possible solutions or policy alternatives have attempted to address the harsh inequalities between First Nations people and other Canadians (see Menzies 2009). First, education and recognition of First Nations issues are important. Most of today's students learn about residential schools and First Nations culture in elementary or high school; this was certainly not the case 30 years ago. Second, movements and campaigns to attempt to redress and compensate for abuse and forced enrolment in residential schools have met with considerable success in Canada—leading to a commission, payment to victims, and apologies by government officials (see Chapter 12).

Third, organizations such as the Assembly of First Nations, created in 1968, work to lobby government on behalf of First Nations people. First Nations people have also organized protest campaigns to respond to the various inequalities they experience. The Idle No More social movement, which has been ongoing since December 2012, is

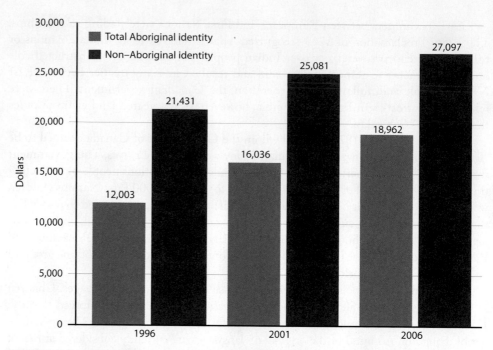

FIGURE 5.1 Median income for Aboriginal people and non-Aboriginal people, Canada, 1996–2006

SOURCE: Wilson, Daniel, and David Macdonald. 2010 (April). "The Income Gap between Aboriginal Peoples and the Rest of Canada," 8. GrowingGap.ca. www.policyalternatives.ca/sites/default/files/uploads/publications/reports/docs/Aboriginal%20 Income%20Gap.pdf.

most famous for the hunger strike led by one of its leaders, Attawapiskat Chief Theresa Spence. However, Idle No More also engages in a variety of campaigns in the hopes of achieving several goals, such as incorporating First Nations people more fully into policy-making, resolving land claims, and halting resource exploitation by the

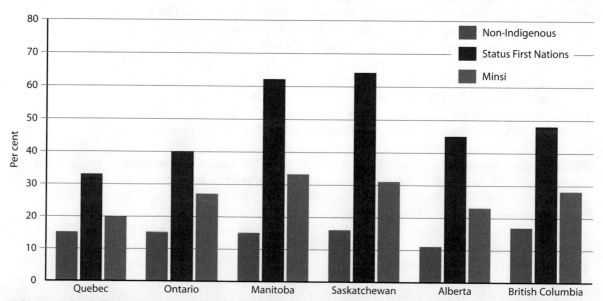

FIGURE 5.2 Child poverty by First Nations status, provinces of Canada

NOTE: MInsI refers to "Métis, Inuit, and non-status First Nations people"
SOURCE: Macdonald, David, and Daniel Wilson. 2013 (June). "Poverty or Prosperity: Indigenous Children in Canada." *Canadian Centre for Policy Alternatives*: 17. www.policyalternatives.ca/sites/default/files/uploads/publications/National%20Office/2013/06/Poverty_or_Prosperity_Indigenous_Children.

government. Social movements and protest as a method of countering inequality are discussed in the final chapter of this book.

Fourth, First Nations groups, the Canadian government, and provincial governments have created a variety of social programs to help facilitate the health, education, and employment of First Nations people. For example, programs facilitating university enrolment among First Nations have been extremely successful in raising the university attendance rate in these communities. Finally, land claim legislation has helped compensate First Nations people for land that was illegally appropriated by the Canadian government. While these issues are extremely complicated and not easily solved, programs, policies, and political activism have helped to address some of these issues.

PHOTO 5.4 In solidarity with the Idle No More movement, Aboriginal and non-Aboriginal people in Montreal participate in a teach-in, an informal, educational forum used to educate the public about a social issue.

Prejudice and Discrimination

One of the important consequences of racial and ethnic distinctions is the rise of prejudice and discrimination. **Prejudice** is a negative attitude toward someone based solely on his membership in a group. If I do not like a person because I think he has an irritating personality, that is not prejudice. However, if I dislike someone because she is Chinese, female, or poor, that is prejudice. Prejudice can lead to **discrimination**, the negative or positive treatment of someone as a result of his belonging (or being perceived as belonging) in a particular group.

HIGHLIGHT

Race and Voting in Canada

1867	Confederation; Only white men with property can vote in federal or provincial elections.
1885	"Indians" west of Ontario are prohibited from voting; Indian males in the east can vote if they own land apart from a reservation and have made at least $150 of improvements to this land; People of Chinese descent are denied the federal vote.
1898	White males without property receive the federal and provincial vote; Indian males east of Manitoba are denied the federal vote regardless of property.
1907	South Asians are denied the federal vote.
1917	People born in "enemy countries" are denied the vote.
1947	Chinese and South Asians are granted the federal vote.
1948	Japanese Canadians are granted the federal vote.
1960	"Indians" are granted the federal vote.
1969	"Indians" are granted the provincial vote in Quebec, the last province to do so.

Academic interest in prejudice increased after the atrocities of World War II against various populations, such as Jewish people, people with physical disabilities, and homosexuals. The extreme implications of anti-Semitism made people around the world ask themselves, "How do people develop prejudice?" and "Who is most likely to develop prejudicial attitudes?" Theodore W. Adorno and his colleagues (1950) wrote some of the earliest research on prejudice. They argued that individuals with a certain personality type, called an **authoritarian personality**, are more likely to develop prejudicial attitudes. People with this personality tend to use strict or oppressive behaviour toward subordinates. They tend to see the world in terms of good and evil and strictly follow rules and orders. Such behaviour existed in the concentration camps, where many Nazi officers treated prisoners horrifically. When asked how they could do such barbaric things, many stated that they were simply following orders and adhering to the Nazi party's rules. Adorno and his colleagues claim that the authoritarian personality was simply more prevalent among the German population than others, such as the French or Belgian, and this is why the Holocaust occurred in Germany.

The idea that someone's personality makes her more or less likely to be prejudiced is very appealing. But most sociologists would question how some countries happen to have more or less of a certain personality type and how the number of people with this personality can rise and fall over time. The World Values Survey is a large international survey that asks citizens of various countries about their lives, values, and political participation. This information allows us to compare the attitudes and behaviours of citizens around the world. Table 5.2 lists, by country, people's responses to one question in the survey: How would you feel about having someone of a different race as a neighbour? Of the countries surveyed, South Koreans would be the most unhappy in this situation; Canadians would be the least unhappy.

RESEARCH METHOD

Survey

TABLE 5.2	Prejudice by country, 2010–2014
Country	**Per cent who would "not like having someone of a different race as a neighbour"**
Canada[1]	2.5
Sweden	2.8
Australia	5.0
Chile	5.6
United States	5.6
Netherlands	8.2
Mexico	10.2
China	10.5
Germany	14.8
Russia	17.2
Ghana	19.9
Japan	22.3
South Korea	34.1

NOTE:
1. Canadian data is from the 2006 wave, as information was not collected in the 2010–2014 wave.
SOURCE: Data compiled from World Values Survey data analysis tool, 2010–2014 wave. www.worldvaluessurvey.org/WVSOnline.jsp.

If prejudice comes from personality, is it simply that nearly 14 times as many South Koreans as Canadians have this trait? Or does something in South Korean society that does not exist in Canada's lead to the development of prejudice? Most sociologists would argue that prejudice, and other attitudes, arises from our social context and socialization.

Lawrence Bobo (1983) was one of the first social scientists to examine how social context shapes people's attitudes, particularly prejudice. He argues that prejudice stems from social groups' competition for valued resources or opportunities. This **realistic conflict theory (RCT)** makes intuitive sense—when groups want access to the same things, they compete with one another and can come to have increasingly negative attitudes toward one another. For example, if there are a limited number of good jobs, spaces in universities, or safe neighbourhoods, many groups will compete for access to them. Over time, these groups in competition come to see the "others" who are vying for similar resources in increasingly negative terms, see more clear boundaries between their own group and the other groups, and view their own group as superior.

To test these ideas, Muzafer Sherif and colleagues (1961) conducted the Robbers Cave experiment, which involved sending twenty-two 11- to 12-year-old boys to summer camp for three weeks. The boys were very similar—they were all healthy, socially well-adjusted, intelligent, white, Protestant, and middle class. One would expect these boys to get along well, as their similarities meant that there was no obvious basis for prejudicial attitudes.

In the first week of camp, the boys were randomly divided into two groups—the Rattlers and the Eagles. The groups lived in far-apart cabins and did not interact with each other. Each group lived and played together for the week and did regular, fun camp activities; the boys swam and hiked and generally enjoyed their camp experience. Just like any summer camp, the kids in each group formed friendships with one another and developed a group identity.

The next week, the Rattlers and Eagles were introduced to one another. The boys from each group were set to participate in a series of competitions, including tug-of-war and capture the flag, to receive a trophy and strongly desired prizes. These competitions led to severe tensions between the groups. First, the groups exchanged verbal taunts (calling boys in the other group "stinkers" and "braggers"—some pretty serious taunts for 1961!). Then, the boys became more aggressive. The Eagles ransacked the Rattlers cabin; the Rattlers responded by burning the Eagles' flag. The boys developed increasingly negative attitudes toward those in the other group. Within one week, two groups of boys who were essentially the same on most dimensions—gender, race, class—and who had never previously met had developed intense animosity and prejudice toward one another. Just as Bobo summarized in Bobo (1983) had predicted, competing over resources led them to develop this prejudice.

After Sherif had created these tensions, he wanted to see how prejudice could be reduced. One popular theory at the time was **contact theory** (Allport 1954). This theory predicts that increasing contact between antagonistic groups will lead to a growing recognition of similarities and alter stereotypes about the other group, thereby reducing prejudice. To test this theory, Sherif created situations where both groups would have to encounter one another. For example, the Rattlers and the Eagles started eating in the cafeteria at the same time. However, instead of leading to more positive attitudes between the groups, this change was just an opportunity to express dislike for the other group. The groups sat separately (think of cliques in your high-school cafeteria) and started a food fight. More contact between the groups was obviously not enough to reduce the conflict.

Sherif then tried to encourage co-operation between the groups. He created situations where the two groups would have to work together for what he called superordinate goals, things that both groups desired but neither could accomplish alone. For example, the boys all wanted a movie night but had to pool their money in order to pay for the movie. Sherif also broke the water pipe that pumped water into the camp, and all the boys

RESEARCH METHOD

Experiment

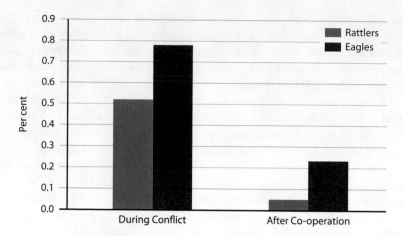

FIGURE 5.3 Per cent of boys who had negative perceptions of all members of the other group

SOURCE: Sherif, M., O. J. Harvey, B. J. White, W. Hood, and C. W. Sherif. 1961. *Intergroup Conflict and Cooperation: The Robbers Cave Experiment*. Norman, OK: University Book Exchange.

had to co-operate in order to fix it. It was only when the boys worked together to achieve these shared goals that their conflict and prejudice diminished. Look at Figures 5.4 and 5.5 to see how co-operation created more positive attitudes and ties between the groups.

What does this experiment tell us about how prejudice arises between groups and how we can reduce it? How can we apply these lessons to the real world? First, we see that the social context is very important for creating and reducing prejudice. It was not simply that some boys were more likely to be prejudiced than others but that all boys were more likely to develop prejudicial attitudes in situations of conflict and to reduce those attitudes in situations that required co-operation. This finding sheds light on prejudice in the real world—it can be increased or reduced by changing elements of the social context.

Second, this study lends some support to realistic conflict theory. When the boys were competing for something that both groups wanted, there was more conflict and prejudicial attitudes between the groups. This situation is similar to the real world, where ethnic, religious, gender, or other groups often compete for jobs, access to education, or other benefits.

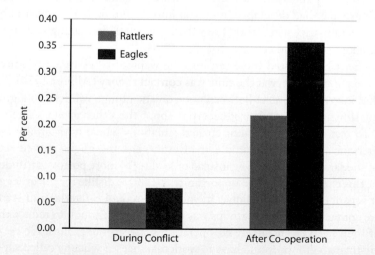

FIGURE 5.4 Per cent of boys who listed a boy in the other cabin as their best friend

SOURCE: Sherif, M., O. J. Harvey, B. J. White, W. Hood, and C. W. Sherif. 1961. *Intergroup Conflict and Cooperation: The Robbers Cave Experiment*. Norman, OK: University Book Exchange.

Third, contact between groups is often not enough to reduce conflict or prejudice. Later research indicates that contact between groups reduces prejudice only when the groups are roughly equal in status, the contact is informal, and the contact permits the disconfirmation of stereotypes. It is also important that the contact involve co-operation, which is the final lesson of this study. Co-operating for the achievement of superordinate goals can lead to increased tolerance and positive attitudes among different groups in society. Think about how these lessons could apply to real-world conflicts between groups such as the Israelis and Palestinians. Can we use experiments such as Sherif's to understand, and potentially alleviate, conflict between groups? If so, how?

ACTIVITY

Canadian Citizenship Test

One of the last steps to becoming a Canadian citizen is taking the citizenship test, which Citizenship and Immigration Canada says, "shows what you know about Canada" (www. cic.gc.ca/english/citizenship/cit-test.asp). Applicants are instructed to prepare for the test by reading the department's study guide, *Discover Canada: The Rights and Responsibilities of Citizenship*. Go to this book's companion website, take the practice citizenship test, and answer the following questions:

1. How did you do on this test? Where did you learn the information covered?

2. What kinds of questions and topics are included in the test? How do they emphasize certain ways that we "imagine" Canada? What, if any, questions would you remove from the test?

3. What other types of questions might you add to the test if you were creating it? What other things should people know before becoming a Canadian citizen?

Now let's look at the symbols and institutions that represent Canada. In a 2012 poll, the Association for Canadian Studies (2013) asked Canadians, "How important are each of the following as a source of personal or collective pride in Canada? Are they very important, somewhat important, not very important or not important at all?"

- universal healthcare
- Canada's reputation in the world
- the Canadian Charter of Rights and Freedoms
- Canada's economic performance
- the Canadian passport
- our history
- the national anthem
- the Armed Forces
- the federal system of governance
- the 1867 Confederation agreements
- multiculturalism
- the policy of official languages and bilingualism
- the War of 1812
- the 1982 patriation of the Constitution
- the monarchy

RESEARCH METHOD

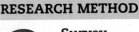

Survey

continued

1. Answer the poll questions by ranking the items in the list very important, somewhat important, not very important, or not important at all.

2. Some of the survey's results are shown in the following table. What are Canadians most and least proud of? How do your results compare? How do people in Quebec agree and disagree with other Canadians?

Responses to "How important are each of the following as a source of personal or collective pride in Canada?" 2013

	Very important	Somewhat important	TOTAL	Quebec only	All provinces other than Quebec	Difference between Quebec and all other provinces
Universal healthcare	74	20	94	92	95	3
Our country's reputation in the world	64	29	93	93	94	1
The Canadian Charter of Rights and Freedoms	60	30	90	89	90	1
Canada's economic performance	57	35	92	90	93	1
The Canadian passport	53	31	84	84	84	0
Our history	52	40	92	89	92	3
The national anthem	44	34	78	58	85	27
The Armed Forces	38	38	76	61	81	20
The federal system of governance	37	42	79	63	84	21
The 1867 Confederation agreements	33	42	75	62	79	17
Multiculturalism	30	38	68	62	70	8
The policy of official languages and bilingualism	26	35	61	82	55	-27
The War of 1812	23	38	61	33	70	37
The 1982 patriation of the Constitution	23	38	61	50	65	15
The monarchy	10	29	39	16	45	30

SOURCE: Association for Canadian Studies. 2013. "Tim Horton Beats the Queen According to Youngest Canadians When Asked about Contribution to Nation Building." www.acs-aec.ca/pdf/polls/Tim%20Horton%20vs%20the%20Queen%20and%20building%20Canada.docx.

3. How might other groups of Canadians answer these questions differently? For example, would men and women answer differently? Would new immigrants have different answers? Why or why not?

Immigration

The movement of people around the world is central to the process of globalization (see Chapter 4). While such movement has occurred throughout history, long-distance human migration for permanent settlement has become increasingly common over the last century. The result is a growing intermingling of the world's people, although not all countries receive or welcome migrants to the same degree.

Canada has one of the highest per capita **immigration** rates in the world, which makes our population very ethnically and culturally diverse. According to the 2006 census, nearly 20 per cent of Canada's population, or 7.2 million people, are born outside Canada (see Figure 5.5). In contrast, some countries (e.g. Japan) have extremely low foreign-born populations (around 1 per cent of the population).

Canada has three broad categories of immigrants: economic, family class, and refugees. Most economic immigrants are skilled workers. Investors and entrepreneurs, who come under the Business Immigration Program, are also in this group. They can have less education and skills than other economic immigrants as long as they have at least $800,000 to invest in the Canadian economy. In 2009, economic immigrants made up over 60 per cent of the total immigration to Canada, an increase from 38 per cent in 1991 (see Figure 5.6).

The Canadian government uses a point system to decide on which skilled workers to accept. An applicant can receive up to 25 points for education, 24 points for proficiency in English and/or French, 21 points for work experience, 10 points for age, 10 points for

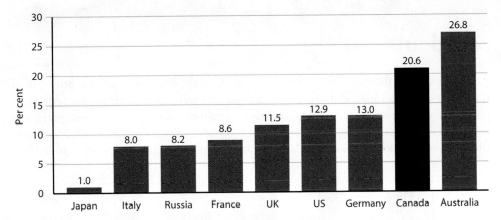

FIGURE 5.5 Per cent foreign born by country, 2013

SOURCE: Based on Statistics Canada data. http://cponline.thecanadianpress.com/graphics/2013/NHS/highlights/index.html.

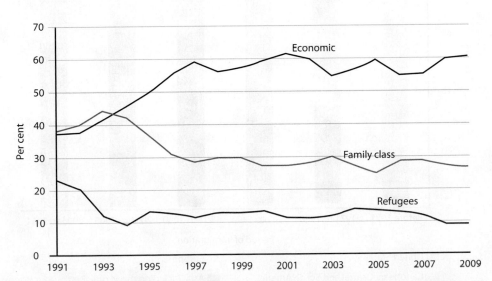

FIGURE 5.6 Immigrants to Canada by category of admission (percentage of landed immigrants)

SOURCE: Statistics Canada. 2012. "Ethnic Diversity and Immigration." Ottawa: Statistics Canada. Catalogue no. 91-209-X. www.statcan.gc.ca/pub/11-402-x/2012000/chap/imm/imm-eng.htm?fpv=30000.

having arranged employment in Canada, and 10 points for indications of being adaptable to Canadian society. Those with over 67 points are eligible to come to Canada.

Canadian citizens and permanent residents can sponsor their family members' immigration. Spouses, children, and parents who receive this sponsorship are family class immigrants. As Figure 5.6 shows, less than 30 per cent of immigrants were from this category in 2009, a decline from a high of about 45 per cent in 1993.

The final group of immigrants is refugees, persons within or outside Canada who fear persecution in their country of origin, based on a variety of reasons such as political beliefs or ethnic identity. Canada accepts thousands of refugees each year. However, the number of immigrants in this group has declined recently, from a high of 23 per cent in 1991 to less than 10 per cent in 2009.

Canada's high immigration rate has changed the country's ethnic landscape considerably over the past 50 years. Figure 5.7 shows regions of immigrants' birth. Before 1971, most immigrants were from Europe. Since 1981, most have been from Asia. The number of immigrants from the Caribbean, Central and South America, and Africa have also increased over this period.

Multiculturalism

As mentioned at the beginning of this chapter, Canada has embraced the principle of **multiculturalism**. Vince Wilson (1993) defined this term as a doctrine that provides a political framework for the official promotion of cultural differences as an integral component of society. Multiculturalism is based on the idea of pluralism, the belief that conflict is a central feature of societies and that ethnicity is an essential aspect of individual

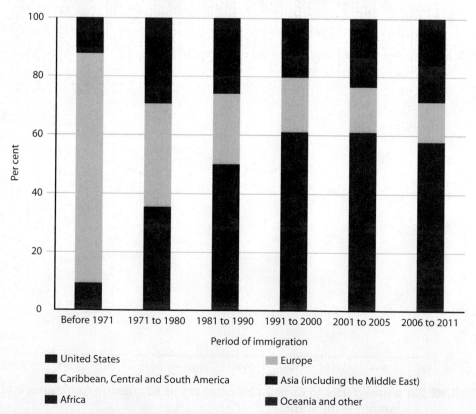

FIGURE 5.7 Region of birth of immigrants by period of immigration, Canada, 2011

SOURCE: www12.statcan.gc.ca/nhs-enm/2011/as-sa/99-010-x/2011001/c-g/c-g02-eng.cfm.

identity and group behaviour. Thus, individuals are encouraged to display and celebrate their ethnicity and distinctness.

Canada has been a pioneer in multiculturalism. It was the first country to make the concept official policy, passing the Canadian Multiculturalism Act in 1988. This Act concerns the management, not the elimination of, racial and ethnic conflict. It pledges federal assistance in "bringing about equal access and participation for all Canadians in the economic, social, cultural and political life of the nation." Canada is one of a handful of countries to adopt such a policy. (Only Australia has officially embraced multiculturalism as robustly.)

Because of its support of multiculturalism and the accompanying belief that immigrants should retain ties to their countries and cultures of origin, Canada is often called a cultural "mosaic." This description directly contrasts with the American "melting pot," in which immigrants are often encouraged to shed their past connections. Instead, they are supposed to assimilate to the "American way of life" by adopting the language, values, norms, and worldview of their new culture.

Canadian sociologist John Porter used the term *vertical mosaic* to describe Canadian society and, particularly, to highlight two of its important parts. First, as we have just discussed, Canada is a mosaic of different ethnicities, languages, regions of residence, and religions. Second, these groupings are unequal in both status and power. In *The Vertical Mosaic: An Analysis of Social Class and Power in Canada*, Porter (1965) describes how the policy of multiculturalism is not benign but benefits certain groups at the expense of others. He argues that some groups, particularly those of British or French origins, have more status and power in Canada and, as a result, enjoy higher incomes and levels of education than other ethnic groups. He calls the British and French in Canada charter groups, the original ethnic groups to settle a previously unoccupied or newly conquered region. These groups have more power than later immigrants and, in fact, get to decide which other groups can enter the territory and under what conditions. This situation leads to great inequality between charter groups and later immigrants. In addition, ethnic differences in a country reproduce class differences and can limit certain groups' social mobility.

Since 1965, several studies have shown that Porter's theory of great inequality within the mosaic continues. Small changes have occurred, including a slight reduction in income inequality based on ethnicity. However, in general, the economic elite is still mostly made up of individuals with British ethnic origins.

PHOTO 5.5 New Canadians celebrate by waving Canadian flags at a citizenship ceremony in 2013. How does this ceremony work to foster a connection to Canada and its symbols? Do these ceremonies also encourage a multicultural view of Canada?

A nation is a group of people who are united by a common fate and who have a shared national character. This is often based on a shared language, ethnicity, and history (Bauer 1907; in Davis 1967, 150). A nation-state is a group of people who share a physical territory and government, although they may not share an ethnicity, language, or history. Canada is a nation-state. It has a common territory made up of a diverse set of peoples from a variety of language, cultural, and ethnic groups. In fact, this multicultural diversity is, for many people, what defines Canada. Benedict Anderson argues that nations are based on **imagined communities** because "the members of even the smallest nation will never know most of their fellow members, meet them, or even hear of them, yet in the minds of each lives the image of their communion." This idea highlights the socially constructed aspect of nations.

READING

Imagined Communities: Reflections on the Origin and Spread of Nationalism

Benedict Anderson

. . . In an anthropological spirit, . . . I propose the following definition of the nation: it is an imagined political community—and imagined as both inherently limited and sovereign.

It is *imagined* because the members of even the smallest nation will never know most of their fellow-members, meet them, or even hear of them, yet in the minds of each lives the image of their communion.[1] Renan referred to this imagining in his suavely back-handed way when he wrote that "Or l'essence d'une nation est que tous les individus aient beaucoup de choses en commun, et aussi que tous aient oublié bien des choses."[2] With a certain ferocity Gellner makes a comparable point when he rules that "Nationalism is not the awakening of nations to self-consciousness: it *invents* nations where they do not exist."[3] The drawback to this formulation, however, is that Gellner is so anxious to show that nationalism masquerades under false pretenses that he assimilates "invention" to "fabrication" and "falsity," rather than to "imagining" and "creation." In this way he implies that "true" communities exist which can be advantageously juxtaposed to nations. In fact, all communities larger than primordial villages of face-to-face contact (and perhaps even these) are imagined. Communities are to be distinguished, not by their falsity/genuineness, but by the style in which they are imagined. Javanese villagers have always known that they are connected to people they have never seen, but these ties were once imagined particularistically—as indefinitely stretchable nets of kinship and clientship. Until quite recently, the Javanese language had no word meaning the abstraction "society." We may today think of the French aristocracy of the *ancien régime* as a class; but surely it was imagined this way only very late.[4] To the question "Who is the Comte de X?" the normal answer would have been, not "a member of the aristocracy," but "the lord of X," "the uncle of the Baronne de Y," or "a client of the Duc de Z."

The nation is imagined as *limited* because even the largest of them, encompassing perhaps a billion living human beings, has finite, if elastic, boundaries, beyond which lie other nations. No nation imagines itself coterminous with mankind. The most messianic nationalists do not dream of a day when all the members of the human race will join their nation in the way that it was possible, in certain epochs, for, say, Christians to dream of a wholly Christian planet.

It is imagined as *sovereign* because the concept was born in an age in which Enlightenment and Revolution were destroying the legitimacy of the divinely ordained, hierarchical dynastic realm. Coming to maturity at a stage of human history when even the most devout adherents of any universal religion were inescapably confronted with the living *pluralism* of such religions, and the allomorphism between each faith's ontological claims and territorial stretch, nations dream of being free, and, if under God, directly so. The gage and emblem of this freedom is the sovereign state.

Finally, it is imagined as a *community*, because, regardless of the actual inequality and exploitation that may prevail in each, the nation is always conceived as a deep, horizontal comradeship. Ultimately it is this fraternity that makes it possible, over the past two centuries, for so many millions of people, not so much to kill, as willingly to die for such limited imaginings.

These deaths bring us abruptly face to face with the central problem posed by nationalism: what makes the shrunken imaginings of recent history (scarcely more than two centuries) generate such colossal sacrifices? I believe that the beginnings of an answer lie in the cultural roots of nationalism.

NOTES

1. Cf. Seton-Watson, *Nations and States*, p. 5: "All that I can find to say is that a nation exists when a significant number of people in a community consider themselves to form a nation, or behave as if they formed one." We may translate "consider themselves" as "imagine themselves."

2. Ernest Renan, "Qu'est-ce qu'une nation?" in *Oeuvres Completes*, 1, p. 892. He adds: "tout citoyen français doit avoir oublié la Saint-Barthelemy, les massacres du Midi an XIIIe siècle. Il n'y a pas en France dix familles qui puissent fournir la preuve d'une origine franque . . ."

3. Ernest Gellner, *Thought and Change*, p. 169. Emphasis added.

4. Hobsbawm, for example, "fixes" it by saying that in 1789 it numbered about 400,000 in a population of 23,000,000. (See his *The Age of Revolution*, p. 78). But would this statistical picture of the noblesse have been imaginable under the *ancien régime*?

CRITICAL Reading Questions

1. What four features does Anderson use to describe nations?

2. How are nations imagined? Who imagines them? How does the idea of imagined communities relate to the theory of social construction?

3. Anderson quotes Ernest Gellner's statement that nationalism "invents nations where they do not exist." What is nationalism and how does it invent nations?

HIGHLIGHT

Ten Most "Canucky" Cities

In 2011, the Martin Prosperity Institute set out to quantify which city in Canada is the most "Canadian." They looked at a host of metrics, such as the labour force share in the fishing, farming, and forestry industries; the number of breweries, Tim Hortons' franchises, syrup producers, fur stores, and CFL and NHL teams; and the distribution of French and English. With these measures in mind, the institute lists the following cities as the "most Canucky."

1. Moncton, NB
2. Owen Sound, ON
3. Rimouski, QC
4. Greater Sudbury, ON
5. Kitchener-Cambridge-Waterloo, ON
6. Brockville, ON
7. Halifax, NS
8. Ottawa-Gatineau, ON-QC
9. Toronto, ON
10. Guelph, ON

What do you think of the criteria used to define Canadian Identity? How does your city or town measure up? What other measures might more accurately represent what it means to be Canadian?

Summary

We began this chapter by examining the differences between race and ethnicity. While race is based on perceived physical traits, ethnicity is based on cultural differences between people. The theory of social construction, introduced by Berger and Luckmann, can help us to understand how we create racial and ethnic categories in our society. The Thomas principle shows how these categories, despite being socially constructed, can have real consequences for individuals. Both theories can be applied to many concepts—such as gender, social class, and sexuality—that we will learn throughout this book. Through Sherif's experiment, we examined how prejudice and discrimination arise in society and how they can be reduced. We also talked about immigration and multiculturalism in Canada and concluded by examining the idea of Canada as an imagined community.

Key Terms

authoritarian personality 148

census 134

contact theory 149

discrimination 147

essentialism 130

ethnicity 130

First Nations 143

imagined communities 156

immigration 153

invisible knapsack 144

multiculturalism 154

prejudice 147

race 130

racism 142

realistic conflict theory 149

social construction 131

symbolic ethnicity 137

Thomas principle 142

vertical mosaic 155

For Further Reading

Anderson, Benedict. 2006. *Imagined Communities: Reflections on the Origin and Spread of Nationalism.* New York: Verso Books.

Berger, Peter L., and Thomas Luckmann. 1966. *The Social Construction of Reality: A Treatise in the Sociology of Knowledge.* New York: Anchor Books.

Koopmans, Ruud. 2013. "Multiculturalism and Immigration: A Contested Field in Cross-National Comparison." *Annual Review of Sociology* 39: 147–69.

Porter, John. 1965. *The Vertical Mosaic: An Analysis of Social Class and Power in Canada.* Toronto: University of Toronto Press.

Waters, Mary C. 1990. *Ethnic Options: Choosing Identities in America.* Berkeley, CA: University of California Press.

6 Gender at the Intersections

Introduction

Caster Semenya won the silver medal in the women's 800-metre final at the 2012 summer Olympics. Three years earlier, the South African runner missed a year of competition while track and field's governing body, the International Association of Athletics Federations (IAAF), investigated claims that her testosterone levels were exceptionally high for a woman. She was cleared to compete, but in April 2011 the IAAF established new gender verification guidelines based on the maximum level of testosterone an athlete can possess to compete as a woman. Semenya's story highlights the somewhat arbitrary cut-offs we use when defining the biology of sex. What does it mean to be a woman? Is it simply having a low level of testosterone? Or does something else distinguish men and women in our society?

Sex and Gender

In the last two chapters, we learned the importance of social class, social status, race, and ethnicity as dimensions of inequality. Another major type of inequality that exists in our society is based on the categories of sex and gender. **Sex** is a biological identity and can be divided into the main categories of male and female. **Gender** is a social concept referring to the entire array of social patterns we associate with men and women in society. Gender exists along the continuum of masculinity and femininity. In many ways, the difference between sex and gender mirrors the difference between race and ethnicity. While sex and race are based on perceived biological differences, gender and ethnicity are rooted in social and cultural constructions and distinctions.

There are certainly biological differences between men and women. For example, men are, on average, taller than women and men and women have different reproductive organs. However, neither of these two distinctions is as clear-cut as it seems. Some women are very tall; some men are very short. Some people are born with the sexual organs of both sexes. Despite these issues, sex is based on perceived physical differences. It is important to note, though, that such differences do not explain gender-based social disparities. In effect, the way we expect men to act (what we deem "masculine" behaviour) and women to act (what we deem "feminine" behaviour) is socially constructed. As with ethnicity (see Chapter 5), our ideas of what is acceptable and laudable behaviour for men and women are socially constructed. The clear division between men/women and masculinity/femininity is, at least partly, an illusion.

Thinking of sex as a dichotomy is problematic in a number of ways. The existence of middle sex categories challenges the male/female binary. For example, some societies have three genders—men, women, and a third group that is variously named. This group is composed of biological males who are allowed to perform the social role of women in their society. They are not women or men but, as a rough translation, "male women." Some African and American-Indian societies have a group of individuals who are "manly hearted women." This group is made up of biological females who perform the social role of men in their society; they have the social responsibilities and privileges usually bestowed on only husbands and fathers. Having the wealth to buy a "wife" bestows the social status of male on these women (Lorber 1994).

Intersex people, those born with the sexual organs of both sexes, also present difficulties for our binary ideas of gender. Approximately 1 per cent of live births in North America are sexually ambiguous based on their anatomy (Fausto-Sterling 2000). Between 0.1 and 0.2 per cent of all births are so sexually ambiguous that specialists medically assign a sex to the child. Today, fewer people with ambiguous genitalia are forced to have this surgery—at least until they are old enough to select for themselves—than people were decades ago.

Individuals who are transgender also test our conceptions of sex and gender. There are a variety of different groups of people within this larger community, such as transgender, gender fluid, and agender people. Advocates for individuals within these groups have coined the term *transgender* (or *trans*) *umbrella* to encompass the variety of different sexual expressions in modern society. The struggles and triumphs of individuals within this community have attracted increased attention recently due to the prominence of transgender characters on shows such as *Orange is the New Black* and *Glee* and the story of Cailtlyn Jenner, who transitioned to living as a woman in 2015 and received an award from ESPY (a sports association) to honour her courage in this process. Figure 6.1 illustrates the term and the groups it encompasses.

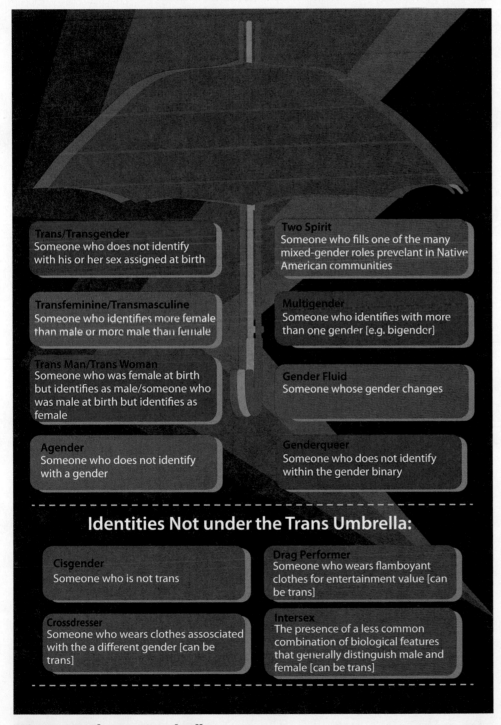

Trans/Transgender
Someone who does not identify with his or her sex assigned at birth

Two Spirit
Someone who fills one of the many mixed-gender roles prevelant in Native American communities

Transfeminine/Transmasculine
Someone who identifies more female than male or more male than female

Multigender
Someone who identifies with more than one gender [e.g. bigender]

Trans Man/Trans Woman
Someone who was female at birth but identifies as male/someone who was male at birth but identifies as female

Gender Fluid
Someone whose gender changes

Agender
Someone who does not identify with a gender

Genderqueer
Someone who does not identify within the gender binary

Identities Not under the Trans Umbrella:

Cisgender
Someone who is not trans

Drag Performer
Someone who wears flamboyant clothes for entertainment value [can be trans]

Crossdresser
Someone who wears clothes asssociated with the a different gender [can be trans]

Intersex
The presence of a less common combination of biological features that generally distinguish male and female [can be trans]

FIGURE 6.1 The trans umbrella

SOURCE: Adapted from Trans Student Educational Resources. www.transstudent.org/graphics.

Gender as a Social Construction

Recall that social construction is a two-step process of classifying experiences and acting on the basis of these categories, followed by forgetting that we have created these divisions and seeing them as natural and unchangeable. When we meet people, one of the first things we do is try to place them into previously learned categories. Are they male or female? Old or young? Rich or poor? Doing so helps us to understand how we should interact with them. Not knowing how to categorize an individual can make your interactions uncomfortable because the societal norms are unclear.

Although it can cause potential struggles with social interactions, some people choose not to identify with a particular sex or not to raise their children with such an identity. In 2011, a Toronto couple announced that they would not reveal the sex of their baby, whom they named Storm. They described this decision as "a tribute to freedom and choice in place of limitation, a stand up to what the world could become in Storm's lifetime—a more progressive place" (Poisson 2013). However, this choice created a huge backlash. Many argued that it was unrealistic and unsustainable in such a gendered society. What institutionalized barriers will these parents face in their attempt to prevent Storm's sex from being disclosed?

There are only a few examples of androgynous characters on television or in film because audiences cannot classify them as male or female and therefore generally find these characters difficult to understand. Androgynous simply refers to sexual ambiguity—a situation where it is difficult to tell if a person is male or female. To find an example, we must look back to the early 1990s, when Julia Sweeney performed her character Pat on *Saturday Night Live*. Pat is intentionally androgynous. The humour came from other people's inability to tell Pat's sex and the resulting difficulty in their interactions, which constantly led to awkward situations.

PHOTOS 6.1 and 6.2 Most sociologists agree that gender—including the binary way in which we think about the concept—is a social construction. Androgynous gender presentation is one way of challenging the gender binary. How does androgyny affect how you think about gender?

Learning, understanding, and viewing one another as male and female are social processes. Our parents hold certain ideas about gender-appropriate behaviour, which they teach us. We later learn to perform our gender through socialization in schools. Expected behaviour is further reinforced within same-sex social circles, during a period when boys tend to play with only other boys and girls with only other girls (Kimmel 2011). The media also informs our sense of gender-appropriate behaviour. This process continues into the workplace and our familial roles. Furthermore, social institutions support and perpetuate gender appropriate behaviour.

In Chapter 2, we talked about social roles, the sets of connected behaviours, beliefs, and norms that individuals perform in a social situation. **Gender roles** are one set of roles that we perform in society. Gender is not a thing that one is born with, but it is situationally constructed through individuals' performances. Goffman's (1959) dramaturgical perspective helped us to see how individuals perform roles in our day-to-day lives. We are actors on the stage of life, performing our gender through our clothes, mannerisms, and behaviours. Remember that the "front stage" is where individuals perform for others, whereas the "back stage" is where individuals do not need to perform. For many individuals, their front stage is living up to the expected gender norms, but their back stage reveals a different set of gender displays.

In her influential book *Gender Trouble*, the feminist scholar Judith Butler (1990) argues that all gender is created and sustained through performances. **Performativity** is "not a singular act, but a repetition and a ritual." What we take to be an "internal essence of gender is manufactured through a sustained set of acts, posited through the gendered stylization of the body"; what we take to be an "internal feature of ourselves is one that we anticipate and produce through certain bodily acts" (xv–xvi). While it appears that our gender is just a natural part of who we are, Butler argues that we create gender through our actions and interactions.

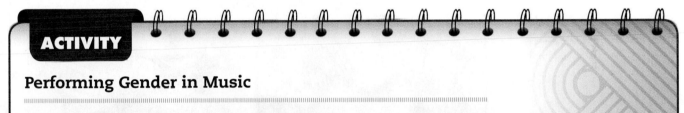

ACTIVITY

Performing Gender in Music

The media is an important avenue for learning about gender norms—how we should act as men and women and what is feminine and masculine behaviour. Music, in particular, is part of how we come to understand the role of men and women in society. However, as we listen to music, we rarely think critically about the messages it contains. In this activity, we will investigate examples of music that support a narrow understanding of masculinity and femininity, as well as music that challenges our ideas of men's and women's roles in society.

Find the lyrics and videos to some songs that talk about gender and answer the following questions. (You can get lyrics to many songs at www.azlyrics.com and find videos on YouTube.)

1. Find a song that you think reproduces gender stereotypes. How do the lyrics or video for this song reproduce these ideas?

2. Find a song that challenges our ideas of gender. How do the lyrics or the video for this song challenge these conceptions?

3. What types of music genres or artists are more likely to challenge gender roles and which are less likely to do so?

4. Why do you think that musicians, record labels, or music sites release gender stereotypical or challenging music?

Butler (1990) argues that labelling a person as male or female is overly restrictive. A person defined as male, for example, is supposed to possess masculine and heterosexual traits (e.g. be sexually active, aggressive, attracted to females). These characteristics are exhibited as a "performance" but are not necessarily voluntary. Some men might naturally want to behave this way, but others might find that these behaviours do not reflect their sense of self. In this way, gender does not automatically stem from inherent personality characteristics but is the result of cultural norms and practices that are subsequently reinforced. The concepts of masculine and feminine, therefore, appear to be just as natural as the sex that they are attached to. And deviations, such as homosexuality or the display of the opposite gendered characteristics, are marginalized as being outside "normality."

Butler also claims that the accepted and "natural" binary composition of two sexes (leaving only the option of male or female) encourages us to see other dichotomies in categorizing people. For example, seeing only two sexes leads to an illusion of only two distinct and opposite genders (masculine or feminine) and two distinct and opposite

HIGHLIGHT

Pointlessly Gendered Products

It seems like almost anything can be gendered in our society. In Chapter 2, we looked at how toys and personal products reflect and reinforce our ideas of gender. Despite the fact that all shampoo has the same basic ingredients, it is marketed very differently to women than it is to men. Ads show men standing stoically in black-and-white industrial settings while women shampoo in vibrant colour in a rain forest.

These two brands of earplugs are essentially the same product. However, Sleep Pretty in Pink Women's Ear Plugs are targeted to female buyers while Skull Screws Ear Plugs are aimed at men. Why do companies advertise and package this product differently for men than for women? How do such products reinforce our ideas of gender?

sexualities (heterosexual or homosexual). Instead, she pushes us to think about gender and sexuality as continuums. While there are certainly men who are very masculine and women who are very feminine, there are also men who are more feminine and women who are more masculine.

Michael Messner (1997) notes that there are many social costs to displaying gender in ways that our society deems inappropriate. Messner particularly focuses on what he calls the **costs of masculinity**. While we often concentrate on the costs of being female (such as lower pay, discrimination, violence, and other factors—discussed in more detail later in this chapter), our society also has a very restrictive idea of what it means to be a man. Messner outlines the rules to masculinity. For example, men must avoid anything feminine. Those who like romantic comedies, music written and/or performed by women, or ballet cannot share these interests with others for fear of seeming less masculine. Masculinity is also defined by external success (money, fast cars, prestigious jobs). And men are expected to show little emotion and to be aggressive.

These rules for behaviour are very limiting for men. Furthermore, men are sanctioned for stepping outside these norms. Men who perform jobs that are considered feminine, such as nurse or day care provider, have to deal with their masculinity being questioned. Men who break the rules might be degraded and lessened to the status of women. A man who fails to live up to gender norms might be called sissy, girlie, or gay, insinuating that he is like a woman or is homosexual and therefore inferior.

Gender and Institutions

Our ideas of sex and gender are socially constructed and created through interacting with agents of socialization (family, friends, peers) who encourage us to present our gender in particular ways. Gender and gender relations are also constantly reinforced through various institutions. Families give different amounts of attention, reward different behaviours, and teach different skills to boys and girls. In this section, we will look at how the institutions of sport, work, and politics reinforce gender distinctions in society.

Gender and Sports

Sports are a social institution. They allow people with a common interest to unite across racial, ethnic, and class distinctions. They also reinforce social norms and values such as hard work, teamwork, and obedience to authority. As Messner (1992, 8) writes, sport is "not an expression of some biological human need, it is a social institution. Like other institutions, such as the economy, politics, and the family, the structure and values of sport emerge and change historically, largely as a result of struggles for power between groups of people."

Sports are an influential institution in many societies. Billions of people play and watch sports worldwide. Almost half of the globe's population, 3.2 billion people, watched at least a minute of the 2010 World Cup in South Africa (FIFA 2014). This figure is only slightly lower than the number of people who watched at least a minute of the 2012 London Olympics (3.6 billion; IOC 2012). The 2014 Super Bowl was watched by 112.2 million people (O'Connell 2014). Needless to say, many people are exposed to professional sports. The content of sports, however, includes more than simply the activity.

PHOTO 6.3 Candace Parker—here playing for the Los Angeles Sparks—is one of the highest-paid players in the WNBA. In the 2013 season, the maximum salary (before endorsements) for an individual player was US$107,000. In comparison, the 2014 minimum salary (before endorsements) for a player in the NBA was $507,336.

As with other institutions in society, sports are highly gendered. On the micro-level, language used in sports is gendered, such as when we refer to defence*men*. Females and femininity can hold negative connotations in sports, such as when someone comments on a man's lack of athletic ability by saying that "he runs (or throws) like a girl." On the macro-level, sports are also gender unequal. The highest paid athlete in the NBA, Kobe Bryant, made US$23.5 million during the 2014–15 season, before endorsements (espn .go.com/nba/salaries). By contrast, Tina Charles, the highest paid athlete in the WNBA, makes US$105,000 per year, without endorsements (Garland 2012). Only 3 of the 100 highest-paid athletes in the world are women (and they are all tennis players): Maria Sharapova is the top-ranking at number 34, with Li Na and Serena Williams at 41 and 55, respectively (www.forbes.com/athletes/). Despite a boom in female athletic participation, sports media is still dominated by coverage of male sports. In 2009, ESPN's popular highlights show *SportsCenter* spent only 1.4 per cent of its airtime on women's sports (Messner and Cooky 2010).

The following article assesses how cheerleading has changed in its gendered norms and expectations. Adams and Bettis (2003, 398) argue that "cheerleading represents a liberating shift in normative femininity while simultaneously perpetuating a norm that does not threaten dominant social values and expectations about the role of girls and women." When reading this article, think about how cheerleading is related to gender norms and how the sport both challenges and reinforces inequality.

RESEARCH METHOD

Participant Observation

READING

Commanding the Room in Short Skirts: Cheering as the Embodiment of Ideal Girlhood

Natalie Adams and Pamela Bettis

. . .

In the United States, the cheerleader is a cultural icon, on one hand, symbolizing "youthful prestige, wholesome attractiveness, peer leadership and popularity," while simultaneously representing "mindless enthusiasm, shallow boosterism, objectified sexuality, and promiscuous availability" (Hanson 1995, 2). A staple of American life and popular culture, the cheerleader has received little scholarly attention.[1] When discussed at all in academic research, as illustrated in the following quote, cheerleading is typically presented as an activity that exploits and demeans girls: "The function of the cheerleader is to encourage the worship of the men—the prettiest, nicest and most lively are selected to show and encourage adoration" (Weis 1997, 83).

. . . Drawing on an ethnographic study of a Midwestern middle school, we discuss cheerleading as one such discursive practice that operates as a socially sanctioned space for a few girls to create multiple gendered subject positions that accommodate the shifting and often contradictory meanings of normative adolescent femininity. Our intent is to offer an examination of cheerleading that acknowledges the multiple meanings embedded in this cultural institution. We argue that cheerleading represents a liberating shift in normative femininity while simultaneously perpetuating a norm that does not threaten dominant social values and expectations about the role of girls and women. . . .

The Changing Face of Cheerleading: A Historical Overview

Originally, cheerleading was an exclusively male activity representing normative masculinity. During the mid- to late 1800s and the early 1900s, cheerleading was an idealized activity for privileged males and was seen as both an athletic and an aesthetic endeavour, as reported by the editors of *The Nation* (Organized cheering 1911, 6), who argued that organized cheering was a noble activity for undergraduates (i.e., males), and the reputation of having been a valiant "cheer-leader" is one of the most valuable things a boy can take away from college. As a title to promotion in professional or public life, it ranks hardly second to that of having been a quarterback.

Girls began entering collegiate organized cheering in small numbers in the late 1920s and early 1930s, but as late as the 1930s, cheerleading was still considered to be a male activity, associated with masculine characteristics of athleticism and leadership (Hanson 1995).

By the 1940s, more than 30,000 American high schools and colleges had cheerleaders, many of whom were girls. The trend to include girls in this previously masculine activity was precipitated in part by World War II. As young men fought in the war, girls were offered entrance into spaces once relegated solely for males. Cheerleading was one of those spaces (Hanson 1995). However, as men returned from the war, they sought to reclaim their place in the public spheres, including cheerleading squads. Thus, by the 1950s, several colleges (e.g., the University of Tennessee) and high schools began to ban girls from the cheering squad (Gonzales 1956).

Despite the ban on women cheerleaders in some squads and the number of men still participating in cheerleading at the collegiate level, by the 1950s, cheerleading was becoming more and more feminized, as illuminated in a 1955 published list of desirable traits for high-school cheerleaders. Gymnastics ability was not included; rather, the important traits were manners, cheerfulness, and good disposition—traits traditionally associated with women and girls (Kutz 1955, 310). Noting the transformation of cheerleading by the 1960s from a masculine activity to a highly feminized activity, McElroy (1999, 15) asserted,

> Cheerleading in the sixties consisted of pom-poms, cutesy chants, big smiles and revealing uniforms. There were no gymnastic tumbling runs. No complicated stunting. Never any injuries. About the most athletic thing sixties cheerleaders did was a cartwheel followed by the splits. . . .

Recognizing the potential of losing profits due to an outdated image of cheerleading, national cheerleading organizations actively sought to reshape this activity as congruent with the newer ideals of normative femininity (Woodmansee 1993). . . . Tight athletic motions, difficult jumps, and pyramid building began to be emphasized in the hundreds of cheerleading camps offered throughout the country. These new cheerleading techniques required girls who not only were strong but also were agile, were well-coordinated, and possessed athletic prowess.

Part of the transformation of cheerleading centred on the introduction of national, state, and regional competitions. Cheerleaders suddenly moved from the sidelines where they were motivational spectators to become the competitors themselves. In 1981, the first national high-school cheerleading competition was held, and in 1983, ESPN televised the event (Hanson 1995). With the introduction and proliferation of national competitions, demands on cheerleading squads increased, with many squads practising 12 months a year, often two or three times a day. Special coaches were often hired to teach squads difficult and often dangerous routines for competition (Argetsinger 1999). . . .

As illuminated in this brief overview of the evolution of cheerleading, the discursive practices of this activity have changed to accommodate the changing nature of gender roles and normative gendered behaviour in our society. From the late 1800s to the 1930s, cheerleading squads comprised primarily of men, and cheerleading signified ideal masculinity. However, by the mid-1950s, cheerleading had changed significantly from an activity representing normative masculinity to one representing ideal femininity. In discussing the shift from a masculine activity to a naturalized feminine activity during this time period, Davis (1990, 155) pointed out that cheerleaders came to symbolize "dominant ideology about how females should look and act in our society." That is, women/cheerleaders were to be pretty, were to possess appealing figures, were to play a secondary role to males, and were not to be taken too seriously. In the aftermath of title IX and the second wave of women's rights, notions of the appropriate role and behaviour of women in society began to shift; thus, cheerleading had to change to reflect new ideals about normative femininity and ideal girlhood. This study illuminates those changes.

Data Collection

In August 1998, along with two other researchers,[2] we began a study focusing on girls and leadership at Powhaton Middle School, a sixth- and seventh-grade school located in a Midwestern town of 26,000.[3] . . . Beginning in January 1999, we began five months of weekly observations of two cheerleading classes the school had instituted to prepare girls for the March cheerleading tryouts. . . .

MASCULINITY AND THE CHEERLEADER ATHLETE: DISCIPLINE, RISK TAKING, AND POWER IN THE PHYSICAL

In the cheerleading preparation classes we observed at Powhaton Middle School, cheerleading as an athletic endeavour was emphasized repeatedly. In preparation for trying out in front of three judges, the cheerleader sponsor continuously instructed the girls to show off their muscular bodies: "All right, girls, make your muscles tight so the judges can see them. Tight across the shoulders. Tomorrow you should hurt. Legs are tight. This is a great time to show off your muscles." In addition to having a muscular, fit body, the ability to tumble and maintain tight motion technique—rigid body movements that some would characterize as almost militaristic in style—were also critical to making the squad. Lisa, a petite blonde who scored the highest number of points at tryouts, explained the importance of being tight:

> Like when you cheer, your arms have to be tight, and your emotions are like aggressive, not like to where you're going to punch someone, just like when they're tight. Like when I get up there, I'm like [hard snapping noise] push my arms down and slap them. . . .

Part of controlling one's emotion means the girls were to act in a way that on the surface seemed inauthentic. As preparation for tryouts, Ms Stone [the teacher] repeatedly told the girls, "Pretend that you are having the time of your life. Show it in your faces, in your smiles." The ability to assume an inauthentic stance was most readily visible in the edicts to the girls to always have a smile on their face. More than any other quality, the ability to smile at all times seemed to be the most prized cheerleading attribute. Yet smiling in this context is not a spontaneous emotional response; rather, the ability to plaster a smile on one's face at a moment's notice was a very disciplined activity requiring a particular mind-set and lots of practice. . . .

FEMININITY AND GIRLIE GIRLS DIVERTING THE GAZE: PLEASURE AND SEXUALIZED SUBJECTIVITY IN CHEERLEADING

> Most of us want to be cheerleaders because we are more into being a girlie girl. (Lisa)

The girls selected cheerleader at Powhaton embraced the public nature of cheerleading, which allowed them to demonstrate to the world that they were confident, assertive, competitive, and athletic. However, the appeal of cheerleading went beyond simply the opportunity to prove they were athletes. In fact, the majority of the girls selected cheerleader were already known at their school as accomplished athletes; many of them had to juggle track and basketball practice with the mandatory cheerleading preparation clinic. This number is in line with recent data from a poll of 2,500 cheerleaders conducted by the Universal Cheerleaders Association, which found that more than 50 per cent of girls who cheer also participate in other athletic activities at their school (Roenigk 2002). Cheerleading was appealing to these girls because it also offered them a space to revel in what they called being a girlie girl. Unlike other athletes, these girls are participating in an activity that remains firmly entrenched within a feminine discourse; thus, they do not have to veil their masculinity nor worry, like other athletes, about being stigmatized as too masculine or as lesbians. These girls embrace cheerleading as a way to have it all—to flirt with the masculine without ever questioning or having someone else question their femininity or their sexual identity. . . .

For the girls in this study, one of the primary joys of being a cheerleader derived from the knowledge that cheerleaders are the object of everyone's gaze—not just males. Most of the girls who were selected cheerleader told stories of how they, as early as four years old, envied and wanted to emulate the cheerleaders they saw from their view in the stands. . . . Being the centre of attention, being the one "others wish they could be," offered these girls a form of power and pleasure not experienced in other activities, such as playing basketball or being in the school orchestra. Milea, the only Native American chosen for the squad, explained the difference between cheerleading and other sports: "Cheerleading is a sport you can have fun at. Sports were invented so that people could have fun, but most sports have turned into work, not fun. But not cheerleading. It's just fun!" The cheerleaders in this study saw themselves as central to the sporting event being observed and believed they had the power to control how the crowd and the players respond to the game on the field or the court . . .

In conveying her implicit understanding of the ideal woman as one who is heterosexual, a wife, and a mother, Ms Stone explicated how cheerleading prepares girls for adult womanhood:

> Cheerleaders are still very feminine, and we work on those characteristics. We have rules, no burping, no farting. You are young ladies. But we build, we jump, we try to get a balance because cheerleading does prepare them for later on in life. They've got to be strong. They've got to bear pain to have children. . . . They've got to be able to stand on their feet and make decisions when it may be mom, or dad, or husband, who's laid out there and you've got to do what is the right thing to do. You've got to support. You've got to lift up. That's the whole role of being an adult woman. . . .

Yet at the same time, cheerleaders at Powhatan were viewed as leaders who serve the interests of the school and community, symbolizing values and traditions deemed positive in American culture (Eckert 1989). As mentioned earlier, cheerleaders were cited as school leaders by almost all of the 61 girls interviewed in the larger study. The girls selected to be cheerleaders took this role seriously and recognized that being a cheerleader meant they would be role models for others. Suzi offered this explanation of the responsibility of cheerleading:

> It's not like it used to be, like popularity and stuff. Now you have to like have what it takes to be a cheerleader. You can't just like get up there and just smile. You have to have tight motions. You have to know what you're supposed to be doing, and you have big responsibility now. You have to be at cheerleading practice on time. If you have to have the tape for the dance, you have to remember to bring it. You have to be responsible. You're going to have a lot of people looking up to you, and so you're going to have lots of responsibility to do right things. . . .

Conclusion

Operating at the juncture of all-American good looks, traditional femininity, and sports-like athleticism, contemporary cheerleading provides a culturally sanctioned space for performing the requisite traits of the ideal girl in the new millennium. Quite literally, cheerleading is a performative act—one that has been traditionally understood as girls performing for the pleasure of others, particularly men. Many would argue, as in the film *American Beauty*, that this performance situates the girl body as the object of the masculine gaze and male fantasy. As Kurman (1986, 58) noted, "the cheerleader is a disturbing erotic icon. . . . She incarnates, in a word, a basic male-voyeuristic fantasy." Yet Kenway et al. (1994, 205), in discussing their work with adolescent girls and gender reform in Australia, offered a different reading of the performance metaphor:

The performance metaphor allows the girls to feel a sense of control over different performance genres, to pick up, discard, play and take risks within them, and even to go beyond them through improvisation, collage, and carnival. Femininity can then become a source of power and pleasure rather than a source of control.

We found ample evidence in our study to suggest that cheerleading offers a critical space for certain girls to take risks, to try on different personas, to delight in the physicality of their bodies, and to control and revel in their own power and desire. In other words, cheerleading offers some girls the opportunity to perform ideal girlhood without being located in a disabling discourse of femininity that equates femininity with exploitation and oppression. In many ways, these girls have embraced cheerleading as a way of accommodating the contradictions of constructing oneself as a feminine subject. Thus, any reading of cheerleading and the new girl order must acknowledge that girls themselves play an active role in reconstituting ideal femininity as they resist, rethink, and re-envision for themselves who they want to be as gendered individuals. . . .

NOTES

1. For notable exceptions, see Davis (1990), Hanson (1995), and Kurman (1986).
2. Drs Deb Jordan and Diane Montgomery, along with the authors, collected the data for the larger study on girls and leadership.
3. Pseudonyms are used for all people and places in this study.

REFERENCES

Argetsinger, Amy. 1999. When cheerleaders are the main event: For private teams, victory is their own. *Washington Post*, 10 July, A1.

Davis, L. 1990. Male cheerleaders and the naturalization of gender. In *Sports, men and the gender order*, edited by Michael Messner and Don Sabo. Champaign, IL: Human Kinetics Books.

Eckert, Penelope. 1989. *Jacks and burnouts*. New York: Teachers College Press.

Gonzales, Arturo. 1956. The first college cheer. *American Mercury* 83: 100–104.

Hanson, Mary Ellen. 1995. *Go! Fight! Win! Cheerleading in American culture*. Bowling Green, OH: Bowling Green University Press.

Kenway, Jane, Sue Willis, Jill Blackmore, and Leonia Rennie. 1994. Making "hope practical" rather than "despair convincing": Feminist poststructuralism, gender reform and educational change. *British Journal of Sociology of Education* 15: 187–210.

Kurman, George. 1986. What does girls' cheerleading communicate? *Journal of Popular Culture* 20: 57–64.

Kutz, F.B. 1955. Cheerleading rules, desirable traits and qualifications. *School Activities* 26: 310.

McElroy, James. 1999. *We've got spirit: The life and times of America's greatest cheerleading team*. New York: Simon & Schuster.

Organized cheering. 1911. *Nation* 92: 5–6.

Roenigk, Alyssa. 2002. Cheer safety: Setting the record straight. *American Cheerleader* 8: 46–48.

Weis, Lois. 1997. Gender and the reports: The case of the missing piece. In *Feminist critical policy analysis: A perspective from primary and secondary schooling*, edited by Catherine Marshall. London: Falmer.

Woodmansee, Ken. 1993. Cheers! Jeff Webb's multicolored world wide spirit machine. *Memphis Business* 3: 14–19.

CRITICAL
Reading
Questions

1. How are ideals of masculinity and femininity seen in the changing nature of cheerleading?

2. How does cheerleading both perpetuate and challenge notions of "ideal girlhood"?

3. To what extent is the changing nature of cheerleading reflective of women's participation in other sports, such as soccer, softball, tennis, and track? Are the changes in cheerleading distinctive to this one sport or do they reflect a larger transformation in the relationship between gender and sports? Give reasons to support your answer.

Gentlemen Prefer Stout

What do men and women tend to drink at parties? Who would you expect to drink wine coolers or Mike's Hard Lemonade? What about beer? Jessica Streeter (2012) argues that even what we drink reinforces ideas of gender. She is particularly interested in the craft beer scene. Craft beer, which comes from small-scale producers, is becoming increasingly popular as drinkers look for options beyond the large-scale breweries such as Molson or Labatt.

Streeter claims that, in the craft beer scene, women and new drinkers are encouraged to try fruit beers, blonde ales, and wheat beers, but men are offered dark India pale ales (IPAs), aged stouts, and a variety of high-alcohol beers. In other words, women and novices are offered light styles of beer. Bolder flavours, such as beers that are hoppy, bitter, or thick, are marketed to men, who are encouraged to advance beyond "girlier offerings."

You can see from this argument that even what we select to eat and drink is, in some ways, a gendered performance. When a woman says that she prefers fruit beers and a man says that he favours stouts, they are reporting their preferences. But their social environments shape these preferences, which reinforce dominant notions of masculinity and femininity. How and why do advertisers and producers reinforce these norms?

Gender and Work

Another major institution of society that reinforces our conceptions of gender and gender inequality is the workforce. Over the last 30 years, women's labour force participation has dramatically increased. In 1979, only 50 per cent of women worked outside the home for pay, while 94 per cent of men did. Thirty years later, the numbers were 81 per cent and 91 per cent, respectively. By 2011, women accounted for 48 per cent of the labour force (Statistics Canada 2011d). This rise in the number of women joining the workforce is the result of changing norms about the role of women in society, a greater need for dual income households, and increased rates of women obtaining higher education. Despite there currently being more women in the workforce than ever before, there remains a great deal of inequality between what men and women earn, the types of jobs they have, and the household tasks they do in addition to their paid labour.

The gap between the income of men and women has fluctuated over time. As Figure 6.2 indicates, this difference has generally narrowed since 1976 but has not been a steady decline. In fact, inequality between men's and women's earnings has widened since 1996, when it was at its lowest level. In 2011, Canadian women made, on average, 66.7 per cent of what men made. Overall, a woman's average income is about two-thirds of the average salary earned by a man.

One reason for this discrepancy is that men and women tend to perform different kinds of jobs. In fact, both groups are disproportionately concentrated in a small number of occupations. Table 6.1 shows the percentage of Canadian women in each type of job from 1987 to 2009. We can see that women are much more likely to work in certain sectors—including nursing, social sciences, teaching, clerical work, and sales. Men are more likely to work in management, natural sciences, primary resource extraction, trades, and construction. Some jobs that men and women perform require less education, such as sales, construction, and clerical work. However, the types of low-education jobs that men perform are usually better paid than those performed by women. This difference is, in part, explained by the higher rate of unionization in construction jobs than in sales work.

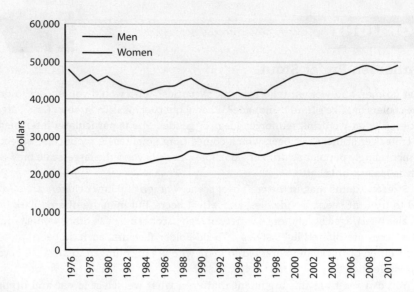

FIGURE 6.2 Average incomes of women and men in Canada, 1976–2011

SOURCE: Statistics Canada, CANSIM table 202-0407. www.statcan.gc.ca/pub/89-503-x/2010001/article/11388/c-g/c-g001-eng.htm.

The table also demonstrates that gender inequalities exist within sectors. For example, while women are generally underrepresented in management, women who are managers are particular unlikely to be senior management (with higher pay and status).

TABLE 6.1	Percentage of women by type of job, Canada, 1987–2009		
Type of Job	**1987**	**1999**	**2009**
Managerial			
Senior Management	21.0	28.2	31.6
Other Management	30.7	35.5	37.4
Total Management	30.1	35.1	37.0
Professional			
Business and Finance	38.3	49.3	51.2
Natural Science/Engineering	19.5	20.7	22.3
Social Science	61.4	67.7	72.5
Teaching	52.3	61.9	65.9
Doctors/Dentists	43.1	47.3	55.2
Nurses/Technicians	87.1	86.3	87.1
Arts/Recreation	48.4	54.1	54.4
Total Professional	50.4	53.4	56.7
Clerical/Administrative	73.9	75.4	75.5
Sales/Service	55.2	57.3	56.9
Primary	19.7	21.6	19.5
Trades, Transportation, Construction	5.2	6.0	6.5
Processing/Manufacturing	32.4	32.2	30.1
TOTAL OCCUPATIONS	43.0	45.9	47.9

SOURCE: Adapted from Ferrao, Vincent. 2010 (December). "Paid Work." *Women in Canada: A Gender-Based Statistical Report*. Ottawa: Minister of Industry. www.statcan.gc.ca/pub/89-503-x/2010001/article/11387-eng.pdf.

Women make up the majority of the professional group but are overrepresented in lower paying professional categories, such as nursing, teaching, and social sciences. Men are more highly represented in the better paying fields of natural sciences, engineering, and business.

There are two main ways that work is gendered. First, there is gender concentration among the people employed in certain kinds of work or among students in particular programs. We saw this occur in certain occupations such as nursing or engineering, which are female and male dominant, respectively. Second, work can also be imbued with gendered meaning and defined in gendered terms. For example, "caring" or "nurturing" professions tend to be seen as more feminine and appropriate for women. Take the difference between doctors and nurses. Nurses are expected to be more caring, whereas doctors (particularly specialists) are expected to focus on the science of medicine. Teaching is another good example. Elementary school teaching is associated with more nurturing; university-level teaching is often seen as a less nurturing job. Think about how many of your elementary school teachers were male and how many were female. Then do the same for your professors. You likely had more female teachers in elementary school and more male professors in university or college. As university professors make more money and have a higher status than elementary school teachers, this inequality could be problematic.

The **feminization** of an occupational sphere occurs when a particular job, profession, or industry becomes dominated by or predominantly associated with women. Such feminized jobs are referred to as "pink collar." Examples of jobs that were previously mostly done by men but have been feminized include bank tellers, secretaries, teachers, and family doctors. The important thing to note is that a feminized occupation tends to lose prestige, wages, required skill levels, and opportunities for promotion. In 1891, only 14.3 per cent of Canada's clerical workers were women. This number has risen steadily; in 2009, 75.5 per cent were women. Meanwhile, the wages and possibilities for promotion in this job have steadily declined.

You might be surprised to learn that clerical work was traditionally a man's job. The male bookkeeper's duties included accounting, note taking, and organizing tasks. As companies grew, there was an increasingly large amount of clerical work to be done and businesses moved toward more efficient systems of managing such tasks. Instead of having one bookkeeper who would do a variety of challenging tasks, companies were hiring many more clerical staff to do smaller parts of the larger job, such as only typing or only answering the phone. This sort of assembly-line office work created very few opportunities for advancement—if all you did was answer the phone all day, how could you move up to other tasks?

In the early 1900s, when this change was happening, the prevalent ideas regarding women's capabilities led to a growing belief that women were ideally suited for this type of narrow and repetitive work. The expectation was that women would work only until

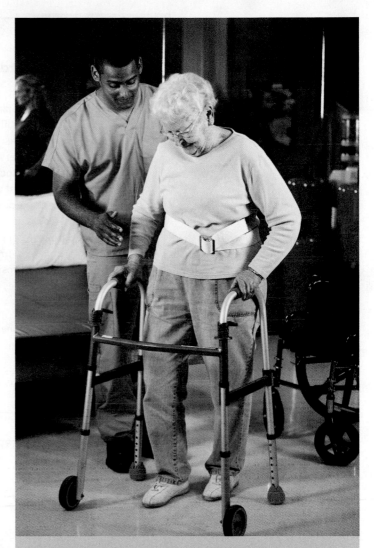

PHOTO 6.4 Because nurturing is considered a feminine trait, nurses who are men challenge our ideas of masculinity and can experience discrimination. What other jobs are associated with feminine or masculine traits?

HIGHLIGHT

Gender Mixed Boards Do Best

Although women are less likely than men to hold top positions in companies, Catalyst Research finds that organizations perform better economically when women serve on their boards. Deborah Gillis, vice-president of Catalyst Canada, says, "[The report] makes the compelling case that gender diversity and financial performance are related" (CanWest News Service 2007).

The researchers focused on data from 2001 to 2004, selecting 132 Fortune 500 companies with the highest average percentage of women board directors (e.g. Merrill-Lynch, Bank of America, Exxon Mobil, Walt Disney, and General Electric—where at least 17 per cent of the board of directors were women) and 129 companies with the lowest percentage (Citigroup, Apple, Time Warner, and General Motors—where less than 8 per cent of the board were women). Companies with the highest percentage of women directors outperformed those with the lowest by an average of 53 per cent. They also had a higher return on sales and return on invested capital (see the figure below).

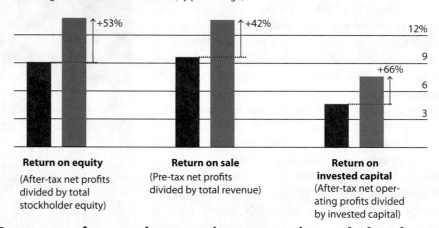

■ Average of the 125 Fortune 500 companies with the fewest females on the board
■ Average of the 125 with the most (by percentage)

Company performance by women's representation on the board

SOURCE: King, Ritchie. 2013 (27 March). "It's Dumb Not to Fill Your Company's Board with Women." Quartz. http://qz.com/67177/its-dumb-not-to-fill-your-companys-board-with-women/.

they married and, if they continued past that point, their jobs would be secondary to their primary roles as mothers and wives. As William Leffingwell (1925, 116) explains:

> A woman is to be preferred for the secretarial position for she is not averse to doing minor tasks, work involving the handling of petty details, which would irk and irritate ambitious men, who usually feel that the work they are doing is of no importance if it can be performed by some person with a lower salary. Most such men are also anxious to get ahead and to be promoted from position to position, and consequently if there is much work of a detail character to be done, and they are expected to perform it, they will not remain satisfied and will probably seek a position elsewhere.

Another concern when talking about the differential incomes and occupations of men and women is the **double shift** that women often perform. This term refers to individuals working outside the home for money and inside the home on unpaid, domestic tasks. Arlie Hochschild (Hochschild and Machung 1990) calls this situation the **second shift**. She finds that, in dual-earner heterosexual couples, women still tend to spend more hours

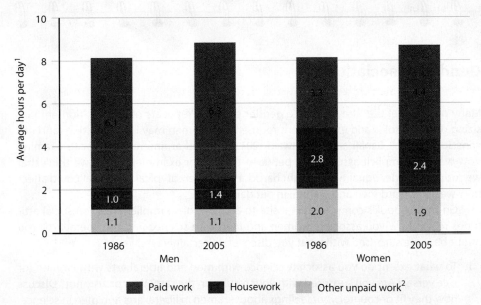

FIGURE 6.3 Time spent on paid and unpaid work by gender, Canada, 1986–2005

1. Numbers may not add due to rounding.
2. Primary childcare and shopping for good and services.
SOURCE: Marshall, Katherine. 2006 (July). "Converging Gender Roles." *Perspectives*. http://www.statcan.gc.ca/pub/75-001-x/10706/9268-eng.pdf

per week on domestic labour (e.g. cleaning, cooking, and caring for children) than do men. This imbalance, she argues, is caused by our traditional understanding of gender roles, where we expect women to do domestic work regardless of their labour outside the home.

As illustrated in Figure 6.3, women tend to work fewer hours outside the home than men. However, this disparity is shrinking. From 1986 to 2005, the amount of time women spent working outside the home increased from 3.3 to 4.4 hours per day. As a result, the difference between men and women in unpaid labour decreased by 0.9 hours. The figure also shows that men are doing more housework than they used to, although they still spend less time on such tasks than women do. In the period under study, the discrepancy in this area went from 2.7 hours a day to 1.8 hours. It is important to note that this sizable decline is primarily a result of men doing more housework and women doing less. The average amount of time women and men spend on childcare is virtually unchanged over the last 20 years.

Gender and Politics

The institution of politics is also affected by and affects gender. While there has been much improvement in women's representation in government, women still make up only 28 per cent of elected officials in Canada. This number is not particularly impressive when compared with other countries; Canada ranks forty-eighth in the world, behind most of Europe and many developing countries. For example, Rwanda (58 per cent), Bolivia (52 per cent), and Cuba (49 per cent) all have considerably higher percentages of women in their parliaments (Inter-Parliamentary Union 2015). See Table 6.2 for the percentage of women who hold elected office in the world's regions.

Why are fewer women elected to political office? Many of the possible answers centre around the organization of politics in Canada and the world. For example, if political parties do not nominate women to be candidates in elections, people will not even have the option to vote for them. Because women are often excluded from informal party networks and do not have the connections to help them get nominated, they are less likely to be put on the ballot. They are also often unable to afford the expense of

ACTIVITY

Gender Associations

Many people feel that they embrace gender equality. Yet years of socialization empha-sizing different roles and expectations for men and women may have a lasting (and un-conscious) effect. Banaji and Greenwald (2013) created an interesting test to examine how we make implicit associations between things. For example, even if we think that we support gender equality, we might harbour some stereotypical ideas that could affect how we act toward men and women in our daily lives.

Go to this book's companion website to access Project Implicit's test on social atti-tudes to see how you associate women and men with science and the liberal arts. You might be quite surprised with what you discover—I certainly was!

1. To what extent do you associate science with men and liberal arts with women (or vice versa)? Are you surprised with your results on the test? Why or why not? Discuss how they fit or counter your feelings about women in liberal arts and men in science.

2. Banaji and Greenwald found that, across every country that they investigated, people usually associated men with science. Countries with the largest sex gap (where people are much more likely to associate science with males), also had the biggest difference between boys' and girls' performances in ninth-grade science. Why do you think this relationship exists?

3. How might we go about changing the associations people have between women and men and science? If they are unconscious ideas, how can we change them?

running for office. As previously discussed, women make less money than men do; they also frequently lack a network of people who could financially support their campaigns. Finally, political office requires considerable travel time, evening and weekend meetings, and other demands that might conflict with family obligations. Although both men and women have these responsibilities, we learned in the preceding section that women tend to spend more hours a day doing household and childcare tasks. Becoming involved in

TABLE 6.2 **Historical comparisons of the percentage of women in parliaments across regions, 1955–2015**

	1955	1965	1975	1985	1995	2005	2015[1]
Scandinavia	10.4	9.3	16.1	27.5	34.4	38.2	41.5
Western Industrial	3.6	4.0	5.5	8.6	12.8	22.7	24.5[2]
Eastern Europe	17.0	18.4	24.7	27.0	8.4	15.7	
Latin America	2.8	2.7	5.2	8.1	10.0	17.1	26.6[3]
Africa	1.0	3.2	5.3	8.0	9.8	16.3	22.2
Asia	5.2	5.3	2.8	5.6	8.8	15.3	18.4
Middle East	1.2	1.2	2.9	3.5	3.9	8.1	16.0

1. 2015 data from the Inter-Parliamentary Union. http://www.ipu.org/wmn-e/world.htm.
2. All European countries combined.
3. Includes all of the Americas.

SOURCE: Kunovich, Sheri, Pamela Paxton, and Melanie M. Hughes. 2007. "Gender in Politics." *Annual Review of Sociology* 33: 263–84. http://digitalrepository.smu.edu/hum_sci_sociology_research/3

HIGHLIGHT

Women and Political Rights in Canada

1867	Only white men with property can vote in federal and provincial elections.
1916	Women in Manitoba, Saskatchewan, and Alberta get the provincial vote.
1917	WWI nurses and female relatives of soldiers get the right to vote.
1918	Canadian women receive the federal vote.
1918	Mary Ellen Smith (British Columbia) becomes the first woman provincial cabinet minister.
1921	Mary Ellen Smith becomes the first woman federal cabinet minister.
1930	Cairine Wilson is named the first woman senator.
1940	Quebec becomes the last province to give women the right to vote provincially.
1951	Charlotte Whitten becomes mayor of Ottawa and the first woman mayor in Canada.
1991	Rita Johnson becomes the first woman premier (British Columbia).
1993	Kim Campbell becomes the first woman prime minister (non-elected).
2008	One province/territory (Nunavut) has a woman premier.
2011	The number of women premiers in Canada rises to four (Nunavut, Newfoundland and Labrador, British Columbia, and Alberta).
2015	There are three women premiers in Canada (British Columbia, Alberta, and Ontario).

a political campaign and holding office could, therefore, create an additional burden for women (Kunovich, Paxton, and Hughes 2007).

Is it a problem that there are few women in Canada's Parliament? Research shows that having more women in government can be important both for the types of policies put forward and for the general perceptions of women's role in society. While it is certainly true that both male and female political leaders can be concerned with issues of gender equality, women are much more likely to prioritize those issues and to put them on the political agenda (Kunovich et al. 2007). For example, policies related to childcare, violence prevention, and pay equity are more likely to be raised by women in political debates. This tendency does not mean that men do not care about these issues, only that they do not tend to be their top legislative priorities. It is important to note that women politicians certainly do not agree on solutions to these issues simply because they are women, but they are more likely to bring these issues into the debate.

Having women as elected officials has also been shown to change the public's perceptions of women's roles and abilities as leaders. Female politicians also provide role models for young women. In places where there are many women in politics, young girls have higher self-esteem and a greater knowledge of and interest in politics than do girls in other places (Kunovich et al. 2007).

Feminism and Feminist Theory

Feminism is concerned with equality between women and men. It focuses on attaining that equality in politics, in the economic system, and through social and cultural change. Feminism exists as a set of ideologies and as groups of people who support these ideologies. These groups seek equality of opportunity for women in multiple areas, including education, the workplace, and the family. Both men and women with these interests can be feminists.

Feminist theory focuses on how gender inequality comes about in society and how men and women's gender roles are created and recreated in society. This theory has been influential in many social sciences and humanities disciplines, including sociology,

PHOTO 6.5 What do you think of this man and his sign? Do you find this message more or less convincing coming from a man? Why or why not? How can men be important allies in the fight for gender equality?

anthropology, political science, history, philosophy, English, and women's studies. In addition, it is rooted in the feminist movement and political action. Many scholars of this movement talk about feminist activism as happening in three distinct periods, or waves.

First-wave feminism began in the nineteenth century and was mostly centred in countries such as Canada, the United States, and the United Kingdom. This wave was focused on *de jure* inequalities, inequalities that are part of the legal and political system. For example, women's rights to vote and to hold property were of primary interest to first-wave feminists.

Second-wave feminism began in the United States in the early 1960s and spread throughout Europe and Canada. Second-wave feminists broadened the movement beyond political and legal rights and sought social change on a wide range of issues, including equality in the workplace and reproductive rights. During this period, women made widespread social gains and moved into a new variety of professions and other areas of society traditionally dominated by males, such as the media, sports, and military. This wave was also concerned with violence against women, including sexual violence and spousal abuse. The women's movement was quite successful at making these issues mainstream, getting marital rape laws passed, and establishing rape crisis centres and shelters for women who have been victims of abuse.

Third-wave feminism began in the early 1990s and continues to the present. This wave, which is a more diverse group of women's movements, arose as a critique of the previous wave. Many activists felt that the second wave was controlled by a small group of white middle-class women and that it did not represent the diverse experiences of women from different racial, ethnic, religious, class, and sexual groups (Staggenborg 2011). Third-wave feminism challenges what it sees as the essentialist nature of second-wave's definition of what it means to be a woman. This third wave also moved away from the focus on social and political rights. Instead, it tends to work in cultural arenas, for example, challenging gender depictions in the media, sexist language, and gendered norms around sexuality.

Intersectionality

The concept of **intersectionality**—the study of how various dimensions of inequality can combine—is one product of feminism's third wave. Kimberlé Williams Crenshaw coined the term in 1989 and explains it with the following metaphor:

> Discrimination, like traffic through an intersection, may flow in one direction, and it may flow in another. If an accident happens in an intersection, it can be caused by cars traveling from any number of directions and, sometimes, from all of them. Similarly, if a Black woman is harmed because she is in an intersection, her injury could result from sex discrimination or race discrimination. But it is not always easy to reconstruct an accident. Sometimes the skid marks and the injuries simply indicate that they occurred simultaneously, frustrating efforts to determine which driver caused the harm. (149)

PHOTO 6.6 At the 2014 MTV Video Music Awards, Beyoncé performed in front of a large sign that said "Feminist." Some praised her performance as a political statement and argued that it raised feminism's profile among young women. Others were more critical of the word being used by a performer who often uses her sexuality to sell her music. Do you think that Beyoncé is a feminist? How does this performance fit into (or challenge) our ideas of what a femInIst is?

The theory came out of Crenshaw's research on work and discrimination in the 1980s. Crenshaw (1989) studied a group of black women in the United States who had filed a workplace discrimination lawsuit. A round of layoffs at their workplace had resulted in all the black women being fired. The trial judge ruled against these women—he said that there was no gender discrimination because white women were not fired and there was no racial discrimination because black men were not fired. As the law saw only two types of discrimination (discrimination against women based on their sex or discrimination against racial minorities based on their race), there was no discrimination in this case.

These black women and Crenshaw understood that the former's experience was rendered invisible by intersectionality. The fact that they were both black and women made the discrimination invisible. The theory of intersectionality highlights how various dimensions of inequality can intersect with one another. For example, we have very different stereotypes about young people who are in wheelchairs than we do about older people in wheelchairs. Perhaps we assume that young people were injured in a sports or car accident and that older people are in poor health. We also have different expectations regarding gay men and lesbian women because of their gender. Seeing the complicated ways that inequalities intersect is a prime feature of third-wave feminist theory.

Table 6.3 uses income to illustrate the intersection of immigration status, education, and sex. We can see that men make, on average, more than women in each category. And those with university degrees make more than those without. Finally, recent immigrants tend to make less money than those either born in Canada or who migrated earlier.

The table is a good example of intersectionality because you can see how the various statuses interact with each other to create different outcomes. While Canadian-born men and women tend to make a lot more money when they earn a university degree (their salary increases by $22,331 and $18,955, respectively), recent immigrants do not get nearly as much of a salary boost by earning a degree (only $5,862 for men and $4,736 for women, on average). These numbers indicate that it is not simply your sex, education

HIGHLIGHT

Marx on Gender

Along with most other classical theorists, Karl Marx has been criticized as being "gender blind"—ignoring the role of gender in creating and perpetuating inequality in society. It is not surprising that none of the classical scholars (such as Marx, Durkheim, and Weber) talked much about gender; we are all a product of our historical period and these men lived in the late 1800s to early 1900s, when gender equality was not a popular topic. At the same time, we can certainly use their theories to understand issues of gender. For example, Marx's theory generally posits that all inequality stems from the capitalist system and the struggle between workers and capitalists. From this perspective, working-class men and women are both equally victimized by capitalists and the capitalist system that exploits their labour.

Feminist scholars have noted that this understanding of women and men as being equally exploited by capitalism misses the unique gender relations that occur within families. They argue that women are exploited not only by the capitalist when working outside the home (just as men are) but also by their spouses when working in the home without pay. Women's unpaid domestic labour benefits the capitalist because it makes it possible for men to return to work the next day, ready to labour for the capitalist. Families are the best and cheapest way to raise new workers. Women (as mothers and wives) keep all family earners (men) and earners-to-be (children) healthy and cared for. They do so at no cost to the capitalist, who later benefits from the surplus value the workers produce.

Marx's theory can be understood, at the broadest level, as a theory that sees the world in terms of those who have power and those who do not. While Marx was primarily concerned with the power of the capitalist over the worker, it is not difficult to see how we could extend this power dichotomy to the inequality that exists between men and women in society. What would other classical theorists, such as Émile Durkheim and Max Weber, say about the role of gender in society?

level, or immigration status that predict your earnings but that these different characteristics can interact and intersect to create more complicated inequalities.

Sexuality

Sexuality is feelings of sexual attraction and behaviours related to them. One important element of sexuality is **sexual orientation**, which involves whom you desire, with whom you want to have sexual relations, and with whom you have a sense of connectedness (Scott and Schwartz 2008). Our ideas about sexuality have changed considerably

TABLE 6.3	Average income by immigration status, education, and sex, Canada, 2006						
	Canadian Born		**Immigrants**		**Recent Immigrants**	
	University Degree	No University Degree	University Degree	No University Degree	University Degree	No University Degree
Men	62,566	40,235	42,998	33,814	30,332	24,470
Women	44,545	25,590	30,633	22,382	18,969	14,233

NOTE: Recent immigrants are those who have migrated to Canada within the last five years.
SOURCE: Adapted from Statistics Canada. 2008. "Earnings and Incomes of Canadians over the Past Quarter Century, 2006 Census," 22. Catalogue no. 97-563-X. Ottawa: Minister of Industry. www12.statcan.gc.ca/access_acces/archive.action-eng.cfm?/english/census06/analysis/income/pdf/97-563-XIE2006001.pdf.

over the past hundred years. In general, there is an increasing openness to diverse sexual behaviours and attitudes, which has led to changing norms surrounding sexuality. For example, people today tend to have sex younger and with more partners, and are more likely to engage in sexual activity outside of marriage than they were in the past. There is also an increasing acceptance of same-sex relationships.

The first systematic study of sex and sexuality was conducted by Alfred Kinsey in the 1940s. Kinsey's initial study interviewed 18,000 adults about their sexual behaviours, interests, and thoughts. Previously, we did not know much about these topics because no one had thought it appropriate (or interesting) to ask these questions. You can imagine how revolutionary (and shocking) this study was at the time!

Kinsey published *Sexual Behavior in the Human Male* in 1948 and *Sexual Behavior in the Human Female* in 1953, which together are known as the **Kinsey Reports**. The reports were highly controversial, but they became bestsellers and made Kinsey a celebrity. His work created a precedent for a legitimate study of human sexuality and laid the groundwork for a body of sexuality research in the social and biological sciences. His research showed that there was much more diversity in sexual desire and behaviour than was previously thought. After seeing this huge diversity, Kinsey argued that people should not think of sexuality as either normal or abnormal. We should define what is normal by looking at what people are doing, not by ideas of morality. For example, if most people have sexual relations before marriage, that is normal, regardless of society's moral ideals about premarital sex.

Perhaps Kinsey's most famous contribution to the study of sexuality is his **Heterosexual–Homosexual Rating Scale**, a seven-point scale of sexual inclinations (see Figure 6.5). After thousands of interviews with men and women, Kinsey argued that people are not simply gay or straight; therefore, we should not categorize people in this way. Instead, we should see that individuals have life histories that express different desires at different times. People can have more or less homosexual or heterosexual desires and experiences, but these things are not always related.

Kinsey's work highlighted social context's importance in shaping sexual desire and behaviours. For example, Kinsey (Kinsey, Pomeroy, and Martin 1948) found that men's sexual behaviours differed by their social class—men of higher social class tended to be more experimental than those of lower social class. Women's behaviour differed by their

RESEARCH METHOD
Interviews

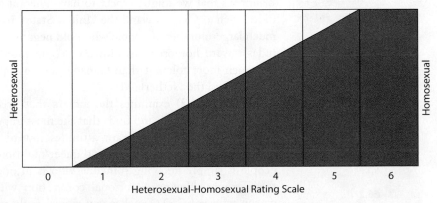

FIGURE 6.4 Kinsey's Heterosexual–Homosexual Rating Scale

0 Exclusively heterosexual with no homosexual tendencies
1 Predominantly heterosexual, only incidentally homosexual
2 Predominantly heterosexual, but more than incidentally homosexual
3 Equally heterosexual and homosexual
4 Predominantly homosexual, but more than incidentally heterosexual
5 Predominantly homosexual, only incidentally heterosexual
6 Exclusively homosexual with no heterosexual tendencies

SOURCE: Courtesy of The Kinsey Institute for Research in Sex, Gender, and Reproduction.

age and their view of gender equality—those who were older and who had a more liberal view of women's role in society were much more likely to experiment sexually and have more partners (Kinsey 1953). In essence, Kinsey showed that what people do sexually is, at least in part, shaped by their characteristics, such as social class and age.

In the 1990s, further research on sexual attitudes and behaviours found that North Americans are fairly sexually conservative. Most people favour monogamy in sexual relationships both in principle and in practice. According to surveys, 93.7 per cent of married persons had been monogamous over the year before the study compared with only 38 per cent of single people. However, about 20–25 per cent of men and 10–15 per cent of women had had at least one extramarital affair during their marriage (Laumann et al. 1994). Surprisingly, this number seems to be declining—by 2000 only about 11 per cent of men and women had had an extramarital affair (Treas and Gieden 2000). If anything, this change shows a more traditional view of sexuality over time.

At the same time, there has been an increase in the percentage of people who identify as gay or lesbian. In the 1990s, 9.1 per cent of men and 4.3 per cent of women say they have had a same-sex sexual experience since puberty, but only 1.4 per cent of men and 2.8 per cent of women reported that they identified as homosexual. By 2010, 7 per cent of men and 7 per cent of women identified as gay, lesbian, or bisexual (NSSHB 2010). The larger number of people identifying as gay, lesbian, and bisexual is, at least in part, a result of declining rates of homophobia in society. **Homophobia** is a set of negative attitudes and beliefs about individuals who are **lesbian, gay, bisexual, transgender, or queer/questioning (LGBTQ)** that can lead to negative behaviours, prejudice, or discrimination. Sometimes these negative attitudes can manifest into behaviours such as hate crimes. According to Dowden and Brennan (2012), 16 per cent of hate crimes are based on sexual orientation, with 65 per cent being violent in nature.

Table 6.4 shows the percentage of people in various countries who say they would not like to live next to someone who is gay. Rates are lower in Canada than in other countries, such as Turkey, Iraq, South Korea, and Ghana. These negative attitudes have declined in Canada, from 29.7 per cent in 1990 to 15.7 per cent in 2006 (the number is presumably still decreasing). Countries that we might expect to have tolerant attitudes, such as Germany and the United States, have a much larger number of people who hold negative attitudes toward homosexuals. However, some countries are much more tolerant than Canada, such as Spain, Sweden, and the Netherlands.

Herek (2002) examines the factors that predict homophobic attitudes and finds that the most important predictor of more tolerant attitudes toward lesbian, gay, bisexual, transgender, and queer/questioning people is simply knowing someone who is in one of these groups. Having a personal connection with a person who is LGBTQ makes you significantly more likely to have a positive attitude toward individuals in these groups. In addition, people who have more education and higher incomes, and live in an urban setting are less likely to be homophobic. Finally, people with higher self-esteem tend to be more tolerant than those with lower self-esteem.

Despite the fact that attitudes toward LGBTQ people are becoming more positive, we still live in a

TABLE 6.4	Percentage of people who responded that they would not like to live next to a homosexual, 2010–2014
Sweden	4.2
Spain	5.1
Netherlands	6.9
Australia	13.4
Canada[1]	15.7
United States	20.4
Germany	22.4
Mexico	23.2
Chile	25.7
Philippines	27.9
China	52.7
Russia	66.2
Ghana	79.7
South Korea	79.8
Iraq	80.3
Turkey	85.4

1. Canadian data is from the 2006 wave, as data were not collected in the later survey wave.

SOURCE: World Values Survey, 2010–2014 wave. www.worldvaluessurvey.org/WVSOnline.jsp.

heteronormative society; our social institutions, practices, and norms support an automatic assumption that other people are or should be heterosexual. For example, the poster shown in Photo 6.7 simply reminds you to be careful on the road. At the same time, it reinforces the idea that a family includes a woman, a man, and children. You might notice that, when you meet a person, he or she might assume that you are heterosexual. For example, if you purchase a bouquet of flowers, the florist might assume that it is for someone of the opposite sex.

Karin A. Martin (2009) conducted a study of how mothers help perpetuate heteronormative ideals. She surveyed 600 mothers of children between the ages of 3 and 6 years and found that the vast majority assumes that their children are heterosexual and interpret their children's behaviours in ways that reinforce this idea. For example, mothers describe the relationship between very young boys and girls as girlfriend–boyfriend, even when the children are too young to understand the relationships in this way.

When Martin asked the mothers to consider the possibility that their child might be gay, she found that two-thirds would "wait to see" what happened or prepare for the possibility by, for example, exposing her to children's books that featured gay characters. However, one-third of the mothers actively tried to prevent their child from developing or expressing a gay identity. As Martin describes, this group said they were parenting in a way that would prevent their child from being gay and therefore did not have to "worry" about it. One respondent said:

> We model a heterosexual healthy marriage life in our family so I believe our daughter sees a correct woman's modeling as do our boys with their dad. Because I believe that it is a sin. . . . I believe that I can teach my children that this is a sin and model a good relationship for them, and this will never be an issue. Because I think if you raise them with good stability and the right surroundings, things like that do not appear to be normal to him so he would realize in his mind that a same-sex marriage just isn't normal nor is it a part of his lifestyle. (Martin 2009, 203)

PHOTO 6.7 Ads such as this one, however unintentional, present a heteronormative idea of the family. What heteronormative images have you seen lately?

RESEARCH METHOD

Survey

These heteronormative sentiments could easily create a situation that makes homophobic attitudes more likely. Heteronormativity persists in our society, but there are also examples of increased tolerance and acceptance for a diversity of lifestyles. For example, American retailer JC Penney released an ad showing a family with two male parents (though the ad did spark some controversy). To avoid assumptions regarding sexual orientation, many individuals use the term *partner* to describe the person with whom they have an intimate relationship. These trends illustrate how our society is moving away from an automatic heteronormative assumption.

Just as gender is socially constructed, so is sexuality. Our ideas about what is normal sexuality, how many groups of sexual orientations there are, and how to delineate sexual preferences is created and reinforced in our society as we interact with one another. These ideas are also historically contingent—they have not always been as they are now. In "The Invention of Heterosexuality," Jonathan Ned Katz outlines how our modern ideas about heterosexuality and homosexuality are socially constructed and how they have changed. We think that heterosexuality is unchanging and universal; however, we create the categories of sexuality and then forget that we made them and see them as unchanging. Moreover, changes in these norms are tied to larger social, historical, economic, and political processes. In fact, heterosexuality is a modern invention and simply one way of perceiving and categorizing the social relations between the sexes.

READING

The Invention of Heterosexuality

Johnathan Ned Katz

Heterosexuality is old as procreation, ancient as the lust of Eve and Adam. That first lady and gentleman, we assume, perceived themselves, behaved, and felt just like today's heterosexuals. We suppose that heterosexuality is unchanging, universal, essential: ahistorical.

Contrary to that common sense conjecture, the concept of heterosexuality is only one particular historical way of perceiving, categorizing, and imagining the social relations of the sexes. Not ancient at all, the idea of heterosexuality is a modern invention, dating to the late nineteenth century. The heterosexual belief, with its metaphysical claim to eternity, has a particular, pivotal place in the social universe of the late nineteenth and twentieth centuries that it did not inhabit earlier. This essay traces the historical process by which the heterosexual idea was created as ahistorical and taken-for-granted. . . .

Contrary to our usual assumption, past Americans and other peoples named, perceived, and socially organized the bodies, lusts, and intercourse of the sexes in ways radically different from the way we do. If we care to understand this vast past sexual diversity, we need to stop promiscuously projecting our own hetero and homo arrangement. Though lip service is often paid to the distorting, ethnocentric effect of such conceptual imperialism, the category heterosexuality continues to be applied uncritically as a universal analytical tool. Recognizing the time-bound and culturally specific character of the heterosexual category can help us begin to work toward a thoroughly historical view of sex. . . .

Before Heterosexuality: Early Victorian True Love, 1820–1860

In the early nineteenth-century United States, from about 1820 to 1860, the heterosexual did not exist. Middle-class white Americans idealized a True Womanhood, True Manhood, and True Love, all characterized by "purity"—the freedom from sensuality.[1] Presented mainly in literary and religious texts, this True Love was a fine romance with no lascivious kisses. This ideal contrasts strikingly with late nineteenth- and twentieth-century American incitements to a hetero sex.[2] . . .

The actors in this sexual economy were identified as manly men and womanly women and as procreators, not specifically as erotic beings or heterosexuals. Eros did not constitute the core of a heterosexual identity that inhered, democratically, in both men and women. True Women were defined by their distance from lust. True Men, though thought to live closer to carnality, and in less control of it, aspired to the same freedom from concupiscence.

Legitimate natural desire was for procreation and a proper manhood or womanhood; no heteroerotic desire was thought to be directed exclusively and naturally toward the other sex; lust in men was roving. The human body was thought of as a means toward procreation and production; penis and vagina were instruments of reproduction, not of pleasure. Human energy, thought of as a closed and severely limited system, was to be used in producing children and in work, not wasted in libidinous pleasures. . . .

Late Victorian Sex-Love: 1860–1892

. . . In the late nineteenth-century United States, several social factors converged to cause the eroticizing of consciousness, behaviour, emotion, and identity that became typical of the twentieth-century Western middle class. The transformation of the family from producer to consumer unit resulted in a change in family members' relation to their own bodies; from being an instrument primarily of work, the human body was integrated into a new economy, and began more commonly to be perceived as a means of consumption and pleasure. . . .

In the late nineteenth century, the erotic became the raw material for a new consumer culture. Newspapers, books, plays, and films touching on sex, "normal" and "abnormal," became available for a price. Restaurants, bars, and baths opened, catering to sexual consumers with cash. Late Victorian entrepreneurs of desire incited the proliferation of a new eroticism, a commoditized culture of pleasure.

In these same years, the rise in power and prestige of medical doctors allowed these upwardly mobile professionals to prescribe a healthy new sexuality. Medical men, in the name of science, defined a new ideal of male–female relationships that included, in women as well as men, an essential, necessary, normal eroticism. Doctors, who had earlier named and judged the sex-enjoying woman a "nymphomaniac," now began to label women's *lack* of sexual pleasure a mental disturbance, speaking critically, for example, of female "frigidity" and "anesthesia."[3]

By the 1880s, the rise of doctors as a professional group fostered the rise of a new medical model of Normal Love, replete with sexuality. The new Normal Woman and Man were endowed with a healthy libido. . . .

Heterosexuality: The First Years, 1892–1900

In the periodization of heterosexual American history suggested here, the years 1892 to 1900 represent "The First Years" of the heterosexual epoch, eight key years in which the idea of the heterosexual and homosexual were initially and tentatively formulated by US doctors. The earliest-known American use of the word *heterosexual* occurs in a medical journal article by Dr James G. Kiernan of Chicago, read before the city's medical society on 7 March 1892 and published that May—portentous dates in sexual history.[4] But Dr Kiernan's heterosexuals were definitely not exemplars of normality. Heterosexuals, said Kiernan, were defined by a mental condition, "psychical hermaphroditism." Its symptoms were "inclinations to both sexes." These heterodox sexuals also betrayed inclinations "to abnormal methods of gratification," that is, techniques to insure pleasure without procreation. . . .

Though Kiernan used the new words *heterosexual* and *homosexual*, an old procreative standard and a new gender norm coexisted uneasily in his thought. His word *heterosexual* defined a mixed person and compound urge, abnormal because they wantonly included procreative and non-procreative objectives, as well as same-sex and different-sex attractions.

. . . The idea of heterosexuality as the master sex from which all others deviated was (like the idea of the master race) deeply authoritarian. The doctors' normalization of a sex that was hetero proclaimed a new heterosexual separatism—an erotic apartheid that forcefully segregated the sex normals from the sex perverts. . . . In 1901, in the comprehensive *Oxford English Dictionary*, *heterosexual* and *homosexual* had not yet made it.

The Distribution of the Heterosexual Mystique: 1900–1930

. . . In its earliest version, the twentieth-century heterosexual imperative usually continued to associate heterosexuality with a supposed human "need," "drive," or "instinct" for propagation, a procreant urge linked inexorably with carnal lust as it had not been earlier. In the early twentieth century, the falling birth rate, rising divorce rate, and "war of the sexes" of the middle class were matters of increasing public concern. Giving vent to heteroerotic emotions was thus praised as enhancing baby-making capacity, marital intimacy, and family stability. . . .

The first part of the new sex norm—hetero—referred to a basic gender divergence. The "oppositeness" of the sexes was alleged to be the basis for a universal, normal, erotic attraction between males and females. The stress on the sexes' "oppositeness," which harked back to the early nineteenth century, by no means simply registered biological differences of females and males. The early twentieth-century focus on physiological and gender dimorphism reflected the deep anxieties of men about the shifting work, social roles, and power of men over women, and about the ideals of womanhood and manhood. . . . The stress on gender difference was a conservative response to the changing social-sexual division of activity and feeling which gave rise to the independent "New Woman" of the 1880s and eroticized "Flapper" of the 1920s. . . .

The Heterosexual Steps Out: 1930–1945

In 1930, in *The New York Times*, heterosexuality first became a love that dared to speak its name. On 20 April of that year, the word *heterosexual* is first known to have appeared in *The New York Times Book Review*. There, a critic described the subject of André Gide's *The Immoralist* proceeding "from a heterosexual liaison to a homosexual one." The ability to slip between sexual categories was referred to casually as a rather unremarkable aspect of human possibility. . . .

In September the second reference to the hetero/homo dyad appeared in *The New York Times Book Review*, in a comment on Floyd Dell's *Love in the Machine Age*. This work revealed a prominent antipuritan of the 1930s using the dire threat of homosexuality as his rationale for greater heterosexual freedom. . . . Young people, Dell said, should be "permitted to develop normally to heterosexual adulthood." . . .

Heterosexual Hegemony: 1945–1965

The "cult of domesticity" following World War II—the reassociation of women with the home, motherhood, and childcare; men with fatherhood and wage work outside the home—was a period in which the predominance of the hetero norm went almost unchallenged, an era of heterosexual hegemony. This was an age in which conservative mental-health professionals reasserted the old link between heterosexuality and procreation. In contrast, sex-liberals of the day strove, ultimately with success, to expand the heterosexual ideal to include within the boundaries of normality a wider-than-ever range of non-procreative, premarital, and extramarital behaviours. But sex-liberal reform actually helped to extend and secure the dominance of the heterosexual idea, as we shall see when we get to Kinsey. . . .

The idea of the feminine female and masculine male as prolific breeders was also reflected in the stress, specific to the late 1940s, on the homosexual as sad symbol of "sterility"—that particular loaded term appears incessantly in comments on homosex dating to the fecund forties.

In 1948, in *The New York Times Book Review*, sex liberalism was in ascendancy. Dr Howard A. Rusk declared that Alfred Kinsey's just published report on *Sexual Behavior in the Human Male* had found "wide variations in sex concepts and behavior." This raised the question: "What is 'normal' and 'abnormal'?" In particular, the report had found that "homosexual experience is much more common than previously thought," and "there is often a mixture of both homo and hetero experience."[5] . . .

Kinsey also explicitly contested the idea of an absolute, either/or antithesis between hetero and homo persons. He denied that human beings "represent two discrete populations, heterosexual and homosexual." The world, he ordered, "is not to be divided into sheep and goats." The hetero/homo division was not nature's doing: "Only the human mind invents categories and tries to force facts into separated pigeon-holes. The living world is a continuum."[6]

With a wave of the taxonomist's hand, Kinsey dismissed the social and historical division of people into heteros and homos. His denial of heterosexual and homosexual personhood rejected the social reality and profound subjective force of a historically constructed tradition which, since 1892 in the United States, had cut the sexual population in two and helped to establish the social reality of a heterosexual and homosexual identity. . . .

HETEROSEXUAL HISTORY: OUT OF THE SHADOWS

. . . Because much stress has been placed here on heterosexuality as word and concept, it seems important to affirm that heterosexuality (and homosexuality) came into existence before it was named and thought about. The formulation of the heterosexual idea did not create a heterosexual experience or behaviour; to suggest otherwise would be to ascribe determining power to labels and concepts. But the titling and envisioning of heterosexuality did play an important role in consolidating the construction of the heterosexual's social existence. Before the wide use of the word *heterosexual*, I suggest, women and men did not mutually lust with the same profound, sure sense of normalcy that followed the distribution of "heterosexual" as universal sanctifier.

According to this proposal, women and men make their own sexual histories. But they do not produce their sex lives just as they please. They make their sexualities within a particular mode of organization given by the past and altered by their changing desire, their present power and activity, and their vision of a better world. That hypothesis suggests a number of good reasons for the immediate inauguration of research on a historically specific heterosexuality. . . .

NOTES

1. Barbara Welter, "The Cult of True Womanhood: 1820–1860," *American Quarterly*, vol. 18 (Summer 1966); Welter's analysis is extended here to include True Men and True Love.

2. Some historians have recently told us to revise our idea of sexless Victorians: their experience and even their ideology, it is said, were more erotic than we previously thought. Despite the revisionists, I argue that "purity" was indeed the dominant, early Victorian, white middle-class standard. For the debate on Victorian sexuality see John D'Emilio and Estelle Freedman, *Intimate Matters: A History of Sexuality in America* (New York: Harper & Row, 1988), p. xii.

3. This reference to females reminds us that the invention of heterosexuality had vastly different impacts on the histories of women and men. It also differed in its impact on lesbians and heterosexual women, homosexual and heterosexual men, the middle class and working class, and on different religious, racial, national, and geographic groups.

4. Dr James G. Kiernan, "Responsibility in Sexual Perversion," *Chicago Medical Recorder*, vol. 3 (May 1892), pp. 185–210.

5. Dr Howard A. Rusk, *New York Times Book Review*, 4 January 1948, p. 3.

6. Alfred Kinsey, Wardell B. Pomeroy, Clyde E. Martin, *Sexual Behavior in the Human Male* (Philadelphia, W. B. Saunders, 1948), pp. 637, 639.

---

1. What are the major periods in the development of the concept of heterosexuality?

2. How did social, historical, economic, and political changes shape the development of our current ideas of heterosexuality? For example, what role did doctors, wars, economic changes, and women's rights play?

3. The time period covered in this article ends at 1965. List three main ways that our ideas about heterosexuality and homosexuality have changed since then.

CRITICAL Reading Questions

Summary

In this chapter, we examined the concepts of sex and gender. Sex is based on perceived biological and physical characteristics and is categorized into the main groups of male and female. Gender is based in cultural and social distinctions and exists along a continuum from masculine to feminine. Both gender and sex are socially constructed and created (and recreated) through performing gender roles in our daily lives. The example of gender in music was used to illustrate how the media and other institutions socialize us to perform our gender roles in particular ways. We discussed three major institutions of society that help to create and perpetuate gender distinctions and inequality in society—sports, the workplace, and politics. Feminist theory and the concept of intersectionality were introduced as ways to understand the importance of gender in our society. We ended this chapter by examining the changing ideas of sexuality in society. The LGBTQ movement has been important in fighting for political, cultural, and social acceptance of the diversity of sexual orientations in modern society. Homophobia has declined, but the generally heteronormative nature of our society as a whole remains.

Key Terms

costs of masculinity 167
double shift (second shift) 176
feminism 179
feminization 175
gender 162
gender roles 165
heteronormative 185
Heterosexual–Homosexual Rating
    Scale 183
homophobia 184

intersectionality 180
intersex 162
Kinsey Reports 183
lesbian, gay, bisexual, transgender,
    or queer/questioning (LGBTQ) 184
performativity 165
sex 162
sexuality 182
sexual orientation 182

For Further Reading

Butler, Judith. 1990. *Gender Trouble: Feminism and the Subversion of Identity*. New York: Routledge.

Collins, Patricia H. 2005. *Black Sexual Politics*. New York: Routledge.

Foucault, Michel. 1976/1998. *The History of Sexuality Vol. 1: The Will to Knowledge*. London: Penguin.

Hochschild, Arlie, and Anne Machung. 1990. *The Second Shift*. New York: Avon Books.

Kimmel, Michael. 2012. *The Gendered Society*, 5th edn. New York: Oxford University Press.

Messner, M.A. 1997. *Politics of Masculinities: Men in Movements*. Lanham, MD: Alta Mira Press.

Smith, Dorothy E. 1987. *The Everyday World as Problematic*. Boston, MA: Northeastern University Press.

PART III

The Role of Institutions

7 Language and the Media

CHAPTER OUTLINE

Introduction

Language is constantly evolving to represent changes in culture. Each year, dictionaries add a list of new words to reflect these changes. In 2005, Merriam-Webster and the American Dialect Society named *truthiness*—coined by Stephen Colbert, then host of *The Colbert Report*—their word of the year. *Truthiness* is the quality of feeling something is true based on instinct rather than facts (Merriam-Webster 2006). The *Oxford English Dictionary* added the following words in 2013: *babymoon, buzzworthy, cake pop, chandelier earring, digital detox, emoji, fauxhawk, girl crush, me time, selfie, squee, street food, twerk,* and *unlike*. Do you know what all these words mean? Do you think your parents would? Are you surprised by any of these additions? Are there any words on this list that you thought were already in the dictionary? This chapter focuses on the importance of language and examines the media's role in society.

Language

The world is filled with language; there are roughly 7,000 languages spoken around the world today. Sociologists have long been interested in this area because, as Durkheim (in Traugott 1978, 102) argued, every language "represents a certain articulation of thought." Languages differ significantly, not just in words but also in ways of making sense of the social world. The difficulties of trying to learn a new language as an adult

PHOTO 7.1 The term *flash mob*—a group of people who have pre-arranged to perform an action, such as a dance, at a specific place and time—was added to the *Oxford English Dictionary* in 2013.

make these differences clear. Similarly, attempting to translate poetry or humour from one language to another is often problematic and meanings can be "lost in translation." It is not enough to simply translate the words—you have to understand how the language and culture work in order to make the joke or poem make sense.

The Sapir–Whorf Hypothesis

Durkheim's understanding of the connection between language and thought was partly stimulated by the work of anthropologists who studied languages in North America. One such anthropologist, Edward Sapir (1884–1939), compared indigenous languages with the European languages with which he was familiar. He argued that these languages are so dissimilar because they are based in cultures that understand the world in very different ways. Based on this idea, Sapir and Benjamin Whorf developed the **Sapir–Whorf hypothesis**, which argues that language impacts thought. Whorf (1956, 212–14) describes this relationship in the following way:

> We dissect nature along lines laid down by our native language. The categories and types that we isolate from the world of phenomena we do not find there because they stare every observer in the face; on the contrary, the world is presented in a kaleidoscope flux of impressions which has to be organized by our minds—and this means largely by the linguistic systems of our minds. We cut nature up, organize it into concepts, and ascribe significances as we do, largely because we are parties to an agreement to organize it in this way—an agreement that holds throughout our speech community and is codified in the patterns of our language . . . all observers are not led by the same physical evidence to the same picture of the universe, unless their linguistic backgrounds are similar, or can in some way be calibrated.

An example of the connection between language and thought is the use of **honorifics** (a linguistic means of conveying respect to a person). Honorifics are not often used in English. When you address another person—no matter if he is your best friend, grandparent, teacher, or the prime minister—you use the word *you*. The French language, however, has two levels of formality. When you initially meet someone or speak to someone older or to whom you owe respect, you use *vous* (the plural for "you"). For your friends, family members, and others with whom you have a more informal relationship, you use the singular *tu*. Many people who learn French later in life find it hard to understand when they should use each term and, especially, when they can move from *vous* to *tu*. When does your relationship transition into a more informal one? This question is not simply a linguistic issue; it is also related to a cultural understanding of whom you should respect and how relationships change.

Korean has seven levels of respect, which are used to mark the formality of the conversation as well as elements of the speaker and listener's relationship. For example, you can use particular noun or verb endings to indicate clearly if your conversation partner has a higher or lower status than you. In other words, you would speak to an older relative, your boss, or your teacher differently than you would to a younger person or an employee. These rules of speech are quite complicated but are very important. If you refer to someone too casually (or too impersonally), you could cause offence.

Sapir and Whorf would argue that these differences in the use of honorifics illustrate something about these cultures as a whole. Because North American or English culture (where English is spoken) tends to pride itself on individualism and equality, there is less need to differentiate people in language based on their status. In cultures that value the role of the collective, respect for authority, and hierarchy (such as Korea), the need to distinguish speakers based on their status and to defer to authorities is a cultural element that is built into the language.

HIGHLIGHT

What's the Problem with Sexist Language, You Guys?

As we learned in the last chapter, our language is filled with gendered terms and there is a lot of discussion about the importance of gendered language. Does it matter if we refer to *mankind, chairman,* or *freshmen* when we really mean *humankind, chair,* or *first-year student?* The people at You All think that it does. They ran a website (http://youall2 .freeservers.com) and created a card, shown below, to explain why using the phrase "you guys" to refer to both women and men is a problem and to offer alternatives. They say:

> We know "you guys" is a habit that's hard to break and the card will help your friends think about why it's worth giving it up. We also leave the card at restaurants if the server has "you guysed" us during the meal. Or drop it in the "suggestion box." The card isn't meant to punish, but to educate, so leave a big tip!

"Hey, You Guys!"

Imagine someone walking up to a group of guys and saying, "Hey, girls, how're ya doing?" We doubt they'd be amused! So isn't it weird that women are supposed to accept – even like – being called "one of the guys?" We're also supposed to like "freshman," "chairman," and "mankind."

Get over it, some people say. Those words are generic. They apply to everyone. But then how come so-called generics are always male?

What if generics ended in "white?" Freshwhite, chairwhite, whitekind, and "Hey, you whiteys!" Would people of color like being called "one of the whites?"

The term "guys" makes women invisible by lumping them in with men. Let's quit doing that. When you're talking to a group of customers, gender really doesn't matter, so why not replace "you guys" with "you all," "folks," or "y'all." Or simply say, "What can I get you?" That would take care of us all.

Thanks for your help.

Source: www.youall2.freeservers.com/home.html

The card is intended to be humorous but also to discuss the issue of gender-biased language. Would you give this card to someone whom you felt was using sexist language? Do you think it is a useful tool? Why or why not?

George Orwell's novel *1984* is based on the idea that language and thought are connected. In the book, Orwell invented the language Newspeak, which removes all words that might lead people to contemplate revolution. For example, the words *freedom* and *love* have been removed. This language is an intentionally extreme version of the Sapir–Whorf hypothesis—it is a novel after all—but it highlights the theory. The principle is that, if you do not have the words to articulate action, you will not be able to act. Without the word for *freedom*, you cannot even contemplate the idea of being free and will not revolt to gain your freedom. As Orwell (1949, 303) describes, "The purpose of Newspeak was not only to provide a medium of expression for the world-view and mental habits proper to the devotees of [the society], but to make all other modes of thought impossible."

Robert B. Moore illustrates the relationship among language, thought, and culture in the following article. Moore argues that "language not only *expresses* ideas and concepts but actually *shapes* thought." His article highlights the use of racist terms and expressions in English and the ways this language reflects an underlying racism in our culture.

Racism in the English Language

Robert B. Moore

. . .

Language and Culture

An integral part of any culture is its language. Language not only develops in conjunction with a society's historical, economic, and political evolution; it also reflects that society's attitudes and thinking. Language not only *expresses* ideas and concepts but actually *shapes* thought.[1] If one accepts that our dominant white culture is racist, then one would expect our language—an indispensable transmitter of culture—to be racist as well. Whites, as the dominant group, are not subjected to the same abusive characterization by our language that people of colour receive. Aspects of racism in the English language that will be discussed in this essay include terminology, symbolism, politics, ethnocentrism, and context. . . .

Depending on one's culture, one interacts with time in a very distinct fashion. One example which gives some cross-cultural insights into the concept of time is language. In Spanish, a watch is said to "walk." In English, the watch "runs." In German, the watch "functions." And in French, the watch "marches." In the Indian culture of the Southwest, people do not refer to time in this way. The value of the watch is displaced with the value of "what time it's getting to be." Viewing these five cultural perspectives on time, one can see some definite emphasis and values that each culture places on time. For example, a cultural perspective may provide a clue to why the negative stereotype of the slow and lazy Mexican who lives in the "Land of Manana" exists in the Anglo value system, where time "flies," the watch "runs," and "time is money."

A Short Play on "Black" and "White" Words

Some may blackly (angrily) accuse me of trying to blacken (defame) the English language, to give it a black eye (a mark of shame) by writing such black words (hostile). They may denigrate (to cast aspersions; to darken) me by accusing me of being blackhearted (malevolent), of having a black outlook (pessimistic, dismal) on life, of being a blackguard (scoundrel)—which would certainly be a black mark (detrimental fact) against me. Some may black-brow (scowl at) me and hope that a black cat crosses in front of me because of this black deed. I may become a black sheep (one who causes shame or embarrassment because of deviation from the accepted standards), who will be blackballed (ostracized) by being placed on a blacklist (list of undesirables) in an attempt to blackmail (to force or coerce into a particular action) me to retract my words. But attempts to blackjack (to compel by threat) me will have a Chinaman's chance of success, for I am not a yellow-bellied Indian-giver of words, who will whitewash (cover up or gloss over vices or crimes) a black lie (harmful, inexcusable). I challenge the purity and innocence (white) of the English language. I don't see things in black and white (entirely bad or entirely good) terms, for I am a white man (marked by upright firmness) if there ever was one. However, it would be a black day when I would not "call a spade a spade," even though some will suggest a white man calling the English language racist is like the pot calling the kettle black. While many may be niggardly (grudging, scanty) in their support, others will be honest and decent—and to them I say, that's very white of you (honest, decent).

The preceding is of course a white lie (not intended to cause harm), meant only to illustrate some examples of racist terminology in the English language. . . .

Colour Symbolism

The symbolism of white as positive and black as negative is pervasive in our culture, with the black/white words used in the beginning of this essay only one of many aspects. "Good guys" wear white hats and ride white horses, "bad guys" wear black hats and ride black horses. Angels are white, and devils are black. The definition of *black* includes "without any moral light or goodness, evil, wicked, indicating disgrace, sinful," while that of *white* includes "morally pure, spotless, innocent, free from evil intent." . . .

Three of the dictionary definitions of white are "fairness of complexion, purity, innocence." These definitions affect the standards of beauty in our culture, in which whiteness represents the norm. "Blondes have more fun" and "Wouldn't you really rather be a blonde?" are sexist in their attitudes toward women generally, but are racist white standards when applied to Third World women. . . .

Passive Voice

Another means by which language shapes our perspective has been noted by Thomas Greenfield,[2] who writes that the achievements of black people—and black people themselves—have been hidden in . . .

> . . . the linguistic ghetto of the passive voice, the subordinate clause, and the "understood" subject. The seemingly innocuous distinction (between active/passive voice) holds enormous implications for writers and speakers. When it is effectively applied, the rhetorical impact of the passive voice—the art of making the creator or instigator of action totally disappear from a reader's perception—can be devastating.

For instance, some history texts will discuss how European immigrants came to the United States seeking a better life and expanded opportunities, but will note that "slaves were *brought* to America." Not only does this omit the destruction of African societies and families, but it ignores the role of northern merchants and southern slaveholders in the profitable trade in human beings. Other books will state that "the continental railroad *was built*," conveniently omitting information about the Chinese labourers who built much of it or the oppression they suffered.

Politics and Terminology

"Culturally deprived," "economically disadvantaged," and "underdeveloped" are other terms which mislead and distort our awareness of reality. The application of the term "culturally deprived" to Third World children in this society reflects a value judgment. It assumes that the dominant whites are cultured and all others are without culture. In fact, Third World children generally are bicultural, and many are bilingual, having grown up in their own culture as well as absorbing the dominant culture. In many ways, they are equipped with skills and experiences which white youth have been deprived of, since most white youth develop in a monocultural, monolingual environment. Burgest[3] suggests that the term "culturally deprived" be replaced by "culturally dispossessed," and that the term "economically disadvantaged" be replaced by "economically exploited." Both these terms present a perspective and implication that provide an entirely different frame of reference as to the reality of the Third World experience in US society.

Similarly, many nations of the Third World are described as "underdeveloped." These less wealthy nations are generally those that suffered under colonialism and neo-colonialism. The "developed" nations are those that exploited their resources and wealth. Therefore, rather than referring to these countries as "underdeveloped," a more appropriate and meaningful designation might be "over exploited." . . . Transpose this term next time you read about "underdeveloped nations" and note the different meaning that results.

Terms such as "culturally deprived," "economically disadvantaged," and "underdeveloped" place the responsibility for their own conditions on those being so described. This is known as "Blaming the Victim."[4] It places responsibility for poverty in the victims of poverty. It removes the blame from those in power who benefit from, and continue to permit, poverty.

Still another example involves the use of "non-white," "minority," or "Third World." While people of colour are a minority in the US, they are part of the vast majority of the world's population, in which white people are a distinct minority. Thus, by utilizing the term minority to describe people of colour in the US, we can lose sight of the global majority/minority reality—a fact of some importance in the increasing and interconnected struggles of people of colour inside and outside the US.

"Loaded" Words and Native Americans

Many words lead to a demeaning characterization of groups of people. For instance, Columbus, it is said, "discovered" America. The word *discover* is defined as "to gain sight or knowledge of something previously unseen or unknown; to discover may be to find some existent thing that was previously unknown." Thus, a continent inhabited by millions of human beings cannot be "discovered." For history books to continue this usage represents a Eurocentric (white European) perspective on world history and ignores the existence of, and the perspective of, Native Americans. "Discovery," as used in the Euro-American context, implies the right to take what one finds, ignoring the rights of those who already inhabit or own the "discovered" thing.

Eurocentrism is also apparent in the usage of "victory" and "massacre" to describe the battles between Native Americans and whites. *Victory* is defined in the dictionary as "a success or triumph over an enemy in battle or war; the decisive defeat of an opponent." *Conquest* denotes the "taking over of control by the victor, and the obedience of the conquered." *Massacre* is defined as "the unnecessary, indiscriminate killing of a number of human beings, as in barbarous warfare or persecution, or for revenge or plunder." *Defend* is described as "to ward off attack from; guard against assault or injury; to strive to keep safe by resisting attack."

Eurocentrism turns these definitions around to serve the purpose of distorting history and justifying Euro-American conquest of the Native American homelands. Euro-Americans are not described in history books as invading Native American lands, but rather as defending *their* homes against "Indian" attacks. Since European communities were constantly encroaching on land already occupied, then a more honest interpretation would state that it was the Native Americans who were "warding off," "guarding," and "defending" their homelands.

Native American victories are invariably defined as "massacres," while the indiscriminate killing, extermination, and plunder of Native American nations by Euro-Americans is defined as "victory." Distortion of history by the choice of "loaded" words used to describe historical events is a common racist practice. Rather than portraying Native Americans as human beings in highly defined and complex societies, cultures, and civilizations, history books use such adjectives as "savages," "beasts," "primitive," and "backward." Native people are referred to as "squaw," "brave," or "papoose" instead of "woman," "man," or "baby.". . .

Speaking English

Finally, the depiction in movies and children's books of Third World people speaking English is often itself racist. Children's books about Puerto Ricans or Chicanos often connect poverty with a failure to speak English or to speak it well, thus blaming the victim and ignoring the racism which affects Third World people regardless of their proficiency in English. Asian characters speak a stilted English ("Honorable so and so" or "Confucius say") or have a speech impediment ("rots or ruck," "very solly," "flied lice"). Native American characters speak another variation of stilted English ("Boy not hide. Indian take boy."), repeat certain Hollywood-Indian phrases ("Heap big" and "Many moons") or simply grunt out "Ugh" or "How." The repeated use of these language characterizations functions to make Third World people seem less intelligent and less capable than the English-speaking white characters.

Wrap-Up

A *Saturday Review* editorial[5] on "The Environment of Language" stated that language . . .

> . . . has as much to do with the philosophical and political conditioning of a society as geography or climate . . . People in Western cultures do not realize the extent to which their racial attitudes have been conditioned since early childhood by the power of words to ennoble or condemn, argue or detract, glorify or demean. Negative language infects the subconscious of most Western people from the time they first learn to speak. Prejudice is not merely imparted or superimposed. It is metabolized in the bloodstream of society. What is needed is not so much a change in language as an awareness of the power of words to condition attitudes. If we can at least recognize the underpinnings of prejudice, we may be in a position to deal with the effects.

To recognize the racism in language is an important first step. Consciousness of the influence of language on our perceptions can help to negate much of that influence. But it is not enough to simply become aware of the effects of racism in conditioning attitudes. While we may not be able to change the language, we can definitely change our usage of the language. We can avoid using words that degrade people. We can make a conscious effort to use terminology that reflects a progressive perspective, as opposed to a distorting perspective. It is important for educators to provide students with opportunities to explore racism in language and to increase their awareness of it, as well as learning terminology that is positive and does not perpetuate negative human values.

NOTES

1. Podiat, S. (1967, March). How bigotry builds through language. *Negro Digest*.
2. Greenfield, T. (1975, April). Race and passive voice at Monticello. *Crisis*.
3. Burgest, D. R. (1973, July). Racism in everyday speech and social work jargon. *Social Work*.
4. Ryan, W. (1971). *Blaming the victim*. Pantheon Books.
5. The environment of language. (1967, April 8). *Saturday Review*.

CRITICAL
Reading
Questions

1. According to Moore, what is the relationship between language and culture?
2. How does Moore explain the relationship between language and culture with reference to the use of black/white terms, "Native Americans," and terms about Africa and developing countries?
3. How could this argument be extended to terms about gender? How are gendered terms used in the English language? How do these terms perpetuate sexist ideas?
4. To what extent and where have you heard these terms before? How much has changed in our use of racist, sexist, and other types of discriminatory language?

Media

Media, the plural of the Latin word *medius* ("middle"), refers to the technological processes that facilitate communication between a sender and a receiver. **Mass media** sends a message from one source to many people. Modern society has many kinds of mass media, including radio, television, books, the Internet, movies, music, and magazines. Using a telephone or writing a letter is not normally understood to be mass media because the contents involve private communication between two people and are not intended for a large audience.

Media are important socializing agents in our society; they teach us about the norms and expectations for different people and situations. The significance of the media is, in part, a result of our very high level of exposure to it. According to a recent study, the average Canadian adult watches 30 hours of television a week (Ryan 2013). Canadians spend an average of about 11 hours per week online, twice the global average (Akkad 2011). In addition, Canadians spend considerable amounts of time listening to the radio and reading newspapers and magazines. In this section, we examine changes in the media and the important role the media play in our society.

One of the most important scholars of media was Marshall McLuhan (1911–1980), a Canadian academic who worked at the University of Toronto and founded the Centre for Culture and Technology. McLuhan (1964) is most famous for the statement **"the medium is the message."** He argued that the content of the medium, such as the words on an Internet news site, is not as important as the physical or psychological effects of that medium. Different media have different effects because of the form of their messages. These various forms alter how we experience the world, how we interact with others, and how we process and communicate information. For example, in print media, our visual sense rules; in radio, our aural; in television, both. In essence, McLuhan argued that the medium's properties (not just the messages' content) affect us as individuals and our social world as a whole. The media can shape and change us; as we develop new technologies, we are changed as a result.

The development of the printing press illustrates how changing mediums can affect individuals and society. The printing press was invented in China in 1041, but the version developed by Gutenberg in 1450 Europe was particularly efficient and easy to use. This new press led to the production of the first mass-produced Bible in 1455. Previously, monks copied Bibles by hand, which took a long time. Not surprisingly, copies were scarce and very expensive.

The invention of the European printing press had significant (and, in some cases, unintended) effects on society. A major consequence was the challenge to the elite's ability to hoard information and knowledge. Before the printing press, only very rich and well-connected individuals had books. The press made it possible for more people to purchase them. It increased the number of books available, as they could be mass-produced relatively quickly. When only monks transcribed books, it was easy for the powerful to control what was printed. The printing press effectively opened a massive communication channel, allowing many groups and interests to promote their messages. One of the first things printed on the printing press in Europe was Martin Luther's *The 95 Theses*—a list of complaints about the Catholic Church that led to the creation of Protestantism. This work certainly challenged the status quo!

The printing press also led to the rise of individualism. Individuals became less reliant on others (especially elites) for information. People gained more access to books, pamphlets, and newsletters on a wide variety of subjects. This shift effectively helped to democratize access to information on, for example, how to cure illnesses, build machines, or start a political movement.

PHOTO 7.2 How has technology changed during your life? Did you have access to any computer devices—such as a tablet or smartphone—when you were a child? How would you have grown up differently if you had or hadn't had access to these devices?

Moreover, literacy rates among different groups of people, including the poor, women, and children, improved.

The invention of the printing press was not simply a change in media; it fundamentally changed the nature of society as a whole. Centuries later, the rise of the Internet did the same. The Internet further democratizes access to information and content. Anyone can now read an almost unlimited number of books, magazines, and newspapers online as well as watch videos, movies, and TV shows. However, as we will discuss later in this chapter, there is still inequality regarding who has access to and knowledge about using computers and the Internet.

Corporate Concentration and the Media

One key concern with modern mass media is the extent to which it is controlled by a limited number of people. Recent decades have seen an increase in the **corporate concentration** of media ownership. In other words, the media is increasingly owned and controlled by fewer huge media corporations and conglomerates. Canada has the most concentrated media ownership of any G8 country. The "Big 10" Canadian media companies control 71 per cent of all mass media in the country (see Table 7.1 for their revenue and market share). This number is a substantial increase from the 56 per cent controlled by these companies in 1992.

For example, Bell Media owns 58 television stations (including CTV, TSN, and MTV Canada) and over 30 radio stations. The company is owned by BCE Inc., which runs Bell Home Telephone, Virgin Mobile, Solo Mobile, Bell Internet, Bell Satellite TV, and Bell Fibe TV. On 13 June 2013, the Canadian Radio-television and Telecommunications Commission (CRTC) approved BCE's application to acquire Astral Media Inc., vastly increasing its media holdings in Canada. It is important to note, however, that this

TABLE 7.1	The "Big 10" Canadian media companies by revenue and market share, 2011							
	Ownership	Market Share	Total Rev.	Cable & Sat. Dist.	Internet Access	Total TV	Radio	Press/ Magazines[1]
Bell/CTV	Diversified	15.3	5,373.1	1,830.0	1,525.0	1,857.6	160.5	
Shaw	Shaw family	15.3	5,356.1	2,432.7	968.6	1,759.1	195.7	
Rogers	Rogers family	11.5	4,039.3	1,874.0	912.0	758.6	220.8	273.9
QMI	Péladeau	8.7	3,046.0	1,040.9	698.2	404.6		902.3
CBC	Public	5.2	1,838.8			1,501.9	336.9	
PostMedia	Godfrey et. al.	3.3	1,168.7					1,168.7
Cogeco	Audet (60%), Rogers (40%)	3.0	1,068.9	639.7	315.6		113.6	
Telus	Diversified	3.0	1,052.4	364.8	687.6			
Astral	Greenberg	2.6	922.5			582.2	340.3	
Bragg	Privately held	1.6	558.5	326.5	232.0			
Total NMI $	35,081.8							

1. Revenues for magazines estimated for 2011 based on extrapolation from 2010 data.

SOURCE: Canadian Media Concentration Research Project. 2012 (21 October). "The Big 10 Canadian Media Companies by Revenue & Market Share, 2011." www.cmcrp.org/2012/10/21/the-big-10-canadian-media-companies-by-market-share-2011/.

approval came with a number of conditions intended to uphold the public interest in a free and open media. As the CRTC (2013) explains:

> There remained a significant risk that BCE could exert its market power to limit choice and competition. To ensure the public interest is served, we are requiring BCE to invest in new Canadian programming and sell more than a dozen services, and we are putting in place a number of competitive safeguards. This will maintain a healthy and competitive broadcasting system that offers more programming choices to Canadian consumers and citizens and more opportunities for Canadian creators.

Such concentration could lead to fewer viewpoints being expressed in the media. Certainly Canada's situation is not the same as having a single state-run newspaper, but how much competition is enough to ensure a free and independent press?

This pattern of media control has long historical roots. The town newspaper was once a family-owned business, as was the dairy, hardware store, and grocery store. Today, provision of these basic items is controlled by large firms—CanWest (newspaper), Saputo (dairy), Home Depot (hardware), and Safeway (groceries). Family-owned businesses have not disappeared, but they are now far less powerful and face continual threat (whether from Walmart, Amazon, or other big-box stores). It may not be significant that we all get our milk or our light bulbs from the same store. However, we may be more concerned that our news and, as a consequence, our information about the world, is filtered by a smaller and smaller group.

This issue is at the core of C. Wright Mills's *The Power Elite* (1956). In this book, Mills argues that the **power elite**, a group of leaders in the military, corporate, and political spheres of society, have interwoven and complementary interests. He also found an interchangeability of top positions within these three institutions and, as a result, the most powerful people in each develop a class consciousness and a similar set of interests.

READING

From *The Power Elite*

C. Wright Mills

. . .

The Nature of the Power Elite

We study history, it has been said, to rid ourselves of it, and the history of the power elite is a clear case for which this maxim is correct. Like the tempo of American life in general, the long-term trends of the power structure have been greatly speeded up since World War II, and certain newer trends within and between the dominant institutions have also set the shape of the power elite. . . .

I. In so far as the structural clue to the power elite today lies in the political order, that clue is the decline of politics as genuine and public debate of alternative decisions—with nationally responsible and policy-coherent parties and with autonomous organizations connecting the lower and middle levels of power with the top levels of decision. America is now in considerable part more a formal political democracy than a democratic social structure, and even the formal political mechanics are weak.

The long-time tendency of business and government to become more intricately and deeply involved with each other has, in the fifth epoch, reached a new point of explicitness. The two cannot now be seen clearly as two distinct worlds. It is in terms of the executive agencies of the state that the rapprochement has proceeded most decisively. The growth of the executive branch of the government, with Its agencies that patrol the complex economy, does not mean merely the "enlargement of government" as some sort of autonomous bureaucracy: it has meant the ascendancy of the corporation's man as a political eminence....

III. In so far as the structural clue to the power elite today lies in the economic order, that clue is the fact that the economy is at once a permanent-war economy and a private-corporation economy. American capitalism is now in considerable part a military capitalism, and the most important relation of the big corporation to the state rests on the coincidence of interests between military and corporate needs, as defined by warlords and corporate rich. Within the elite as a whole, this coincidence of interest between the high military and the corporate chieftains strengthens both of them and further subordinates the role of the merely political men. Not politicians, but corporate executives, sit with the military and plan the organization of war effort....

The power elite is composed of political, economic, and military men, but this instituted elite is frequently in some tension: it comes together only on certain coinciding points and only on certain occasions of "crisis": In the long peace of the nineteenth century, the military were not in the high councils of state, not of the political directorate, and neither were the economic men—they made raids upon the state but they did not join its directorate. During the thirties, the political man was ascendant. Now the military and the corporate men are in top positions.

Of the three types of circle that compose the power elite today, it is the military that has benefited the most in its enhanced power although the corporate circles have also become more explicitly entrenched in the more public decision-making circles. It is the professional politician that has lost the most, so much that in examining the events and decisions, one is tempted to speak of a political vacuum in which the corporate rich and the high warlord, in their coinciding interests, rule.

It should not be said that the three "take turns" in carrying the initiative, for the mechanics of the power elite are not often as deliberate as that would imply. At times, of course, it is—as when political men, thinking they can borrow the prestige of generals, find that they must pay for it, or, as when during big slumps, economic men feel the need of a politician at once safe and possessing vote appeal. Today all three are involved in virtually all widely ramifying decisions. Which of the three types seems to lead depends upon "the tasks of the period" as they, the elite, define them. Just now, these tasks centre upon "defence" and international affairs. Accordingly, as we have seen, the military are ascendant in two senses: as personnel and as justifying ideology. That is why, just now, we can most easily specify the unity and the shape of the power elite in terms of the military ascendancy....

Neither the idea of a "ruling class" nor of a simple monolithic rise of "bureaucratic politicians" nor of a "military clique" is adequate. The power elite today involves the often uneasy coincidence of economic, military, and political power.

The Composition of the Power Elite

Despite their social similarity and psychological affinities, the members of the power elite do not constitute a club having a permanent membership with fixed and formal boundaries. It is of the nature of the power elite that within it there is a good deal of shifting about, and that it thus does not consist of one small set of the same men in the same positions in the same hierarchies. Because men know each other personally does not mean that among them there is a unity of policy; and because they do not know each other personally does not mean that among them there is a disunity. The conception of the power elite does not rest, as I have repeatedly said, primarily upon personal friendship.

As the requirements of the top places in each of the major hierarchies become similar, the types of men occupying these roles at the top—by selection and by training in the jobs—become similar. This is no mere deduction from structure to personnel. That it is a fact is revealed by the heavy traffic that has been going on between the three structures, often in very intricate patterns. The chief executives, the warlords, and selected politicians came into contact with one another in an intimate, working way during World War II; after that war ended, they continued their associations, out of common beliefs, social congeniality, and coinciding interests. Noticeable proportions of top men from the military, the economic, and the political worlds have during the last 15 years occupied positions in one or both of the other worlds: between these higher circles there is an interchangeability of position, based formally upon the supposed transferability of "executive ability," based in substance upon the co-optation by cliques of insiders. As members of a power elite, many of those busy in this traffic have come to look upon "the government" as an umbrella under whose authority they do their work. . . .

Given the formal similarity of the three hierarchies in which the several members of the elite spend their working lives, given the ramifications of the decisions made in each upon the others, given the coincidence of interest that prevails among them at many points, and given the administrative vacuum of the American civilian state along with its enlargement of tasks—given these trends of structure, and adding to them the psychological affinities we have noted—we should indeed be surprised were we to find that men said to be skilled in administrative contacts and full of organizing ability would fail to do more than get in touch with one another. They have, of course, done much more than that: increasingly, they assume positions in one another's domains. . . .

These men are not necessarily familiar with every major arena of power. We refer to one man who moves in and between perhaps two circles—say the industrial and the military—and to another man who moves in the military and the political, and to a third who moves in the political as well as among opinion-makers. These in-between types most closely display our image of the power elite's structure and operation, even of behind-the-scenes operations. To the extent that there is any "invisible elite," these advisory and liaison types are its core. Even If—as I believe to be very likely—many of them are, at least in the first part of their careers, "agents" of the various elites rather than themselves elite, it is they who are most active in organizing the several top milieux into a structure of power and maintaining it. . . .

The Interests of the Power Elite

The conception of the power elite and of its unity rests upon the corresponding developments and the coincidence of interests among economic, political, and military organizations. It also rests upon the similarity of origin and outlook, and the social and personal intermingling of the top circles from each of these dominant hierarchies. This conjunction of institutional and psychological forces, in turn, is revealed by the heavy personnel traffic within and between the big three institutional orders, as well as by the rise of go-betweens as in the high-level lobbying. The conception of the power elite, accordingly, does *not* rest upon the assumption that American history since the origins of World War II must be understood as a secret plot, or as a great and coordinated conspiracy of the members of this elite. The conception rests upon quite impersonal grounds.

There is, however, little doubt that the American power elite—which contains, we are told, some of the greatest organizers in the world—has also planned and has plotted. The rise of the elite, as we have already made clear, was not and could not have been caused by a plot; and the tenability of the conception does not rest upon the existence of any secret or any publicly known organization. But, once the conjunction of structural trend and of the personal will to utilize it gave rise to the power elite, then plans and programs did occur to its members and indeed it is not possible to interpret many events and official policies of the fifth epoch without reference to the power elite. "There is a great difference," Richard Hofstadter has remarked, "between locating conspiracies in history and saying that history is, in effect, a conspiracy. . . "

So far as explicit organization—conspiratorial or not—is concerned, the power elite, by its very nature, is more likely to use existing organizations, working within and between them, than to set up explicit organizations whose membership is strictly limited to its own members. But if there is no machinery in existence to ensure, for example, that military and political factors will be balanced in decisions made, they will invent such machinery and use it, as with the National Security Council. Moreover, in a formally democratic polity, the aims and the powers of the various elements of this elite are further supported by an aspect of the permanent war economy: the assumption that the security of the nation supposedly rests upon great secrecy of plan and intent. Many higher events that would reveal the working of the power elite can be withheld from public knowledge under the guise of secrecy. With the wide secrecy covering their operations and decisions, the power elite can mask their intentions, operations, and further consolidation. Any secrecy that is imposed upon those in positions to observe high decision-makers clearly works for and not against the operations of the power elite.

There is accordingly reason to suspect—but by the nature of the case, no proof—that the power elite is not altogether "surfaced." There is nothing hidden about it, although its activities are not publicized. As an elite, it is not organized, although its members often know one another, seem quite naturally to work together, and share many organizations in common. There is nothing conspiratorial about it, although its decisions are often publicly unknown and its mode of operation manipulative rather than explicit.

Conclusion

The idea of the power elite rests upon and enables us to make sense of (1) the decisive institutional trends that characterize the structure of our epoch, in particular, the military ascendancy in a privately incorporated economy, and more broadly, the several coincidences of objective interests between economic, military, and political institutions; (2) the social similarities and the psychological affinities of the men who occupy the command posts of these structures, in particular the increased interchangeability of the top positions in each of them and the increased traffic between these orders in the careers of men of power; (3) the ramifications, to the point of virtual totality, of the kind of decisions that are made at the top, and the rise to power of a set of men who, by training and bent, are professional organizers of considerable force and who are unrestrained by democratic party training. . . .

As a result, the political directorate, the corporate rich, and the ascendant military have come together as the power elite, and the expanded and centralized hierarchies which they head have encroached upon the old balances and have now relegated them to the middle levels of power. Now the balancing society is a conception that pertains accurately to the middle levels, and on that level the balance has become more often an affair of entrenched provincial and nationally irresponsible forces and demands than a centre of power and national decision.

CRITICAL
Reading
Questions

1. Who are the power elite? What are the three types of institutions that make up the power elite?

2. How do the interests of these three groups coincide and how do they conflict? How do they come to share these commonalities?

3. Does Mills think that the power elite has control because of a conspiracy? How do they continue to exist?

Effects of Media Concentration

As mentioned in the previous section, corporate concentration in the media and other areas can limit the free exchange of ideas and the diversity of content we receive as media consumers. The two main types of media diversity that can be affected are idea diversity and demographic diversity.

Idea diversity refers to the range of viewpoints expressed in the media marketplace of ideas. Media conglomerates have the power to censor information according to their interests. In *Manufacturing Consent: The Political Economy of the Mass Media*, Noam Chomsky and Edward S. Herman (2002) argue that wealthy and powerful people control the mass media. Because the mass media are one of the primary means of socialization and persuasion in our society, elites are able to create news that reflects their own interests. Herman and Chomsky also argue that elites can use this media control to legitimize the class system and other inequalities in our society.

Demographic diversity refers to how the media represents and addresses the interests of a diversity of people from a variety of races, ethnicities, genders, sexual orientations, and classes. One might argue that a way to ensure demographically diverse content is to support demographically diverse ownership (Gamson and Latteier 2004). In the United States, where more data is collected on this issue, less than 5 per cent of the media is owned by women or ethnic minorities (Byerly 2006). This lack of diversity in ownership could limit the variety of characters and shows presented. However, it is possible that a homogeneous group of media owners could be showing a range of characters.

A GLAAD study of diversity on US television found that ethnic minorities, women, and gay and lesbian characters are underrepresented in the media (Elber 2013). This study examined all 796 regular characters on prime-time broadcast dramas and comedies airing in the United States in the 2013 television season. It found that, while ethnic minorities make up 28 per cent of the country's population, they account for only 23 per cent of characters on American television. Women, who make up 56 per cent of the population, account for only 43 per cent of television characters (down from 45 per cent from the previous season). LGBTQ people account for only 3.3 per cent of all characters, a decline from 4.4 per cent the season before. Mainstream cable television currently has only one regular transgender character, on *Glee* (Kane 2013).

The depiction of gay and lesbian characters in the media is further complicated by the different rating standards that these shows often incur. The documentary *This Film Is Not Yet Rated* (2006) discusses the rating system of the Motion Picture Association of America (MPAA) and finds that movies depicting gay intimacy are much more likely to have an NC-17 rating than do movies with sexually explicit scenes between a heterosexual pair. Just having LGBTQ characters or themes in a movie makes the MPAA more likely to increase the age restrictions because of "sexual references," despite the fact that heterosexual sexual activity is less likely to be so restricted.

This lack of diversity has many serious implications for viewers. For example, it can have negative effects on the self-esteem of various groups. Martins and Harrison (2012) surveyed 396 black and white preteens in the United States to examine television's effect on children's self-esteem. They found that television exposure led to decreased self-esteem for white and black girls and black boys. However, it was associated with increased self-esteem among white boys.

PHOTO 7.3 *Black-ish*, which debuted on ABC in 2014, attempts to show demographic diversity both in front of and behind the camera. Is it important to depict diversity in television shows? Can this lead to more inclusiveness in society as a whole?

HIGHLIGHT ///////////////////////////////

Adbusters and Buy Nothing Day

In Vancouver in 1989, Kalle Lasn and Bill Schmalz founded Adbusters, a non-profit, anti-consumerist organization that publishes an activist magazine of the same name. The organization promotes, among other things, Buy Nothing Day, a day of anti-consumerist protest that asks people not to purchase anything for 24 hours. Started in 1992 by Vancouver artist Ted Dave, this event is intended to illustrate that we do not necessarily need to buy as many products as we do and to question consumerism in society as a whole. Adbusters created many advertisements for this day and tried to buy airtime on MTV, FOX, ABC, NBC, and CBS. None of these channels agreed to air the ad, but you can access it and an interview with Lasn at this book's companion website.

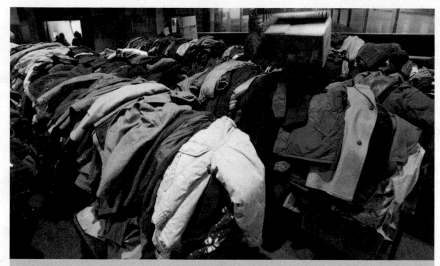

On Buy Nothing Day, some organizations encourage activities such as donation drives in order to demonstrate opposition to consumerism. How does donating or purchasing used clothing challenge our consumerist culture?

While we are constantly inundated with advertisements that sell both products and ideas (e.g. consumerism, the importance of physical appearance, disregard for the environment), different perspectives, such as the one put forth by this campaign, are silenced. What is the implication for free speech?

Such forms of protesting consumerism have been critiqued. For example, *Adbusters* is sold, turning its counterculture claims into a commodity. Buy Nothing Day also sells t-shirts to promote the movement. Does this situation negate the power of the message or is it just a natural by-product of capitalist society?

RESEARCH METHOD

Survey

The study shows that children from certain groups (females and ethnic minorities) suffer lower self-esteem when they are not exposed to TV role models who look like them. When individuals who share their racial and gender characteristics are shown, they are engaging in negative behaviours, which can also cause the viewer's feelings of self-worth to drop. The study authors found that white male characters are mostly portrayed as powerful, strong, rational, and central to the storyline. Female characters are more likely to appear emotional, sensitive, and as a sidekick or love interest. Black male characters are shown as threatening or unruly; black female characters are exotic and sexually available (Martins and Harrison 2012). As a result, young white boys had a better set of positive media representation than the children in the other groups.

A UCLA study found that there are benefits to having more diversity in the media. Hunt (in Lee 2013) analyzed shows from the 2011–2012 TV season (over 1,000 shows across 67 networks). Shows with a more diverse cast tended to have higher ratings than other shows—in fact, shows with casts that were between 31 per cent and 40 per cent minority did the best in ratings measures. Shows with very low levels of diversity (10 per cent or less) tended to have lower ratings. Clearly, diversity is not only important for audiences, but it also benefits media corporations.

New Media and Social Media

The media environment has undergone widespread change over the past 20 to 30 years with the rise in new media. **New media** is accessible on demand, is digital, and is interactive, encouraging user comments and feedback. Some examples of new media are the Internet, websites, video games, CDs, and DVDs. Wikipedia combines a number of features of new media: it is digitally based, incorporates images and video links, and allows interactive and creative participation among users.

Social media, a type of new media, allows the creation and online sharing of information in communities and networks. According to Kaplan and Haenlein (2010), social media technologies can be classified into six types: collaborative projects (Wikipedia), blogs and microblogs (Twitter), content communities (YouTube), social networking sites (Facebook), virtual game worlds (*Clash of Clans*), and virtual social worlds (*Minecraft* or *Second Life*). However, the boundaries between the different types are increasingly blurred.

Social media is used mainly for social interaction. The high usage rates of these technologies indicate that they are filling important social functions for many people. In fact, many argue that technology is transforming how we engage with others and how we spend our time. More and more people are willing to make social connections and seek companionship through social media such as Tinder or Grindr. The Internet is also an effective way for users to connect with people across great distances, such as through Skype. Moreover, our expectations and norms about love, friendship, and identity are strongly informed by our use of social media. What it means to "friend" someone, for example, is very different in the Facebook era than it was 50 years ago.

With the largest concentration of Internet users in the world, state investment in technological infrastructure, and high use of technology, South Korea is often seen as the first digital democracy. Many commentators have credited the strong role of the Internet and television for changing Korean social norms. For example, previous taboos, including divorce, extramarital affairs, and cohabitation, are changing. In the last 10 years, South Korea's divorce rate increased by 250 per cent (Onishi 2003). Koreans' changing attitudes about these issues are reflected in television programs, many of which are centred on the lives of women. *The Woman Next Door* focuses on the marriages and affairs of three women in their thirties and challenges traditional norms in Korean society, where men were allowed to engage in affairs and wives were expected to remain faithful.

We can also see that social media has created many large-scale changes in Canada. The biggest change is in the scale of our social networks—we can interact with many more people than was possible in the past. Traditionally, our social networks were limited by our geography, but physical presence is no longer a precondition for establishing a friendship or tie. Think about how you show friends your vacation photos. Twenty years ago, you would have had to meet in person, flip through hard copies of the photos, and explain them. Doing this with all your Facebook friends would take a long time. Now you can simply upload all your photos to Facebook and add descriptions; your friends can view the photos at their leisure, increasing this interaction of photo-sharing. Although you can certainly share your photos with a larger group of people, the quality of the interaction is possibly lower. Not all your Facebook friends will commit the half hour they might have spent looking at your photos in the past.

Social Media and the Arab Spring

The Arab Spring was a widespread movement of protests and civil wars that occurred across the Arab world beginning in December 2010. This call for political rights and democracy created great social change. For example, the protests deposed rulers in Egypt, Libya, Tunisia, and Yemen; inspired large-scale demonstrations in Algeria, Bahrain, Iraq, Jordan, Kuwait, Morocco, Syria, and Sudan; and led to minor protests in Mauritania, Oman, Saudi Arabia, Djibouti, Western Sahara, and the Palestinian Authority.

The widespread use of social media during the Arab Spring is unique and noteworthy. Access to social media was particularly important in countries where the government controls the media. As Lindsey (2013) reports, "an individual blogger can affect an election, an Internet posting can recruit a terrorist and an audiotape can incite fear in the strongest of nation-states, all with little capital investment and certainly without bureaucratic rules or censorship."

The ability of activists to use social media enabled individuals to spread news of events and issues both locally to mobilize people and internationally to foster support for the movement. The use of Facebook and other social media sites is credited with helping to facilitate messaging and outreach and to mobilize events such as the 18-day occupation of Tahrir Square. As Wael Ghonim, an Egyptian activist, said, "If you want to liberate [a people], give them the Internet" (in Lindsey 2013). Facebook use has risen dramatically in Egypt, from 450,000 before the revolution to an estimated 3 million users in the six months after. While we tend to focus on its more social and frivolous aspects—for example, taking pictures of our lunch—social media can be a powerful tool for social change (see Chapters 12 and 13).

Social media also places fewer restrictions on your communication. Previously, the only way to get your message to a large group of people was to talk with them face to face (perhaps in a speech to a large crowd); otherwise, you could be censored. For example, if you write a letter to the editor, the publication has the power to select (or not select) your letter for printing. If you wanted to air your advertisement on TV, the station could refuse your ad or make you change its content. But with social media, you can distribute your message to a virtually unlimited number of people with very little censorship (at least in Canada). If you're upset with something the prime minister does, you can post your feelings on a blog, Twitter, or Facebook, where all your friends and followers can read it.

There are obvious benefits to social media. However, we must not overestimate the diversity of social media networks. While it might seem that we can have contact and communication with virtually anyone, we know that individuals tend to create online communities of similar people who share their opinions. It is not surprising that, just as in face-to-face friendships, we tend to seek out others like us online. As a result, we are exposed to a limited number of views. People who hold very different beliefs or perspectives than we do are unlikely to be in our online circle of friends. Perhaps you are part of a political or religious group online. These groups will likely only have other members who share your political or religious ideology, which could simply reinforce the opinions you already have instead of exposing you to new ideas and information.

The ability to spread information about ourselves and others so easily has created a lack of privacy, which can be a particular problem for young people. A 2011 Kids Help Phone study found that the majority of young people (aged 13–15) did not realize that social media was not private and that information put online could not always be removed (Knighton et al. 2012). This age group is also particularly susceptible to

cyber-bullying, the use of the Internet and related technologies to deliberately harass, intimidate, or threaten a person. The same survey revealed that 70 per cent of participants reported being bullied online and 44 per cent reported having bullied someone else at least once. This bullying was most rampant on social networking sites.

Digital Divide

The percentage of Canadians who use the Internet has increased over time. In 2005, 74 per cent reported using the Internet in the past year. Six years later, this number had increased to 86 per cent (CRTC 2013). However, use of the Internet and other communication technologies is not equally distributed across all groups. The **digital divide** is the inequality between groups with regard to their access to information and communication technologies (ICTs) and to their use of such technologies (OECD n.d.). The divide within one country occurs between individuals, households, and geographic areas at different socio-economic levels. The divide between countries, referred to as the global digital divide, measures the gap between the digital access and use of technologies across countries.

Age is a major dimension of the digital divide in Canada. Figure 7.1 illustrates the role of age, gender, and education level in the digital divide. Individuals under the age of 35 are most likely to use the Internet—96.5 per cent had done so in 2009. Those over 65 are much less likely to have done so, with only about 40 per cent having used the Internet in the past year (Statistics Canada 2012).

Women and men are roughly equal in terms of Internet use, at 79.7 and 81.0 per cent, respectively (Statistics Canada 2012). However, their usage patterns are very different. Women are more likely to frequent social networking websites, with 37 per cent using such sites daily compared with only 24 per cent of men (Ipsos Reid 2012).

A strong urban/rural digital divide also exists. Urban Canadians are much more likely to use the Internet for personal reasons (outside of work use) than are rural Canadians (76 per cent compared with 65 per cent). When they do go online, urban Canadians do a more diverse set of activities than their rural counterparts. There are a variety of reasons for such disparities; one is simply that high-speed service is less reliable or even unavailable in rural regions (Dewing 2012).

Finally, and perhaps most significantly, there is a large digital divide between the richest and poorest Canadians. While 97 per cent of Canadians in the highest income bracket (over $87,000 a year) have access to the Internet, just 54 per cent in the lowest income bracket (less than $30,000 a year) have access (Dewing 2012).

As illustrated in Figure 7.2, the digital divide is much more extreme across countries. While North America, Europe, and Australia have near universal access to computers and Internet technology (from 80–100 per cent of all citizens), many areas of Africa and Asia have levels closer to 10–20 per cent. The situation in Ghana, where

PHOTO 7.4 Internet cafés like this one often provide people's only link to the Internet. What are the implications of having such limited access to the Internet? How does accessing the Internet through a café, instead of at home, change the types of activities one can engage in online and the benefits of Internet access?

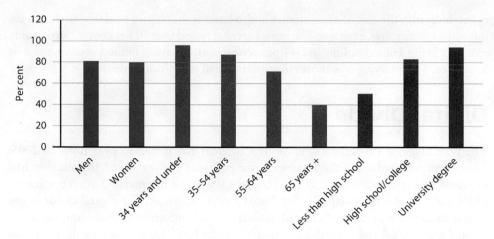

FIGURE 7.1 Rates of Internet use by gender, age, and education, Canada, 2009

SOURCE: www.statcan.gc.ca/tables-tableaux/sum-som/l01/cst01/comm35a-eng.htm.

the Internet is delivered through phone connections, illustrates the challenges of the global digital divide. The country has only 240,000 phones for its 20 million people, and the phone lines are spread across a nation the size of Great Britain. A business phone line costs about $1,000, as much as office rent would cost for a year. Even if a person has access to a phone, about half of all calls do not go through because of system failures. Cellphones are available (300,000 in total), but they are very costly (about 10 times the cost of one in Canada) and also frequently drop calls because of the relatively few cellphone towers. This situation makes it clear that we cannot simply eliminate the digital

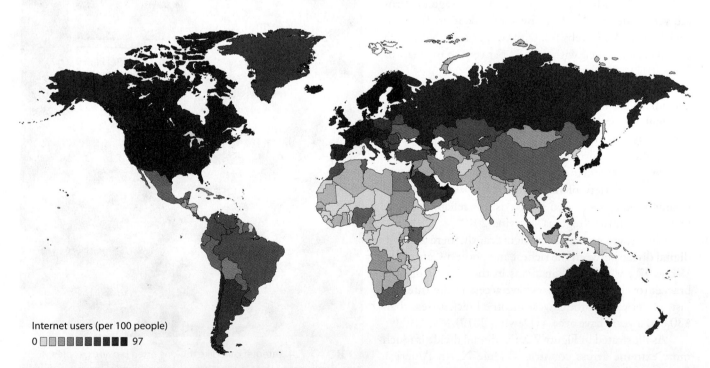

Internet users (per 100 people)

0 ▢▢▢▢▢▢▢▢▢▢ 97

FIGURE 7.2 Internet users per 100 people, 2011–2015

SOURCE: http://data.worldbank.org/indicator/IT.NET.USER.P2/countries?display=map.

The Reality of Reality TV

Another major change in the media over the past 20 years is the rise of reality programming. The first reality television show was *Cops*, which has run since 1989. This show uses actual video footage of police officers in their daily work and shows arrests, car chases, and investigations as they happen.

Technological advancements helped make reality TV possible. The availability of less expensive and smaller cameras allowed crew members to follow the action as it happened. In the case of *Cops*, cameras could be mounted on police cars to catch police work in real time. This programming was very appealing to television stations and production studios because it was relatively inexpensive. There was no need to pay writers, actors, or costume designers. TV crews could simply film real people on the ground, in the course of their daily lives.

As other reality shows followed, people began to wonder how "real" these shows were. In many ways, *Cops* is real. The people are not actors; they are real police officers and real suspects. The show is based on real situations (e.g. actual arrests) that are not scripted. There is minimal narration and no host. In fact, it was originally seen by some as educational programming about the police and their work. However, its content and narratives are edited to fit into a 30-minute time slot (including commercial breaks). The editors use story-telling devices, such as featuring heroes and villains without ambiguity. They also select the most interesting and dramatic police work—there is no episode of officers giving out parking tickets!

These manipulated aspects of the show have important consequences. They exaggerate the rate and severity of certain types of crimes in the public's mind. There is much more coverage, for example, of assault and other violent crimes than of white-collar crimes such as tax evasion. To keep viewership, the show also focuses on crimes that are committed by strangers and that are particularly dramatic, even though these crimes are relatively rare. *Cops* also distorts reality by depicting those who are arrested for crimes as violent, stupid, poor, and visible minorities. While some criminals fall into these stereotypes, many are non-violent, smart, rich, and white. Police officers are depicted as heroes who are always doing the right thing, which ignores the reality of police brutality and excessive force. (Chapter 11 discusses these issues in more detail.)

In this activity, we will look at other types of reality programming, including shows based on survival (*Survivor*, *The Amazing Race*), biography (*Keeping Up with the Kardashians*, *The Real Housewives* franchise), competition (*Dancing with the Stars*, *America's Next Top Model*), and love (*The Bachelor* and *The Millionaire Matchmaker*). With these shows in mind, answer the following questions.

1. Go to this book's companion website to access an interview with Troy DeVolld, a producer of *The Osbournes*, *The Surreal Life*, *The Bachelor*, and *Dancing with the Stars*. Based on this article, how "real" are reality shows? How are they cast and scripted? What is a Frankenbite and how could it distort the reality of these shows?

2. Watch the *Jersey Shore* and *American Idol* clips on this book's companion website. To what extent does it matter that these shows are scripted? How do they distort our image of reality?

3. What types of values and behaviours do reality shows display? Should we be concerned about these shows purporting to represent reality? Why or why not?

divide in a country such as Ghana by sending computers. Even if there were staff that knew how to use them, computers are useless without an Internet connection or stable power supply (Oppong-Tawiah and Boateng 2011; Zachary 2002).

The digital divide has important consequences, both within Canada and around the world. First, it creates unequal access to information. For example, in countries with limited access, schools must rely on expensive books that quickly become outdated instead of using Internet resources that are cheaper and more current. Access to the Internet and computers can also allow people to learn computer skills that are useful for employment and job training. Second, Internet access is important for commerce. Businesses that are able to get online can sell their products to a larger group of people. Consumers with Internet access can purchase a larger variety of products, usually for less money, than those who can access only local businesses. Third, the Internet can be an important social outlet for people. For certain groups of Canadians, such as the elderly, rural people, and those who have lower incomes, the lack of access can reduce feelings of social connection with others. Finally, the Internet can provide important means of political organizing. In countries with non-democratic political regimes, the Internet can provide access to information that the government might censor. It can also provide a way of organizing people into activism, such as in the Arab Spring (see p. 210).

How do we address these significant inequalities? Close the Gap is an international non-profit organization that "aims to bridge the digital divide by offering high-quality, pre-owned computers donated by European companies to educational, medical, and social projects in developing and emerging countries" (http://close-the-gap.org/discover-us/mission/). The organization also works with local groups to bring software and training to recipients.

Violence in the Media

The prevalence of violent images in modern media is a major concern. The Harvard School of Public Health (2004) found that violence, sexual content, and profanity in the media have significantly increased between 1992 and 2003 and have most likely continued to rise since this time. Violence has increased most in PG and PG-13 movies, which are targeted to children and teens. Surprisingly, there is considerably more violence in animated films than in non-animated movies. In addition, video games and television are becoming increasingly violent. Many wonder about the effects of watching this amount of violent content.

The killing of Jamie Bulger in Merseyside, England, drew attention to the potential problem of violence in the media. In 1993, 10-year-olds Robert Thompson and Jon Venables kidnapped, abused, and murdered Bulger, who was only 2 years old. Prior to committing this crime, Thompson and Venables had reportedly seen *Child's Play 3*, a horror movie involving a doll (Chucky) possessed by a serial killer. Many news reports argued that the Bulger killing imitated the murder in the movie. While this event is extremely tragic and horrific, more systematic studies are needed to understand violent media's effect on behaviour. How can we know that this movie was a catalyst for murder when many other people who saw it did not engage in violence?

PHOTO 7.5 Should we be concerned about children playing violent video games? Are they just entertainment or are they also teaching lessons about how to interact with others?

Nathanson and Cantor (2000) used experimental methods to examine the effect of media violence on children. They examined the behaviour of 24 children; half watched a violent Woody Woodpecker cartoon and the other half watched a non-violent cartoon. Immediately afterward, the children who had seen the violent cartoon were more likely to hit other children or break toys in play than were those who watched the non-violent cartoon. Later research on young adults finds that exposure to media violence, including violent video gaming, can have a desensitization effect, lowering concern for others in need. In one study, researchers looked at 780 young adults (average age 19.6 years old) from four American universities. They found that those who played violent video games had lower levels of concern for others and were less likely to help strangers in need (Fraser et al. 2012).

Most research finds that viewing violence in the media can have serious implications for viewers' attitudes and behaviours (Murray 2008). Viewing violence is associated with more aggressive behaviour and a more tolerant attitude toward the use of violence to solve problems. As we have just seen, being exposed to high levels of media violence may lead individuals to become desensitized to violence. Finally, exposure to media violence may lead viewers to overestimate their risk of victimization and be more fearful of crime. In light of the increased prevalence of media violence and its serious effects for individuals and society, these issues are of concern to the public and policy-makers.

RESEARCH METHOD

Experiment

Media Literacy

In light of the serious implications of the media in the socialization process, many critics have argued that we should increase **media literacy** in an effort to regain control over our media consumption. Media literacy is an educational tool that helps individuals analyze and evaluate the messages they receive from the media. It works to empower people to examine and think more critically about the media messages they receive.

Media literacy programs can take place in schools, online, or at community centres. Even a parent who watches television with his or her child and talks critically about what they are seeing engages in media literacy training. There are three main stages in media literacy education. First, one must become aware of one's media "diet"—the media that one consumes. It is obvious to think about the television shows that you watch, the radio that you listen to, or the Internet news you read. However, it is also important to consider all the more incidental media to which you are exposed—billboards on the highway, advertisements on Google, or radio in the background at a store.

The second stage is to learn specific skills of critical viewing, which requires you to analyze both what is shown on television and what is left out. Perhaps you notice that the TV shows you watch feature a lot of upper-class characters and that very few poor or homeless characters are depicted. Or perhaps you notice a lot of white lead characters but not many visible minority lead characters in the movies you see.

Finally, media literacy pushes you to question what is behind the media and why certain messages are relayed while others are not. For example, TV shows might focus on upper-class characters because producers think that audience members will find them more interesting and compelling. But seeing so many upper-class characters also distorts our idea of how much money most people in society have, what regular jobs and careers are, and what we should aspire to be. Seeing so many extremely thin women or muscular men on television might distort our idea of beauty and a "regular" body shape. This can have severe implications for individual self-esteem and lead to eating disorders and other health issues. By thinking critically about who produces the media for what purpose and who benefits from media images, we can better understand what we see. This comprehension can help individuals to be more critical about the media messages they receive.

Using Media Literacy with Alcohol and Tobacco Ads

Advertising is all around us, and our exposure to it is increasing. The market research firm Yankelovich estimates that a person living in New York City was exposed to about 2,000 advertisements a day 30 years ago. Today, a New Yorker sees an average of 5,000 ads a day (Story 2007). Clearly, one of the primary purposes of these ads is to sell products; however, they also communicate other messages and rely on certain techniques. Look at these ads and answering the following questions.

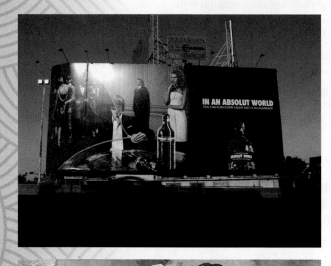

1. What techniques are used in these ads? Do they focus on the quality of the products or on other things?

2. Do all these ads show the product that they are selling? How prominent is the product in the ad? Why would you show (or not show) a product in an ad?

3. What message are these ads trying to send about the products? What type of person uses each product? What would the advertisers like you to associate their product with?

4. Research has shown that cigarette ads, in particular, tend to exploit people's desire for freedom and/or adventure. Can you see the use of these concepts in the ads presented here? What other types of products focus on freedom or adventure?

5. The Dos Equis advertisements, the Dove "Real Beauty" campaign, and others either make fun of or challenge our conventional ideas of how advertising should be done. To what extent do you think these ads are effective? Why do you think advertisers would use such ads?

6. *Adbusters* creates "spoof ads" that challenge advertising messages. Visit www .adbusters.org/spoofads (or access the direct link available on this book's companion website) to see some of these ads. What do you think of them? Are they effective at pointing out some of the problematic messages in advertising? How could they be more effective?

Alternative Media

As we have discussed in this chapter, one major concern with media concentration is a potential decline in the diversity of perspectives available to consumers. One way to address this issue is **alternative media**, which provides "alternative information to the mainstream media in a given context, whether the mainstream media are commercial, publicly supported, or government-owned" (Atton 2002). Blogs, websites such as Indymedia, community- or student-run newspapers, public broadcasting radio and television stations, and pirate stations are examples of alternative media.

Alternative media is defined by four main characteristics. The message is not corporately controlled and is not based on a profit motive, as alternative media is non-profit. The message's content tends to be anti-establishment, subversive, and change-centred. Alternative media is usually distributed in a creative way, focusing on being visually appealing and interesting. Finally, the relationship between the producer and consumer is fundamentally different. Traditional or corporate media is unidirectional—as a consumer you simply receive the message, but you do not have the opportunity to shape it. Alternative media has a two-way relationship; consumers can comment on and shape the media they consume. Alternative media, then, provides an interesting way to exert power and control over the media messages and content you receive.

Summary

Language is everywhere—without it you could not even be able to read this book! We began this chapter by examining the importance of language and how language shapes thought and is shaped by culture. These connections were illustrated by examining racist terms in the English language. The chapter then discussed the mass media's role as a mode of communication. We looked at the evolution of the media, using Marshall McLuhan's famous idea that "the medium is the message," and discussed the rise in corporate concentration and its effects on the diversity of ideas available. C. Wright Mills's concept of the power elite illuminated how an increasingly small group of people holds power in the major political, military, and corporate institutions of society. This chapter also examined the rising importance of new media and social media, the digital divide, violence in the media, the need for media literacy, and alternative media.

Key Terms

alternative media 217	media 218
corporate concentration 202	media literacy 215
cyber-bullying 211	"the medium is the message" 201
demographic diversity 207	new media 209
digital divide 211	power elite 203
honorifics 195	Sapir–Whorf hypothesis 195
idea diversity 207	social media 209
mass media 218	

For Further Reading

Chomsky, Noam, and Edward S. Herman. 2002. *Manufacturing Consent: The Political Economy of the Mass Media*. New York: Pantheon Books.

McLuhan, Marshall. 1964. *Understanding Media: The Extensions of Man*. New York: McGraw Hill.

Mills, C. Wright. 1956. *The Power Elite*. New York: Oxford University Press.

Whorf, Benjamin. 1956. *Language, Thought, and Reality: Selected Writings of Benjamin Lee Whorf*. Cambridge, MA: MIT Press.

8 The Family

CHAPTER OUTLINE

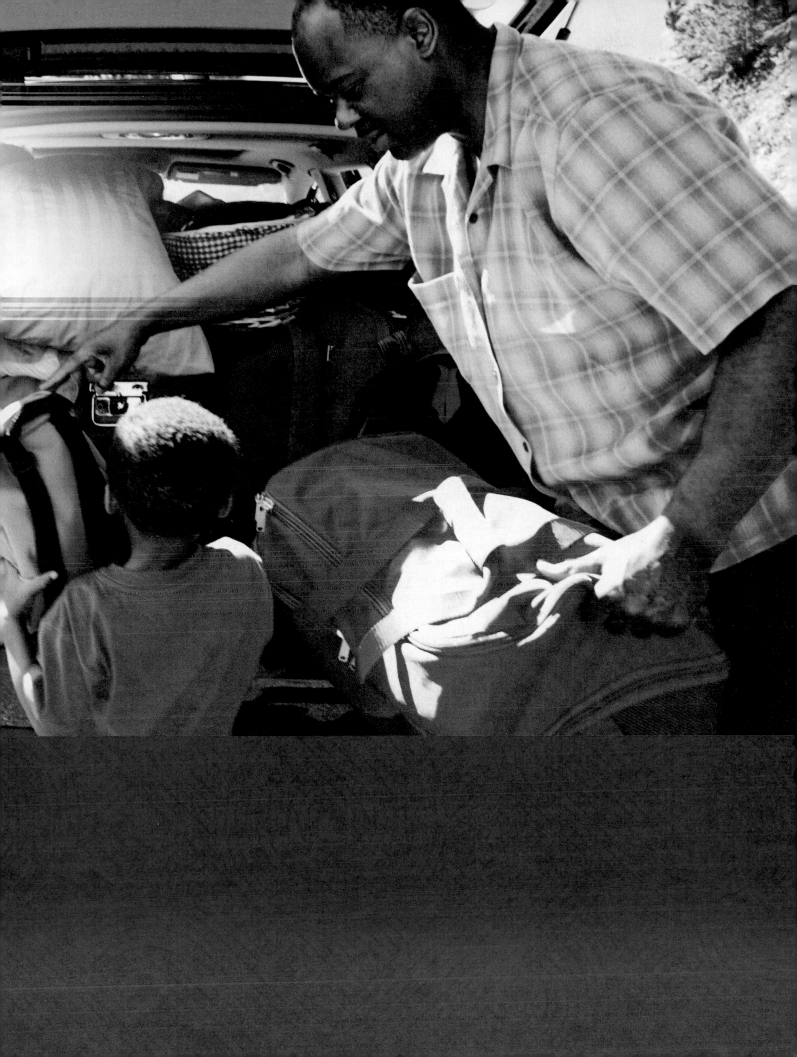

Introduction

One challenge that sociologists face is trying to make sense of things we are very familiar with but might not have examined critically. As quoted in Chapter 1, Peter Berger (1963) argued that sociology helps us see "the general in the particular" and the "strange in the familiar." Each of us has a lifetime of experiences in society and each of us comes from a family context. From all these experiences, we come to generalize about how families function. However, sometimes this familiarity can be a challenge; it can be quite hard to study an institution such as the family because it is all around us. We also all have a very particular experience of family life—your family surely shares some features with your friends' families, but it is probably different as well. If you compare your family with others you see on television, in the newspaper, or in the larger community, you probably notice even starker differences.

In this chapter, we will examine the family in a larger comparative perspective. What major changes are happening to the family? What are the functions of the family in society and how are these functions changing? How is the institution of the family related to issues of social inequality and social change? By taking a step back from our own particular experiences, we can come to understand the family's role in society as a whole.

What Is the Family?

Families are groups of people related by birth, affinity, or cohabitation. Families clearly differ radically from one another, and what people think of as a family has changed. In general, we think of an individual's **family household** as a group of people who share a relationship by blood, marriage, or legal adoption living together. **Marriage** is the legal union of two people, allowing them to live together and to have children. A **nuclear family** consists of two adults living with one or more children. An **extended family** moves beyond the nuclear, or immediate, family and consists of two or more generations who share the same residence.

PHOTO 8.1 This image depicts the traditional nuclear family. To what extent is this image representative of the diversity of families in Canada today?

ACTIVITY

Comedy and the TV Family

Society has many stereotypes about men's and women's roles in romantic relationships and parenting. Think of the jokes you have heard about husbands and wives. Here are a few examples (from www.funnigurl.com):

How many men does it take to change a roll of toilet paper?
Who knows? It hasn't happened yet!!

What do you instantly know about a well-dressed man?
His wife is good at picking out clothes.

I married Miss Right.
I just didn't know her first name was "Always."

I haven't spoken to my wife for 18 months:
I don't like to interrupt her.

The general themes of these and similar jokes—that husbands and fathers are lazy and unable to do anything for themselves and that wives are bossy and nagging—are part of the overarching repertoire of how we understand men's and women's roles in relationships and families. You don't typically hear, for example, a joke about wives being lazy or men nagging.

Think about television shows such as *Leave it to Beaver*, *The Brady Bunch*, *The Cosby Show*, *Roseanne*, *Married with Children*, *The Simpsons*, and *Modern Family*. (If you have not seen some of these shows, watch some clips on YouTube or read about the show on Wikipedia.) As you answer the following questions, keep in mind how jokes may be used to perpetuate and exaggerate stereotypes of gendered roles in the family.

1. How have depictions of the family changed? How did the earliest show on our list (*Leave it to Beaver*) depict the role of husbands and wives and their relationship with their children? How does this show portray the functions of the family and the role of the family in society? How does this depiction relate to the larger social context in which this show existed?

2. How did later shows (*The Brady Bunch*, *The Cosby Show*, and *Roseanne*) challenge some earlier depictions of the family? How are these challenges related to our changing ideas of gender norms and family relationships in society?

3. How do the most recent shows (*The Simpsons* and *Modern Family*) further expand or change our perception of the role of spouses and parents in society? How do these shows reflect the times in which they are made? Are these positive reflections of the family today?

4. What shows do you watch that depict a positive view of the family and spousal relationships? What shows have negative depictions? What are the larger social implications of television shows presenting families in these ways?

The Canadian family is undergoing some widespread changes, as illustrated in Figure 8.1. These trends reflect a changing set of norms and expectations surrounding the family, particularly marriage and children, in modern Canadian society. Note the decline in the traditional nuclear family and the growth in the number of unmarried couples living together.

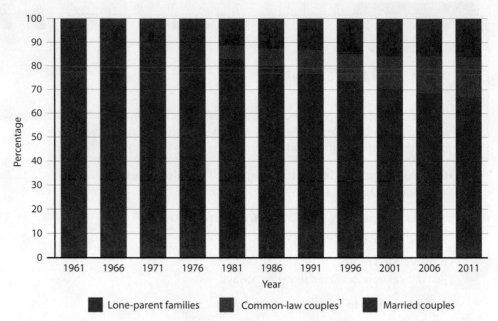

FIGURE 8.1 **Distribution (in percentage) of census families by family structure, Canada, 1961–2011**

NOTES: Historical comparisons for census families, particularly lone-parent families, must be interpreted with caution due to conceptual changes in 2001. For more information, see "Concepts and Definitions" in *Family Portrait: Continuity and Change in Canadian Families and Households in 2006, 2006 Census.*
1. Data on common-law couples are not available prior to the 1981 census.
SOURCE: Statistics Canada. 2012. "Fifty Years of Families in Canada: 1961 to 2011." Ottawa: Minster of Industry, 2. www12.statcan. gc.ca/census-recensement/2011/as-sa/98-312-x/98-312-x2011003_1-eng.pdf.

Andrew Cherlin (2004) argues that modern society is characterized by the "**deinstitutionalization of marriage**." Our understanding of the norms and rules surrounding marriage has changed, and people are increasingly questioning the role of marriage in their lives and society as a whole. There are five main ways that marriage is becoming deinstitutionalized. First, fewer people are getting married because they are choosing to remain single or to **cohabitate** (i.e. same-sex or opposite-sex couples who live together without being legally married). Cohabitation gained popularity in the 1970s and the rate accelerated into the twenty-first century. Many cohabitating couples in Canada become common law, a relationship that Canadian law treats as analogous to marriage.

These unions are especially popular in Quebec, where almost twice as many people live common law as in the rest of the country. The number is also higher than that of many other countries (see Table 8.1). Many attribute the high rate of common-law marriage in Quebec to the province's Quiet Revolution in the 1960s–1970s, a period of significant social and cultural upheaval. In particular, there was a widespread rejection of the Catholic Church and a questioning of this institution's extremely powerful role in Quebec society at this time. Others argue that factors such as greater access to contraception, the strength of the women's movement, and the comparatively high rate of women's participation in the paid labour force might account for the higher rates of common-law couples in Quebec. In addition, Quebec law has more liberal divorce laws and common-law legislation, making cohabitation a more attractive choice for couples (Milan, Vézina, and Wells 2007).

Second, the roles of individuals in couples (married or not) have become increasingly questioned in modern society. As women enter the labour force in larger numbers, the division of labour in the home can be challenged. We no longer simply assume

TABLE 8.1	Common-law couples in Quebec, Canada, and selected countries by year	
	Percentage of All Couples	**Reference Year**
Canada	18.4	2006
Quebec	34.6	2006
Other provinces and territories	13.4	2006
Sweden	25.4	2005
Finland	23.9	2006
New Zealand	23.7	2006
Denmark	22.2	2007
Iceland	19.9	2006
United Kingdom	15.5	2004
Australia	14.8	2006
Ireland	14.1	2006

SOURCE: www12.statcan.gc.ca/census-recensement/2006/as-sa/97-553/table/t8-eng.cfm.

that women will be homemakers and men breadwinners. Since there are more women working outside the home and more men staying home to raise children, the traditional gender roles in marriage are questioned. Our basic understanding of what men and women "do" in a relationship is eroding, leading to a lack of clarity about how marriages and the family work in modern society. Chapter 6 discussed the large-scale changes to gender roles in society; this increased flexibility of gender roles in marriages can lead to a greater diversity of family arrangements, including the rise of lone-parent families and same-sex marriages.

Third, norms about having children have also changed. In the past, it was socially acceptable only to have children in a marital relationship. Today, many people are single parents and many unmarried couples have children. Furthermore, more people choose to remain childless.

Fourth, divorce rates rose steeply between 1970 and 1990, although they have stabilized since this time. These heightened divorce rates challenge the idea that individuals should remain married "till death do us part"—even if they are unhappy or the relationship is abusive. It is also associated with a declining stigma associated with divorce and a waning of religious influences that traditionally prohibited this act.

Finally, there is a rising diversity in the forms of marriages in modern society. With the rise of marriages between couples from different ethnic, racial, religious, and class backgrounds, couples are becoming more diverse than ever before. Mixed unions in Canada saw a 33 per cent increase from 2001 to 2006, according to the 2006 census (Milan, Maheux, and Chui 2010). The legalization of gay marriage in Canada and other countries further adds to the diversity of marriage as an institution in modern society. Table 8.2 and Figure 8.2 give more information about gay marriage.

The first four trends have challenged the traditional idea of marriage in a way that many argue undermine it as an institution. However, many claim that the fifth change supports and reinforces traditional ideas of marriage as new groups of people opt into and support the institution.

HIGHLIGHT

Teen Mom and the Reality of Teenage Pregnancy

Why do you think shows depicting teen pregnancy are increasingly popular even though teenage pregnancy is on the decline?

Shows such as *Teen Mom* and *16 and Pregnant* follow teens through their pregnancies and their first years of motherhood. Many argue that these shows, and the popularity of their stars, glorify **teen pregnancy** (pregnancy of a woman who is under the age of 20 at the time the pregnancy ends) and worry that they could lead to more incidents. In reality, teen pregnancy rates are declining (or at least stabilizing). In fact, a US study published in 2014 claims that watching these shows has significantly lowered teen birth rates in the country (see the figure below). Watching the shows led to a 5.7 per cent decrease in teen births, which the study's authors say accounted for around one-third of the overall decline in US teen births in that year and half of the decline since the shows were introduced in 2009 (Gallant 2014). Do you think these shows act as a deterrent and cautionary tale rather than glorification? Can reality television serve a social purpose and help deal with social problems?

Rates of teenage pregnancy are relatively low in Canada and have been steadily declining since the 1970s. Many attribute this change to rising gender equality, which can empower young women and, as a result, make them less likely to become pregnant as teens. For the last 10 years, the rate of teen pregnancy has been relatively stable, hovering around 28 pregnancies per 100,000 women. However, this figure masks a spike of more than 15 per cent in Manitoba, New Brunswick, Newfoundland and Labrador, and Nova Scotia during this period (DeMara 2013). What accounts for the higher rates in these provinces? One explanation is that teen pregnancy indicates larger economic troubles in a province; all four of these provinces have economic problems. Teenage girls are more likely to get pregnant when they have fewer education or employment prospects (Bielski 2013).

Canada's rate of teen pregnancy is approximately half that of the United States. (For a comparison of rates around the world, see the following figure.) This difference can be explained by Canada's universal healthcare system, easier access to contraception, more widespread sex education in schools, and lower rates of youth poverty (Bielski 2013). In the United States, many young women, particularly those with low incomes, have no access to contraception or healthcare that could prevent pregnancy.

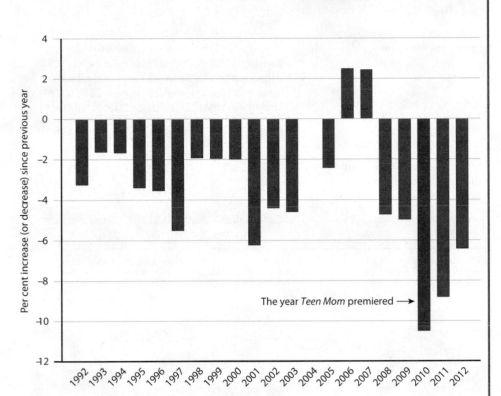

The year *Teen Mom* premiered →

Teen pregnancy rates in the United States and the premiere of *Teen Mom*

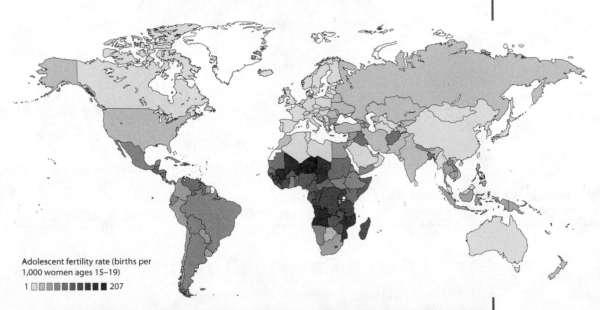

Adolescent fertility rate (births per 1,000 women ages 15–19)

1   207

Adolescent fertility rate, 2011–2015 (births per 1,000 women ages 15–19)

TABLE 8.2	Gay marriage around the world
First place gay marriage was legalized	Netherlands (2001)
Countries that currently allow same-sex marriage	Netherlands (2001), Belgium (2003), Spain (2005), Canada (2005), South Africa (2006), Norway (2009), Sweden (2009), Portugal (2010), Iceland (2010), Argentina (2010), Denmark (2012), Brazil (2013), France (2013), Uruguay (2013), New Zealand (2013), United Kingdom (2014), United States (2015)
Countries where same-sex marriage is legal in some regions	Mexico
Per cent of world's population living in areas where same-sex marriage is legal	10
Per cent of same-sex couples by country	Canada (0.8%), Australia (0.7%), United Kingdom (0.4%), United States (0.6%)

SOURCES: Freedom to Marry. 2015. "The Freedom to Marry Internationally." www.freedomtomarry.org/landscape/entry/c/international; Lindell, Rebecca. 2012. "Number of Gay Marriages in Canada Triples: Census." Global News. http://globalnews.ca/news/288323/number-of-gay-marriages-in-canada-triples-census/; CNN Library. 2015. "Same-Sex Marriage Fast Facts. www.cnn.com/2013/05/28/us/same-sex-marriage-fast-facts.

Status
- Legal or pending legalization
- Legal in some places
- Not legal

FIGURE 8.2 Gay marriage around the world, 2015
SOURCE: Based on www.cbc.ca/news/interactives/map-same-sex-marriage-world/index.html.

Larger Social Changes That Impact the Family

Changes in marriage and the family can be tied to many larger social changes. As we have already seen, the rise of women's rights is a major change in Canadian society. This movement accounts for rising rates of university enrolment and graduation among women and an increased number of women in the paid workforce. These changes, in turn, are

HIGHLIGHT

Arranged Marriages

In an **arranged marriage**, a third party selects the bride and groom. Parents or others might make the match without consulting the children. However, the children usually have some level of control over choosing among partners deemed appropriate by their parents. This type of marriage was common worldwide until the eighteenth century and remains prevalent in many areas, including parts of Asia, Africa, the Middle East, and Latin America. Arranged marriages also occur in Canada, particularly among certain ethnic minorities.

Our modern ideas about marriage, and the role of romantic love within it, seem inconsistent with arranged marriage. But research shows that these marriages might be more likely to develop into lasting love than previously thought (Bentley 2011). According to research conducted by Robert Epstein (in Bentley 2011), individuals in arranged marriages tend to feel more in love over time while individuals in non-arranged marriages (most people in North America) tend to feel less in love. Epstein interviewed 30 individuals in 22 marriages and found that, within 10 years, the self-rated satisfaction among individuals in arranged marriages was twice as high as it was for those in non-arranged marriages. There are many possible reasons for this. Arranged marriages are carefully planned and considered by families and communities, while non-arranged marriages can be spontaneous and may be less thought out. As a result, individuals in arranged marriages may be more likely to remain married, even if times are difficult, because they have the interests of their extended families to consider. Those in non-arranged marriages tend to be more focused on romantic love and can often overlook other critical compatibility issues. It is also possible, however, that those in arranged marriages might be more likely to report being in love because of different expectations. These different levels of reporting may not reflect true differences in feelings.

Epstein's research shows that, the more parents are involved in the selection process, the more successful the resulting marriage tends to be. Parents can help weed out potential mates with "deal breaker" features—perhaps an incompatibility on values, the number of children they want, or where they want to live. Parents are also important because their support can help solidify the marriage. This support can come in the form of financial help for the wedding, for one or both spouses to attend school, for a home, or for help with children. Along with emotional support, this assistance can provide the resources needed to help single people transition into being married and, perhaps, being parents.

RESEARCH METHOD

Interviews

associated with lower levels of marriage, later age at the birth of a first child, and a higher divorce rate. Divorce, for example, is much more likely among women who make money independently from the family unit.

Our society is also becoming increasingly tolerant of diversity. This development partly explains the rise of marriages between people from different racial, ethnic, or religious backgrounds. This more inclusive ideology in modern society is also a factor in the mobilization for legalizing same-sex marriage.

Another major change that has affected the family is the declining levels of religiosity in Canada and other Western nations. Religions are generally strong supporters of a traditional view of marriage and childrearing. With the decline of religiosity in a society, we tend to see higher rates of cohabitation without marriage, more children raised by unmarried parents, and a rise in divorce rates.

Finally, modern society is characterized by a rising tide of individualism. In essence, we are more concerned with individual happiness and fulfillment than we were in the past. In Canada, most people pick jobs and romantic partners based on their own interests and preferences. Young people usually resist the idea that they are simply expected to perform the same job as their parents or that their parents will select their mate for them. This surge in individualism occurred at the same time as religion's power over individuals was waning; both trends have radically altered our ideas about the nature of marriage.

Originally, marriage was seen as a way to bind larger families and communities. **Institutional marriages** have a collective focus; that is, they focus on how a marriage will solidify ties between families and communities and benefit society as a whole. Think about how spouses were selected historically in royal weddings. No one cared if a prince and princess from different countries liked one another or would fall in love. All that mattered was that the marriage would lead to a coalition between their countries. Institutional marriages are about the needs of society, not the individuals' need to be happy and fulfilled (Wilcox and Nock 2006).

Over time, people began to think that marriages should be based on bonds of sentiment, friendship, and sexual ties. **Companionate marriages** make a clear division of labour between breadwinner (usually the husband) and the homemaker (usually the wife). Consequently, husbands and wives are expected to be one another's companions. They are friends and confidants who need and rely on one another to perform the role that they cannot. In companionate marriages, romantic love is very important (Wilcox and Nock 2006). These relationships are based on the satisfaction of the couple, the family as a whole, and the roles the couple plays within the family.

Lauer and Yodanis (2011) argue that we now live in a time of **individualized marriages**. These marriages are focused on each spouse's satisfaction, ability to develop and express his or her sense of self, happiness, and fulfillment. Individualized marriages tend to be more flexible than the other types described because they attempt to meet the varied needs of individual spouses. Despite these challenges to traditional ideas of marriage and the rise of individualized marriages, the vast majority of people still get married at some point in their lives, even if these marriages don't last as long as past unions.

The many changes in marriage and the family in North America have led to a heated debate about whether governments or other institutions in society should try to promote traditional ideas of marriage and the family. The following reading examines evidence for the supposed "decline of marriage." It also assesses the evidence for the

PHOTO 8.2 In modern society, some intimate partner relationships still include a strong division of labour. As individualism in relationships has increased, the variety of partnership options has also risen, with individuals being more able to negotiate their roles within their partnerships.

media's prevalent claim that the rising divorce rate and incidence of single-parent families is problematic for children.

Should the Government Promote Marriage?

Andrew J. Cherlin

. . . Is getting parents to marry the answer to the difficulties that children in single-parent families face? . . .

On one side is the "marriage movement"—a loose group of conservative and centrist activists, religious leaders, and social scientists who want to strengthen the institution of marriage. Some of them advocate marriage because they are morally certain that it provides the best kind of family. Others, including most of the social scientists in this camp, favour it because they believe children's well-being would improve if more of their parents were married.

On the other side are "diversity defenders"—liberal activists, feminists, and sympathetic social scientists who argue that single-parent families can be just as good for children if they receive the support they need. The marriage movement favours public policies that encourage marriage. The diversity defenders favour policies that provide services and economic opportunities to low-income parents, whether married or not, and their children. In the end, the evidence suggests that the benefits of marriage promotion would be marginal. But the real debate may be far more about symbols than substance.

The Decline of Marriage

Most observers on both sides agree that the social institution of marriage is substantially weaker than it was 50 years ago. In mid-twentieth-century America, marriage was the only acceptable context for having a sexual relationship and for bearing and raising children. In 1950, just 4 per cent of children were born to unmarried women. (Fifty years later, the figure was 33 per cent.) Most women, and many men, abstained from sexual intercourse until they were engaged to be married. When an unmarried woman became pregnant, relatives pressured her and her partner to agree to a "shotgun wedding." Once married, couples were less likely to divorce—approximately one in three marriages begun in the 1950s ended in divorce, compared to one in two today. Consequently, even among the poor, most families had two parents.

In the ensuing decades, however, the likelihood that a child would spend a substantial portion of time in a single-parent family grew. More adults had children outside of marriage, choosing either to remain single or live with their partners without marrying. Divorce became more common. As a result, about half of all children are projected to spend some time in a single-parent family while growing up. Although these trends cut across class, racial, and ethnic lines, poor children and black children are more likely to be raised in single-parent families than are middle-class children and white children, respectively.

Statistics and Politics

. . .

THE STATISTICAL DEBATE

Most social scientists would agree that, on average, children who grow up in a one-parent family are more disadvantaged than children who grow up with two parents. As Sara McLanahan wrote in the spring 2002 issue of *Contexts*:

They are more likely to drop out of high school, less likely to attend college, and less likely to graduate from college than children raised by both biological parents. Girls from father-absent families are more likely to become sexually active at a younger age and to have a child outside of marriage. Boys who grow up without their fathers are more likely to have trouble finding (and keeping) a job in young adulthood. Young adult men and women from one-parent families tend to work at low-paying jobs.

But we cannot conclude from these differences that growing up in a single-parent family causes these unwanted outcomes. Both conditions—the number of parents in the home while growing up and problems in adulthood—could be caused by other factors. For example, poverty could cause parents to divorce and also prevent their children from attending college. Research by McLanahan and Gary Sandefur suggests that as much as half of the apparent disadvantage of growing up in a single-parent family is due to the lower incomes these families typically have. . . .

STATE OF LEGISLATION

The federal welfare reform legislation, the Personal Responsibility and Work Opportunity Reconciliation Act of 1996, must be reauthorized by Congress in 2003. In February, the House of Representatives passed a reauthorization bill that included $300 million per year in state funds for marriage promotion. A wide range of activities would be allowed, including training in marriage and relationship skills, conflict resolution programs, public advertising campaigns, education in high schools on the value of marriage, and research and demonstration projects. In the spring, the Senate held hearings on reauthorization and prepared to vote on its own bill. Most observers expect the Senate bill to include at least some of the marriage promotion funds approved by the House.

In addition, some families have pre-existing problems, such as genetic predispositions to depression, that raise both the probability that parents will divorce and the probability that their children will have mental health problems. In these cases, the divorce would not be the reason for the children's misfortunes. Several colleagues and I examined an extensive British study that followed individuals from birth to adulthood. As expected, we found that people whose parents had been divorced had poorer mental health as adults. But by looking at records of their childhood, we found that some portion, although not all, of their difficulties could be accounted for by behaviour problems and psychological distress that were visible early in their lives, before their parents had divorced. Our study and others like it suggest that being short a parent in the home is not responsible for all the ills these children show. Therefore, a policy aimed at reducing single-parent families and increasing two-parent families would most likely not eliminate such problems.

Nevertheless, family structure has something to do with the difficulties children experience. Our study and others do find some differences that could be due to divorce or birth outside of marriage. Only a minority of children in single-parent families actually experience problems later, but divorce and childbearing outside of marriage are so common that this minority still represents a large number of children. Taken together, all of these findings suggest that while the number of parents matters, it matters less than most people think; and it matters less than many other factors for how children fare.

THE POLITICAL DEBATE

If the debate ended with social scientific studies and statistics, marriage promotion policies would not be so contentious. But there is a deeper level to the controversy. The politics of single parenting involve not simply disagreements about data, but about how Americans view the autonomy of women, the authority of men, and the imposition of a particular moral view of family life on those who choose other lifestyles. Until the mid-twentieth century, marriage was taken for granted as the central institution of family life. Men held considerable power in marriages because of social norms and because they typically earned more money. In the stereotypical mid-twentieth-century marriage, women restricted themselves to home and family. As recently as 1977, two-thirds of those interviewed in the General Social Survey—a national sample of adults repeated every year or two—agreed that "It is much better for everyone involved if the man is the achiever outside the home and the woman takes care of the home and family." By 1998, just one-third agreed with the same statement.

Since mid-century, new options have made it possible for women to live full lives outside of marriage. New job opportunities provide independent income and welfare provides an income floor (although the recent welfare reform now limits reliance on that floor to five years). The birth control pill allows for sexual activity without unwanted pregnancies, and the greater acceptability of raising a child outside of marriage allows single women to have children if they want. At the same time, the economic fortunes of men without college educations have diminished, reducing the attractiveness of marriage for many women. All told, alternative paths to parenthood other than long-term marriage are more feasible and more attractive. Feminists fought for these gains in women's autonomy, and many of them see the pro-marriage movement as an attempt to reassert men's control over women's lives. Being a single parent may not be easy, but it is a more viable alternative than it used to be and many feminists defend women's freedom to follow this path. Other liberals argue that gay and lesbian parents, whether single or partnered, should receive the same acceptance and support as heterosexual parents. These diversity defenders argue for public policies that would provide more income support, child-care options, and flexible work arrangements for single-parent families to minimize any remaining disadvantages of these non-marital choices. But it can be difficult to disentangle the political debate from the statistical debate. Often the political debate constitutes the unspoken subtext of a seemingly statistical argument. In an influential 1972 book, *The Future of Marriage*, Jessie Bernard argued that men get most of the rewards in marriage because women do most of the work in the home while being denied (at least in the 1950s and 1960s) the opportunity to work outside the home. Bernard claimed, for example, that married women are more depressed than single women, whereas married men are less depressed than single men. The subtext is that marriage, at least in its current form, oppresses women, and that policies that promote marriage should be resisted by feminists. More recently, Linda J. Waite and journalist Maggie Gallagher argued in their book, *The Case for Marriage: Why Married People Are Happier, Healthier, and Better Off Financially*, that marriage is just as beneficial for women as it is for men. The subtext here is that because marriage is not an oppressive institution, opposition to pro-marriage policies is misguided. Although Waite and Gallagher persuasively demonstrate that marriage is not all bad for women, their attempt to show that it benefits women as much as men is less convincing.

Marriage and Morality

In some writing on marriage, the political and moral claims are in plain view. Consider *The Marriage Problem: How Our Culture Has Weakened Families*, a recent book by political scientist James Q. Wilson. He endorses an evolutionary model in which men are by nature promiscuous and women are by nature more interested in raising children. Marriage, he argues, is the cultural invention that restrains men and provides mothers and children with support and protection. Wilson concludes that more women need to emphasize marriage over career, even though this may limit their autonomy. He offers sympathy, but little more, for the difficulty of this choice. Postponing marriage, Wilson writes, is risky. "Older women lose out in the marriage race much faster than do men. It may be unfair, but that is the way the world works" (p. 12). Women's lot in life, the book implies, is to make the selfless choice to marry for the good of their children.

Even if one agreed with Wilson's view of the need for marriage, his exhortations are increasingly out of step with Americans' moral views. Although most Americans still value marriage, they hesitate to impose their preferences on others. Rather, the American philosophy, Alan Wolfe argues, is "moral freedom": each person should be free to decide what is a good and virtuous life. Each is free, in other words, to choose his or her own morality. For example, Americans view divorce as a serious and unwelcome step. But they tend to believe that each person should be allowed to decide when a marriage no longer works. As Grace Floro, a Dayton housewife and one of Wolfe's interview subjects said: "How loyal can you be if somebody's wronged you? When is loyalty appropriate and when isn't it? You can be loyal to a fault just like you can be honest to a fault. That's what makes life so difficult. Nothing is black and white and every circumstance merits its own judgment" (p. 55).

Americans' view of marriage was also apparent in a 1999 *New York Times* national survey. Respondents were presented with a list of values and asked how important each was to them. After the replies were tallied, the values were ranked by the percentage of people who said each was "very important." The top-ranking values largely reflected self-reliance ("Being responsible for your own actions," "Being able to stand up for yourself") and self-expression ("Being able to communicate your feelings"). "Having children" came in sixth. "Being married" ranked tenth—below "Being a good neighbour." Marriage, it would seem, is valued as long as it is consistent with the expressive individualism that Americans hold most dear. That is why pro-marriage policies that seem to interfere with individual decisions and self-expression are not broadly popular. . . .

CRITICAL Reading Questions

1. What are the **marriage movement** and the **diversity defenders**? Why does each group take its respective position concerning the promotion of marriage? What specific policies would each group like to see?

2. Does being in a single-parent family cause poor educational and occupational outcomes for children? What other factors could account for these outcomes?

3. This article uses US data. Are these trends the same in Canada? Begin by comparing the rates of divorce and single-parent families in each country. Is this issue more or less of a concern in Canada? Why or why not?

To this point, we have been discussing marriage as a **monogamous** relationship. However, certain cultures practise **polygamy** (having one or more spouse at the same time). Canada's most famous case of polygamy is in Bountiful, British Columbia. Based on the Fundamentalist Church of Jesus Christ of Latter Day Saints, an offshoot of the Mormon Church, this polygamous commune has been criticized for what some argue are forced marriages of underage women and the abuse of women and children. Polygamy is illegal in Canada, but this law had not been implemented in Bountiful. In 2011, the government attempted to prosecute members of the community for polygamy. The case went to the BC Supreme Court, which had to adjudicate between two contradicting principles—the right of individuals to practise their religion and the illegality of polygamy.

A woman from Bountiful, who shares a husband with her sister and has nine children, testified about her experience:

> I did not know him well, I knew he was in good standing in the church. . . . He [my father] told me, "You do not have to marry him if you don't want to." I felt good about him, and I married him. My sister wife and I have lived at times in the same home, we've lived in different homes. I feel that we are both very committed in having a good relationship with each other. . . . I feel that my husband really supported me

through my years of education and he really has been a life-long friend to me, as well as watched my children when I went to school. . . . I believe that there's so many people in mainstream society that make so many assumptions about us that we are treated with bias and prejudice, and that affects my everyday life. If I wanted to go anywhere and get any sort of counseling in mainstream society, I feel like I would not be accepted. . . . My beliefs are that living in plural marriage isn't for everyone. . . . (Canadian Press 2011)

The courts found in favour of the government and ruled that the polygamous marriages could not continue. The community members' religious freedom was seen as less important than the necessity of protecting women and children from abuse.

A 2011 University of British Columbia study demonstrated that a link exists between polygamous relationships (typically men with many female partners) and other social problems. The study found that this intra-sexual competition between men to find multiple female partners and the resources to support these multiple partners and children leads to greater gender inequality, poverty, and crime (including sexual assault and murder) than occurred in societies that practise solely monogamous relationships. This situation illustrates support for the court's decision that polygamous relationships harm society (Henrich, Boyd, and Richerson 2012). What do you think of polygamous marriages and families? Do they have to be associated with abuse of women and children? How do they challenge our ideas about marriage and the family?

ACTIVITY

Increasing or Decreasing Fertility in Quebec and China

We often hear about the low **fertility rates**, the average number of children per woman over her lifetime, in many Western countries. These countries (including Canada and the United States) are below the replacement rate of fertility, meaning that people are not having enough children to replace the population. Other countries worry that their fertility rates are too high and face the difficult social problem of overpopulation. In certain cases, such as Quebec and China, the government has implemented policies to affect fertility rates.

Go to this book's companion website, read the Population Change and Lifecourse Strategic Cluster's policy brief, and answer the following questions:

1. Why would the Quebec government, or any government, want to increase the fertility rate? What are the benefits of higher fertility rates?

2. What specific policies have been enacted in Quebec to try to increase the fertility rate? Why might policy-makers think that these measures would increase fertility?

3. How successful have these policies been at increasing fertility in Quebec? What are the other implications of these policies?

Now go to this book's companion website to read a BBC article about recent changes to China's **one-child policy**. After you read the article, answer these questions:

1. Why would China want to reduce its fertility rate? How can high fertility be a problem?

2. What specific policies have been enacted by the Chinese government to try to limit fertility? Are there exceptions to these policies? If so, why might they have been created?

3. What consequences have arisen from this policy? What are the unintended consequences?

Theorizing the Family

Our ideas about the family depend, to a large extent, on the theoretical perspective we use to understand it. Two theoretical traditions used to explain the family's role in society are structural functionalism and conflict theory, which are discussed throughout this book. Each approach paints a very different picture of the family's role and impact in modern society.

Structural functionalists focus on the functions of the family and the ways families can help create stability and order in society as a whole. From a structural functionalist perspective, the family performs a wide variety of important roles that fall into four main categories: reproduction, socialization, support, and regulation. In terms of reproduction, families help maintain the population by having and raising children. The family also cares for children's physical and emotional needs. The essential process of socializing children into the larger culture and teaching them the norms and rules of society begins in the family. Families are also important because they can share resources. Parents support children when they are young (and sometimes later in life); children often support parents in their old age. Families work to regulate behaviour as well. For example, the family traditionally helps to control sexual behaviour. This function might be declining as more people engage in sexual activity before and outside marriage.

Talcott Parsons was instrumental in developing structural functionalist theory in the 1950s and 1960s (Parsons and Bales 1955). He argued that the nuclear family was very important (particularly for American society, where his research was based) because its structure frees individuals from the obligations of an extended family. It gives individuals in family units the mobility needed in industrial society, where people often have to move from place to place for work. Without the same close ties to extended families and the need to consider them in one's life plans, it is easier to move nuclear families. Parsons also argued that the nuclear family system works well to distinguish clearly between the "expressive" roles of women and the "instrumental" roles of men (Kimmel 2011).

The structural functionalist perspective of the family has great appeal. It makes sense to think about the important functions the family performs for individuals and society. All societies are based on family units that provide important resources, support, and socialization for children. However, many argue that this theory overemphasizes the family's harmonious elements and tends to ignore the disharmony—such as the discord between parents and children, between siblings, and between spouses. Clearly, not everyone enjoys the functionality and stability of the family setting! This approach also focuses on the positive nature of the family, which promotes and rationalizes the family as it is. However, many social problems arise, such as abuse and mistreatment, that might be ignored by looking at only the functions of families.

Conflict theory offers a different lens on the family and its role in society. At its root, this approach is always concerned with the unequal distribution of resources between those with and without power. Not surprisingly, conflict theorists do not see the family as the harmonious institution that structural functionalists do. Instead, they

PHOTO 8.3 How do same-sex marriages fit into traditional theoretical understandings of the family? Do we have to tailor these theories in order to understand same-sex marriages or can they be easily applied? Why or why not?

HIGHLIGHT

Renting Families in Japan

Family members are an important part of our lives—they provide care and company, as well as help to mark important events such as holidays, weddings, and religious ceremonies. But what if you don't have a family? How can these functions be fulfilled when the number of people living alone, getting divorced, or migrating to other parts of the world is rising? In Japan, companies are stepping in to help people deal with these new circumstances.

In the early 1990s, Japan Efficiency Corporation was "doing the booming business [of] renting families to the lonely," especially the elderly (Kubota 2009). With the declining number of children per couple and the higher propensity of children to live far away from their aging parents, the elderly had fewer people to care for their physical and emotional needs. Office Agents, a Tokyo firm, offers friends and family for rent as event guests. They have about a thousand "fakes" available for occasions such as weddings and funerals. The company reports that many brides and grooms do not even know which of their guests are real and which ones are rented.

Perhaps most interestingly, the Hagemashi Tai agency rents temporary "husbands" to single mothers. Having a husband can be socially useful in many situations, for example, in day care or elementary school admission interviews. Single mothers can even rent a "dad" to help children with homework, resolve issues with neighbours, or take children to events (Kubota 2009).

At a purely rational level, the idea of renting family members to serve particular social purposes makes sense, as it may be the most efficient way to fulfill the short-term goal of appearing to have family or friends. However, to many Canadians, renting a family might seem odd and perhaps even offensive because it challenges our fundamental ideas about the nature of the relationship between family members. Do you see this trend catching on in Canada? Why or why not? How is it similar to, or different from, renting an escort to attend an event? What does it say about our emphasis on idealized notions of the nuclear family and the pressure to conform?

see the family as an arena for a wide variety of conflicts. For example, women and men have differing levels of power within the family as do older and younger family members. Such conflicts are related to power within the family, who has it and how it is used.

Arguing from a conflict perspective, Collins (1975) states that the family is an arena for gender conflict in which males have historically been more powerful. This causes discord among opposite-sex partners who struggle with their different roles in the relationship and the division of power and labour in the family unit. For example, many couples argue about who will do housework or control the finances.

Age-based conflict is also prevalent in the family. Parents have more power in the family than children do because of their greater access to resources. As children try to influence their parents' decisions or become autonomous, conflicts can arise. Although they can be benign, such as when children want to eat dessert and parents say no, they can be much more serious, such as when parents abuse their children physically, emotionally, or sexually. This abuse is possible only because of the differential levels of power and resources in the family.

Conflict theorists agree with structural functionalists that the family works to socialize young people. However, the conflict theorists argue that this socialization is problematic as it reproduces existing inequalities, particularly class inequalities. Melvin Kohn (1959) was particularly interested in how parents socialize their children differently depending on their social class and how these various emphases in socialization help to reproduce social class distinctions. He compared 200 white, working-class American families who had children in the fifth grade with 200 white middle-class families. He

HIGHLIGHT

Family Violence

Conflict theorists posit that a dire consequence of family power struggles is **family violence**, defined by the Canadian government as "any form of abuse, mistreatment, or neglect that a child or adult experiences from a family member, or from someone with whom they have an intimate relationship" (Department of Justice 2013). Family violence can take the form of physical, sexual, emotional, and financial abuse of a spouse, child, or elder. Honour killings and forced marriage are also included in this term.

These women are part of a support group that works to help individuals recover from domestic violence. Why might it be important for individuals who have been victims of violence to be able to participate in these type of programs?

RESEARCH METHOD

Interviews

showed the parents a list of characteristics that most parents would want to foster in their children: honest, happy, considerate, obedient, dependable, good manners, self-control, popular, good student, neat, curious, ambitious, able to defend self, affectionate, liked by adults, able to play by self, and act in a serious way. He asked them to rank the ones that they considered most important for their child's age. He also asked which traits the parents thought were most important for girls of that age and for boys of that age.

In general, Kohn (1959) found that most mothers from both groups wanted their children to display these traits. However, when choosing the most important characteristics, middle- and working-class mothers differed. Middle-class mothers were more likely to say that internal factors and an ability to be self-directed was important. For example, they were more likely to rank happiness, self-control, and curiosity as important characteristics for children. Working-class mothers were more likely to value obedience and neatness.

Such differences could have serious implications for the children's educational and career prospects. High-status and well-paying jobs tend to emphasize curiosity and self-control. For example, lawyers, doctors, and CEOs must be curious and self-directed. However, lower-status jobs tend to be more focused on obedience to authority and superiors. People who work in a factory are expected to follow orders, not to think outside the box. If a lawyer, business leader, or doctor just followed orders, she might be fired.

Family violence is a widespread problem around the world. According to the General Social Survey on Victimization (Statistics Canada 2009), 6 per cent of individuals reported experiencing physical or sexual spousal abuse in the preceding five years. Family violence is so prevalent that 25 per cent of police-reported crime involves family violence, half of which **are** spousal abuse and half child abuse. Most researchers assume that family violence is much more widespread than even these alarming numbers suggest, given that as few as 25 per cent of victims of spousal abuse report the incident to the police.

It is hard to imagine making light of family violence or abuse. However, look at this 2012 ad, part of a campaign called "Victim of Beauty" printed in 12 magazine. These ads drew harsh criticism from groups against domestic violence, who suggested that the campaign undermines a serious issue by using images of women with black eyes, broken noses, and burn marks

Does this image glorify violence against women? Does it trivialize the issue by using these images to draw attention? Why or why not?

to draw readers to a magazine. Editor-in-chief Huben Hubenov disagreed and argued that readers were the ones associating the images with domestic violence but that this link was not intended by the magazine or photographer (Murray 2012).

Kohn also found that middle-class mothers tended to value the same things in boys and girls. However, working-class mothers valued different things for each sex. They rated school performance and ambition as more important for boys but neatness and good manners as more important for girls. Think about how encouraging these different values in boys and girls reproduces a gendered division of labour and directs women and men into different types of occupations. This study highlights both how the family socializes children and how this socialization can work to reproduce societal inequalities.

The process of mate selection and dating creates the conditions for marriage, cohabitation, and family. Research shows that men and women tend to look for different features in spouses. This is, in part, because of gender stereotypes about how men and women should act and what role they should play in a relationship. These differences are also related to how we understand the marital (or spousal) relationship. Is it one where partners engage in very different roles, with one partner (often the woman) staying at home to raise children and the other partner (often the man) working? Or is it one of equal partners?

In the following reading, Simon Davis examines personal ads, comparing what men and women look for in a romantic partner. While you read this article, think about the different expectations that the men and women in the study have about marital and spousal relationships.

Men as Success Objects and Women as Sex Objects:
A Study of Personal Advertisements

Simon Davis

A study was made of 328 personal advertisements sampled from a major daily Canadian newspaper. It was found that gender differences for desired companion attributes were consistent with traditional sex role stereotypes. Relative to the opposite sex, women emphasized employment, financial, and intellectual status, as well as commitment, while men emphasized physical characteristics. Physical characteristics were the most desired, regardless of sex. Secondary findings were that, for this sample, considerably more men than women placed ads, and that the mean age for both sexes was relatively high. The main findings were similar to those from earlier studies.

Previous research has indicated that, to a large extent, selection of opposite-sex partners is dictated by traditional sex stereotypes (Urberg, 1979). More specifically, it has been found that men tend to emphasize sexuality and physical attractiveness in a mate to a greater extent than women (e.g., Harrison & Saeed, 1977; Deaux & Hanna, 1984; Nevid, 1984); this distinction has been found across cultures, as in the study by Stiles and colleagues (1987) of American and Icelandic adolescents.

The relatively greater preoccupation with casual sexual encounters demonstrated by men (Hite, 1987, p. 184) may be accounted for by the greater emotional investment that women place in sex; Basow (1986, p. 80) suggests that the "gender differences in this area (different meaning attached to sex) may turn out to be the strongest of all gender differences."

Women, conversely, may tend to emphasize psychological and personality characteristics (Curry & Hock, 1981; Deaux & Hanna, 1984), and to seek longevity and commitment in a relationship to a greater extent (Basow, 1986, p. 213).

Women may also seek financial security more so than men (Harrison & Saeed, 1977). Regarding this last point, Farrell (1986, p. 25) suggests that the tendency to treat men as success objects is reflected in the media, particularly in advertisements in women's magazines. On the other hand, men themselves may reinforce this stereotype in that a number of men still apparently prefer the traditional marriage with working husband and unemployed wife (Basow, 1986, p. 210).

Men have traditionally been more dominant in intellectual matters, and this may be reinforced in the courting process: Braito (1981) found in his study that female coeds feigned intellectual inferiority with their dates on a number of occasions. In the same vein, Hite, in her 1981 survey, found that men were less likely to seek intellectual prowess in their mate (p. 108).

The mate selection process has been characterized in at least two ways. Harrison and Saeed (1977) found evidence for a matching process, where individuals seeking particular characteristics in a partner were more likely to offer those characteristics in themselves. This is consistent with the observation that "like attracts like" and that husbands and wives tend to resemble one another in various ways (Thiessen & Gregg, 1980). Additionally, an exchange process may be in operation, wherein a trade-off is made with women offering "domestic work and sex for financial support" (Basow, 1986, p. 213).

With respect to sex stereotypes and mate selection, the trend has been for "both sexes to believe that the other sex expects them to live up to the gender stereotype" (Basow, 1986, p. 209).

Theoretical explanations of sex stereotypes in mate selection range from the sociobiological (Symons, 1987) to radical political views (Smith, 1973). Of interest in recent years has been demographic influences, that is, the lesser availability of men because of population shifts and marital patterns (Shaevitz, 1987, p. 40). Age may differentially affect women, particularly when children are desired; this, combined with women's generally lower economic status [particularly when unmarried (Halas, 1981, p. 124)], may mean that the need to "settle down" into a secure, committed relationship becomes relatively more crucial for women.

The present study looks at differential mate selection by men and women as reflected in newspaper companion ads. Using such a forum for the exploration of sex stereotypes is not new; for instance, in the study by Harrison and Saeed (1977) cited earlier, the authors found that in such ads women were more likely to seek financial security and men to seek attractiveness; a later study by Deaux and Hanna (1984) had similar results, along with the finding that women were more likely to seek psychological characteristics, specific personality traits, and to emphasize the quality and longevity of the relationship. The present study may be seen as a follow-up of this earlier research, although on this occasion using a Canadian setting. Of particular interest was the following: Were traditional stereotypes still in operation, that is, women being viewed as sex objects and men as success objects (the latter defined as financial and intellectual accomplishments)?

Method

Personal advertisements were taken from *The Vancouver Sun*, which is the major daily newspaper serving Vancouver, British Columbia. *The Sun* is generally perceived as a conservative, respectable journal—hence it was assumed that people advertising in it represented the "mainstream." It should be noted that people placing the ads must do so in person. For the sake of this study, gay ads were not included. A typical ad would run about 50 words, and included a brief description of the person placing it and a list of the attributes desired in the other party. Only the parts pertaining to the attributes desired in the partner were included for analysis. Attributes that pertained to hobbies or recreations were not included for the purpose of this study.

The ads were sampled as follows: only Saturday ads were used, since in *The Sun* the convention was for Saturday to be the main day for personal ads, with 40–60 ads per edition—compared to only 2–4 ads per edition on weekdays. Within any one edition *all* the ads were included for analysis. Six editions were randomly sampled, covering the period of 30 September 1988 to 30 September 1989. The attempt to sample through the calendar year was made in an effort to avoid any unspecified seasonal effect. The size of the sample (six editions) was large enough to meet goodness-of-fit requirements for statistical tests.

The attributes listed in the ads were coded as follows:

1. *Attractive:* specified that a partner should be, for example, "pretty" or "handsome."
2. *Physique*: similar to 1; however, this focused not on the face but rather on whether the partner was "fit and trim," "muscular," or had "a good figure." If it was not clear if body or face was being emphasized, this fell into variable (1) by default.
3. *Sex*: specified that the partner should have, for instance, "high sex drive," or should be "sensuous" or "erotic," or if there was a clear message that this was an arrangement for sexual purposes ("lunchtime liaisons—discretion required").
4. *Picture*: specified that the partner should include a photo in his/her reply.
5. *Profession*: specified that the partner should be a professional.
6. *Employed*: specified that the partner should be employed, e.g., "must hold steady job" or "must have steady income."
7. *Financial*: specified that the partner should be, for instance, "financially secure" or "financially independent."
8. *Education*: specified that the partner should be, for instance, "well educated" or "well read," or should be a "college grad."
9. *Intelligence*: specified that the partner should be "intelligent," "intellectual," or "bright."
10. *Honest*: specified, for instance, that the partner should be "honest" or have "integrity."

11. *Humour*: specified "sense of humour" or "cheerfulness."

12. *Commitment*: specified that the relationship was to be "long term" or "lead to marriage," or some other indication of stability and longevity.

13. *Emotion*: specified that the partner should be "warm," "romantic," "emotionally support- ive," "emotionally expressive," "sensitive," "loving," "responsive," or similar terms indicating an opposition to being cold and aloof.

In addition to the 13 attribute variables, two other pieces of information were collected: the length of the ad (in lines) and the age of the person placing the ad. Only if age was exactly specified was it included; if age was vague (e.g., "late 40s") this was not counted.

Variables were measured in the following way: any ad requesting one of the 13 attributes was scored once for that attribute. If not explicitly mentioned, it was not scored. The scoring was thus "all or nothing," e.g., no matter how many times a person in a particular ad stressed that looks were important it was only counted as a single score in the "attractive" column; thus, each single score represented one person. Conceivably, an individual ad could mention all, some, or none of the variables. Comparisons were then made between the sexes on the basis of the variables, using percentages and chi-squares. Chi-square values were derived by cross-tabulating gender (male/female) with attribute (asked for/not asked for). Degrees of freedom in all cases equalled one. Finally, several of the individual variables were collapsed to get an overall sense of the relative importance of (a) physical factors, (b) employment factors, and (c) intellectual factors.

Results

A total of 329 personal ads were contained in the six newspaper editions studied. One ad was discarded in that it specified a gay relationship, leaving a total sample of 328. Of this number, 215 of the ads were placed by men (65.5 per cent) and 113 by women (34.5 per cent).

The mean age of people placing ads was 40.4. One hundred and twenty seven cases (38.7 per cent) counted as missing data in that the age was not specified or was vague. The mean age for the two sexes was similar: 39.4 for women (with 50.4 per cent of cases missing) and 40.7 per cent for men (with 32.6 per cent of cases missing).

Sex differences in desired companion attributes are summarized in Table I. It will be seen that for 10 of the 13 variables a statistically significant difference was detected. The three largest differences were found for attractiveness, professional, and financial status. To sum- marize the table: in the case of attractiveness, physique, sex, and picture (physical attributes) the men were more likely than the women to seek these. In the case of professional status, employment status, financial status, intelligence, commitment, and emotion (nonphysical attributes) the women were more likely to seek these. The women were also more likely to specify education, honesty, and humour, however, not at a statistically significant level.

The data were explored further by collapsing several of the categories: the first four variables were collapsed into a "physical" category. Variables 5–7 were collapsed into an "employment" category, and variables 8 and 9 were collapsed into an "intellectual" category. The assumption was that the collapsed categories were sufficiently similar (within the three new categories) to make the new larger categories conceptually meaningful; conversely, it was felt the remaining variables (10–13) could not be meaningfully collapsed any further.

Sex differences for the three collapsed categories are summarized in Table II. Note that the Table II figures were not derived simply by adding the numbers in the Table I categories: recall that for variables 1–4 a subject could specify all, one, or none; hence simply adding the Table I figures would be biased by those individuals who were more effusive in specifying various physical traits. Instead, the Table II categories are (like Table I) all or nothing: whether a subject specified one or all four of the physical attributes it would only count once. Thus, each score represented one person.

In brief, Table II gives similar, although more exaggerated results to Table I. (The exag- geration is the result of only one item of several being needed to score within a collapsed category.) The men were more likely than the women to specify some physical attribute. The women were considerably more likely to specify that the companion be employed, or have a profession, or be in good financial shape. And the women were more likely to emphasize the intellectual abilities of their mate.

One can, incidentally, also note from this table an overall indication of attribute importance by collapsing across sexes, i.e., it is apparent that physical characteristics are the most desired regardless of sex.

Discussion

SEX DIFFERENCES

This study found that the attitudes of the subjects, in terms of desired companion attributes, were consistent with traditional sex role stereotypes. The men were more likely to emphasize stereotypically desirable feminine traits (appearance) and deemphasize the nonfeminine

TABLE I Gender comparison for attributes desired in partner

Variable	Desired by men (n = 215)	Desired by women (n = 113)	Chi-square
1. Attractive	76 (35.3%)	20 (17.7%)	11.13[1]
2. Physique	81 (37.7%)	17 (23.9%)	6.37[1]
3. Sex	25 (11.6%)	4 (3.5%)	6.03[1]
4. Picture	74 (34.4%)	24 (21.2%)	6.18[1]
5. Profession	6 (2.8%)	19 (16.8%)	20.74[1]
6. Employed	8 (3.7%)	12 (10.6%)	6.12[1]
7. Financial	7 (3.2%)	22 (19.5%)	24.26[1]
8. Education	8 (3.7%)	8 (7.1%)	1.79 (ns)
9. Intelligence	22 (10.2%)	24 (21.2%)	7.46[1]
10. Honest	20 (9.3%)	17 (15.0%)	2.44 (ns)
11. Humour	36 (16.7%)	26 (23.0%)	1.89 (ns)
12. Commitment	38 (17.6%)	31 (27.4%)	4.25[1]
13. Emotion	44 (20.5%)	35 (31.0%)	4.36[1]

1. Significant at the 0.05 level
SOURCE: Copyright © 1990, Plenum Publishing Corporation

TABLE II Gender comparison for physical, employment, and intellectual attributes desired in partner

Variable	Desired by men (n = 215)	Desired by women (n = 113)	Chi-square
Physical (variables 1–4)	143 (66.5%)	50 (44.2%)	15.13[1]
Employment (variables 5–7)	17 (7.9%)	47 (41.6%)	51.36[1]
Intellectual (variables 8 and 9)	29 (13.5%)	31 (37.4%)	9.65[1]

1. Significant at the 0.05 level
SOURCE: Copyright © 1990, Plenum Publishing Corporation

traits (financial, employment, and intellectual status). One inconsistency was that emotional expressiveness is a feminine trait but was emphasized relatively less by the men. Women, on the other hand, were more likely to emphasize masculine traits such as financial, employment, and intellectual status, and valued commitment in a relationship more highly. One inconsistency detected for the women concerned the fact that although emotional expressiveness is not a masculine trait, the women in this sample asked for it, relatively more than the men, anyway. Regarding this last point, it may be relevant to refer to Basow's (1986, p. 210) conclusion that "women prefer relatively androgynous men, but men, especially traditional ones, prefer relatively sex-typed women.". . .

REFERENCES

Basow, S. (1986). *Gender stereotypes: Traditions and alternatives*, Brooks/Cole Publishing Co.

Braito. R. (1981). The inferiority game: Perceptions and behavior. *Sex Roles*, 7, 65–72.

Curry. T., & Hock. R. (1981). Sex differences in sex role ideals in early adolescence. *Adolescence*, 16, 779–789.

Deaux, K., & Hanna, R. (1984). Courtship in the personals column: The influence of gender and sexual orientation. *Sex Roles*, 11, 363–375.

Farrell, W. (1986). *Why men are the way they are*. New York: Berkley Books.

Green, S., & Sandos, P. (1983). Perceptions of male and female initiators of relationship. *Sex Roles*, 9, 849–852.

Halas, C. (1981). *Why can't a woman be more like a man?* New York: Macmillan Publishing Co.

Harrison, A., & Saeed, L. (1977). Let's make a deal: An analysis of revelations and stipulations in lonely hearts advertisements. *Journal of Personality and Social Psychology*, 35, 257–264.

Hite, S. (1981). *The Hite report on male sexuality*. New York: Alfred A. Knopf.

Hite, S. (1987). *Women and love: A cultural revolution in progress*. New York: Alfred A. Knopf.

Nevid. J. (1984). Sex differences in factors of romantic attraction. *Sex Roles*, 11, 401–411.

Shaevitz, M. (1981). *Sexual Static*. Boston: Little, Brown & Co.

Smith, D. (1973). Women, the family and corporate capitalism. In M. Stephenson (Ed.), *Women in Canada*. Toronto: New Press.

Stiles, D., & Gibbon, J., Hardardottir, S., & Schnellmann, J. (1987). The ideal man or women as described by young adolescents in Iceland and the United States. *Sex Roles*, 11, 313–320.

Symons, D. (1987). An evolutionary approach. In J. Geer & W. O'Donohue (Eds.). *Theories of human sexuality*. New York: Plenum Press.

Thiessen, D., & Gregg, B. (1980). Human assortive mating and genetic equilibrium: An evolutionary perspective. *Ethology and Sociology*, 1, 111–140.

Urberg, K. (1979). Sex role conceptualization in adolescents and adults. *Developmental Psychology*, 15, 90–92.

CRITICAL Reading Questions

1. According to Davis's study, what do men and women look for in romantic partners? How can these findings help us to understand the different views that men and women have about marriage and the family? What can this study tell us about gender roles in society?

2. How was this study conducted? What are the benefits of the data used and how might this data influence the trends found in this study? Would different data be better? Why or why not?

3. How would the findings of this study be different if it were conducted today? How have larger social changes (e.g. changing gender roles and the rise in the number of gay couples) affected what men and women look for in romantic partners?

Summary

This chapter critically examined the role of the family in society. We began by talking about major changes in the family, including Andrew Cherlin's argument regarding the deinstitutionalization of marriage. These changes are related to larger social processes, such as the rise of women's rights and individualism and the decline of religiosity. We

HIGHLIGHT ///////////////////////////////////

The Incest Taboo

Despite all the variability in marriage and family within and across cultures, it seems that there may be one cultural universal in these institutions: the **incest taboo**. This norm of behaviour forbids certain relatives from having sexual relationships or marrying. While there are a few exceptions, such as ancient Peruvian and Egyptian royal families that allowed marriages between brothers and sisters of noble blood, the vast majority of societies and situations forbid these types of relationships.

What accounts for this cultural universal when almost everything else about marriage and the family differs from place to place and over time? One explanation is biological. When people of the same bloodline procreate, the offspring have a higher risk of mental or physical problems. For example, intermarrying among European royalty over many generations led to higher rates of diseases such as hemophilia (even though these were not marriages between direct relatives).

Other explanations for this universal taboo are social. Limiting sexual relationships between close relatives has a number of important functions for families and society as a whole. The rule that sex can occur only between spouses restricts sexual competition in families and makes people's rights and obligations toward each other clearer. For example, if you marry a sibling, you are both a spouse and a sibling to each other. This situation complicates family relationships and issues such as inheritance. Finally, encouraging people to marry outside their family helps to make connections with larger groups of people and thereby integrate larger societies.

discussed how structural functionalism and conflict theory understand the family's role in society. The chapter also explored the depiction of the family on television, teen pregnancy, and fertility rates.

Key Terms

arranged marriage 229
cohabitation 224
companionate marriage 230
deinstitutionalization of marriage 224
diversity defenders 234
extended family 222
family 222
family household 222
family violence 238
fertility rate 235

incest taboo 245
individualized marriage 230
institutional marriage 230
marriage 222
marriage movement 234
monogamy 234
nuclear family 222
one-child policy 235
polygamy 234
teenage pregnancy 227

For Further Reading

Cherlin, Andrew J. 2004. "The Deinstitutionalization of Marriage in America." *Journal of Marriage and the Family* 66: 848–61.

Engels, Friedrich. 1894/1946. *The Origin of the Family, Private Property and the State.* New York: International Publishers.

Kimmel, Michael. 2012. *The Gendered Society*, 5th edn. New York: Oxford University Press.

Lauer, Sean, and Carrie Yodanis. 2011. "Individualized Marriage and the Integration of Resources." *Journal of Marriage and the Family* 73: 669–83.

Parsons, Talcott, and Robert F. Bales. 1955. *Family Socialization and Interaction Process.* Glencoe, IL: Free Press.

9 Education

CHAPTER OUTLINE

Introduction

You are very familiar with the institution of education. The average Canadian youth spends 30 per cent of each weekday in schooling. (The only other activity in which they spend this much time is sleeping!) If you are the typical undergraduate student, you have been in this system almost your whole life. Perhaps you started in pre-school when you were three or four years old, moved through elementary and high school, and now are in a university or college. You might have also attended other classes outside school—perhaps piano, tennis, or Japanese lessons. Unless you took some time off between high school and post-secondary education, you probably cannot even remember when the majority of your waking hours were spent somewhere other than in school. And you are currently gaining even more schooling. Why did you make the decision to continue your education? What is the role of the education system in society as a whole?

The Schooled Society

Schooling and the education system have fundamentally changed in modern society. Scott Davies and Neil Guppy (2010) outline three major changes that have created the modern "**schooled society**" in which we live. First is the growth in modern schooling. Today, there is mass post-secondary enrolment in Canada, with more than half of graduating high-school seniors attending college or university (Canadian Council on Learning 2006). The high rates of post-secondary completion in this country are illustrated in Figures 9.1 and 9.2.

Second, schooling has become increasingly integral to modern life. Individuals with a post-secondary degree earn higher incomes, on average, and are less likely to experience unemployment (Davies and Guppy 2010). (We will discuss these important implications later in this chapter.) Governments have become more interested in education's role in improving national productivity and have called for a focus on the development of highly educated "knowledge workers." Many countries, including Canada, previously emphasized manual labour and resource extraction. These changes can be linked to the decline in the primary sector (where jobs did not usually require much education). The evolution of working conditions and employment sectors in Canada is discussed in more detail in Chapter 10.

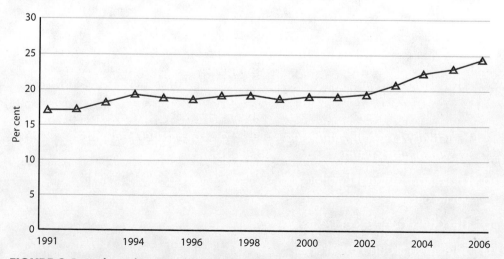

FIGURE 9.1 University enrolment in Canada 18–24-year-olds, 1992–2006 (per cent)

SOURCE: Calculations of HRSDC based on special data request from Statistics Canada, Labour Force Survey, 2006. Ottawa, Statistics Canada, 2006. http://www4.hrsdc.gc.ca/.3ndic.1t.4r@-eng.jsp?iid=56#M_1.

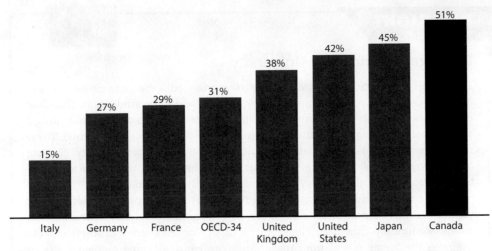

FIGURE 9.2 Completion of post-secondary education, population 25–64 years, countries and OECD average, 2010

SOURCE: OECD (2012), *Education at a Glance 2012: OECD Indicators*, OECD Publishing. http://dx.doi.org/10.1787/eag-2012-en.

Finally, the forms and functions of education are increasing and diversifying in our modern schooled society. Historically, schools focused on reading, writing, and basic math. The current system is expected to teach these skills as well as a host of additional subjects, such as physical education, media literacy, drug and alcohol awareness, environmental responsibility, and sex education. Modern schools are seen as ways to solve a myriad of social problems. For example, French immersion programs were established across Canada in the 1970s as a means of dealing with issues of national integration and supporting new policies of bilingualism. These programs also attempted to foster national solidarity and entrench bilingualism. French immersion has been highly successful, enrolling approximately 300,000 students across Canada (or 7 per cent of eligible students; Davies and Guppy 2010). Mandarin immersion programs have been established in Alberta and British Columbia to further the national policy of multiculturalism.

The Functions of Education

The education system has several functions. The obvious and intended ones, such as teaching students basic knowledge and skills, are known as **manifest functions**. While learning to read, write, and do math are certainly part of education, sociologists have also focused on the **latent functions** of education, which are unintended. These functions fall into three broad categories: **socialization** of young people, **selection** of people into employment, and **legitimation** of certain types of knowledge and divisions in society. Durkheim, Marx, and Weber were all interested in these functions of education and saw them as integral to modern society. Let's explore each one and see how these three theorists understood education's role in society.

Socialization

Durkheim focused on the socializing role of the education system. The common theme in Durkheim's work is a fundamental concern with the functioning of society and what accounts for its solidarity and cohesion. This is the basis for his structural functionalist theory and is the core of his interest in the education system.

Durkheim (1956) argued that universal education serves the needs of society in a number of ways. Tasked with providing individuals with training for life in broader

HIGHLIGHT

Pressure to Perform in University

The importance placed on obtaining a post-secondary education can cause stress in many students. According to Bradshaw (2013), more and more students in Canadian universities deal with this pressure by using illegal prescription drugs. "Study drugs" are increasingly being sold, particularly in times of anxiety (such as exams). These medications are usually for patients with attention deficit hyperactivity disorder (ADHD); however, nearly 4 per cent of students take these drugs to improve focus and to study longer, even though they do not suffer from the condition.

These drugs can have serious health risks if not taken properly under medical guidance. Stimulants such as methylphenidate, amphetamine, and dextroamphetamine—commonly known as Ritalin, Adderall, or Concerta—have after-effects. For example, the "come down" from these drugs can cause sleeping problems. Use of these drugs can also cause loss of appetite and dehydration. Besides health risks, possessing these drugs without a prescription is a violation of the Controlled Drugs and Substances Act, an offence that carries a maximum prison sentence of seven years (http://laws-lois.justice.gc.ca/eng/acts/C-38.8/).

Two years ago, Duke University made the non-prescription use of these types of study drugs an offence under its rules on academic dishonesty. Yet most students interviewed for Bradshaw's (2013) article disagreed with this decision. One second-year University of British Columbia student argues that "it's still your work, . . . because you're still studying, you're just doing it with an increased mental capacity."

Why do you think study drugs are becoming increasingly popular? Are they a legitimate way of dealing with the increased stress of university life or a way of cheating?

society, schools convey basic knowledge and skills that will be useful for a society's members. In addition, individuals need specialized training for the specific roles that they will occupy in life, such as an occupation. Durkheim argued that, in the complex division of labour that characterizes modern society, education should be aligned with one's future occupational aspirations; that is, teachers should learn how to teach and lawyers should learn how to practise the law.

Education also socializes children into the mainstream. Each society has unique needs; schools can provide the guidelines that help us fit into that society. Education acts as the social "glue" that helps a highly differentiated society remain normatively coherent by offering a "moral education," where young people learn the norms and values of their society and the importance of following these rules of behaviour. Moral education is "the means by which society perpetually re-creates the conditions of its very existence" and schooling is about the "systematic socialization of the young generation" (Durkheim 1956, 123, 124). Socialization occurs when children are given grades and gold stars for following the rules. This practice helps bring together children of different backgrounds by tying them into the cohesive whole of society.

Remember that Durkheim argued that there are two types of societies, those based on mechanical solidarity (everyone is similar) and those based on organic solidarity (people are dissimilar but interdependent). From a structural functionalist perspective, Durkheim saw religion as a source of moral guidance in societies based on mechanical solidarity. However, with the cultural diversity in modern society and waning of religion's influence on our daily lives, Durkheim claimed that education is the new way to morally integrate people into our modern society, which is based on organic solidarity.

Durkheim focused on the education system's part in training young people to play roles in and to fit into society. As a result, he saw the education system as an important part of how society reproduces itself. He explained that education "is only the image and reflection of society . . . it does not create it" (Durkheim 1897/1951, 371). For Durkheim and others who focus on the socializing role of the education system, education plays a fundamental role in promoting social order and in creating stability in society.

Selection

A second major function of the education system is to select individuals by awarding badges of ability through "sorting, differentially rewarding, and certifying graduates of elementary, secondary, and post-secondary schools" (Davies and Guppy 2010). Focusing on this element of the education system, Weber argued that schools are based on bureaucracies and work to confer status and prestige.

Weber was interested in the rise of rationalization in society, particularly the development of bureaucracies in a number of different areas. (We will discuss this topic in more detail in the next chapter.) The education system—including your university or college—is filled with bureaucracies. There are many positive aspects of the bureaucratization of the education system. For example, universities are very efficient systems for producing degrees. It is clear what classes and grades students need to graduate, and most earn degrees in four years. These educational bureaucracies also strive to be fair. Student numbers, not names, are often used on exams so that the professor or teaching assistant grades the tests without regard to his personal opinion of the student.

Just as they are efficient at producing degrees, universities and colleges can be frustrating in the amount of red tape students have to go through to fulfill all the requirements. They can limit your choice of classes—you need certain courses in a certain order to get your degree, regardless of your interests or abilities. They can also be very depersonalizing. The use of those student numbers, which is efficient and perhaps fairer, might make you feel as though you are not being treated as a unique individual.

PHOTO 9.1 Think about how you felt when you received your report card at school. Why are reports cards used and what are the potential problems with this form of evaluation?

A consequence of the rise of bureaucracies in society as a whole, including in the education system, is a growing need for individuals to have specialized certifications linked to specific occupations. Instead of providing a general education to all young people, modern society requires individuals to be trained in particular tasks, such as medicine, engineering, or social work. Weber highlighted how this specialization leads to an increasingly complicated set of certifications and degrees that can prevent certain people from entering a trade or profession. While it makes sense for certain professionals to earn a specialized degree, the practice also allows these individuals to gain significant control over entrance to their respective fields and to monopolize access to the elite positions and status.

Randall Collins (1979) called Weber's observation **credentialing**, the attestation of a qualification or competence issued to an individual by a party with authority to do so, such as a university. As low- and high-status groups both pursue upward mobility, the latter maintain their social position by acquiring more education and educational credentials. Occupational groups have an obvious interest in making it difficult to enter their occupations (making it so that you need a BSc before entering medical school or a bachelor's degree before entering teaching college). By limiting the number of people who may practise in their area, they can reduce competition and keep their pay and job security high.

Legitimation

The third major function of the education system is to legitimate certain kinds of knowledge and divisions in society. In 1846, Canadian educational reformer Egerton Ryerson (after whom Ryerson University is named) began promoting the idea of a free and compulsory universal school system. He argued that this system would help to produce order, facilitate social control, and avert potential conflict arising from a new wave of immigrants to Canada at the time. Ryerson warned that new Irish labourers entering Canada were dangerous: "the physical disease and death which have accompanied their influx among us may be the precursor of the worst pestilence of social insubordination and disorder" (in Schecter 1977, 373). He claimed that education could assimilate these "alien" labourers into the dominant Protestant culture.

Karl Marx (Marx and Engels 1964) noted the general tendency of dominant groups to subdue the masses. He argued that education maintains social inequality and preserves the power of capitalists and others who are already in control of society. This position is consistent with Marx's overall theory that society's dominant institutions (including schools, religions, and the state) support and reproduce the capitalist system. In essence, Marx argued that schools work to systematically reproduce class relations and the capitalist order with each new generation of students.

As we have learned from Marx earlier in this book, "the ruling ideas of each age have ever been the ideas of its ruling class" (Marx and Engels 1964, 125). This class diffuses its ideas throughout society in several ways, such as by setting the school curriculum. In formal education, a **curriculum** is the planned interaction of pupils with instructional content, materials, resources, and processes for evaluating the attainment of educational objectives (Adams and Adams 2003). Marx claimed that ideas are disseminated through both the official and what he called the **hidden curriculum**, the lessons that are not normally considered part of the academic program but that schools unintentionally or secondarily provide. He argued that, along with teaching social studies, English, and science, schools teach students to be submissive, docile, punctual, and hard-working—all the traits that make for "good" workers in the capitalist system. In this way, education dulls the lower classes into obedient workers. Individual traits, such as punctuality, perseverance, and obedience, are rewarded with high grades and praise in school. For example, students are told to be quiet when the teacher is talking and to raise their hand when they would like to speak. The education system encourages and fosters this conformity to authority, which benefits the overarching interests of the society's powerful.

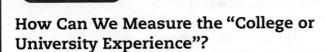

ACTIVITY

How Can We Measure the "College or University Experience"?

Universities and colleges are increasingly interested in comparing post-secondary institutions and students' on-campus experiences. How do we judge the "best" university, professor, or campus? How you answer this question depends on who you are within the institution (a university president, professor, or student) and what you think the role of a university is in society at large.

Looking at online resources that attempt to quantify and compare universities and professors pushes us to think critically about what we value in a university education and how to best assess how well your school or professors provide your education. Go to this book's companion website to access three measures of the university experience: *Maclean's* system of ranking Canadian universities and colleges, Rate My Professors' criteria, and *Playboy's* selection of the top party schools in North America. After you've examined these sites, answer the following questions:

1. How do these organizations judge a "good" school? What criteria do they use? How do their criteria differ?

2. Based on the criteria of each measure, what are the most important things about universities and the role of universities in society as a whole?

3. Who makes each of these lists? On whose interests do each of these rankings focus?

4. Which ranking do you think is best? Which is worst? What would you include in the perfect ranking?

5. How could you use these rankings? What problems or unintended consequences could arise from measuring post-secondary education in these ways?

In "A Matter of Degrees," William Beaver examines the various theories that sociologists use to explain education's role in modern society. When reading this article, try to connect the theories Beaver discusses with the ideas of Durkheim, Weber, and Marx.

READING

A Matter of Degrees

William Beaver

Americans value few things more than college degrees. Right now, 29 per cent of adults over age 25 have a bachelor's or higher. That figure has more than doubled since the 1970s, and many within the educational establishment argue it will have to increase significantly for the United States to remain globally competitive.

The number of graduate degrees also continues to rise—masters' have doubled since 1980 and record numbers are enrolled in master's programs, a recent article in *The New York Times* reported.

In many ways these numbers aren't surprising. Early on, students learn that a college degree is the starting point to making it in American society. . . .

Media reports periodically reinforce such beliefs, reminding us that degree-holders have important income advantages. A recent news story in *The Washington Post* reported that in tough economic times, those with college degrees are much more likely to avoid lay-offs and maintain their incomes than those with high-school diplomas or less.

But what exactly do degrees do for people? The conventional wisdom holds that college graduates acquire skills that better prepare them for the world of work, which makes them more attractive to employers. Thus, students and parents are willing to pay the continually rising costs of higher education, assuming the pay-off will be worth it.

Although college graduates do have higher incomes, the reasons why, and our ever-increasing need to acquire educational credentials, are tied to larger social forces that sociologists have explored—forces that will continue to impact all those trying to climb the ladder of success.

The most popular view on the purpose of a college degree is known as the human capital model, which argues students attend college to acquire the knowledge and skills modern societies require, and that this allows them to obtain meaningful employment.

It's the model most students seem to accept, too. For example, surveys conducted by UCLA's Higher Education Research Institute found that 72 per cent of college freshman cite "to get a better job" as the major reason for going to college.

However, if the human capital model is correct, it must be assumed students acquire skills in the classroom that are directly transferable to the job. One can certainly argue certain majors like accounting and computer science offer more skill-training than others, and research indicates that with these types of majors, employers do tend to hire on the basis of perceived skills.

The fact of the matter is, though, most college students don't major in areas that teach job skills. Some 22 per cent of students currently major in business, but even within the business curriculum not all areas of study focus on acquiring specific skills. Moreover, many students continue to major in the social sciences and liberal arts, where there is little or no skill-training.

Along these lines, it would be logical to assume those possessing the necessary job skills, as indicated by their college major, would be more productive. Yet, the research that does exist on this idea suggests job productivity isn't significantly related to major. . . .

Why We Credential

Max Weber is credited with being the first sociologist to closely examine the function of degrees. He concluded educational credentials had much less to do with acquiring job skills than providing occupational and professional groups with a way of excluding certain individuals. The ability to exclude not only gives these groups power but helps ensure those hired will be loyal to the organization.

Weber's basic insights provided the foundation for modern credentialing theory, the most important work about which remains Randall Collins's *The Credentialed Society*. His detailed historical and social analysis supported Weber's contention that degrees allow certain occupational groups to exclude individuals, and that even business degrees seldom provide actual job training but do serve as indicators that a potential employee possesses the correct values that make compliance with organizational standards more likely.

There are always uncertainties about how new hires will adjust. The last thing most employers want is for them to "rock the boat," which could threaten stability within the organization. It's assumed individuals with the appropriate college degree will be more likely to fit in, but why? Part of the answer is self-selection. That is, students choose a college major that appeals to them, hoping to land a job and the start of a career, and hence are more than willing to conform. On the other hand, it's also likely that being exposed to a curriculum socializes students to acquire values associated with a profession. For years sociologists have investigated this so-called hidden curriculum.

For example, prospective managers are taught that their interests and the interests of workers are often in conflict and that their loyalties should be tied to management. Credentialing theorists have also suggested possessing the appropriate values is particularly important in higher-level positions, where individuals are often given more autonomy and are less likely to be closely monitored. So perhaps it isn't surprising that business researchers Nasrollah Ahadiat and Kenneth Smith discovered employers considered "professional conduct" the most important attribute when hiring accounting graduates.

Besides conformity and control, credentialing theory emphasizes that degrees also confer status on those who hold them. Along these lines, sociologist David K. Brown traced the development of the credentialing system to the late nineteenth century and the rise of large-scale bureaucratic organizations where individuals with management skills were needed.

It was assumed college graduates possessed the cognitive and verbal abilities good managers needed, which also reduced the uncertainty associated with hiring. Interestingly, studies do show college tends to increase cognitive abilities, so in many cases these assumptions weren't unfounded. Nonetheless, degrees provided a claim of competence or status that came to be taken for granted.

Thus credentials, as David Labaree points out in his book *How to Succeed in College Without Really Learning*, have exchange value because they allow students to obtain employment based largely on the status a degree confers. However, much less use value is apparent because the connection between degrees and actual job performance is questionable.

The Pay Gap

Many students pursue a degree to position themselves to earn a higher income, and it has been well established that college graduates earn more. In fact, four-year degree holders earn nearly 45 per cent more per year than high-school graduates, according to the U.S. Census Bureau.

Indeed, the pay gap is one of the strongest arguments for the conventional wisdom of the human capital model, because it seems to demonstrate that employers are willing to pay for the skills college graduates possess. On the other hand, it's difficult to know exactly how much degrees are really worth because the most capable students go to college. As a result, there's no control group of equally capable, non-degree students available for comparison.

Nonetheless, credentialing theorists would agree that income and degrees are clearly related. Research by Ross Boylan found the largest gains in income occur soon after obtaining a degree. In this regard, reports from the Bureau of Labor Statistics show income gains for students are small unless they obtain a credential, even though students could certainly acquire job skills without earning a degree.

Consider that the median weekly income of individuals with some college but no degree in 2004 was $574, compared to $916 for those with a bachelor's. This suggests degrees do serve as status indicators. Just as important, Boylan found income gains experienced by degree holders are often relative. That is, as the number of people with degrees increase, degree holders take jobs formerly held by high-school graduates. Hence, the relative value of a degree actually increases because non-degree holders are forced into even lower-paying jobs.

One result, according to D.W. Livingstone in his book *The Education–Jobs Gap*, is that workers are often underemployed, because employers have increased the educational requirements for jobs whose basic content hasn't changed. Research by Stephen Vaisey discovered that nearly 55 per cent of workers are overqualified, which has produced increasing levels of job dissatisfaction, to say nothing of the fact that workers are forced to pursue even higher, increasingly expensive credentials (which is particularly burdensome to lower income groups) if they want a chance to be hired.

This phenomenon has been termed "defensive credentialing," where students attend college to keep from losing ground to degree holders. As one student recently put it, "I don't like college much, but what kind of job can I get without a degree?" Similarly, as the number of bachelor's degrees climbs, more have pursued graduate degrees, hoping to gain some advantage. This also helps explain the increase in the number of master's degrees.

Credentialing and Higher Education

The role of higher education in a credentialing system seems obvious—to grant degrees to those who earn them. But there's still more involved. Although higher education certainly responds to the demands of industry and students for credentials, colleges haven't just been passive participants waiting for students to enroll. They've used the credentialing system to their advantage, having relied on demographic changes.

By the late 1970s, higher education faced a troubling reality. The education of the baby boom generation that had produced the so-called golden years of higher education, when enrolments tripled, was coming to an end. The last of the boomers would be graduating in a few years and the future looked grim. The Carnegie Council warned enrolments could decline by as much as 50 per cent, while others predicted 30 per cent of colleges might have to close or merge. To survive, they would have to recruit more students from a dwindling pool.

Hence, colleges began to enroll a more academically diverse group of students and recruit more women and minorities, many of whom represented first-generation college students. To a lesser extent, the situation was helped by the fact that more students were completing high school. According to the U.S. Department of Education, between 1972 and 1985 high-school completion rates increased by roughly 2.6 per cent, and then climbed by about 3 per cent by 1999.

Moreover, the curriculum, particularly at less prestigious institutions, was expanded and further vocationalized. In fact, W. Norton Grubb and Marvin Lazerson in their book *The Education Gospel and the Economic Power of Schooling* maintain that expansion in higher education has only occurred when more occupational majors have been added to the curriculum.

In the early 1970s, 58 per cent of majors were considered occupational and by the late 1980s that figure had climbed to 65 per cent. These types of degrees can be particularly appealing to first-generation college students, who often come from working- and lower-class backgrounds and want a degree that seems to improve their chances for employment and justifies the considerable investment.

New degree programs were often in subject areas that in the past hadn't required a bachelor's degree for employment. For example, females who might have needed a certificate or an associate degree to secure work as a secretary could now earn a four-year degree in office management. Such was also true for other areas, ranging from various medical technologies to the performing arts, which reinforced the credentialing system in two significant ways. First, a more diverse group of students earned degrees, many of whom might not have obtained them in the past. Second, by creating new majors, credentialing was expanded into vocational areas not traditionally associated with a four-year degree, while at the same time reinforcing the notion that a college degree imparts job skills. . . .

RECOMMENDED RESOURCES

Ross D. Boylan. "The Effect of the Number of Diplomas on Their Value," *Sociology of Education* (1993) 66: 206–221. Shows how the relative value of college degrees has increased while their absolute value has not.

David K. Brown. *Degrees of Control: A Sociology of Educational Expansion and Occupational Credentialism* (Teachers College Press, 1995.) Documents the development of the credentialing system to the late nineteenth century and how it came to be assumed that degree holders had certain traits that made them more attractive to employers.

Randall Collins. *The Credentialed Society: An Historical Sociology of Education and Stratification* (Academic Press, 1979). A detailed historical account of the credentialing system and its implications for American society.

W. Norton Grubb and Marvin Lazerson. *The Education Gospel and the Economic Power of Schooling* (Harvard University Press, 2004). Discusses the rise of vocationalism and its continuing impacts on higher education.

D.W. Livingstone. *The Education–Jobs Gap: Underemployment or Economic Democracy* (Westview Press, 1998). Suggests workers are increasingly underemployed because the educational credentials required for jobs has risen even though the content of most jobs has not essentially changed.

Eric Margolis, ed. *The Hidden Curriculum in Higher Education* (Routledge, 2001). One of the first attempts to describe and analyze the hidden curriculum at colleges and universities.

CRITICAL
Reading
Questions

1. What evidence does Beaver use to support the **human capital model**? Does he find this theory convincing? Which classical theory (Durkheim's, Weber's, or Marx's) does this theory most closely resemble?

2. What classical theory discussed in this book is related to the screening and sorting theory? What evidence supports this theory and how accurate does Beaver think this theory is?

3. What is **defensive credentialing**?

4. Why has there been an expansion in the number and types of degrees?

Education and Social Inequality

Canadians pride themselves on living in a meritocracy, a society where individuals achieve based on their personal merit. While Canada has many features of a meritocracy, not all individuals are equally likely to succeed in our society. In the previous chapters, we learned the importance of social class, race, ethnicity, and gender in shaping people's opportunities. Despite the significance of these individual characteristics in shaping our lives, we are not simply passive agents who are doomed to certain kinds of lives. Many individuals who come from disadvantaged backgrounds achieve great things and many people who come from positions of advantage do not have high-paying jobs or high-status degrees.

The education system is a centrally important institution in a meritocracy because it has the potential to level the playing field and provide equal opportunities for individuals to work hard and move up the social hierarchy. Yet all Western countries have a clear pattern of inequality that suggests that the educational system is not meritocratic. For example, children from lower-class families tend to do worse in the education system than those from higher-class backgrounds.

It is important to note that not all dimensions of inequality work in relation to educational outcomes as we might expect. For example, when it comes to gender inequality, one would guess that men would be advantaged in the education system. However, women tend to perform better than men in schools and are more likely to earn degrees. In addition, some visible minority groups perform better than the majority white population, although this trend varies across racial and ethnic groups.

Education and Social Class

The largest and most persistent inequality in educational outcomes is based on social class. The relationship between these two factors is persistent over time, robust across measures, and consistent across country contexts. According to Statistics Canada (2011b), high-income Canadians are much more likely to earn degrees than those from low-income backgrounds. In fact, 67 per cent of the top 1 per cent of income earners graduated from university. Comparatively, only 21 per cent of all Canadians ages 15 and over have graduated.

There are a variety of reasons that individuals from low-income backgrounds are less likely to perform well in schools and achieve degrees. Lower-class families might have **different expectations** and values than upper-class families. A second reason could be **differential association**; that is, children from lower-class backgrounds are less likely to have role models who were high achievers in school or who attended university or college. As a result, these children lack the knowledge of how to work within the educational system (e.g. how to apply to university, what classes to take in high school to get into university). **Differential preparation** is another possible explanation. Children from families with more money are more likely to have private tutors, go on educational trips, have educational toys, and have books and newspapers around the home. These resources help to prepare them for school and to succeed in the educational system.

Social class is also important because it can help determine your position within the organization of a school. **Streaming**, also sometimes called **tracking**, is the practice of placing students with comparable skills or needs together. Streaming includes putting students in specific schools for high or low achievement or in specific classes such as enriched/advanced or applied/basic or giving students harder or easier work within one class.

Streaming students into groups with similar skill levels has many advantages. It allows students to advance according to their ability, thus helping to preserve their interest and incentive to perform. Because bright students are not bored by the slow participation of others, they also are more likely to continue to engage in the class. Moreover, teachers can adapt their teaching styles and materials to the type of students in their classes and the abilities of these students. This approach can be beneficial to students, as they will have material targeted to their ability level.

These purported advantages explain why streaming remains popular in schools in Canada and around the world. However, streaming also has some noteworthy disadvantages. The stigma attached to being assigned to the lower-ability group might discourage the learning of children labelled in this way. This situation can create a **self-fulfilling prophecy**. Robert K. Merton (1968, 477) coined this term in *Social Theory and Social Structure* and defined it in the following way:

PHOTO 9.2 By adapting their teaching specifically to their students, teachers offer a more tailored educational experience, which leads to even better performance from high-achieving pupils. What are some of the practical effects of streaming on lower-level students?

> The self-fulfilling prophecy is, in the beginning, a *false* definition of the situation evoking a new behaviour which makes the original false conception come "true." This specious validity of the self-fulfilling prophecy perpetuates a reign of error. For the prophet will cite the actual course of events as proof that he was right from the very beginning. (emphasis in original)

In other words, a strongly held belief thought to be true (even if it is false) may have such an influence on a person that his actions ultimately realize the belief (Merton 1949). This idea might remind you of the Thomas principle (see Chapter 5). Both stress the importance of our perceptions of a situation and how (even if they are not based in reality) they can change our "real" experiences.

A famous experiment showing the self-fulfilling prophecy's effect in the education system involved students in a San Francisco elementary school (Wineburg 1987). The researchers selected 60 children at random and told their teachers that, based on IQ tests, they were "expected to bloom." The researchers returned a year later to conduct new IQ tests. The 60 children enjoyed significant gains, far above the students who had not been labelled as particularly intelligent or with high potential. Remember that the two groups were the same—the label was unrelated to actual performance on the test. However, the teachers' belief that certain students were smarter *made* these students smarter (or at least perform better on the second IQ test).

RESEARCH METHOD

Experiment

How do students who are expected to do better end up performing better, even when their ability is no greater than others'? Barr and Dreeben (1983) looked at first-grade classes in which students were grouped by their reading ability at the beginning of the year. Students in higher-ability groups learned more new words and improved their reading skills more rapidly than students in the low-ability groups. Better readers were placed in high-ability groups at the beginning of the year, and they received more instructional time, were exposed to more new words, and experienced a faster pace of instruction than students in the low-ability groups. In short, higher-performing students received more learning opportunities than lower-performing students; consequently, the gap between high- and low-achieving students grew larger over the course of the year.

These experiments show the powerful effect of positive expectations. Many researchers and observers have generalized these findings to argue that there must be powerful negative effects of negative expectations. However, running an experiment with negative expectations would be unethical. Suppose you told teachers that certain students are slow learners. They might hold the pupils back or spend less time instructing them. Because we cannot test this directly, it is important to question whether the effect of the positive expectation experiments would hold true of students expected to perform poorly. Would it really hold students back in the same way that positive expectations can benefit students?

If all students are equally likely to make it into the high- and low-ability streams and student placement is based solely on their ability, streaming would not reproduce inequalities. However, when students with the same test scores and grades are compared, students from higher socio-economic status (SES) families are still more likely than low SES students to be enrolled in high-track classes (Gamoran and Mare 1989). Thus, the former are advantaged regardless of their ability and test scores; they are not only more likely to be prepared for school, but they are also more likely to be placed in the high-ability stream, with all its benefits.

Annette Lareau's (2003) *Unequal Childhoods: Class, Race, and Family Life* addresses this issue. Through interviews and observations of 10 families, Lareau examined the factors that lead to different educational outcomes across SES groups. First, parents who went to university are more knowledgeable regarding which classes are the "best" and most likely to prepare children for higher education. Parents with higher SES have the means to send their children to enrichment schools and to enroll them in extracurricular activities. Second, university-educated parents are better integrated into school networks—through

RESEARCH METHOD

Interviews

Parent Teacher Associations and volunteering—which gives them more information about classes and teachers. Finally, these parents influence their children's class selection by encouraging them to challenge themselves and to think about the long-term consequences of their choices, such as which classes best prepare them for university.

Streaming seems to have serious benefits for some students at the cost of others. Students in the advanced classes do better, in part because they tend to be taught by more experienced teachers (Kelly 2004). In fact, research shows that similar students will perform quite differently if they are placed into a high or a low stream. Being put into the latter will reduce their learning, while being in the former will increase it, even if these students have similar abilities at the beginning. Streaming also has long-term implications. For example, high-streamed students are more likely to attend university. Streaming can create what is referred to as a cumulative disadvantage; the most advanced individuals are awarded the best opportunities, which increases inequality (DiPrete et al. 2006).

Education and Gender

When we discuss inequality, we are sometimes tempted to think that certain groups are always disadvantaged. For example, we know that women tend to make less money than men and are more likely to live in poverty. It therefore seems logical to assume that women, and other groups who are similarly disadvantaged, are disadvantaged in all realms of society, including education. Yet, as previously mentioned, Canadian women currently tend to do better, on average, than men in the educational system (see Figure 9.3). For example, since 1990, women have earned more degrees (both undergraduate and advanced) than men in Canada.

How can we understand this **gender reversal in educational outcomes**? Since the 1960s, the women's movement has had many important implications for society in Canada, the United States, and Western Europe. These movements were instrumental in gaining women more opportunities to enter higher education. Furthermore, women in this period were entering the workforce at higher rates than ever before and were becoming involved in more professionalized occupations, which required more education.

The declining influence of religion, something we talked about in Chapter 1, changed our expectations about the need for men and women to marry and the timing and number of children couples had. With delayed marriages, a rise in the number of people choosing to remain single, and a decline in the number of children per couple, women

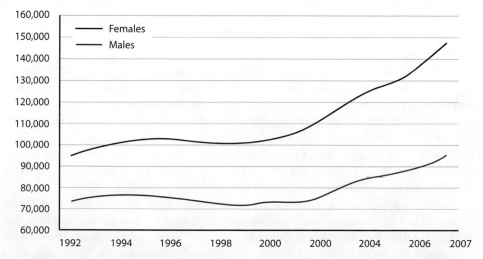

FIGURE 9.3 Number of university graduates by sex, Canada, 1992–2007

SOURCE: Statistics Canada. 2009. "Trends in University Graduation, 1992 to 2007." Ottawa: Statistics Canada. www.statcan.gc.ca/pub/81-004-x/2009005/article/11050-eng.htm.

had more time and ability to attend higher education. The invention of modern birth control methods, particularly the birth control pill, was also very important. The pill, first approved for contraceptive use in the United States in 1960 and in Canada a few years later, is currently used by more than 100 million women worldwide (Shader and Zonderman 2006). The pill's invention and availability was a major development in women's engagement in the education system. Now that women could control when and how many children they had (at least to some extent), they could remain in education longer and pursue degrees with fewer interruptions.

While women have made large gains in terms of attendance and completion of university degrees, women still make less than men once they have completed school. In fact, women earn about 15 per cent less than men early in their careers (Blau 1998). These early income inequalities are important because they tend to grow over time (Marini 1989). One of the main reasons given for women earning less than men even though they are more likely to earn a degree is the different majors that women and men select. Men are overrepresented in majors such as engineering, which are more likely to lead to high-paying jobs. In addition, women are not able to translate their degrees into earnings the same way that men do.

Educational attainment also varies widely by race and ethnic group. As we learned in Chapter 5, racial and ethnic groups have very different rates of high-school and university graduation. However, as with gender, these inequalities do not always follow the general trends of discrimination that we observe in society as a whole. For example, only 17 per cent of white Canadians earn a university degree, a much lower rate than other groups (see Table 5.1, p. 143). Ann Mullen discusses how men's and women's performances in higher education differ by social class and ethnicity. As you read Mullen's article, keep in mind the concept of intersectionality (introduced in Chapter 6).

PHOTO 9.3 Despite the gender reversal of education outcomes, the wage gap between men and women continues. Based on what you have learned in this chapter, how do you explain this situation?

READING

The Not-So-Pink Ivory Tower

Ann Mullen

Since 1982, women in the United States have been graduating from college at higher rates than men; they currently earn 57 per cent of all bachelor's degrees. Some view this trend as a triumphant indicator of gender egalitarianism, while others sound the alarm about the supposed "male crisis" in higher education and the problem of increasingly "feminized" universities. . . .

Who's Getting Degrees

During the past 40 years, the gender distribution of bachelor's degrees reversed. In 1970, men earned 57 per cent of all degrees; today, women do. This trend leads some to conclude that women are squeezing men out of higher education, and that women's success has led to men's decline. In fact, this zero-sum scenario is incorrect: the college-going rates for both men and women have increased substantially. Both genders are far more likely to graduate from college now than at any previous point in time. Women's increasing graduation rate isn't due to a decrease in the number of graduating male students, but to the fact that women's increases occurred faster than men's. Particularly between 1970 and 1990, as employment opportunities for women expanded, their college graduation rates grew more rapidly than did those of men.

The rates of growth for men and women have now equalized. Over the past decade, the number of degrees earned by both men and women actually increased by the identical rate of 38 per cent. The U.S. Department of Education predicts that over the course of the next decade women's share of bachelor's degrees will rise by only one percentage point, to 58 per cent of all degrees. In looking at these figures, we see that women's successes did not come at the expense of men, and that the gender gap is not growing uncontrollably. It has in fact stabilized, and has held steady for more than 10 years.

To fully assess the gender distribution of bachelor's degrees, we also need to look at what kinds of men and women graduate from college, and whether men and women of different racial, ethnic, and class backgrounds have the same chances of graduating. Among 25- to 29-year-olds, across all racial and ethnic groups, more women than men hold bachelor's degrees. The gap is just over 7 per cent among whites and Hispanics, 6 per cent among blacks, and about 10 per cent for Asians.

But in terms of race and ethnicity, the gaps in college completion far exceed that of gender: 56 per cent of Asians between 25 and 29 years old hold bachelor's degrees, compared to only 39 per cent of whites, 20 per cent of blacks, and nearly 13 per cent of Hispanics. Both white and Asian men are far more likely than black or Hispanic students of either gender to earn a bachelor's degree. These racial gaps are actually larger now than they were in the 1960s: while students from all backgrounds are now more likely to graduate from college, the rates have increased more quickly for whites and Asians.

Social class continues to be the strongest predictor of who will attend and graduate from college—one that far outweighs the effects of either gender, or race and ethnicity. Surveys by the U.S. Department of Education show that 70 per cent of high-school students from wealthy families will enter four-year colleges, compared to only 21 per cent of their peers from low-income families. Gender differences also vary by social class background. According to education policy analyst Jackie King, for the wealthiest students, the gender gap actually favours men. (For families in the highest income quartile, men comprise 52 per cent of college students, compared to 44 per cent in the lowest income quartile, and 47 per cent in the middle two quartiles). Age also plays a role: among adults 25 years and older, women are far more likely than men to return to college for a bachelor's degree. But among those 24 and under, women make up only 55 per cent of all students, and the gender difference among enrolment rates for recent high-school graduates is small (41 per cent of men and 44 per cent of women).

In other words, women's overall advantage in earning college degrees is not shared equally among all women. White women, Asian women, and wealthy women outpace women from other backgrounds. Gender differences are largest among students 25 years and up, Asians, and low-income students. But differences in relation to class, race, and ethnicity greatly overshadow gender gaps in degree attainment.

Not at Caltech

In assessing gender equity in higher education, it's also necessary to take into account where men and women earn their degrees. While more women than men tend to graduate from college, women are disproportionately represented in less competitive institutions. Sociologist Jayne Baker and I found that women earned more than 60 per cent of degrees in the least selective institutions, but only slightly more than half in the most selective institutions. Women's gains have been greatest at institutions with lower standardized test scores and higher acceptance rates, while men and women are roughly on par with each other at elite institutions. Women are also underrepresented at the top science and engineering institutions, like Caltech and MIT. So, while women may be in the majority overall, their integration into higher education has been uneven, and they are more likely to attend lower-status institutions.

Perhaps the most striking disparities are in the choice of college majors. In spite of their overall minority status, men still earn 83 per cent of all degrees in engineering, 82 per cent in computer and information sciences, 70 per cent in philosophy, and 69 per cent in economics. Women, on the other hand, continue to earn the lion's share of degrees in traditionally female-dominated fields: 77 per cent in psychology, 80 per cent in education, and 85 per cent in nursing and other health professions. About a third of all men (or women) would have to change majors in order to achieve gender parity across majors today. This hasn't changed much in the last 25 years. (Through the 1970s and early 1980s, fields moved steadily toward becoming more integrated, but in the mid-1980s, this trend slowed and then stalled, shifting very little since then.)

Sociologists Paula England and Su Li found that most of the decrease in segregation came from the growth of gender-integrated fields, like business, and from the flow of women into previously male-dominated fields. Men are much less likely to move into female-dominated fields. They also found that women's entrance into predominantly male fields discourages later cohorts of men from choosing those fields. Women gain status and pay by entering predominantly male fields, while men lose out when they enter devalued, predominantly female fields of study.

Women and men are ostensibly free to select any field they wish, and they no longer face the blatant kinds of barriers to entry that have historically existed. But, other factors influence students' choices subtly, but powerfully. Sociologist Shelly Correll has done innovative experiments with undergraduate students that demonstrate how cultural beliefs about gender shape individuals' career aspirations. When exposed to the idea that men are better at certain tasks, male participants in the study rated their own abilities higher than the women, even though they were all given the same scores. These subjective assessments of their own competencies then influenced students' interest in related careers. Correll argues that widely shared cultural beliefs about gender and different kinds of competencies (like math and science) bias men's and women's perceptions of their own abilities, and their interest in pursuing these fields. She finds that men assess their own capabilities in math more generously than do women, which then encourages them to go into math and science fields. . . .

After College

Paradoxically, women's success in closing the gender gap in higher education has not closed the gender gaps in the labour market. Men and women still generally work in different kinds of jobs, and women still earn considerably less than men (even with the same levels of education). Occupational segregation remains high and the trend toward narrowing the gender gap in pay has slowed. Currently, young, college-educated, full-time working women can expect to earn only 80 per cent of the salaries of men ($40,000 annually compared to $49,800), a ratio identical to that of 1995. In fact, women with bachelor's degrees earn the same as men with associate degrees. Some of this pay gap can be attributed to students' undergraduate fields of study. Engineering graduates, for example, earn about $55,000 annually in their first year after graduation, while education majors bring home only $30,500. However, even after taking into account fields of study, women still earn less than men.

These pay disparities suggest an economic rationale for women's vigorous pursuit of higher education. Not only do women need to acquire more education in order to earn the same salaries as men, they also receive higher returns on their educational investments. Education scholar Laura Perna has found that even though women's salaries are lower than men's, women enjoy a greater pay-off in graduating from college than men do. In the early years after graduating, a woman with a college degree will earn 55 per cent more than a woman with a high-school degree. For men, that difference is only 17 per cent. What's more, men with only a high-school education earn a third more than women do, and are more likely to find work in traditionally male blue-collar jobs that offer healthcare and other benefits—which are not available in the sales and service jobs typically held by women.

Though men with high-school educations enjoy higher salaries and better benefits than do women, they are also more vulnerable to unemployment. In general, the rates of unemployment are twice as high for high-school graduates as they are for college graduates. They are also slightly higher for men than for women at all educational levels below the bachelor's degree. According to data from a 2010 U.S. Census survey, the unemployment rate for high-school graduates was 11.3 per cent for men versus 9 per cent for women (compared to 4.8 per cent and 4.7 per cent, respectively, for those with at least a bachelor's degree), due in part to the effects of the recent recession on the manufacturing sector.

Along with offering access to better jobs, higher salaries, and less risk of unemployment, going to college offers a host of other advantages. College graduates live longer, healthier lives. They are less likely to smoke, drink too much, or suffer from anxiety, depression, obesity, and a variety of illnesses. They are more likely to vote, to volunteer, and to be civically engaged. Because of this broad array of social and economic benefits, we should be concerned about patterns of underrepresentation for any group.

Incomplete Integration

To some, the fact that women earn 57 per cent of all degrees to men's 43 per cent suggests the gender pendulum has swung too far. They claim that if the ratio still favoured men, there would be widespread protest. But such claims fail to see the full picture: though women earn more degrees than men, the gender integration of higher education is far from complete. Men and women still diverge in the fields of study they choose, their experiences during college, and the kinds of jobs they get after graduating.

In the early 1970s, when men earned 57 per cent of college degrees, women faced exclusion and discrimination in the labour market and earned less than two-thirds of what men earned. Many professions, and most positions of power and authority, were almost completely closed to women. While the ratio of college graduates now favours women, women are not benefiting from more education in ways that men did 40 years ago. In terms of the economic rewards of completing college, women are far from matching men, let alone outpacing them.

By paying exclusive attention to the gender ratio, we tend to overlook much more serious and enduring disparities of social class, race, and ethnicity. This lessens our ability to understand how gender advantages vary across groups. If there is a crisis of access to higher education, it is not so much a gender crisis, as one of race and class. Young black and Hispanic men and men from low-income families are among the most disadvantaged, but women from these groups also lag behind their white, Asian, and middle-class counterparts. Addressing the formidable racial and economic gaps in college access will improve low-income and minority men's chances far more than closing the gender gap would.

The higher proportion of degrees earned by women does not mean that higher education is feminizing, or that men are getting crowded out. It seems that if women hold an advantage in any area, even a relatively slim one, we jump to the conclusion that it indicates a catastrophe for men. In the case of access to college degrees, that's simply not true.

RECOMMENDED RESOURCES

1. England, Paula, and Su Li. "Desegregation Stalled: The Changing Gender Composition of College Majors, 1971–2002," *Gender & Society* (2006), 20: 657–677. Reviews trends in the gender segregation of fields of study and the reasons behind shifts toward integration as well as the stalling of desegregation.

2. Sax, Linda J. *The Gender Gap in College: Maximizing the Developmental Potential of Women and Men* (Jossey-Bass, 2008). Examines the impact of college experiences, peer groups, and faculty on a comprehensive array of student outcomes.
3. U.S. Department of Education, National Center for Education Statistics, Institute of Education Sciences. (Washington DC, various years). *Digest of Education Statistics and The Condition of Education*. Comprehensive compendiums of education statistics, including a wide range of gender, race, ethnicity, and class indicators.

CRITICAL Reading Questions

1. How has the percentage of women and men earning degrees changed? What would you expect the situation to be in 10 years?

2. What is the role of race and ethnicity in the relationship between gender and degrees? Do all ethnic groups have the same gap between men and women in terms of the number of degrees earned?

3. What is the role of social class in the relationship between gender and degrees?

4. Why is it important to assess men's and women's majors when talking about inequality in education? How is this factor related to the types of jobs that men and women perform?

ACTIVITY

Critically Analyzing School Curriculum

Every province and territory in Canada outlines a specific curriculum for each grade in order to standardize what is taught to students across all the schools in the area. These curricula, along with the teaching resources on which they rely, are given to teachers at all levels to help them plan their classes. As we have learned in this chapter, the decisions of what will and will not be taught shape what students learn and their worldview. Consequently, a curriculum is not neutral in its effect on students.

In this activity, we will explore the grade 9/10 curriculum in Ontario. Go to this book's companion website to access this curriculum or search online for your preferred province and grade. Then answer the following questions:

1. What topics and materials are covered that might not have been 50 or 100 years ago?

2. What topics and materials might have been dropped from earlier curricula? What does this difference tell us about the changing ideas of education's role in modern society?

3. How does this curriculum tackle issues of social inequality? Looking at the specific subject areas and the additional resources on the web page, how do the curriculum designers address gender, ethnic, and class inequality?

4. How does this curriculum address the value of multiculturalism in Canadian society? Where are ideas about multiculturalism and diversity included in this curriculum?

5. How does this curriculum deal with other social issues, such as concerns with the environment or the changing importance of technology in society? Where do these concerns appear in the curriculum?

6. How does this curriculum reflect larger changes in society?

Education, Cultural Capital, and Social Capital

One reason that education can perpetuate social inequality, or lead to social mobility, is its relationship to different forms of capital. When we think about capital, we tend to think about economic capital, things that have a monetary or exchange value (see Chapter 3). However, there are other kinds, such as social and cultural capital; these resources can be acquired through the education system and affect one's chance of future success.

Cultural capital is the non-economic social assets that promote social mobility. For example, we can earn degrees, learn a more refined style of speech, or adopt elite social tastes, which can make us appear to belong to a higher social class than the one to which we were born. To Pierre Bourdieu, who developed the concept, cultural capital is essentially the cultural knowledge that we learn over the course of our lives that confers power and status (Bourdieu and Passeron 1973). Cultural capital is comprised of the behaviours, knowledge, and values that indicate your social class. For example, liking the theatre and classical music is considered more sophisticated than liking action movies and heavy metal. Some individuals or families are more likely to possess sophisticated tastes and styles. In addition, this cultural capital is taught and institutionalized in the education system.

Social capital is the collective value of all of one's social networks. Essentially, it is about who you know and the "norms of reciprocity" that develop between people who know one another. Social capital is important because it can provide a wide variety of benefits. For example, having wide social networks can help foster trust among people, provide resources and information, and lead to co-operation. Both cultural and social capital can be acquired through the education system (Bourdieu and Passeron 1990).

An example of social capital in education is the Greek system. Rushing a fraternity or sorority is a very common social activity in American, and in some Canadian, schools. The networks afforded through membership in these communities help individuals expand their social capital and gain access to social circles, which can influence their future success in work and other realms. For example, 85 per cent of Fortune 500 CEOs have been in the Greek system, and the majority of US presidents were in fraternities (University of Missouri 2013).

According to Marx and other conflict theorists, the education system reflects the interests and experiences of the dominant class in society. Children from the dominant class in a society tend to do better in the education system because they enter that system already having certain types of cultural and social skills that facilitate their progress. Children from the working class, however, must learn these skills in schools, which can slow down their progress in other areas of the curriculum. Marx also argued that, even if children from the working class can learn the social and cultural skills that upper-class children naturally possess, these skills will never be natural for them. Teachers, principals, employers, and other children detect who innately possesses these social and cultural skills and tend to reward those students, perhaps by streaming them into advance placement classes or other special educational opportunities.

The Consequences of Degrees

A person's level of education has many serious and important consequences. We have already indicated two of the most important effects: earning more money and being less likely to fall into unemployment. According to the *US News and World Report*, individuals with bachelor's degrees earn about $2.27 million over the course of their lifetime (Burnsed 2011). This amount is considerably more than that of individuals with some college education ($1.55 million) or a high-school diploma ($1.30 million). People who earn master's, doctoral, and professional degrees earn, on average, $2.67 million, $3.25 million, and $3.65 million, respectively (see Figure 9.4).

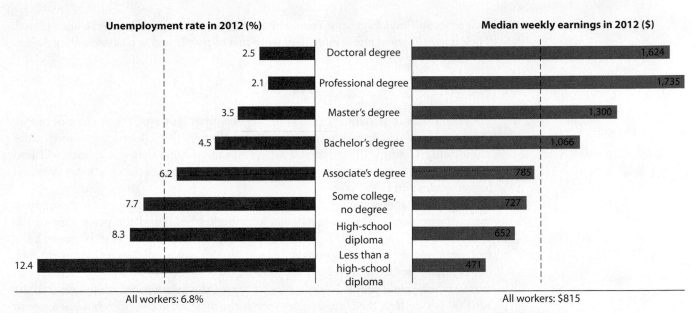

Unemployment rate in 2012 (%)		Median weekly earnings in 2012 ($)
2.5	Doctoral degree	1,624
2.1	Professional degree	1,735
3.5	Master's degree	1,300
4.5	Bachelor's degree	1,066
6.2	Associate's degree	785
7.7	Some college, no degree	727
8.3	High-school diploma	652
12.4	Less than a high-school diploma	471
All workers: 6.8%		All workers: $815

FIGURE 9.4 Earnings and unemployment rates by education attainment, United States

SOURCE: Bureau of Labor Statistics. 2015 (2 April). "Employment Projections." www.bls.gov/emp/ep_chart_001.htm.

The report showed, however, that the benefit of earning a degree is not equally distributed across groups. For example, whites earn more than any other ethnic group. The only exception is that Asian Americans with master's, doctoral, or professional degrees are able to out-earn white workers with degrees of the same level. Latinos and African Americans need to earn a master's degree in order to make the same amount of money over the course of their lives as a white worker with a bachelor's degree (i.e. complete two more years of post-secondary education) (Burnsed 2011).

Women are also less likely to reap the rewards of degrees, just as Mullen described in her article earlier in this chapter. The *US News Report* finds that, on average, women have to earn a PhD to make more money over their lifetimes ($2.86 million) than men with only a bachelor's degree ($2.60 million; Burnsed 2011). In summary, while university and college degrees clearly increase the lifetime earnings of all groups, not all individuals are equally able to turn their degrees into earnings.

Another benefit of education is that it can protect individuals from unemployment. Figure 9.5 shows the unemployment rate for 25–64 year olds in OECD countries based on

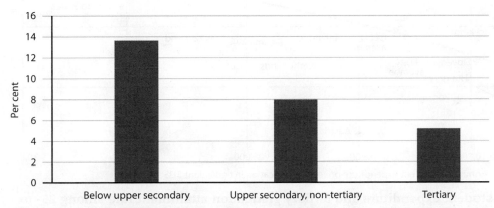

FIGURE 9.5 Percentage of 25- to 64-year-olds who are unemployed, by education level, OECD average, 2013

SOURCE: Data from OECD. 2015. "Unemployment rates by education level (indicator)." https://data.oecd.org/unemp/unemployment-rates-by-education-level.htm.

their education level. In general, those with less education are more likely to be unemployed. Their unemployment rate is more than twice that of people with a post-secondary degree.

Education around the World

Education is an important institution in every country. However, the amount of money countries spend on the education system and the results from these expenditures differ significantly. Countries that spend a lot on education hope that this money will lead to better educational outcomes, such as higher achievement on international tests and higher graduation rates.

Figure 9.6 shows the relationship between the amounts of money a government spends on tertiary education (education after high school) and the percentage of the population ages 25–34 with a post-secondary degree. You can see that, in general, the more money a government spends on education, the higher its degree attainment rate. For example, Sweden and Norway spend more than Mexico and Italy on education and more of their young people have degrees. However, this relationship is not universal. At $26,000 per student, the United States spends the most of all countries but has a rate of completion similar to Chile, which spends only about $6,000 per student.

Another exception is Korea, a remarkable success story in educational attainment. The country spends relatively little per student but has one of the highest rates of education completion in the world: 64 per cent of Koreans between the ages of 25 and 34 have a university or college degree (van Damme 2013). The Korean government spent 7.6 per cent of its 2010 GDP on education, a much higher level of spending than the OECD average of 6.3 per cent. Higher education in Korea received 2.6 per cent of this amount, again above the OECD average (1.6 per cent). Yet student expenditures are quite low because the Korean education system serves a very sizeable population.

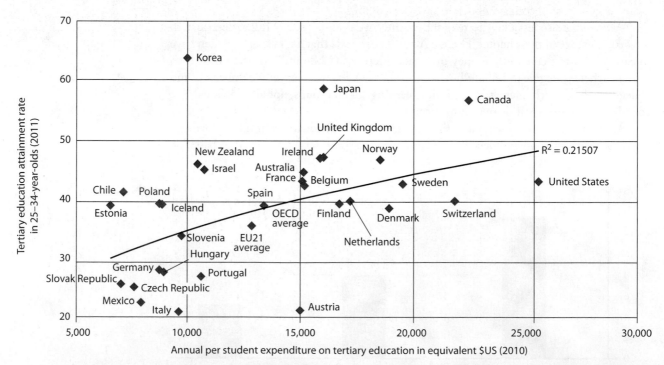

FIGURE 9.6 Annual per student expenditure and tertiary graduation attainment rate among 25- to 34-year-olds

SOURCE: OECD. 2013 (October). "How Can Countries Best Produce a Highly-qualified Young Labour Force?", *Education Indicators in Focus*, No. 16, OECD Publishing. http://dx.doi.org/10.1787/5k3wb8khp3zn-en

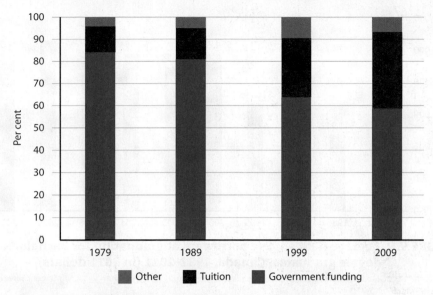

FIGURE 9.7 University operating revenue by source, Canada

SOURCE: Ivanova, Iglika. 2012 (29 May). "Seven Reasons Why You Should Support a Move to Low Tuition Fees for Higher Education." Policy Note. Statistics Canada and CAUBO. www.policynote.ca/seven-reasons-why-you-should-support-a-move -to-low-tuition-fees-for-higher-education/.

Most universities in Canada are publicly funded and operated. The federal government is the majority funder, but its share is decreasing. As shown in Figure 9.7, government funding accounted for 84 per cent of universities' operating budget in 1979. Today, that amount has declined to about 58 per cent. To return to the funding levels of the early 1980s, the government would have to invest an additional $4 billion in post-secondary education.

Most of the remaining money used to run post-secondary education in Canada comes from higher tuition fees. In 1979, about 10 per cent of university budgets came from tuition fees; the number is currently 35 per cent. The average tuition fee in Canada was about $1,100 per year in 1991. Now, average tuition is about $5,300 a year (see Figure 9.8). As a result, students leaving university have larger debts than ever before. As shown in Figure 9.9, the average student debt has increased by 300 per cent between 1982 and 2011.

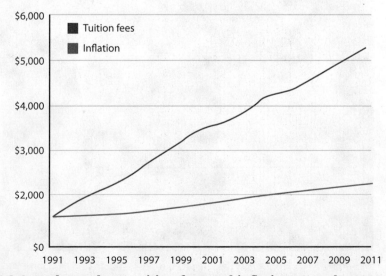

FIGURE 9.8 Undergraduate tuition fees and inflation, Canada, 1991–2011

SOURCE: CNW. 2011 (16 September). "Tuition Fees Increase in Most Provinces: Students Call for Federal Leadership on Education." www.newswire.ca/en/story/842221/tuition-fees-increase-in-most-provinces-students-call-for-federal-leadership-on-education.

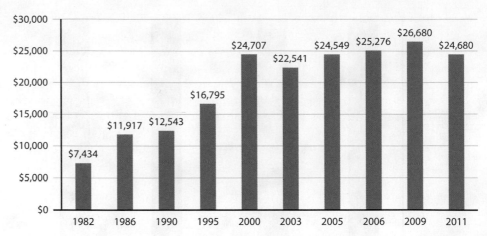

FIGURE 9.9 **Average debt among borrowers at graduation for bachelor's degree graduates, Canada, 1982–2011 (in 2011 dollars)**

SOURCE: Statistics Canada's National Graduate Surveys, Canadian University Survey Consortium Graduating Student Surveys. http://higheredstrategy.com/a-closer-look-at-student-debt-part-1/.

The Corporatization of Universities

With reduced government funding and the unpopularity of increasing tuition fees, creating corporate partnerships and running universities with business or management techniques have become more popular. This **corporatization** can take the form of naming campus buildings after major donors or corporate sponsors (e.g. the Clayton H. Riddell Faculty of Environment, Earth, and Resources at the University of Manitoba; the K.C. Irving Chemistry Centre at the University of Prince Edward Island; and the Wayne & William White Engineering Design Centre at the University of British Columbia). In many cases,

In 2007, Ryerson University renamed its business school the Ted Rogers School of Management, after receiving a $15 million donation from the media mogul and his wife, Loretta.

Rising tuition and debt also occurs in other countries, including the United States and UK. The US government drastically cut funding for public universities and colleges between 1988 and 1998. As a result, tuition fees are now 50 per cent of the average income of a middle-class family (Canadian Federation of Students 2013).

The history of tuition fees in Germany is quite different. Traditionally, university tuition was free in Germany. When the governments of 7 out of Germany's 16 states began to charge fees, there was much opposition, including large protests held by students and unions. By 2012, all but two states had returned to the previous system of free higher education (Canadian Federation of Students 2013).

Canadian students concerned with rising tuition fees and student debt have followed this success and have started the Education is a Right campaign. This campaign pushes for increased funding for education and reduced tuition fees. It involves a range of tactics, including an annual student protest in February. (For more information on this movement, see http://cfs-fcee.ca/take-action/education-is-a-right/.)

Quebec students have been particularly active in fighting to stop tuition fee increases. In 2012, students held a series of large protests in response to the province's plan to raise university tuition from $2,168 to $3,793 over six years (Venton-Rublee and Wray 2013). These protests, which attracted both students and others who were concerned about cuts

these donations are from wealthy alumni or successful community members who simply want to support higher education. However, these relationships become controversial when donors seek to influence the research or teaching at the institution.

In 2013, GEO Group, a private, for-profit prison company, paid Florida Atlantic University $6 million over 12 years in return for having the school's stadium named after it (Rush 2013). This deal led to protests on campus and across the United States. Students argued that the school should not take money from a company that runs prisons and that such naming contracts can create problematic relationships that might taint the values and identity of the university and its students.

Universities also make money by signing deals with companies that give the latter a monopoly on selling products on campus. For example, perhaps you can buy only Coca-Cola or Pepsi products at your school. It is not difficult to imagine why a company would want to sign such a deal with a university—it exposes its products to thousands of captive students who are making consumer choices that will continue throughout their lives. For example, if you become a Coke drinker early, you will probably remain one for life!

Exclusive deals between universities and companies gained popularity in the 1990s. Twenty-one Canadian and many American universities have signed such exclusive—and very lucrative—deals with the cola giants. In its 11-year contract with Coca-Cola, McGill University received a small fee every time a Coke product was sold on its campus. While the exact amount could not be revealed, the estimated revenue was over $1.5 million, money that was used to renovate the student union building (Chester 1999). Other universities have earned even more. The University of Missouri received $16 million for its 10-year deal with Coke in 1995; the University of Minnesota was given $28 million in its 10-year contract with Coke the same year; and the University of Maryland received $58 million from Pepsi in a 15-year deal.

Have you noticed any of these arrangements at your university or college? What do you think of such agreements? What are the benefits and drawbacks to accepting money from large corporations?

PHOTO 9.4 At this Montreal demonstration against tuition hikes, many people wore red or displayed a red square, the symbol of the protest. Have there been protests against tuition fee increases on your campus?

to social programs more generally, were successful. Following an election, the new government stopped the planned increase in tuition fees.

Summary

The education system is one of modern society's central institutions and permeates many aspects of our day-to-day lives. This system works to socialize, select, and legitimize knowledge in our society. It is clear that not all individuals have equal access to or perform equally well in the education system. In this chapter, we have critically examined the role of this system in perpetuating, and potentially alleviating, social inequality, including the role of cultural and social capital in this relationship. We also discussed education around the world, comparing funding in various countries. The issues of rising tuition fees and the corporatization of the university illustrate the widespread changes occurring in education in Canada and around the world, changes that have important implications for educational outcomes across groups.

Key Terms

corporatization 270
credentialing 252
cultural capital 266
curriculum 252
defensive credentialing 257
different expectations 257
differential association 257
differential preparation 258
gender reversal in educational
   outcomes 260
hidden curriculum 252

human capital model 257
latent functions 249
legitimation 249
manifest functions 249
schooled society 248
selection 249
self-fulfilling prophecy 258
social capital 266
socialization (function of
   education) 249
streaming (tracking) 258

For Further Reading

Bourdieu, Pierre, and Jean Claude Passeron. 1990. *Reproduction in Education, Society and Culture*, 2nd edn. London: Sage.

Coleman, James. 1990. *Foundations of Social Theory*. Cambridge, CA: Harvard University Press.

Collins, Randall. 1979. *The Credential Society: An Historical Sociology of Education and Stratification*. New York: Academic Press.

Davies, Scott, and Neil Guppy. 2014. *The Schooled Society: An Introduction to the Sociology of Education*, 3rd edn. Don Mills, ON: Oxford University Press.

Durkheim, Émile. 1956. *Education and Sociology*. Glencoe, IL: Free Press.

10 Work and Rationalization

CHAPTER OUTLINE

Introduction

Sociologists have long been interested in the changing nature of society. Max Weber, in particular, focused on the rise of rationality in society and the character of modernized, bureaucratic, secularized Western society, which focuses on scientific understanding and processes oriented toward rational goals. He described how this new world contrasts with earlier faith-based societies, where the world seemed unknowable and mystical. This chapter will discuss this process of rationalization in society. It will also look at the role of work and occupations in society and how they are becoming increasingly rationalized. We will examine a number of key changes in the Canadian labour market, including the rise of scientific management, the rise in precarious employment, and the prevalence of emotional labour.

The Rationalized World

Weber (1965) argued that, prior to the Enlightenment (a period in Europe in the late seventeenth and eighteenth centuries), we lived in an enchanted world. People had very little understanding of why natural events occurred—at this time, they still believed that the sun rotated around the earth. They saw the world as magical and invested with other worldly forces. They explained droughts and plagues by claiming that the gods were angry or Mother Nature was out of sync. The only way to "solve" these events was to appease the gods, such as by performing a ritual or sacrifice.

The Enlightenment, or age of reason, was an exciting period in Europe—people came to embrace new ideas of science, logic, and reasoning, as well as the use of evidence to make sense of the world. This era came with new ways of understanding the natural and social worlds. For example, people used to think that things fall to the ground because it was simply in their nature to do so. As the seventh-century Indian mathematician Brahmagupta stated, "Bodies fall towards the earth as it is in the nature of the earth to attract bodies, just as it is in the nature of water to flow." Through experiments and logic, people discovered gravity.

The age of reason also marked a decline in religion's role in society. Instead of always looking to religious institutions and leaders to make sense of the world, people increasingly looked to science. For example, while the Church tells us to have faith that humans were created in God's image because that is what the Bible says, Darwin demonstrated that humans have evolved over millennium through the process of natural selection. This new way of seeing the world—through science and the principles of rationality—weakened the influence of religious authorities. Weber called this process the **disenchantment of the world**.

Rationalization is a way of solving problems that is based on four main factors: predictability, calculability, efficiency, and control. Predictability means that things can be repeated with the expectation of the same results. When a scientist does an experiment, for example, she will replicate it many times to make sure that the findings are correct. Calculability focuses on things that can be counted and quantified. In modern society, we tend to like to measure things with numbers and to compare things numerically—we assess athletic ability by comparing performance statistics and academic ability by comparing grades, even though there are other, less tangible ways to measure them. Rationality is also based on efficiency, the best means to a given end. For instance, it would seem nonsensical to drive from Vancouver to Toronto through Mexico. The route might be more enjoyable, but it is not efficient because it would take longer and therefore does not fit with our modern principles of rationality. Finally, rationality is based on ideas of control and an enhanced certainty of outcomes, such as knowing exactly how long a trip will take, thus providing a basis for choosing how to undertake the task.

Rationalization has changed many aspects of society and permeates modern life. For example, the economy is run on its principles. The rise of factories and assembly lines, which we will discuss later in this chapter, was an important part of this process. Living in such a world has many benefits. Most important, rational systems are very efficient. Rationalization and the rise of science help us solve certain problems. When we thought that the plague was caused by bad humours or evil natures, we were ill-equipped to stop it. When we realized that vermin living in the city caused the plague, we could address the problem by improving sanitation. The age of reason allowed us to make sense of the world and afforded us some control over it.

In this rationalized world, we tend to live longer and healthier lives, partly because of our understanding of science. However, rationalization is not without its downsides. Weber (1965) argued that the process of disenchantment is a process of disillusionment. As the world becomes less enchanted and less magical, it also becomes less meaningful for people. Part of what makes us human is our ability to be creative, emotional, and spontaneous. None of these qualities makes sense in a rationalized world. Creativity is absent from mass-produced consumer goods, and the worker is unable to express individuality or make unique additions to the product. In this way, the rise of rationality might be robbing us of our very humanity.

The prototype of rationalization in modern society is the **bureaucracy**. The word originated in 1789 and is based on the French root *bureau*, which means "office or desk," and the Greek root *kratia*, which means "power or rule." Bureaucracy, then, is the rule of the office or desk and is essentially a machine made of humans. Bureaucracies rose to prominence as an organizational form in the twentieth century. Examples in modern society include non-profit organizations (such as your university, Big Brothers and Big Sisters of Canada, and the United Nations) and for-profit companies (such as Starbucks, Microsoft, or Apple).

According to Weber (1965), bureaucracies have six core features:

1. They are based on hierarchically organized "offices."
2. They have a vertical chain of command. Your university probably has professors who report to a chair who reports to the dean.

PHOTO 10.1 The UN has a clear, hierarchical division of labour and written rules of organization. What bureaucratic features does your university or college display?

3. They have a clear, formal division of labour. In your university, there are people who teach classes (professors), those who run the library (librarians), and those who clean and maintain the buildings (janitors and maintenance staff). The university could not run without these and many other individuals. However, they do not switch from one task to the other—there is a clear separation of roles, with different people doing different tasks.

4. They are dominated by technical qualifications. Specific degrees and qualifications are needed to perform each job.

5. They have impersonal decision-making. All prospective students submit the same application that is judged without knowing the student's name or identifying features.

6. They are staffed by full-time, salaried employees.

A prototypical bureaucracy is McDonalds, which has more than 30,000 restaurants in 118 countries (James 2009). In the following article, George Ritzer applies Weber's ideas about the rise of rationality to the emergence of fast-food restaurants and discusses how these establishments have affected society (a process he calls **McDonaldization**).

READING

The "McDonaldization" of Society

George Ritzer

A wide-ranging process of *rationalization* is occurring across American society and is having an increasingly powerful impact in many other parts of the world. It encompasses such disparate phenomena as fast-food restaurants, TV dinners, packaged tours, industrial robots, plea bargaining, and open-heart surgery on an assembly-line basis. As widespread and as important as these developments are, it is clear that we have barely begun a process that promises even more extraordinary changes (e.g. genetic engineering) in the years to come. We can think of rationalization as a historical process and rationality as the end result of that development. As an historical process, rationalization has distinctive roots in the Western world. Writing in the late nineteenth and early twentieth centuries, the great German sociologist Max Weber saw his society as the centre of the ongoing process of rationalization and the bureaucracy as its paradigm case. The model of rationalization, at least in contemporary America, is no longer the bureaucracy, but might be better thought of as the fast-food restaurant. As a result, our concern here is with what might be termed the "McDonaldization of Society." While the fast-food restaurant is not the ultimate expression of rationality, it is the current exemplar for future developments in rationalization.

A society characterized by rationality is one which emphasizes *efficiency, predictability, calculability, substitution of non-human for human technology*, and *control over uncertainty*. In discussing the various dimensions of rationalization, we will be little concerned with the gains already made, and yet to be realized, by greater rationalization. These advantages are widely discussed in schools and in the mass media. In fact, we are in danger of being seduced by the innumerable advantages already offered, and promised In the future, by rationalization. The glitter of these accomplishments and promises has served to distract most people from the grave dangers posed by progressive rationalization. In other words, we are ultimately concerned here with the irrational consequences that often flow from rational systems. Thus, the second major theme of this essay might be termed "the irrationality of rationality."

In spite of the emphasis here on the problems posed by rationalization, this will not be one of those pleas for a return to a less rationalized way of life. Although there is certainly room for less rationalized pockets in a rational society, in most cases we cannot, and should not, try to reverse the process of rationalization. In our rush to critique rationalization we cannot ignore its many advantages (McDonald's does offer a lot of tasty food at relatively low cost). Furthermore, we should not romanticize the "noble" life of the pre-rational society with its many problems and disadvantages. We would not, in most cases, want to recreate a life beset by these problems, even if it was possible to do so. Instead, what we need [to] do is gain a better understanding of the process of rationalization so that we can come to exercise more and better control over it. . . .

Efficiency

The process of rationalization leads to a society in which a great deal of emphasis is placed on finding the best or optimum means to any given end. Whatever a group of people define as an end, and everything they so define, is to be pursued by attempting to find the best means to achieve the end. . . .

The modern American family, often with two wage earners, has little time to prepare elaborate meals. For the relatively few who still cook such meals, there is likely to be great reliance on cookbooks that make cooking from scratch much more efficient. However, such cooking is relatively rare today. Most families take as their objective quickly and easily prepared meals. To this end, much use is made of pre-packaged meals and frozen TV dinners.

For many modern families, the TV dinner is no longer efficient enough. To many people, eating out, particularly in a fast-food restaurant, is a far more efficient way of obtaining their meals. Fast-food restaurants capitalize on this by being organized so that diners are fed as efficiently as possible. They offer a limited, simple menu that can be cooked and served in an assembly-line fashion. The latest development in fast-food restaurants, the addition of drive-through windows, constitutes an effort to increase still further the efficiency of the dining experience. The family now can simply drive through, pick up its order, and eat it while driving to the next, undoubtedly efficiently organized, activity. The success of the fast-food restaurant has come full circle with frozen-food manufacturers now touting products for the home modelled after those served in fast-food restaurants.

Increasingly, efficiently organized food production and distribution systems lie at the base of the ability of people to eat their food efficiently at home, in the fast-food restaurant, or in their cars. Farms, groves, ranches, slaughterhouses, warehouses, transportation systems, and retailers are all oriented toward increasing efficiency. A notable example is chicken production where they are mass bred, force fed (often with many chemicals), slaughtered on an assembly line, iced or fast frozen and shipped to all parts of the country. Some may argue that such chickens do not taste as good as the fresh-killed, local variety, but their complaints are likely to be drowned in a flood of mass-produced chickens. . . .

The fast-food restaurant is certainly not the only place one can spend money. The centre of spending is now the modern shopping centre and the supermarket. These are organized in a highly efficient manner in order to aid business. Supermarkets have grown even more efficient recently with the advent of computer scanning devices which expedite the checkout process and, at the same time, make the work of stockpeople more efficient by eliminating the need to stamp prices on the items.

When our shoppers return home (in efficiently produced cars and on efficiently built roads) they are likely to enter apartments or suburban tract houses which have been efficiently constructed. Among other things, this means there is little or nothing to distinguish one apartment or house from many others. In constructing such dwellings, esthetic elements like trees or hills are likely to be levelled if they stand in the way of efficient construction. . . .

If the family is unhappy with the efficiency that pervades virtually every facet of daily life, it might seek relief in leisure-time activities that it may assume to be immune from the process of rationalization. However, even in these areas, the principles of efficiency are omnipresent. International travel is affordable for many only through organized tours that efficiently transport large groups of tourists from one site to another. The modern amusement park is often little more than a vast, elaborate people-moving machine designed to transport people through the park and its various attractions as efficiently as possible. Campgrounds, trout farms, sporting events, and night clubs are other examples of entertainment that have grown increasingly efficient. . . .

Predictability

A second component of rationalization involves the effort to ensure predictability from one place to another. In a rational society, people want to know what to expect when they enter a given setting or acquire some sort of commodity. They neither want nor expect surprises. They want to know that if they journey to another locale, the setting they enter or the commodity they buy will be essentially the same as the setting they entered or product they purchased earlier. Furthermore, people want to be sure that what they encounter is much like what they encountered at earlier times. In order to ensure predictability over time and place a rational society must emphasize such things as discipline, order, systemization, formalization, routine, consistency, and methodical operation. . . .

Fast-food restaurants rank very high on the dimension of predictability. In order to help ensure consistency, the fast-food restaurant offers only a limited menu. Predictable end-products are made possible by the use of similar raw materials, technologies, and preparation and serving techniques. Not only the food is predictable; the physical structures, the logo, the "ambience," and even the personnel are as well.

The food that is shipped to our homes and our fast-food restaurants is itself affected by the process of increasing predictability. Thus our favourite white bread is indistinguishable from one place to another. In fact, food producers have made great efforts to ensure such predictability. . . .

Other leisure-time activities have grown similarly predictable. Camping in the wild is loaded with uncertainties—bugs, bears, rain, cold, and the like. To make camping more predictable, organized grounds have sprung up around the country. Gone are many of the elements of unpredictability replaced by RVs, paved over parking lots, sanitized campsites, fences, and enclosed camp centres that provide laundry and food services, recreational activities, television, and video games. Sporting events, too, have in a variety of ways been made more predictable. The use of artificial turf in baseball makes for a more predictable bounce of a ball. . . .

Calculability or Quantity Rather than Quality

It could easily be argued that the emphasis on quantifiable measures, on things that can be counted, is *the* most defining characteristic of a rational society. Quality is notoriously difficult to evaluate. How do we assess the quality of a hamburger, or a physician, or a student? Instead of even trying, in an increasing number of cases, a rational society seeks to develop a series of quantifiable measures that it takes as surrogates for quality. . . .

. . . One of the most obvious examples in the university is the emphasis given to grades and cumulative grade point averages. With less and less contact between professor and student, there is little real effort to assess the quality of what students know, let alone the quality of their overall abilities. Instead, the sole measure of the quality of most college students is their grade in a given course and their grade point averages. Another blatant example is the emphasis on a variety of uniform exams such as SATs and GREs in which the essence of an applicant is reduced to a few simple scores and percentiles.

Within the educational institution, the importance of grades is well known, but somewhat less known is the way quantifiable factors have become an essential part of the process of evaluating college professors. For example, teaching ability is very hard to evaluate. Administrators have difficulty assessing teaching quality and thus substitute quantitative scores. Of course each score involves qualitative judgments, but this is conveniently ignored. Student opinion polls are taken and the scores are summed, averaged, and compared. Those who score well are deemed good teachers while those who don't are seen as poor teachers. There are many problems involved in relying on these scores such as the fact that easy teachers in "gut" courses may well obtain high ratings while rigorous teachers of difficult courses are likely to score poorly. . . .

Sports in general, and baseball in particular, are dominated by an emphasis on numbers. However, in sports there is a closer relationship between quantity and quality than in many other areas of life. The earned run average of a pitcher or the batting average of a batter are fairly good measures of the quality of their play. But even here a number of intangible qualities of play do not show up. For example, a player may be very valuable, even though his statistics are not particularly good, for his ability to make a clutch play, inspire his teammates, or be a leader. . . .

Politics offers a number of interesting examples of the substitution of quantitative for qualitative measures. Presidential candidates are obsessed by their ratings in the polls and often adjust what they say or do to what the pollsters tell them is likely to increase their ratings. Even sitting presidents (and other politicians) are highly attuned to the polls. The emphasis often seems to be on their impact on the polls of taking a specific political position rather than the qualities of that position. . . .

Substitution of Non-Human Technology

In spite of Herculean efforts, there are important limits to the ability to rationalize what human beings think and do. Seemingly no matter what one does, people still retain at least the ultimate capacity to think and act In a variety of unanticipated ways. Thus, in spite of great efforts to make human behaviour more efficient, more predictable, more calculable, people continue to act in unforeseen ways. People continue to make home cooked meals from scratch, to camp in tents in the wild, to eat in old-fashioned diners, and to sabotage the assembly lines. Because of these realities, there is great interest among those who foster increasing rationality in using rational technologies to limit individual independence and ultimately to replace human beings with machines and other technologies that lack the ability to think and act in unpredictable ways.

McDonald's does not yet have robots to serve us food, but it does have teenagers whose ability to act autonomously is almost completely eliminated by techniques, procedures, routines, and machines. There are numerous examples of this including rules which prescribe all the things a counterperson should do in dealing with a customer as well as a large variety of technologies which determine the actions of workers such as drink dispensers which shut themselves off when the cup is full; buzzers, lights, and bells which indicate when food (e.g. French fries) is done; and cash registers which have the prices of each item programmed in. One of the latest attempts to constrain individual action is Denny's use of pre-measured packages of dehydrated food that are "cooked" simply by putting them under the hot water tap. Because of such tools and machines, as well as the elaborate rules dictating worker behaviour, people often feel like they are dealing with human robots when they relate to the personnel of a fast-food restaurant. When human robots are found, mechanical robots cannot be far behind. Once people are reduced to a few robot-like actions, it is a relatively easy step to replace them with mechanical robots. Thus Burgerworld is reportedly opening a prototypical restaurant in which mechanical robots serve the food.

Much of the recent history of work, especially manual work, is a history of efforts to replace human technology with non-human technology. Scientific management was oriented to the development of an elaborate and rigid set of rules about how jobs were to be done. The workers were to blindly and obediently follow those rules and not to do the work the way they saw fit. The various skills needed to perform a task were carefully delineated and broken down into a series of routine steps that could be taught to all workers. The skills, in other words, were built into the routines rather than belonging to skilled craftspersons. Similar points can be made about the assembly line which is basically a set of non-human technologies that have the needed steps and skills built into them. The human worker is reduced to performing a limited number of simple, repetitive operations. However, the control of this technology over the individual worker is so great and omnipresent that individual workers have reacted negatively manifesting such things as tardiness, absenteeism, turnover, and even sabotage. We are now witnessing a new stage in this technological development with automated processes now totally replacing many workers with robots. With the coming of robots we have reached the ultimate stage in the replacement of human with non-human technology. . . .

Control

This leads us to the fifth major dimension of rationalization—control. Rational systems are oriented toward, and structured to expedite, control in a variety of senses. At the most general level, we can say that rational systems are set up to allow for greater control over the uncertainties of life—birth, death, food production and distribution, housing, religious salvation, and many, many others. More specifically, rational systems are oriented to gaining greater control over the major source of uncertainty in social life—other people. Among other things, this means control over subordinates by superiors and control of clients and customers by workers. . . .

At a more specific level, the rationalization of food preparation and serving at McDonald's gives it great control over its employees. The automobile assembly line has a similar impact. In fact, the vast majority of the structures of a rational society exert extraordinary control over the people who labour in them. But because of the limits that still exist on the degree of control that rational structures can exercise over individuals, many rationalizing employers are driven to seek to more fully rationalize their operations and totally eliminate the worker. The result is an automated, robot-like technology over which, barring some *2001* rebellion, there is almost total control.

In addition to control over employees, rational systems are also interested in controlling the customer/clients they serve. For example, the fast-food restaurant with its counter, the absence of waiters and waitresses, the limited seating, and the drive-through windows all tend to lead customers to do certain things and not to do others.

Irrationality of Rationality

Although not an inherent part of rationalization, the *irrationality of rationality* is a seemingly inevitable by-product of the process. We can think of the irrationality of rationality in several ways. At the most general level it can simply be seen as an overarching label for all the negative effects of rationalization. More specifically, it can be seen as the opposite of rationality, at least in some of its senses. For example, there are the inefficiencies and unpredictabilities that are often produced by seemingly rational systems. Thus, although bureaucracies are constructed to bring about greater efficiency in organizational work, the fact is that there are notorious inefficiencies such as the "red tape" associated with the operation of most bureaucracies. Or, take the example of the arms race in which a focus on quantifiable aspects of nuclear weapons may well have made the occurrence of nuclear war more, rather than less, unpredictable.

Of greatest importance, however, is the variety of negative effects that rational systems have on the individuals who live, work, and are served by them. We might say that *rational systems are not reasonable systems*. As we've already discussed, rationality brings with it great dehumanization as people are reduced to acting like robots. Among the dehumanizing aspects of a rational society are large lecture classes, computer letters, pray TV, work on the automobile assembly line, and dining at a fast-food restaurant. Rationalization also tends to bring with it disenchantment leaving much of our lives without any mystery or excitement. Production by a band craftsman is far more mysterious than an assembly-line technology where each worker does a single, very limited operation. Camping in an RV tends to suffer in comparison to the joys to be derived from camping in the wild. Overall a fully rational society would be a very bleak and uninteresting place.

In addition to being dehumanizing and disenchanting many rational systems which are supposedly constructed to help people, in the end often have very negative effects. Thus to produce massive amounts of food, producers are driven to rationalize food production in a number of ways including the use of more and more pesticides and artificial ingredients. While such rational technologies are capable of producing a lot of food, they often produce foods that are not as nourishing as their natural counterparts and, in some cases, include chemicals that may be harmful, dangerous, and even fatal. McDonald's seemingly rational way of feeding people quickly and cheaply has had many unforeseen and irrational consequences such as weight gain because of the highly caloric nature of the food, increased cholesterol levels, heightened blood pressure as a result of the high salt content of the food, and it has played a key role in the destruction of the family meal and perhaps ultimately the nuclear family....

1. How do McDonalds and other fast-food restaurants embody the ideas of rationalization?
2. What are the benefits of McDonaldization?
3. What are the costs of McDonaldization?
4. Ritzer outlines many other examples of things that have become "McDonaldized" in modern society, including camping, education, work, politics, and television. Take one of these examples and outline how it has become more efficient, predictable, calculable, and controlled.

CRITICAL
Reading
Questions

Undoubtedly, the process of rationalization occurs in modern society. As Ritzer notes, we cannot and should not try to stop it. There are many important benefits to rationalization. It allows us to produce a wider range of goods and services and to make them available to a much larger portion of the population. These goods are convenient and cheaper alternatives to higher-priced customized goods. Rationalization also allows us to create goods of uniform quality and to provide a sense of familiarity and stability for the consumer.

Does this mean that everything in modern society is rationalized or McDonaldized? Ritzer (2011) argues that two main types of organizations are not. Ones that are traceable to an earlier "premodern" age, such as independent corner stores or lemonade stands (unless they are from pre-packaged stand kits available at Walmart), are not McDonaldized. Moreover, some businesses are in direct opposition to McDonaldized companies. People who do not want to stay at a Holiday Inn or other chain hotel can stay at a bed and breakfast, where they get personalized attention and a homemade breakfast from a friendly proprietor. If you do not want to go to the rationalized Tim Hortons or Starbucks, you can go to an independent coffee shop.

Despite the existence of some non-rationalized parts of society, the general trend is toward increasing rationalization. Ritzer highlights how this can create what Weber referred to as the **irrationality of rationality**. On a general level, the irrationality of rationality is simply that rationalized systems can create negative outcomes. For example, the rationalized education system, in which you have a student number and are judged based on your grade point average, can be alienating and frustrating. While it may be "fairer" to give each student a standardized test, doing so ignores a student's individuality. It is also irrational to think that each student understands the material in the same way.

The irrationality of rationality can also be seen in the fact that rationalized systems are sometimes unreasonable, which leads to negative effects. As previously mentioned, bureaucracies involve a lot of red tape (an excessive adherence to formal rules that hinders the functioning of organizations). Anyone who has filled out student loan forms has had first-hand experience with this phenomenon. If you have ever worked on a committee such as student council, think of the issues (such as decorations for a dance) that were long debated and went through an unnecessarily tedious approval process that was disproportionate to its significance.

Returning to Ritzer's main example, it is easy to see that the rationalized system of McDonald's has negative consequences. For example, McDonald's (and other fast-food restaurants) produces huge amounts of waste, which is bad for the environment. It also produces food which, although cheap and plentiful, leads to obesity and other health problems.

The 2004 documentary *Super Size Me* focuses on the negative health effects of McDonald's. The film follows Morgan Spurlock as he eats only McDonald's food for 30 days and experiences drastic changes to his physical and psychological well-being. Spurlock, then 32 years old, consumed an average of 5,000 calories a day. He gained 24.5 pounds, increased his body mass by 13 per cent, and experienced mood swings and sexual dysfunction. It took only 30 days to gain the weight but 14 months to lose it.

One of the goals of McDonaldization is to make consumers' lives easier, yet rationalized systems also get consumers to do more of the labour originally assigned to workers. This practice allows corporations to save money on labour. For example, as we discussed in Chapter 4, consumers now pump their own gas, check out their own groceries, and do online banking, all under the façade that it is more efficient to do so.

Another potential drawback of rationalization and McDonaldization is that it produces a focus on efficiency and calculability that spreads to all aspects of our lives. In a rationalized world, we are encouraged to see everything through the lens of rationalization. For example, we come to see things that previously were viewed as having no monetary value as having a price.

Commodities are products that have some monetary value, are standardized, and are mass-produced by many different producers. Consumer goods, such as clothing, cars, and food, are commodities. **Commodification** is the transformation of what is normally a non-commodity into a commodity, that is, the assigning of monetary value. Commodification refers to the process through which social relations are reduced to an exchange relation, or as Karl Marx (Marx and Engels 1964) called it, "callous 'cash payment.'" Marx focused on the commodification of the labour process, in which the real, material activity of labour by individual workers was transformed into abstract labour, just another cost in the process of production. The cost labour could be measured in terms of hours and dollars.

Modern society has many examples of commodification. When we bottle water, we take something that was not seen as a commodity (it was something everyone could get free) and make it into one (something that is bought and sold). There are even oxygen bars where you can buy air. Imagine trying to explain to your grandparents that even air has to be bought! Other things that were never thought of as having a cash value are also now commodified. For example, human organs are bought and sold around the world and people can pay women to be a surrogate mother for them. In a rationalized world, more and more realms of life are controlled by and valued with money.

In modern society, culture can also be commodified. The process can reduce these ideas, customs, and behaviours to items that can be bought and sold. When culture is commodified, it becomes mass-produced and removed from its original meaning and significance.

ACTIVITY

The Commodification of Love

According to a Pew Research study on men's and women's attitudes and behaviours, 93 per cent of married people and 84 per cent of unmarried people say love is a very important reason to get married (Cohn 2013). The survey also found that men and women were equally likely to report that love is a very important reason to get married. People are clearly looking for love, which can be time-consuming. In a world where we are trying to accomplish tasks in the most efficient way possible, even the search for love can be commodified and rationalized.

The American novelist Jonathan Franzen (2012) wrote:

> You can all supply your own favorite, most nauseating examples of the commodification of love. Mine include the wedding industry, TV ads that feature cute young children or the giving of automobiles as Christmas presents, and the particularly grotesque equation of diamond jewelry with everlasting devotion. The message, in each case, is that if you love somebody you should buy stuff.

Visit these websites and then answer the following questions:

- eHarmony (www.eharmony.ca)
- J-Date (www.jdate.com)
- Gay Dating (www.gaydating.com)
- Ashley Madison (www.ashleymadison.com)
- Just Lunch (www.itsjustlunch.com)

1. What features do these websites emphasize in the matching process? (How should you be picking a partner?)
2. How do these sites emphasize the four major components of rationality and McDonaldization?
3. How do the sites commodify love and sexuality?
4. Think of four more examples of how love is commodified and rationalized in modern society.
5. What are the benefits of this process of commodification and rationalization of love?
6. What are the costs of this process?

There are many examples of the commodification of culture. Katy Perry's 2013 American Music Awards performance involved the use of Japanese cultural symbols, such as the kimono, traditional fans, and parasols (See Photo 10.2). This use, which was unrelated to the song Perry performed ("Unconditionally"), was widely criticized. Critics argued that she was using Japanese culture to sell her song while misrepresenting it (for example, she dressed as a geisha without representing the historic and cultural meaning and altered her kimono to show her legs and cleavage). Miley Cyrus was also criticized for twerking at the 2013 MTV Video Music Awards. Critics claimed that Cyrus appropriated this dance—which is associated with African-American culture—to make money and presented it as novel despite the fact that it was borrowed. Another common and recognizable cultural commodification is the t-shirt featuring a picture of Che Guevara, a major figure in the Cuban Revolution who subsequently became a symbol of rebellion and counterculture.

PHOTO 10.2 Katy Perry performs at the 2013 American Music Awards in Los Angeles. Do you agree that her use of Japanese symbols is cultural commodification? Should performers be able to use cultural symbols in this way? Why or why not?

Aboriginal symbols have long been appropriated and commodified. For example, sports teams such as the Cleveland Indians and the Washington Redskins have been criticized for their racist and negative depictions of Aboriginal people. The clothing company Urban Outfitters has also caused controversy through its use of Navajo tribe patterns in their clothing designs. Use of Aboriginal symbols in the 2010 Vancouver Olympics, particularly the Inuksuk (used by Inuit people to mark paths), was also criticized. Do you think that this instance is cultural commodification? Is it a positive or negative use of the symbol? Is it similar to, or different from, Katy Perry's or Miley Cyrus's appropriation of cultural symbols?

The Division of Labour in Society

The question of what holds society together has long intrigued sociologists and other social scientists. As a structural functionalist, Émile Durkheim (1960) was interested in examining how things come to function as they do. His work focused on how the glue that holds society together has changed. We have moved from a time characterized by mechanical solidarity to one characterized by organic solidarity. As you will recall from Chapter 4, in a society exhibiting the former, cohesion and integration come from the fact that individuals are all the same. Small-scale "traditional" societies are based on mechanical solidarity. Think of a small village society in 1500. Most people in that village would do similar sorts of jobs, would have the same level of education (which would probably be quite low), and would be from the same religious and ethnic group.

Modern and industrial societies, such as Canada, are characterized by organic solidarity. In these societies, we are not tied together because we are so similar but because we are so different. People in modern societies are very diverse—they have different religious beliefs, come from different cultural traditions, and have different interests and values. However, we need one another because we are so specialized that we cannot survive without others who do different tasks.

For Durkheim, one of the major differences between societies based on mechanical solidarity and those based on organic solidarity is the extent to which these societies have a complex **division of labour** (the specialization of labour into specific and distinct tasks). Societies based on mechanical solidarity have very little division of labour—most people perform a variety of tasks to navigate their daily life. Everyone grows their own food, sews their own clothes, and makes their own candles.

A society based on organic solidarity has a much more complex division of labour, which has a number of advantages. If tasks are split into smaller and simpler units, we can hire cheaper unskilled labour to perform them. For example, if you no longer need to hire a tailor to design, measure, and sew your clothes but can have one person who only designs, one who only cuts material, and one who only sews, you can have people with fewer skills doing each job. Moreover, one worker is no longer instrumental to a whole factory. If your tailor quits, you are left with no means to obtain clothes. However, if the fabric cutter in a factory leaves, you can easily find another unskilled worker to do the job and the overall production is not devastatingly affected. It is also possible to use more machinery when the tasks are broken down—a machine can cut material, but it cannot do all the parts of production. A high degree of division of labour is therefore a very efficient and cheap way of making products.

Scientific Management

Frederick Taylor developed the principle of **scientific management** (also known as **Taylorism**) within the manufacturing industries of the 1880s and 1890s. This theory applies scientific principles and methods to labour management and involves creating divisions in the labour process. Its methods sought to rationalize work and make it more efficient by dividing it into smaller and smaller tasks. Henry Ford, the founder of the Ford Motor Company, helped to perfect these ideas of scientific management at the turn of the nineteenth century. Ford developed the modern method of mass-production, in particular, the assembly line. Although Ford's methods of scientific management were used to improve the speed and standardization of production in the automotive industry, his principles have been applied to many manufacturing processes and other workplaces (Bonanno 2012).

Ford practised two main principles of scientific management: the standardization of products and the use of specialized equipment. Using scientific management, products are not handmade or unique. Instead, they are made with machines using moulds and models without the need for skilled craftspeople. This system of production relies on the use of specific machines and tools designed so that workers do not need specialized skills to work on the assembly line. A worker can easily be trained to do a small repetitive task and can be replaced without much difficulty (Beyon and Nichol 2006).

Increased efficiency and productivity are the two main benefits to scientific management. However, the system also has many disadvantages. For example, Taylor (1947) found that the workers he studied often became dissatisfied with the work environment and angry at their treatment by management. This was partly because, under scientific management, the conception of work was separated from its execution. Managers—with the help of efficiency experts—conceived of how the work was to be done, while the workers were expected to do what they were told in an unthinking and uncreative manner. Because workers were asked to do only one or a few repetitive tasks, most of their skills and abilities (including the ability to think) were not used. In general, scientific management separates "head" work from "hand" work. Before Taylor and other innovators of scientific management, the skilled worker performed both head and hand work by exercising control and creativity at work. Taylor took the time to understand the head work that skilled workers were doing and then divided it into simpler, repetitive tasks that anyone could easily learn. As a result, workers had to do only easy and monotonous hand work.

Later repercussions of scientific management were many. The system led to **automation**, where

PHOTO 10.3 The Ford Motor Company's assembly lines are a classic example of mass-production. Such scientific management made it possible to create the Ford Model T, the first automobile that a wide range of consumers could afford.

HIGHLIGHT

Outsourcing Phone Centres

When you call a customer service number, you probably speak with an operator from halfway around the world. India was one of the first locations of such phone centres, but many of these services are now located in the Philippines. As Bajaj (2011) notes:

> It helps that Filipinos learn American English in the first grade, eat hamburgers, follow the NBA, and watch the TV show *Friends* long before they enter a call center. In India, by contrast, public schools introduce British English in the third grade, only the urban elite eat American fast food, cricket is the national pastime, and *Friends* is a teaching aid for Indian call center trainers.

> Some Canadian employers are moving call centre jobs back to Canada. Between 2009 and 2011, Primus Telecommunications Canada moved 125 jobs from Mumbai, India, to call centres in New Brunswick and Ontario (Silcoff 2012). In the early 2000s, Primus had outsourced and "got qualified, college-educated employees with accent neutralization training. But over the years [they] felt the quality of agents started to decline." Accent neutralization training was one way that companies such as Primus tried to deal with angry customers in countries, including Canada, who did not like talking to customer service help overseas. Andrew Day, Primus's CEO, reports that, now that the jobs have returned to Canada, about 83 per cent of customers say they are satisfied with their customer service experience. This figure marks an increase of 10 per cent from the period when customer service calls were answered internationally. The higher rate raises interesting questions about why Canadians might feel more satisfied with customer service representatives who they feel are "local."

control systems for operating equipment are run with minimal or reduced human activity. The benefit of automation is that it saves labour (and, as a result, money for business owners) and can help to improve the quality and precision of the labour process. **Outsourcing** is another major implication of scientific management. Companies often

PHOTO 10.4 What are some of outsourcing's implications for Canadian workers? What are some of the implications for the workers doing the outsourced labour?

move their manufacturing division, telephone call centre, or their entire business to other countries in an attempt to save money.

In scientific management, the worker is merely a cog in the machine. In fact, Taylor had a negative view of the worker. When describing the "average worker," he explains (Taylor 1947, 59):

> Now one of the very first requirements for a man . . . is that he shall be so stupid and so phlegmatic that he more nearly resembles in his mental make-up the ox than any other type . . . He is so stupid that the word "percentage" has no meaning to him, and he must consequently be trained by a man more intelligent than himself into the habit of working in accordance with the laws of this science before he can be successful.

Henry Ford also had a fairly dim view of the worker. In his autobiography, he explains that "repetitive labor—the doing of one thing over and over again and always in the same way—is a terrifying prospect to a certain kind of man. It is terrifying to me . . . The average worker, I am sorry to say, wants a job in which he does not have to think" (Ford 1922, 103).

The Alienation of Labour

Marx, who spent his life examining the role of social class in society, feared the effect of these types of labour changes on the worker. He clearly notes that work in capitalism, using scientific management and rationalized techniques, is very productive (Marx and Engels 1964). Under capitalism, we can create more goods faster than ever before. However, Marx also notes that capitalism is a problem because it distorts the process of work, something that should be creative and enjoyable for the worker.

This distortion occurs in four main ways. First, capitalism transforms a naturally social and collective activity into a process that is about pursuing one's own interests. Workers compete with each other for jobs or promotions while capitalists try to maximize profits by exploiting workers. Second, in capitalism, workers create wealth through their labour and the goods they produce, but they get only a small portion of this money. If a person works faster or more productively, the additional profit (surplus) does not go to him but to the capitalist.

Third, as the division of labour in jobs increases, more surplus is created for capitalists. However, this change reduces that natural enjoyment of labour. Before the rise of factories, workers could labour in their own small cottage industries. A cobbler making shoes in her own family business has creative control over the process and the enjoyment of creating the whole product. In modern factories or other work settings, we all perform smaller portions of jobs that are less enjoyable. It is much less satisfying to add the sole to a hundred identical shoes a day in a factory than to make three beautiful unique pairs of shoes in your independent business.

Finally, according to Marx, capitalism distorts work because it separates the worker from the product they make, the production process, other workers, and themselves. Workers are **alienated** from the product because they have no creative control over what they make. They are alienated from the production process because they have no control over how they work—they do not create the assembly lines or stores in which they labour or have any control over how they make their products. They are alienated from other workers because they are separated from others on the assembly line and are forced to compete with the other workers. They are alienated from themselves because the process of work has become routine and exploitative. These four types of alienation were, for Marx, the by-product of capitalism. The rise of scientific management, spearheaded by people such as Taylor and Ford, furthered these problems.

Changes in Work in Canada

The nature of work in the Canadian economy has changed significantly over the past hundred years. One major change is in the types of jobs that workers perform and the economic sector in which they work. The economy has three major sectors. The **primary sector** extracts or harvests resources. Activities associated with the primary sector include mining, forestry, farming, and fishing. This sector has seen a sharp decline over the last 50 years. While 48 per cent of the 1951 workforce was engaged in this type of work (mostly in the extraction of natural resources), only 5 per cent was employed in the primary sector in 2014 (see Figure 10.1).

The **secondary sector** manufactures finished goods. This part of the economy includes automobile production, textile manufacturing, and construction. This sector has also declined, although not to the same extent as the primary sector. As Figure 10.1 shows, the amount of the population involved in this sector has dropped to approximately 11 per cent.

The **tertiary sector** of the economy is the service industry, including services to individuals and businesses. Retail sales, transportation and distribution, entertainment, the hospitality industry, tourism, banking, healthcare, and law are all part of this sector. The service sector is increasing rapidly in Canada—from 21 per cent of employees in 1951 to 78 per cent in 2014. For more detail on Canadians' specific occupations, see Table 10.1.

Service sector jobs tend to have lower wages than other occupations. Canadians working in goods-producing industries make, on average, 35 per cent more than people who work in the service sector. However, the service sector includes a great level of diversity in earnings. Some jobs, such as healthcare, teaching, and management, require high levels of education and training. These jobs tend to pay considerably more than those in manufacturing and other goods-producing jobs. Occupations within the service sector requiring less education, such as hospitality and retail services, tend to make very low wages. For example, restaurant workers are among the lowest paid of all workers, with an average wage of only $317 per week (Statistics Canada 2007).

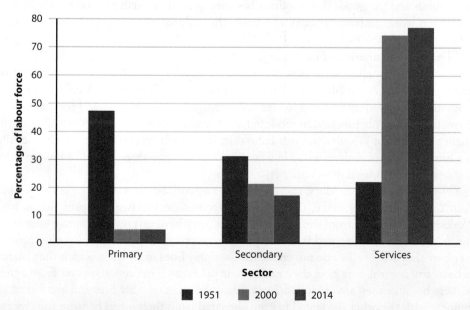

FIGURE 10.1 Growth by sector of the economy, Canada, 1951–2014

SOURCES: O'Halloran, Chris. "Workers of Tomorrow: A Position Paper on the Promise and Problem of Young Workers and Unions." www.congressboard.ab.ca/workplace_2004/cohalloran.htm; Statistics Canada. 2015. "Employment by Industry and Sex." http://www.statcan.gc.ca/tables-tableaux/sum-som/l01/cst01/labor10a-eng.htm.

Even Kids Have a Wage Gap

The wage gap appears to begin in childhood. According to a 2009 University of Michigan survey, girls spend an average of two more hours per week on household chores than boys do. Another survey found that boys tend to make more money for completing chores than do girls. This is, in part, because boys tend to perform different types of chores than girls and these chores earn better pay. For example, mowing the lawn or shovelling snow (chores that boys are more likely to perform) earns higher allowance wages than folding laundry or helping with cooking (chores associated with girls).

While it is clear that these divisions are not rigid, and many girls and boys perform each type of chore, this division perpetuates larger-scale inequalities in the labour force (Chemaly 2013).

RESEARCH METHOD

Survey

TABLE 10.1 Employment by sector, Canada, 2014	
Industry	**Number Employed (%)**
Goods-producing sector	**21.7**
Agriculture	1.7
Forestry, fishing, mining, oil, and gas	4.1
Utilities	0.9
Construction	7.4
Manufacturing	9.7
Services-producing sector	**78.2**
Trade	30.3
Transportation	5.0
Finance, insurance, and real estate	12.5
Professional, scientific, and technical	7.7
Business and support services	4.0
Educational services	7.3
Healthcare and social assistance	12.5
Information, culture, and recreation	4.4
Accommodation and food services	6.5
Other services	4.3
Public administration	5.3

SOURCE: Statistics Canada. 2015. "Labour Force Survey Estimates (LFS), by North American Industry Classification System (NAICS), Sex and Age Group Annual (Persons X 1,000)." Table 282-0008. www5.statcan.gc.ca/cansim/a26?lang=eng&retrLang=eng&id=2820008&pattern=&csid=.

Precarious Employment

Service sector jobs vary considerably not only in their wages but also in their stability and potential for promotion. Government jobs, teaching, and business are considered "good" service jobs because of their higher pay, job security, and possibility for advancement.

Service jobs in retail sales and food services tend to lack these advantages. This second set of jobs, sometimes called McJobs, is **precarious employment**. Precarious work typically gives employers full control over their workers' labour process. Companies are able to hire and fire employees with ease and frequency since the kind of work they typically do makes them readily replaceable. Precarious labour is characterized by the "three Ds"—dirty, dangerous, and demeaning.

A large study conducted at McMaster University in 2013 combined data from a survey of 3,244 workers and 82 interviews (PEPSO, McMaster University, and United Way Toronto 2013). The study found that at least 20 per cent of Canadians work in precarious employment and that this area has grown by nearly 50 per cent in the last 20 years. Research also shows that immigrants, visible minorities, and women tend to be overrepresented in these types of jobs.

Access Alliance Canada's (2013) report *Where Are the Good Jobs?* highlights the serious consequences of precarious employment (see also Shakya and Janczur 2013). This research shows how being stuck in these jobs causes harmful economic, social, and health effects. The researchers interviewed precariously employed individuals and found that, despite working multiple jobs, most of them were living close to the poverty line. They reported that the precarious nature of their employment spilled into other areas of their lives, making decisions about things such as family, housing, and relationships difficult. The health impacts—workplace injuries, as well as depression, chronic pain, diabetes, and heart disease—are particularly concerning. These issues are even more difficult to deal with as most precariously employed individuals do not tend to have health benefits, including extended health coverage or sick leave.

RESEARCH METHOD

Interviews

RESEARCH METHOD

Survey

RESEARCH METHOD

Interviews

Emotional Labour

Another challenge of service sector work is the need to engage in **emotional labour** (the emotional management done by workers and a process of commodifying emotional displays at work). Arlie Russell Hochschild (1983) defines the term as the result of work that involves direct contact with the public. Through this contact, the employee is expected to not only provide the public with a product or service but also to make the customer feel a certain way. Employees are trained to do this by employers and, as a result, the employer controls the emotional responses of employees. Through the process of emotional labour, workers must control their own feelings to achieve the desired effect in others.

RESEARCH METHOD

Interviews

Nurses, servers, and telemarketers, among others, must perform emotional labour. It is not enough that a nurse takes your blood; he must chat and smile while doing it. A server is expected to welcome you warmly and treat you like a friend, not just bring you your dinner. The service sector often requires workers to engage in emotional labour. Hochschild (1983) argues that this emotional labour leads service workers to become alienated from themselves and their own emotions in the workplace.

Hochschild (1983) looks at a variety of professions that engage in emotion work. One of the best examples is flight attendant. As you read about Hochschild's research on this job, think about the service work that you have done (in a restaurant, as a babysitter, as a camp counsellor) and how you might have engaged in emotional labour in this job.

PHOTO 10.5 Along with customer service professionals and nurses, psychologists, counsellors, social workers, and therapists perform emotional labour as a major part of their daily responsibilities.

Feeling Management:
From Private to Commercial Uses

Arlie Russell Hochschild

> If they could have turned every one of us into sweet quiet Southern belles with velvet voices like Rosalyn Carter, this is what they would want to stamp out on an assembly line.
>
> —Flight attendant, Delta Airlines

... When rules about how to feel and how to express feeling are set by management, when workers have weaker rights to courtesy than customers do, when deep and surface acting are forms of labour to be sold, and when private capacities for empathy and warmth are put to corporate uses, what happens to the way a person relates to her feelings or to her face? When worked-up warmth becomes an instrument of service work, what can a person learn about herself from her feelings? And when a worker abandons her work smile, what kind of tie remains between her smile and her self?

Display is what is sold, but over the long run display comes to assume a certain relation to feeling. As enlightened management realizes, a separation of display and feeling is hard to keep up over long periods. A principle of *emotive dissonance*, analogous to the principle of cognitive dissonance, is at work. Maintaining a difference between feeling and feigning over the long run leads to strain. We try to reduce this strain by pulling the two closer together either by changing what we feel or by changing what we feign. When display is required by the job, it is usually feeling that has to change; and when conditions estrange us from our face, they sometimes estrange us from feeling as well.

Take the case of the flight attendant. Corporate logic in the airline industry creates a series of links between competition, market expansion, advertising, heightened passenger expectations about rights to display, and company demands for acting. When conditions allow this logic to work, the result is a successful transmutation of the private emotional system we have described. The old elements of emotional exchange—feeling rules, surface acting, and deep acting—are now arranged in a different way. Stanislavski's *if* moves from stage to airline cabin ("act as if the cabin were your own living room") as does the actor's use of emotion memory. Private use gives way to corporate use....

Behind the Demand for Acting

"A market for emotional labour" is not a phrase that company employees use. Upper management talks about getting the best market share of the flying public. Advertising personnel talk about reaching that market. In-flight service supervisors talk about getting "positive attitude" and "professional service" from flight attendants, who in turn talk about "handling rates." Nevertheless, the efforts of these four groups, taken together, set up the sale of emotional labour....

As competition grew from the 1930s through the early 1970s, the airlines expanded that visible role [with the customer]. Through the 1950s and 1960s the flight attendant became a main subject of airline advertising, the spearhead of market expansion.[1] The image they chose, among many possible ones, was that of a beautiful and smartly dressed Southern white woman, the supposed epitome of gracious manners and warm personal service.[2]

Because airline ads raise expectations, they subtly rewrite job descriptions and redefine roles....

The ads promise service that is "human" and personal. The omnipresent smile suggests, first of all, that the flight attendant is friendly, helpful, and open to requests. But when words are added, the smile can be sexualized, as in "We really move our tails for you to make your every wish come true" (Continental), or "Fly me, you'll like it" (National). Such innuendos lend strength to the conventional fantasy that in the air, anything can happen. As one flight attendant put it: "You have married men with three kids getting on the plane and suddenly they feel anything goes. It's like they leave that reality on the ground, and you fit into their fantasy as some geisha girl. It happens over and over again." . . .

Behind the Supply of Acting: Selection

Even before an applicant for a flight attendant's job is interviewed, she is introduced to the rules of the game. Success will depend in part on whether she has a knack for perceiving the rules and taking them seriously. Applicants are urged to read a preinterview pamphlet before coming in. In the 1979–1980 *Airline Guide to Stewardess and Steward Careers*, there is a section called "The Interview." Under the subheading "Appearance," the manual suggests that facial expressions should be "sincere" and "unaffected." One should have a "modest but friendly smile" and be "generally alert, attentive, not overly aggressive, but not reticent either." Under "Mannerisms," subheading "Friendliness," it is suggested that a successful candidate must be "outgoing but not effusive," "enthusiastic with calm and poise," and "vivacious but not effervescent." As the manual continues: "Maintaining eye contact with the interviewer demonstrates sincerity and confidence, but don't overdo it. Avoid cold or continuous staring." Training, it seems, begins even before recruitment. . . .

Different companies favour different variations of the ideal type of sociability. Veteran employees talk about differences in company personality as matter-of-factly as they talk about differences in uniform or shoe style. United Airlines, the consensus has it, is "the girl-next-door," the neighbourhood babysitter grown up. Pan Am is upper class, sophisticated, and slightly reserved in its graciousness. PSA is brassy, fun-loving, and sexy. . . .

The trainees, it seemed to me, were also chosen for their ability to take stage directions about how to "project" an image. They were selected for being able to act well—that is, without showing the effort involved. They had to be able to appear at home on stage. . . .

Somewhat humbled and displaced, the worker was now prepared to identify with Delta. Delta was described as a brilliant financial success (which it is), an airline known for fine treatment of its personnel (also true, for the most part), a company with a history of the "personal touch." Orientation talks described the company's beginnings as a family enterprise in the 1920s, when the founder, Collett Woolman, personally pinned an orchid on each new flight attendant. It was the flight attendant's job to represent the company proudly, and actually identifying with the company would make that easier to do.

Training seemed to foster the sense that it was safe to feel dependent on the company. Temporarily rootless, the worker was encouraged to believe that this company of 36,000 employees operated as a "family." The head of the training centre, a gentle, wise, authoritative figure in her fifties, appeared each morning in the auditorium; she was "mommy," the real authority on day-to-day problems. Her company superior, a slightly younger man, seemed to be "daddy." Other supervisors were introduced as concerned extensions of these initial training parents. (The vast majority of trainees were between 19 and 22 years old.) As one speaker told the recruits: "Your supervisor is your friend. You can go to her and talk about anything, and I mean *anything*." The trainees were divided up into small groups; one class of 123 students (which included 3 males and 9 blacks) was divided into four subgroups, each yielding the more intimate ties of solidarity that were to be the prototype of later bonds at work. . . .

Beyond this, there were actual appeals to modify feeling states. The deepest appeal in the Delta training program was to the trainee's capacity to act as if the airplane cabin (where she works) were her home (where she doesn't work). Trainees were asked to think of a passenger *as if* he were a "personal guest in your living room." The workers' emotional memories of offering personal hospitality were called up and put to use, as Stanislavski would recommend. As one recent graduate put it:

> You think how the new person resembles someone you know. *You see your sister's eyes in someone sitting at that seat.* That makes you want to put out for them. I like to think of the cabin as the living room of my own home. When someone drops in [at home], you may not know them, but you get something for them. You put that on a grand scale—thirty-six passengers per flight attendant—but *it's the same feeling.*

On the face of it, the analogy between home and airplane cabin unites different kinds of experiences and obscures what is different about them. It can unite the empathy of friend for friend with the empathy of worker for customer, because it assumes that empathy is the *same sort of feeling* in either case. Trainees wrote in their notebooks, "Adopt the passenger's point of view," and the understanding was that this could be done in the same way one adopts a friend's point of view. The analogy between home and cabin also joins the worker to her company; just as she naturally protects members of her own family, she will naturally defend the company. Impersonal relations are to be seen *as if* they were personal. Relations based on getting and giving money are to be seen *as if* they were relations free of money. The company brilliantly extends and uses its workers' basic human empathy, all the while maintaining that it is not interfering in their "personal" lives. . . .

Collective Emotional Labour

To thwart cynicism about the living room analogy, to catch it as it collapses in the face of other realizations, the company eye shifts to another field of emotion work—the field in which flight attendants interact with each other. This is a strategic point of entry for the company because if the company can influence how flight attendants deal with each other's feeling on the job, it can assure proper support for private emotion management.

As trainers well know, flight attendants typically work in teams of two and must work on fairly intimate terms with all others on the crew. In fact, workers commonly say the work simply cannot be done well unless they work well together. The reason for this is that the job is partly an "emotional tone" road show, and the proper tone is kept up in large part by friendly conversation, banter, and joking, as ice cubes, trays, and plastic cups are passed from aisle to aisle to the galley, down to the kitchen, and up again. Indeed, starting with the bus ride to the plane, by bantering back and forth the flight attendant does important relational work: she checks on people's moods, relaxes tension, and warms up ties so that each pair of individuals becomes a team. She also banters to keep herself in the right frame of mind. As one worker put it, "Oh, we banter a lot. It keeps you going. You last longer." . . .

Once established, team solidarity can have two effects. It can improve morale and thus improve service. But it can also become the basis for sharing grudges against the passengers or the company. Perhaps it is the second possibility that trainers meant to avoid when in Recurrent Training they offered examples of "bad" social emotion management. One teacher cautioned her students: "When you're angry with a passenger, don't head for the galley to blow off steam with another flight attendant." In the galley, the second flight attendant, instead of calming the angry worker down, may further rile her up; she may become an accomplice to the aggrieved worker. Then, as the instructor put it, "There'll be *two* of you hot to trot."

The message was, when you're angry, go to a teammate who will calm you down. Support for anger or a sense of grievance—regardless of what inspires it—is bad for service and bad for the company. Thus, the informal ways in which workers check on the legitimacy of a grievance or look for support in blowing off steam become points of entry for company "suggestions." . . .

Achieving the Transmutation

To the extent that emotion management actually works—so that Bloody Marys do not spill "by accident" on white pantsuits, and blowups occur in backstage offices instead of in airplane aisles—something like alchemy occurs. Civility and a general sense of well-being have been enhanced and emotional "pollution" controlled. Even when people are paid to be nice, it is hard for them to be nice at all times, and when their efforts succeed, it is a remarkable accomplishment.

What makes this accomplishment possible is a transmutation of three basic elements of emotional life: emotion work, feeling rules, and social exchange.

First, emotion work is no longer a private act but a public act, bought on the one hand and sold on the other. Those who direct emotion work are no longer the individuals themselves but are instead paid stage managers who select, train, and supervise others.

Second, feeling rules are no longer simply matters of personal discretion, negotiated with another person in private but are spelled out publicly—in the *Airline Guide to Stewardess and Steward Careers*, in the *World Airways Flight Manual*, in training programs, and in the discourse of supervisors at all levels.

Third, social exchange is forced into narrow channels; there may be hiding places along shore, but there is much less room for individual navigation of the emotional waters.

The whole system of emotional exchange in private life has as its ostensible purpose the welfare and pleasure of the people involved. When this emotional system is thrust into a commercial setting, it is transmuted. A profit motive is slipped in under acts of emotion management, under the rules that govern them, under the gift exchange. Who benefits now, and who pays? . . .

In relation to each issue, emotional labour poses a challenge to a person's sense of self. In each case, the problem was not one that would cause much concern among those who do not do emotional labour—the assembly line worker or the wallpaper machine operator, for example. In each case the issue of estrangement between what a person senses as her "true self" and her inner and outer acting becomes something to work out, to take a position on.

When a flight attendant feels that her smile is "not an indication of how she really feels," or when she feels that her deep or surface acting is not meaningful, it is a sign that she is straining to disguise the failure of a more general transmutation. It indicates that emotion work now performed on a commercial stage, with commercial directors and standardized props, is failing to involve the actors or convince the audience in a way that it once did.

When feelings are successfully commercialized, the worker does not feel phony or alien; she feels somehow satisfied in how personal her service actually was. Deep acting is a help in doing this, not a source of estrangement. But when commercialization of feeling as a general process collapses into its separate elements, display becomes hollow and emotional labour is withdrawn. The task becomes one of disguising the failed transmutation. In either case, whether proudly or resentfully, face and feelings have been used as instruments. An American Airlines worker said: "Do you know what they call us when we get sick? *Breakage*. How's that for a 'positive attitude'? Breakage is what they call people that go to the complaint service to cancel for illness." Or again, as a San Francisco base manager at United remarked ruefully: "And we call them bodies. Do we have enough 'bodies' for the flight?" Feeling can become an instrument, but whose instrument?

NOTES

1. When an airline commands a market monopoly, as it is likely to do when it is owned by government, it does not need to compete for passengers by advertising friendly flight attendants. Many flight attendants told me that their counterparts on Lufthansa (the German national airline) and even more on El Al and Aeroflot (the Israeli and Russian national airlines) were notably lacking in assertive friendliness.

2. A black female flight attendant, who had been hired in the early 1970s when Delta faced an affirmative action suit, wondered aloud why blacks were not pictured in local Georgia advertising. She concluded: "They want that market, and that market doesn't include blacks. They go along with that." Although Delta's central offices are in Atlanta, which is predominantly black, few blacks worked for Delta in capacity.

1. Why do organizations want workers to perform emotional labour? What function does it serve?

2. What are the costs of emotional labour for the employee? How can these problems be dealt with by the employee?

3. How does the performance of emotional labour relate to Goffman's dramaturgical perspective (see Chapter 2)?

ACTIVITY

Training Employees for Emotional Labour

Organizations in a variety of industries actively work to teach their employees to engage in emotional labour. Go to this book's companion website to watch a customer service training video and then answer the following questions:

1. What is the point of this video? How does it relate to the concept of emotional labour?

2. In the longer version of this video, the narrator explains that customer service representatives should aim to show they care, show they understand, and make the customer feel that he can trust them to take care of the situation. How are each of these tasks related to emotional labour?

3. The videos often discuss the need to apologize. Why do the trainers feel that apologizing is important? How could apologizing cause problems for an employee?

The next set of questions relates to a University of Memphis study of how effective employees are at emotional labour. Go to this book's companion website to watch a video regarding this research.

1. Do you think Julianne Pierce's test to assess an employee's ability to perform emotional labour is useful? What does this test measure well and how could it be improved?

2. What is the difference between **surface acting** and **deep acting**? What are the costs of surface acting for the employee? How do these concepts relate to what you learned from Hochschild's article?

3. How does the video suggest that employees could be more satisfied at work? Do you think that this plan would work? Why or why not?

4. If you've had a service industry job such as a restaurant server or salesperson, how did you feel about performing emotional labour? Did you have to represent a certain type of identity as a representative of your company?

5. How do employees sometimes resist companies' attempts to force them to engage in emotional labour? Are these techniques effective? Why or why not?

Summary

We began this chapter by learning about Weber's theory of rationalization in modern society and examining the rise of bureaucracies as a prototype of this process. George Ritzer built on Weber's theory by applying the idea of rationalization to the development of McDonald's and showing how much of modern society is becoming "McDonaldized." One of the by-products of this situation is the increasing commodification of many elements of our lives, from products and our labour to culture and love. We then turned to another major change in modern society, discussed by Durkheim—the increased division of labour over time. This division of labour is seen in processes of scientific management, developed by Taylor and Ford, and, according to Marx, can lead to feelings of alienation for workers. Finally, we discussed changes in work in Canada, including the rise of the service sector, precarious employment, and emotional labour.

Key Terms

alienation 289
automation 287
bureaucracy 277
commodification 284
commodity 284
deep acting 297
disenchantment of the world 276
division of labour 286
emotional labour 292
irrationality of rationality 283

McDonaldization 278
outsourcing 288
precarious employment 292
primary sector 290
rationalization 276
scientific management (Taylorism) 287
secondary sector 290
surface acting 297
tertiary (service) sector 290

For Further Reading

Hochschild, Arlie Russell. 1983. *The Managed Heart: Commercialization of Human Feeling.* Berkeley, CA: University of California Press.

Marx, Karl, and Friedrich Engels. 1964. *The Communist Manifesto.* New York: Modern Reader Paperbacks.

Ritzer, George. 2011. *The McDonaldization of Society*, 6th edn. Los Angeles: Sage.

Weber, Max. 1965. *The Sociology of Religion.* London: Methuen.

———. 1968. *Economy and Society*, Volume 1, Chapters 2–4. New York: Bedminster.

The Changing Social Construction of Deviance

Even within the same society, individuals have different ideas about what counts as deviance and the seriousness of various deviant acts. Consider the items in this list and answer the following questions:

- downloading music without paying
- cheating on your romantic partner
- using steroids to improve athletic performance
- hitting a child as punishment
- taking Adderall to study late for an exam
- dating someone from a different ethnic group
- abstaining from alcohol in any context
- hitting your spouse
- getting a tattoo
- killing someone
- having sex before marriage
- punching someone in a fight
- driving after drinking alcohol

1. Rank these acts in terms of their severity. Which ones do you consider to be the most and least serious acts of deviance?

2. Which of these acts are illegal in Canada? Which are legal in Canada but illegal elsewhere?

3. What acts are now considered less serious than they were in the past? Which are considered more serious?

4. How do different groups of people vary in their attitudes about the seriousness of these acts? How would your grandparents, religious leader, friends, or other people in your life answer these questions differently?

5. Would you answer these questions differently in a different context? If yes, give an example. Which deviant acts in the list might be acceptable in certain contexts?

Why Are People Deviant?

Scholars have developed many theories in an attempt to explain why people are deviant or commit crimes. Some of these theories look at individual-level explanations. Most of the theories that sociologists use, however, are based on broader social explanations for an individual's propensity to engage in deviance or break the law.

Individual Explanations of Deviance and Crime

Individual-level explanations of crime generally focus on the deviant or criminal's character (Collins 1992). The logic behind these explanations is, for example, that thieves steal because they are greedy and murderers kill because they are aggressive. Some arguments are grounded in biology, such as the theory that criminals are genetically defective, predisposed to crime, or have too much testosterone. The idea that criminals are "simply bad people" and their deviant propensities come from within generally leads to support for severe punishments, such as the death penalty or long jail sentences. After all, if criminals are just "bad apples," nothing can be done to rehabilitate them; therefore, we should reduce the potential harm they can do by removing them from society. However, as Collins notes, there is little empirical evidence to support the claim that more punitive reactions to crime significantly reduce crime rates. We will discuss punishment and its effects later in this chapter.

Social Explanations of Deviance and Crime

Unlike individual explanations, social explanations seek to understand criminal activity as a product of the criminal's environment, particularly how it shapes his actions. Sociologists use a wide variety of these explanations, which originate from the different theoretical perspectives we have discussed throughout this book.

Strain theory argues that some individuals' goals and opportunities for success do not match (Merton 1957). If, for example, criminals come from broken homes and low-income neighbourhoods and lack opportunities to change their social conditions, they may experience strain. An individual might want to make enough money to be self-sufficient but be unable to get a well-paying job. Thus, he could turn to crime to fulfill this aspiration.

PHOTO 11.3 On 2 June 2012, a gang-related shooting occurred at the Toronto Eaton Centre; five people were shot, two of whom died. Many youth-led anti-violence groups responded to the shooting, represented here by (from left to right) Keegan Henry-Mathieu, director of community engagement with the Toronto Youth Cabinet; Kofi Hope, director of the Black Youth Coalition Against Violence; Joel Reodica, representing Justice4Jeffery; and Saeed Selvam, director of youth–police relations with the Toronto Youth Cabinet.

Subcultural theory focuses on the role of culture in crime. Stanley Cohen (2011) argues that gangs and other criminal organizations are subcultures with different norms and values than the larger culture. As such, we can understand these gangs as a collective adaptation to social conditions and a rejection of the establishment's cultural goals. For example, beating someone up to defend a friend might be seen as both legitimate and necessary within gang subculture.

Elijah Anderson's (1999) famous study, *Code of the Streets*, uses both strain and subcultural theories to explore the street-oriented subculture of American inner-city ghettos. Through participant observation, Anderson tries to understand how young minority men living in these ghettos search for respect and how this search can create the need for aggressive, violent, and criminal behaviour. He explains that the consequence of this relentless pursuit of respect is a vicious cycle that begins with the hopelessness and alienation many inner-city youth feel at the hands of joblessness and racism in mainstream culture and leads to violence as a means of gaining respect. This violence, in turn, reinforces the negative perceptions many whites and middle-class individuals have about the ghetto poor, thus legitimating the code of the streets in the eyes of the minority youths.

Anderson (1999, 9) writes that the code's basic requirement is "the display of a certain predisposition to violence" and "mayhem," which may include fighting, exacting revenge, or stealing "trophy" objects (such as clothes or girlfriends). Young men ascribing to the code of the streets often use violence and the threat of violence to "campaign for respect." Children from street-oriented homes, for example, spend a great deal of time "hanging" with their peers on the streets, thus making their primary social bonds and social interactions with their friends rather than their parents. The toughest person in this context is often the one who garners the most respect.

Consistent with subcultural theory, this important work highlights how the norms and values that groups follow can be quite different, even within the same society, and how the social context can influence individuals' behaviour. In many ways, it is rational for young minority men living in US ghettos to act violently and criminally if that is what it takes to survive. These same behaviours would be irrational in a middle-class suburban context.

Developed by Edwin Sutherland (1947), **learning theory** is an extension of strain and subcultural theories. Sutherland argued that different environments provide opportunities to learn to engage in deviance and crime. The saying "The best place to learn how to be a criminal is in jail" epitomizes the logic behind learning theory—if people interact with and are exposed to criminals, they learn to engage in criminal behaviour. Via the social interaction that occurs in jail, for example, individuals learn a new set of skills. Sitting in a prison cafeteria might lead to a conversation about how best to steal a car without getting caught or how to justify to oneself that committing crimes is acceptable. This argument is based on ideas about the importance of socialization (see Chapter 2).

Travis Hirschi's (2004) **control theory** also focuses on social context's role in deviant and criminal behaviour. He argues that weak social control can lead individuals to engage in deviant or criminal acts. A number of factors can result in weak control. An individual might not have close relationships with her parents, teachers, or peer group. Or individuals can have weak institutional involvement if they are not actively engaged in organizations such as religious institutions, schools, sports teams, or other groups. Individuals can also have weak beliefs in traditional values. Finally, individuals can have limited opportunities for success if, for example, there is high unemployment or a lack of access to education where they live. Most people are integrated in these four ways and thus are less likely to engage in deviance. This theory might remind you of Durkheim's theory of suicide. Remember, Durkheim argued that individuals who are well integrated into their community and peer groups are less likely to commit suicide, arguably an act of deviance because it breaks a social norm.

RESEARCH METHOD

Participant Observation

These social explanations of crime focus on why individuals might be more or less likely to commit crimes based on their social environment. **Labelling theory** (just like symbolic interactionist theory) explores how we respond to deviant or criminal acts and how this reaction (or label) can either increase or decrease an individual's propensity to engage in further deviance. This theory originated in the work of Howard Becker (1963), who argues that almost all young people engage in deviant behaviour but only some get caught. If a young person is apprehended by authorities and is actually arrested, charged, convicted, and sentenced, her life can be significantly affected in a negative way. It is not the deviant behaviour, per se, that leads to the later problems. Instead, being labelled deviant can create a deviant or criminal identity for the young person. Once an individual is labelled a criminal, she may find it difficult to get a job and may turn to illegitimate means, such as crime, to make money. Labelling involves a process by which identifying someone as a criminal can produce a self-fulfilling prophecy. Collins (1992, 99) explains that the response to deviance is critical in labelling theory:

> The labelling theory declares that crime is actually created by the process of getting caught. Unlike the previous types of theories that we looked at, the personal characteristics of the individuals, or their social class or ethnic or neighborhood background, is not a crucial point. It is assumed that all sorts of people violate the law. But only some of them get caught, are prosecuted, labeled and all the rest, thereby becoming full-fledged criminals. If criminals who go through the courts and the prisons are so often likely to be disproportionately poor, black, or otherwise fit someone's idea of "social undesirables" or the "socially deprived," it is because these are the types of people who are most likely to be apprehended and prosecuted.

In sum, labelling theory posits that, when a person is caught and labelled as a deviant or a criminal, they become stigmatized and viewed as a criminal by others. This situation also creates a process of identity formation—people begin to adopt the identity of "deviant." As a result, individuals sometimes change the way they view themselves and engage in deviant or criminal behaviour to fulfill this social role or identity.

It is important, from a labelling theory perspective, to differentiate between primary and secondary acts of deviance. **Primary deviance** includes early, random acts of deviance. This sort of deviance is very common and most people have, at some point, engaged in primary deviant activity. **Secondary deviance**, however, is much more serious. The result of persistent deviant behaviour, it can often cause an individual to organize his life and identity around being "deviant."

Take, for example, a young boy who gets into a fight at school. If this is his first act of deviance, labelling theory would encourage us not to label him a deviant or criminal. But if the boy was arrested for his behaviour, he would likely be labelled a deviant and a "bad kid" by others. Over time, it would be hard for him to find a job or other opportunities because everyone knows he is a "bad seed." In this way, it is not so much the act of deviance, but how we as a society respond to it, that leads to more (or less) deviance.

The Canadian Youth Criminal Justice Act recognizes the importance of labelling. Under this Act, it is illegal to publish the identity of a young offender. One of the purposes of this legislation is to help young people avoid being labelled as deviant and stigmatized. Keeping a young offender's identity private could help prevent primary deviance from being translated into secondary deviance and increase the chance that youthful deviance will not lead to a life of crime.

Social explanations generally advocate for rehabilitative punishments and crime prevention by focusing on contextual factors, such as reducing concentrated poverty and facilitating access to education and employment. Some of these theories, including labelling theory, shift the emphasis away from the offender and his environment and toward

The Media and Labelling the "Deviant"

In examining labelling theory, it is interesting to consider how we may label primary deviance differently depending on the offender's characteristics. Are we more likely to think of a young woman engaging in deviance as an aberration but a young man engaged in the same activity as an indication of more serious problems? Do we understand early deviance differently depending on the race or ethnicity of the offender?

Ann Arnett Ferguson (2001) argues that black children, especially boys, are stereotyped as pre-criminals. They are not seen as "adorably naughty," like white boys, but as dangerously bad from the beginning. Let's compare news reports of two stories of seven-year-old boys—one black, one white—who each stole his family's car and went for a joyride. The coverage of the stories, the responses of the boys' families, and the ways the boys understood this primary deviance highlight how labelling occurs. (The interviews referred to in the following paragraphs can be seen at http://thesocietypages. org/socimages/?s=deviance.)

In 2008, CNN reported on the story of Latarian Milton, a black boy from Florida. The story begins with the announcer commenting that Milton is "not your typical seven-year-old." The interviewer, off-camera, asks Milton why he took the car. He replies: "I wanted to do it 'cause it's fun, it's fun to do bad things." The interviewer asks, "Did you know that you could perhaps kill somebody?" He replies: "Yes, but I wanted to do hoodrat stuff with my friends." According to *The Huffington Post*, the police planned to charge Milton with grand theft. The reporter indicates that, while he's "too young to go into any type of juvenile facility, police say they do want to get him into the system, so that they can get him some type of help" (Wade 2013). This response treats the boy as a young man who needs to be in the criminal justice system. Milton also embraces the deviant identity—he revels in doing a bad thing and the way that it shows his street smarts and credibility. He internalizes the stereotypes that others have of him.

A year later, Preston Scarborough, a white boy from Utah, appeared on *The Today Show* with his family to talk about his joyride. This story and the media coverage stands in stark contrast to Milton's. During this interview, the boy's father calls the incident "funny" and argues that if his "cotton candy all-American" son could do something like this then any child could. Even the interviewer, Meredith Vieira, does not consider the incident serious. When she asks Preston why he hid from the police, he simply responds, "cause I wanted to." Vieira says, "I don't blame you actually." Preston's mother explains that "he just wanted to know what it felt like to drive a car." The boy's punishment was a four-day grounding without TV or video games. Vieira ends the segment by saying that the incident shows that "you never know what can happen!" The story is presented as a light-hearted, human interest story with a happy ending and the child as a fundamentally good kid who was simply curious and impulsive. How do these two stories illustrate the concept of labelling and how this process differs based on gender, race, and social class?

the response to the deviant act. Proponents of labelling theory tend to promote programs that divert youths caught engaging in criminal acts from the courts and into community service as a means to avoid labelling them as a criminal too hastily.

D.L. Rosenhan's article illustrates the process of labelling. Rosenhan had eight mentally and physically healthy volunteers admitted to a mental hospital to see how they would be treated once they were labelled insane, as well as how long it would take for them to be labelled sane and released.

RESEARCH METHOD

Experiment

On Being Sane in Insane Places

D.L. Rosenhan

If sanity and insanity exist, how shall we know them?

The question is neither capricious nor itself insane. However much we may be personally convinced that we can tell the normal from the abnormal, the evidence is simply not compelling. It is commonplace, for example, to read about murder trials wherein eminent psychiatrists for the defence are contradicted by equally eminent psychiatrists for the prosecution on the matter of the defendant's sanity. . . .

To raise questions regarding normality and abnormality is in no way to question the fact that some behaviours are deviant or odd. Murder is deviant. So, too, are hallucinations. Nor does raising such questions deny the existence of the personal anguish that is often associated with "mental illness." Anxiety and depression exist. Psychological suffering exists. But normality and abnormality, sanity and insanity, and the diagnoses that flow from them may be less substantive than many believe them to be.

At its heart, the question of whether the sane can be distinguished from the insane (and whether degrees of insanity can be distinguished from each other) is a simple matter: Do the salient characteristics that lead to diagnoses reside in the patients themselves or in the environments and contexts in which observers find them? . . .

Gains can be made in deciding which of these is more nearly accurate by getting normal people (that is, people who do not have, and have never suffered, symptoms of serious psychiatric disorders) admitted to psychiatric hospitals and then determining whether they were discovered to be sane and, if so, how. If sanity of such pseudopatients were always detected, there would be prima facie evidence that a sane individual can be distinguished from the insane context in which he is found. Normality (and presumably abnormality) is distinct enough that it can be recognized wherever it occurs, for it is carried within the person. If, on the other hand, the sanity of the pseudopatients were never discovered, serious difficulties would arise for those who support traditional modes of psychiatric diagnosis. Given that the hospital staff was not incompetent, that the pseudopatient had been behaving as sanely as he had been outside of the hospital, and that it had never been previously suggested that he belonged in a psychiatric hospital, such an unlikely outcome would support the view that psychiatric diagnosis betrays little about the patient but much about the environment in which an observer finds him.

This article describes such an experiment. Eight sane people gained secret admission to 12 different hospitals. . . .

Pseudopatients and Their Settings

The eight pseudopatients were a varied group. One was a psychology graduate student in his twenties. The remaining seven were older and "established." Among them were three psychologists, a pediatrician, a psychiatrist, a painter, and a housewife. Three pseudopatients were women, five were men. All of them employed pseudonyms, lest their alleged diagnoses embarrass them later. Those who were in mental health professions alleged another occupation in order to avoid the special attentions that might be accorded by staff, as a matter of courtesy or caution, to ailing colleagues. With the exception of myself (I was the first pseudopatient and my presence was known to the hospital administrator and chief psychologist and, so far as I can tell, to them alone), the presence of pseudopatients and the nature of the research program was not known to the hospital staffs.

The settings were similarly varied. In order to generalize the findings, admission into a variety of hospitals was sought. The 12 hospitals in the sample were located in 5 different states on the East and West coasts. Some were old and shabby, some were quite new. Some were research-oriented, others not. Some had good staff–patient ratios, others were quite understaffed. Only one was a strictly private hospital. All of the others were supported by state or federal funds or, in one instance, by university funds.

After calling the hospital for an appointment, the pseudopatient arrived at the admissions office complaining that he had been hearing voices. Asked what the voices said, he replied that they were often unclear, but as far as he could tell they said "empty," "hollow," and "thud." The voices were unfamiliar and were of the same sex as the pseudopatient. The choice of these symptoms was occasioned by their apparent similarity to existential symptoms. Such symptoms are alleged to arise from painful concerns about the perceived meaninglessness of one's life. It is as if the hallucinating person were saying, "My life is empty and hollow." The choice of these symptoms was also determined by the absence of a single report of existential psychoses in the literature.

Beyond alleging the symptoms and falsifying name, vocation, and employment, no further alterations of person, history, or circumstances were made. The significant events of the pseudopatient's life history were presented as they had actually occurred. Relationships with parents and siblings, with spouse and children, with people at work and in school, consistent with the aforementioned exceptions, were described as they were or had been. Frustrations and upsets were described along with joys and satisfactions. These facts are important to remember. If anything, they strongly biased the subsequent results in favour of detecting sanity, since none of their histories or current behaviours were seriously pathological in any way.

Immediately upon admission to the psychiatric ward, the pseudopatient ceased simulating any symptoms of abnormality. In some cases, there was a brief period of mild nervousness and anxiety, since none of the pseudopatients really believed that they would be admitted so easily. Indeed, their shared fear was that they would be immediately exposed as frauds and greatly embarrassed. Moreover, many of them had never visited a psychiatric ward; even those who had nevertheless had some genuine fears about what might happen to them. Their nervousness, then, was quite appropriate to the novelty of the hospital setting, and it abated rapidly.

Apart from that short-lived nervousness, the pseudopatient behaved on the ward as he "normally" behaved. The pseudopatient spoke to patients and staff as he might ordinarily. Because there is uncommonly little to do on a psychiatric ward, he attempted to engage others in conversation. When asked by staff how he was feeling, he indicated that he was fine, that he no longer experienced symptoms. He responded to instructions from attendants, to calls for medication (which was not swallowed), and to dining-hall instructions. Beyond such activities as were available to him on the admissions ward, he spent his time writing down his observations about the ward, its patients, and the staff. Initially these notes were written "secretly," but as it soon became clear that no one much cared, they were subsequently written on standard tablets of paper in such public places as the dayroom. No secret was made of these activities.

The pseudopatient, very much as a true psychiatric patient, entered a hospital with no foreknowledge of when he would be discharged. Each was told that he would have to get out by his own devices, essentially by convincing the staff that he was sane. The psychological stresses associated with hospitalization were considerable, and all but one of the pseudopatients desired to be discharged almost immediately after being admitted. They were, therefore, motivated not only to behave sanely, but to be paragons of co-operation. That their behaviour was in no way disruptive is confirmed by nursing reports, which have been obtained on most of the patients. These reports uniformly indicate that the patients were "friendly," "co-operative," and "exhibited no abnormal indications."

The Normal Are Not Detectably Sane

Despite their public "show" of sanity, the pseudopatients were never detected. Admitted, except in one case, with a diagnosis of schizophrenia,[1] each was discharged with a diagnosis of schizophrenia "in remission." The label "in remission" should in no way be dismissed as a formality, for at no time during any hospitalization had any question been raised about any pseudopatient's simulation. Nor are there any indications in the hospital records that the pseudopatient's status was suspect. Rather, the evidence is strong that, once labelled schizophrenic, the pseudopatient was stuck with that label. If the pseudopatient was to be discharged, he must naturally be "in remission"; but he was not sane, nor, in the institution's view, had he ever been sane.

The uniform failure to recognize sanity cannot be attributed to the quality of the hospitals, for, although there were considerable variations among them, several are considered excellent. Nor can it be alleged that there was simply not enough time to observe the pseudopatients. Length of hospitalization ranged from 7 to 52 days, with an average of 19 days. The pseudopatients were not, in fact, carefully observed, but this failure speaks more to traditions within psychiatric hospitals than to lack of opportunity.

Finally, it cannot be said that the failure to recognize the pseudopatients' sanity was due to the fact that they were not behaving sanely. While there was clearly some tension present in all of them, their daily visitors could detect no serious behavioural consequences—nor, indeed, could other patients. It was quite common for the patients to "detect" the pseudopatient's sanity. During the first three hospitalizations, when accurate counts were kept, 35 of a total of 118 patients on the admissions ward voiced their suspicions, some vigorously. "You're not crazy. You're a journalist, or a professor [referring to the continual note-taking]. You're checking up on the hospital." While most of the patients were reassured by the pseudopatient's insistence that he had been sick before he came in but was fine now, some continued to believe that the pseudopatient was sane throughout his hospitalization. The fact that the patients often recognized normality when staff did not raises important questions.

Failure to detect sanity during the course of hospitalization may be due to the fact that physicians operate with a strong bias toward what statisticians call the type 2 error.[2] This is to say that physicians are more inclined to call a healthy person sick (a false positive, type 2) than a sick person healthy (a false negative, type 1). The reasons for this are not hard to find: it is clearly more dangerous to misdiagnose illness than health. Better to err on the side of caution, to suspect illness even among the healthy.

But what holds for medicine does not hold equally well for psychiatry. Medical illnesses, while unfortunate, are not commonly pejorative. Psychiatric diagnoses, on the contrary, carry with them personal, legal, and social stigmas.[3] It was therefore important to see whether the tendency toward diagnosing the sane insane could be reversed. . . .

The Stickiness of Psychodiagnostic Labels

Beyond the tendency to call the healthy sick—a tendency that accounts better for diagnostic behaviour on admission than it does for such behaviour after a lengthy period of exposure—the data speak to the massive role of labelling in psychiatric assessment. Having once been labelled schizophrenic, there is nothing the pseudopatient can do to overcome the tag. The tag profoundly colours others' perceptions of him and his behaviour. . . .

Once a person is designated abnormal, all of his other behaviours and characteristics are coloured by that label. Indeed, that label is so powerful that many of the pseudopatients' normal behaviours were overlooked entirely or profoundly misinterpreted. Some examples may clarify this issue. . . .

As far as I can determine, diagnoses were in no way affected by the relative health of the circumstances of a pseudopatient's life. Rather, the reverse occurred: the perception of his circumstances was shaped entirely by the diagnosis. A clear example of such translation is found in the case of a pseudopatient who had had a close relationship with his mother but was rather remote from his father during his early childhood. During adolescence and beyond, however, his father became a close friend, while his relationship with his mother cooled. His present relationship with his wife was characteristically close and warm.

Apart from occasional angry exchanges, friction was minimal. The children had rarely been spanked. Surely there is nothing especially pathological about such a history. Indeed, many readers may see a similar pattern in their own experiences, with no markedly deleterious consequences. Observe, however, how such a history was translated in the psychopathological context, this from the case summary prepared after the patient was discharged.

> This white 39-year-old male . . . manifests a long history of considerable ambivalence in close relationships, which begins in early childhood. A warm relationship with his mother cools during his adolescence. A distant relationship to his father is described as becoming very intense. Affective stability is absent. His attempts to control emotionality with his wife and children are punctuated by angry outbursts and, in the case of the children, spankings. And while he says that he has several good friends, one senses considerable ambivalence embedded in those relationships also . . .

All pseudopatients took extensive notes publicly. Under ordinary circumstances, such behaviour would have raised questions in the minds of observers, as, in fact, it did among patients. Indeed, it seemed so certain that the notes would elicit suspicion that elaborate precautions were taken to remove them from the ward each day. But the precautions proved needless. The closest any staff member came to questioning those notes occurred when one pseudopatient asked his physician what kind of medication he was receiving and began to write down the response. "You needn't write it," he was told gently. "If you have trouble remembering, just ask me again."

If no questions were asked of the pseudopatients, how was their writing interpreted? Nursing records for three patients indicate that the writing was seen as an aspect of their pathological behaviour. "Patient engaged in writing behaviour" was the daily nursing comment on one of the pseudopatients who was never questioned about his writing. Given that the patient is in the hospital, he must be psychologically disturbed. And given that he is disturbed, continuous writing must be a behavioural manifestation of that disturbance, perhaps a subset of the compulsive behaviours that are sometimes correlated with schizophrenia.

One tacit characteristic of psychiatric diagnosis is that it locates the sources of aberration within the individual and only rarely within the complex of stimuli that surrounds him. Consequently, behaviours that are stimulated by the environment are commonly misattributed to the patient's disorder. For example, one kindly nurse found a pseudopatient pacing the long hospital corridors. "Nervous, Mr. X?" she asked. "No, bored," he said.

The notes kept by pseudopatients are full of patient behaviours that were misinterpreted by well-intentioned staff. Often enough, a patient would go "berserk" because he had, wittingly or unwittingly, been mistreated by, say, an attendant. A nurse coming upon the scene would rarely inquire even cursorily into the environmental stimuli of the patient's behaviour. Rather, she assumed that his upset derived from his pathology, not from his present interactions with other staff members. Occasionally, the staff might assume that the patient's family (especially when they had recently visited) or other patients had stimulated the outburst. But never were the staff found to assume that one of themselves or the structure of the hospital had anything to do with a patient's behaviour. One psychiatrist pointed to a group of patients who were sitting outside the cafeteria entrance half an hour before lunchtime. To a group of young residents he indicated that such behaviour was characteristic of the oral-acquisitive nature of the syndrome. It seemed not to occur to him that there were very few things to anticipate in a psychiatric hospital besides eating.

A psychiatric label has a life and an influence of its own. Once the impression has been formed that the patient is schizophrenic, the expectation is that he will continue to be schizophrenic. When a sufficient amount of time has passed, during which the patient has done nothing bizarre, he is considered to be in remission and available for discharge. But the label endures beyond discharge, with the unconfirmed expectation that he will behave as a schizophrenic again. Such labels, conferred by mental health professionals, are as influential on the patient as they are on his relatives and friends, and it should not surprise anyone that the diagnosis acts on all of them as a self-fulfilling prophecy. Eventually, the patient himself accepts the diagnosis, with all of its surplus meanings and expectations, and behaves accordingly.[4] . . .

REFERENCES AND NOTES

1. Interestingly, of the 12 admissions, 11 were diagnosed as schizophrenic and 1, with the identical symptomatology, as manic-depressive psychosis. This diagnosis has a more favourable prognosis, and it was given by the only private hospital in our sample. On the relations between social class and psychiatric diagnosis, see A. deB. Hollingshead and F. C. Redlich, *Social Class and Mental Illness: A Community Study* (Wiley, New York, 1958).
2. T. J. Scheff, *Being Mentally Ill: A Sociological Theory* (Aldine, Chicago, 1966).
3. J. Cumming and E. Cumming, *Community Men. Health* 1, 135 (1965); A. Farina and K. Ring, *J. Abnorm. Psychol.* 70, 47 (1965); H. E. Freeman and O. G. Simmons, *The Mental Patient Comes Home* (Wiley, New York, 1963); W. J. Johannsen, *Ment. Hygiene* 53, 218 (1969); A. S. Linsky, *Soc. Psychiat.* 5, 166 (1970).
4. Scheff, *Being Mentally Ill*.

CRITICAL Reading Questions

1. How is this article an example of labelling theory? How did the diagnosis of "insane" lead to the symptoms observed by the staff?

2. Why does a false positive diagnosis of mental illness generally have more serious repercussions than a false positive diagnosis of physical illness?

3. What is the significance of the fact that many patients, but none of the staff, managed to detect pseudopatients?

4. What can this study teach us about why people engage in deviant acts and/or crime? How can it help us to better deal with people labelled deviant?

The Power of the Situation

In April 2004, dramatic images of US military personnel's abuse and torture of Iraqi prisoners at Abu Ghraib appeared in newspapers and magazines around the world. The photographs, which showed smiling soldiers with naked, scared, and wounded prisoners, shocked citizens and led to calls for the participating soldiers to be punished. Eleven soldiers were eventually convicted for these crimes. The commanding officer, Brigadier General Janis Karpinski, was reprimanded and demoted. She denied knowledge of the abuses and claimed that the soldiers' actions were authorized by her superiors. The military argued that these incidents were isolated events involving a few "bad apples."

Two famous experiments have investigated how individuals who often have no past history of deviant or criminal behaviour can do such heinous things. Perpetrators sometimes justify their actions by saying that they were simply "following orders." In the 1960s, Stanley Milgram tested whether individuals are more likely to blindly follow orders from authority figures in certain conditions and, if so, how this behaviour affected people's treatment of one another. Ten years later, Philip Zimbardo conducted the Stanford Prison experiment, which explored how individuals' behaviours are shaped by the social context and social roles.

Milgram's (1963) experiment involved three people: an experimenter (an authoritative role), a volunteer (who acted as a teacher), and a learner (who was an actor paid by Milgram). The volunteer and the learner drew slips of paper to determine their roles; however, unknown to the volunteer, both slips said "Teacher." The actor would always

RESEARCH METHOD

Experiment

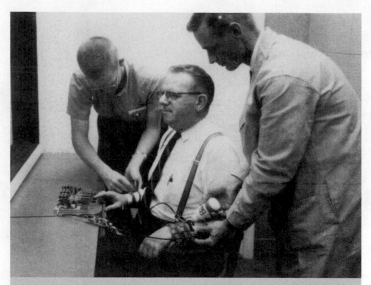

PHOTO 11.4 The Milgram experiment, "teacher" role. The teacher is being instructed how to give electrical shocks to the "learner" (who is, unbeknown to them, an actor).

PHOTO 11.5 Students in the roles of prisoners and guard in the Stanford Prison experiment.

play the learner role and the volunteer would always be the teacher. Throughout the experiment, the learner and teacher were placed in different rooms so that they could talk to but not see one another (see Photo 11.4). The teacher was instructed to teach the learner a list of word pairs. Each time the learner made a mistake, the teacher was to give him an electrical shock. The teacher was given a sample shock to get a sense of how strong it felt. After each wrong answer, the teacher was to increase the shock by 15 volts. In reality, there were no shocks. The learner set up a tape recorder integrated with the electroshock generator, which played pre-recorded sounds for each shock level. Part way through the experiment, after receiving several "shocks," the learner began to bang on the wall between him and the teacher. He then began complaining of a heart condition. Finally, there was silence from the learner's room.

As the learner demonstrated more serious signs of distress, most of the teachers wanted to stop the experiment. But the experimenter urged them to go on, saying "The experiment requires that you continue"; "It is absolutely essential that you continue"; and "You have no other choice, you must go on." Milgram and his colleagues thought that most people would not continue to administer the shocks after hearing the distress of the learner, but 65 per cent (26 of 40) of the volunteers in the first set of the experiment administered the final, massive 450-volt shock, though many were very uncomfortable doing so. Milgram concluded that being assigned the role of teacher and having an authority figure giving instructions led many people to administer much stronger shocks than they would have otherwise.

In the Stanford Prison experiment, Zimbardo (Zimbardo, Maslach, and Haney 1999) recruited 24 mentally and physically healthy, middle-class, white males with no history of crime or emotional, physical, or social problems. Half of the participants were randomly assigned to the role of prisoner and half to the role of guard. Zimbardo placed these young men in a simulated prison in the basement of Stanford University to see how they would adapt to their assigned roles in this unfamiliar environment.

Zimbardo was astonished by the extent to which the participants adopted their roles. The guards enforced their authority over the prisoners, sometimes engaging in psychological torture. Many prisoners passively accepted the abuse. Those who resisted the guards were harassed by the other prisoners. In fact, the treatment of the prisoners was so dire that two of the prisoners quit the experiment early and the experiment as a whole was stopped after only six days. As Zimbardo (in Aronson and Aronson 2011, 127) explains, "in less than a week the experience of imprisonment undid (temporarily) a lifetime of learning, human values were suspended, self-concepts were challenged and the ugliest, most base, pathological side of human nature surfaced."

These studies highlight how deviant behaviours are more likely and more severe in certain social settings. Both push us to understand that it is not just that some people are "bad" but that some situations can make people act in ways contrary to their usual selves. As Zimbardo (in Aronson and Aronson 2011, 128) argues, "individual behavior is largely under the control of social forces and environmental contingencies rather than personality traits, character, will power or other empirically unvalidated constructs." We thus expect that deviance is more likely in certain situations, such as when individuals enjoy anonymity (in Milgram's study, the volunteer is in a separate room from the person he is shocking; in Zimbardo's, the guards wear the same uniform and reflective glasses so prisoners cannot see their eyes). Consider how the theories of crime and deviance we have learned about in this chapter support or contradict the findings of these studies.

Crime Rates

Crime has consequences at both the micro-individual level as well as the macro-social level. People who have been victims of crime are clearly affected by their experience; however, the existence of crime in a community can also affect residents' well-being and health (HRSDC 2013; Pittman et al. 2012). These serious implications are one reason that governments spend large amounts of money on trying to prevent and reduce crime.

RESEARCH METHOD

Survey

To this end, governments must know how much and what types of crimes occur in their country. Conducted by Statistics Canada since 1962, the **Uniform Crime Reporting (UCR) Survey** collects information on all criminal incidents reported to, and substantiated by, Canadian police services. Using data from the UCR Survey, Figure 11.2 shows crime rates in Canada from 1962 to 2012. The crime rate is the incidents of a particular type of crime per 100,000 people in a population. The figure separates crimes that are violent, such as murder and sexual assault, from property crimes, such as robbery and breaking and entering. You will notice that crime rates were at their highest in 1991 and have been declining steadily since. Property crime experienced a particularly sharp drop; violent crimes decreased at a slower rate, although they have always occurred at much lower rates than property crime.

Measuring the severity of crime is also important. The **Crime Severity Index (CSI)** assigns each offence a weight based on the severity of the sentences handed down by the courts. For example, petty theft is less serious and has shorter sentences than homicide. As shown in Figure 11.3, the CSI has declined every year since 2003. Figures 11.4 and 11.5 show the rates of homicide (arguably the most severe crime) and break and enter/motor vehicle theft (less serious crimes). Although both offences are declining, the rate is much steeper for the property crimes.

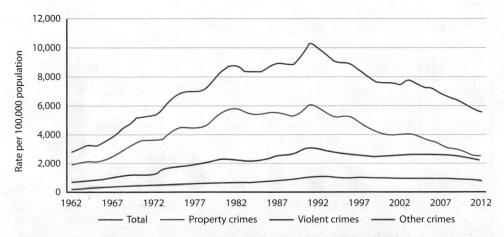

FIGURE 11.2 Police-reported crime rates, Canada, 1962–2012

SOURCE: Perreault, Samuel. 2013. "Police-Reported Crime Statistics in Canada, 2012." Statistics Canada, 25 July. www.statcan.gc.ca/pub/85-002-x/2013001/article/11854-eng.htm.

HIGHLIGHT ///

Comparing Crime around the World

Comparing crime rates across countries is difficult because laws, police practices, and crime classifications often differ. For example, marijuana possession is legal in the Netherlands, illegal but only selectively prosecuted in Canada, and can lead to jail time in the United States.

Murder is reported and tracked in all countries. Figure A shows that most of the Western world has relatively low murder rates compared to other regions. High murder rates tend to occur in countries with high levels of poverty, inequality, and discrimination. These differences partly account for the higher rates of murder in certain countries. Although this global comparison makes Canadian murder rates appear relatively low, many argue that comparing Canada with countries experiencing high levels of poverty and underdevelopment may not be a fair comparison. Figure B compares Canada's murder

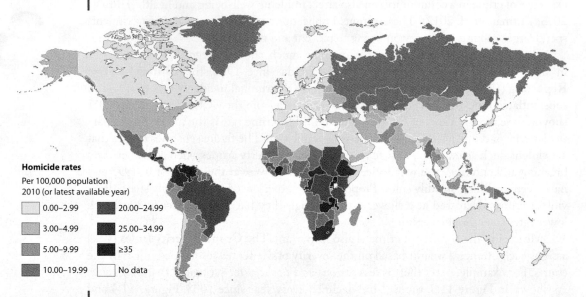

Homicide rates

Per 100,000 population
2010 (or latest available year)

0.00–2.99	20.00–24.99
3.00–4.99	25.00–34.99
5.00–9.99	≥35
10.00–19.99	No data

FIGURE A Murder rates across the world, country by country, per 100,000

SOURCE: Chapman, Mark. 2011. "Murder Rates across the World, Country by Country." *Knifecrime* (blog), 7 October. http://knifecrime.blogspot.ca/2011/10/murder-rates-across-world-country-by.html.

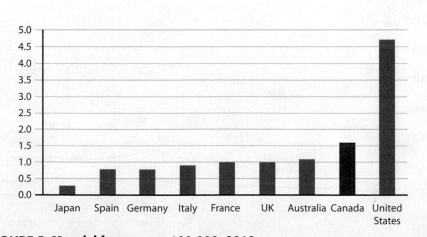

FIGURE B Homicide rate per 100,000, 2013

SOURCE: Based on data from the United Nations Office on Drugs and Crime. 2014. *Global Study on Homicide 2013: Trends, Contexts, Data*. Vienna: UNODC. www.unodc.org/documents/gsh/pdfs/2014_GLOBAL_HOMICIDE_BOOK_web.pdf.

rate with that of some other industrialized countries. We can see that the Canadian murder rate, while much lower than the rate in the United States, is still relatively high when compared with most other European countries, Australia, and Japan.

The rate of gun ownership is another explanation given for higher crime rates in certain countries, particularly murder rates. Many more Americans than Canadians own guns—the number of guns per 100 people in the United States is about three times higher than it is in Canada (see Figure C). The US murder rate is also about three times higher. While these statistics are interesting, we have to be cautious about drawing a connection between them. For example, gun ownership in the UK is about the same as it is in Canada; however, Britain's murder rate is much lower than ours.

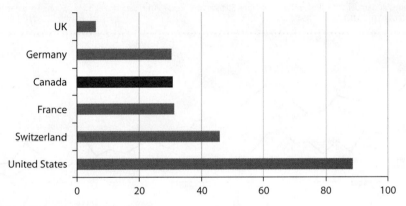

FIGURE C Guns per 100 civilians

SOURCE: Based on data from MacQueen, Ken. 2009. "The Lowdown on Crime in Canada: We Have a Higher Murder Rate than Germany and a Lower One than Scotland." *Maclean's*, 1 July. www.macleans.ca/news/canada/the-lowdown-on-crime-in-canada-compared-to-other-countries/.

It is also instructive to look at the prison population across countries. We can see in Figure D that the Canadian prison population is similar to the rate in the UK and France, and much lower than that in the United States and Russia, which have six to seven times more prisoners. Comparing rates across countries allows us to assess the extent to which Canada's laws, criminal justice system, and culture as a whole effectively handle and reduce crime.

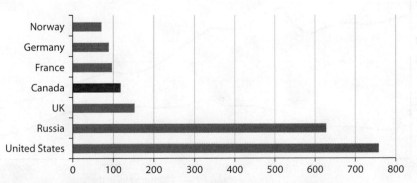

FIGURE D Prisoners per 100,000 population

SOURCE: Based on data from MacQueen, Ken. 2009. "The Lowdown on Crime in Canada: We Have a Higher Murder Rate than Germany and a Lower One than Scotland." *Maclean's*, 1 July. www.macleans.ca/news/canada/the-lowdown-on-crime-in-canada-compared-to-other-countries/.

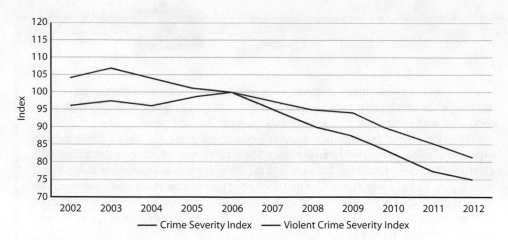

FIGURE 11.3 Police-reported Crime Severity Indexes, 2002–2012

SOURCE: Perreault, Samuel. 2013. "Police-Reported Crime Statistics in Canada, 2012." Statistics Canada, 25 July. www.statcan.gc.ca/pub/85-002-x/2013001/article/11854-eng.htm.

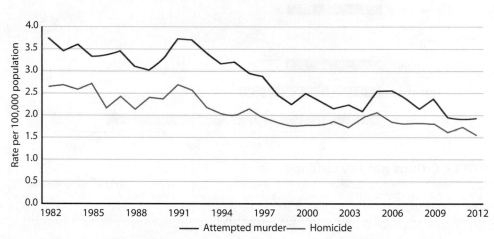

FIGURE 11.4 Attempted murder and homicide, police-reported rates, Canada, 1982–2012

SOURCE: Perreault, Samuel. 2013. "Police-Reported Crime Statistics in Canada, 2012." Statistics Canada, 25 July. www.statcan.gc.ca/pub/85-002-x/2013001/article/11854-eng.htm.

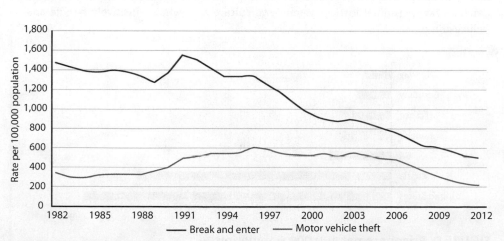

FIGURE 11.5 Break and enter and motor vehicle theft, police-reported rates, Canada, 1982–2012

SOURCE: Perreault, Samuel. "Police-Reported Crime Statistics in Canada, 2012." 2013. Statistics Canada, 25 July. www.statcan.gc.ca/pub/85-002-x/2013001/article/11854-eng.htm.

Crime Rates by Group

Looking at a country's overall crime rate can demonstrate whether crime is increasing or decreasing and what types of crimes are most prevalent. However, these overall statistics mask some important differences between groups. Crime rates vary widely by age of the accused perpetrators. Individuals are most likely to commit crimes between the ages of 15 and 24 (see Figure 11.6). These youth crimes are usually acts of primary deviance and tend to be of low severity, such as drug use, shoplifting, and petty theft. In most cases, criminal behaviour ends with the onset of adulthood and adult responsibilities. After 60, people are highly unlikely to engage in criminal activity!

Crime rates also differ significantly by gender. In Canada, men are much more likely to be arrested than women and account for four out of every five adults charged with crime in Canada (Brennan 2013). This imbalance is particularly evident in sexual crimes; men accounted for 98 per cent of all persons charged with sexual assault, child pornography, and sexual violations against children in 2011. Women tend to be more evenly represented in crimes such as abduction (49 per cent), prostitution (47 per cent), and theft under $5,000 (37 per cent).

Interestingly, trends in crime for men and women have diverged over time. Crime by men has been declining for 20 years in Canada; however, crime by women has been increasing (Brennan 2013). Violent crime among women, in particular, has seen a notable increase. While the rate of male violent crime has decreased by 32 per cent since 1991, female violent crime has increased by 34 per cent. That said, women have always been less likely than men to commit violent crimes, accounting for only 20 per cent of this type of crime in 2011.

Finally, there is a wide difference in crime rates by ancestry and race. A disproportionate number of Aboriginal and black Canadians are in the criminal justice system. Aboriginal people represent 3 per cent of the population but account for 17 per cent of federal inmates (CBC News 2008). Black people account

PHOTO 11.6 Why are crimes such as shoplifting generally considered less serious? Would your opinion of someone change if you found out that she had shoplifted as a teenager? Why or why not?

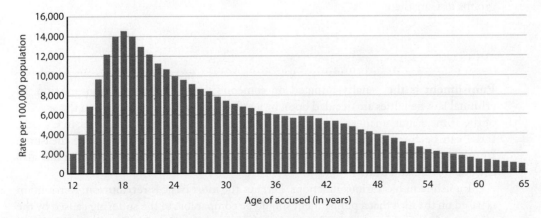

FIGURE 11.6 Crime rate by age of accused, Canada, 2011

SOURCE: Brennan, Shannon. 2013. "Police-reported crime statistics in Canada, 2011." Statistics Canada, 25 July. www.statcan.gc.ca/pub/85-002-x/2012001/article/11692-eng.htm#a15.

Calculating Crime Rates

The Government of Canada and the criminal justice system calculate the crime rate to give us a sense of the amount of types of crimes that occur in Canada. However, official statistics do not necessarily report *actual* rates of crime because not every criminal activity is reported and some activities reported to police are not crimes. Instead, these statistics are collected by using particular methods with particular limitations, constraints, and complications. Go to this book's companion website to access Samuel Perreault's "Police-Reported Crime Statistics in Canada, 2012." Read the article and then answer the following questions:

1. How is the crime rate calculated? What is good about this traditional crime rate and what is missed?

2. How is the CSI better or worse than the traditional crime rate that Canada has used? (See Statistics Canada's "Section: 1 The Crime Severity Index," available at this book's companion website.)

3. Beyond the traditional crime rate and CSI, what other methods could be used to construct as comprehensive a crime rate as possible?

4. What are the benefits of using **victimization surveys** instead of a traditional crime rate? Why do victimization surveys usually show evidence of higher crime rates than do official statistics?

for only 2 per cent of the population yet represent more than 6 per cent of the federal prison population (COP 2008).

Conflict theorists argue that the higher crime rates in these populations could be the result of low SES, lack of education, as well as high rates of victimization, substance abuse, and gang participation in Aboriginal and African-Canadian communities (Latimer and Foss 2004). In this way, the real predictor of engagement in crime is poverty and other social problems, not race or ethnicity. Demographics could be another cause (Latimer and Foss 2005). Because Canada's Aboriginal population is significantly younger than its non-Aboriginal population, and younger people commit more crime than older people, Aboriginal people have a higher probability of being in the age group most associated with offending. In this way, crime rates by group can indicate other inequalities between groups of Canadians.

Punishment

Punishment is the penalty inflicted on someone for committing a transgression. In criminal law, penalties are decided upon by a judge and/or jury, depending on the severity of the crime. Punishments are a denial of certain privileges, abilities, or rights; in Canada, these can be fines, community service, imprisonment, or restorative justice measures. In other countries (and historically in Canada), penalties for transgressing the law also include torture and death.

Punishment has various functions. Perhaps the most basic is **retribution**. Retribution is based on the idea that a punishment should be comparable to the suffering caused by the crime (i.e. "an eye for an eye"). The thinking is that a crime upsets society's moral balance. By punishing the criminal in equal measure, this balance and moral order can be restored. Retributive justice must be proportionate to the crime committed so that criminals suffer the pain that they have inflicted on others. A murderer can be executed, but someone who commits robbery should not be. Proponents of retributive justice argue that it can help to satisfy the resentment felt by the victim or victim's family.

The second main function of punishment is **deterrence**, the process of dissuading someone from future wrongdoing by making the "cost" of punishment outweigh the "benefit" of committing the crime. Deterrence assumes that offenders conduct a rational cost–benefit analysis before committing an offence. There are two types of deterrence: general and specific. **General deterrence** involves making an example out of deviants to deter others from committing crimes. **Specific deterrence** aims to discourage specific individuals by convincing them that engaging in crime does not benefit them. For example, if an individual is charged with drug trafficking and sentenced to a long jail sentence, he may decide that remaining in the drug trade is not worth the risk of future (and longer) jail terms.

Many people consider the death penalty the ultimate deterrent. The idea is that the high cost of potentially being executed is greater than any benefit from committing a crime. Canada abolished the death penalty in 1976 but has not executed anyone since 1962. Many other countries have also abol-

PHOTO 11.7 Ankle monitors are usually used in conjunction with house arrest. How are they punishments and how might they deter future crimes?

ished the death penalty, including the UK, France, and Germany. However, there are many countries that still use it: China, Iran, North Korea, Yemen, and the United States have the most executions per year (Rogers and Chalabi 2013). While many people support the death penalty, some believe that it is morally wrong to kill in all contexts. Others worry that some innocent people are executed, which is particularly problematic given the strong evidence of bias, especially racial bias, in capital punishment. For example, studies show that blacks, and non-whites more generally, who are convicted of killing whites are more likely to get the death penalty than whites who kill other whites (Paternoster 2007).

The next major function of punishment is **rehabilitation**, a newer focus of the criminal justice system. Rehabilitation is not simply about punishing criminals but aims to reform, or "heal," them and help them reintegrate into society so that they will not reoffend. If you believe, for example, that crime originates from the social environment, rehabilitation might be an appropriate response to deviance. If offenders learn to be deviant, they can learn to conform. However, rehabilitation is needed to transform the "deviant" into this new identity. Rehabilitation does so by motivating constructive improvement on the part of the offender.

Parole, the supervised early release of a prisoner for such things as good behaviour, can be thought of as part of rehabilitation. Parole officers work with parolees to help them adjust to life outside prison and to ensure that they do not violate the conditions of their release. If they do breach those terms, they can be sent back to prison. **Probation** is a possibility for individuals who are convicted of less serious crimes. These individuals are released into the community under supervision and certain conditions, such as attending and completing a substance abuse program or having a curfew. If the offender does not adhere to these conditions or is arrested, the probation can be revoked.

Punishment is also about **societal protection**. When we incapacitate criminals, we physically prevent them from committing crimes. For example, when criminals are put in jail or are equipped with electronic monitoring devices, we limit their ability to commit crimes and try to protect other members of society from crime. Incapacitation can include imprisonment, the death penalty, or castration of sex offenders.

Punishment is also used for boundary-setting, education, and norm re-enforcement. The logic is that, if wrongdoing goes unpunished, citizens will become demoralized and will not respect laws, thus ultimately threatening the "moral fabric" of society. Historically, societies pursued these goals by holding executions in public. Doing so reinforced the sovereign's power (i.e. the state's power to punish those that violate its laws) in the minds of the people. Punishment thus aided in boundary-setting by illustrating what the population is or is not allowed to do and publicly demonstrated that the state is the ultimate enforcer of power. A very effective way to increase solidarity in a society is to have its members collectively agree that something is wrong. For example, when people comment on what a "monster" a high-profile murderer is, they implicitly emphasize the collective opinion that murder is wrong and that those who commit murder are deviant and lie outside society's norms. This theory of punishment is consistent with Durkheim's argument about the functions of crime, which include creating solidarity and clarifying social norms.

Finally, punishment can lead to **restoration**. Offenders restore order by compensating or fixing the injustice caused by their crime. Restorative justice requires that the offender must first accept guilt. Examples of restorative justice include vandals cleaning up their graffiti and offenders participating in Aboriginal healing circles. In Chapter 12, we will learn about a recent and prominent incident of restorative justice, the Truth and Reconciliation Commission of Canada.

Individuals who ascribe to individual-level explanations for crime tend to favour harsher punishments, while those that use social explanations tend to support less punitive responses. Regardless of whether the punishments are harsh or lenient, **recidivism rates** (the rates at which individuals reoffend) are generally quite high. For example, Langan and Levin (2002) found that approximately 67.5 per cent of released prisoners were rearrested within three years. This number should make us question how well the current system rehabilitates individuals who have entered the criminal justice system.

The following excerpt from Michel Foucault's *Discipline and Punish: The Birth of the Prison* examines two types of punishment: torture and incarceration. The comparison of the public torture of Robert-François Damiens, who was convicted of attempted murder in the mid-eighteenth century, with the daily routine of inmates in a nineteenth-century prison illustrates the dramatic changes that have occurred in punishment in Western societies. Foucault also discusses the reasons for these changes and the issue of the most humane way to punish a criminal.

READING

The Body of the Condemned

Michel Foucault

On 2 March 1757 Damiens the regicide was condemned "to make the *amende honorable* before the main door of the Church of Paris," where he was to be "taken and conveyed in a cart, wearing nothing but a shirt, holding a torch of burning wax weighing two pounds"; then, "in the said cart, to the Place de Grève, where, on a scaffold that will be erected there, the flesh will be torn from his breasts, arms, thighs and calves with red-hot pincers, his right hand, holding the knife with which he committed the said parricide, burnt with sulphur, and, on those places where the flesh will be torn away, poured molten lead, boiling oil, burning resin, wax and sulphur melted together and then his body drawn and quartered by four horses and his limbs and body consumed by fire, reduced to ashes and his ashes thrown to the winds" (*Pièces originales . . .*, 372–4).

"Finally, he was quartered," recounts the *Gazette d'Amsterdam* of 1 April 1757. "This last operation was very long, because the horses used were not accustomed to drawing; consequently, instead of four, six were needed; and when that did not suffice, they were forced, in order to cut off the wretch's thighs, to sever the sinews and hack at the joints . . .

"It is said that, though he was always a great swearer, no blasphemy escaped his lips; but the excessive pain made him utter horrible cries, and he often repeated: 'My God, have pity on me! Jesus, help me!' The spectators were all edified by the solicitude of the parish priest of St Paul's who despite his great age did not spare himself in offering consolation to the patient."

Bouton, an officer of the watch, left us his account: "The sulphur was lit, but the flame was so poor that only the top skin of the hand was burnt, and that only slightly. Then the executioner, his sleeves rolled up, took the steel pincers, which had been especially made for the occasion, and which were about a foot and a half long, and pulled first at the calf of the right leg, then at the thigh, and from there at the two fleshy parts of the right arm; then at the breasts. Though a strong, sturdy fellow, this executioner found it so difficult to tear away the pieces of flesh that he set about the same spot two or three times, twisting the pincers as he did so, and what he took away formed at each part a wound about the size of a six-pound crown piece.

"After these tearings with the pincers, Damiens, who cried out profusely, though without swearing, raised his head and looked at himself; the same executioner dipped an iron spoon in the pot containing the boiling potion, which he poured liberally over each wound. Then the ropes that were to be harnessed to the horses were attached with cords to the patient's body; the horses were then harnessed and placed alongside the arms and legs, one at each limb.

"Monsieur Le Breton, the clerk of the court, went up to the patient several times and asked him if he had anything to say. He said he had not; at each torment, he cried out, as the damned in hell are supposed to cry out, 'Pardon, my God! Pardon, Lord.' Despite all this pain, he raised his head from time to time and looked at himself boldly. The cords had been tied so tightly by the men who pulled the ends that they caused him indescribable pain. Monsieur Le Breton went up to him again and asked him if he had anything to say; he said no. Several confessors went up to him and spoke to him at length; he willingly kissed the crucifix that was held out to him; he opened his lips and repeated: 'Pardon, Lord.'

"The horses tugged hard, each pulling straight on a limb, each horse held by an executioner. After a quarter of an hour, the same ceremony was repeated and finally, after several attempts, the direction of the horses had to be changed, thus: those at the arms were made to pull towards the head, those at the thighs towards the arms, which broke the arms at the joints. This was repeated several times without success. He raised his head and looked at himself. Two more horses had to be added to those harnessed to the thighs, which made six horses in all. Without success.

"Finally, the executioner, Samson, said to Monsieur Le Breton that there was no way or hope of succeeding, and told him to ask their Lordships if they wished him to have the prisoner cut into pieces. Monsieur Le Breton, who had come down from the town, ordered that renewed efforts be made, and this was done; but the horses gave up and one of those harnessed to the thighs fell to the ground. The confessors returned and spoke to him again. He said to them (I heard him): 'Kiss me, gentlemen.' The parish priest of St Paul's did not dare to, so Monsieur de Marsilly slipped under the rope holding the left arm and kissed him on the forehead. The executioners gathered round and Damiens told them not to swear, to carry out their task and that he did not think ill of them; he begged them to pray to God for him, and asked the parish priest of St Paul's to pray for him at the first mass. . . .

Eighty years later, Léon Faucher drew up his rules "for the House of young prisoners in Paris":

Art. 17. The prisoners' day will begin at six in the morning in winter and at five in summer. They will work for nine hours a day throughout the year. Two hours a day will be devoted to instruction. Work and the day will end at nine o'clock in winter and at eight in summer.

Art. 18. *Rising.* At the first drum-roll, the prisoners must rise and dress in silence, as the supervisor opens the cell doors. At the second drum-roll, they must be dressed and make their beds. At the third, they must line up and proceed to the chapel for morning prayer. There is a five-minute interval between each drum-roll.

Art. 19. The prayers are conducted by the chaplain and followed by a moral or religious reading. This exercise must not last more than half an hour.

Art. 20. *Work.* At a quarter to six in the summer, a quarter to seven in winter, the prisoners go down into the courtyard where they must wash their hands and faces, and receive their first ration of bread. Immediately afterwards, they form into work-teams and go off to work, which must begin at six in summer and seven in winter.

Art. 21. *Meal.* At ten o'clock the prisoners leave their work and go to the refectory; they wash their hands in their courtyards and assemble in divisions. After the dinner, there is recreation until twenty minutes to eleven.

Art. 22. *School.* At twenty minutes to eleven, at the drum-roll, the prisoners form into ranks, and proceed in divisions to the school. The class lasts two hours and consists alternately of reading, writing, drawing and arithmetic.

Art. 23. At twenty minutes to one, the prisoners leave the school, in divisions, and return to their courtyards for recreation. At five minutes to one, at the drum-roll, they form into work-teams.

Art. 24. At one o'clock they must be back in the workshops: they work until four o'clock.

Art. 25. At four o'clock the prisoners leave their workshops and go into the courtyards where they wash their hands and form into divisions for the refectory.

Art. 26. Supper and the recreation that follows it last until five o'clock: the prisoners then return to the workshops.

Art. 27. At seven o'clock in the summer, at eight in winter, work stops; bread is distributed for the last time in the workshops. For a quarter of an hour one of the prisoners or supervisors reads a passage from some instructive or uplifting work. This is followed by evening prayer.

Art. 28. At half-past seven in summer, half-past eight in winter, the prisoners must be back in their cells after the washing of hands and the inspection of clothes in the courtyard; at the first drum-roll, they must undress, and at the second get into bed. The cell doors are closed and the supervisors go the rounds in the corridors, to ensure order and silence (Faucher, 274–82).

We have, then, a public execution and a timetable. They do not punish the same crimes or the same type of delinquent. But they each define a certain penal style. Less than a century separates them. It was a time when, in Europe and in the United States, the entire economy of punishment was redistributed. It was a time of great "scandals" for traditional justice, a time of innumerable projects for reform. It saw a new theory of law and crime, a new moral or political justification of the right to punish; old laws were abolished, old customs died out. "Modern" codes were planned or drawn up: Russia, 1769; Prussia, 1780; Pennsylvania and Tuscany, 1786; Austria, 1788; France, 1791, Year IV, 1808 and 1810. It was a new age for penal justice.

Among so many changes, I shall consider one: the disappearance of torture as a public spectacle. Today we are rather inclined to ignore it; perhaps, in its time, it gave rise to too much inflated rhetoric; perhaps it has been attributed too readily and too emphatically to a process of "humanization," thus dispensing with the need for further analysis. And, in any case, how important is such a change, when compared with the great institutional transformations, the formulation of explicit, general codes and unified rules of procedure; with the almost universal adoption of the jury system, the definition of the essentially corrective character of the penalty and the tendency which has become increasingly marked since the nineteenth century, to adapt punishment to the individual offender? Punishment of a less immediately physical kind, a certain discretion in the art of inflicting pain, a combination of more subtle, more subdued sufferings, deprived of their visible display, should not all this be treated as a special case, an incidental effect of deeper changes? And yet the fact remains that a few decades saw the disappearance of the tortured, dismembered, amputated body, symbolically branded on face or shoulder, exposed alive or dead to public view. The body as the major target of penal repression disappeared.

By the end of the eighteenth and the beginning of the nineteenth century, the gloomy festival of punishment was dying out, though here and there it flickered momentarily into life. In this transformation, two processes were at work. They did not have quite the same chronology or the same raison d'être. The first was the disappearance of punishment as a spectacle. The ceremonial of punishment tended to decline; it survived only as a new legal or administrative practice. . . . The use of prisoners in public works, cleaning city streets or repairing the highways, was practised in Austria, Switzerland, and certain of the United States, such as Pennsylvania. These convicts, distinguished by their "infamous dress" and shaven heads, "were brought before the public. The sport of the idle and the vicious, they often become incensed, and naturally took violent revenge upon the aggressors. To prevent them from returning injuries which might be inflicted on them, they were encumbered with iron collars and chains to which bombshells were attached, to be dragged along while they performed their degrading service, under the eyes of keepers armed with swords, blunderbusses and other weapons of destruction" (Roberts Vaux, *Notices*, 21, quoted in Teeters, 1937–24). This practice was abolished practically everywhere at the end of the eighteenth or the beginning of the nineteenth century. . . .

Punishment, then, will tend to become the most hidden part of the penal process. This has several consequences: it leaves the domain of more or less everyday perception and enters that of abstract consciousness; its effectiveness is seen as resulting from its inevitability, not from its visible intensity; it is the certainty of being punished and not the horrifying spectacle of public punishment that must discourage crime; the exemplary mechanics of punishment changes its mechanisms. . . .

The disappearance of public executions marks therefore the decline of the spectacle; but it also marks a slackening of the hold on the body. . . . One no longer touched the body, or at least as little as possible, and then only to reach something other than the body itself. It might be objected that imprisonment, confinement, forced labour, penal servitude, prohibition from entering certain areas, deportation—which have occupied so important a place in modern penal systems—are "physical" penalties: unlike fines, for example, they directly affect the body. But the punishment–body relation is not the same as it was in the torture during public executions. The body now serves as an instrument or intermediary: if one intervenes upon it to imprison it, or to make it work, it is in order to deprive the individual of a liberty that is regarded both as a right and as property. The body, according to this penalty, is caught up in a system of constraints and privations, obligations and prohibitions. Physical pain, the pain of the body itself, is no longer the constituent element of the penalty. . . . As a result of this new restraint, a whole army of technicians took over from the executioner, the immediate anatomist of pain: warders, doctors, chaplains, psychiatrists, psychologists, educationalists; by their very presence near the prisoner, they sing the praises that the law needs: they reassure it that the body and pain are not the ultimate objects of its punitive action. . . .

The modern rituals of execution attest to this double process: the disappearance of the spectacle and the elimination of pain. . . .

. . . But a punishment like forced labour or even imprisonment—mere loss of liberty—has never functioned without a certain additional element of punishment that certainly concerns the body itself: rationing of food, sexual deprivation, corporal punishment, solitary confinement. Are these the unintentional, but inevitable, consequence of imprisonment? In fact, in its most explicit practices, imprisonment has always involved a certain degree of physical pain. The criticism that was often levelled at the penitentiary system in the early nineteenth century (imprisonment is not a sufficient punishment: prisoners are less hungry, less cold, less deprived in general than many poor people or even workers) suggests a postulate that was never explicitly denied: it is just that a condemned man should suffer physically more than other men. It is difficult to dissociate punishment from additional physical pain. What would a non-corporal punishment be? . . .

The reduction in penal severity in the last 200 years is a phenomenon with which legal historians are well acquainted. But, for a long time, it has been regarded in an overall way as a quantitative phenomenon: less cruelty, less pain, more kindness, more respect, more "humanity." In fact, these changes are accompanied by a displacement in the very object of the punitive operation. Is there a diminution of intensity? Perhaps. There is certainly a change of objective.

If the penalty in its most severe forms no longer addresses itself to the body, on what does it lay hold? . . . It seems to be contained in the question itself: since it is no longer the body, it must be the soul. The expiation that once rained down upon the body must be replaced by a punishment that acts in depth on the heart, the thoughts, the will, the inclinations. . . .

. . . They are punished by means of a punishment that has the function of making the offender "not only desirous, but also capable, of living within the law and of providing for his own needs"; they are punished by the internal economy of a penalty which, while intended to punish the crime, may be altered (shortened or, in certain cases, extended) according to changes in the prisoner's behaviour; and they are punished by the "security measures" that accompany the penalty (prohibition of entering certain areas, probation, obligatory medical treatment), and which are intended not to punish the offence, but to supervise the individual, to neutralize his dangerous state of mind, to alter his criminal tendencies, and to continue even when this change has been achieved. . . . During the 150 or 200 years that Europe has been setting up its new penal systems, the judges have gradually, by means of a process that goes back very far indeed, taken to judging something other than crimes, namely, the "soul" of the criminal. . . .

. . . A corpus of knowledge, techniques, "scientific" discourses is formed and becomes entangled with the practice of the power to punish. . . .

REFERENCES

Faucher, L. *De la réforme des prisons*, 1838.

Pièces originales et procédures du procès fait à Robert-François Damiens, III, 1757. Teeters, N. K., *They Were in Prison*, 1937.

Vaux, Roberts, *Notices*, 1768.

CRITICAL
Reading
Questions

1. How did punishment change over time, according to Foucault? How are these changes related to evolving ideas of punishing the body versus punishing the soul?

2. What is the public's role in punishment and how has it changed?

3. What is the purpose of punishment? How did the purpose change from the eighteenth to the nineteenth centuries?

4. Who decides and enacts punishment in Foucault's analysis? How is this person/institution related to ideas about why people commit crimes, the function of the criminal justice system, and the reasons for punishment?

PHOTO 11.8 Are these people vandalizing a building or creating art? What would make this act a crime and what would make it an artistic impression? Why does such categorization matter?

Summary

This chapter discussed the different kinds of deviance and crime that exist in society and how these categories are socially constructed. Explanations for these acts can be made at the individual level, by looking at a person's biology or personality, or at the social level, by focusing on a person's social environment. Most sociological work in this area focuses on social explanations. We also examined labelling theory and Rosenhan's experiment regarding the powerful impact of labelling someone a deviant. This chapter explored crime rates in Canada and around the world, including how these numbers are calculated. We ended by considering punishment's different functions in society and Foucault's famous discussion of changes in punishment.

Key Terms

consensus crimes 303
control theory 308
Crime Severity Index (CSI) 317
deterrence 323
deviance 302
general deterrence 323
labelling theory 309
learning theory 308
lesser crimes 302
normality of crime 304
parole 323
primary deviance 309
probation 323
punishment 322

recidivism rate 324
rehabilitation 323
restoration 324
retribution 322
secondary deviance 309
societal protection 323
specific deterrence 323
strain theory 307
subcultural theory 308
Uniform Crime Reporting (UCR)
    Survey 317
victimization survey 322
white-collar crime 303

For Further Reading

Anderson, Elijah. 1999. *Code of the Street*. New York: Norton.

Becker, Howard. 1963. *Outsiders: Studies in the Sociology of Deviance*. New York: Free Press.

Downes, David, Paul Rock, and Chris McCormick. 2013. *Understanding Deviance: A Guide to the Sociology of Deviance and Rule Breaking*, 2nd Canadian edn. Don Mills, ON: Oxford University Press.

Foucault, Michel. 1995. *Discipline and Punish: The Birth of the Prison*. New York: Vintage.

Goffman, Erving. 1986. *Stigma: Notes on the Management of Spoiled Identity*. New York: Simon and Schuster.

PART IV

Social Change

12 Change through Policy and the Law

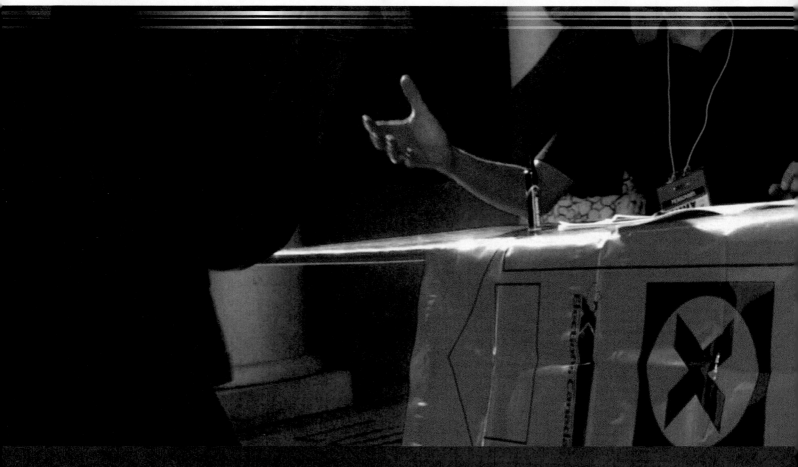

CHAPTER OUTLINE

Introduction

Throughout this book, we have learned about how our society operates. We began by examining how we learn to fit into society through socialization, the ways we differentiate people and how doing so can lead to inequality, and the major social institutions and their roles. The final core area of sociology is the study of social change. For many students, learning about the inequality that exists in our society and how societal institutions often help to perpetuate that inequality can be frustrating. They ask: How can we change our society and make it more equal and just? How can we alter institutions to address important social problems? In this chapter and the next, we will learn about the major routes to social change.

How Does Society Reproduce Itself?

We all want to change things about society. Yet, for a variety of reasons, society generally stays the same. We are all socialized to follow the rules and norms of society and to fit in. Those who question or resist the social order are punished for their deviance. A child who will not listen to the teacher in class, who does not like to do the activities usually associated with her age group or gender, or who does not dress in a conventional way might be punished by being suspended, receiving poor grades, or being isolated or bullied by other children. Even later in life, we are rewarded for doing what we are "supposed to"—going to university, getting a "good" job, finding a partner, and raising a family. In general, we are taught not to question why things are as they are and to simply accept that the way our society is set up is the natural order. If formal laws and regulations are not enough to encourage us to conform, informal social sanctions such as exclusion and shaming ensure that we follow the rules.

PHOTO 12.1 In Ottawa in 1938, a plaque commemorating the Famous Five, whose work led to the Persons Case and women's right to hold public office in Canada, was unveiled. From left to right in the front row are Muir Edwards, daughter-in-law of Henrietta Muir Edwards; J.C. Kenwood, daughter of Judge Emily Murphy; Prime Minister Mackenzie King; and Nellie McClung. In the rear row, from left to right, are Senators Iva Campbell Fallis and Cairine Wilson.

Despite these disincentives, social change does happen. **Social change**, at a general level, is the transformation of culture and social institutions over time. Sometimes this change occurs quite quickly, such as in the invention of new computer technology that revolutionized how we interact with one another. At other times, things happen more slowly, such as shifting gender norms (see Chapter 6). Social change can be intentional, for example, when a new law is passed to legalize abortion or gay marriage. However, social change is often unintentional. The printing press, discussed in Chapter 7, was not invented to create social change but still altered many facets of society and social interaction.

Finally, while we tend to think of many social changes as natural and inevitable, they were often quite contentious at the time. The women's suffrage movement required the dissolution of many informal norms about women's behaviour, such as the idea that it was natural for women to remain within the domestic sphere and that they did not belong in the public sphere. The removal of formal laws restricting women's roles in public life also brought about gradual social change. Women's suffrage, the legalization of marriage between people of different races, and the abolition of slavery seem like things that everyone would have surely supported. However, these were very controversial proposals and many people fought vigorously against them.

The Routes to Social Change

Social change can happen through institutional channels, particularly through the state. The state provides an important arena for creating social change through elections, laws, and social policy. Social change can also occur outside the state's institutions, through cultural change or the work of social movements. This chapter focuses on state-based social change; the next examines social change outside the state.

To consider the general routes to social change, let's think about the expansion of LGBTQ rights. If you are interested in these rights and are working within the state, you could elect political leaders who are also interested in gay rights—perhaps those who advocate for the passing of same-sex marriage laws. You could also challenge the legality of discriminating against gays and lesbians. The latter is, in fact, how gay marriage became legal in Canada. Gay couples argued in court that not being allowed to marry simply because of their sexual orientation was discriminatory. The Supreme Court of Canada agreed, finding the law unconstitutional and instructing Parliament to change it. Another approach is to change the policies of government or government agencies. For example, gay and lesbian people used to have more trouble adopting children than heterosexual people did. During this time, passing a policy in adoption agencies that excludes sexual orientation as a basis for determining who would be a good parent would have made the process easier.

The Rise of the State

The **state** is a set of institutions that includes four components: political decision-makers, who are either elected or appointed; administrative units or bureaucracies, such as a ministry of health or education; a judiciary or legal system; and security services (police within a country and armies outside). States are also attached to a geographic territory and maintain a monopoly and autonomy on rule-making, coercion, and violence within that territory. The state is, arguably, the most powerful institution in contemporary society. It is the only institution with the legal right to tax you, use violence on you through the police, military, and court systems; permit or force you to kill by sending you to war; legally hold you in prison; and, in some places, kill you via capital punishment (Stanbridge and Ramos 2012).

The state's right to use violence is considered justifiable because it works to maintain social order and to defend the nation's interests. As Max Weber famously said, the power of the state ultimately flows from its monopoly on the legitimate use of violence (in Gerth and Mills 1946). However, the state cannot wield these powers in any way it chooses. If people feel that it uses violence in an illegitimate way, they can resist through civil unrest. The state can also be subject to sanctions from the international community and, eventually, a decline in state power.

The state is also powerful because it can set policies and laws governing your behaviour—how you can buy or sell a car, rent a house, or become licensed to work as a teacher or doctor; whom you can marry; and many other facets of your daily life. We permit the state to do these things because they provide us with services such as schools, roads, and healthcare, ensure a safe and orderly society, and protect our national interests (Stanbridge and Ramos 2012).

States, like other institutions in society, change over time. The state emerged in its modern form between the twelfth and eighteenth centuries in Western Europe. The three major explanations for this rise focus on the importance of the state for managing increasingly large territories, enacting war, and controlling the economy. Let's examine each function in turn.

From 1100 to 1600 in Europe, there was a rise of "political units persisting in time and fixed in space, the development of permanent, impersonal institutions, agreement on the need for an authority which can give final judgments, and the acceptance of the idea that this authority should receive the basic loyalty of its subjects" (Strayer 1970, 10). As territories grew in geographic size and population, the state was needed to better manage and control these larger areas and groups of people. This **managerial perspective** focuses on the evolving practices relating to the recruitment, training, and employment of administrators needed to manage these new bureaucracies. The individual bureaucrats who occupy these offices are important because they convince the population that a central state can fulfill the needs and interests of the people, who often have intense local loyalties. It makes sense that individuals of this time would be much more connected to their local communities, which were filled with people they knew personally and who tended to be similar to them, instead of a distant, impersonal state. However, communities came to accept the obligations created by the individual bureaucrats through centralized state government.

The state was also instituted to create a monopoly on the acceptable use of violence, particularly in relation to the ability to wage war. This **militaristic perspective** is related to Weber's earlier claim that the state is the only legitimate user of violence within a territory. Early European states developed through war, particularly through conquering neighbouring lands. The states with the better bureaucracies were more financially equipped to wage war because they were more efficient at taxation (they knew who lived where, the amount of property people owned, and what people were doing that could be taxed). In addition, knowing the population enabled these states to conscript soldiers more effectively.

From the beginning, the modern state was essentially intended for war-making and was centrally concerned with establishing and maintaining its military might. Wars and who won them created the national boundaries in Europe and the original context of the state system (Poggi 2004). As Charles Tilly (1985, 42) argues, "War made the state, and the state made war." His central claim is that the state is a "protection racket"—it trades security in exchange for revenues. Essentially, co-operation between people is difficult without a third party; citizens therefore cede to the state their rights to do whatever they want in return for a guarantee of protection.

As Tilly (1985, 172) explains:

> The pursuit of war involved them willy-nilly in extraction of resources for war-making from the populations over which they had control and in the promotion of capital accumulation by those who could help them borrow and buy. War-making, extraction, and capital accumulation interacted to shape European State making. Power holders did not undertake those three momentous tasks with the intention of creating national states—(centralized, differentiated, autonomous, extensive political organizations). Nor did they forsee that national states would emerge from war-making, extraction and capital accumulation . . . instead, they warred in order to check or overcome their competitors and thus to enjoy the advantages of power within a secure or expanding territory. To make more effective war, they attempted to locate more capital. In the short run, they might acquire that capital by conquest, by selling off their assets, or by coercing or dispossessing accumulators of capital. In the long run, the quest inevitably involved them in establishing regular access to

capitalists who could supply and arrange credit and in imposing one form of regular taxation or another on the people and activities within their spheres of control.

To have military might, states must engage in four things: war-making (eliminating or neutralizing their rivals outside the territories), state-making (eliminating or neutralizing their rivals inside their territory), protection (eliminating or neutralizing their clients' enemies), and extraction (acquiring the means of carrying out the first three activities).

Finally, the state is the result of class struggle in capitalism and works to regulate economic relations. This perspective is related to Marx's theories and can be termed the **economic perspective**, which argues that the state is needed to regulate economic interests and the clashing of these interests between groups in a capitalist society. Marx argued that the state usually "resolves" these conflicts by siding with capitalists (Marx and Engels 1964). For Marx, the state—what he called "the executive committee of the bourgeoisie"—is just an extension of the dominant capitalist class.

From the economic perspective, the state manages economic relations to facilitate the work of capitalists. The formation of states allows for a power centre to have an increasing reach. The state is able to standardize and secure relations between many individuals across wide spaces. This capacity is important for capitalism as it makes both the production and exchange of goods easier and more calculable. The state also imposes rules of law about property, which helps in the exchange of goods and services between partners.

The Welfare State

To this point, our discussion of the state has highlighted its many important functions and its origins. However, this depiction emphasizes the negative things that the state can do (coerce you and make you pay taxes). Why do humans create states and why do we, as individuals, give them power even when we know that doing so restricts our individual freedoms? One of the main reasons has already been mentioned: the state offers many important benefits, such as healthcare, education, and clean water, that we cannot enjoy as isolated individuals. Without people joining to create these services, we would not all have access to these important things.

These benefits are part of the **welfare state**, a particular type of state that performs three basic functions. It attempts to provide a minimum income for individuals; to reduce the potential economic insecurity that could come from events such as illness, old age, and unemployment; and to give the public a range of social services (Briggs 2000). In a welfare state, the government plays a primary role in the promotion of its citizens' economic and social well-being. Such states expand their bureaucracies in order to provide a variety of programs that reduce economic inequality in society (Peoples 2012).

The twentieth century saw the development of welfare states around the world. The expenditures of these states vary greatly (see Table 12.1). The countries of Europe, particularly Sweden, France, Germany, the Netherlands, Italy, and Greece, have the highest spending on welfare programs as a percentage of their overall GDP. Spending is much lower in the United States, Ireland, Mexico, and South Korea.

We might expect that countries with higher GDPs would spend more on welfare. Yet the group of countries that spend 24 per cent or more of their GDPs on welfare have GDPs from $21,956 to $60,430, whereas the countries that spend less than 20 per cent of their GDPs on welfare have GDPs from $25,977 to $67,458. There does not seem to be a direct relationship between a county's overall GDP and its welfare spending. Canada is a case in point. The Canadian welfare state is weak in comparison with European countries. Expenditures are only 17 per cent of our GDP even though we are a relatively wealthy country.

TABLE 12.1	Welfare expenditures by country, 2013–2014	
Nation	**Welfare expenditure (% of GDP)**	**GDP per capita (PPP US$)**
France	31.9	42,503
Italy	28.6	35,926
Sweden	28.1	60,430
Spain	26.8	29,863
Germany	25.8	46,269
Netherlands	24.7	50,793
Greece	24.0	21,956
United Kingdom	21.7	41,787
Ireland	21.0	50,503
Poland	20.6	13,648
United States	19.2	53,042
Australia	19.0	67,458
Canada	**17.0**	**51,958**
Iceland	16.5	47,461
South Korea	10.4	25,977

SOURCES: Welfare Expenditure (2014) OECD Statistics Extractor. http://stats.oecd.org/Index.aspx?DataSetCode=SOCX_AGG#; GDP Per capita. The World Bank (2013). http://data.worldbank.org/indicator/NY.GDP.PCAP.CD.

The Welfare State in Canada

A hundred years ago, care for those in need, including health and welfare services, was provided at the local community level. Community groups and charities attempted to provide minimal social services. One of Canada's first government social programs was the Mothers' Pension Act, passed in Manitoba in 1916 to provide widowed, divorced, or deserted mothers with an income. During the Great Depression, the unemployment rate reached 30 per cent, and the federal government was under considerable pressure to become involved in dealing with this important social issue. This widespread unemployment and poverty created many social problems that touched a huge proportion of Canadians. For example, access to healthcare, which had long been seen as a problem for only the poor, became a concern for the majority of the population. When these problems were seen as public issues instead of personal troubles (as C. Wright Mills explained), the government responded in the form of social programs.

The rise of the welfare state in Canada occurred around the time of World War II, when the federal government instituted a group of wide-reaching welfare measures. By the beginning of the war, Canadians increasingly accepted the idea that the state had a responsibility to help provide economic

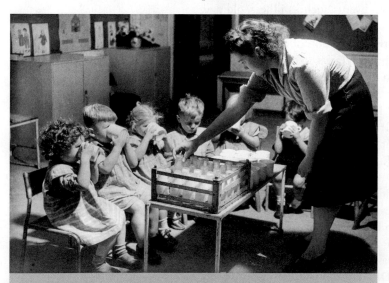

PHOTO 12.2 Canadian schoolchildren receive their milk ration in 1947. During World War II, adequate nutrition became a priority for the Canadian state. The country's first national nutrition education program arose as a result of the rise of the welfare state.

and social security and expected these social programs to continue after the war. In the 1950s and early 1960s, permanent programs for the funding of hospitals higher education, and vocational training were introduced or extended. In the 1960s, Liberal Prime Minister Lester B. Pearson introduced three major pieces of social legislation that have been pivotal to the Canadian welfare state: the Canada Pension Plan, the Canada Assistance Plan, and Medicare. The last was based on a program created by Saskatchewan Premier Tommy Douglas, who later became the leader of the New Democratic Party.

In the 1970s, the number and type of social programs provided by the Canadian government grew. Consequently, the government began spending more money on social expenditures. These new investments improved income security, particularly for the elderly, persons with disabilities, single parents, and the unemployed. For example, the Family Allowance benefit provided income to parents, post-secondary education covered a wider section of the population, and healthcare became widely available for the first time. As unemployment grew in the 1970s, programs such as unemployment insurance and social assistance automatically expanded. The impact of this greater spending was particularly evident from the mid-1970s, when the economy entered a period of decline after 10 years of growth. These conditions ushered in a call to decrease government spending, particularly for social programs.

Similar calls in the 1980s led the federal and provincial governments to make a number of changes. The governments changed eligibility and benefits, particularly for unemployment insurance and social assistance. They also privatized many provincial social programs by outsourcing responsibility for social services, attempted to raise revenues through Medicare premiums and user fees, and moved to decrease social-program budgets and terminate some social programs, such as the aforementioned Family Allowance.

In many countries, including Canada, the welfare state has declined. Evidence includes less generous benefits and more rigorous eligibility tests (van den Berg et al. 2008). Many countries around the world, including in Europe, are retrenching their social welfare programs. Even countries with very strong and entrenched programs, such as Sweden, have decreased their social spending.

The Welfare State and Social Inequality

Social programs enacted through the welfare state are important for a variety of reasons. We have already mentioned that they are instrumental in dealing with and reducing inequality. A wide body of evidence shows the significant effects of welfare programs on inequality. For example, taxes and transfers considerably reduce poverty in most countries whose welfare spending constitutes at least a fifth of their GDP (Kenworthy 1999; Bradley et al. 2003).

Most welfare states have considerably lower poverty rates than they had before the implementation of welfare programs. Table 12.2 lists a selection of countries and the percentage of their populations that live under the absolute poverty line before and after welfare policies were enacted. Through the implementation of welfare policies, all the countries included cut their poverty rate by at least half. For example, Canada's poverty rate fell from 22.5 per cent to 6.5 per cent.

Social Policy: Universal and Means-Tested Programs

Social programs in the welfare state can be categorized as either universal or means tested. **Universal programs** are available to all citizens, regardless of income or wealth. These programs tend to be very popular because everyone benefits equally. All people over 60 get the Canada Pension Plan (CPP), all children get access to public education, and all Canadians have access to healthcare. Because these programs are available to

TABLE 12.2 Absolute poverty by country

| Country | Absolute Poverty Rate (Threshold set at 40% of US median household income) | |
	Pre-welfare	Post-welfare
Australia	23.3	11.9
Belgium	26.8	6.0
Canada	22.5	6.5
Denmark	26.4	5.9
Finland	11.9	3.7
France	36.1	9.8
Germany	15.2	4.3
Italy	30.7	14.3
Netherlands	22.1	7.3
Norway	9.2	1.7
Sweden	23.7	5.8
Switzerland	12.5	3.8
United Kingdom	16.8	8.7
United States	21.0	11.7

SOURCES: Kenworthy, L. 1999. "Do Social-Welfare Policies Reduce Poverty? A Cross-National Assessment." *Social Forces* 77 (3): 1119–39; Bradley, D., E. Huber, S. Moller, F. Nielson, and J. D. Stephens. 2003. "Determinants of Relative Poverty in Advanced Capitalist Democracies." *American Sociological Review* 68 (3): 22–51.

everyone, all citizens have a stake in seeing them continue and thrive. However, universal programs might not be the most efficient way to deal with issues such as poverty. If some of the money allocated to addressing poverty among the elderly goes to rich seniors who do not need the CPP payment, we have less money for seniors who are living at or near the poverty line. In other words, these misallocated payments create inefficiencies in the system by assisting people who are not at risk of living in poverty.

A **means-tested program** relies on a determination of whether an individual or family needs government assistance. In Canada, means tests are used for student finance (for post-secondary education), legal aid, and welfare (direct transfer payments to individuals to combat poverty). Compared to universal programs, means-tested programs are a more efficient way to address inequality. By simply giving more money to people who have less and giving no benefit to people who already have enough, you can reduce the gap between the rich and the poor.

Yet means-tested programs are often less popular than universal programs. The former tend to have less political support because they are seen to benefit only a small group of people. In contrast, universal programs are viewed as something that all citizens share. Some people also argue that means-tested programs carry a

PHOTO 12.3 According to Gaetz and colleagues (2013, 25), 47.5 per cent of Canada's homeless population are single adult men between the ages of 25 and 55. Despite the existence of social programs that address poverty, homelessness remains an often life-threatening state for many Canadians, with at least 200,000 experiencing homelessness in any given year (5).

stigma. For example, many schools have free lunch programs for students from low-income homes. Children who participate in this program may be teased by other students. To combat this social stigma, many schools make it difficult to tell which students get lunch for free and which pay.

Means-tested programs are also often criticized based on access issues. Means tests, particularly complicated ones, can make accessing social programs difficult. Sometimes individuals cannot easily decipher whether they qualify for different programs and under which conditions. The work required to verify that the tests are satisfied can increase administrative costs. Some argue that these costs can offset part of the savings from not giving the benefit universally.

Despite these drawbacks, means-tested programs such as the **Guaranteed Income Supplement (GIS)** can decrease inequality. Like the CPP, the GIS is a pension benefit for seniors, but it is for only those who make below a certain income level. In 1961, before the CPP and GIS were implemented, the incidence of poverty for families headed by individuals over 65 years of age was 43.9 per cent. Seniors between the ages of 65 and 69 who were living alone had a 64.1 per cent chance of being low income and those over the age of 70 had a 72.5 per cent chance. These figures are all substantially higher than the number for the overall Canadian population, which was 25.3 per cent at the time (Perry 1989, 701–9). After the CPP and GIS were instituted, poverty among seniors declined sharply, from approximately 30 to 5 per cent (see Figure 12.1). These programs have been critical in decreasing poverty among seniors (Osberg 2001).

Another group of Canadians very likely to live in poverty is children. This pressing issue has serious long-term consequences, particularly for children who experience extended periods of poverty. These children are more likely to have health problems, delayed social and intellectual development, and behavioural problems. They also have lower levels of educational attainment, on average, than children who have not experienced poverty (Frenette 2007) and a higher chance of being poor as adults (Fleury 2008). As the OECD (2005, 1) notes, "Failure to tackle the poverty and exclusion facing millions of families and their children is not only socially reprehensible, but it will also weigh heavily on countries' capacity to sustain economic growth in years to come."

Looking at Figure 12.2, we can see that the rate of child poverty has remained at around 15 per cent since the 1970s. Canada does quite poorly in cross-national comparisons of poverty rates among children. Out of 17 peer countries, only the United States

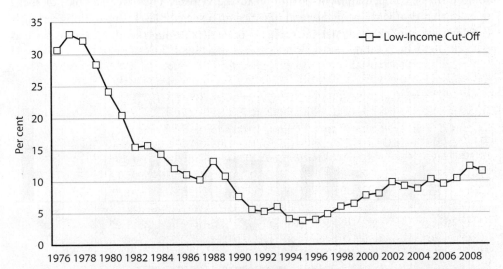

FIGURE 12.1 Low-income rates for seniors, Canada, 1976–2009 (per cent)

NOTE: Low-income rates are calculated using three low-income thresholds: the low-income cut-off (LICO), the low-income measure (LIM), and the market basket measure (MBM).
SOURCE: Survey of Consumer Finances (1976–1995) and Survey of Labour and Income Dynamics (1996–2009), Statistics Canada. http://www.statcan.gc.ca/pub/75f0002m/2012001/fig/fig3.2-eng.htm

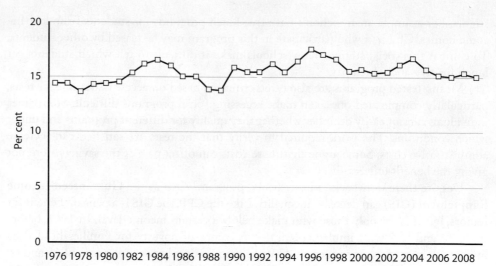

FIGURE 12.2 Low-income rates for children, Canada (per cent)

NOTE: Low-income rates and gap ratios are calculated using three low-income thresholds: the low-income cut-off (LICO), the low-income measure (LIM) and the market basket measure (MBM).
SOURCE: Survey of Consumer Finances (1976–1995) and Survey of Labour and Income Dynamics (1996–2009), Statistics Canada. http://www.statcan.gc.ca/pub/75f0002m/2012001/fig/fig3.1-eng.htm.

and Italy have higher rates of child poverty than Canada. Countries such as Denmark, Sweden, and Finland have rates less than one-third the Canadian rate (see Figure 12.3).

Reparation Programs

In Chapter 11, we learned about restorative justice, in which offenders restore order by compensating or fixing the injustice caused by their crime. One part of restorative justice can be the payment of reparations. **Reparation programs** are measures taken by the state to redress gross and systematic violations of human rights or humanitarian law through some form of compensation or restitution to the victims. They are examples of social policies that deal with inequality and injustice on a societal level. Reparations seriously consider and publicly recognize the suffering of victims through symbolic means, such as an apology, or material means, such as monetary payments.

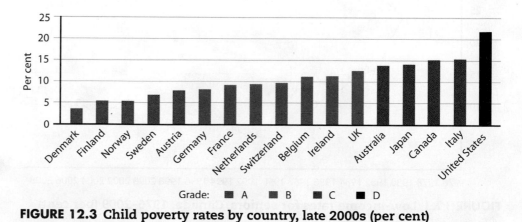

FIGURE 12.3 Child poverty rates by country, late 2000s (per cent)

SOURCE: The Conference Board of Canada. 2013. "Child Poverty." http://www.conferenceboard.ca/hcp/details/society/child -poverty.aspx.

HIGHLIGHT

Programs to Deal with Child Poverty in Canada

Canada has a number of social programs designed to assist families with children. Such programs include a child tax benefit (a monthly payment to help families pay for the extra costs associated with having children, about $120 per child per month to the age of 18), the universal childcare benefit ($100 per month per child until the age of 6 years), and the child fitness tax credit (for the payment of children's fitness activities such as hockey, soccer, or dance class). These are all universal benefits; thus, families with very high incomes get the same benefits as those with very low incomes. In fact, high-income families are more likely to benefit from the child fitness tax credit because they are more likely to be able to afford the cost of sports teams and dance lessons.

These programs tend to be very popular among the Canadian population because all individuals with children can benefit from them. However, Campaign 2000 argues that, if the government eliminated these benefits, it could substantially reduce child poverty (Jones 2012). The group claims that an estimated 174,000 children would be lifted out of poverty if the government allocated the money spent on these benefits toward ones for families making less than $25,000 a year.

This result has obvious advantages for the people who would emerge from poverty. Reducing child poverty also has many social benefits. Sid Frankel, a member of Campaign 2000 and University of Manitoba social work professor, explains that it would be a boost to the economy because children living in poverty are less likely to obtain higher education, which makes them more likely to be unemployed later in life (Jones 2012). Children who grow up in poverty tend to have more health problems throughout their lives and, as a result, use the healthcare system more than children who grow up with higher incomes. In this way, reallocating money to those most in need assists both individuals and society.

Reparations have been made to several groups, including Japanese Canadians and Japanese Americans after their forced internment in World War II, Jewish people after the Holocaust, black South Africans after apartheid, and, most recently, Aboriginal people in Canada after the residential school system (see the activity on pp. 347–348). Another prominent situation in which reparations have been discussed is slavery in the United States. After slavery was abolished, there were proposals about giving each freed slave 40 acres of land and a mule. This reparation never happened, creating an interesting situation where issues of restorative justice and social policy come together in the debate over how to deal with the injustice of slavery and the resulting inequality. Dalton Conley addresses this issue in the following article.

READING

Forty Acres and a Mule: What if America Pays Reparations?

Dalton Conley

In the present political climate, slavery reparations remain a remote dream of activists. But it is still worthwhile to do the math, if not for the purpose of actual payments, at least for what the numbers reveal about race and equal opportunity in America. . . .

Contemporary Debates

The issue of reparations has recently made another comeback. Armed with precedents such as payments to Japanese Americans for internment during World War II and the claims of Holocaust victims on Swiss banks for lost accounts, the most recent discourse on slavery restitution is more legalistic in tone and, as such, has been the most effective to date. . . .

There are several important issues to sort out in this debate. Practical concerns—who would receive payments and how much they would get—blend with larger issues about race and ascription (that is, assignment to a social status by virtue of birth). Had the proverbial 40 acres and a mule been real rather than rhetorical compensation, many of these issues would not have to be addressed. Back in the mid-nineteenth century, for example, payments could have been extracted from Southern plantations, targeting most directly those who benefited from the chattel labour. Most important, payments could have been made directly to the victims of slavery rather than to their descendants. Fourteen decades later everything gets a lot more complicated.

How Much?

Perhaps the simplest argument for reparations is that they are payment of back wages for slave labour. This was the underlying rationale the black power movement used in the 1970s. One researcher took slave prices during the period from 1790 to 1860 as proxies for the value of slave capital and projected that, given compound interest, the total value in 1970 was from $448 billion to $995 billion. Merely adjusted for inflation, this sum would translate to a range of $2 trillion to almost $4 trillion today (which, incidentally, was within budget surplus estimates in 2000, if paid out over six to eight years). The 1970 price happened to match the $400 billion sum that was being demanded around the same time by a prominent black separatist movement called the Republic of New Africa (RNA). The RNA also demanded sovereignty over five southern states: Alabama, Georgia, Louisiana, Mississippi, and South Carolina (which the researcher estimated to be worth $350 billion at the time).

If reparations were paid directly to the ex-slaves themselves, one might follow this strategy of imputing a fair wage, or splitting the profits made from the industries in which they toiled, then adding on sums for pain and suffering and lost future earnings. Even one generation later, the heirs of the slaves could be compensated as representatives of the estate.

However, this approach presents a number of difficulties six or more generations later. Using compound interest only works when we assume an unbroken chain of birth from slaves to the current African-American population, from slaveholders to today's white Americans. Would whites who immigrated after slavery ended have to pay? Would their black counterparts be entitled to payments? And what about the descendants of blacks who lived as free individuals during the antebellum period? The free blacks who owned slaves themselves? Then, of course, there is the issue of racial mixing. Would children born to a white parent and a black parent pay a reparations tax or receive a reparations payout?

Is Slavery a Proxy for Race, or Race a Proxy for Slavery?

These questions raise the larger issue of whether being black is a good proxy for descending from slaves and, therefore, being entitled to restitution. On the one hand, Americans of all races have ancestors of various races. On the other hand, the way that race has long been classified in the United States, commonly known as the one-drop rule, suggests that African-American racial identity should act as a proxy for slave ancestry since it is socially defined that way by the government. (The one-drop rule states that if either parent of a child has any black "blood" the child is classified as black.) Or, to turn this question around, we could assume that slavery stands for the sum total of oppression and discrimination that blacks have experienced in America, both before and after 1865. Are these other disadvantages not to be remedied through financial restitution as well?

One approach to the question stresses that slavery was a foundation of America's current wealth. Whether people's families arrived in 1700 or in 2000, they benefit today from businesses, such as the cotton garment industry, that profited from slave labour. Conversely, blacks in America, regardless of when their families arrived, live with the stigma and burdens that are the legacy of slavery (while gaining a disproportionately small share of its benefits).

One could persuasively argue that most black–white inequality in contemporary America is a direct result of slavery because it stripped African Americans of their ethnic honour. All other Americans are linked to a particular immigrant (or Native American) group and therefore to a particular nation of peoples. Slavery wiped out this sense of nationhood as slaveholders purposely mixed slaves of various tribal origins. This lack of national heritage and ethnic honour places African Americans at the bottom of the racial-ethnic hierarchy in the United States. Combined with other stigmatizing aspects of slavery, this loss of ethnicity may make all black–white inequality today directly attributable to slavery, whether or not particular individual blacks or whites had ancestors in the United States before abolition. This wider interpretation of the legacy of slavery would legitimate a claim for "symbolic damages" or "group pain and suffering" in addition to back wages.

Calculating Reparations from the Wealth Gap

Given a rationale for paying reparations to twenty-first-century blacks without having to link particular individuals back to slave ancestors, we can turn to calculating the right amount. Property values offer a potentially simple procedure because they are often used as a direct measure of tort damages. For instance, if a chemical company spills its wares in my community, making my home unlivable, I am entitled to the home's full value (plus some amount for pain and suffering). Similarly, one could choose to view the wealth gap between blacks and whites as a result of slavery, both lost wages and long-term consequences.

In fact, if there were one statistic that captured the persistence of racial inequality in the United States, it would be net worth—also known as wealth, equity, or assets. (If you want to know your net worth, add up everything you own and subtract from this figure your outstanding debt.) The typical white family enjoys a net worth more than seven times greater than that of a typical non-white family. The wealth gap cannot be explained by annual income differences alone and is therefore distinct from current racial or class conditions. That is, while African Americans as a group earn less than whites, even when we compare black and white families that earn the same income, differences in assets remain large. For instance, among families earning under $15,000, the typical African-American family has a net worth of zero, while the typical white family holds $10,000 worth of equity. This is also true among the often-heralded new black middle class. The typical white family that earns $40,000 per year enjoys a nest egg of around $80,000. Its African-American counterpart has less than half that amount.

Why are these gaps so large, even among families with the same income levels? Some pundits—and many white Americans—believe that blacks perpetuate an oppositional culture that works to their own disadvantage. This culture, they argue, encourages spending at the cost of savings, an anti-intellectual attitude in school, and overall hostility to mainstream social institutions including the financial sector. Some theorists believe that this culture arose from slavery and oppression but has now become self-perpetuating. Others see what they often call "underclass" behavioural patterns as genetically determined. The overwhelming majority of evidence, however, refutes these claims. Several studies have shown that black and white savings rates, for example, are indistinguishable. Surveys also show that blacks value education as much as, if not more than, whites.

Rather, wealth, more than other measures of economic status, captures the long-term, multigenerational scars of prior inequality and is not easily erased by measures intended to guarantee equal opportunity. "Equity inequity" is, in part, the result of the head start that whites have enjoyed in accumulating and passing on assets. Whites not only earn more now, but they have always earned more than African Americans—a lot more—which, in turn, feeds wealth differences. Some researchers estimate that up to 80 per cent of lifetime wealth results from gifts in one form or another from past generations of relatives. These gifts can range from the down payment on a first home, to a free college education, to a bequest upon the death of a parent. Over the long run, small racial differences in wealth holdings widen rapidly, especially when combined with barriers to black property accumulation (such as the "black codes" of the nineteenth century and the housing and credit discrimination of the twentieth and twenty-first centuries). Even if equal opportunity was finally here, equal wealth would take a while to achieve.

If we take the broad view that all wealth inequality between blacks and whites today is directly or indirectly a result of slavery, then there might be an argument that whites should transfer 13 per cent of their private wealth to blacks to close the gap. However, we may wish to distinguish between the earnings of the current generation and the legacy of past injustice (since we already have some policies in place to address current conditions, i.e. affirmative action). Since about half of the black–white wealth gap is attributable to current income and demographic differences, this would suggest a payment half as large. We could use another, yet more conservative approach. Using the estimate mentioned earlier that 80 per cent of our wealth can be attributed in one form or another to our parents' generation, we would find that six generations after 1865, about 25 per cent of the distribution of wealth today is explained by the distribution of wealth at the time of emancipation. Correcting for this much of the gap would rectify only the wealth inequalities associated directly with slavery, not with Jim Crow, sharecropping, racial violence, housing segregation, or labour, educational, and credit discrimination that has occurred since 1865. . . .

RECOMMENDED RESOURCES

Browne, Robert. "The Economic Case for Reparations to Black America." *American Economic Review* 62 (1/2) (1972): 39–46. A calculation of the value of slave labour.

Conley, Dalton. *Being Black, Living in the Red: Race, Wealth and Social Policy in America*. Berkeley: University of California Press, 1999. An overview of the centrality of wealth to understanding racial dynamics in other arenas.

Conley, Dalton. "Decomposing the Black–White Wealth Gap: The Role of Parental Resources, Inheritance and Investment Dynamics." *Sociological Inquiry* 71 (Winter 2001): 39–66. Evidence on the persistence of the wealth gap that challenges *Being Black, Living in the Red*.

Kotlikoff, Laurence J., and Lawrence H. Summers. "The Role of Intergenerational Transfers in Aggregate Capital Accumulation." *Journal of Political Economy* 89 (August 1981): 706–32. High-end estimate of the role of progenitors in wealth accumulation.

Menchik, Paul L., and Nancy A. Jianakoplos. "Black–White Wealth Inequality: Is Inheritance the Reason?" *Economic Inquiry* 35 (April 1997): 428–42. A detailed analysis of the role of inheritance, narrowly construed.

Modigliani, Franco. "The Role of Intergenerational Transfers and Life Cycle Saving, in the Accumulation of Wealth." *Journal of Economic Perspectives* 2 (Spring 1988): 15–40. A more conservative accounting of the role of past wealth in explaining current wealth.

Oliver, Melvin, and Thomas Shapiro. *Black Wealth/White Wealth*. London: Routledge, 1994. A good summary of the history of the asset gap.

Robinson, Randall. *The Debt: What America Owes to Blacks*. New York: Dutton, 2000. A well-argued polemic making the case for reparations.

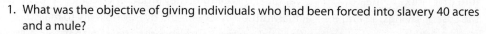

CRITICAL Reading Questions

1. What was the objective of giving individuals who had been forced into slavery 40 acres and a mule?

2. One of the major issues in reparations is how much individuals should be paid. In what ways does the article suggest the reparation payment for slavery could be determined?

3. Another central issue in the payment of reparations is to determine who should receive payments and who should pay. What are the different arguments for which groups should be recompensed for slavery? Who should pay these reparations?

4. How successful are reparation programs, either the proposed reparation for slavery or other programs, at repairing damage to specific individuals affected by injustices and at creating a more equal society? Give reasons to support your answer.

PHOTO 12.4 In September 2013, the Truth and Reconciliation Commission of Canada held a one-week national event in Vancouver that culminated in the Walk for Reconciliation. Tens of thousands of people participated in the walk.

ACTIVITY

The Truth and Reconciliation Commission of Canada

Since the 1870s, there have been over 130 residential schools located across Canada, the last of which closed in 1996. Paid for by the government and operated by churches, the intention of the schools was to eliminate parental involvement in the intellectual, cultural, and spiritual development of Aboriginal children. More than 150,000 Aboriginal children attended these schools, often against their own will and their parents' wishes. At these schools, the children were forbidden from speaking their language or practising their own culture. Many were also subjected to physical, sexual, and psychological abuse. The significant impact of these schools goes beyond the students; it has also affected subsequent generations and contributed to a host of ongoing social problems.

It is difficult to imagine what could be done to address the intense and widespread injustice of the residential schools. With the assistance of the Assembly of First Nations and Inuit organizations, former students have sued the Canadian federal government and the churches responsible for the schools. These cases led to the Indian Residential Schools Settlement Agreement, the largest class-action settlement in Canadian history, in 2007. This agreement seeks to repair the harm caused by residential schools by compensating former students and calling for the establishment of the **Truth and Reconciliation Commission of Canada (TRC)**.

The TRC worked for six years, collecting documents and over 6,000 accounts from those who funded the schools, officials of the institutions that operated the schools, survivors, their families, communities, and anyone else personally affected by the residential

continued

school experience. The TRC's final report, released on 2 June 2015, includes 94 recommendations, such as legislation for education, child welfare, and Aboriginal languages and the implementation of the UN's Declaration on the Rights of Indigenous Peoples (Watters 2015).

Explore the TRC's website (www.trc.ca) and then answer the following questions. (A direct link to the commission's final report is available on this book's companion website.)

1. Why was the TRC established and what did it hope to accomplish?

2. Who are the commissioners? How were they selected and why is their selection important?

3. What is the truth and reconciliation part of the agreement (particularly the national public events, the "It Matters to Me" Twibbon Campaign, and the National Research Centre)? What is its purpose and how was it achieved? What was the public's role in this process?

4. What types of reparations are being paid? What is the purpose of these reparations and who receives them? What is the difference between the Common Experience Payment and the Independent Assessment Payment?

5. Go to this book's companion website to access apologies made to the Aboriginal people by Stephen Harper, the Anglican Church, the Catholic Church, and the United Church. What is the role of apologies in this process? Why are they important (or not important)?

How the State Involves the Public

One of the primary ways that the state engages the public is through regular **elections**, a formal decision-making process in which eligible citizens select individuals for public office. Elections are a critical part of representative democracies such as Canada. That said, the percentage of Canadians who vote in elections has declined significantly (see Figure 12.4). The 1950s and 1960s were a high point of voting in Canada, with almost 80 per cent of registered voters going to the polls during those years. The federal election of 2011 saw a voting rate of only 61.1 per cent of eligible voters. Figure 12.5 illustrates that these trends are not unique to Canada. Of the 39 countries listed, 32 have seen a decline in voting rates since 1980. Voting in the United States has declined by 29 per cent in this period and rates in Europe by around 10 to 15 per cent.

Along with the overall decline in voting in Canada, it is important to note that the rates of voting differ by group. For example, young people are much less likely to vote than older people: only 39 per cent of people ages 18 to 24 vote, while about 75 per cent of people ages 65 to 74 do so (see Figure 12.6). Voting rates decline again for those 75 years and over. The reasons for not voting are many, as illustrated in Figure 12.7.

Research on voter turnout indicates two main theories to explain changing voting patterns, the **life-cycle effect** and **generational replacement**. The life-cycle effect argues that fewer young people vote because of a variety of structural, social, and economic circumstances. As these young non-voters age, they become more likely to vote. A number of recent studies have pushed us to question this theory. For example, an Elections Canada study finds "not only are young people participating less than their elders, their willingness to participate appears to be declining over time" (Barnes and Virgint, 2013).

Generational replacement studies have grouped the electorate into approximate "generations" according to age and tracked their voting propensities. These studies find that voters of the middle generations (born between 1945 and 1959) and those of the oldest generations (born before 1945) have a high propensity to vote. These generations are being replaced by younger ones (born after 1960) that have a lower propensity to engage in this way. Some of the studies' authors have proposed that this generational

PHOTO 12.5 Highly visible and simple Elections Canada signage attempts to draw the eye and to reduce barriers to voting that depend on literacy or language skills. What other methods could increase voter turnout in Canada?

replacement could account for the decrease in voter turnout (Barnes and Virgint 2013). If so, voting should continue to drop.

Following the 2011 general election, Blais and Loewen (2011) used census data to examine youth electoral engagement in Canada. They found that today's young people are better educated, earn less income, and are more likely to have been born in Canada

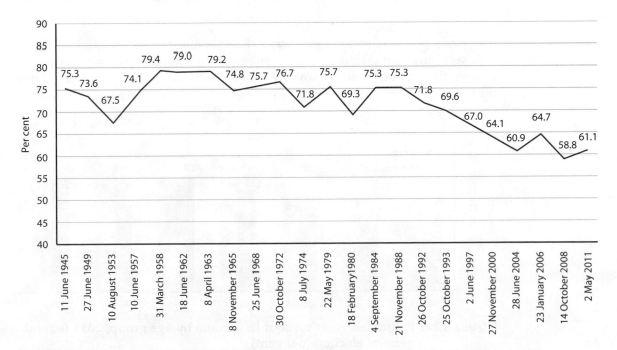

FIGURE 12.4 Voting in Canada, 1945–2011 (per cent)

SOURCE: Elections Canada. This reproduction is a copy of the version available at www.elections.ca. Reproduced with the permission of Elections Canada.

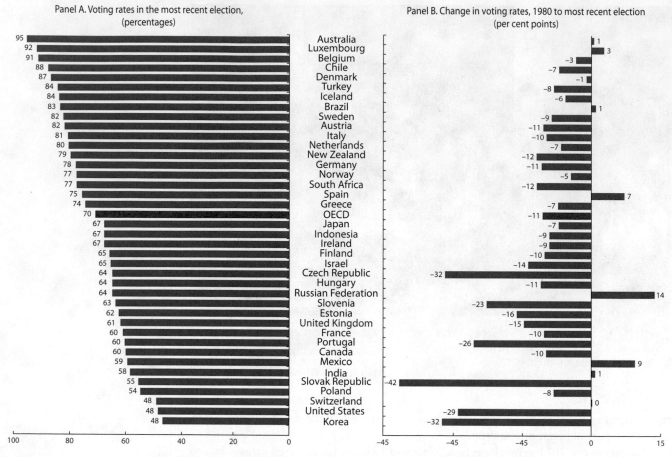

FIGURE 12.5 Changing voting rates by country

SOURCE: OECD. 2011. "Society at a Glance 2011: OECD Social Indicators." http://www.oecd-ilibrary.org/sites/soc_glance-2011-en/08/04/g8_co4-01.html?contentType=&itemId=/content/chapter/soc_glance-2011-29-en&containerItemId=/content/serial/19991290&accessItemIds=/content/book/soc_glance-2011-en&mimeType=text/html.

than young people of previous generations. Education and being born in Canada are both very important predictors of one's propensity to vote. Comparing young people between the ages of 18 and 24 who are students with those who are not shows that the former are 9 per cent more likely to participate in politics. Young people in this age

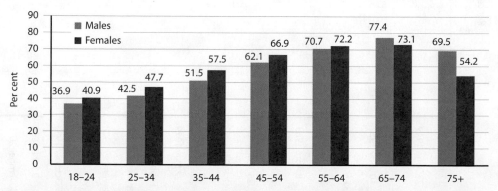

FIGURE 12.6 Estimated voter turnout in Canada by age group, 2011 federal general election (per cent)

SOURCE: Elections Canada. 2014. "Estimation of Voter Turnout by Age Group and Gender at the 2011 Federal General Election." This reproduction is a copy of the version available at www.elections.ca. Reproduced with the permission of Elections Canada.

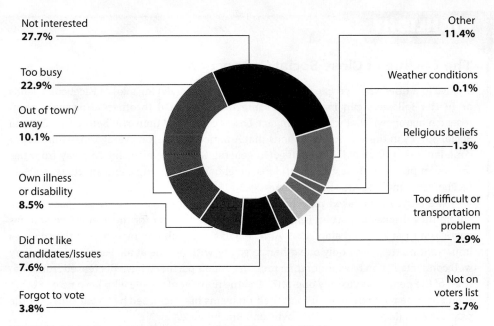

Not interested
27.7%

Too busy
22.9%

Out of town/
away
10.1%

Own illness
or disability
8.5%

Did not like
candidates/Issues
7.6%

Forgot to vote
3.8%

Other
11.4%

Weather conditions
0.1%

Religious beliefs
1.3%

Too difficult or
transportation
problem
2.9%

Not on
voters list
3.7%

FIGURE 12.7 Reasons for not voting, Canada, 2011

SOURCE: Barr, Andrew. 2011. "Infographic: Why People Didn't Vote in the 2011 Federal Election." *National Post*, 5 July. http://news.nationalpost.com/2011/07/05/infographic-why-people-didnt-vote-in-the-2011-federal-election/.

group who are born in Canada are 12 per cent more likely to vote than those not born in the country. Blais and Loewen argue that this difference is because "those who are born outside of Canada take slightly longer than their Canadian-born counterparts to come to socialize into Canadian politics." In addition to the importance of these socio-demographic factors, they found that interest in and information about politics have an even greater effect on youth voting behaviour. Why do you think that young people vote at a relatively low rate? What are the implications for society at large?

RESEARCH METHOD

Survey

Challenges Facing the Modern State

Declines in voting rates in Canada and other countries challenge the government's ability to engage citizens. Many argue that these low voting levels are the result of the lower level of social capital and civic engagement in our society. Social capital is the social resources that individuals can draw on in making decisions and taking action (Coleman 1990). This type of capital is based on people's social relations and their sense of underlying trust and confidence in one another.

Social capital is illustrated in the "**rotating credit associations**" described by cultural anthropologist Clifford Geertz (1962). These associations are co-operative economic ventures practised among people in Southeastern Asian societies. Individuals pool their resources and then rotate in drawing on the general fund of credit. The method provides people with a means to begin an economic enterprise, and they are required to pay back into the pool from their earnings. These rotating credit associations require trust and co-operation between people and would be impossible without social capital. You would never contribute to the pool if you did not trust that you could take out money later when you needed it. We can also find examples of social trust and co-operation in other groups, particularly families. These feelings, which are at the heart of social capital, provide an important resource on which individuals can draw.

Robert D. Putnam's (1993) influential study of regional government in Italy, *Making Democracy Work*, helped illustrate the importance of social capital. In the early 1970s,

HIGHLIGHT //

The Decline of Close Social Connections

We live in a time when people often feel very connected. Having a lot of Facebook friends or Twitter followers can make us feel integrated and tied to others. However, recent research has shown that we might, in fact, be *less* connected than ever before. The General Social Survey in the United States finds that Americans have, on average, one-third fewer confidants than they did 30 years ago. In general, they have also shifted away from ties formed in places such as churches, clubs, neighbourhood groups, and sports teams (see McPherson, Smith-Lovin, and Brashears 2008).

The survey also asked respondents how many "discussion partners" (people with whom they discuss important issues) they have. The number for the average person has decreased from 2.9 to 2.1 since 1985. Almost half the population reports that they discuss important matters with only one other person or with no one at all. People who are very well connected, who have more than four discussion partners, have decreased from one-third of the population to only one-fifth. And the number of people who have no one other than a spouse with whom to discuss their problems has increased by 50 per cent over the past 30 years (McPherson, Smith-Lovin, and Brashears 2008).

One interesting trend to note is that highly educated people tend to have more confidants than those with less education. As the following figure shows, each additional year of education increases the number of discussion partners. Highly educated people also

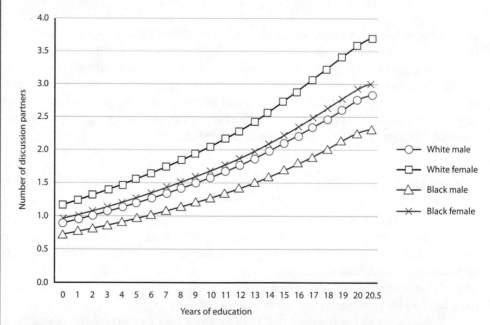

Projected number of discussion partners by sex, race, and level of education

SOURCE: Brashears, Matthew E. 2011. "Small Networks and High Isolation? A Reexamination of American Discussion Networks." *Social Networks* 33 (4): 331–41. Copyright © 2011 Elsevier B.V. All rights reserved.

Italy created a new system of 20 regional governments, which were all set up in the same way and had the same institutions. However, the citizens in some regions were more satisfied with their governments and some governments were able to institute policies and function more effectively than others. The question was, "Why were some regional have a smaller proportion of family in their networks than people with less education, which means that the former are more likely than others to be exposed to new perspectives by talking outside their family circle.

The decline in the number of confidants seems surprising in light of the highly interconnected nature of modern society, including the widespread use of social media on the Internet. But some researchers argue that Internet use might interfere with communication in the home and neighbourhood. While the Internet can help us to interact with people across larger geographical areas, these looser ties might be replacing the stronger ones to confidants that we had in the past. For instance, we might be connected to a lot of people on Facebook, but these contacts are what sociologists call weak ties—friends of friends or acquaintances. They might expose us to a greater range of information than close ties, but they are less likely to provide emotional support because we cannot rely on most of them when we are in need or confide in them when we have a problem.

However, not everyone sees the creation of this wider net of weak ties as a negative thing. According to Veenhof et al. (2008), Internet users may be at least as socially engaged as non-users. Their study found that, although Internet users have larger networks and more frequent interactions with friends and family, they tend to spend less in-person time and, of course, more time online. However, a large number of Internet users are civically and politically engaged, using the Internet for these types of activities.

In particular, the researchers examined how Internet use might be particularly important for certain groups of Canadians. They found, for example, that recent immigrants are especially likely to use the Internet to maintain ties with family and friends in their country of origin and to integrate into larger Canadian society.

What are the differences between "friends" on Facebook and friends in real life? Why does it matter that we are replacing real-world friends with online friendships?

governments more effective than others?" Putnam and his colleagues worked to answer this query by comparing all 20 governments, using such sources as survey data of citizen engagement and participation. They found that wealth was not the most important predictor of regional success. Instead, governments tended to work more effectively and

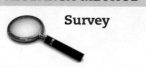
citizens were more satisfied and engaged in regions with strong civic traditions. Regions with more "**civicness**"—the fabric of values, norms, institutions, and associations—have higher levels of solidarity, mutual trust, and tolerance among citizens (Putnam 1993). This greater social capital, in turn, made for more effective governance.

Putnam and others claim that voting rates are declining because of the decrease in social capital and civicness in modern society. Individuals are less likely to trust one another, less likely to participate together in social groups and organizations, and less likely to co-operate with one another. In the influential *Bowling Alone: The Collapse and Revival of American Community*, Putnam (2000) argues that American society has seen a decline in social capital and **civic engagement**, activities that address social issues. This change is particularly concerning because social capital and civic engagement are related to a number of positive social outcomes. For example, societies with high amounts of social capital tend to have lower levels of crime, healthier people, less poverty and unemployment, and many other benefits. Can we apply Putnam's arguments to the Canadian case? Keep this question in mind when reading the following excerpt.

READING

Bowling Alone: America's Declining Social Capital

Robert D. Putnam

Many students of the new democracies that have emerged over the past decade and a half have emphasized the importance of a strong and active civil society to the consolidation of democracy. Especially with regard to the postcommunist countries, scholars and democratic activists alike have lamented the absence or obliteration of traditions of independent civic engagement and a widespread tendency toward passive reliance on the state. To those concerned with the weakness of civil societies in the developing or postcommunist world, the advanced Western democracies and above all the United States have typically been taken as models to be emulated. There is striking evidence, however, that the vibrancy of American civil society has notably declined over the past several decades. . . .

. . . Researchers in such fields as education, urban poverty, unemployment, the control of crime and drug abuse, and even health have discovered that successful outcomes are more likely in civically engaged communities. Similarly, research on the varying economic attainments of different ethnic groups in the United States has demonstrated the importance of social bonds within each group. These results are consistent with research in a wide range of settings that demonstrates the vital importance of social networks for job placement and many other economic outcomes . . .

The norms and networks of civic engagement also powerfully affect the performance of representative government. That, at least, was the central conclusion of my own 20-year, quasi-experimental study of subnational governments in different regions of Italy.[1] Although all these regional governments seemed identical on paper, their levels of effectiveness varied dramatically. Systematic inquiry showed that the quality of governance was determined by long-standing traditions of civic engagement (or its absence). Voter turnout, newspaper readership, membership in choral societies and football clubs—these were the hallmarks of a successful region. In fact, historical analysis suggested that these networks of organized reciprocity and civic solidarity, far from being an epiphenomenon of socio-economic modernization, were a precondition for it.

. . . Social scientists in several fields have recently suggested a common framework for understanding these phenomena, a framework that rests on the concept of social capital.[2] By analogy with notions of physical capital and human capital—tools and training that enhance individual productivity—"social capital" refers to features of social organization such as networks, norms, and social trust that facilitate coordination and co-operation for mutual benefit.

For a variety of reasons, life is easier in a community blessed with a substantial stock of social capital. In the first place, networks of civic engagement foster sturdy norms of generalized reciprocity and encourage the emergence of social trust. Such networks facilitate coordination and communication, amplify reputations, and thus allow dilemmas of collective action to be resolved. When economic and political negotiation is embedded in dense networks of social interaction, incentives for opportunism are reduced. At the same time, networks of civic engagement embody past success at collaboration, which can serve as a cultural template for future collaboration. Finally, dense networks of interaction probably broaden the participants' sense of self, developing the "I" into the "we," or (in the language of rational-choice theorists) enhancing the participants' "taste" for collective benefits.

I do not intend here to survey (much less contribute to) the development of the theory of social capital. Instead, I use the central premise of that rapidly growing body of work—that social connections and civic engagement pervasively influence our public life, as well as our private prospects—as the starting point for an empirical survey of trends in social capital in contemporary America. I concentrate here entirely on the American case, although the developments I portray may in some measure characterize many contemporary societies.

Whatever Happened to Civic Engagement?

We begin with familiar evidence on changing patterns of political participation, not least because it is immediately relevant to issues of democracy in the narrow sense. Consider the well-known decline in turnout in national elections over the last three decades. From a relative high point in the early 1960s, voter turnout had by 1990 declined by nearly a quarter; tens of millions of Americans had forsaken their parents' habitual readiness to engage in the simplest act of citizenship. Broadly similar trends also characterize participation in state and local elections.

It is not just the voting booth that has been increasingly deserted by Americans. A series of identical questions posed by the Roper Organization to national samples 10 times each year over the last two decades reveals that since 1973 the number of Americans who report that "in the past year" they have "attended a public meeting on town or school affairs" has fallen by more than a third (from 22 per cent in 1973 to 13 per cent in 1993). Similar (or even greater) relative declines are evident in responses to questions about attending a political rally or speech, serving on a committee of some local organization, and working for a political party. By almost every measure, Americans' direct engagement in politics and government has fallen steadily and sharply over the last generation, despite the fact that average levels of education—the best individual-level predictor of political participation—have risen sharply throughout this period. Every year over the last decade or two, millions more have withdrawn from the affairs of their communities.

Not coincidentally, Americans have also disengaged psychologically from politics and government over this era. The proportion of Americans who reply that they "trust the government in Washington" only "some of the time" or "almost never" has risen steadily from 30 per cent in 1966 to 75 per cent in 1992 . . .

Religious affiliation is by far the most common associational membership among Americans. Indeed, by many measures America continues to be . . . an astonishingly "churched" society. For example, the United States has more houses of worship per capita than any other nation on earth. Yet religious sentiment in America seems to be becoming somewhat less tied to institutions and more self-defined.

How have these complex crosscurrents played out over the last three or four decades in terms of Americans' engagement with organized religion? The general pattern is clear: the 1960s witnessed a significant drop in reported weekly churchgoing—from roughly 48 per cent in the late 1950s to roughly 41 per cent in the early 1970s. Since then, it has stagnated or (according to some surveys) declined still further. . . .

For many years, labour unions provided one of the most common organizational affiliations among American workers. Yet union membership has been falling for nearly four decades, with the steepest decline occurring between 1975 and 1985. . . .

Next, we turn to evidence on membership in (and volunteering for) civic and fraternal organizations. These data show some striking patterns. . . .

. . . Evidence on "regular" (as opposed to occasional or "drop-by") volunteering is available from the Labor Department's Current Population Surveys of 1974 and 1989. These estimates suggest that serious volunteering declined by roughly one-sixth over these 15 years, from 24 per cent of adults in 1974 to 20 per cent in 1989. . . .

Fraternal organizations have also witnessed a substantial drop in membership during the 1980s and 1990s. Membership is down significantly in such groups as the Lions (off 12 per cent since 1983), the Elks (off 18 per cent since 1979), the Shriners (off 27 per cent since 1979), the Jaycees (off 44 per cent since 1979), and the Masons (down 39 per cent since 1959). In sum, after expanding steadily throughout most of this century, many major civic organizations have experienced a sudden, substantial, and nearly simultaneous decline in membership over the last decade or two.

The most whimsical yet discomfiting bit of evidence of social disengagement in contemporary America that I have discovered is this: more Americans are bowling today than ever before, but bowling in organized leagues has plummeted in the last decade or so. Between 1980 and 1993 the total number of bowlers in America increased by 10 per cent, while league bowling decreased by 40 per cent. (Lest this be thought a wholly trivial example, I should note that nearly 80 million Americans went bowling at least once during 1993, *nearly a third more than voted in the 1994 congressional elections* and roughly the same number as claim to attend church regularly. Even after the 1980s' plunge in league bowling, nearly 3 per cent of American adults regularly bowl in leagues.) . . . The broader social significance, however, lies in the social interaction and even occasionally civic conversations over beer and pizza that solo bowlers forgo. Whether or not bowling beats balloting in the eyes of most Americans, bowling teams illustrate yet another vanishing form of social capital.

Countertrends

At this point, however, we must confront a serious counterargument. Perhaps the traditional forms of civic organization whose decay we have been tracing have been replaced by vibrant new organizations. For example, national environmental organizations (like the Sierra Club) and feminist groups (like the National Organization for Women) grew rapidly during the 1970s and 1980s and now count hundreds of thousands of dues-paying members. An even more dramatic example is the American Association of Retired Persons (AARP), which grew exponentially from 400,000 card-carrying members in 1960 to 33 million in 1993, becoming (after the Catholic Church) the largest private organization in the world. The national administrators of these organizations are among the most feared lobbyists in Washington, in large part because of their massive mailing lists of presumably loyal members.

These new mass-membership organizations are plainly of great political importance. From the point of view of social connectedness, however, they are sufficiently different from classic "secondary associations" that we need to invent a new label—perhaps "tertiary associations." For the vast majority of their members, the only act of membership consists in writing a cheque for dues or perhaps occasionally reading a newsletter. Few ever attend any meetings of such organizations, and most are unlikely ever (knowingly) to encounter any other member. The bond between any two members of the Sierra Club is less like the bond between any two members of a gardening club and more like the bond between any two Red Sox fans (or perhaps any two devoted Honda owners): they root for the same team and they share some of the same interests, but they are unaware of each other's existence. Their ties, in short, are to common symbols, common leaders, and perhaps common ideals, but not to one another. The theory of social capital argues that associational membership should, for example, increase social trust, but this prediction is much less straightforward with regard to membership in tertiary associations. From the point of view of social connectedness, the Environmental Defense Fund and a bowling league are just not in the same category. . . .

Within all educational categories, total associational membership declined significantly between 1967 and 1993. Among the college-educated, the average number of group memberships per person fell from 2.8 to 2.0 (a 26-per-cent decline); among high-school graduates, the number fell from 1.8 to 1.2 (32 per cent); and among those with fewer than 12 years of education, the number fell from 1.4 to 1.1 (25 per cent). In other words, at *all* educational (and hence social) levels of American society, and counting *all* sorts of group memberships, *the average number of associational memberships has fallen by about a fourth over the last quarter-century.* . . .

Americans are also less trusting. The proportion of Americans saying that most people can be trusted fell by more than a third between 1960, when 58 per cent chose that alternative, and 1993, when only 37 per cent did. The same trend is apparent in all educational groups; indeed, because social trust is also correlated with education and because educational levels have risen sharply, the overall decrease in social trust is even more apparent if we control for education.

Our discussion of trends in social connectedness and civic engagement has tacitly assumed that all the forms of social capital that we have discussed are themselves coherently correlated across individuals. This is in fact true. Members of associations are much more likely than nonmembers to participate in politics, to spend time with neighbours, to express social trust, and so on.

The close correlation between social trust and associational membership is true not only across time and across individuals, but also across countries. Evidence from the 1991 World Values Survey demonstrates the following:[3]

. . . Across the 35 countries in this survey, social trust and civic engagement are strongly correlated; the greater the density of associational membership in a society, the more trusting its citizens. Trust and engagement are two facets of the same underlying factor—social capital. . . .

Why Is US Social Capital Eroding?

As we have seen, something has happened in America in the last two or three decades to diminish civic engagement and social connectedness. What could that "something" be? Here are several possible explanations, along with some initial evidence on each. . . .

Mobility: The "re-potting" hypothesis. Numerous studies of organizational involvement have shown that residential stability and such related phenomena as homeownership are clearly associated with greater civic engagement. Mobility, like frequent re-potting of plants, tends to disrupt root systems, and it takes time for an uprooted individual to put down new roots. It seems plausible that the automobile, suburbanization, and the movement to the Sun Belt have reduced the social rootedness of the average American, but one fundamental difficulty with this hypothesis is apparent: the best evidence shows that residential stability and homeownership in America have risen modestly since 1965, and are surely higher now than during the 1950s, when civic engagement and social connectedness by our measures was definitely higher.

Other demographic transformations. A range of additional changes have transformed the American family since the 1960s—fewer marriages, more divorces, fewer children, lower real wages, and so on. Each of these changes might account for some of the slackening of civic engagement, since married, middle-class parents are generally more socially involved than other people. Moreover, the changes in scale that have swept over the American economy in these years—illustrated by the replacement of the corner grocery by the supermarket and now perhaps of the supermarket by electronic shopping at home, or the replacement of community-based enterprises by outposts of distant multinational firms—may perhaps have undermined the material and even physical basis for civic engagement.

The technological transformation of leisure. There is reason to believe that deep-seated technological trends are radically "privatizing" or "individualizing" our use of leisure time and thus disrupting many opportunities for social-capital formation. The most obvious and probably the most powerful instrument of this revolution is television. Time-budget studies in the 1960s showed that the growth in time spent watching television dwarfed all other changes in the way Americans passed their days and nights. Television has made our communities (or, rather, what we experience as our communities) wider and shallower. In the language of economics, electronic technology enables individual tastes to be satisfied more fully, but at the cost of the positive social externalities associated with more primitive forms of entertainment. The same logic applies to the replacement of vaudeville by the movies and now of movies by the VCR. The new "virtual reality" helmets that we will soon don to be entertained in total isolation are merely the latest extension of this trend. Is technology thus driving a wedge between our individual interests and our collective interests? It is a question that seems worth exploring more systematically. . . .

NOTES

1. Robert D. Putnam, *Making Democracy Work: Civic Traditions in Modern Italy* (Princeton: Princeton University Press, 1993).

2. James S. Coleman deserves primary credit for developing the "social capital" theoretical framework. See his "Social Capital in the Creation of Human Capital," *American Journal of Sociology* (Supplement) 94 (1988): S95–S120, as well as his *The Foundations of Social Theory* (Cambridge: Harvard University Press, 1990), 300–21. See also Mark Granovetter, "Economic Action and Social Structure: The Problem of Embeddedness," *American Journal of Sociology* 91 (1985): 481–510; Glenn C. Loury, "Why Should We Care about Group Inequality?" *Social Philosophy and Policy* 5 (1987): 249–71; and Robert D. Putnam, "The Prosperous Community: Social Capital and Public Life," *American Prospect* 13 (1993): 35–42. To my knowledge, the first scholar to use the term *social capital* in its current sense was Jane Jacobs, in *The Death and Life of Great American Cities* (New York: Random House, 1961), 138.

3. I am grateful to Ronald Inglehart, who directs this unique cross-national project, for sharing these highly useful data with me. See his "The Impact of Culture on Economic Development: Theory, Hypotheses, and Some Empirical Tests" (unpublished manuscript, University of Michigan, 1994).

CRITICAL
Reading
Questions

1. According to Putnam, what is social capital and why is it important?

2. How is bowling an example of declining civic engagement? What are some other pieces of evidence, aside from lower voting rates?

3. What are some of the arguments Putnam gives for the decreasing levels of social capital? What might he say about the rise of the Internet (e.g. social networking sites, online activism, etc.) for the development of social capital?

Civil Society on Campus and among the Young

It is clear from the work of Coleman, Putnam, and others that social capital and civicness are very important. How actively involved are students on your campus in comparison with other Canadian campuses? Why do you think this is the case? What are the implications of having an active (or inactive) campus?

Look for measures of engagement at your college or university, Including the number of students who voted in recent student elections, the existence of clubs on campus, social events on campus, student athletics, student newspapers, alumni associations, and other groups and activities.

1. Do you think that your university administration encourages this kind of social capital? If so, how? Why do you think they encourage it?

2. What are the implications of this engagement on your campus? Is civicness related to such things as your campus's score on student satisfaction, graduation rates, or student achievement? Why or why not?

3. What factors make your campus engaged or not? How does the size of the campus, its location, number of students living on campus, or diversity of students impact student engagement?

Now compare your school to another Canadian college or university. Select one that differs from yours in terms of size, location, student body, or some other factor and find the measures listed above. Note the similarities and differences between the two campuses.

1. Why is one campus more or less active than the other? What features seem to lead to higher engagement?

2. What are the implications of these differences for student satisfaction and educational outcomes?

3. If you think that engagement on campus is a positive thing, how could you encourage more students to engage in campus life and activities?

4. How could colleges and universities support your efforts to increase civicness?

Summary

This chapter began by examining how society changes over time. Social change can happen either through the state, the focus of this chapter, or outside the state, the focus of the next chapter. Because of the state's significance in social change, we examined the rise of the state and its components. We then looked at the development of the welfare state, both internationally and in Canada. The welfare state provides many goods to citizens, particularly social programs. Through examining both universal and means-tested programs, we assessed how government programs can reduce social inequality and deal with particular social issues, such as poverty among the elderly and children. We also explored the role of reparation programs, particularly the TRC, as a means by which the state addresses social inequality. The chapter ended with a discussion of a key issue facing the modern state, the decline of social capital. This weaker connectedness between people can make the state's ability to engage citizens and effectively institute social change difficult.

Key Terms

civic engagement 354
civicness 354
economic perspective 337
election 348
generational replacement 348
Guaranteed Income Supplement
  (GIS) 341
life-cycle effect 348
managerial perspective 336
means-tested program 340

militaristic perspective 336
reparation programs 342
rotating credit association 351
social change 334
state 335
Truth and Reconciliation Commission
  of Canada (TRC) 347
universal program 339
welfare state 337

For Further Reading

Evans, Peter B., Dietrich Rueschemeyer, and Theda Skocpol. 1985. *Bringing the State Back In.* New York: Cambridge University Press.

Inglehart, Ronald. 1997. *Modernization and Postmodernization: Cultural, Economic and Political Change in 43 Nations.* Princeton, NJ: Princeton University Press.

Putnam, Robert D., with Robert Leonardi and Raffaella Y. Nanetti. 1993. *Making Democracy Work: Civic Traditions in Modern Italy.* Princeton, NJ: Princeton University Press.

Stanbridge, Karen, and Howard Ramos. 2012. *Seeing Politics Differently: A Brief Introduction to Political Sociology.* Don Mills, ON: Oxford University Press.

Tilly, Charles. 1992. *Coercion, Capital, and European States (990–1992).* Cambridge, MA: Basil Blackwell.

Introduction

In November 2012, Nina Wilson, Sheelah Mclean, Sylvia McAdam, and Jessica Gordon held a teach-in in Saskatoon to educate the public about the impact of Bill C-45. Many activists claim that measures contained in the bill could harm the environment, particularly the waterways that pass through reserve land. This teach-in set off a series of events called Idle No More, an ongoing social movement originating with both the Aboriginal people of Canada and their supporters. The movement has involved a number of tactics to raise awareness and to advance its goals, the most prominent strategy being Attawapiskat Chief Theresa Spence's hunger strike. There were also coordinated social media campaigns, flash mobs dancing in shopping malls, and blockades of the Trans-Canada Highway. Just a month after the teach-in, there had been a hundred protest events across Canada and 30 across the United States and around the world. These events attracted thousands in cities such as London, Berlin, and Cairo.

In Chapter 12, we learned how social change can occur through the state. For example, we can elect leaders who will pass laws and policies that create social change. However, not all social change happens in this way. Sometimes the state is not responsive to certain groups' interests or needs. When the state is indifferent or unable to act, social movements such as Idle No More can arise. In this chapter, we will learn about social movements, specifically how people come to participate in them and how they can lead to social change.

Social Movements

Social movements are sustained challenges to existing holders of power in the name of a wronged population. This population could be a group who feels that its rights have not been respected, such as women, LGBTQ people, ethnic minorities, immigrants, First Nations, individuals with disabilities, the young, or the homeless. Their members engage in activities such as **protesting** in the streets, occupying buildings, sending e-mails to political leaders, striking, going to benefit concerts, and **boycotting** products. Through these actions, the wronged population and/or sympathetic allies work to demonstrate that they are worthy of being listened to, united in their cause, numerous, and committed to social change (Tilly 1997).

In many ways, social movements are similar to routine politics, such as elections. Groups use both to gain public support for their opinions and interests. For example, a social movement group might work to increase public support for gay marriage. In election campaigns, political leaders sometimes also discuss gay rights; they try to convince the electorate that their perspective on this issue matches voters' opinion and therefore merits votes. In addition, the interests of social movement groups can be incorporated into party policy and government. For example, the Green Party has taken up many of the environmental movement's concerns. And the federal government has created large bureaucracies, such as Environment Canada, to deal with these issues, often after much pressure from the environmental movement.

There are also important differences between elections and social movements. Elections and political parties are often run by powerful political insiders. Social movements, however, tend to represent the interests of outsiders who have less power. Elections are also routine, occurring at set times. Engagement in social movements is less predictable and involves different strategies depending on the situation. Participation in elections is also low cost, as going to the polls does not require risky behaviour or a great amount of time. Participating in social movements requires more energy and commitment from members and activists.

According to Charles Tilly (1997), social movements require five main elements. They must involve a sustained challenge; challenge power holders; act on behalf of a

HIGHLIGHT

Pride Parades and the LGBTQ Movement

The LGBTQ movement has been an important part of changing attitudes toward gays and lesbians in Canada and around the world. One of the most prominent events staged by this movement is the annual pride parade, which celebrates LGBTQ culture. In Canada, the three biggest pride parades are held in Toronto (close to a million participants), Vancouver (600,000), and Montreal (200,000). The next largest parades occur in the following cities:

Halifax, NS (100,000)
Ottawa, ON (38,000)
Calgary, AB; Edmonton, AB; and Winnipeg, MB (30,000)
Quebec City, QC, and Saskatoon, SK (15,000)
London, ON (10,000)
Kitchener-Cambridge-Waterloo, ON (7,000)
Durham, ON (6,000)

SOURCE: Compiled from various sources.

wronged population; work to demonstrate worthiness, unity, numbers, and commitment; and engage in unauthorized action. Let's examine each of these components separately.

The first major component of a social movement is that it involves a sustained challenge. One protest event does not make a social movement. If there is a protest on your campus to reduce tuition fees but no other event ever materializes, it is not a social movement. However, once the issue of tuition fees is taken up by an organization such

PHOTO 13.1 Demonstrators in Grand Central Terminal, New York City, participate in a "die-in" on 6 December 2014 to protest the acquittal of the white police officer responsible for the choking death of Eric Garner, an African American, in July of the same year. Such protests, associated with the Black Lives Matter movement, which began on Twitter, originated after George Zimmerman was acquitted of the murder of Trayvon Martin in 2013.

as the Canadian Federation of Students and/or is the source of repeated protests, e-mail campaigns, and media advertisements, it fulfills Tilly's first requirement. This sustained challenge involves repeated collective claims to power holders, which demonstrate to the public that the movement is committed to the issue at hand.

As discussed, social movements tend to involve people with less power challenging those with more. For example, social movements can try to convince government leaders to change laws. Activists can also work to get business leaders to alter their practices, perhaps by paying their workers higher wages. Movements can encourage other institutions, such as churches, the media, or schools, to change how they operate. For example, activists could call for the media to be more inclusive of people from various ethnic and racial backgrounds. In all these examples, social movements focus their actions on trying to get power holders to change elements of society with which they disagree.

We mentioned at the beginning of this section that social movements represent a wronged population. For example, the women's movement fights for the rights of women, including the right to vote, to get equal pay, to be protected from physical and sexual violence, and to have access to daycare. First Nations movements in Canada fight for treaty rights, better schools on reserves, social programs for First Nations people, and for reparation for past injustices.

Movements are composed of both the wronged population and **conscience constituencies**, other people who are sympathetic to the group's plight. Many men support groups such as Take Back the Night, a feminist organization that works to raise awareness of sexual assault against women. Many non–First Nations people support the payment of reparations to those who were forced to attend residential schools. Conscience constituents do not directly benefit from the movement's success, yet they support the cause and efforts.

To gain attention, social movements have to disrupt daily routines. Holding a protest against clear-cut logging in the middle of an old growth forest far from any towns or cities will neither be seen by many people nor cause a disruption. As a result, it probably will not create social change. Conversely, the activists of the Greensboro sit-ins, a major part of the US civil rights movement, protested in busy stores. Because of this disruption, the sit-ins gained public attention and were instrumental in creating mass social change. In fact, they were a major reason that businesses in the American South were desegregated. Social movement activists must engage in action that is outside regular politics—not just voting or donating money to political parties. They must also protest, boycott, or do other unconventional activities to gain media and public attention.

Finally, the strength of a social movement is based on the worthiness, unity, numbers, and commitment (**WUNC**) of its members. Worthiness is showing that your group or interests are worth listening to—that you are important enough to deserve the attention of the public and those in power. Endorsements from moral authorities, such as religious or community leaders, can show worthiness. Having the pope or Dalai Lama support your cause, for example, would be a sure demonstration of your worthiness! Groups exhibit unity by sharing similar values, interests, and goals. A group that seems fragmented will not be as strong as one that is united. Wearing the same shirts, having the same signs, or singing the same songs shows that the group belongs together and is unified in its cause. A group also needs to demonstrate that it has the support of a large number of people. Leaders and the public will be much more likely to care about social issues if they are brought forth by a large group instead of a small circle of friends. A group can show their numbers by holding large public demonstrations that fill the streets, sending **petitions** with many signatures, or having a large number of members in their organization. Finally, a group must show that their members are committed to the cause. When members are willing to persist in costly or risky behaviour, they show their commitment. For example, if your members are willing to be arrested, go to jail, or camp out in the cold for long periods, they are highly committed to the cause.

Tilly (1997) says that the strength of a social movement is the result of the formula W x U x N x C. If any of these numbers is zero, the movement will have no strength, even if it has a lot of the other three components. However, you can make up for less of one with more of another. If you do not have many people interested in your cause but the people in your group are highly committed, you might engage in a more radical tactic, such as having them chain themselves to a gate at a military base. Even though there are only 10 people at your event, you can still garner attention through this risky behaviour. If many people are interested in your cause but not intensely committed to it, you might want to launch a Facebook campaign. People do not have to be very committed to a cause to "like" it; if you can get a thousand people to respond, you can show that your issue is important.

There are many significant social movements in Canada and around the world. The environmental movement has been particularly prominent in Canada and effective at getting its issues on the political agenda. In the following reading, Suzanne Staggenborg discusses the rise of this movement in Canada and the support for its work.

READING

The Environmental Movement

Suzanne Staggenborg

. . .

Origins of the Environmental Movement

. . . Conservation movements emerged in a number of countries in the nineteenth century to promote national parks, wilderness preservation, resource management, and the exploration of nature (Lowe and Goyder, 1983: 15–17). . . . Canada's first conservation organization, the Canadian Nature Foundation, was founded in the 1930s (Paehlke, 1997: 254). . . .

Greenpeace, founded in Canada in 1971, quickly became an international organization that is perhaps best known for its use of media-oriented direct-action tactics. The founders of Greenpeace were Canadian and American peace activists and journalists from the protest movements of the 1960s who had originally organized themselves as a committee of the Canadian branch of the Sierra Club (Dale, 1996: 16). The political context of the student New Left and anti-Vietnam War protest was critical to Greenpeace's first action in 1971, when activists sailed an old fishing boat from Vancouver to the site of a planned US nuclear test on the island of Amchitka in the Aleutian Islands. Because this underground test might create tidal waves on Canada's west coast, the Greenpeace organizers called themselves the Don't Make a Wave Committee. Although the Greenpeace campaign was framed to appeal to mainstream Canadian nationalism, it was also calculated to build on previous peace movement and student protests against US military tests. Exploiting both Canadian patriotism and anti-American sentiment caused by the Vietnam War, Greenpeace took off during a period of expanded activism that had been generated by the movements of the 1960s. . . .

Public Support for Environmentalism

Public interest in the environment and membership in environmental organizations have ebbed and flowed over the years, as has media attention to environmental issues. Anthony Downs (1972) argues that there is an "issue attention cycle" whereby the public becomes alarmed about a problem and very concerned with its amelioration. Once the public comes to realize the cost of significant advances, however, enthusiasm for solutions to the problem dampens. Eventually, the decline in public interest is followed by a "post-problem phase" during which the problem may sporadically recapture public interest. In 1972, Downs wrote that the public was already starting to realize the enormity of the social and financial costs involved in cleaning up the environment. Between 1965 and 1970, numerous environmental groups had formed in North America, and there had been a great sense of urgency about environmental issues (McKenzie, 2002: 89). After extensive North American media interest in the environment in the early 1970s, however, stimulated in part by the large Earth Day demonstrations in the United States in 1970, media coverage of environmental issues would drop off dramatically by the late 1970s (Steinhart, 1987).

Media attention is one factor that affects public concerns, and although there have been periods of heightened media attention to the environment in North America since the early seventies, the movement has struggled to maintain ongoing, serious coverage of environmental problems. Media coverage of environmental issues tends to focus on dramatic events such as oil spills and nuclear power accidents. For example, the 1989 *Exxon Valdez* oil spill in Alaska and the confrontation over logging in British Columbia in the 1990s were major stories (Hacket and Gruneau, 2000: 169). As Downs (1972) suggests, coverage also tends to go in cycles. For example, one study shows that coverage of global warming by *The New York Times* and *The Washington Post* increased dramatically in the late 1980s but declined in the 1990s (McComas and Shanahan, 1999). Systematic, ongoing coverage that does not involve major crises or movement-created drama is generally lacking in the North American media; the media have difficulty sustaining interest in idea-based issues, and this has important consequences for public attention to environmental issues.

The extent of public concern about the environment also depends on competition from other concerns, such as economic problems. During periods of economic recession and high unemployment, for example, environmental concerns tend to be less salient than economic ones, meaning that they take on less immediate personal importance for members of the public . . .

It is clear that public support for environmentalism has risen to strikingly high levels worldwide. The 1990–1993 World Values Survey (WVS) found that on average 96 per cent of people in over 40 countries approved of the ecology movement. Ten years later, another World Values Survey, carried out in a larger number of countries, together with other global surveys, again found very high levels of environmental concern (Leiserowitz et al., 2005). And support for environmentalism remains high even when it is seen as costly. For example, 65 per cent of the combined global sample in the 1990–1993 World Values Survey said they would agree to a tax increase if the money went toward preventing environmental pollution (Inglehart, 1995: 59). In the 1999–2001 World Values Survey, 52 per cent of respondents worldwide agreed that environmental protection should take priority over economic growth and job creation. Moreover, Dunlap and York (2008) found in their analysis of this more recent WVS that people in poor countries were even more willing to make sacrifices for the environment than those in affluent countries. . . .

. . . Concern about climate change has remained high in Canada; in a 2010 Angus Reid poll, 61 per cent of Canadians said that protecting the environment is more important than economic growth and 60 per cent said global warming is a fact, compared to 47 per cent of Britons and 42 per cent of Americans (Angus Reid Public Opinion, 2010). For the environmental movement, the challenge is to convert this base of public support into the major changes that are necessary to limit the impacts of the global warming crisis and other environmental problems.

Participation in the Environmental Movement

Attitudinal support for the environmental movement does not necessarily translate into environmentally conscious behaviour or support for environmental organizations. Because environmental protections are a public good and because individual contributions to the reversal of large-scale environmental degradation are not likely to make a dent in the problem, the movement is, not surprisingly, faced with a free-rider problem. Many more people believe in environmental goals than actively support the movement, and recent surveys suggest that only 10–13 per cent of the worldwide public supports the movement by donating to environmental organizations, writing letters, and signing petitions (Leiserowitz et al., 2005: 28–9). . . . Global surveys also show differences between richer and poorer societies with regard to behaviours such as recycling and selecting "green" products. For example, one survey found that among respondents from high-income countries 67 per cent reported buying green products and 75 per cent reported recycling, compared to only 30 per cent of respondents from low-income countries reporting buying green and 27 per cent reporting recycling. However, such results may reflect the lack of facilities and markets in lower-income countries, and it is unlikely that surveys adequately represent the very poor, "who are most likely to reuse and recycle as part of survival" in low-income countries (ibid., 28). Moreover, residents of wealthier countries engage in high levels of consumption and use large amounts of energy. And, as environmental activism becomes more common in many poor countries and as international environmental organizations work to spread environmental values around the world (Wapner 2002), multinational survey evidence shows that activism is viewed favourably by residents of poor countries (Dunlap and York, 2008: 542). . . .

The Clayoquot Sound Protests

In 1993, after the British Columbia provincial government announced that it would allow clear-cut logging in much of the old-growth forests of Clayoquot Sound, on the west coast of Vancouver Island, one of the most dramatic direct-action campaigns in the history of the environmental movement was organized in British Columbia. As many as 12,000 protesters blocked access to a logging road, and some 800 people were arrested in largely non-violent protests. A local group called Friends of Clayoquot Sound, which had been fighting for preservation of the forests for over a decade, established a peace camp, and this became one base for protesters involved in the blockades. The protests drew attention from around the world, and numerous environmental organizations, including Greenpeace and the Sierra Club, became involved. A countermovement also mobilized; in the spring of 1994, as many as 20,000 forestry workers and their families lobbied the provincial legislature, and in July of that year, thousands of people held a festival designed to celebrate "timber culture," which they felt was threatened by the protests (*The Globe and Mail*, 14 July 1994).

Nevertheless, public opinion was strongly opposed to clear-cutting, and the environmental campaign employed both market-based tactics and direct action, using the resources of large international organizations as well as those of local groups. After Greenpeace threatened to boycott their products, two British paper companies cancelled contracts to buy pulp from the Canadian timber company MacMillan Bloedel. The BC government eventually set stricter limits on logging in Clayoquot Sound, and the direct-action protests ended.

The struggle over clear-cutting, however, continued. In a boycott campaign led by the Sierra Club and Greenpeace against Home Depot, the huge home improvement and building supplies retailer based in the United States, environmentalists deluged the company with postcards, sent an exhibit on the Great Bear Rainforest (located on the central mainland BC coast) to a shareholder meeting, and erected a Home Depot protest billboard over a clear-cut patch near Vancouver. The campaign resulted in a major victory when Home Depot, which has over 850 stores worldwide and sells 10 per cent of the world's market supply of wood, announced in 1999 that it would phase out sales of wood from endangered forests by 2002 (*The New York Times*, 22 October 1999). Boycotts also forced timber companies to agree to more sustainable practices, although conflicts over logging in British Columbia continue. Overall, the movement campaign made important gains by building on favourable public opinion, using the resources of large environmental organizations, and harnessing the energies of grassroots activists with direct-action tactics. . . .

Conclusion

The modern environmental movement has endured for decades despite ebbs and flows in its organizational strength and activity. The movement's organizational and strategic diversity is one important reason for the continued salience of environmentalism. Large national organizations have created green lobbies in numerous countries. International organizations have spread to many countries and are capable of mounting both national and transnational campaigns. Greenpeace, in particular, has become expert at generating media coverage. Local and regional groups, such as Friends of Clayoquot Sound and Earth First!, have demonstrated the potential of non-violent direct action for the environmental movement. Networks of environmental activists and collective identities endure, even when particular organizations and campaigns decline. The movement has provoked significant countermovement activities, but these responses are an indicator of environmentalism's appeal, even though they seek to harm the movement's cause.

Strong public support for environmentalism helps the movement endure by creating financial support for movement organizations and political support for movement positions. Environmental problems are subject to issue attention cycles, but the movement continues to be relevant to the public because critical environmental problems are ongoing and local populations are often affected by environmental devastation. Public support creates the potential for a greater use of market-based strategies, but also the risk that only strategies that appeal to the mainstream public will be developed. Strategies that are difficult to convey through the mass media and that involve slow and complicated solutions may be difficult to sell to the public. Organizations that depend on donations from a great many people may fail to develop solutions that require lifestyle sacrifices on the part of the public. Moreover, even with public support to combat such enormous problems as global warming, economic interests and financial costs create major barriers. Industry's opposition to the movement and an industry-backed countermovement have stymied progress. Coalitions with labour unions and other groups are clearly necessary, as are international efforts to address the global scope of environmental problems. Many environmentalists are involved in such efforts, including the global justice movement . . .

REFERENCES

Angus Reid Public Opinion. 2010. "Americans and Britons Becoming More Skeptical of Climate Change." http://www.visioncritical.com/category/global-opinions-and-trends.

Dale, Stephen. 1996. *McLuhan's Children: The Greenpeace Message and the Media.* Toronto: Between the Lines.

Downs, Anthony. 1972. "Up and Down with Ecology—The 'Issue-Attention Cycle,'" *Public Interest* 28: 38–50.

Dunlap, Riley E., and Richard York. 2008. "The Globalization of Environmental Concern and the Limits of the Postmaterialist Values Explanation: Evidence from Four Multinational Surveys," *Sociological Quarterly* 49: 529–63.

The Globe and Mail. 1994. "Myth of Eternal Forest Toppled," 14 July, A1, A3.

Hacket, Robert A., and Richard Gruneau. 2000. *The Missing News: Filters and the Blind Spots in Canada's Press.* Aurora, ON: Garamond Press.

Inglehart, Ronald. 1995. "Public Support for Environmental Protection: Objective Problems and Subjective Values in 43 Societies," *PS: Political Science and Politics* 28, 1: 57–72.

Leiserowitz, Anthony A., Robert W. Kates, and Thomas M. Parris. 2005. "Do Global Attitudes and Behaviors Support Sustainable Development?" *Environment* 47, 9: 22–38.

Lowe, Philip, and Jane Goyder. 1983. *Environmental Groups in Politics.* London: George Allen & Unwin.

McComas, Katherine, and James Shanahan. 1999. "Telling Stories about Global Climate Change," *Communication Research* 26, 1: 30–57.

McKenzie, Judith I. 2002. *Environmental Politics in Canada: Managing the Commons into the Twenty-First Century.* Toronto: Oxford University Press.

The New York Times. 1999. "Loggers Find Canadian Rain Forest Flush with Foes," 22 Oct.

Paehlke, Robert. 1997. "Green Politics and the Rise of the Environmental Movement," in Thomas Fleming, ed., *The Environment and Canadian Society.* Scarborough, ON: ITP Nelson, 252–74.

Steinhart, Peter. 1987. "The Longer View," *Audubon* 89, 2: 10–13.

Wapner, Paul. 2002. "Horizontal Politics: Environmental Activism and Global Cultural Change," *Global Environmental Politics* 2, 2: 37–62.

1. What are **issue attention cycles**? Why might they be important for social movements?
2. Aside from protesting, how could you support the environmental movement and its cause?
3. What is the level of support for the environmental movement generally? How does this support differ in poor versus rich countries?
4. What was the Clayoquot campaign? What types of tactics, groups, and people were involved in it? To what extent was this campaign successful?

The Collective Action Problem

Early work on social movements argued that participation is irrational. If you think about the costs and benefits of participating, it is clear that the former are relatively high and the latter relatively low. The costs of participating include finding information about a cause, a group involved in that cause, and an event that the group is putting on. In addition, you have to spend the time and energy to go to the protest event, sign the petition, or boycott the product. All these activities are pretty costly in terms of time and energy. If you believe that there is a relatively small chance that you will help the group be successful, perhaps it does not make rational sense to participate in social movements.

This sort of reasoning is very familiar. Everyone has heard the argument that people do not vote because they feel that it will not make a difference. Even if they care about the cause, people might not go to a protest event because they think that their individual participation will not contribute to the group's success. This perspective, first articulated by Mancur Olson (1965), is called the **collective action problem** (or the **free-rider problem**). Olson argued that people tend to avoid participating in collective action (e.g. social movements) because they still benefit from whatever is gained whether or not they contribute to the cause. Therefore, collective action is unlikely to occur even when large groups of people have common interests.

Social movements often fight for **public goods**, things which are non-excludable (one person cannot reasonably prevent another from consuming the good) and non-rivalrous (one person's consumption of the good does not affect another's). Clean air is a public good that illustrates the collective action problem. Environmental activists lobby the government to pass laws restricting pollution and they boycott companies that pollute. If these tactics are successful, we will have cleaner and better quality air. Once the air is cleaner, I (as an environmental activist) cannot stop you (a free rider) from breathing my clean air, even though you never went to any of my protest events to fight for it. Voting rights is another example of a public good. Once women got the right to vote, all women—those who fought for it and those who did nothing—can enjoy this right.

Olson's argument makes some intuitive sense, but it also poses some important problems. If everyone sat at home and waited for others to push for social change, nothing would ever happen. (You need someone fighting for clean air and voting rights!) Also, if Olson's theory is true, how do we explain all the social movement events and campaigns that have occurred? Are all social movements simply a bunch of irrational people getting together? The next section considers the variety of reasons why someone might join a social movement.

HIGHLIGHT

Occupy

On 3 January 2012, Canadians learned that, by noon that day, each of the 100 top CEOs in the country had already earned as much as the average Canadian makes in an entire year. Using 2010 figures, Mackenzie (2012) reported that the average Canadian earned $44,300 annually, while the top CEOs earned $8.4 million. These figures clearly indicate a great inequality between Canada's workers and top earners. If we were to compare these top salaries with the incomes of Canadians living in poverty, the imbalance would be even starker.

Many people feel that this level of inequality in a relatively rich country is unacceptable. The recent Occupy protests illustrate this view. While the protesters focused on a number of issues, they were primarily concerned with the growing gap between society's rich and poor. They argued that large corporations and wealthy individuals exert a disproportionate amount of control over society and the economy; the resulting system benefits these individuals at the expense of the larger population.

The Occupy movement was initiated by *Adbusters*, an anti-consumerist magazine discussed in Chapter 7 (see p. 208). The magazine and its founders called for individuals concerned about inequality, democracy, and the environment to come together and challenge the power of the small group that owns much of the Canadian economy. The first protests, called Occupy Wall Street, began on 17 September 2011 in New York City's Zuccotti Park. A month later, similar protests were occurring in 95 cities across 82 countries. The movement eventually spread to over 900 cities around the world.

The Occupy protesters camped out at city parks, sometimes for more than a month, and used the slogan "We are the 99 per cent" to highlight the concentration of society's wealth among the top 1 per cent of earners and the lack of benefits for the remaining population. The statement mirrors Marx's (1982, 660–1) sentiment that "Accumulation of wealth at one pole is at the same time accumulation of misery, agony of toil, slavery, ignorance, brutality, mental degradation, at the opposite pole."

A group of protesters at an Occupy rally in Toronto hold up signs bearing the group's slogans. How do such protests showcase the issues of inequality and social class discussed in this book?

Trends in Social Movement Participation

Many people participate in social movements, and they do so in various ways. Some are members of social movement organizations (SMOs). Others never join groups but go to social movement events, such as protests or marches. Still others simply do things that support social movement causes. For example, composting or biking to school both support the environmental movement.

These different methods of engaging in social movements vary along two main dimensions that have already been introduced—the risk associated with the activity and the cost of engaging (Corrigall-Brown 2013). Most activism in Canada is not particularly risky. For example, there is little danger in attending a peaceful protest or signing a petition. Some Canadian activists do participate in risky activities, such as occupying a building or breaking into military bases, which can lead to jail time or social stigma. Engaging in social movement activities in other contexts (particularly non-democratic countries) can be quite dangerous. Participation can also be more or less costly, in terms of how difficult the activity is for an individual. If you have to travel a far distance or take time away from work or school to engage, the activity has a higher cost than other, easier activities.

Risk and cost are usually related. Signing a petition is both low risk and low cost. Camping out at an Occupy protest for weeks is both risky (in that you could be arrested) and costly (in terms of time and energy). However, quitting your job to volunteer for Greenpeace is costly but not very risky. Attending a protest event in a country that does not permit protest is not very costly (does not take a lot of time) but is extremely risky (could lead to a jail sentence).

Using World Values Survey data, Table 13.1 compares three social movement activities: protesting, signing a petition, and boycotting a product. Protesting is the most contentious of these activities, although it is legal in all the countries listed (the survey does not ask about protest participation in countries where it is illegal, such as China). Boycotting is the least contentious of the three acts because it requires only that you avoid

PHOTO 13.2 Members of the Hong Kong Federation of Students boycotted classes in September 2014 as part of a larger pro-democracy, pro-universal suffrage movement. These protesters challenged the proposed voting limits that would allow the Chinese government to screen candidates for the post of Hong Kong's head of government.

TABLE 13.1 Participation in social movement activities by country, 2010–2014 (per cent)

Country	Protested	Signed a Petition	Boycotted a Product
France	38	67	14
Germany	31	50	9
Canada	26	73	24
Netherlands	20	46	14
Australia	20	79	15
India	19	29	15
Great Britain	17	68	17
Mexico	16	21	3
United States	15	70	20
Rwanda	14	9	4
South Africa	13	12	10
Japan	10	60	7
Turkey	6	12	5

SOURCE: Data from World Values Survey Data analysis tool, Wave 6 (data collected from 2010–2014). http://www.worldvaluessurvey.org/WVSOnline.jsp.

doing something. For example, if you are concerned with sweatshop labour, you might refuse to buy clothing from companies that use sweatshops. If you are an advocate of animal rights, you might not buy products from companies that engage in animal testing.

You can see from the table that, in most countries, people are more likely to sign a petition or boycott a product than attend a protest event. And, they are also usually more apt to sign a petition than boycott a product. This is partly because signing a petition is a one-time activity while boycotting requires a sustained commitment not to buy something.

In comparison with the other countries in the chart, Canadians are fairly active in social movements. Over the past 50 years, the character of protest in modern industrial democracies, such as Canada and the United States, has changed radically. Since the 1960s and 1970s, the frequency of protest events and the levels of individual participation in protest activity have increased (Meyer and Tarrow 1998). This trend is evident in Canada—Canadians, as a group, have increased their propensity to participate in social movements (see Table 13.2). In the United States, the percentage of people who have attended a demonstration has also increased, from 11 per cent in 1975 to 15 per cent in 2014. Over the last quarter of the twentieth century, most advanced industrial democracies have seen a rise in protest participation (Inglehart 1997; Norris 2002).

TABLE 13.2 Social movement participation, Canada, 1982–2008 (per cent)

	1982	1990	2000	2008
Demonstration	14	21	20	25
Petition	62	77	73	58
Boycott	15	22	21	16

SOURCE: Data from World Values Survey Data analysis tool. http://www.worldvaluessurvey.org/WVSOnline.jsp.

Explaining Social Movement Participation

The survival and success of social movements is based on the participation of individuals. With this in mind, what predicts who will participate in a social movement? What leads certain individuals to participate in social movements while others do not? Participation requires four main elements: ideology, resources, biographical availability, and social ties and identity.

Ideology

Individuals need to be committed to the goals of a movement in order to participate in a social movement (Klandermans 1997). Not all individuals who believe in a cause become activists. However, it is equally true that individuals who are not sympathetic to the cause are highly unlikely to join a movement. Ideological commitment is important because it makes people at least cognitively available to participate in a movement.

Ideology is also a very significant part of why many people participate in protests. We mostly think of a protest as something in which liberals engage. Research supports this argument, showing that leftists are more apt to attend protests (Dalton, Van Sickle, and Weldon 2010). However, protest is clearly no longer just for people on the political left. The prominence of conservative movements in Canada and the United States has brought people from across the political spectrum into social movements.

Religious ideologies are also important predictors of engagement. Religious beliefs can motivate individuals to come together to create social change. Belonging to and participating in a religious institution can lead individuals to develop social networks, political knowledge, and resources. Such factors make these individuals more prone to join social movements than those not tied to religious institutions (Diani 2004; McAdam 1986).

However, ideology alone is not enough to predict engagement. Individuals must also feel that their participation will yield results. This sense of **efficacy** is the belief that one is capable of the specific behaviours required to produce a desired outcome in a given situation (Gecas 2000). Individuals who are efficacious are self-confident and feel that they can produce the changes in the world that they desire. Not surprisingly, these individuals are more likely to participate in protest activities (Rosenstone and Hansen 1993).

Resources

Along with ideologies, individuals must have the resources that allow them to engage in social movements. For example, individuals with more money are much more apt to protest than people with less money. This difference is not because those with more money believe more strongly in social movement goals but because money helps individuals to translate their beliefs into action.

Socio-economic status (SES) is one of the most important predictors of an individual's propensity to protest (Verba, Schlozman, and Brady 1995). Individuals with high SES tend to have other resources, such as free time and certain skills that enable them to participate in social movements. As a result, they are more likely than other people to engage in groups of all kinds, including social movement organizations (see also Rosenstone and Hansen 1993).

Other non-financial resources, such as education and political knowledge, also predict engagement (Wilkes 2004). Putnam's (2000, 35) work on political participation and general group membership finds that political knowledge is a "critical precondition for active forms of participation" and that those who know more about politics are more disposed to engage in protest.

PHOTO 13.3 The Raging Grannies, who started out as anti-nuclear cam-
paigners in the late 1980s, are activist groups comprised of older women. Older
people are less likely to be targets for arrest—if you were a police officer, would
you want to be seen arresting these women? Why or why not?

Biographical Availability

When individuals are **biographically available** to participate in social movements, they
have the opportunity to convert their ideology and resources into action (Beyerlein and
Hipp 2006). Life changes make individuals more or less available to participate. For
example, if you are married or have children, you might be less inclined to attend protests
because you have less free time to engage and you might be more fearful of the risks of
participation (McAdam 1986, 70). Students are often considered particularly biographically available as many do not have spouses, children, full-time jobs, or other constraints
on their time (Wiltfang and McAdam 1991). Older people are also frequently biographically available because they are usually retired and do not have children living at home
(Nepstad and Smith 1999).

Social Ties and Identity

Having social ties to other activists is another central component of participating in
social movements. If you have many close friends who are active in social movements, you
are much more likely to join (McAdam 1986).

One of the main reasons that social ties are so important is that they can help create
identities that facilitate and encourage social movement engagement. **Identities** are the
names that people give to themselves and others in the course of social interaction (Snow
2001). Some sociologists argue that a collective identity, a sense of "we-ness" that comes
from shared attributes or experiences among a group (Melucci, Keane, and Mier 1989), is
a pre-requisite for collective action (Klandermans and de Weerd 2000). By participating
in social movements, individuals can come to change their identities, sometimes adopting an "activist identity" (Taylor and Raeburn 1995).

Political Context/Critical Events

Social movement participation is also shaped by the context in which it happens. Some
contexts are more facilitative to the growth of social movement mobilization than
others. These facilitative contexts are called **free spaces**, the small-scale settings within a

SlutWalk

While speaking at Toronto's York University in 2011, Police Constable Michael Sanguinetti suggested that "women should avoid dressing like sluts" in order to remain safe from sexual assault (Rush 2011). Many criticized Sanguinetti (who later apologized) for suggesting that women who were raped were at fault and for excusing the behaviour of rapists. This statement is a form of victim blaming; the individual who suffers at the hand of another is viewed as responsible for or contributing to the wrong committed against her.

Women and men who disagree with such claims organized a set of marches, which they called SlutWalk, to protest these stereotypes (Church 2011). The first walk occurred in Toronto on 3 April 2011 and inspired additional protests in over 60 cities across the world. The use of the salacious term in the name is intentional. Organizers argued that, instead of allowing others to label them, they would reclaim the word so that it could not be used against them. Some feminists, the media, and the public have criticized the movement for reappropriating a term that many people feel is degrading to women.

What do you think of calling the movement SlutWalk? Does the attention the name garners justify its use or undermine the cause? Can degrading words ever truly be reclaimed?

community or movement that are removed from the direct control of dominant groups, are voluntary, and generate the cultural challenge that precedes or accompanies political mobilization (Polletta 1999). These free spaces protect activists from those in power who might oppose them. Student lounges, union halls, and neighbourhood groups are examples of free spaces (Fantasia and Hirsch 1995).

In his research on Beijing's pro-democracy student movement, Zhao (1999) conducted 70 interviews with student activists. He found that free spaces were critical to the movement's success. In particular, universities acted as safe places that allowed students to meet and organize.

RESEARCH METHOD

Interviews

Consequences of Participation

Participating in a social movement or protest activities can have long-term transformative effects for individuals. A group of studies (e.g. Whalen and Flacks 1989) that interviewed people who were active in social movements of the 1960s found that participating in protest had important consequences for the later lives of individuals. Activists tended to maintain the same ideology over the course of their lives and to remain politically active. There were many interesting personal consequences to their participation as well. Former activists are concentrated in teaching and other helping professions; have lower incomes; are more likely to have divorced, married later, or remained single; and are more apt to have experienced an episodic or nontraditional work history than non-activists (Giugni 2004).

The Media and Social Movements

Most of what we learn about social movement causes and campaigns comes from the media, which works to frame social movements. **Frames** are ways of interpreting the world that allow individuals to understand and label occurrences in their daily lives. There are simply too many things happening in the world "out there"; we need frames to condense the world into a smaller set of ideas designed to attract and mobilize potential participants. The process of framing is about selecting certain parts of the world to emphasize and others to de-emphasize. Think of a photograph. When you take a picture, you capture some of what is happening, but some elements are left out. In the same way, a frame focuses on some aspects of reality to promote a particular interpretation of an event or issue. Activists use frames to inspire and legitimate social movement activity. The media might pick up these frames and make them available to the public.

Frames have three key parts: diagnostic, prognostic, and motivational. First, the social movement and activists "diagnose" the problem. In terms of the environmental movement, a group could argue that environmental problems are the result of weak laws that do not prevent or restrict pollution. Second, a social movement tries to propose a solution to the problem. If we think that the government's environmental laws are too weak, the prognosis is that we should lobby the government to pass firmer legislation. Third, social movement activists try to get individuals to do something to solve the problem. Perhaps we should start a petition, go to a protest event on Parliament Hill, or create a Facebook page for environmental protection. A different group might argue that individual consumers cause environmental problems by buying too much stuff and using too many resources (diagnosis). It might suggest that consumers should buy less or recycle/reduce/reuse (prognosis) and start a campaign such as Buy Nothing Day (as discussed in Chapter 7) or a campaign to encourage recycling (motivational). Even though both groups are interested in protecting the environment, their different diagnostic frames lead to different solutions and calls to action.

Selection and Description Bias

One way for the public to be exposed to social movements' frames is by attending their events or going to SMOs' websites. We can also learn of social movement activities and causes through media coverage of protests and campaigns. Because so many events occur every day, the media must select which are the most "important" to cover. Many social movement groups stage events that get no coverage at all!

Media editors must pick a limited number of events to observe and report because there is only so much space in the paper, on the website, or in the broadcast. **Selection bias** involves media editors' choices of a small number of protest events from a much larger pool. Media agendas can influence this selection, independent of an event's characteristics. With the exception of size, objective matters such as the form of the protest or its timing are unrelated to whether an event is reported in the mass media (Smith et al. 2001).

Events are more likely to be reported if their substantive focus can be used to illustrate an issue that is already on the media's radar. A group concerned with gun control has a better chance of getting media attention after a large-scale incident of gun violence. Such issue attention cycles, which Staggenborg discussed in her reading, are the specific times when the public is more apt to become concerned about a problem and attempt to solve it. Once the public realizes the cost of addressing a problem, however, enthusiasm for solutions often dampens. Eventually, the decline in public interest is followed by (as Staggenborg says) a post-problem phase.

Once a group has secured media coverage (no small feat!), activists become concerned with **description bias**, or how they and their actions are depicted. We can make sense of how the media selects what to cover and how they frame that coverage in a variety of ways. These explanations are generally based on either organizational or ideological models (Smith at al. 2001).

From the perspective of **organizational models of the media**, the media acts as gatekeepers. These gatekeepers do not just choose the most important events to cover. Instead, they also give more coverage to events that are seen to be changing. For example, in the last chapter we learned about the very serious problem of child poverty in Canada. Getting coverage for this issue is difficult because it is relatively stagnant over time (i.e.

the rates remain high and unchanging). Why would the media cover child poverty today or tomorrow instead of something that is considered more current? For social movement activists to get this issue covered, they must connect it to some event or matter that is seen to be increasing, spreading, or intensifying to make it sufficiently interesting. A UN report stating that child poverty in Canada is higher than most other Western countries or a story of a particular child and his plight can capture the public's interest and therefore draw media attention to the larger issue.

Economics also shape what is covered in the media. Newspapers, television stations, and news websites are experiencing budget cuts. Consequently, editors tend to favour generalist reporters rather than specialists. Generalists can write a story on transit today, education tomorrow, and health the next day, which eliminates the need to have one reporter (who might not have anything to cover on a given day) for each area. Generalists are cheaper and more efficient to hire; however, by their very nature, they do not know as much about each area that they cover because they are forced to move from one to another. As a result, they are more reliant on official government sources for information. A reporter who covers a transit strike, the education system, and healthcare wait lines can call up a government contact and get a quote to include in the article on any of these topics. She is less apt to contact social movement activists or others (such as bus drivers, teachers, or nurses) because she lacks contacts in all these different areas. This means that the news is more likely to represent the interests and perspectives of officials and those in power than of challengers.

The organizational perspective does not argue that journalists and editors conspire against coverage of social movements and other critical groups. Reporters and editors want to get the best and most accurate story out to the public. The structure and organization of news collection simply makes it so that reporters write and editors choose stories that tend to support the status quo and undermine activists.

The **ideological model of media coverage** argues that there is a more concerted effort on the part of the media, political, and corporate elites to control the information in the news. This model says that broader structures of power relations in society affect the portrayal of social movements and protest. Such structures lead to increased privatization, commercialization, and concentration of ownership, which severely limits the range of ideas conveyed in the media (see Chapter 7).

The media makes money through advertising; therefore, it tends to cover issues that will get the most attention, regardless of their importance. Articles about Kim Kardashian having a baby or Taylor Swift dating someone new are not really "important," but they attract many readers. As a result, the news outlet can charge more for advertisements. Publishing sensational stories in order to draw the public's attention is also the basis of the saying "If it bleeds, it leads." News coverage of crime often focuses on particularly gruesome murders. Such articles frequently appear on the front page or as the top item on a broadcast or website and include dramatic photographs of the accused killer or innocent victim. Despite the fact that the overall crime rate in Canada is declining, coverage that emphasizes these dramatic crimes is selected because it attracts attention and makes money for the news outlet.

Because of the importance of advertising revenue, journalists must be very aware of advertisers' interests. Thus, from the perspective of the ideological model, the media works to reproduce broader power relationships. For example, it tends to focus on individual responsibility for social problems and neglect social causes. Instead of reporting on the overall reasons that crime rates are higher in some areas or groups, the media tends to centre on one individual criminal or victim. This approach encourages a shallow understanding of these issues and discourages the critical engagement of audiences.

As our discussion has indicated, media framing is important because the media plays a powerful role in educating the public about social issues. It sends signals about who is legitimate and sympathetic and to whom we should listen. Consequently, the media can affect public opinion and government policy. In terms of social movements, the media

ACTIVITY

Media Images of Protest—The Oka Crisis and Occupy

To see how the media depicts protest events, let's look at two examples—the Oka Crisis and the Occupy protests.

The Oka Crisis

The **Oka Crisis** is Canada's largest and longest standoff between First Nations people and the government. On 11 July 1990, several dozen Mohawk people from Kanesatake, Quebec, set up a barricade to stop the town of Oka's plans to expand a golf course in the area. The development included land that was supposed to be held in trust for the Mohawks, who had a symbolic and spiritual connection to it. Oka's mayor responded to the protest by calling in the provincial police, who stormed the barricade. In the ensuing conflict, one police officer was killed and the police retreated. The barricade continued, and the event received extensive media coverage in Canada and around the world. Protest events supporting the Mohawks were held across Canada and a peace camp was set up at Oka Park.

Frustrated by the long standoff, Prime Minister Brian Mulroney called in 2,500 Canadian soldiers to replace the Quebec police. On 26 September, the remaining Mohawks burned their weapons and walked away. Most of the protesters were charged with various offences, although only two were convicted of any crime. In 1997, the Canadian government purchased the land and "gave" it to the Mohawk people.

With this background in mind, do an Internet image search for the Oka Crisis. Use the photos you find to answer the following questions.

1. How do the images represent the Mohawks, the Quebec police, the Canadian military, and others? Do the photos reflect a positive or negative view of these groups? How is the relationship between these various groups depicted?

2. Why would these images have been selected for publication? Answer this question using the organizational model, then the ideological model.

3. The following image, "Face to Face," appeared over a hundred times in Canadian newspapers, becoming the most reprinted image of the Oka Crisis. How does it depict the Canadian soldier and the Mohawk protester? Who elicits more sympathy? How would the image affect public opinion about this event?

4. The following two images were also taken during the Oka Crisis but did not appear in newspapers. How do these photos depict the protesters and the officials? Do they convey a different message about this event and the participants than the others you've seen? How would the organizational and ideological models explain why these other images were not shown in the media?

Occupy

1. Now look online for images of the Occupy protests. How are the protesters depicted in these images? How are officials depicted (if they are shown)?

2. Why were these images selected? How do they relate to the organizational or ideological theories of the media? Do these images support or challenge the idea of the protest paradigm?

3. Are the depictions of protesters and officials the same or different than they were in the Oka Crisis? If so, why?

HIGHLIGHT

Independent Media and Social Movements— The Arab Spring

The mainstream media—newspapers, television news, and news websites—often discredits and marginalizes protest events, with journalists relying on the protest paradigm. To combat these negative portrayals, activists often turn to alternative media outlets or create their own media.

Social media and alternative media have become a recognized—and sometimes reviled—tool for activism. On 4 February 2011, the Egyptian government cut off most Internet and cellphone access in an attempt to inhibit anti-government protesters, many of whom were using social media platforms such as Twitter to organize their efforts and spread word of their protests internationally.

In Chapter 7, we looked at the significant role that social media played in reporting events during the Arab Spring. Harlow and Johnson (2011) examined how these new tools are similar to, or different from, traditional media. They compared protest coverage of the Arab Spring in *The New York Times*, the Twitter feed of reporter Nick Kristof, and the citizen media site Global Voice. They found that *The Times* closely emphasized the spectacle, quoted official sources, and devalued protesters. In contrast, Global Voices and Kristof's Twitter feed legitimized protesters. Global Voices also provided more opportunities for reader interactivity. This research shows that alternative and social media offer activists the chance to shape the coverage that they receive and to get their message to the public.

coverage of protests generally tends to be limited and, when it does occur, negative. These findings are consistent with both the organizational and ideological perspectives: the media tends to emphasize officials' views at the expense of activists' and other challengers' and centre on individual-level explanations instead of the social explanations most movements try to convey. In addition, because the media tries to attract attention and emphasize drama in order to increase circulation and revenue, they tend to focus on the violence, drama, and "wackiness" at a protest event.

The specific way that the media tends to cover protest events is known as the **protest paradigm** (McLeod and Hertog 1999). This template uses a particular framing and relies on official sources. Together, these elements lead to the delegitimization, marginalization, and even demonization of protesters.

Success in Social Movements

Social movement groups often call for large-scale social changes. A women's group that calls for equality between the sexes will find that the goal is pretty hard to achieve. How can full equality be attained? If men and women make the same salaries, is that equality? What about access to education or depictions in the media? When groups have large and broad goals, it is frequently hard to determine if they have been successful. Moreover, groups with a variety of goals tend to achieve only some of them.

Another reason that success is hard to measure is that politicians, business leaders, and others in power are often reluctant to admit being influenced by social movement groups. Leaders might feel that doing so makes them seem weak and easily swayed by public opinion. They often do not want to encourage more protest or campaigns. A very active and engaged population is certainly harder to govern than one that sits at home and only comes out to vote once every four years. With these issues in mind, how can we measure social movement success? William Gamson has created a typology of outcomes, which he details in the following article.

READING

The Meaning of Success

William Gamson

Success is an elusive idea. What of the group whose leaders are honoured or rewarded while their supposed beneficiaries linger in the same cheerless state as before? Is such a group more or less successful than another challenger whose leaders are vilified and imprisoned even as their program Is eagerly implemented by their oppressor? Is a group a failure if it collapses with no legacy save inspiration to a generation that will soon take up the same cause with more tangible results? And what do we conclude about a group that accomplishes exactly what it set out to achieve and then finds its victory empty of real meaning for its presumed beneficiaries? Finally, we must add to these questions the further complications of groups with multiple antagonists and multiple areas of concern. They may achieve some results with some targets and little or nothing with others.

It is useful to think of success as a set of outcomes, recognizing that a given challenging group may receive different scores on equally valid, different measures of outcome. These outcomes fall into two basic clusters: one concerned with the fate of the challenging group as an organization and one with the distribution of new advantages to the group's beneficiary. The central issue in the first cluster focuses on the *acceptance* of a challenging group by its antagonists as a valid spokesman for a legitimate set of interests. The central issue in the second cluster focuses on whether the group's beneficiary gains *new advantages* during the challenge and its aftermath.

Both of these outcome clusters require elaboration, but, for the moment, consider each as if it were a single, dichotomous variable. Assume a group that has a single antagonist and a single act which they wish this antagonist to perform—for example, a reform group which desires a particular piece of national legislation. We ask of such a group, did its antagonist accept it as a valid spokesman for the constituency that it was attempting to mobilize or did it deny such acceptance? Secondly, did the group gain the advantages it sought—for example, the passage of the legislation that it desired?

By combining these two questions, as in [the following table], we acquire four possible outcomes: full response, co-optation, preemption, and collapse. The full response and collapse categories are relatively unambiguous successes and failures—in the one case the achievement of both acceptance and new advantages, in the other, the achievement of neither. The remainder are mixed categories: co-optation is the term used for acceptance without new advantages and preemption for new advantages without acceptance.

Outcome of resolved challenges		Acceptance	
		Full	**None**
New	**Many**	Full response	Pre-emption
Advantages	**None**	Co-optation	Collapse

[The table] is the paradigm for handling outcomes of challenging groups, but it requires additional complexity before it can be used to handle as diverse a set of groups as the 53 represented here. Acceptance must be given a special meaning for revolutionary groups, for example, which seek not a nod of recognition from an antagonist but its destruction and replacement. Similarly, new "advantages" are not always easy to define. We must deal with cases in which a group seeks, for example, relatively intangible value changes, shifts in the scope of authority, or a change in procedures as well as the simpler case of material benefits for a well-defined group.

The Endpoint of a Challenge

The outcome measures used refer to "ultimate" outcome, to the state of the group at the end of its challenge. A given group might achieve significant new advantages at one point without receiving acceptance, but we would not consider that preemption had occurred as long as it continued to press an active challenge. Only when it eventually collapsed or ceased activity would we classify its outcome as preemption. Or, if it eventually won acceptance, its outcome would be full response instead. Similarly, the new advantages might be withdrawn and the group brutally crushed, making "collapse" the appropriate outcome. Thus, during its period of challenge, a group might appear to be in one or another cell of [the table] at different times, but the outcome measures only consider its location at the end.

A challenge period is considered over when one of the following occurs:

1. *The challenging group ceases to exist as a formal entity.* It may officially dissolve, declaring itself no longer in existence. Or, it may merge with another group, ceasing to maintain a separate identity. Note, however, that a group does not cease to exist by merely changing its name to refurbish its public image. Operationally, we consider that two names represent the same challenging group if and only if:

   a. The major goals, purposes, and functions of the two groups are the same.

   b. The constituency remains the same.

   c. The average challenging group member and potential member would agree that the new-name group is essentially the old group relabelled.

2. *The challenging group, while not formally dissolving, ceases mobilization and influence activity.* A five-year period of inactivity is considered sufficient to specify the end of the challenge. If, after such a dormant period, the group becomes active again, it is considered a new challenging group in spite of its organizational continuity with the old challenger. This occurred, in fact, with 2 of the 53 challengers in the sample. In each case the period of dormancy was quite a bit longer than the required five years, and, in one case, the geographical location of activity was different as well.

Marking the end of a challenge is more difficult with groups that continue to exist and be active. The line between being a challenging group and an established interest group is not always sharp. The essential difference lies in how institutionalized a conflict relationship exists between the group and its antagonists. When this conflict becomes regulated and waged under some standard operating procedures, the challenge period is over. Operationally, this can be dated from the point at which the group is accepted. Hence, for continuing groups, the challenge period is over when:

3. *The challenging group's major antagonists accept the group as a valid spokesman for its constituency and deal with it as such.* In the case of unions, this is indicated by formal recognition of the union as a bargaining agent for the employees. In other cases, the act of acceptance is less clear, and, even in the case of unions, different companies extend recognition at different times. Issues such as these are dealt with in the discussion of measures of acceptance below.

With continuing groups, then, there is some inevitable arbitrariness in dating the end of a challenge. The compiler was instructed to err, in ambiguous cases, on the side of a later date. Thus, where acute conflict continues to exist between the group and important antagonists, the challenge is not considered over even when some other antagonists may have begun to deal with the challenger in a routinized way. Furthermore, by extending the challenge period, we include new benefits that might be excluded by using a premature termination date.

Measuring Outcomes

ACCEPTANCE

Did the relationship between the challenging group and its antagonists change from the beginning to the end of the challenge? Although more than 75 per cent of the groups here are more complicated, we will begin the discussion of this question with the simplest case of a group with a single antagonist. This antagonist necessarily begins with a relationship of active or passive hostility toward the challenging group or, at best, indifference. Acceptance involves a change from hostility or indifference to a more positive relationship.[1]

There are four indicators of this more positive relationship:

1. *Consultation.* This must involve some degree of initiative by the antagonist. For example, if a legislative body has opened hearings on a matter of importance to the challenging group, the antagonist might invite representatives of the group to testify. On the other hand, if the group asks to testify and is permitted, this would not by itself be considered consultation. Similarly, if the antagonist issues a subpoena to force the group to testify, no consultation would be coded because the group is not being treated in such an instance as a legitimate spokesman for a constituency.

2. *Negotiations.* If the antagonist is willing to enter into negotiations with the group on a continuing basis, not simply at the height of a particular crisis, this also implies acceptance of the group as a spokesman for a constituency. To be coded as acceptance, the negotiations must imply that the antagonist is dealing with the challenging group's negotiators as representatives of a constituency. The outcome of the negotiations is not relevant here; the two parties may fail to reach an acceptable settlement. But the mere fact of a continuing negotiating relationship implies acceptance.

3. *Formal recognition.* This form of acceptance is characterized by the antagonist making explicit, typically in writing, that it recognizes the challenging group as a legitimate spokesman for a designated constituency. This is the functional equivalent of diplomatic recognition of a government in international politics. Nothing needs to be implied about general mutuality of interests or approval of the challenging group and its actions.

4. *Inclusion.* This form of acceptance is characterized by the inclusion of challenging group leaders or members in positions of status or authority in the antagonist's organizational structure. It is essential, however, that the included challenging group members maintain their status, formally or informally, as group members. If serving in the antagonist's organization requires repudiating membership in the challenging group as a condition of office, it is not coded as acceptance through inclusion. . . .

NEW ADVANTAGES

Did the potential beneficiaries of the challenging group receive what the group sought for them? No assumption is made that the challenging group necessarily caused the benefits. We asked only whether desired results were forthcoming, for whatever reason, during and immediately after the period of challenge. . . .

How is the achievement of new advantages actually measured? First, consider the simplest case of a group with a single goal or area of concern. Four perceptions of goal achievement were coded: the perception of degree of achievement (1) by historians, (2) by the challenging group, and (3) by its antagonist, and (4) the challenging group's level of satisfaction with its achievement at the end of the challenge. In many cases, we were unable to get sufficient information on one or more of these perceptions, in which case we coded what we could. The codes covered changes both during the period of the challenge and in the following 15 years.[2]

Since many groups had multiple goals and since sources sometimes disagreed on how well the goals were achieved, each group had multiple measures of new advantages. To reduce this complexity for analysis, a summary measure was essential. We ended up using the following four categories:

1. *Twenty groups (38 per cent) received no new advantages.* These groups had minuses and zeroes on all clusters.

2. *Twenty-six groups (49 per cent) received new advantages.* These groups had at least one positive field (i.e. pluses, no more than two zeroes, and no minuses) in a majority of their areas of concern. In other words, on most of their goals, these groups received a positive response on at least one major aspect.

3. *Four groups (7 per cent) received peripheral advantages.* These were groups that had some positive fields but did not meet the full definition of a group receiving new advantages.

4. *Three groups (6 per cent) received equivocal advantages.* These were groups with mixed fields (some pluses and some minuses concerning the same goal). In other words, these were groups on which disagreement existed among different observers on whether goals had been realized or not.

The seven groups in the last two categories will be combined with the no-advantage group for analysis purposes. [The following table] shows the distribution of the 53 groups in the four outcome categories described above. In many analyses, we will examine each summary measure separately as we explore the relative influence of some variable of interest on these different measures of outcome. . . .

Outcomes for the sample of challenging groups based on summary measure of acceptance and new advantages

		Minimal Acceptance Relationship	
		Yes	**No**
New	**Yes**	Full response = 20 38%	Pre-emption = 6 11%
Advantages	**No** (or equivocal and peripheral)	Co-optation = 5 9%	Collapse = 22 42%
		n = 53	

NOTES

1. If acceptance existed from the very beginning, the group would not qualify as a challenging group.

2. Since most groups had multiple goals and multiple areas of concern within each goal cluster, a challenger's goal achievement was covered by a code consisting of many columns. We first broke goals down into specific clusters for separate evaluation. Then, for each cluster, we gave a challenger a plus for each source (that

is, an historian, challenging group, or antagonist) who agreed that at least half of the relevant targets had responded in the desired fashion. We recorded a minus when a source asserted that less than half of the targets responded as desired or the group was no more satisfied at the end of the challenge than when it began. If there was insufficient information on the perceptions of one or another source, a zero was recorded.

1. What are the different ways that social movements can achieve success? What is the difference between **acceptance** and **new advantage**?

2. Explain what Gamson means by full response, co-optation, pre-emption, and collapse.

3. According to Gamson, when do social movement challenges end? Is a social movement ever really "over"? Why or why not?

Public Sociology and Using Our Sociological Imagination

Recently, there have been calls for sociologists to engage more with the public and bring sociological ideas to the larger community. **Public sociology**, a term introduced by Herbert Gans in 1988, uses the sociological imagination to engage with wider audiences

ACTIVITY

Using Our Sociological Imagination for Social Change

Patricia Hill Collins, an important feminist scholar, has long been concerned with her work's impact on different communities of people. She and many other sociologists hope that their work and a sociological understanding of the world can be used to improve society. Collins (2013) discusses intellectual activism and how it can help us use our sociological imagination to improve society and the lives of individuals. This idea is similar to public sociology. She argues that, as sociologists, we should both "speak truth to power" and "speak truth to people." The former uses the power of ideas to confront existing power relations in order to change the foundations of social hierarchy—the less powerful take on the ideas and practices of the powerful, often armed solely with their ideas. The latter means talking to the masses and is based on the idea that sociologists should communicate how sociological knowledge can help improve individuals' daily lives (Collins 2013).

To learn more about public sociology, go to this book's companion website to read an excerpt from Herbert Gans. Then answer the following questions:

1. What is public sociology, according to Gans? What four kinds of public sociology should academic sociologists undertake?

2. How can sociology students engage in these activities? Is it possible to be a public sociology student? Why or why not?

3. Take one of the main theories or research findings that you have learned in this book. How could you use this information to engage in public sociology?

4. Who would you want to know about your public sociology research? How would you try to get this information to them? How could it create social change and a more equitable world?

outside traditional academic circles. Promoters of public sociology have sought to encourage sociologists to engage with social issues in explicitly public and political ways. This movement uses the theories and findings of sociology in debates about not just what is or what has been in society but also what could be.

Summary

In this final chapter, we examined social change as it can occur through social movements. We began by learning about the core features of social movements and examining the rise of the Canadian environmental movement. The collective action problem helped us to understand why we might not expect individuals to engage in social movements. Despite this problem, Canadian participation is relatively high and is increasing. Therefore, it is important to know why some individuals might take part in protest and social movement events. We discussed the media's importance in social movements, particularly regarding issues of selection and description bias. We also considered how to measure success for social movements. We ended this chapter, and this book, by thinking about public sociology and intellectual activism.

Key Terms

acceptance 387
biographical availability 376
boycott 364
collective action problem (or free-rider
  problem) 371
commitment xx
conscience constituency 366
description bias 378
efficacy 375
frames 377
free spaces xx
identities 376
ideological model of media coverage 379

issue attention cycles 371
new advantage 387
Oka Crisis 380
organizational model of media
  coverage 378
petition 366
protest 364
protest paradigm 382
public good 371
public sociology 387
selection bias 378
social movement 364
WUNC 366

For Further Reading

Klandermans, B. 1997. *The Social Psychology of Protest*. Oxford: Blackwell.

McAdam, Doug. 1988. *Freedom Summer*. New York: Oxford University Press.

McCarthy, J., and M. Zald. 1973. *The Trend of Social Movements in America: Professionalization and Resource Mobilization*. Morristown, NJ: General Learning Press.

Meyer, David S., and Sidney Tarrow, eds. 1998. *The Social Movement Society: Contentious Politics for a New Century*. Lanham: Rowan and Littlefield.

Staggenborg, Suzanne, and Howard Ramos. 2016. *Social Movements*, 3rd edn. Don Mills, ON: Oxford University Press.

Glossary

acceptance According to Gamson, a measure of social movement success in which a movement is considered a valid representative for a legitimate set of interests.

achievement-based stratification system A system that ranks individuals based on their accomplishments.

agents of socialization The various societal groups that help us learn to become members of society (e.g. family, peer groups, the education system, the mass media, and religion).

alienation Generally, the separation of things that naturally belong together. According to Marx, workers become alienated from the product they make, the process of production, other workers, and themselves.

alternative media Media that is non-profit, anti-establishment, and creative and is based on a two-way relationship between the producer and the consumer.

anticipatory socialization The process of individuals rehearsing roles that they may have to perform in the future.

arranged marriage A marital union in which a third party selects the bride and groom. Arranged marriage was common in certain cultures and areas throughout history and remains so in South Asia, Africa, the Middle East, Latin America, Southeast Asia, and parts of East Asia.

ascription-based stratification system A system that ranks individuals based on a person's ascribed features (e.g. race or sex).

authoritarian personality Adorno's term for a personality that is more likely to develop prejudicial attitudes. People with this type of personality tend to see the world in terms of good and evil and strictly follow rules and orders.

automation The operation of equipment with minimal or reduced human intervention.

biographical availability A main predictor of social movement engagement. Individuals with fewer responsibilities and constraints, such as young people, students, single people, and those without children, are more likely to have the time, energy, and inclination to engage in contentious political activity.

bourgeoisie (capitalist) One of the two primary classes in Marx's theory; the owners of the means of production.

boycott The minimally contentious act of withdrawing from commercial or social relations with a country, organization, or person as a form of protest.

breaching experiments Experiments that intentionally break a social rule or norm in order to reveal the common work done by individuals to maintain social order in day-to-day life.

bureaucracy Literally, "the rule of the office or desk," an organizational form that predominates in modern society and focuses on rationality. Weber described bureaucracies as human machines.

Canada Pension Plan (CPP) A universal social program available to all Canadians over the age of 60, regardless of financial means.

cash crops Crops that are sold for profit. This type of agriculture contrasts with subsistence farming, in which farmers grow crops for their own consumption.

census The systematic collecting and recording of information about members of a given population.

civic engagement The individual and collective actions designed to identify and address issues of public concern. The decline of civic engagement is the core concern of Robert D. Putnam's work.

civicness Putnam's term for the values, norms, institutions, and associations that allow and foster civic commitment, solidarity, mutual trust, and tolerance.

class consciousness An awareness of what is in the best interests of one's class. Marx argued that this awareness is an important pre-condition for organizing into a "class for itself" and advocating for class interests.

class struggle The conflict between those who own the means of production (bourgeoisie) and those who own only their labour power (workers).

cohabitation The state of a heterosexual or homosexual couple living together and having a sexual relationship without being legally married.

collective action problem (free-rider problem) The idea, posited by Olson, that people tend to avoid participating in collective action (e.g. social movements) because they will benefit from whatever is gained whether or not they contribute to the cause.

commodification The process of reducing social relations to an exchange relation (i.e. assigning them with a monetary value).

commodity An item of value and uniform quality produced in large quantities by many producers. Consumer goods, such as clothing, cars, and food, are commodities.

commodity chain A process used by companies to gather resources, transform them into goods or commodities, and distribute them to consumers; the connected path from which a good travels from producers to consumers.

companionate marriage A marriage based on the satisfaction of the couple, the family as a whole, and the different roles each person plays in the family. Companionate marriages include a clear division of labour between the breadwinner (usually the husband) and the homemaker (usually the wife). Husbands and wives are seen as friends and confidants who need and rely on one another to perform the roles that each cannot.

conflict theory The idea that human behaviour and social relations result from the underlying conflicts that arise from the power differences between competing groups in society.

conscience constituency A sympathetic ally who is outside the "wronged population" represented by the social movement.

consensus crimes Deviant acts that are illegal, perceived to be very harmful to society, and have a high level of public agreement regarding their severity. Murder and sexual assault are examples of consensus crimes.

contact theory Allport's theory that increasing contact between antagonistic groups can reduce prejudice, lead to a growing recognition of similarities, and alter stereotypes about the other group.

control theory Hirschi's theory that weak social control contributes to an individual engaging in deviant or criminal acts. Weak controls can be the result of having few social connections and relationships.

core countries The most economically diversified, wealthy, and powerful nations in the world. Core countries are highly industrialized and tend to produce manufactured goods rather than extract raw materials for export.

corporate concentration The extent to which an industry, such as the media, is increasingly owned and controlled by fewer large corporations and conglomerates.

corporatization The process of using business or management techniques to transform institutions and services previously managed by government. Corporatization occurs in universities with the naming of buildings and scholarships after major donors and the signing of exclusive contracts with companies.

costs of masculinity Messner's concept that there are rules to masculinity and what men can be and do. For example, masculinity is defined by external success; men must avoid everything feminine and are expected to be aggressive and show little emotion.

counterculture A group, such as an anti-consumerist organization, that rejects certain elements of the dominant culture.

credentialing Collins's term to describe an authority, such as a university, issuing a qualification or competence to an individual. This practice is used to exclude some people from certain jobs or opportunities.

Crime Severity Index (CSI) A measurement of the severity of police-reported crime, calculated by assigning each offence a weight based on its perceived seriousness (as measured by the sentences handed down by the courts).

cultural capital Bourdieu's term for the non-financial social assets that promote social mobility. For example, individuals can gain degrees, learn a more refined style of speech, or adopt elite social tastes, which can make them appear to belong to a higher social class than the one they were born into.

culture A system of behaviour, beliefs, knowledge, practices, values, and materials that shape how we act and the physical elements of our society.

curriculum The standardized content, materials, resources, and processes used to teach students. Each province in Canada outlines a specific curriculum for each grade.

cyberbullying The use of technology, such as the Internet, to deliberately harass, intimidate, or threaten a person.

cycle of poverty The causes and elements of poverty that trap people in this situation and require outside intervention.

deep acting Based on Hochschild's work on emotional labour, the modification of an employee's inner feelings to match the expressions required by the employer.

defensive credentialing The process of attending college or university and/or enrolling in graduate and professional programs in order to avoid losing job opportunities to degree holders and to gain an advantage in employment.

deinstitutionalization of marriage The term used by Cherlin to describe the weakening of social norms concerning marriage and people's resulting doubt of their actions, and those of others, within this institution.

demographic diversity The extent to which the media represents and addresses the interests of people from a variety of groups such as races, ethnicities, genders, and classes.

description bias In terms of social movements, the media's positive or negative depiction of a protest event or activist.

deterrence The process of dissuading someone from committing future wrongdoings by making the "cost" of punishment outweigh the "benefit" of the offence. The idea is based on the assumption that individuals conduct a rational cost–benefit analysis before committing a crime.

deviance The act of breaking a social norm.

differential association The idea that children from the lower class are less likely than other children to have role models who have achieved at school or attended university. As a result, these children lack the knowledge of how to work within the system and are less successful in it.

differential expectations The different values and outlooks that families have, based on their social class. The different education expectations of low-income and high-income families could explain why individuals from the former are less likely to perform well in schools or earn degrees than people from the latter.

differential preparation The various ways that individuals can be prepared for an aspect of society, depending on their social class. For example, children from families with more money probably have more access to private tutors, educational trips, educational toys, and books and newspapers than do poorer children. These resources help to prepare them for school and to do well in the educational system.

digital divide An inequality between groups' ability to access, use, or learn about information and communication technologies. Within countries, this term refers to inequalities between individuals, households, and geographic areas at different socio-economic levels. The global digital divide examines the gap in digital access across countries.

discrimination The unfair treatment of an individual based on his actual or perceived membership in a certain group or category.

disenchantment of the world The term used by Weber to describe the change from explaining phenomenon through magical or other-worldly forces to using rational thought and science.

diversity defenders Individuals (such as liberal activists, feminists, and sympathetic social scientists) who believe that social support makes single-parent families as beneficial to children as the traditional nuclear family. These individuals support policies that provide low-income parents and children with services and economic opportunities.

division of labour A focus of Durkheim's work, the specialization of co-operating individuals who perform specific tasks and roles.

dominant culture The culture that, through its political and economic power, is able to impose its values, beliefs, and behaviours on a given society.

double shift (second shift) Hochschild's concept that women in heterosexual dual-income households often spend significantly more time on household tasks and caring work than their partners do in addition to their work in the paid workforce.

dramaturgical perspective Goffman's theory that social life is like a stage and individuals are actors on it, performing roles for others.

ecological footprint A measure of a person's or community's impact on the earth's ecosystems; the amount of land and sea area required to sustain the use of natural resources and to process the associated waste.

economic perspective Based on Marxist theory, the argument that the state is needed to regulate economic interests and the clashing of those interests between groups. Marx argued that the state usually "resolves" these conflicts by siding with capitalists.

efficacy The belief that one is capable of the specific behaviours required to produce a desired outcome in a given situation. Efficacy is an important predictor of social movement engagement.

emotional labour Work, especially in the service sector, that requires emotional performances from employees. This labour is commodified and controlled by management.

essentialism The theory that some "essential" element makes a person part of a particular race or ethnic group. From this perspective, ethnic groups and nationalities are based on biological factors (similar appearance, skin colour, or eye colour) and a territorial location (region or country).

ethnicity The shared language, religion, customs, and history of a particular group. The core difference between race and ethnicity is that race is based on perceived biological traits and ethnicity is based on cultural differences.

experiment A process that allows researchers to examine a specific factor's effect on individual behaviour by comparing two groups: the experimental (which is exposed to the factor) and the control (which is not exposed to it).

extended family Two or more generations of a family living in the same household or in close proximity to one another; often contrasted with the nuclear family.

false consciousness A willingness among the working class to support ideologies that are advantageous to the ruling class but disadvantageous to working-class interests. Marx argued that false consciousness is part of the reason that the working class does not unite and overthrow the capitalist system.

family A group of people who are related by birth, affinity, or cohabitation.

family household A residential unit of people who are related by blood, marriage, or adoption.

family violence Any abuse, mistreatment, or neglect in which the victim and perpetrator are related or have an intimate relationship. Types of family violence include physical, sexual, emotional, and financial abuse.

feminism The various movements and ideologies that seek to define, confirm, and protect equal political, economic, and social rights for women. Feminism is sometimes understood as occurring over three waves of activism.

feminization The process of a particular job, profession, or industry being dominated by or predominantly associated with women (e.g. nurses, secretaries, teachers, and family doctors). Feminized jobs tend to lose prestige, wages, required skill levels, and opportunities for promotion.

fertility rate The average number of children born to a woman over her lifetime.

First Nations A term of ethnicity that refers to the Aboriginal people in what is now Canada who are neither Inuit nor Métis.

frames Interpretation schemes that enable individuals to understand and label occurrences in their daily lives. Framing is composed of three parts: diagnostic, prognostic, and motivational.

free spaces The small-scale settings of a community or movement that are outside dominant groups' direct control, are voluntary, and create the cultural challenge preceding or accompanying political mobilization. Social movements need free spaces so that activists can have some protection from authorities.

gender A social concept that includes all social patterns associated with being male or female and that ranges from masculine to feminine. Gender focuses on differences that are social and cultural, not biological.

gender reversal in educational outcomes The trend, which seems to have stabilized, of more women than men obtaining post-secondary degrees. In the past, men were much more likely than women to attend and graduate from university or college.

gender roles The behaviours and mannerisms that people learn as being appropriate to their respective genders and that are reinforced by cultural norms.

gender socialization The process of learning how to behave consistently with society's gender rules and norms.

general deterrence A type of deterrence that makes examples of deviants in order to discourage others from committing crimes.

generational replacement A main theory in voter turnout research that seeks to explain declining voting rates by examining how the emergence of new generations of voters (who vote less) are replacing older generations of voters (who vote more).

Gini index A measure used to compare income inequality across countries. The index ranges from zero (perfect equality) to one (total inequality).

globalization The increasing interconnectedness of people and places that results from advances in transport, communication, and information technologies and causes political, economic, and cultural convergence or integration of different people and places around the world. Globalization has three major dimensions: physical, spatio-temporal, and cognitive.

Guaranteed Income Supplement (GIS) A Canadian mean-tested program that provides money to seniors whose income is below a certain level.

heteronormative The social institutions, practices, and norms that support the assumption that people are or should be heterosexual.

Heterosexual–Homosexual Rating Scale Kinsey's seven-point scale of sexual inclinations. Instead of thinking of people as either gay or straight, Kinsey argued that they simply have life histories that express different desires. People can have more or less homosexual or heterosexual desires and more or less homosexual or heterosexual experiences, but these things are not always related.

hidden curriculum Marx's term for lessons that are not normally considered part of the academic curriculum and that schools unintentionally or secondarily provide. These lessons teach students to be submissive, punctual, and hard-working—all the traits that make "good" workers in the capitalist system.

high culture The culture of the elite, which may generally be difficult to appreciate without having cultivated a palate for it. High culture is often juxtaposed with popular culture, the culture of the majority.

homophily The propensity of individuals to make friendships and other social ties with people who share their characteristics, such as race, class, or religious beliefs.

homophobia The negative attitudes and feelings, ranging from antipathy to hatred, toward homosexuality or people who identify as or are perceived to be LGBTQ.

honorifics A form of address or reference that shows esteem or respect toward a person.

human capital model The argument, related to Durkheim's theory, that schools are organized largely to nurture productive skills needed in the economy.

Human Development Index (HDI) A number that combines a variety of measures (e.g. life expectancy, education, and income) regarding the health and quality of life in a country.

idea diversity The diversity of viewpoints expressed in the media.

identities The names that people give to themselves and others in the course of social interaction. Identity is central to social movement participation as both a cause and outcome of engagement.

ideological model of media coverage The perspective that media, political, and corporate elites make a concerted effort to control the information released through the media. This model argues that broader structures of power relations in society affect the portrayal of social movements and protest.

ideology A system of conscious and unconscious ideas that shape a person's or group's objectives, expectations, and actions. Marx argues that a society's dominant ideologies come from the dominant class and serve to perpetuate the capitalist system.

imagined communities Anderson's term to describe members of a nation feeling a sense of community even though they will never know most of their fellow citizens.

immigration The movement of people around the world. Canada has three major categories of immigrants: economic, family class, and refugees.

incest taboo An almost universally enforced norm that forbids sexual relations and marriage between certain family members.

individualized marriage A marriage that focuses on the individual's satisfaction and ability to develop and express a sense of self. These marriages are more flexible than other types, as they attempt to meet the varied needs of each spouse.

infant mortality rate A common measure of health in a country; reflects the number of deaths in the first year of a child's life, per thousand live births.

institutional marriage A marriage that is less concerned with whether spouses are in love or are good companions to each another and more focused on how the marriage solidifies family and community ties and benefits society as a whole.

intergenerational income elasticity The statistical relationship between a parent's and child's economic standings; the higher the elasticity, the less social mobility a society offers. In this situation, childhood upbringing plays a larger role than individual talents and capabilities in predicting later income.

intersectionality Crenshaw's term for the study of how various dimensions of inequality can combine.

intersex People who are born with both male and female sexual organs.

interview A qualitative research technique whereby a researcher asks subjects questions, records their answers, and then analyzes the responses. Interviews allow the researcher to ask questions that require longer answers and to follow up by asking for more detail.

invisible knapsack Coined by McIntosh, an unseen collection of unearned assets that white people use in their daily lives but about which they are expected to remain oblivious.

irrationality of rationality Weber's concept that rationalized systems can create negative outcomes.

issue attention cycles The idea that the public is more likely to become alarmed about a problem and concerned with its amelioration at certain times. Learning the cost of addressing the problem can quash this enthusiasm, followed by a "post-problem phase" of sporadic recaptured interest.

Kinsey Reports The name given to Kinsey's two books on human sexuality, *Sexual Behavior in the Human Male* (1948) and *Sexual Behavior in the Human Female* (1953).

labelling theory Becker's theory on how we label and think about individuals who engage in deviance. Becker argues that the important element is not the behaviour but the label of being deviant, which can create a deviant or criminal identity and produce a self-fulfilling prophecy that leads to more deviance.

latent functions Unintended functions.

learning theory Developed by Sutherland, who argued that different environments or social milieu, such as a jail,

provide opportunities to learn to engage in crime. This theory claims that we are socialized into deviance and criminality through learning from others.

legitimation A major function of the education system, aimed at legitimating certain kinds of knowledge and divisions in society. This process is consistent with Marx's conflict theory.

lesser crimes Acts of deviance that are illegal; however, their perceived harmfulness and severity of public response are moderate. An example of a lesser crime is speeding.

LGBTQ Lesbian, gay, bisexual, transgender, and queer/questioning.

life-cycle effect A main theory in voter turnout research that seeks to explain turnout by illustrating that there is usually an increase in the propensity to vote among older people.

looking-glass self Cooley's theory that we refine our sense of self over time in light of how others react to us.

low-income cut-offs (LICOs) Income thresholds, created by Statistics Canada, below which a family will likely spend more than the average amount of its income on basic necessities (i.e. food, shelter, clothing).

McDonaldization Ritzer's term to describe the movement from traditional to rational methods of thought. Where Weber used the model of the bureaucracy to represent this change, Ritzer sees the fast-food restaurant as representing this transformation.

managerial perspective One of the major lenses used to understand the rise of the state. This perspective argues that the state was established to politically administer increasingly large territories more effectively.

manifest functions Obvious and intended functions.

marriage The legal union of two people in an intimate relationship.

marriage movement A loose group of conservative and centrist activists, religious leaders, and social scientists who want to strengthen the institution of marriage because they believe that it is a morally superior family structure and/or benefits children. These advocates often propose and support marriage promotion programs.

mass media A message that originates from one source but is intended for many people.

means-tested program A type of social program that bases eligibility for government assistance on whether an individual or family possesses the means to do without that help. In Canada, means tests are used for student finance (for post-secondary education), legal aid, and welfare (direct transfer payments to individuals to combat poverty).

mechanical solidarity The type of solidarity that involves societies being held together by similarities among people. Durkheim argued that, in early societies, people shared a collective consciousness that created solidarity, despite the fact that each unit (such as a family) basically provided for its own production and consumption needs and subunits could survive in isolation from one another.

media The technological processes facilitating communication between a sender and a receiver.

media literacy The framework used to access, analyze, and evaluate media messages and thus create an understanding of the media's role in society.

"medium is the message" Marshall McLuhan's famous statement that argues that the content of the medium is less important than the physical or psychological effects of that medium.

microfinancing A system of offering financial services to individuals who are not served by the traditional financial system. These services provide small amounts of start-up capital to assist people with their entrepreneurial projects and thus help lift individuals, families, and communities out of poverty.

militaristic perspective One of the main lenses used to understand the rise of the state. From this perspective, the state was instituted to create a monopoly on the legitimate use of violence, particularly in relation to the ability to wage war.

modernization theory One of the main theories of globalization, which contends that countries are poor because they cling to traditional and inefficient attitudes, technologies, and institutions. Modern societies embrace industrial capitalism, modern technologies, and modern institutions. This theory predicts that, given enough time and with the "correct" behaviours, all societies can become modernized and develop like Western societies.

monocropping The agricultural practice of producing high yields by growing a single crop on the same land each year. Corn, soybeans, and wheat are three common monocrops.

monogamy An exclusive relationship between two people (one man and one woman, two women, or two men).

multiculturalism Based on the idea of pluralism, support for having various cultural or ethnic groups in a society; the belief that conflict is a central feature of societies and that ethnicity is an essential aspect of individual identity and group behaviour.

new advantage According to Gamson, a measure of social movement success in which a group gains benefits, such as a new policy or law, during a challenge and its aftermath.

new media On-demand access to content, interactive user feedback, and creative contribution on any digital device. New media technologies are digital and interactive and can be manipulated, networked, and compressed.

normality of crime Durkheim's argument that crime is necessary, functional, and even good for a society. According to Durkheim, all societies have crime and deviance, which allow groups to define and clarify their collective beliefs.

nuclear family A family consisting of two adults living with one or more children.

Oka Crisis A standoff, occurring in 1990, between the Mohawk First Nations and the Quebec police/Canadian army over the contested use of an area of land called the Pines.

one-child policy A policy enacted in China in 1979 to reduce population growth by restricting part of the population to having only one child. Exemptions include families with twins, rural couples, ethnic minorities, and couples who were both only children.

organic solidarity The type of solidarity formed by people who are quite different. Durkheim argued that modern societies tend to lack adherence to a collective conscience. What holds these societies together, despite the differences between people, is the fact that people need one another because they are so specialized.

organizational model of media coverage The perspective that the media acts as a gatekeeper that determines what events are newsworthy and, because of the way it is set up, tends to rely on official sources and generalist journalists, leading to a particular type of coverage of protest.

outsourcing Contracting work, usually manufacturing or supporting processes, to another country.

parole The supervised early release of a prisoner for such things as good behaviour. Parolees work with parole officers to adjust to life outside prison and to ensure that they do not violate the conditions of their release. If they do, their parole can be revoked and they can be sent back to prison.

participant observation (ethnography) A qualitative research method in which a researcher attempts to deeply understand a given group of individuals and their practices by becoming intensely involved in their cultural environment, usually over an extended period of time.

party In Weber's theory, organizations that attempt to influence social action and focus on achieving some political goal.

performativity Judith Butler's term to describe the repeated rituals that create and sustain gender through performance.

periphery countries The world's least economically diversified and industrialized nations. These countries focus on one type of economic activity (mostly extracting and exporting raw materials to core nations).

personal troubles Problems that individuals face in their personal lives.

petition A document signed by many people, requesting an authority (usually a government official or public entity) to do something in regards to a particular cause.

polygamy The practice of having multiple spouses. Polygamy is illegal in Canada and the United States.

popular culture The culture of the majority or the masses; often juxtaposed with high culture, the culture of the elite.

poverty A condition in which material or cultural resources are lacking. Relative poverty describes the deprivation of some people in relation to those who have more; absolute poverty is a life-threatening deprivation of resources.

power According to Weber, the chance that a person or group can realize its own will in a communal action, even against the resistance of others participating in the same action. The idea is based on a person's or group's economic class, social status, and party.

power elite C. Wright Mills's name for the interwoven interests of society's military, corporate, and political leaders.

precarious employment Employment in dead-end, low-paying, and insecure jobs (sometimes called McJobs). In this area, employers have full control over the labour process; they are able to hire and fire employees with ease and frequency, as the kind of work makes them readily replaceable.

prejudice A negative attitude toward someone, based solely on her membership in a particular group.

primary deviance In labelling theory, early acts of deviance. Isolated acts of primary deviance rarely lead to the successful application of a deviant label.

primary sector The economic sector concerned with extracting or harvesting products from the earth. Agriculture (both subsistence and commercial farming), mining, forestry, and fishing are primary sector activities.

primary socialization The earliest stage of socialization, in which we learn how to be a member of society and what attitudes, values, and actions are culturally and socially appropriate.

probation A community release that can be granted to individuals convicted of less serious crimes. Probation entails supervision and certain conditions, such as being involved in and completing a substance abuse program. If the offender does not adhere to these conditions or is re-arrested, the probation can be revoked.

proletariat (worker) One of the two primary classes in Marx's theory. Proletariats own only their capacity to labour, which they must sell to the capitalist.

property Any resource that can be used to produce things of value and to generate wealth. In Marxist theory, property is owned by the capitalist.

protest An organized and public demonstration against an event, policy, or action.

protest paradigm The particular way that the media tends to cover protest events, which works to delegitimate and marginalize protesters and focuses on the spectacle by highlighting sensational details such as violence, visible drama, and deviant or strange behaviour.

public good Things that are non-excludable (a person cannot reasonably prevent another from consuming the good) and non-rivalrous (a person's consumption of the good does not affect another's). Clean air is an example of a public good.

public issues Social problems that a society faces as a whole.

public sociology A sociological approach that attempts to interact with audiences outside academia by encouraging sociologists to engage publicly and politically with issues concerning public policy, political activism, and the institutions of civil society.

punishment The penalty (e.g. denial of certain privileges, abilities, or rights) inflicted on someone for committing a transgression. In criminal law, a judge and/or jury decide punishments.

qualitative research A set of research techniques, including interviews and participant observation, in which the researcher intensely studies a smaller number of cases. This research tends to focus on process questions, including how and why certain things happen, and to look at how actions affect individuals and groups.

quantitative research A set of research techniques that focus on things that can be counted and examine how variables relate to one another and test relationships with statistical models. This type of research explores what, where, when, how often, and how long social phenomena occur.

race A social distinction based on perceived physical or biological characteristics.

racism The systematic belief, which operates at every level of society, that races have particular characteristics or abilities that make them inferior or superior to others.

rationalization According to Weber, rationalization and rationality are ways of solving problems by focusing on the optimal means toward an end. The process is based on predictability, calculability, efficiency, and control.

realistic conflict theory Based on the work of Bobo, the theory that prejudice originates from social groups competing over valued resources or opportunities.

recidivism rate The rate at which individuals recommit crimes after an initial offence.

rehabilitation The attempt to reform (or "heal") an offender so that she will not commit further offences.

religiosity A measure of how religious a person is, sometimes based on attendance at religious services or intensity of belief.

reparation programs Measures taken by the state to redress gross and systematic human rights violations through some form of compensation or restitution to the victims. Governments enact these programs to deal with injustices on a societal level.

resocialization The process in which individuals take on new roles and discard former behaviours, attitudes, and values.

restoration An aspect of restorative justice that requires offenders to accept their guilt and to restore the moral order by compensating or fixing the injustice they caused.

retribution Based on "an eye for an eye," punishment that makes offenders undergo suffering that is comparable to that which they have inflicted.

roles The associated behaviours, beliefs, and norms that individuals perform and/or display in social situations.

rotating credit association An example of social capital, a co-operative association that operates in Southeast Asia. In these organizations, people pool their resources and then take turns drawing on the general fund of credit.

Sapir–Whorf hypothesis Developed by Edward Sapir and Benjamin Whorf, the idea that language influences thought.

schooled society A term used by Davies and Guppy to describe the education system in modern society, particularly how mass education has expanded from elementary to high schools and to high post-secondary enrolment in Canada; how schooling has become increasingly integral to modern life; and how the forms and functions of education are increasing and diversifying.

scientific management (Taylorism) The application of scientific principles and methods to the management of labour. These practices were popularized by Frederick Taylor in order to rationalize work and make it more efficient by dividing it into increasingly smaller tasks.

secondary deviance In labelling theory, deviant acts that persist, become more common, and eventually cause people to organize their lives and identities around their deviant status.

secondary sector The economic sector that manufactures finished goods. Metalwork, automobile production, textile production, and engineering industries are part of this sector.

secondary socialization The second stage of socialization, in which people learn the appropriate behaviours and attitudes of a smaller group—a subculture—within larger society.

secularization A process whereby society as a whole moves away from religious explanations, institutions, and values to secular ones.

selection A major function of the education system; the sorting, differentially rewarding, and certifying graduates of elementary, secondary, and post-secondary schools. According to Weber, schools use this function to confer status and prestige.

selection bias In regards to the media and social movements, the gatekeepers' (editors') choice to report on a small number of protest events. Media agendas can influence this selection, independent of the events' characteristics.

self-fulfilling prophecy Defined by Merton as a strongly held belief that a person thinks of as true, regardless of whether it actually is, which so influences the person that his reactions ultimately fulfill the prophecy.

semi-periphery countries Countries that are moving toward industrialization and a more diversified economy. During this transition, such countries are not usually dominant in international trade.

sex A biological identity that is based on physical or biological differences and that can be divided into the main categories of male and female.

sexuality Feelings of sexual attraction and behaviours related to them.

sexual orientation A person's sexual identity, expressed in terms of whom a person desires, wants to have sex with, and feels a sense of connectedness with.

significant others Key individuals, such as parents, whom young children imitate and model themselves after in the process of socialization.

social capital From the work of Bourdieu, Coleman, and Putnam, the collective value of all social networks. Social capital is essentially about whom you know and the "norms of reciprocity" that develop between people who know one another.

social change The alteration of culture and social institutions over time.

social construction According to Berger and Luckman, a process that involves two steps: 1) people categorize experience and then act on the basis of those classifications; 2) they eventually forget the social origins of the categories and come to see them as natural and unchangeable.

social fact Larger structures of society and norms that shape individuals' actions.

social inequality According to Grabb, the result of social differences that have consequences for individuals. This inequality shapes the rights individuals enjoy, their opportunities, and the privileges that they can exercise in society.

social institutions The norms, values, and rules of conduct that structure human interactions.

socialization The lifelong process of developing a sense of identity and self, as well as of inheriting and transmitting norms, customs, and ideologies that provide the skills and habits required to participate in society.

socialization (function of education) A major function of the education system that helps children learn the specialized tasks that they will perform in society as well as the values and behaviours required to fit into the mainstream.

social media Websites and other means that allow users to create, share, and/or exchange information and ideas.

social mobility The upward or downward movement in a

stratification system, such as the class system. Social mobility can be intergenerational (occur between generations) or intragenerational (occur within a single generation).

social movement An organized and sustained challenge to existing power holders on behalf of a wronged population.

social protection An element of punishment that protects members of a society from harm. For example, we can limit a criminal's ability to commit crimes by placing the offender in prison.

society Human groupings that are based in a defined geographic area and share common institutions.

socio-economic status (SES) A measure of a person's or family's income, educational attainment, and occupational prestige that is used to determine one's social and economic position in relation to others'.

sociological imagination A worldview that sees the connections between our individual lives (and personal troubles) and the larger society (with its public issues) in which we live.

sociology The systematic study of human society.

specific deterrence A type of deterrence that aims to discourage the specific individual by convincing him that engaging in crime has no benefits.

stages of role-taking Outlined by George Herbert Mead, the four stages that occur in socialization and teach people to take the role of the other. The stages are preparatory, role-taking, game, and taking the perspective of the generalized other.

state A set of institutions that include four groups of people: political decision-makers, who can be either elected or appointed; administrative units or bureaucracies; a judiciary or legal system; and security services. States are attached to a geographic territory and maintain a monopoly on rule-making, coercion, and violence within that area.

status group Weber's term for a group that is based on social honour or prestige and that has a "style of life." Honour refers to any distinction, respect, or esteem that is accorded to an individual by others.

strain theory Merton's theory that some individuals experience a poor fit between cultural goals and opportunities for success. For example, these individuals might want to earn enough money to support themselves but cannot get a well-paying job. Thus, they turn to illegitimate means (i.e. crime) to make money.

streaming (tracking) The placing of students with those of similar skills or needs, such as in specific classes or groups within a class.

structural functionalism A theory that, by looking at how societal structures or institutions work together to create consensus and social cohesion, focuses on explaining how society functions effectively.

subcultural theory A theory that focuses on the role of culture in crime. Cohen argues that gangs and other criminal organizations are subcultures with different norms and values than the larger culture.

subculture A group that differs from the dominant culture in some way but is not necessarily critical of it.

surface acting In Hochschild's theory of emotional labour, the situation of a worker presenting emotions without actually feeling them.

surplus value In Marx's theory, the new value created by workers that is in excess of their own labour-cost and is available to be appropriated by the capitalist. This value is the amount of money that the capitalist keeps after paying the worker's wages.

survey research A major tool of quantitative research that involves learning about people's characteristics, attitudes, or behaviours by having a large group complete a questionnaire.

symbolic ethnicity Waters's term for the individualistic type of ethnicity that some people can adopt with little social cost.

symbolic interactionism A theory that argues that meanings do not naturally attach to things—we derive meaning from and come to understand our society and our role in it through interacting with other people.

teenage pregnancy Any pregnancy of a woman under the age of 20 at the time that the pregnancy ends.

tertiary (service) sector The economic sector that provides services to the general population and to businesses. Retail sales, transportation and distribution, entertainment, banking, healthcare, and law are part of the tertiary sector.

Thomas principle Thomas and Thomas's theory that, if we define a situation as real, it is real in its consequences.

trade union density The percentage of a population's wage earners who are members of a union.

Truth and Reconciliation Commission of Canada (TRC) Part of Canada's reparation program for Aboriginal people who were forced to attend residential schools. By examining school records and collecting thousands of personal testimonies, the commission sought to learn the truth about what happened in the schools. Its six years of work culminated in the release of its final report in June 2015.

types of suicide According to Durkheim, suicide has four variations, which differ based on the level of integration or regulation in society as a whole. The types are egoistic (low integration), altruistic (high integration), anomic (low regulation), and fatalistic (high regulation).

Uniform Crime Reporting (UCR) Survey Collected by Statistics Canada since 1962, a survey that records information on all criminal incidents reported to and confirmed by Canadian police services.

universal program A type of social program available to all citizens, regardless of income or wealth. The Canada Pension Plan (CPP) is a universal program.

vertical mosaic John Porter's term that describes a society, such as Canada, that contains different ethnic, language, regional, and religious groups with unequal levels of status and power.

victimization survey A survey that asks respondents if they have been victims of crimes and other related questions. In Canada, the General Social Survey is such a survey.

visible minority A Canadian term used to designate a person or group that is visibly not of the majority race in a given population.

welfare state A system in which the state provides a range of social services, including a minimum income and economic assistance to the ill, elderly, and unemployed, to ensure the health and well-being of its citizens. Canada became a welfare state after the passage of social welfare reforms in the 1960s.

white-collar crime A type of crime that occurs in a work setting and is motivated by monetary gain but does not involve intentional or direct acts of violence.

world society theory A main theory of globalization that emphasizes the significance of institutions and culture in forming the structure and behaviour of nation-states, organizations, and individuals worldwide. This theory seeks to explain global change (especially the dispersion of Western policies) as a result of the post–World War II emergence of global institutions and international organizations, as well as an increasingly shared world culture.

world systems theory A main theory of globalization that views the world as a transnational division of labour, which classifies countries as core, semi-periphery, or periphery.

WUNC (worthiness, unity, numbers, commitment) According to Tilly, the criteria that determine the strength of a social movement.

References

Access Alliance. 2013. *Where Are the Good Jobs?: Ten Stories of "Working Rough, Living Poor."* Toronto: Access Alliance Multicultural Health and Community Services. http://accessalliance.ca/sites/accessalliance/files/Summary_Where%20are%20the%20Good%20Jobs%20Report%202013.pdf.

Adams, Kathy L., and Dale E. Adams. 2003. *Urban Education: A Reference Handbook*. Santa Barbara, CA: ABC-CLIO.

Adams, Natalie, and Pamela Bettis. 2003. "Commanding the Room in Short Skirts: Cheering as the Embodiment of Ideal Girlhood." *Gender & Society* 17: 73–91.

Adorno, T. W., E. Frenkel-Brunswik, D. J. Levinson, and R. N. Sanford. 1950. *The Authoritarian Personality*. New York: Norton.

Akkad, Omar El. 2011. "Canadians' Internet Usage Nearly Double Worldwide Average." *The Globe and Mail*, 8 March.

Alberta Energy. 2014. "Facts and Statistics." http://www.energy.alberta.ca/oilsands/791.asp.

Allport, G. W. 1954. *The Nature of Prejudice*. Cambridge, MA: Perseus.

Anderson, Elijah. 1999. *Code of the Street*. New York: Norton.

Aronson, Joshua, and Elliot Aronson, eds. 2011. *Readings about the Social Animal*. New York: Worth Publishers.

Association for Canadian Studies. 2013. "Tim Horton Beats the Queen According to Youngest Canadians When Asked about Contribution to Nation Building." www.acs-aec.ca/pdf/polls/Tim%20Horton%20vs%20the%20Queen%20and%20building%20Canada.docx.

Atton, Chris. 2002. *Alternative Media*. Thousand Oaks, CA: Sage.

Bajaj, Vikas. 2011. "A New Capital of Call Centers." *The New York Times*, 25 November.

Banaji, Mahzarin R., and Anthony G. Greenwald. 2013. *Blind Spot: Hidden Biases of Good People*. New York: Delacorte.

Barnes, Andre, and Erin Virgint. 2013. "Youth Voter Turnout in Canada." Publication No. 2010-19-E. 7 April 2010. Revised August 9, 2013. Ottawa: Library of Parliament.

Barr, Rebecca, and Robert Dreeben. 1983. *How Schools Work*. Chicago: University of Chicago Press.

Becker, Howard. 1963. *Outsiders*. New York: Free Press.

Bennett, Dinah, Michael Sharpe, Chris Freeman, and Alan Carson. 2004. "Anorexia Nervosa among Female Secondary Students in Ghana." *British Journal of Psychiatry* 185: 312–17.

Bentley, Paul. 2011. "Why an Arranged Marriage 'Is More Likely to Develop into Lasting Love.'" *Daily Mail*, 4 March. http://www.dailymail.co.uk/news/article-1363176/Why-arranged-marriage-likely-develop-lasting-love.html.

Berger, Peter. 1963. *Invitation to Sociology*. Garden City, NY: Doubleday.

———, and Thomas Luckmann. 1966. *The Social Construction of Reality: A Treatise in the Sociology of Knowledge*. New York: Anchor Books.

Beyerlein, K., and J. R. Hipp. 2006. "A Two-Stage Model for a Two-Stage Process: How Biographical Availability Matters for Social Movement Mobilization." *Mobilization* 11: 299–320.

Beyon, Huw, and Theo Nichol, eds. 2006. *The Fordism of Ford and Modern Management: Fordism and Post-Fordism*. Cheltenham, UK: Elgar.

Bibby, Reginald. 2011. *Beyond the Gods and Back: Religion's Demise and Rise and Why it Matters*. Lethbridge, AB: Project Canada Books.

Bielski, Zosia. 2013. "Why Teen Pregnancy Is on the Rise Again in Canada (and Spiking in These Provinces)." *The Globe and Mail*, 29 January.

Blais, André, and Peter Loewen. 2011 (January). "Youth Electoral Engagement in Canada." Working Paper Series. Ottawa: Elections Canada.

Blau, Francine D. 1998. "Trends in the Well-Being of American Women, 1970–1995." *Journal of Economic Literature* 36: 112–65.

Blumer, Herbert. 1969. *Symbolic Interactionism: Perspective and Method*. Englewood Cliffs, NJ: Prentice-Hall.

Bobo, Lawrence. 1983. "Whites' Opposition to Busing: Symbolic Racism or Realistic Group Conflict?" *Journal of Personality and Social Psychology* 45 (6): 1196–1210.

Bonanno, Allessandro. 2012. "Fordism Post Fordism." In *The Encyclopedia of Globalization*, edited by George Ritzer, 680–2. Malden, MA: Wiley-Blackwell.

Bourdieu, Pierre, and Jean Claude Passeron. 1973. "Cultural Reproduction and Social Reproduction." In *Knowledge, Education and Cultural Change*, edited by Richard K. Brown, 71–112. London: Tavistock.

———, and ———. 1990. *Reproduction in Education, Society and Culture*, 2nd edn. London: Sage.

Bradley, D., E. Huber, S. Moller, F. Nielson, and J. D. Stephens. 2003. "Determinants of Relative Poverty in Advanced Capitalist Democracies." *American Sociological Review* 68 (3): 22–51.

Bradshaw, James. 2013. "Students Reaching for ADHD Drugs to Deal with Academic Stress." *The Globe and Mail*, 18 October.

Brennan, Shannon. 2013. "Police-Reported Crime Statistics in Canada, 2011." Ottawa: Statistics Canada. http://www.statcan.gc.ca/pub/85-002-x/2012001/article/11692-eng.htm.

Briggs, Asa. 2000. "The Welfare State in a Historical Perspective." In *The Welfare State Reader*, edited by C. Pierson and F. Castles, 1–31. Cambridge: Polity Press.

Burnsed, Brian. 2011. "How Higher Education Affects Lifetime Salary: College Degrees Significantly Boost Earnings, but Women and Minorities Benefit Less." *US News and World Report*, 5 August 5.

Butler, Judith. 1990. *Gender Trouble: Feminism and the Subversion of Identity*. New York: Routledge.

Byerly, Carolyn. 2006. "Gender and Race in Media Ownership." *WIMN's Voices* (blog), 28 October. www.wimnonline.org/WIMNSVoicesBlog/?p=302.

Canadian Council on Learning. 2006. *Canadian Post-Secondary Education: A Positive Record–An Uncertain Future*. Ottawa: Canadian Council on Learning.

Canadian Federation of Students. 2013. "International Comparisons." http://cfs-fcee.ca/the-issues/tuition-fees-and-access-to-education/international-comparisons/.

Canadian Press. 2011 (27 January). "Plural Wife Describes Life in Bountiful Commune." www.ctvnews.ca/plural-wife-describes-life-in-bountiful-commune-1.600642.

Canadian Radio-television and Telecommunications Commission (CRTC). 2013 (27 June). "CRTC Approves BCE's Bid to Acquire Astral's Television and Radio Services." (Press Release). http://www.crtc.gc.ca/eng/com100/2013/r130627.htm.

CanWest News Service. 2007. "Boards Do Best When Women Sit on Them." *The Province*, 28 October, A48.

Cazenave, Noel A., and Darlene Alvarez Maddern. 1999. "Defending the White Race: White Male Faculty Opposition to a White Racism Course." *Race and Society* 2: 25–50.

CBC News. 2008 (15 December). "Rise in Female, Aboriginal Inmates Alters Prison Population: Stats Can." http://www.cbc.ca/news/canada/rise-in-female-aboriginal-inmates-alters-prison-population-statscan-1.737175.

Central Intelligence Agency (CIA). 2013. *The World Factbook, 2013–14*. Washington, DC: Central Intelligence Agency.

Charon, Joel M. 2012. *Ten Questions: A Sociological Perspective*. Belmont, CA: Wadsworth Publishing.

Chemaly, Soroya. 2013 (15 August). "Even Little Kids Have a Wage Gap." Salon.com. www.salon.com/2013/08/15/even_little_kids_have_a_wage_gap/.

Cherlin, Andrew J. 2004. "The Deinstitutionalization of Marriage in America." *Journal of Marriage and the Family* 66: 848–61.

Chester, Bronwyn. 1999. "McGill and Coke Set to Ink Deal." *The McGill Reporter*, 9 September. http://reporter-archive.mcgill.ca/Rep/r3201/coke.html.

Chomsky, Noam, and Edward S. Herman. 2002. *Manufacturing Consent: The Political Economy of the Mass Media*. New York: Pantheon Books.

Church, Elizabeth. 2011. "SlutWalk Sparks Worldwide Protest Movement." *The Globe and Mail*, 10 May. http://www.theglobeandmail.com/news/toronto/ slutwalk-sparks-worldwide-protest-movement/article583076/.

Cohen, Stanley. 2011. *Folk Devils and Moral Panic*. New York: Routledge.

Cohn, D'Vera. 2013. "Love and Marriage." Pew Research Social and Demographic Trends. www.pewsocial trends.org/2013/02/13/love-and-marriage/.

Coleman, James S. 1990. *Foundations of Social Theory*. Cambridge, MA: Belknap Press.

Collins, Patricia Hill. 2013. "Truth-Telling and Intellectual Activism." *Contexts* 12 (1): 36–41.

Collins, Randall. 1975. *Conflict Society: Towards an Explanatory Science*. New York: Academic Press.

———. 1979. *The Credential Society: An Historical Sociology of Education and Stratification*. New York: Academic Press.

———. 1992. *Sociological Insight: An Introduction to Non-Obvious Sociology*, 2nd edn. New York: Oxford University Press.

———. 1994. *Four Sociological Traditions: Selected Readings*. New York: Oxford University Press.

Colour of Poverty (COP). 2008. "Colour of Poverty Fact Sheet #7: Understanding the Racialization of Poverty in Ontario in Justice and Policing in 2007." www.colourofpoverty.ca.

Cooley, Charles Horton. 1902. *Human Nature and the Social Order*. New York: Scribner's.

Corak, Miles. 2006. "Do Poor Children Become Poor Adults? Lessons from a Cross Country Comparison of Generational Earnings Mobility." *Research on Economic Inequality* 13 (1): 143-188.

Corrigall-Brown, C. 2013. "Participation in Social Movements." In *The Wiley-Blackwell Encyclopedia of Social and Political Movements*, edited by D. A. Snow, D. della Porta, B. Klandermans, and D. McAdam. Oxford: Wiley-Blackwell.

Crenshaw, Kimberlé W. 1989. "Demarginalizing the Intersection of Race and Sex: A Black Feminist Critique of Antidiscrimination Doctrine, Feminist Theory and Antiracist Politics, 1989." *University of Chicago Legal Forum* 139–67.

Crockett, Zachary. 2014. "The Great Toilet Paper Scare of 1973." *priceonomics* (blog), 9 July. http://priceonomics.com/the-great-toilet-paper-scare-of-1973/.

Dalton, R. J., A. Van Sickle, and S. Weldon. 2010. "The Individual–Institutional Nexus of Protest Behaviour." *British Journal of Political Science* 40: 51–73.

Davies, Scott, and Neil Guppy. 2010. *The Schooled Society: An Introduction to the Sociology of Education*. Don Mills, ON: Oxford University Press.

Davis, Horace B. 1967. *Nationalism and Socialism: Marxist and Labor Theories of Nationalism to 1917*. New York: Monthly Review Press.

Davis, Kingsley. 1940. "Extreme Social Isolation of a Child." *American Journal of Sociology* 45 (4): 554–65.

DeMara, Bruce. 2013. "Teen Pregnancy Rates Level off in Canada, Study Shows." *Toronto Star*, 29 January.

Department of Justice. 2013. "Family Violence." www.justice.gc.ca/eng/cj-jp/fv-vf/.

Dewing, Michael. 2012. "Social Media: Who Uses Them?" Ottawa: Library of Parliament. www.parl.gc.ca/Content/LOP/ResearchPublications/2010-05-e.pdf.

Diani, M. 2004. "Networks and Participation." In *The Blackwell Companion to Social Movements*, edited by D.A. Snow, S. A. Soule, and H. Kreisi, 339–59. Malden, MA: Blackwell Publishing.

DiPrete, Thomas A., Gregory M. Eirich, Karen S. Cook, and Douglas S. Massey. 2006. "Cumulative Advantage as a Mechanism for Inequality: A Review of Theoretical and Empirical Developments." *Annual Review of Sociology* 32: 271–97.

Dowden, Cara, and Shannon Brennan. 2012. "Police-Reported Hate Crime in Canada, 2010." *Juristat*, 12 April. http://www.statcan.gc.ca/pub/85-002-x/2012001/article/11635-eng.pdf.

Durkheim, Émile. (1897/1951). *Suicide: A Study in Sociology*. Glencoe, IL: Free Press.

———. 1956. *Education and Sociology*. Glencoe, IL: Free Press.

———. 1960. *The Division of Labour in Society*. Glencoe, IL: Free Press.

———. 1982. *The Rules of the Sociological Method*. Edited by Steven Lukes, Translated by W. D. Halls. New York: The Free Press.

Ebaugh, Helen Rose Fuchs. 1988. *Becoming an Ex: The Process of Role Exit*. Chicago: University of Chicago Press.

Elber, Lynn. 2013 (11 October). "GLAAD Study Finds Fewer Gay Characters on Network TV this Season." CTV News. http://www.ctvnews.ca/entertainment/glaad-study-finds-fewer-gay-characters-on-network-tv-this-season-1.1493495.

Environics. 2012. "Focus Canada: Final Report." www.environicsinstitute.org.

Fantasia, R., and E. L. Hirsch. 1995. "Culture in Rebellion: The Appropriation and Transformation of the Veil in the Algerian Revolution." In *Social Movements and Culture*, edited by H. Johnston and B. Klandermans, 144–62. Minneapolis: University of Minnesota Press.

Fausto-Sterling, Anne. 2000. *Sexing the Body: Gender Politics and the Construction of Sexuality*. New York: Basic Books.

Ferguson, Ann Arnett. 2001. *Bad Boys: Public Schools in the Making of Black Masculinity*. Ann Arbor, MI: University of Michigan Press.

Festa, Lauren. 2011. "'Look Good In All You Do' or Not . . ." *Contra*. http://www.thinkcontra.com/look-good-in-all-you-do-or-not/

FIFA. 2014. "2010 FIFA World Cup South Africa: Television Audience Report." http://www.fifa.com/mm/document/affederation/tv/01/47/32/73/2010fifaworldcupsouthafricatvaudiencereport.pdf.

Fiss, Peer C., and Paul M. Hirsch. 2005. "The Discourse of Globalization: Framing and Sensemaking of an Emerging Concept." *American Sociological Review* 70: 29–52.

Fleury, Dominique. 2008. "Low-Income Children." *Perspectives on Labour and Income* 9 (5): 14–23.

Ford, Henry. 1922. *My Life and Work*. Garden City, NY: Doubleday.

Frank, David John, Bayliss J. Camp, and Steven A. Boutcher. 2010. "Worldwide Trends in the Criminal Regulation of Sex, 1945 to 2005." *American Sociological Review* 75 (6): 867–93.

Franzen, Jonathan. 2012. *Farther Away: Essays*. New York: Farrar, Straus, and Giroux.

Fraser, Ashley M., Laura M. Padilla-Walker, Sarah M. Coyne, Larry J. Nelson, and Laura A. Stockdale. 2012. "Associations between Violent Video Gaming, Empathetic Concern, and Prosocial Behavior Towards Strangers, Friends, and Family Members." *Journal of Youth and Adolescence* May: 636–49.

Frenette, Marc. 2007. *Why Are Youth From Lower-Income Families Less Likely to Attend University?* Ottawa: Statistics Canada.

Gaetz, Stephen, Jesse Donaldson, Tim Richter, and Tanya Gulliver. 2013. *The State of Homelessness in Canada 2013*. Toronto: Canadian Homelessness Research Network Press. http://www.homelesshub.ca/ResourceFiles/SOHC2103.pdf

Gallant, Jacques. 2014. "Reality Shows *Teen Mom* and *16 and Pregnant* Lead to Drop in Teen Birth Rates." *Toronto Star*, 14 January.

Gamoran, A., and R. Mare. 1989. "Secondary School Tracking and Educational Inequality: Compensation, Reinforcement, or Neutrality?" *American Journal of Sociology* 94: 1146–83.

Gamson, Joshua, and Pearl Latteier. 2004. "Do Media Monsters Devour Diversity?" *Contexts* 3 (3): 26–31.

Garland, Maurice. 2012 (28 December). "Top WNBA Salaries vs NBA Salaries: Who Gets Paid More?" Black Enterprise. http://www.blackenterprise.com/lifestyle/wnba-player-salaries-vs-nba-salaries/.

Garfinkel, Harold. 1991. *Studies in Ethnomethodology*. Malden, MA: Polity Press/Blackwell Publishing.

Gecas, V. 2000. "Value Identities, Self-Motives, and Social Movements." In *Self, Identity, and Social Movements*, edited by S. Stryker, T. J. Owens and R. W. White, 93–109. Minneapolis, University of Minnesota Press.

Geertz, Clifford. 1962. "The Rotating Credit Association: A 'Middle Rung' in Development." *Economic Development and Cultural Change* 10: 240–63.

Gerth, H. H., and C. Wright Mills, eds and trans. 1946. *From Max Weber: Essays in Sociology*. New York: Oxford University Press.

———, and ———, eds. 2009. *From Max Weber: Essays in Sociology*. New York: Routledge.

Giugni, Marco G. 2004. "Personal and Biographical Consequences." In *The Blackwell Companion to Social Movements*, edited by David A. Snow, Sarah A. Soule, and Hanspeter Kriesi, 489–507. Malden, MA: Blackwell.

Goffman, Erving. 1959. *The Presentation of Self in Everyday Life*. New York: Anchor Books.

Government of Canada. 1995. Employment Equity Act. http://laws-lois.justice.gc.ca/eng/acts/E-5.401/.

Grabb, Edward. 2006. *Theories of Social Inequality*, 5th edn. Toronto: Nelson.

Grant, Tavia, and Janet McFarland. 2012. "Generation Nixed: Why Canada's Youth Are Losing Hope for the Future." *The Globe and Mail*, 27 October, B6–7.

Harlow, Summer, and Thomas J. Johnson. 2011. "Overthrowing the Protest Paradigm? How *The New York Times*, Global Voices and Twitter Covered the Egyptian Revolution." *International Journal of Communication* 5: 1359–74.

Harvard School of Public Health. 2004 (13 July). "Study Finds: 'Ratings Creep.'" (Press Release). http://archive.sph.harvard.edu/press-releases/archives/2004-releases/press07132004.html.

Heibling, Marc. 2008. *Practising Citizenship and Heterogeneous Nationhood*. Amsterdam: Amsterdam University Press.

Henrich, Joseph, Robert Boyd, and Peter J. Richerson. 2012. "The Puzzle of Monogamous Marriage." *Philosophical Transactions of The Royal Society of Biological Sciences* 367: 657–69.

Herek, G. M. 2002. "Heterosexuals' Attitudes toward Bisexual Men and Women in the United States." *Journal of Sex Research* 39 (4): 264–74.

Hirschi, Travis. 2004. "Self-Control and Crime." In *The Handbook of Self-Regulation Research, Theory, and Application*, edited by R. F. Baumeister and K. D. Vohs, 537–52. New York: Guilford.

Hochschild, Arlie, and Anne Machung. 1990. *The Second Shift*. New York: Avon Books.

Hochschild, Arlie Russell. 1983. *The Managed Heart: Commercialization of Human Feeling*. Berkeley, CA: University of California Press.

Hollander, Jocelyn A., and Rachel L. Einwohner. 2004. "Conceptualizing Resistance." *Sociological Forum* 19 (4): 533–54.

Human Resources and Skills Development Canada (HRDC). 2013. *Indicators of Well-being in Canada—Security*. Ottawa: HRSDC.

Inglehart, Ronald. 1997. *Modernization and Postmodernization: Cultural, Economic and Political Change in 43 Nations*. Princeton, NJ: Princeton University Press.

International Olympic Committee (IOC). 2012. "London 2012 Olympic Games: Global Broadcast Report." http://www.olympic.org/Documents/IOC_Marketing/Broadcasting/London_2012_Global_%20Broadcast_Report.pdf.

Inter-Parliamentary Union. 2015. "Women in National Parliaments." http://www.ipu.org/wmn-e/classif.htm.

Ipsos Reid. 2012. "The IpsosCanadian inter@ctive Reid Report: 2012 Fact Guide." http://www.ipsos.ca/common/dl/pdf/Ipsos_InteractiveReidReport_FactGuide_2012.pdf.

James, Randy. 2009 (28 October). "A Brief History of McDonalds Abroad." Times.com. http://content.time.com/time/world/article/0,8599,1932839,00.html.

Jones, Allison. 2012 (21 November). "Anti-Poverty Group Urges End of Child Tax Benefits." CTVNews.ca. http://www.ctvnews.ca/canada/anti-poverty-group-urges-end-of-child-tax-benefits-1.1047052.

Kane, Matt. 2013. "Transgender Characters That Changed Film and Television #TransWk." GLAAD (blog post), 12 November. http://www.glaad.org/blog/transgender-characters-changed-film-and-television-transwk.

Kaplan, Andreas M., and Michael Haenlein. 2010. "Users of the World, Unite! The Challenges and Opportunities of Social Media." *Business Horizons* 53 (1): 61.

Kay, Barbara. 2011. "Barbara Kay: Multiculturalism 'Is Not a Quebec Value.'" *National Post*, 19 January. http://news.nationalpost.com/full-comment/barbara-kay-multiculturalism-is-not-a-quebec-value.

Keay, Douglas. 1987. "Aids, Education and the Year 2000." *Woman's Own*, 31 October, 8–10. http://www.margaretthatcher.org/document/106689.

Kelly, William, ed. 2004. *Fanning the Flames: Fans and Consumer Culture in Contemporary Japan*. New York: SUNY.

Kenworthy, L. 1999. "Do Social-Welfare Policies Reduce Poverty? A Cross-National Assessment." *Social Forces* 77 (3): 1119–39.

Kimmel, Michael. 2011. *The Gendered Society*. New York: Oxford University Press.

Kinsey, Alfred C. 1953. *Sexual Behavior in the Human Female*. Philadelphia: WB Saunders.

———, Wardell B. Pomeroy, and Clyde E. Martin. 1948. *Sexual Behavior in the Human Male*. Philadelphia: W B Saunders.

Klandermans, B. 1997. *The Social Psychology of Protest*. Oxford: Blackwell.

———, and M. de Weerd. 2000. "Group Identification and Political Protest." In *Self, Identity, and Social Movements*, edited by S. Stryker, T. J. Owens, and R. W. White. Minneapolis: University of Minnesota Press.

Knighton, Lila, Alisa Simon, Janice Kelly, and Alexandra Kimball. 2012. "Cyberbullying: Reality Check." http://dev.kidshelpphone.ca/main-data/uploads/2014/11/2012-cir-cyberbullying1.pdf.

Kohn, Melvin L. 1959. "Social Class and Parental Values." *American Journal of Sociology* 64 (4): 337–51.

Kubota, Yoko. 2009 (8 June). "Tokyo Firm Rents Fake Family, Friends for Weddings." Reuters. http:www.reuters.com/article/2009/06/08/us-japan-weddings-isUSTRE55771IY20090608.

Kuhn, Manfred, and Thomas S. McPartland. 1954. "An Empirical Investigation of Self-Attitudes." *American Sociological Review* 19 (1): 68–74.

Kunovich, Sheri, Pamela Paxton, and Melanie M. Hughes. 2007. "Gender in Politics." *Annual Review of Sociology* 33: 263–84.

Langan, Patrick A., and David J. Levin. 2002 (June). "Recidivism of Prisoners Released in 1994." Bureau of Justice Statistics Special Report. http://www.aci-adc.com/images/Recidivism/RecidivismofPrisonersReleased1994.pdf.

Lareau, Annete. 2003. *Unequal Childhoods: Class, Race, and Family Life*. Berkeley, CA: University of California Press.

Latimer, J., and L. Foss. 2004. *Havens in a Heartless World*. New York: Basic Books.

———, and ———. 2005. "The Sentencing of Aboriginal and Non-Aboriginal Youth under the YOA: A Multivariate Analysis." *Canadian Journal of Criminology and Criminal Justice* 47 (3): 481–500.

Lauer, Sean, and Carrie Yodanis. 2011. "Individualized Marriage and the Integration of Resources." *Journal of Marriage and the Family* 73: 669–83.

Laumann, Edward O., John H. Gagnon, Robert T. Michael, and Stuart Michaels. 1994. *The Social Organization of Sexuality*. Chicago: University of Chicago Press.

Lee, Cynthia. 2013 (8 October). "Study Finds TV Shows with Ethnically Diverse Casts, Writers Have Higher Ratings." UCLA Newsroom.

http://newsroom.ucla.edu/releases/study-finds-that-tv-shows-with-248757.

Leffingwell, William. 1925. *Office Management: Principles and Practice.* Chicago: A. W. Shaw.

Lemieux, Thomas, and David Card. 1998. "Education, Earnings, and the 'Canadian G.I. Bill.'" NBER Working Paper Series, Working Paper 6718. Cambridge, MA: National Bureau of Economic Research. http://www.nber.org/papers/w6718.pdf.

Library of Parliament. 2011. "41st Parliament: Current and Emerging Issues." http://www.parl.gc.ca/content/lop/researchpublications/currentemergingissues-e.pdf.

Linden, Greg, Kenneth L. Kraemer, and Jason Dedrick. 2009. "Who Captures Value in a Global Innovation Network? The Case of Apple's iPod." *Communications of the ACM* 52 (3): 140–4.

Lindsey, Richard. 2013 (29 July). "What the Arab Spring Tells Us About the Future of Social Media in Revolutionary Movements." *Small Wars Journal.* http://smallwarsjournal.com/jrnl/art/what-the-arab-spring-tells-us-about-the-future-of-social-media-in-revolutionary-movements.

Lorber, Judith. 1994. *Paradoxes of Gender.* New Haven, CT: Yale University Press.

McAdam, D. 1986. "Recruitment to High-Risk Activism—The Case of Freedom Summer." *American Journal of Sociology* 92: 64–90.

McIntosh, Peggy. 1988. "White Privilege and Male Privilege: A Personal Account of Coming To See Correspondences through Work in Women's Studies." Wellesley College Center for Research on Women, Working Paper 189. Wellesley, MA: Wellesley College.

McKenna, Barrie. 2012. "In Canada, Unlike the U.S., the American Dream Lives On." *The Globe and Mail*, 15 January.

Mackenzie, Hugh. 2012. "Canada's CEO Elite 100: The 0.01%." Ottawa: Canadian Centre for Policy Alternatives. http://www.policyalternatives.ca/sites/default/files/uploads/publications/National%20Office/2012/01/Canadas%20CEO%20Elite%20100FINAL.pdf.

McLeod, D. M., and Hertog, J. K. 1999. "Social Control, Social Change and the Mass Media's Role in the Regulation of Protest Groups." In *Mass Media, Social Control and Social Change: A Macrosocial Perspective,* edited by D. Demers and K. Viswanath, 305–30. Ames, IA: Iowa State University Press.

McLuhan, Marshall. 1964. *Understanding Media: The Extensions of Man.* New York: McGraw-Hill.

McPherson, Miller, Lynn Smith-Lovin, and Matthew Brashears. 2008. "The Ties That Bind Are Fraying." *Contexts* 7 (3): 32–6.

Marini, Margaret Mooney. 1989. "Sex Differences in Earnings in the United States." *Annual Review of Sociology* 15: 343–80.

Martin, Karin A. 2009. "Normalizing Heterosexuality: Mothers' Assumptions, Talk, and Strategies with Young Children." *American Sociological Review* 74 (2): 190–207.

Martin Prosperity Institute. 2011. "The Canucky-est City." www.martinprosperity.org/images/stories/jmc/cache/mpi-canuck-city.pdf.

Martins, Nicole, and Kristen Harrison. 2012. "Racial Differences in the Relationship between Children's Television Use and Self-Esteem: A Longitudinal Panel Study." *Communication Research.* 39 (3): 338–57.

Marx, Karl. 1867/2000. *Das Kapital.* Washington, DC: Regenery Publishing.

———. 1907. *The Eighteenth Brumaire of Louis Bonaparte.* Chicago: Charles H. Kerr.

———. 1975. "Critique of Hegel's Doctrine of State." In *Karl Marx: Early Writings,* translated by Rodney Livingstone and Gregor Benton. New York: Vintage.

———. 1982. *Capital.* London: Sonnenschein.

———. 2004. *The German Ideology.* New York: International Publishers.

———, and Friedrich Engels. 1848. "Manifesto of the Communist Party." In *Marx/Engels Selected Works, Volume One,* 98–137. Moscow: Progress Publishers.

———, and ———. 1964. *The Communist Manifesto.* New York: Modern Reader Paperbacks.

Mead, George Herbert. 1934. *Mind, Self, and Society.* Chicago: University of Chicago Press.

Mead, Margaret. 1928. *Coming of Age in Samoa.* New York: W. Morrow.

Melucci, A., J. Keane, and P. Mier. 1989. *Nomads of the Present: Social Movements and Individual Needs in Contemporary Society.* Philadelphia: Temple University Press.

Menzies, Charles R. 2009. "First Nations, Inequality, and the Legacy of Colonialism." In *Social Inequality in Canada,* 5th edn, edited by Edward Grabb and Neil Guppy, 295–304. Toronto: Pearson.

Merriam-Webster. 2006. "New Words and Slang: Archives." http://nws.merriam-webster.com/opendictionary/newword_search.php?word=truthiness.

Merton, Robert K. 1949. *Social Theory and Social Structure.* New York: Free Press.

———. 1957. *Social Theory and Social Structure,* rev. edn. New York: Free Press.

———. 1968. *Social Theory and Social Structure,* enlarged edn. New York: Free Press.

Messner, Michael A. 1992. *Power at Play: Sports and the Problem of Masculinity.* Boston: Beacon Press.

———. 1997. *Politics of Masculinities: Men in Movements.* Lanham, MD: AltaMira Press.

———, and Cheryl Cooky. 2010. "Gender in Televised Sports: News and Highlights Shows, 1989–2009." Center for Feminist Research, University of Southern California.

Meyer, David S., and Sidney Tarrow, eds. 1998. *The Social Movement Society: Contentious Politics for a New Century.* Lanham, MD: Rowan and Littlefield.

Meyer, John W., John Boli, George M. Thomas, and Francisco O. Ramirez. 1997. "World Society and the Nation-State." *American Journal of Sociology* 103: 144–81.

Milan, Anne, Hélène Maheux, and Tina Chui. 2010. "A Portrait of Couples in Mixed Unions." Ottawa: Statistics Canada. http://www.statcan.gc.ca/pub/11-008-x/2010001/article/11143-eng.htm.

———, Mireille Vézina, and Carrie Wells. 2007. 2006 *Census: Family Portrait: Continuity and Change in Canadian Families and Households in 2006: Findings.* Ottawa: Statistics Canada. http://www12.statcan.ca/census-recensement/2006/as-sa/97-553/index-eng.cfm.

Milgram, S. 1963. "Behavioral Study of Obedience." *Journal of Abnormal and Social Psychology* 67: 371–8.

Mills, C. Wright. 1956. *The Power Elite.* New York: Oxford University Press.

———. 1959/2000. *The Sociological Imagination.* New York: Oxford University Press.

Mintz, Steven. 2004. *Huck's Raft: A History of American Childhood.* Cambridge, MA: Belknap Press.

Murray, John P. 2008. "Media Violence: The Effects Are Both Real and Strong." *American Behavioral Scientist.* 51(8): 1212–30.

Nathanson, A. I., and J. Cantor. 2000. "Reducing the Aggression-Promoting Effect of Violent Cartoons by Increasing Children's Fictional Involvement with the Victim." *Journal of Broadcasting and Electronic Media* 44: 125–42.

National Survey of Sexual Health and Behavior (NSSHB). 2010. Special Issue: *Findings from the National Survey of Sexual Health and Behavior, Centre for Sexual Health Promotion, Indiana University. Journal of Sexual Medicine* 7 (5): 243–373

Nepstad, S. E., and C. Smith. 1999. "Rethinking Recruitment to High-Risk/Cost Activism: The Case of the Nicaragua Exchange." *Mobilization* 4: 25–40.

Norris, Mary Jane. 2014. "Aboriginal Languages in Canada: Emerging Trends and Perspectives on Second Language Acquisition." Ottawa: Statistics Canada. http://www.statcan.gc.ca/pub/11-008-x/2007001/9628-eng.htm.

Norris, Pippa. 2002. *Democratic Phoenix: Reinventing Political Activism.* Cambridge: Cambridge University Press.

O'Connell, Michael. 2014. "TV Ratings: Super Bowl XLVIII Is Most Watched in History with 112.2 Million Viewers." *The Hollywood*

Reporter, 3 February. http://www.hollywoodreporter.com/live-feed/tv-ratings-super-bowl-xlviii-676651.

Olson, Mancur. 1965. *The Logic of Collective Action: Public Goods and the Theory of Groups*. Cambridge, MA: Harvard University Press.

Onishi, Norimitsu. 2003. "Divorce in South Korea: Striking a New Attitude." *The New York Times*, 21 September. www.nytimes.com/2003/09/21/world/divorce-in-south-korea-striking-a-new-attitude.html.

Oppong-Tawiah, D., and Boateng, R. 2011. "ICT and Bridging the Digital Divide in Ghana: A Culture, Policy & Technology Approach." Paper presented at Africa Digital Week, Accra, Ghana, 25–29 July.

Organisation for Economic Co-operation and Development (OECD). 2005 (March). "*Combating Poverty and Social Exclusion Through Work.*" *Paris*: OECD. http://78.41.128.130/dataoecd/62/35/34598300.pdf.

———. n.d. "Bridging the Digital Divide." http://www.oecd.org/site/schoolingfortomorrowknowledgebase/themes/ict/bridgingthedigitaldivide.htm.

Ortiz, Isabel, and Matthew Cummins. 2011 (April). "Global Inequality: Beyond the Bottom Billion." Social and Economic Policy Working Paper. New York: UNICEF. http://www.unicef.org/socialpolicy/files/Global_Inequality.pdf.

Orwell, George. 1949. *Nineteen Eighty-Four*. New York: Harcourt, Brace & World, Inc.

Osberg, Lars. 2001. "Poverty among Senior Citizens: A Canadian Success Story." In *The State of Economics in Canada: Festschrift in Honour of David Slater*, edited by Patrick Grady and Andrew Sharpe, 151–81. Ottawa: Centre for the Study of Living Standards and John Deutsch Institute.

Parsons, Talcott. 1955. *Family, Socialization, and Interaction Process*. Glencoe, IL: Free Press.

———, and Robert F. Bales. 1955. *Family Socialization and Interaction Process*. Glencoe, IL: Free Press.

Paternoster, Ray. 2007. "Capital Punishment." In *The Blackwell Encyclopedia of Sociology*, vol. 2, edited by George Ritzer, 385–8. Malden, MA: Blackwell.

Pay Equity Commission. 2012. "Gender Wage Gap." http://www.payequity.gov.on.ca/en/about/pubs/genderwage/wagegap.php.

Peoples, Clayton D. 2012. "Welfare State." In *The Encyclopedia of Globalization*, edited by George Ritzer, 2218–21. Malden, MA: Wiley-Blackwell.

Perry, J. H. 1989. "A Fiscal History of Canada: The Post War Years." Canadian Tax Paper no. 85. Toronto: Canadian Tax Foundation.

Pittman, Tyler, Candace Nykiforuk, Javier Mignone, Piush Mandhane, Allan Becker, and Anita Kozyrskyj. 2012. "The Association between Community Stressors and Asthma Prevalence of School Children in Winnipeg, Canada." *International Journal of Environmental Research and Public Health* 9 (2): 579–95.

Poggi, Gianfranco. 2004. "Formation and Form: Theories of State Formation." In *The Blackwell Companion to Political Sociology*, edited by Kate Nash and Alan Scott, 95–106. Malden, MA: Blackwell Publishing.

Poisson, Jamie. 2013. "Remember Storm? We Check In On the Baby Being Raised Gender-Neutral." *Toronto Star*, 15 November. http://www.thestar.com/life/parent/2013/11/15/remember_storm_we_check_in_on_the_baby_being_raised_genderneutral.html.

Polletta, F. 1999. "'Free Spaces' in Collective Action." *Theory and Society* 28: 1–38.

Porter, John. 1965. *The Vertical Mosaic: An Analysis of Social Class and Power in Canada*. Toronto: University of Toronto Press.

Poverty and Employment Precarity in Southern Ontario (PEPSO), McMaster University, and United Way Toronto. 2013. "It's More than Poverty: Employment Precarity and Household Well-Being." Toronto: United Way.

Putnam, R. D. 2000. *Bowling Alone: The Collapse and Revival of American Community*. New York: Simon & Schuster.

———, with Robert Leonardi and Raffaella Y. Nanetti. 1993. *Making Democracy Work: Civic Traditions in Modern Italy*. Princeton, NJ: Princeton University Press.

Rankin, Jim, and Patty Winsa. 2012. "Known to Police: Toronto Police Stop and Document Black and Brown People Far More Than Whites." *Toronto Star*, 9 March.

Rigler, David. 1993. "Letters: A Psychologist Portrayed in a Book about an Abused Child Speaks Out for the First Time in 22 Years." *The New York Times Book Review*, 13 June, 35.

Ritzer, George. 2011. *The McDonaldization of Society*, 6th edn. Los Angeles: Sage.

Rogers, Simon, and Mona Chalabi. 2013. "Death Penalty Statistics, Country by Country." *The Guardian*, 13 December. http://www.theguardian.com/news/datablog/2011/mar/29/death-penalty-countries-world.

Rosenstone, S. J., and J. M. Hansen. 1993. *Mobilization, Participation, and Democracy in America*. New York: Macmillan.

Rostow, W. W. 1991. *The Stages of Economic Growth: A Non-Communist Manifesto*. Cambridge: Cambridge University Press.

Rousseau, Jean-Jacques. 2011. "Discourse on the Origin of Inequality." In *The Basic Political Writings*, 2nd edn, translated by Donald A. Cress. Indianapolis: Hackett.

Roy, William G. 2001. *Making Societies*. Boston: Pine Forge Press.

Rush, Curtis. 2011. "Cop Apologizes for 'Sluts' Remark at Law School." *Toronto Star*, 18 February. http://www.thestar.com/news/gta/2011/02/18/cop_apologizes_for_sluts_remark_at_law_school.html.

———. 2013. "Controversy at Florida Atlantic University over Prison Company's Stadium-Naming Deal." *Toronto Star*, 6 March.

Ryan, Andrew. 2013. "30 Hours a Week and Then Some: When Did Canada Become a Nation of TV Watching Zombies?" *The Globe and Mail*, 25 April.

Samuel, John, and Kogalur Basavarajappa. 2006. "The Visible Minority Population in Canada: A Review of Numbers, Growth and Labour Force Issues." *Canadian Studies in Population* 33 (2): 241–69. http://www.canpopsoc.ca/CanPopSoc/assets/File/publications/journal/CSPv33n2p241.pdf.

Scanlan, Stephen J., J. Craig Jenkins, and Lindsey Peterson. 2010. "The Scarcity Fallacy." *Contexts* 9 (1).

Schecter, Stephen. 1977. "Capitalism, Class, and Educational Reform in Canada." In *The Canadian State: Political Economy and Political Power*, edited by L. Panitch. Toronto: University of Toronto Press.

Schneider, Michael. 2014. "America's Most Watched: The Top 50 Shows of the 2013–2014 TV Season." *TV Guide*, 6 June. http://www.tvguide.com/news/most-watched-shows-2013-2014-1082628/.

Scott, Barbara Marliene, and Mary Ann A. Shwartz. 2008. *Sociology: Making Sense of the Social World*. Boston: Allyn and Bacon.

Sesay, Isha, and Teo Kermeliotis. 2013 (1 February). "The American Secretary Who Became King: A Woman's Journey to Royalty." CNN.com. http://www.cnn.com/2013/01/31/world/africa/king-peggy-otuam-ghana/.

Shader, Laurel, and Jonathan Zonderman. 2006. *Birth Control Pills*. New York: Infobased Publishing.

Shah, Anup. 2005. "The Scale of the Debt Crisis." Global Issues.org. http://www.globalissues.org/article/30/the-scale-of-the-debt-crisis.

Shakya, Yogendra B., and Axelle Janczur. 2013. "Where Are the Good Jobs?" *Toronto Star*, 30 July.

Sherif, M., O. J. Harvey, B. J. White, W. Hood, and C. W. Sherif. 1961. *Intergroup Conflict and Cooperation: The Robbers Cave Experiment*. Norman, OK: University Book Exchange.

Shimer, William Allison. 1946. "Review of *From Max Weber*." *The American Scholar* 15.

Siddiqui, Haroon. 2011. "Siddiqui: On Multiculturalism, Harper's Got It Right." *Toronto Star*, 16 April.

Silcoff, Sean. 2012. "Canadian Call Centers Ring Up New Job Growth." *The Globe and Mail*, 13 March.

Smith, Jackie, John D. McCarthy, Clark McPhail, and Boguslaw Angustyn. 2001. "From Protest to Agenda Building: Description Bias in Media Coverage of Protest Events in Washington, D.C." *Social Forces* 79 (4): 1397–1423.

Snow, D. A. 2001. "Collective Identity and Expressive Forms." In *The International Encyclopedia of the Social and Behavioral Sciences*, edited by N. J. Smelser and P. B. Blates. Oxford: Elsenier Selpin.

———, and Cynthia L. Phillips. 1982. "The Changing Self-Orientations of College Students: From Institution to Impulse." *Social Science Quarterly* 63 (3): 462–76.

Staggenborg, Suzanne. 2011. *Social Movements*, 2nd edn. Toronto: Oxford University Press.

Stanbridge, Karen, and Howard Ramos. 2012. *Seeing Politics Differently: A Brief Introduction to Political Sociology*. Don Mills, ON: Oxford University Press.

Statistics Canada. 2006. "Low-Income Cutoffs for 2005 and Low-Income Measures for 2004." *The Daily*, 6 April. http://www.statcan.gc.ca/daily-quotidien/060406/dq060406d-eng.htm.

———. 2007. "Are Average Wages Higher in Services?" Ottawa: Statistics Canada. http://www41.statcan.gc.ca/2007/0163/ceb0163_004-eng.htm.

———. 2009. "General Social Survey—Victimization." Ottawa: Statistics Canada. http://www23.statcan.gc.ca/imdb/p2SV.pl?Function=getSurvey&SurvId=51198&InstaId=49195&SDDS=4504.

———. 2011a. "Indicators of Well-Being in Canada: Financial Security—Income Distribution." Ottawa: Statistics Canada. http://well-being.esdc.gc.ca/misme-iowb/.3ndic.1t.4r@-eng.jsp?iid=22.

———. 2011b. *National Household Survey*. Catalogue no. 99-010-X2011032. Ottawa: Statistics Canada.

———. 2011c. "Canadians in Context: Aging Population." Ottawa: Statistics Canada. http://www4.hrsdc.gc.ca/.3ndic.1t.4r@-eng.jsp?iid=33.

———. 2011d. "Portrait of Canada's Labour Force." Ottawa: Statistics Canada. www12.statcan.gc.ca/nhs-enm/2011/as-sa/99-012-x/99-012-x2011002-eng.pdf.

———. 2012. "Internet Use by Individuals, by Selected Characteristics." Ottawa: Statistics Canada. http://www.statcan.gc.ca/tables-tableaux/sum-som/l01/cst01/comm35a-eng.htm.

———. 2013. "Aboriginal Peoples in Canada: First Nations People, Métis and Inuit." Ottawa: Statistics Canada. http://www12.statcan.gc.ca/nhs-enm/2011/as-sa/99-011-x/99-011-x2011001-eng.pdf.

———. 2014. "Employment by Industry." CANSIM, table 282-0008. Ottawa: Statistics Canada. http://www.statcan.gc.ca/tables-tableaux/sum-som/l01/cst01/econ40-eng.htm.

Story, Louise. 2007. "Anywhere the Eye Can See, It's Likely to See an Ad." *The New York Times*, 15 January.

Strayer, J. R. 1970. *On the Medieval Origins of the Modern State*. Princeton, NJ: Princeton University Press.

Streeter, Jessica. 2012. "Gentlemen Prefer Stouts." *Contexts* (Summer): 5.

Sutherland, Edwin H. 1947. *Criminology*, 4th edn. Philadelphia: Lippincott.

Taylor, Frederick W. 1947. *The Principles of Scientific Management*. New York: Harper & Row.

Taylor, V., and N. C. Raeburn. 1995. "Identity Politics as High-Risk Activism: Career Consequences for Lesbian, Gay, and Bisexual Sociologists." *Social Problems* 42: 252–73.

This Film Is Not Yet Rated. 2006. Directed by Kirby Dick. New York: Independent Film Channel.

Thomas, W. I., and D. S. Thomas. 1928. *The Child in America*. New York: Knopf.

Tilly, Charles. 1985. "War Making and State Making as Organized Crime." In *Bringing the State Back In*, edited by Peter Evans, Dietrich Rueschemeyer, and Theda Skocpol, 169–87. Cambridge: Cambridge University Press.

———. 1997. "Social Movements as Political Struggle." Working Paper, Center for Advanced Study in the Behavioral Sciences at Stanford University. https://www.ciaonet.org/wps/tic03/.

Tjepkema, Michael, Russell Wilkins, and Andrea Long. 2013. "Cause-Specific Mortality by Income Adequacy in Canada: A 16-Year Follow-Up Study." Ottawa: Statistics Canada. http://www.statcan.gc.ca/pub/82-003-x/2013007/article/11852-eng.htm.

Traugott, Mark, ed. 1978. *Émile Durkheim: On Institutional Analysis*. Chicago: University of Chicago Press.

Treas, J., and Gieden, D. 2000. "Sexual Infidelity among Married and Cohabiting Americans." *Journal of Marriage and the Family* 62 (1): 48–60.

Tucker, Robert C., ed. 1978. *The Marx-Engels Reader*. London: Norton.

United Nations. 1948. Convention on the Prevention and Punishment of the Crime of Genocide. https://treaties.un.org/doc/Publication/UNTS/Volume%2078/volume-78-I-1021-English.pdf.

University of Missouri. 2013. "Student Involvement: National Statistics." http://www.umkc.edu/getinvolved/fsa-national-statistics.asp.

Van Damme, Dirk. 2013. "Smart Policies Matter in Education." *OECD Education Today* (blog), 23 October. http://oecdeducationtoday.blogspot.ca/2013/10/smart-policies-matter-in-education.html.

Van den Berg, Alex, Claus-H von Restorff, Daniel Parent, and Anthony Masi. 2008. "From Unemployment to Employment Insurance: Towards Transitional Labour Markets in Canada." In *Flexibility and Employment Security in Europe: Labour Markets in Transition*, edited by Rudd J. Muffels, 308–35. Cheltenham, UK: Edward Elgar.

Veenhof, B., B. Wellman, C. Quell, and B. Hogan. 2008. "How Canadians' Use of the Internet Affects Social Life and Civic Participation." Catalogue no. 56F0004M—no. 016. Ottawa: Statistics Canada. http://www.statcan.gc.ca/pub/56f0004m/56f0004m2008016-eng.htm.

Venton-Rublee, Jordan, and Dana Wray. 2013. "One Year Later: The PQ Government." *The McGill Daily*, 9 September. http://www.mcgilldaily.com/2013/09/one-year-later-the-pq-government/.

Verba, S., K. L. Schlozman, and H. E. Brady. 1995. *Voice and Equality: Civic Voluntarism in American Politics*. Cambridge, MA: Harvard University Press.

Wade, Lisa. 2013. "Two 7-Year-Old Boys, Two Dramatically Different News Stories." *The Huffington Post*, 22 July. http://www.huffingtonpost.com/2013/07/22/media-kids-racial-stereotypes_n_3624740.html.

Wallerstein, Immanuel. 2011. *The Modern World System*. Berkeley, CA: University of California Press.

Warner, Kris. 2013. "The Real Reason for the Decline of American Unions." *BloombergView*, 23 January. http://www.bloombergview.com/articles/2013-01-23/the-real-reason-for-the-decline-of-american-unions.

Watters, Haydn. 2015 (3 June). "Education 'only way forward,' says Gov. David Johnston as TRC ends." CBCNews.ca. http://www.cbc.ca/news/politics/education-only-way-forward-says-gov-gen-david-johnston-as-trc-ends-1.3098297.

Weaver, Mathew. 2010. "Angela Merkel: German Multiculturalism Has 'Utterly Failed.'" *The Guardian*, 17 October. http://www.theguardian.com/world/2010/oct/17/angela-merkel-german-multiculturalism-failed.

Weber, Max. 1965. *The Sociology of Religion*. London: Methuen.

———. 1978. *Economy and Society*. Berkeley, CA: University of California Press.

Wells, Spencer. 2002. *The Journey of Man: A Genetic Odyssey*. Princeton, NJ: Princeton University Press.

Whalen, J., and R. Flacks. 1989. *Beyond the Barricades: The Sixties Generation Grows Up*. Philadelphia: Temple University Press.

Whorf, Benjamin. 1956. *Language, Thought, and Reality: Selected Writings of Benjamin Lee Whorf*. Cambridge, MA: MIT Press.

Wilcox, W. Bradford, and Steven L. Nock. 2006. "What's Love Got To Do With It? Equality, Equity, Commitment and Women's Marital Quality." *Social Forces* 84 (3): 1321–45.

Wilkes, Rima. 2004. "First Nation Politics: Deprivation, Resources, and Participation in Collective Action." *Sociological Inquiry* 74: 570–89.

Wilkinson, Richard, and Kate Pickett. 2010. *The Spirit Level: Why More Equal Societies Almost Always Do Better*. New York: Bloomsbury.

Wilson, Vince Seymour. 1993. "The Tapestry Vision of Canadian Multiculturalism." *Canadian Journal of Political Science* 26 (4): 657.

Wiltfang, G. L., and D. McAdam. 1991. "The Costs and Risks of Social Activism—A Study of Sanctuary Movement Activism." *Social Forces* 69: 987–1010.

Wineburg, Samuel. 1987. "The Self-Fulfillment of the Self-Fulfilling Prophecy." *Educational Researcher* 16: 28–44.

World Hunger Education Service. 2015. "2015 World Hunger and Poverty Facts and Statistics." http://www.worldhunger.org/articles/Learn/world%20hunger%20facts%202002.htm.

World Public Opinion. 2007 (25 April). "World Public Favors Globalization and Trade but Wants to Protect Environment and Jobs." www.worldpublicopinion.org/pipa/articles/btglobalizationtradera/349.php?lb=btgl.

Zachary, G. Pascale. 2002. "Ghana's Digital Dilemma." *MIT Technology Review*, 1 July. http://www.technologyreview.com/featuredstory/401607/ghanas-digital-dilemma/.

Zhao, D. 1999. "Ecologies of Social Movements: Student Mobilization during the 1989 Pro-Democracy Movement in Beijing." *American Journal of Sociology* 103: 1493–529.

Zimbardo, P. G., C. Maslach, and C. Haney. 1999. *Reflections on the Stanford Prison Experiment: Genesis, Transformations, Consequences.* http://www.prisonexp.org/pdf/blass.pdf.

Credits

Literary Credits

Chapter 1
Horace Miner, "Body Ritual Among the Nacirema," *American Anthropologist*, Vol. 58(3), pp. 503–7, June 1956.

C. Wright Mills, *The Sociological Imagination*, pp. 3–24. Oxford University Press, Inc., 1959.

Chapter 2
"Review of *Albert Schaeffle, Bau und Leben des Sozialen Körpers: Erster Band* by Émile Durkheim." Mark Traugott (translator). From *Emile Durkheim On Institutional Analysis*, pp. 93–114. The University of Chicago Press, 1978.

Furstenberg, F.F. Jr, Kennedy, S., McLoyd, V.C., Rumbaut, R.G., Settersten, R.A. Jr (2004), "Growing Up is Harder to Do," *Contexts* Vol. 3(3), pp. 33–41. Copyright © 2004 by American Sociological Association. Reprinted by permission of SAGE Publications, Inc.

Excerpt(s) from THE PRESENTATION OF SELF IN EVERYDAY LIFE by Erving Goffman, copyright © 1959 by Erving Goffman. Used by permission of Doubleday, an imprint of the Knopf Doubleday Publishing Group, a division of Penguin Random House LLC. All rights reserved.

Chapter 3
Excerpted from: Robert Tucker, ed. *The Marx-Engels Reader*, 2e (WW Norton & Company, 1978, 1972) pp. 473–83.

Barbara Ehrenreich, "Nickel-and-Dimes: On (not) getting by in America," *Harper's Magazine*, January 1999; 298, 1784; Research Library Core, pp. 37–52.

Chapter 4
"The Uses of Global Poverty: How Economic Inequality Benefits the West," by Daina Stukuls Eglitis. Used by permission of Daina Eglitis.

"The Record of Microfinance," by Jon Westover, in the *Electronic Journal of Sociology* (2008) ISSN: 1198 3655, http://www.sociology.org/content/2008/_westover_finance.pdf

Chapter 5
From Pedraza/Rumbaut, *Origins and Destinies*, 1st edition. © 1996 South-Western, a part of Cengage Learning, Inc. Reproduced by permission. www.cengage.com/permissions.

Excerpt from the *Johnny Carson Tonight Show* monologue, by permission of the Carson Entertainment Group.

"Imagined Communities," by Benedict Anderson, from *Imagined Communities: Reflections on the Origin and Spread of Nationalism*, Revised edition. Verso (2006), pp. 5–7.

Chapter 6
"Commanding the Room in Short Skirts," by Natalie Adams and Pamela Bettis. Copyright © 2003, © SAGE Publications.

Abridged version of Jonathan Ned Katz, "The Invention of Heterosexuality," *Socialist Review* 20 (Jan–Mar, 1990), 7–34.

Chapter 7
"Racism in the English Language," by Robert B. Moore, reprinted from *Council on Interracial Books for Children*, 1976, by permission of the Lawrence Jordan Agency, 345 West 121st Street, NY, NY 10027.

C. Wright Mills, *The Power Elite*, Oxford University Press, Inc. (1956) pp. 269–97.

Chapter 8
Cherlin, A.J. (2003), "Should the Government Promote Marriage?," *Contexts*, Vol. 2(4) pp. 22–9. Copyright © 2003 by American Sociological Association. Reprinted by permission of SAGE Publications, Inc.

"Men as Success Objects and Women as Sex Objects: A Study of Personal Advertisements," by Simon Davis. Copyright © 1990, Plenum Publishing Corporation.

Chapter 9
Beaver, W. (2009), "A Matter of Degrees?," *Contexts* Vol. 8(2) pp. 22–6. Copyright © 2009 by American Sociological Association. Reprinted by permission of SAGE Publications, Inc.

Mullen, A. (2012), "The Not-So-Pink Ivory Tower," *Contexts* Vol. 11(4) pp. 34–8. Copyright © 2012 by American Sociological Association. Reprinted by permission of SAGE Publications, Inc.

Chapter 10
"The 'McDonaldization' of Society," by George Ritzer. Copyright © 2004, John Wiley and Sons.

Arlie Russell Hochschild, "Feeling Management: From Private to Commercial Uses," *The Managed Heart: Commercialization of Human Feeling*, University of California Press (1983, 2009) pp. 89–136.

Chapter 11
"On Being Sane in Insane Places," by D.L. Rosenhan, in *Science*, Vol. 179, 19 January 1973, pp. 250–8.

DISCIPLINE AND PUNISH by Michel Foucault. English Translation copyright © 1977 by Alan Sheridan (New York: Pantheon). Originally published in French as *Surveiller et Punir*. Copyright © 1975 by Editions Gallimard. Reprinted by permission of Georges Borchardt, Inc., for Editions Gallimard.

Chapter 12
Conley, D. (2002). "Forty Acres and a Mule: What if America Pays Reparations?," *Contexts* Vol. 1(3) pp. 13–20. Copyright © 2002 by American Sociological Association. Reprinted by permission of SAGE Publications, Inc.

"Bowling Alone: America's Declining Social Capital," by Robert D. Putnam, in *Journal of Democracy*, 6.1 (1995) 65–78.

Chapter 13
Suzanne Staggenborg, "The Environmental Movement," from *Social Movements*, 2nd edition. © Oxford University Press Canada 2012. Reprinted by permission of the publisher.

William Gamson, from *The Strategy of Social Protest*, 2nd edition, Wadsworth Publishing Company (1990, 1975) pp. 28–37.

Photo Credits

Index